THE PROCEDURE OF THE UN SECURITY COUNCIL

THE PROCEDURE OF THE UN SECURITY COUNCIL

THIRD EDITION

SYDNEY D. BAILEY
and
SAM DAWS

CLARENDON PRESS · OXFORD
1998

Oxford University Press, Great Clarendon Street, Oxford OX2 6DP
Oxford New York
Athens Auckland Bangkok Bogota Buenos Aires
Calcutta Cape Town Chennai Dar es Salaam
Delhi Florence Hong Kong Istanbul Karachi
Kuala Lumpur Madrid Melbourne Mexico City
Mumbai Nairobi Paris São Paolo Singapore
Taipei Tokyo Toronto Warsaw
and associated companies in
Berlin Ibadan

Oxford is a registered trade mark of Oxford University Press

Published in the United States
by Oxford University Press Inc., New York

First published 1975
2nd edition 1988
3rd edition 1998

British Library Cataloguing in Publication Data
Data available

Library of Congress Cataloging in Publication Data
Data available
ISBN 0–19–828073–4

Set by Hope Services (Abingdon) Ltd.
Printed in Great Britain
on acid-free paper by
Biddles Ltd
Guildford & King's Lynn

PREFACE TO THE THIRD EDITION

Much has changed since the second edition of this book went to press in 1987. The end of the Cold War ushered in new possibilities for international co-operation, and increased recourse to the United Nations. The last decade has seen the Gulf War and a plethora of new and often complex peace-keeping operations, from Bosnia to Rwanda. Such increased demands and associated expectations have placed a spotlight on the role and functioning of the Security Council. Recent years have seen a greater recourse to informal consultations of Council members prior to Council meetings. The search for consensual Council decision-making has led to differences of opinion on both procedural and substantive matters being dealt with largely during such consultations. This has produced calls from non-members for greater Council transparency. Other proposals, both from within and outside the United Nations, have advocated reforms to the Council's composition or working methods to ensure its continued effectiveness and legitimacy.

This new edition attempts to reflect the many recent developments in the procedure of the Security Council while faithfully reflecting the considerable continuity that exists with the past. In particular, to illustrate and illuminate aspects of Council procedure, we have used many examples from the UN's early years, since this was the time when many of the original precedents were created. In keeping with the last two editions we have also retained some of the anecdotes that touch on the human side of Council diplomacy. This edition includes new information on the following: the Provisional Rules of Procedure; public and private meetings; consultations and briefings with non-members and troop-contributors; informal consultations and 'Arria formula' meetings; the appointment of the Secretary-General; relationships with the General Assembly, the International Court of Justice, the Trusteeship Council, and the Military Staff Committee; subsidiary organs, including sanctions committees; the veto; Chapter VII resolutions, UN peace-keeping and UN-authorized enforcement; Council enlargement and *de jure* and *de facto* Charter amendment; changes in Council documentation; and *ad hoc* and regional groupings in the Council.

We are indebted to the editorial and marketing staff of Oxford University Press for their patience and professionalism, especially Sophie Ahmad, Dominic Byatt, and Andrea Nicholls, and to our ever vigilant proof-reader Marie Diaz. We are also deeply grateful to those diplomats, international officials, academics, and librarians who have assisted with information and the occasional indiscretion, in the preparation of this, and previous editions. In particular we would like to acknowledge the help of Fatma Ashour, Paul Bentall, Barbara Blenman, Neil Briscoe, Norma Chan, Hannah Chandler, Noel Dorr, David Gore-Booth, Sir Marrack Goulding, Solonge Habib, Judge Rosalyn Higgins, Diane Jumet, Roy Lee, Caroline Lombardo, Donald Maitland, Alemayehu Makonnen, David Malone, Sally Morphet, Sir Anthony Parsons, Lord Ivor Richard, Adam Roberts, Robert Rosenstock, Bruce Russett, Sir Brian Urquhart, and Elizabeth Wilmshurst. A particular debt of gratitude is owed to Neylan Bali and Michael Wood who generously gave of their time and knowledge in the preparation of this manuscript.

S.D.B. & S.B.D.

Postscript

Sydney D. Bailey died on 26 November 1995. It was a special privilege and personal pleasure to work with Sydney on what was to be his final book. The revising of this book has been continued after his death, and the information in this third edition has been updated to 1 January 1997. Developments after this date have been included where this has been possible.

S.B.D. 1 August 1997

NOTES ON THE AUTHORS

Sydney D. Bailey (1916–1995) wrote extensively on the United Nations and peacemaking. Among his books were *The UN Security Council and Human Rights*, *The General Assembly of the United Nations*, *The Secretariat of the United Nations*, *How Wars End*, *The Making of Resolution 242*, *Four Arab–Israeli Wars and the Peace Process*, *The Korean Armistice*, and *The United Nations: A Concise Political Guide* (with Sam Daws). In 1985 he was awarded the Lambeth Degree of Doctor of Civil Law. As a Quaker representative, he was involved in various international mediation efforts. His personal philosophy on peacemaking was summarized in the 1993 Swarthmore Lecture, published as *Peace is a Process*. He worked on the third edition of *The Procedure of the UN Security Council* right up until a few weeks before his death on 26 November 1995.

Sam Daws (b. 1965) is a consultant on UN affairs. He was previously head of the UN and Conflict Programme at the United Nations Association in London and has worked for the Quaker UN Office in Geneva, as a Parliamentary researcher at the House of Commons, and as President of Sussex University Students' Union. He has served as a Consultant to the UN Department of Political Affairs in New York, and on working attachment to the British Foreign and Commonwealth Office. He was a Visiting Fellow at Yale in 1995, has degrees in Social Anthropology and International Conflict Analysis, and is currently completing a doctorate on UN Security Council reform at New College, Oxford. This is his fifth co-authored book on the United Nations.

CONTENTS

List of Tables and Charts xv
List of Abbreviations and Acronyms xvii

1. THE CONSTITUTIONAL FRAMEWORK 1

1. The role of the Security Council 3
2. The Charter 6
3. The rules of procedure 9
4. Custom 17
5. Functions 18

2. THE COUNCIL MEETS 21

1. Formal meetings and informal consultations 21
2. Convening a meeting 22
3. Notice of meetings 37
4. Place of meeting 40
5. 'Periodic' meetings 45
6. 'Orientation' and 'exchange of views' meetings 50
7. Private (closed) meetings 53
8. Informal consultations 60
9. Duration of meetings 75
10. The agenda 76
11. Rejection of items 89
12. Interpretation and translation 91
13. Documents and records 94
14. Communications 102

3. THE PEOPLE 110

1. Secretary-General 110
2. President 124
3. Permanent members 137
4. Non-permanent members 141
5. Other participants 154

6. Permanent missions 166
7. Groups 168
8. Regionalism 173
9. Credentials 175
10. Representation of China 179
11. Precedence 187

4. DIPLOMACY AND DEBATE 188

1. Order of speakers 189
2. Interrupting the speaker 192
3. Right of reply 196
4. Motions, proposals, suggestions 197
5. 'Precedence motions' (Rule 33) 201
6. Amendments 212
7. Statements before or after the vote 218

5. VOTING 221

1. Procedural motions 225
2. Substantive decisions 226
3. The veto 227
4. The double veto 240
5. The 'hidden veto' 249
6. Abstentions 250
7. Absence 257
8. Non-participation in the vote 258
9. Consensus and unanimity 259
10. When are decisions binding? 263

6. RELATIONS WITH OTHER ORGANS 274

1. Military Staff Committee 274
2. General Assembly 281
3. Economic and Social Council 301
4. Trusteeship Council 303
5. International Court of Justice 307
6. Non-Governmental Organizations 320
7. Appointment of the Secretary-General 321

7. SUBSIDIARY ORGANS 333

1. Organs concerned with Council procedure 334
 (a) Committee of Experts 334
 (b) Committee on Council Meetings away from Headquarters 335
2. Organs concerned with membership 338
 (a) Committee on Admission of New Members 338
 (b) Committee of Experts established at its 1506th meeting (mini-States) 350
3. Organs concerned with the maintenance of international peace and security 353
 (a) Fact-finding missions 353
 (b) Peace-keeping operations 356
 (c) International tribunals 363
 (d) Sanctions committees 365
 (e) UN peace-enforcement 374
 (f) Other miscellaneous organs for the maintenance of international peace and security 377
4. Other subsidiary bodies 377
 (a) Informal Working Group of the Security Council concerning the Council's documentation and other procedural questions 377

8. NEW CHARTER, NEW MEMBERS, NEW RULES, NEW WORKING PRACTICES, OR NEW NATIONAL POLICIES? 379

1. New Charter? 379
2. New members? 382
3. New rules? 390
4. New working practices? 410
5. New national policies? 411

APPENDICES 413

I. (a) Extracts from the UN Charter 413
 (b) Extracts from the Statute of the International Court of Justice 437
II. Provisional Rules of Procedure of the Security Council, as amended 21 Dec. 1982 441

III. The Yalta formula on voting in the Security Council, 8 June 1945 455

IV. (a) Opinion of the Legal Counsel on relations between the General Assembly and the Security Council, 10 Sept. 1964 459

(b) Opinion of the Legal Counsel on relations between the General Assembly and the Security Council, 12 Dec. 1968 473

V. Memorandum by the Secretary-General on the procedure to be followed in the election of a member of the International Court of Justice, 24 January 1996. Extract 474

VI. United Nations Peace-keeping Operations 1948–96. Details of authorizing resolutions, function, location and duration. 477

VII. Matters of which the Security Council is seized, 10 January 1997. S/1997/40. 518

VIII. Communications received from private individuals and non-governmental bodies relating to matters of which the Security Council is seized, 3 February 1997. S/NC/1996/4. 529

IX. The Secretariat's tentative forecast of the programme of work of the Security Council for the month of August 1995 533

X. Resolutions, Notes, and Letters related to procedural developments in the documentation of the Security Council 542

(a) Presidential Note of 30 June 1993 concerning the annual report of the Security Council to the General Assembly, S/26015. 542

(b) Presidential Note of 27 July 1993 concerning the forecast of the programme of work of the Council, S/26176. 544

(c) Presidential Note of 31 August 1993 concerning Council documentation, S/26389. 545

(d) Letter dated 2 June 1995 from Argentina concerning changes to the nomenclature of statements made by the President of the Security Council, S/1995/456. 546

(e) General Assembly resolution 51/193 of 17 December 1996 concerning the annual report of the Security Council 549
(f) Note by the President [concerning the format of the annual report of the Council to the General Assembly], 12 June 1997. S/1997/451. 551
(g) Informal briefing note on Blue Draft Resolutions, prepared by the Secretariat, July 1995 553

XI. *Aide-mémoire* concerning the working methods of the Security Council from the Permanent Representative of France, 11 November 1994, A/49/667 and S/1994/1279. 556

XII. Presidential Statements related to procedural developments in UN peace-keeping:

Peace-keeping general:

(a) Presidential Statement of 3 May 1994. Improving UN capacity for peace-keeping, S/PRST/1994/22. 563
(b) Presidential Statement of 22 February 1995. Consideration of Supplement to 'An Agenda for Peace', S/PRST/1995/9. 568

Peace-keeping consultations and transparency:

(c) Presidential Statement of 4 November 1994. Meetings between members of Security Council, troop-contributing countries and Secretariat, S/PRST/1994/62. 573
(d) Presidential Statement of 16 December 1994. Increased recourse to open meetings of Security Council in order to improve flow of information and exchange of ideas between Security Council and other UN Member States, S/PRST/1994/81. 575
(e) Presidential Statement of 28 March 1996. Strengthening consultation procedures with troop-contributing countries, S/PRST/1996/13. 576

Peace-keeping stand-by arrangements:

(f) Presidential Statement of 27 July 1994. Stand-by arrangements for peace-keeping operations, S/PRST/1994/36. 579
(g) Presidential Statement of 19 December 1995. Peace-keeping stand-by arrangements, S/PRST/1995/61. 580

XIII. Notes by the President concerning Sanctions Committees of the Security Council
(a) Note by the President dated 29 March 1995, S/1995/234. 581
(b) Note by the President dated 31 May 1995, S/1995/438. 582
(c) Note by the President dated 24 January 1996, S/1996/54. 583
XIV. Letter from the permanent members of the Security Council on the humanitarian aspects of sanctions, 13 April 1995, S/1995/300. 584
XV. Note dated 26 February 1997 by the Secretary-General, circulated to the Security Council, on the adoption of General Assembly resolution 51/208, entitled 'Implementation of the provisions of the Charter of the United Nations related to assistance to third States affected by the application of sanctions', S/1997/161. 586
XVI. Presidential Statement of 26 September 1995. Fiftieth anniversary of the United Nations, S/PRST/1995/48. 587
XVII. Security Council resolution 984 (1995) of 11 April 1995. Assurances to non-nuclear weapons States. 589
XVIII. Statute of the International Tribunal for Rwanda. Annex to Security Council resolution 955 (1994) of 8 November 1994. 592
XIX. The first Sydney Bailey Memorial Lecture. Address given by his Royal Highness Crown Prince Hassan bin Talal of the Hashemite Kingdom of Jordan, Westminster Abbey, London, 10 March 1997. 606

Select bibliography 611
References 616
Index 671

LIST OF TABLES AND CHARTS

Tables

1. The evolution of the Rules of Procedure 14
2. Number of Council meetings and resolutions, 17 January 1946–31 December 1996 34
3. Symbols of documents of main subsidiary organs of the Security Council 101
4. Cession of the presidency under Rule 20, 1946–1996 126
5. Non-permanent members of the Security Council, 1946–1997 148
6. UN Members by region, 1 January 1997 169
7. Some cases of simple adjournment under Rule 33, 1946–1996 206
8. Vetoes cast in the Security Council, 16 February 1946–1 August 1997 231
9. Summary of vetoes in the Security Council, 16 February 1946–1 August 1997 239
10. Absence from the Council when a resolution has been voted on, 1946–1996 258
11. Non-participation in votes on resolutions, 1946–1996 259
12. Security Council resolutions adopted 'without a vote' or 'by consensus', 1946–1996 260
13. Five decades of Chapter VII resolutions, 1946–31 December 1995 272
14. Military Staff Committee: chronology, 1946–1996 278
15. Voting for the International Court of Justice, 1963 312
16. Appointment of the Secretary-General, 1946–1996 325
17. Tasks entrusted to the Committee of Experts and Reports of the Committee, 1946–1996 336
18. Work of the Committee on Council meetings away from Headquarters, 1972–1996 338

19. Applications for UN membership referred to the Committee on Admission of New Members, 1946–1949, 1971–1984, and 1990–1996 339
20. Meetings of Security Council sanctions committees 367
21. Enforcement Action by Member States authorized by the Security Council, 1946–1996 375

Charts

1. General Assembly voting on the representation of China, 1961–71 184
2. Council resolutions: degree of unanimity, 1946–1996 264
3. UN membership, 1946–96 349

LIST OF ABBREVIATIONS AND ACRONYMS

Add.	Addendum (addition of text to the main document)
ASEAN	Association of South-East Asian Nations
Corr.	Corrigendum (to correct errors, revise wording, reorganize text, whether for substantive or technical reasons)
Charter Committee	Special Committee on the Charter of the United Nations and on the Strengthening of the Role of the Organization
CIS	Commonwealth of Independent States
DOMREP	Mission of the Representative of the Secretary-General in the Dominican Republic
ECOSOC	Economic and Social Council
FRUS	Foreign Relations of the United States
GA	General Assembly
GA res.	General Assembly resolution
GAOR	General Assembly Official Records
IAEA	International Atomic Energy Agency
ICJ	International Court of Justice
IFOR	Implementation Force
ILC	International Law Commission
JIU	Joint Inspection Unit
MICIVIH	International Civilian Mission to Haiti
MINUGUA	United Nations Human Rights Verification Mission in Guatemala
MINURSO	United Nations Mission for the Referendum in Western Sahara
MINUSAL	Mission of the United Nations in El Salvador
MSC	Military Staff Committee
NATO	North Atlantic Treaty Organization
NGO	Non-Governmental Organization
NPT	Nuclear Non-Proliferation Treaty

OAS	Organization of American States
OAU	Organization of African Unity
ONUC	United Nations Operation in the Congo
ONUCA	United Nations Observer Group in Central America
ONUMOZ	United Nations Operation in Mozambique
ONUSAL	United Nations Observer Mission in El Salvador
ONUV	United Nations Office of Verification
OEWG	Open-Ended Working Group on the Question of Equitable Representation on and Increase in the Membership of the Security Council and other matters related to the Security Council
OSCE	Organization for Security and Co-operation in Europe
PC	Document of the Preparatory Commission of the United Nations
PC/EX	Document of the Executive Committee of the Preparatory Commission of the United Nations
PIP	Peace Implementation Programme
PLO	Palestine Liberation Organization
PV.	Provisional Verbatim Record (Procès-Verbal) (mimeo.)
Rev.	Revision (new text superseding and replacing a previously issued document)
SC	Security Council
SC res.	Security Council resolution
SCOR	Security Council Official Records
UNAMIC	United Nations Advance Mission in Cambodia
UNAMIR	United Nations Assistance Mission for Rwanda
UNASOG	United Nations Aouzou Strip Observer Group
UNAVEM	United Nations Angola Verification Mission
UNCIO	United Nations Conference on International Organizations
UNCIP	United Nations Commission for India and Pakistan
UNCRO	United Nations Confidence Restoration Operation in Croatia
UNDOF	United Nations Disengagement Observer Force
UNEF	United Nations Emergency Force
UNFICYP	United Nations Peace-keeping Force in Cyprus

UNGOMAP	United Nations Good Offices in Afghanistan and Pakistan
UNIDIR	United Nations Institute for Disarmament Research
UNIFIL	United Nations Interim Force in Lebanon
UNIIMOG	United Nations Iran–Iraq Observer Group
UNIKOM	United Nations Iraq–Kuwait Observation Mission
UNIPOM	United Nations India–Pakistan Observation Mission
UNITAR	United Nations Institute for Training and Research
UNMIBH	United Nations Mission in Bosnia and Herzegovina
UNMIH	United Nations Mission in Haiti
UNMOGIP	United Nations Military Observer Group in India and Pakistan
UNMOP	United Nations Mission of Observers in Prevlaka
UNMOT	United Nations Mission of Observers in Tajikistan
UNOGIL	United Nations Observation Group in Lebanon
UNOMIG	United Nations Observer Mission in Georgia
UNOMIL	United Nations Observer Mission in Liberia
UNOMUR	United Nations Observer Mission Uganda–Rwanda
UNOSOM	United Nations Operation in Somalia
UNPF	United Nations Peace Forces
UNPREDEP	United Nations Preventive Deployment Force
UNPROFOR	United Nations Protection Force
UNSCOM	United Nations Special Commission
UNSF	United Nations Security Force in West New Guinea (West Irian)
UNSMIH	United Nations Support Mission in Haiti
UNTAES	United Nations Transitional Administration for Eastern Slavonia, Baranja and Western Sirmium
UNTAC	United Nations Transitional Authority in Cambodia
UNTAG	United Nations Transition Assistance Group
UNTS	United Nations Treaty Series
UNTSO	United Nations Truce Supervision Organization
UNU	United Nations University
UNYOM	United Nations Yemen Observation Mission
WEO	Western European and Other States

The first meeting of the UN Security Council held at the level of Heads of State and Government, 31 January 1992
UN Photo 179210/M. Grant

CHAPTER 1

THE CONSTITUTIONAL FRAMEWORK

> There is no durable treaty which is not founded on reciprocal advantage, and indeed a treaty which does not satisfy this condition is no treaty at all and is apt to contain the seeds of its own dissolution.

WHEN a new body meets for the first time, it usually has a clean procedural slate, except for the rules which customarily govern bodies of that kind, be it a political party, a religious congregation, or a golf club. But when the UN Security Council met for the first time just after 3 p.m. on Thursday 17 January 1946, the procedural slate was not clean. The Council had to operate within the framework of the UN Charter, which had been approved at San Francisco seven months previously. Moreover, the UN Preparatory Commission had drafted some tentative rules of procedure for the Council and had drawn up a provisional agenda of thirteen items for the first meeting, which the Secretariat placed before the Council after making some slight adjustments in the order of items.[1]

The Security Council met in Church House, London, close to Westminster Abbey and the bomb-scarred Houses of Parliament. The Council's membership included five permanent members:* the Republic of China, France, the Soviet Union (now the Russian Federation), the United Kingdom, and the United States, represented respectively by Wellington Koo, Vincent Auriol, Andrei Andrevich Gromyko, Ernest Bevin, and Edward Stettinius, Jr. The previous Saturday, the General Assembly had elected six non-permanent members: Australia, Brazil, Egypt, Mexico, the Netherlands, and Poland.

* In this book, we refer to members of the Security Council, but Members (with a capital M) of the United Nations.

It was a distinguished company. Paul-Boncour was a former Prime Minister and veteran of French public life. Vincent Auriol was to become President of the Fourth French Republic. Wellington Koo (China), Badawi (Egypt), Cordova (Mexico), and Padilla Nervo (Mexico) were to become members of the International Court of Justice. Padilla Nervo and van Kleffens (the Netherlands) were to become Presidents of the UN General Assembly. Modzelewski (Poland) was in 1950 to be the Soviet candidate to succeed Trygve Lie as UN Secretary-General. Bidault (France) was to become Prime Minister; Bevin (United Kingdom) was Foreign Minister, and Cyro de Freitas-Valle (Brazil), Andrei Gromyko (Soviet Union), van Kleffens (the Netherlands), and Andrei Vyshinsky (Soviet Union) were later to reach that rank; Massigli (France) was a future Secretary-General at the Quai d'Orsay; Cadogan (United Kingdom) and Stettinius (USA) were their countries' first ambassadors at the United Nations. Abdel Fattah Amr (Egypt), Foo Ping-sheung (China), W. R. Hodgson (Australia), Alfonso de Rosenzweig Diaz (Mexico), Henrique Valle (Brazil), and Jonkheer Michiels van Verduynen (the Netherlands) were or were soon to become senior diplomats. Philip Noel-Baker (United Kingdom) was to be awarded the Nobel Peace Prize.

But it was Norman Makin, a former Australian Minister for Navy and Munitions, who by the accident of the alphabet was to become the Security Council's first presiding officer. The Council established a tradition, which it has respected ever since, by starting late. Modzelewski presented part of the report of the Preparatory Commission (item 2 of the agenda), after which the Council adopted a rule by which the presidency was to rotate on a monthly basis in the English alphabetical order of names of the Council's members. Makin then changed from being 'temporary chairman' to becoming President, and addressed the Council briefly about the political and organizational tasks which lay ahead and the need to base the work of the Council on the Charter. Other members of the Council then made agreeable remarks appropriate to a formal historic occasion, Bevin taking special pride in the fact that a British Dominion (as the jargon then was) had been called upon to preside. The Council approved the provisional agenda, adopted the remaining rules of procedure on an interim basis, and appointed a committee of experts to consider procedural matters. At 4.15 p.m., Stettinius moved that the Council should adjourn, and one minute later the motion was approved. The Council had disposed of six of its first thirteen agenda items.

By the time the Council met again eight days later, substantive problems had started to accumulate. Iran had complained of Soviet interference in its internal affairs. The Soviet Union alleged that the presence of British troops in Greece endangered world peace. The Ukrainian Soviet Socialist Republic (as then called) drew attention to military operations against the people of Indonesia. Albania had applied for UN membership. The Council was thus faced at an early date with some of the characteristic issues of the Cold War.

1. THE ROLE OF THE SECURITY COUNCIL

There are four chapters in the Charter relating to the Security Council: V on composition, functions, and procedure; VI on the pacific settlement of disputes; VII on threats to or breaches of the peace, and acts of aggression; and VIII on regional arrangements. Chapters VI and VII deal with disputes or situations of like nature, whereas the former includes an Article (33(1)) which sets out methods open to the Council for settling disputes peacefully.

There has always been tension between the Security Council, with its unprecedented powers and limited membership plus the right of five permanent members to veto substantive proposals, and the General Assembly, comprising all UN Members and with the right to recommend. In order to limit rivalry between the Security Council and the General Assembly, the founders included in the Charter a provision stating that when the Security Council is exercising in respect of any matter the functions assigned to it in the Charter, the General Assembly shall not make any recommendation with regard to the matter 'unless the Security Council so requests' (Article 12 (1)). In practice, this Article has been interpreted with flexibility.

The United Nations was created to advance human welfare; in particular, by the avoidance of war through co-operative efforts among sovereign States. But the avoidance of war is a negative goal, and in positive terms the United Nations was to devote its efforts, or should devote them, to creating the conditions of peace in which disputes do not arise or, if they do, are resolved without recourse to armed force; in which basic human rights are protected on a non-discriminatory basis, economic and social advancement for all is promoted, international law is respected, and nations co-operate in those technical matters which affect the universal common good.

It is sometimes said that the United Nations has had more success in dealing with economic and social problems than in the field of peace and security. This is an assessment which it is difficult to substantiate in a scientific way, but we doubt whether the Organization will have a useful future in the long term if it is manifestly failing to do what it should to preserve world peace. It is on the Security Council that this primary responsibility rests. The phrase 'international peace and security' occurs twenty-seven times in the Charter;[2] the next most important goal, 'human rights', is mentioned seven times.[3]

Five facts about the Security Council are especially relevant at this stage of our study.

First, although the Council consists of only a limited number of UN Members (originally eleven, now fifteen), it acts on behalf of them all (Article 24(1) of the Charter).

Second, the Council has the authority to take decisions which bind not only its own members but all the Members of the Organization (Articles 2(5), 25, and 49) and, to some extent, even non-members (Article 2(6)).

Third, this right of decision is restricted by the rule of unanimity, or veto, by which all five permanent members have the right to block non-procedural proposals in the Security Council and amendments to the Charter (Articles 27(3) and 108). We would interject at this point that Article 27(3) is concerned with non-procedural decisions ('. . . all other matters . . .'), but we will in this book often use the more handy terms 'substantive proposals' or 'substantive decisions'.*

Fourth, the Council must be able to function at all times (Article 28(1)). Other UN organs, such as the General Assembly, in principle, meet at prescribed times of the year, and the machinery for calling

*It may be noted that in the General Assembly the distinction is not between procedure and substance but between 'important' and 'other' questions, the former requiring a two-thirds majority (Article 18(2)).

emergency or special sessions is relatively cumbersome. The Security Council can and does meet at only an hour or two's notice.

Fifth, the Charter gives to the Council the right to adopt its own rules of procedure (Article 30) subject, of course, to the UN Charter itself.

The Charter, like any basic constitutional document, expresses the views and expectations of the founders at a particular point in time. The long process of planning an international organization to keep the peace began in national capitals more than fifty years ago, leading to the Dumbarton Oaks meeting in 1944, the summit consultations in Malta and Yalta in 1945, culminating in the San Francisco Conference in 1945 and the formal signing of the Charter on 26 June.

The Charter consists of 111 Articles divided into 19 Chapters, occupying about fourteen pages of medium octavo text. Attached to the Charter and integral to it is the Statute of the International Court of Justice (Article 92). Relevant articles from the two documents are reproduced in Appendix 1.

It is possible to rank the issues which come before the Security Council according to their gravity, beginning with those which are described as matters, questions or situations, and proceeding through disputes, to threats to or breaches of the peace, and (most serious of all) acts of aggression. The more threatening the issue, the more likely it is that the Security Council will be involved.

Some of these semantic differences are not now of great importance, but parties to a 'dispute' must abstain from voting on substantive proposals under Chapter VI or Article 52(3) in the Security Council (Article 27(3)), and measures under Chapter VII can be taken only if international peace is seriously endangered. In this book we use the full Charter expression 'the maintenance of international peace and security' only when a shorter expression might cause confusion; in other cases, we do not hesitate to use more crisp language such as 'Members look especially to the Security Council to preserve world peace', whereas the full language of the Charter is 'Members confer on the Security Council primary responsibility for the maintenance of international peace and security' (Article 24(1)).

2. THE CHARTER

All constitutions are imperfect, but some are more imperfect than others. The UN Charter is based on some assumptions in 1945 which are not valid over fifty years later. As a former Secretary-General has put it,

> some of the assumptions on which the United Nations was based have proved unfounded . . . The Organization has, for example, proved to be of limited value as an instrument of collective security . . . The idea of maintaining peace and security in the world through a concert of great Powers . . . would seem to belong to the nineteenth rather than to the twentieth century.[4]

Other Secretaries-General have said much the same thing.[5]

This imperfect UN Charter contains contradictions, such as its assertion of the equality of States (Article 2(1)) while at the same time having conferred on five Members the right to veto substantive proposals in the Security Council and amendments to the Charter (Articles 27(3) and 108), as well as originally giving one State three seats in the General Assembly (the Soviet Union and the Byelorussian and Ukrainian Soviet Socialist Republics); or the ban on intervening in matters which are essentially within the domestic jurisdiction of any State (Article 2(7)) while at the same time requiring Members to take joint action to achieve universal observance of human rights and fundamental freedoms for all (Articles 55–6). There are expressions in the Charter which are ambiguous or the meaning of which is not absolutely clear, such as 'expenses of the Organization' in Article 17(2), or the relationship between Articles 25 and 49 regarding the unconditional obligation of UN Members to implement resolutions of the Security Council. Some provisions of the Charter, such as the references to 'any state which during the Second World War [had] been an enemy of any signatory of the present Charter' (Articles 53, 77, and 107) are now clearly out of date, and on 15 December 1995 the General Assembly accepted a recommendation from the Special Committee on the Charter to delete the relevant 'enemy State clauses' at its earliest appropriate future session.[6]

There have been some *de facto* amendments to the Charter, such as the interpretation of Article 12(1) so as to permit the General Assembly to make recommendations about matters of which the Security Council is seized; or the practice whereby an abstention by a permanent member in the Security Council on a substantive proposal is not regarded as a veto, which would appear on the face of it to be inconsistent with the natural meaning and intention of Article 27(3).

It is, however, the only UN Charter we have, and none of the Members which have the right to veto proposals to amend the Charter (Article 108) has given much encouragement to the idea that major amendments are at present (1997) feasible. The challenge, then, is to use whatever flexibility the Charter allows so as to adapt the Organization to a world which differs greatly from that of 1942–5, when statesmen were taking their minds momentarily off the prosecution of war in order to cope with the hazards of world politics once victory had been achieved. The fault (and the United Nations has more than its share of faults) is not primarily in the Charter: Charles Yost, a US ambassador of vast experience and wise judgement, exonerated the Charter and blamed the Members. 'I do not think the fault really lies primarily in the Charter. I think it lies in the policies of the various governments.'[7]

Whether or not one is now disenchanted with the United Nations depends to a large extent on how enchanted one was in the first place. Robert E. Riggs conducted a rigorous examination of whether the United Nations was 'oversold' in the United States, and he found that a close examination of statements by US supporters of the United Nations in the early days 'belies the allegation that the campaign was based on unrealistic promises of a brave new world'.[8] Our own examination of public governmental statements in the UK, as well as the published documents on US Foreign Relations for 1946 to 1960, point in the same direction. In March 1946, Adlai Stevenson wrote:

> The atmosphere of the General Assembly . . . was one of sobriety, of relentless realism, in marked contrast with the boundless optimism that prevailed after the last war, at the time of the League's birth . . . There were no illusions, no slap-happy optimism. There was just sober restraint, not melancholy pessimism. On balance, I think it was generally agreed . . . that the

startling candor and vigor of the debates in the Security Council was wholesome.[9]

At private meetings of the five permanent members of the Security Council later in 1946, British Foreign Minister Ernest Bevin said bluntly that something must be done to increase confidence in the United Nations 'as, quite frankly, we haven't much confidence now'; Paul-Henri Spaak of Belgium noted that 'the atmosphere . . . fell far short of our hopes'; and US Senator Warren Austin told a meeting of the US delegation that an effort was needed 'to revive the spirit of our people with regard to the United Nations'.[10] A year later, a US State Department official was expressing 'serious concern . . . as to whether the Organization will survive'.

It was those with less information or less experience or less contact with the realities of the embryonic Organization who were most bemused in the early days and who soon either abandoned their faith in or support for an Organization which had proved such a bitter disappointment to them, or who were wilfully blind to its palpable defects and failures. The fact is that peace is a process to engage in, not a goal to be reached.[11]

We have noted how the Cold War intruded itself into the work of the Security Council almost from the word 'go', but it is interesting that the one thing on which the major powers were agreed was that the Charter must be upheld. This did not guarantee that they agreed on what the Charter meant or intended. 'When we are translating paper documents into living institutions,' said Philip Noel-Baker of Britain three weeks after the Council had begun work, 'difficulties in interpretation and procedure must inevitably arise.'[12]

One of us has remarked elsewhere that most diplomats enjoy arguing about procedure, for a time at least, because it is the one subject on which they are without instructions from headquarters and are on their own, as it were. Once a UN organ becomes involved in a procedural discussion, representatives are able to freewheel.

One can sense the atmosphere of liberation which sweeps over a meeting [one of us has written] when debate on the substance of a question is temporarily put aside so that some knotty procedural point can be resolved. One observes representatives closing their folders of papers and lighting cigarettes so as to deal in a thoroughly relaxed and level-headed way with a matter which requires initiative, tact, and imagination rather than fidelity to official instructions.[13]

[M]any delegates welcomed debates on procedure [a Canadian diplomat has written] since these debates gave them opportunities to display their debating talents on issues which they considered themselves to be expert. It was for them a relief from questions of substance.[14]

Resolving procedural questions can be very time-consuming, but 'sometimes procedure is more important than time, especially when you are creating precedents'.[15]

Not that the distinction between procedure and substance is always clear and unambiguous.[16] If it were, Article 27(3) of the Charter would doubtless read 'Decisions of the Security Council on substantive matters shall be made . . .', and the problem of the double veto would never have arisen. Canada pointed out in 1973 that 'procedural problems cannot be pursued very far before they encounter political and substantive difficulties'.[17]

3. THE RULES OF PROCEDURE[18]

The Executive Committee of the Preparatory Commission had prepared a first draft of thirty-four rules of procedure, plus nine supplementary rules on the conduct of debate which had the support of a majority of the Committee but not the requisite two-thirds majority. There had been a division of opinion in the Committee, some members believing that 'the Council would have mainly to operate in the light of its own day-to-day experience and of certain guiding principles', while others favoured 'a complete set of rules of procedure and other detailed guidance'. Neither school of thought prevailed, and the rules drafted by the Committee were a 'not entirely satisfactory' compromise.

The Committee reported that the draft rule to the effect that the President would represent the Council 'in its corporate capacity' was intended to allow the President 'to nominate committees and to conclude agreements on behalf of the Council'. The presidency was 'deemed to attach to the member state concerned and not to the person of its representative'. In special circumstances, the President should be able to cede his office to 'the representative whose State is next in the alphabetical line of succession', a matter which is now covered by Rule 20. Australia reserved the right to reopen the discussion of the method of selecting the President, and France thought that rotating the presidency in French alphabetical order, or even drawing lots, would be preferable to using English alphabetical order. Yugoslavia considered that applicants for UN membership should indicate the constitutional organ which would have to consent to ratification of the Charter.[19]

The Preparatory Commission dropped most of the rules on languages drafted by its Executive Committee (now Rules 41 to 47) and one rule about verbatim records, as well as the proposed rules for the conduct of debate,[20] and then got completely bogged down in the question of whether a rule providing for private (closed) meetings of the Security Council was or was not a reversion to the discredited idea of secret diplomacy. As so often happens in matters of this kind, the positions became more extreme, even more absurd, the more trivial the issue and the longer the debate continued.

The matter was first raised by Syria, which considered that all UN Members should have the right to be acquainted with the Council's proceedings. The proposal that the Council could meet in private was 'unconstitutional and contrary to the provisions of the Charter'. Cuba insisted that 'the United Nations should have no secret documents', adding the curious suggestion that the Council might well be permitted to reach private *decisions* so long as the *debates* which preceded those decisions were open. Another member, unidentified in the summary record, said that the whole purpose of the United Nations was to minimize secret diplomacy: States making honest and sincere decisions had no reason to be afraid of publicity. Another unidentified member said, with doubtful relevance, that if enemy States were to be admitted to UN membership, it was important that they should not have equal status with the others.

Britain was surprised at the fuss over 'a routine article of rather minor importance'. The Soviet Union said that there was no implication of secret diplomacy in the draft rule, adding that if a member of the Council should choose not to attend a Council meeting which was private, it should clearly have the right to see the record. Norway thought that if the Council could not hold closed meetings, informal meetings would be held, and this would tend to even greater secrecy.

This issue of 'transparency' was to come to the fore in discussions on Council procedure some fifty years later, and we address these debates in detail later.

The Preparatory Commission appended a summary of its somewhat heated debates to the draft rules.[21] These rules were then adopted on a provisional basis at the first meeting of the Council, and a Committee of Experts consisting of all members of the Council was asked to review the draft rules.[22]

Within three weeks, the Committee had done as it was asked. Many draft rules were revised, one (no. 23) was divided into two (becoming nos. 32 and 36), and fourteen new rules were added: one (no. 2) stated the right of the President to call a meeting of the Council at the request of any member; four (nos. 9–12) dealt with representation and credentials; two (nos. 37–8) required the President to approve and sign the records of meetings; and the rules about languages which had been proposed by the Executive Committee but dropped by the Preparatory Commission itself (nos. 18–25) were revised along lines decided upon by the First Committee of the General Assembly and reinstated (nos. 22–9).[23]

The rules thus revised were issued on 5 February 1946, but the Council was too preoccupied with substantive business to examine the draft with the necessary care. On 18 March, the Secretariat issued a working paper drawing attention to a number of new procedural problems which had arisen,[24] as a result of which the Committee of Experts prepared a fresh draft. Two rules relating to the languages of summary records (nos. 26 and 27) were dropped, twenty-seven rules were retained unchanged or with only minor textual amendments, eleven rules were considerably revised, nineteen further rules were added (twelve of them dealing with the conduct of business and being very much like the rules originally considered by the Executive Committee of the Preparatory Commission); and an annex was added setting out a procedure for dealing with communications from non-governmental organizations. On 9 April, the Council turned its attention to the first twenty-three of the new draft rules as well as the proposed annex.

The debate was surprisingly low-keyed. The Committee of Experts had been unable to agree how often there should be high-level 'periodic' meetings under Article 28(2) of the Charter (Rule 4), and the

Council decided that the number should be two a year. The chairman of the Committee of Experts was asked to clarify the difference between the Council's agenda and the matters of which it was seized, and the word 'also' was inserted in the last sentence of Rule 12. In Rule 13 on credentials, 'Prime Minister' was changed to 'Head of Government'.[25]

The Committee of Experts then encountered serious difficulties over the rule or rules about voting. The rule on voting provisionally approved in February (rule 30, now Rule 40) had read:

Voting in the Security Council shall be in accordance with the relevant Articles of the Charter and of the Statute of the International Court of Justice.

The Soviet Union wanted a more precise rule for applying Article 27(3) of the Charter, which deals with the veto and the obligation of parties to a dispute to abstain from voting. The Soviet Union proposed that:

1. a distinction should be made between a dispute within the scope of Article 33 'the continuance of which is likely to endanger the maintenance of international peace and security', and disputes and situations under Article 34 or other Articles of the Charter;
2. the veto should apply when the Council had to decide (a) whether a question was procedural or substantive, (b) whether the question was a dispute or a situation, and (c) in the event that it was a dispute, whether or not it was 'of the nature referred to in Article 33 of the Charter', in which case a party would have to abstain from voting.

This proposal caused consternation in Washington, and the US representative on the Committee of Experts was instructed to stall. On 13 April, the US delegation received from Washington the text of three draft rules on voting 'to promote discussion' but not representing a firm US position. The debate continued in the Committee of Experts until 25 April. On 13 May, the Committee reported that 'certain members' took the view that the rules should contain 'detailed provisions covering both the mechanics of the vote and the majorities by which the various decisions of the Council should be taken'. The Committee recommended to the Council that the provisional rule should be retained for the time being, pending further study. This further study is still pending (1997), because the matter was soon submerged by the General Assembly's concern about the veto. John Ross, Alger Hiss's deputy in the State Department, was later to comment that the United States had perhaps been indulging in 'a large amount of shadow-boxing with the technicalities of rules of procedure without having first formulated our broad policies with regard to the veto'. [26]

The Council considered the remaining thirty-seven rules at four further meetings between 16 May and 24 June. Britain proposed, and the Council agreed, to bring the wording of draft rule 25 (now Rule 28) into line with draft rule 26 (now Rule 29). Following proposals of the Netherlands, Poland, the United Kingdom, and China, the last five words of present Rule 32 were added. The United Kingdom wanted to know the difference between substantive motions, principal motions, proposed resolutions, and draft resolutions in draft rules 28 and 29 (present Rules 31 and 32), and was given contradictory explanations. Two new rules were adopted on the rights of the Secretary-General (now Rules 22 and 23) and one on the cession of the presidency (now Rule 20). The United States expressed a wish to have a rule providing for the closure of debate, and Australia repeated the objections to holding private (closed) meetings of the Council. Australia also made an impassioned speech about the procedure for admitting new Members, arguing that 'the General Assembly is the only body which . . . can make the final and binding decisions on the subject of admission'; but an Australian proposal to defer the adoption of rules 55–7 (now Rules 58–60) was defeated by ten votes to one.[27] After five months' work, the Council had adopted sixty Provisional Rules of Procedure and a short Appendix, and these were issued shortly thereafter under the symbol S/96.

> Because of obstruction by the Soviet Union and the United States, supported fitfully by the other permanent members of the Security Council—Britain, France and China—we were able to produce only curtailed and unsatisfactory provisional rules of procedure . . . The failure of the Preparatory Commission to recommend clear and precise draft rules of procedure for the Security Council was unfortunate . . .[28]

Only minor changes in the Rules have been made since 1946. A new Rule (61) was added in 1947 in the hope that this would clarify the

TABLE 1

The evolution of the Rules of Procedure

Draft of Executive Committee of Preparatory Commission, PC/EX/113/REV. 1, 12 Nov. 1945: rule no.	Draft of Preparatory Commission, PC/20, 23 Dec. 1945 (also issued as SCOR, 1st year, 1st series, Supplement no. 1, pp. 3–6, S/28): rule no.	First revision by Committee of Experts, SCOR, 1st year, 1st series, Supplement no. 2, pp. 3–8, S/6, 5 Feb. 1946: rule no.	Second revision by Committee of Experts, SCOR, 1st year, 1st series, 31st meeting (9 April 1946), pp. 103–18, S/29, and Supplement no. 2, pp. 25–30, S/57 (13 May 1946): rule no.	Further revisions by the Committee of Experts, SCOR, 1st year, 1st series, Supplement no. 20, pp. 40, 42–3, S/71, S/88: rule no.	Present rule adopted, SCOR, meeting and page or para. no.	Present Rule no.
1	1	1	1		31, pp. 103–7	1
		2	2		31, pp. 103–7	2
3, 15	3, 15	3	3		31, pp. 103–7	3
2	2	5	4		31, pp. 103–7	4
			5		21, pp. 103–7	5
			6		31, pp. 108–11	6
4	4	7	7		31, pp. 108–11	7
5	5	4	8		31, pp. 108–11	8
8	8	8	9		31, pp. 108–11	9
			10		31, pp. 108–11	10
			11		31, pp. 108–11	11
6, 7	6, 7	6	12		31, pp. 108–11	12
		9	13		468, pp. 9–11	13
			14		31, pp. 111–15	14
		10	15		31, pp. 111–15	15
		11	16		31, pp. 111–15	16
		12	17		31, pp. 111–15	17
9	9	13	18		31, pp. 115–16	18
10	10	14	19		31, pp. 115–16	19
				20	48, p. 382	20
11	11	15	20		44, pp. 310–11	21
				21		22
				22	44, pp. 310–11	23
12	12	16	21		31, p. 116	24

13	13	17	22	31, p. 116	25
14	14	18	23	31, p. 116	26
A			24	41, pp. 254–60	27
B			25	41, pp. 254–60	28
			26	41, pp. 254–60	29
C			27	41, pp. 254–60	30
D			28	41, pp. 254–60	31
E			29	41, pp. 254–60	32
			30	41, pp. 254–60	33
			31	41, pp. 254–60	34
			32	41, pp. 254–60	35
F, H			33	41, pp. 254–60	36
			34	41, pp. 254–60	37
			35	41, pp. 254–60	38
I	17	20	36	41, pp. 254–60	39
26	19	30	37	41, pp. 260–1	40
17	18	21	38	{ Res. 263 (1969), 345	41
18		22	39	(1974), 528 (1982)	42
19		23	40	deleted	43
20		24	41	1761, para. 140	44
22		25	42	1761, para. 140	45
24		28	43	1761, para. 140	46
21, 25		29	44	1761, para. 140	47
16, 27	16, 20	19, 31	45	41, p. 261	48
30	23	{ 32	46	1761, para. 140	49
		36	47	41, p. 261	50
31	24	35	48	41, p. 261	51
		37	49	41, p. 261	52
		36, 38	50	41, p. 261	53
29	22	33	51	41, p. 261	54
28	21	34	52	41, p. 261	55
			55	41, p. 261	56
			54	41, p. 261	57
32	25	39	55	222, p. 2771	58
33	26	40 }	{ 56	42, p. 278	59
34	27	41 }	57	222, p. 2771	60
				138, pp. 949–52	61
			Annex A	31, pp. 117–18	Appendix

procedure for electing members of the International Court of Justice, and Rules 58 and 60 concerning the admission of new Members were also revised in 1947.[29] Rule 13 regarding credentials was revised in 1950 following disagreements about the seating of China.[30] Russian and Spanish were added to the Council's working languages in 1969, Chinese in 1974, and Arabic in 1982.[31] The Rules thus amended are now issued under the symbol S/96/Rev. 7.

The Rules are still only provisional, but it would be tedious to remind the reader of this fact every time one of the Rules is cited. We have therefore often omitted 'Provisional', and refer to particular Rules parenthetically.

The Charter refers to 'members of the Security Council'. Some of the Rules of Procedure do the same, especially where the Rule is based on a provision of the Charter and also in connection with the rotation of the presidency in the alphabetical order of members (Rules 2, 5, 12–14, 18, 20, 37, 59): in other Rules, the words 'representative(s) on' are used rather than 'member(s) of' (Rules 8, 11, 15–17, 27, 30–2, 34, 35, 44–6, 49, 50, 52, 59, and Appendix).

There are thus three ways in which one can refer to the people who comprise the Council. One can use the name of the State—Afghanistan, say, or Zambia; one can write each time 'the representative of Afghanistan' or 'the representative of Zambia'; or one can be even more personal and refer to 'ambassador Zarif' or 'ambassador Lusaka'. We have not tried to follow a consistent usage in this book.

An understanding of the Rules of Procedure and the accepted practice of the Council is an important diplomatic asset. In April 1982, the Council was debating the dangerous situation in the Falkland Islands (Islas Malvinas) following the invasion by Argentina and the British decision to dispatch a modern armada to the South Atlantic to liberate the occupied terrritory. The Council was convened at the request of the United Kingdom, and the UK submitted a draft resolution that would have demanded the immediate withdrawal of all Argentine forces. The Argentine representative maintained that the United Kingdom, as a party to the dispute, should not be allowed to vote on its own draft resolution as, according to Article 27(3) of the Charter, parties to a dispute shall abstain from voting. Sir Anthony Parsons, the British ambassador, immediately took the floor to explain that his draft resolution was not submitted under Chapter VI, but was a provisional measure under Article 40.

During the course of the meeting the proceedings were suspended for one hour and five minutes, ostensibly so that 'Islas Malvinas' could be added to 'the Falkland Islands' in the British text. That hour and five minutes could, of course, be used for a variety of purposes: to make the text more accurate or less offensive to one of the parties, to get in touch with one's capital for further instructions, to exercise persuasive powers with colleagues, to argue with the President about procedure, to have a drink. Later in the meeting, the revised British text was put to the vote and approved.[32]

4. CUSTOM

Any committee or similar body soon begins to adopt habits, and in due course habits become customs, and customs become traditions, traditions become rules, and rules become law.

Nowhere in the Charter or the Provisional Rules of Procedure is it decreed that the Secretary-General shall sit at the right of the President at Council meetings.

Nowhere is it stipulated that the President shall, or indeed shall not, thank the President for the previous month for discharging his or her responsibilities in so exemplary a manner.

There is no Rule which states where a non-member of the Council invited to participate in the discussion of any matter shall be seated. There is not even a Rule requiring members of the Council to refrain from physically assaulting one another: the Charter prohibition of the threat or use of force applies only if the victim is a State (Article 2(4)).

There are, to be sure, general customs governing the conduct of diplomatic business, and there are special customs dealing with conference diplomacy. Much of the practice of the Security Council is based on custom, some of it so deeply rooted and generally respected as to virtually have the force of law. But just as statute law can be changed by constitutional means, so can custom so long as those affected agree to, or at least acquiesce in, the change. Sometimes a change is accepted implicitly rather than explicitly, as when the Council during the course of 1972 gave up what had been the almost invariable practice of consecutive interpretation of speeches into all the working languages.

The procedure and practice of the Council has continued to evolve since the first edition of this book went to press twenty-three years ago, particularly regarding the increased use of informal consultation before an open meeting is convened. Much of the record of day-to-day procedural practice in the Council is now obscured as substantive debate occurs behind closed doors. Much that was written about the veto when it was a Soviet instrument reads quaintly in an era when the veto is rarely overtly used. Aspects of the Council's procedure and practice which now seem sacrosanct will no doubt change in the years ahead.

A living institution is always in course of development. We have tried in this book to examine the procedure and practice of the Security Council as it was at a particular point in time: 1 January 1997. It would be astonishing if the Council were to have stopped evolving on that date. This, therefore, is a provisional book about an organ of the United Nations which still conducts its work according to Provisional Rules of Procedure. Perhaps *Il n'y a que le provisoire qui dure*.

5. FUNCTIONS

It is convenient to envisage the functions of the Security Council in three main groups as laid down in the Charter: recommendations to the parties to a dispute, recommendations to the General Assembly, and mandatory (binding) decisions.

Recommendations to the parties: The Security Council '*shall*, when it deems necessary, call upon the parties' to a dispute to settle it by peaceful means (Article 33(2)); it *may*, in order to prevent an aggravation of the situation, call upon the parties to a dispute to comply with such provisional measures as it deems necessary or desirable (Article 40); it *may*, at any stage of a dispute or a situation of like nature, recommend appropriate procedures or methods of adjustment (Article 36(1) or such terms of settlement as it *may* consider appropriate (Article 37(2)) or, if all the parties to any dispute so request, make recommendations to the parties with a view to pacific settlement (Article 38). It '*shall* encourage the development of pacific settlement of local disputes' through regional arrangements or agencies (Article 52(3)). It *shall* be kept fully informed about activities undertaken or in contemplation by States under regional arrangements (Article 54). It *may* make recommendations or decide on measures not involving the use of armed force (Articles 39 and 41) or decide on such military action as may be necessary to maintain or restore international peace and security (Articles 39 and 42).

Recommendations to the General Assembly: The Security Council *may* make recommendations to the General Assembly about the admission, suspension, or expulsion of Members (Articles 4 to 6), about the appointment of the Secretary-General (Article 97), about the election of members of the International Court of Justice (Article 4.3 of the Statute of the Court), about amendments to the Statute of the Court (Article 69 of the Statute), about compliance with judgments of the Court (Article 94(2)), and about the terms on which a State which is not a Member of the United Nations may become a party to the Statute of the Court.

Mandatory (binding) decisions: As the Security Council acts on behalf of all UN Members when it is carrying out its duties for the maintenance of international peace and security (Article 24(1)), it follows that UN Members should accept and carry out the Council's decisions in accordance with the Charter (Article 25). They should give 'every assistance' in any action the Council takes 'in accordance with the . . . Charter' (a positive obligation) 'and shall refrain from giving assistance to any State against which the United Nations is taking preventive or enforcement action' (a negative obligation) (Article 2(5)). This is one of the basic principles on which the Organization is based; it is to be found in the introductory Chapter of the Charter and is reinforced by an article in Chapter VII which states that UN Members 'shall' join in affording mutual assistance in carrying out the measures decided upon by the Security Council (Article 49).

When the Council wishes to take a mandatory (binding) decision, it may not be strictly necessary to cite any of the three relevant

Articles (Articles 2(5), 25, and 49), but the practice has been to refer to or to cite Chapter VII or to use its precise language in the resolution, and failure to cite Chapter VII may cast doubts on whether or not the Council intends the decision to be binding on UN Members. The *Repertoire,* with appropriate delicacy, comments that resolution 246 (S/8429) on Namibia 'might be considered as containing an implied reference to Article 49',[33] though we would take leave to question this implication since the reference to 'effective steps or measures in conformity with the relevant provisions of the Charter' is only a conditional threat.

The arrangements for the use of force provided for in the Charter cannot be utilized as the founders envisaged, as there have not been concluded agreements under Article 43 for making armed forces and facilities available to the Security Council. In the absence of such agreements, the Security Council has resorted to *ad hoc* expedients on each occasion. The details of UN peace-keeping operations carried out under Chapter VII of the Charter, and enforcement action authorized by the Council but carried out by Member States are to be found in Chapter 7.

CHAPTER 2

THE COUNCIL MEETS

> Most men in handling public affairs pay more attention to what they themselves say than what is said to them . . . Menaces always do harm to negotiations, and they frequently push one party to extremities to which they would not have resorted without provocation.

1. FORMAL MEETINGS AND INFORMAL CONSULTATIONS

There are two kinds of meetings of the Security Council:

(a) Public meetings. These are usually held in the Security Council Chamber at the UN building in New York, unless the Council has taken a decision to meet in another conference room or away from Headquarters. These meetings are held in public, invariably with the world's media in attendance, and States that are not members of the Council can request permission to participate without the right to vote.

(b) Private meetings. These are also usually held in the Security Council Chamber, but are not open to the public, or the media. The Council always meets in private (often referred to as a 'closed' meeting) to discuss its recommendation on the appointment of the UN Secretary-General, and invariably until 1993 its draft annual report to the General Assembly. The Council has held occasional private meetings to address other issues. Official records are kept of private meetings, but the Council may decide that only one copy of the verbatim record is made by the Secretariat, and kept by the Secretary-General, to be viewed only by those who attended the meeting, and others given specific permission. Whatever is decided on the issuing of a verbatim record, an official *communiqué* is always issued by the Secretary-General after the close of the meeting. On some occasions the Council has published a verbatim record of a private meeting, in addition to a communiqué. There are no provisions in the Rules of Procedure of the Council for non-members to request permission to attend private meetings.

In addition, there are 'informal consultations'. There has been some argument over the status of informal consultations, and whether they may properly be described as 'meetings' of the Council, but their existence *per se* is not in doubt. They are in fact 'meetings of Council members'. In this book we distinguish between 'consultations of the whole' and a variety of other consultations involving a sub-set of the Council's membership. No official record is kept of informal consultations, but Council members have developed a number of methods by which information about such consultations is communicated to non-members and to the public. Informal consultations are considered in detail later in this chapter.

2. CONVENING A MEETING

Members of the United Nations, by virtue of Article 24(1) of the Charter, have conferred on the Security Council primary responsibility for the maintenance of international peace and security and have agreed that, in carrying out this responsibility, the Council 'acts on their behalf'. The Security Council, thus, does not act simply on behalf of its fifteen (originally eleven) members; it acts for the whole membership of the United Nations. Moreover, all UN Members have agreed 'to accept and carry out the decisions of the Security Council in accordance with the . . . Charter' (Article 25). If peace is threatened or breached, or if an act of aggression occurs, UN Members *shall* (not 'may') join in affording mutual assistance in carrying out the measures decided upon by the Council (Article 49). That, at any rate, is what the Charter says.

In order to discharge its primary responsibility for international peace and security, the Council must be ready to meet at short notice—or, to use the words of the Charter, 'shall be so organized as to be able to function continuously'. All members of the Council must be represented at all times at the seat of the Organization (Article 28(1)), that is to say, New York, and it is this requirement which first led to the establishment of permanent diplomatic missions at the Headquarters of the United Nations.[1]

The responsibility for convening a public meeting of the Council is laid upon the President for the time being (Rules 1–3), the presidency rotating monthly in English alphabetical order of the Council's members (Rule 18). The formal procedure for calling meetings is laid down in the Rules of Procedure, but in practice the President's decisions are virtually always taken after informal consultations. The decision to hold informal consultations of the whole, in which much of the substantive work of the Council is now prepared, is also taken by the President, after consultation with Council members. Except when time does not permit doing so due to unforeseen developments, the date, time, and proposed programme for such consultations of the whole are listed in the UN *Journal*. It is usually during such consultations of the whole that the Council members decide whether and when to hold a public or private meeting, and approve a draft provisional agenda for such a meeting. The Rules provide that ordinary meetings of the Council shall be held at any time deemed necessary by the President, 'but the interval between meetings shall not exceed fourteen days' (Rule 1). The *Repertoire* of Security Council practice states that when no particular item on the Council's agenda requires immediate consideration, it has become customary for the President to consult representatives regarding the waiver of the fourteen-day requirement.[2] We know of only one case which, by implication, challenged the practice of regularly waiving the fourteen-day requirement. The matter at issue concerned the appointment of a Governor for Trieste, a matter which had been placed on the agenda of the Security Council on 20 June 1947, two years previously. Yakov Malik of the Soviet Union pointed out that it was 'more than a month now' since the Council had met. The Soviet representative did not expressly cite the fourteen-day Rule, but rather the Charter requirement that the Council should be in a position to function continuously. The Egyptian President for the previous month stated that he had been in constant touch with the Council's members and that no one had asked for a meeting. As for continuous functioning, the Egyptian representative added sardonically, 'I imagine that no one assumes that we sit here day and night.'[3] The Soviet representative did not press his point.

2. *The Council Meets*

Rule 1 states that the President calls a meeting of the Council 'at any time he deems necessary'. Rules 2 and 3 state that he 'shall' call a meeting:

1. At the request of any member of the Council (Rule 2);
2. If the General Assembly makes recommendations to the Council or refers to it any question relating to the maintenance of international peace and security under Article 11(2) of the Charter (Rule 3);
3. If the Secretary-General brings to the attention of the Council any matter which in his opinion may threaten the maintenance of international peace and security, under Article 99 of the Charter (Rule 3);
4. If a dispute or situation is brought to the attention of the Council under Article 35 of the Charter (disputes, or situations which might lead to international friction or give rise to disputes) or Article 11(3) of the Charter (situations which are likely to endanger international peace and security) (Rule 3).

If the matter were not serious, one might think that Rules 1 to 3 had been deliberately drafted so as to give rise to misunderstanding and confusion. Does Rule 1 empower the President to call a meeting of the Council simply when the fancy takes him, or only when he deems that one of the requirements of Rules 2 and 3 have been met? If there were only Rule 1 to go by, it might be argued that complete discretion to call meetings had been conferred on the President. Were Rules 2 and 3 added, then, to limit or to extend the President's discretion? If the second interpretation is accepted, does that mean that if any of the requirements are met, the President *must* call a meeting, even if he deems such an action to be unnecessary or even dangerous? Are there any contingencies not covered by Rules 2 and 3 which would fall within the scope of Rule 1? Is the crux of Rule 1 the words 'at any *time*' (our italics), so that the discretion granted to the President relates only to the precise timing of the meeting?

All this may seem typical UN niggling; and so it is. But lack of clarity about Rules 1 to 3 provides a convenient device for filibustering if a Council member has not yet received instructions from his capital, or if he wishes to delay Security Council debate and decision until anticipated events have become *faits accomplis*.

In an emergency, the President sometimes convenes a meeting even if he has not been able to consult all the members, and if the emergency is real, this normally gives rise to no difficulty.[4] But if a member, or indeed the President himself, wishes for substantive political reasons to have a meeting of the Council either sooner or later than other members desire, the Council can be prevented from getting down to business by a discussion regarding the President's discretion and, in particular, the relationship between Rule 1 and Rules 2 and 3.

In September 1959, Italy was the President for the month, and received from Secretary-General Hammarskjold a request to 'convene urgently' a meeting of the Council to consider Hammarskjold's report on a request for the dispatch to Laos of 'an emergency force . . . to halt an aggression'. Hammarskjold had deliberately not cited in his request Article 99 of the Charter, which empowers the Secretary-General to bring to the attention of the Council any matter which in his opinion may threaten the maintenance of international peace and security. The President convened a meeting, claiming to be acting under the discretionary Rule 1.

The Soviet representative had apparently been kept in the dark as to the full purpose of the meeting, and probably did not know that his attempt to exercise a double veto was about to be thwarted by a presidential ruling. Be that as it may, the Soviet representative took the first opportunity to challenge what he called 'a number of irregularities' in the convening of the meeting.

It is quite obvious that it is not rule 1 of the Council's rules of procedure that is applicable in the present case, but rules 2 and 3.

The President replied that his decision was based on the rule which 'gives to the President of the Security Council complete discretion in calling meetings at any time he deems necessary'.[5] The Soviet representative did not persist in his objection, and the matter was allowed to lapse.

A similar situation arose in 1965, when the President (the United States) called a meeting to consider the fighting which had broken out between India and Pakistan in Kashmir. The President distinguished between the practice of the Council and the Rules of Procedure. There had, he said, been 'extensive consultations', and he had been in touch personally with 'most' members of the Council. In view of the urgency of the situation, and simply citing Rules 1 to 3, he had felt justified in calling a meeting. The Soviet representative, as in 1959, challenged the attempt to separate Rule 1 from Rules 2 and 3. Before a meeting could be called, he said, there had to be a specific request as provided in Rules 2 and 3; 'meetings of the Council cannot be called as it were "anonymously".' There followed an inconclusive discussion, but there was a general wish to proceed with the business of the Council, and the Soviet representative did not persist with his objection.[6]

The practice of the Council, as the President hinted in September 1965, is clearer than the wording of the Rules of Procedure. If the Council has not itself decided on the date and time of its next meeting, an agreed decision is usually reached, on the initiative of the President for the month, by informal consultation among the members of the Council. If agreement by this means is not possible, the President acts in accordance with the wishes of the majority and, in any public reference to his decision, uses some such wording as that he has met the wishes of 'some members' or 'most members' of the Council.[7] Often in such cases the minority is not unconditionally opposed to the calling of a meeting, but is in favour of its being held later or earlier than the time favoured by the majority.

Two other types of difficulty can theoretically arise. The first would be if a non-member of the Council were to desire a meeting to consider a matter not qualifying as a dispute or situation under Articles 11(3) or 35 of the Charter, and if no member of the Council, nor the Secretary-General, were to request a meeting to consider the matter, and if the President for the month did not deem it necessary to convene a meeting under his discretionary powers (Rule 1). It is, however, difficult to imagine such a situation arising: some means would surely be found to call a meeting, even if in the end the Council should not place the matter on its agenda—as, indeed, happened in the case of Ireland's request in 1969 for an urgent meeting of the Council in connection with 'the situation in the six counties of Northern Ireland'.[8]

The other kind of difficulty would arise if one or more members of the Council were to consider that there has been an unreasonable delay in convening a meeting. The Australian representative made such a charge in 1948 in connection with the Indonesian question, but the response of the President (Belgium) suggested that the charge could not be substantiated.[9]

A more serious case arose in 1966 when a new member of the Council, Ambassador Keita of Mali, was President for the month of April. At 10 a.m. on 7 April 1966, the United Kingdom requested an urgent meeting to consider the question of Rhodesia and, in particular, the possibility that the tanker *Joanna V* might try to discharge oil at Beira in Mozambique for transmission to Southern Rhodesia, contrary to the Council's sanctions policy. A majority of the Council's members were prepared to meet that day and, indeed, assembled in the Council chamber. The representative of Mali, who alone could call a meeting of the Council, could not be found, although there was reason to think that he was closeted with some of his colleagues from the African Group. Members of the Council were notified that the Council would meet at 5 p.m., but later, without consultation, were told that the meeting had been cancelled. A confused situation then ensued, and some members of the Council were under the impression that the meeting had been reinstated. At 7.20 p.m., eight members of the Council requested Secretary-General Thant to inform the ambassador of Mali 'formally and urgently' that they were holding themselves ready to meet, and two other members of the Council had separately informed U Thant that they agreed that a meeting of the Council should be held that day. More than forty-eight hours were in fact to elapse between the request for an emergency meeting and the actual opening of the meeting (which, as it happened, was on Easter Saturday).

The representative of New Zealand described the situation as follows:

> Under Rule 2, the President is obliged to call a meeting at the request of any Council member. The obligation is mandatory, not permissive. The one element of discretion given to the President is the precise timing.
>
> In this instance . . . a request was made for the Council to meet urgently on Thursday afternoon . . . Almost all members of the Council were willing to meet at the time requested. They were unable to do so despite repeated efforts and the assistance, at the request of a majority of Council members, of the Secretary-General. Yet a meeting was fixed much later for another time upon which most members . . . were not consulted at all.

The explanation given by the ambassador of Mali and his supporters was unconvincing. The representative of Uganda, for example, referring to the Charter requirement that the Security Council should be so organized as to function continuously, had this to say:

> The word 'continuously' . . . does not really mean 'continuously' in the usual sense. The Security Council does not sit or function without stop: it does stop from time to time.

The Soviet representative simply said that the representative of Mali had acted 'absolutely correctly and effectively, in full conformity with the rules of procedure and in observance of all necessary standards'. The representative of Mali, in a telephone message to an official in the UN Secretariat, the substance of which was circulated as an official document of the Security Council, said he was following 'the customary procedure by engaging in consultations', that he hoped to conclude these the following day (Good Friday), and that he would then 'announce a time and date for the Security Council meeting'.[10]

This unhappy, and unprecedented, incident led to a sharp exchange of written communications between the United States and Mali.'[11]

In a letter dated 21 April 1966 the United States representative wrote to the President of the Council expressing his government's view that Rule 2 of the Provisional Rules of Procedure was mandatory and did not give the President the choice of convening or not convening the Council when a member so requested. The United States requested that its letter to the President of the Council be incorporated in the next edition of the official *Repertoire* of Security Council practice.[12] In its letter the US stated:

1. The Security Council is given primary responsibility for the maintenance of international peace and security, according to Article 24 of the United Nations Charter, 'in order to ensure prompt and effective action'. It is required by Article 28 to be 'so organized as to be able to function continuously'. These two articles established the responsibility of the Council to be available for emergency action to maintain peace and security. The provisional rules of procedure of the Security Council are designed and must be interpreted so as to ensure that the Council can fulfil the responsibilities these Articles place upon it.
2. The dominant paragraph of the provisional rules of procedure of the Security Council accordingly is rule 2, which states that 'The President

shall call a meeting of the Security Council at the request of any member of the Security Council'. This ruling is mandatory and does not give the President the choice of convening or not convening the Council when a member so requests . . . Even if a majority of Council members are opposed to a meeting, the meeting must be held. Those members opposed to the meeting may express their views on the agenda when the meeting is convened, may seek to adjourn the meeting, or to defeat proposals submitted to it, but the President is bound to convene the Council on a request under rule 2, unless that request is not pressed.

3. . . . A request for an urgent meeting must be respected and decided upon on an urgent basis, and the timing established responsive to the urgency of the situation . . . The President's obligation to act promptly on urgent requests is, of course, further underlined if on consultation he finds that a majority [of Council members] favour an immediate convening of the Council.[13]

The representative of Mali, as President, was the only Council member to submit a written reply to the United States, and it is therefore a fair assumption that the other members of the Council accepted that the US letter accurately described what had been the practice of the Council. The representative of Mali said that he had acted entirely in accordance with the Rules of Procedure—adding, somewhat confusingly: 'Consequently, the President cannot think that the procedure followed at the latest meeting of the Security Council can be regarded as setting a precedent.'

Western members of the Council were inclined to attribute Ambassador Keita's behaviour to inexperience and concluded that no useful purpose would be served by revising the Rules of Procedure. The issue lay dormant for nearly 25 years, before a number of requests concerning Rules 1 to 3 arose in the 1990s.

A relatively minor instance arose on 20 November 1990 when four non-aligned members of the Council requested, for the following day, a meeting of the Council to consider the subject of the safety and protection of Palestinian civilians under Israeli occupation. After much debate in the course of informal consultations, a meeting of the Council was eventually held on 8 December. Citing the long wait before the Council had been convened, Cuba ironically charged that the Council's Provisional Rules of Procedure appeared to have developed 'a somewhat subversive character'.[14] It was apparent when the Council did convene that the holding of a substantive debate did not have the support of the majority of the Council at that time, and the meeting was adjourned and suspended a number of times before a compromise solution in the form of a resolution and a presidential statement was agreed on 20 December.

A more significant dispute over Rules 1 to 3 arose in the early months of 1991, during the attempt of the international community to reverse Iraq's invasion and attempted annexation of Kuwait. On 23 January five members of the Arab Maghreb Union (Algeria, Libya, Mauritania, Morocco, and Tunisia) wrote to the President of the Council (Zaire) requesting that he 'convene an urgent meeting of the Security Council to consider the grave situation in the Gulf region'.[15] Requests using identical language were made by Sudan[16] on the same day, Yemen,[17] at that time a member of the Council, on 24 January, and Jordan[18] on 25 January. In the absence of a meeting of the Council being called, Cuba, like Yemen a member of the Council, wrote on 28 January to the President of the Council requesting the convening of the Council, in similar language to that employed by the United States in 1966:

> Cuba believes that the Council must assume its responsibilities under the Charter . . . for the maintenance of international peace and security . . . the only legitimate way to do this is to hold a formal debate in the Security Council so that the Council can take appropriate steps to end the hostilities . . .
>
> The request . . . makes it necessary to implement the relevant regulatory measures immediately, particularly article [*sic*] 2 of the provisional rules of procedure . . . Under this rule the Security Council is compelled to take action when requested to do so by a member state. It is also required to act under rule 3 of its provisional rules of procedure, which authorizes any State member . . . to request the Security Council to call a meeting . . . to consider a dispute or situation . . . under Article 35.[19]

What became clear through revelations in later meetings of the Council was that Council members had been meeting regularly during January under the Presidency of Zaire, but in informal consultations of the whole.[20] Austria revealed that there had been a deadlock between States who opposed the holding of a Council meeting as long as Iraq failed to abide by previous Security Council resolutions, and others who sought an immediate public debate. At informal consultations on 24 January Austria proposed a compromise—a private meeting of the Council would be held, but with the relevant rules of procedure waived so that all members that wished to could participate, and so that a verbatim record of the meeting could be distributed as if it was a public meeting. Austria made this proposal:

to uphold rule 2 of the provisional rules of procedure, since we consider this rule to be of particular importance for the protection of the rights of members of the Security Council who find themselves in a minority.[21]

The Council met seven days later, on 30 and 31 of January, but simply to extend the mandates of the UN Interim Force in Lebanon and the UN Iran–Iraq Military Observer Group. Yemen and Cuba challenged the proposed agenda of the meeting on 31 January, to draw attention to the failure of the Council to accede to their requests: 'I find it most regrettable that the Security Council has to date been unable to agree to my request in accordance with rule 2 of the provisional rules of procedure'.[22] Yemen added, not strictly accurately, that 'this is the first time in the history of the Security Council that, regrettably, a request of this kind has not been accepted'.

With just over two hours left of his Presidency, since the meeting had begun at 9.40 p.m., the ambassador of Zaire replied to this implied criticism. He argued that he had 'duly applied' Rule 2, on the basis that he had

received a mandate from all members of the Council to conduct consultations. It is clearly understood that members of the Council are unanimous *in supporting the principle of* convening a formal meeting of the Council. The President has therefore received a mandate to convene to agree on the date of that meeting. Hence the President of February will continue the consultations that his predecessor, in my person, began, and will prepare for that formal meeting in terms of form, substance and content. . . . (our italics).[23]

Yemen wrote again on the day of this meeting, alluding to its refusal, during informal consultations, to accept the Austrian compromise proposal:

Today, one full week having elapsed since the submission of our request for an immediate meeting of the Council . . . Our concern is increased by the fact that our request for an immediate meeting *has been made subject to procedures and conditions* that have no relation to the provisional rules of procedure of the Council and the underlying objective of which is no more than to provide a means for procrastination, without any legal grounds, at a time when the situation in the Gulf region is becoming ever more serious owing to the fact that the scope of the military operations in the region has gone beyond that stipulated in Security Council resolution 678 (1990).[24] (our italics)

The new Presidency (Zimbabwe) coincided with an escalation of fighting in the Gulf. After a gap of two weeks, on 13 February, the President convened a public meeting of the Council to address 'the situation between Iraq and Kuwait'. At this meeting, the delegate of India revealed that it was he who first suggested that the Council 'keep the matter [of the Gulf War] under review through the instrumentality of informal consultation meetings',[25] and that while they had been useful, the failure to hold a formal meeting had damaged the prestige of the Council and the UN. The Indian representative also revealed that Secretary-General Pérez de Cuéllar had relayed his personal concern over the prestige issue in a statement to Council members in informal consultations the previous week. At the start of the 13 February meeting the UK proposed that the Austrian compromise be adopted. After lengthy debate it was, and the Council began its private session the following day (see Section 5 below).

The failure of the Council to meet until 13 February has been cited by some as evidence that the Council had passed effective control of the Gulf War to the States supporting the Government of Kuwait. Those Coalition forces considered that the Council had, through its resolutions under Chapter VII, delegated authority to them to implement Council resolutions. Interference in the conduct of the war, once begun, would not have been welcome. The impression of general assent from the Council for the execution of Desert Storm was certainly viewed as desirable for the war effort. As we show later in this chapter, this was also an important factor in the compromise formula agreed when the Council chose to continue its 13 February meeting in private.

At this point we turn to the question of whether the two Presidents acted properly in delaying the convening of the meeting. First, we deduce from the evidence available that the Presidents in January and February 1991 *would* have convened the Council if nine or more of the Council members had demanded this. Such support did not appear to be forthcoming, and so we turn to the question of whether there is an obligation on the President to convene the Council even if the requisite majority is not in favour. We agree with the view expressed in the 1966 US letter that the Council must be called in this circumstance. This was emphasized by Austria when it stated that its compromise proposal was made in order to uphold Rule 2, particularly to safeguard the rights of States in a minority. Assuming that the Council must *eventually* be called, the key question becomes how *promptly* the President is required to convene a meeting. The apparent absence of requisite support may serve to reduce the need for promptness. The 1966 letter of the US read: '*Even* if a majority of Council members are opposed . . . the meeting must be held' (our italics), unintentionally highlighting that while the meeting must be called, a distinction is inevitably made between popular and unpopular requests. It is to be expected that a President would spend additional time consulting before convening an unpopular meeting, but a wait of over two weeks, as occurred in 1991, would surely fall beyond the outer limits of delay permitted. It can be argued from this that the onus remains on the President to convene the Council promptly in response to all requests, even when a public debate would not appear to be helpful to the work of the Council. Members are then free to vote for an immediate adjournment when it does meet, as occurred in the 1990 case outlined earlier.

On the question of the *nature* of the meeting, once a public meeting has been convened at the request of a member or a non-member of the Council, there is nothing to prevent the Council from continuing the meeting in private if the requisite number of Council members so decide.

In April 1993, in the aftermath of events in Srebrenica, the Contact Group on Bosnia and Herzegovina of the Organization of the Islamic Conference requested an urgent meeting of the Council so that its members could voice their concerns.[26] The failure of the Council to convene brought a strong riposte from Malaysia which expressed

> serious concern over the actions of certain Council members in obstructing repeated desperate attempts for emergency meetings of the Council to address the growing deterioration of the situation in Bosnia. Those actions

are tantamount to applying a surreptitious veto . . . [it may become necessary] for members of the United Nations to consider working towards a 'Uniting for Peace' resolution at a special meeting of the General Assembly.[27]

The President will often, with the support of other Council members, persuade those who request a meeting to accept a delay or even to abandon their request.

TABLE 2

Number of Council meetings and resolutions, 17 January 1946–31 December 1996

Year	Council meetings	Resolution no. from	to	Total number of resolutions
1946	88	1	15	15
1947	137	16	37	22
1948	171	38	66	29
1949	62	67	78	12
1950	72	79	89	11
1951	39	90	96	7
1952	42	97	98	2
1953	43	99	103	5
1954	32	104	105	2
1955	23	106	110	5
1956	50	111	121	11
1957	49	122	126	5
1958	36	127	131	5
1959	5	132	132	1
1960	71	133	160	28
1961	68	161	170	10
1962	38	171	177	7
1963	59	178	185	8
1964	104	186	199	14
1965	81	200	219	20
1966	70	220	232	13
1967	46	233	244	12
1968	76	245	262	18
1969	64	263	275	13
1970	38	276	291	16
1971	59	292	307	16
1972	61	308	324	17
1973	76	325	344	20
1974	52	345	366	22
1975	57	367	384	18
1976	113	385	402	18

Year	Council meetings	Resolution no. from	to	Total number of resolutions
1977	73	403	422	20
1978	52	423	443	21
1979	77	444	461	18
1980	77	462	484	23
1981	60	485	499	15
1982	89	500	528	29
1983	98	529	545	17
1984	57	546	559	14
1985	74	560	580	21
1986	91	581	593	13
1987	58	594	606	13
1988	67	607	626	20
1989	53	627	646	20
1990	59	647	683	37
1991	64	684	725	42
1992	92	726	799	74
1993	151	800	892	93
1994	159	893	969	77
1995	130	970	1035	66
1996	114	1036	1092	57

The Council has held meetings on average 72 times a year. The pattern of meetings for the last five decades has been as follows (average of each ten-year period appears in brackets): 1946–55 (71); 1956–65 (56); 1966–75 (60); 1976–85 (77); 1986–95 (92). However, the proliferation of the use of informal 'consultations of the whole' for the preparation of much of the substantive business of the Council since the late 1980s means that less can now be deduced from statistics based on actual meetings.

At one period, the Council seemed to be in danger of running out of business, and one scholar noted that, without Palestine and Kashmir, 'the Council would have been practically moribund throughout most of the 1950s'.[28]

For most of the Council's history meetings rarely began on time. Ambassador Farah of Somalia commented in 1961:

> I doubt whether the Security Council has ever met on time since it was established . . . I would suggest that we maintain our traditions of the past 25 years, schedule the meeting for 10.30, and begin at 11.30.[29]

As this book went to press there had been some attempts to change this practice. The President in December 1996 took an uncompromising stance. He would begin informal consultations of the whole at the time published in the UN *Journal*, even if all Council members were not present. Soon delegates could be seen running to the Consultation Chamber to be present when Council members began consultations. Whilst this approach was threatened, but not actually extended, to meetings of the Council itself, it had a similar effect in ensuring greater promptness.[30] A similar level of promptness was temporarily maintained by subsequent Presidents, with consultations of the whole and formal meetings scheduled for 10.30 a.m. usually beginning just five or ten minutes later. Times when the Council meets more than 20 minutes late are usually occasioned by the need for minor changes to draft resolutions (agreed immediately prior to a meeting) to be translated into the six official languages. Because of the delay that this causes the President may instead read out the proposed amendments, thus benefiting from simultaneous translation into the six languages, and then propose that the resolution be put to the vote 'as orally revised'.

A rigid insistence on the Council meeting on time may not always be constructive. Extra time in which to receive instructions from capitals or to conduct bilateral consultations with other delegations prior to the meeting can at times facilitate more effective Council decision-making.

There has been perhaps just one occasion when the Council meeting was convened too *early*. It occurred at a meeting at which the representative of Palestine had requested that he could show a videotape relating to the Occupied Territories. The President convened the meeting at 11.20 a.m. and the representative of Palestine objected, citing the 11.30 a.m. time listed in the *Journal*. The President apologized, and whilst replying that he had been under the impression that contrary to the *Journal*, they had agreed to meet immediately following the preceding informal consultations, he delayed the start of the meeting for 10 minutes.[31]

In 1947, the United Kingdom proposed that the Council should normally break at 1 p.m. and 6 p.m., and should try to arrange that it would not meet at all for two three-week periods a year, one being in August.[32] Unfortunately for Council delegates, the pressures of international politics do not follow so predictable a pattern. In the months following Iraq's invasion of Kuwait (which inconveniently took place on 2 August), Council meetings were invariably held on weekends and in the middle of the night.[33] This was partly due to the pressure of events in the Gulf occurring in a time zone eight hours divergent, and partly due to the pressures on delegations to communicate constantly with their capitals and to engage in frequent consultations.

3. NOTICE OF MEETINGS

Once a decision to convene a meeting has been taken, and the date and time have been fixed by the President, a notice of the meeting is sent to 'representatives on the Security Council'.

The responsibility for convening meetings falls on the Secretary-General (Rule 25). The Secretary-General is also required to communicate to representatives the provisional agenda. This should be done at least three days before the meeting, although, in urgent circumstances, the provisional agenda may be communicated simultaneously with the notice of the meeting (Rule 8).

By the very nature of the Council's primary responsibility for international peace and security, 'circumstances' are frequently 'urgent', and the Council has usually been willing to dispense with the 'three days' notice' requirement. In the first fifty one years of its existence, the Security Council met 3,728 times. We have come across eight occasions when the Council failed to accept the item proposed or decided to adjourn without adopting an agenda. The first four of these instances took place during the years when the Council was almost continuously facing procedural difficulties. In the first case, the Council's decision to restrict the agenda did not prevent members from discussing the excluded item; and the seventh case was surely pre-arranged.

The eight cases were as follows:

1. The Council met on 9 January 1947 to consider the question of disarmament, and the provisional agenda included two resolutions of the General Assembly as well as proposals for the implementation of one of the resolutions, together with a letter from the Chairman

of the UN Atomic Energy Commission transmitting the Commission's first report. This letter was not included in the agenda because it had not been circulated in sufficient time, but this did not prevent members of the Council (who were members of the Atomic Energy Commission anyway) from referring to the contents of the Commission's report. The letter transmitting the Commission's report was included in the agenda of a later meeting.[34]

2. The Council met on 30 August 1948 under the Presidency of the Soviet Union, the provisional agenda including both the India–Pakistan question and the Palestine question. The United States objected to the provisional agenda on the ground that it had been agreed that no further meetings would be held in New York (the General Assembly was due to convene in Paris on 21 September) unless an emergency arose, and he did not regard either of the items in question as constituting an emergency. Two other members considered it inexpedient to discuss the Palestine question at that time. The Council did not adopt the provisional agenda (two votes in favour, nine abstentions).[35]

3. The Council had agreed informally that there would be no meetings during the second half of December 1948 unless urgent problems arose. The Council met, nevertheless, on 17 December to consider Israel's application for UN membership. Syria proposed that an additional item be added to the agenda concerning attacks by Israel on Egyptian forces in the Faluja area. The Soviet representative said he did not object in principle to the Syrian proposal, but that advance notice was required, and it would be premature to include the matter in the agenda of that meeting. The Syrian proposal was put to the vote but was not adopted (two in favour, nine abstentions). At the end of the meeting, the Soviet representative asked the President of the Council for 'three days' notice in the event of an extraordinary meeting being called during the next few days'.[36]

4. The Council met on 18 November 1949 to consider the Indonesian question. The Ukrainian representative pointed out that he had received the documents for the meeting only that day, and he required time to study them. Other members expressed similar views, and the Council adjourned without adopting an agenda.[37]

5. The Council had been called to meet on the evening of 3 December 1960 under the Presidency of the Soviet Union to consider

Mauritania's application for UN membership, dated 28 November 1960. Just before the meeting, a revised provisional agenda was circulated containing, as an additional sub-item, a letter from the Soviet Union proposing that the Council consider also Mongolia's application for UN membership, which had been first submitted in 1946. When the Council met, the Soviet representative, speaking in that capacity and not as President, proposed that the Mongolian application should be considered first. Several representatives opposed this proposal, and Italy pointed out that the provisional agenda had to be circulated at least three days before the meeting, except in urgent circumstances. The Soviet proposal was rejected (four votes in favour, five against, two abstentions).[38]

6. In January 1962, the Soviet Union requested that an urgent meeting of the Council be convened to consider the situation in the Congo (Leopoldville). After the usual New Year felicitations, the Council turned its attention to the provisional agenda, and US ambassador Adlai Stevenson proposed the adjournment of the meeting. The Soviet Union objected, and the Council spent the next two hours discussing the procedural situation until, shortly before lunch, it approved the motion to adjourn.[39]

7. On 20 August 1969, Ireland requested an urgent meeting to consider 'the situation in the six counties of Northern Ireland'. The United Kingdom maintained that the matter was one of domestic jurisdiction. Ireland then addressed the Council. Britain replied, whereupon Zambia proposed that the Council adjourn, and the Council approved the proposal unanimously.[40]

8. In a series of meetings in December 1990 the Council was adjourned three times before the adoption of the agenda, at the request of the Soviet Union (on 8, 10, and 12 December). This was despite resistance from Colombia, Cuba, and Malaysia who regarded this as a tactic to water down, in informal consultations, a draft resolution that they had sponsored on the protection of Palestinians. This meeting is addressed in more detail in Chapter 4. On 19 December 1990 the President forgot that the British ambassador, Sir David Hannay, had asked to raise a point of order before the adoption of the agenda. Once the agenda had been adopted Sir David successfully proposed the suspension of the meeting under Rule 33.1 of the Provisional Rules of Procedure.

We recall only one occasion when a member has complained about the lack of three days' notice and was outvoted. This was on 14 October 1948, when Syria objected to the adoption of the agenda (the Palestine question) on the ground that he had received the notice of the meeting only the previous evening, and that no emergency had arisen to justify abandoning the requirement of three days' notice. The agenda was, nevertheless, adopted (eight votes in favour, three abstentions).[41]

On 9 November 1984, the United States complained that an evening meeting to discuss a Nicaraguan complaint had been called with undue haste, but the provisional agenda was adopted without a vote.[42]

The 'three days' notice' requirement arose by implication on one other occasion. The Council had met to consider two complaints by Israel against Egypt (4 February 1954). Lebanon suggested that an Egyptian complaint that Israel was violating the General Armistice Agreement should be added as a sub-item. The Soviet Union stressed that the Council had the right to deal with urgent matters without the usual notice. The sub-item proposed by Lebanon was approved on the understanding that the two complaints would not be discussed simultaneously. But the discussion about the agenda had lasted more than two hours, and no sooner had the agenda been adopted than the Council adjourned.[43]

In practice, nowadays, the provisional agenda is invariably approved in advance in informal consultations of the whole. If there is time, the provisional agenda so approved is printed in the *Journal.*

4. PLACE OF MEETING

The Charter and Rules of Procedure provide that:

1. Meetings of the Council shall normally be held at the seat of the United Nations (Rule 5);
2. The Council may decide to meet elsewhere if to do so will 'facilitate its work' (Article 28(3) and Rule 5);
3. A proposal to meet other than at United Nations Headquarters may be made by any member of the Council or by the Secretary-General (Rule 5).

Place of Meeting

Six groups of meetings have been held away from New York. Meetings were held in London in 1946 and in Paris in 1948 and 1951–2, where the General Assembly was in session, the decision to meet in Paris being taken informally. Meetings were held in Addis Ababa in 1972 to give special attention to African questions. Meetings were held in Panama City in 1973, ostensibly to consider peace and security in Latin America, but in reality to enable Panama to ask for a new Canal treaty with the United States. One meeting was held in Geneva in 1990 to discuss 'The situation in the Occupied Arab Territories'.

There had previously been a number of proposals that the Council should meet in cities away from Headquarters. On 8 September 1960, the Government of the Congo (Leopoldville) invited the Security Council to meet in the Congo so that the members could 'see for themselves . . . the United Nations authorities' interference in the Congo's domestic problems'. This proposal was supported by the Soviet Union and Poland and—with reservations—by Ceylon (Sri Lanka), but was rejected by the Council. In February 1961, Liberia suggested that the Council should meet in the Congo, but the idea was not pressed.[44]

In 1965, the Soviet Union proposed that the Council should meet in Santo Domingo to consider the situation in the Dominican Republic, but the United States thought the proposal frivolous and mischievous, and Jordan wanted more time to consider the idea. The proposal was not put to a vote.[45]

The initiative for the meetings held in Africa in 1972 came from thirty-six African States and was considered by the General Assembly in 1971. By a vote of 113 to 2, the Assembly invited the Security Council 'to consider the request of the Organization of African Unity concerning the holding of meetings of the Council in an African capital'. There were reservations about this proposal on the part of some Western delegations, partly on grounds of expense; partly because the Council might find it difficult to 'function continuously' if a crisis erupted while the Council and its staff were *en route* to Africa or while returning to New York; and partly because to meet in Africa might increase anti-Western sentiment.

The Security Council held thirteen meetings in Addis Ababa in the space of a week. The Council was addressed by Emperor Haile

Selassie of Ethiopia, President Ould Daddah of Mauritania (Chairman of the OAU Assembly), and the UN Secretary-General. The Council also heard representatives of nine liberation movements, two spokesmen for the OAU, a representative of the International Defence and Aid Fund, and the General Secretary of the All Africa Conference of Churches, all under Rule 39, which permits the Council to invite competent persons to supply it with information or to give other assistance.[46] Perhaps the most impressive statement was that made by the late Amilcar Cabral, President of the African Party for the Independence of Guinea Bissau and the Cape Verde Islands (PAIGC).

The Council adopted resolutions concerning Namibia (South West Africa), apartheid, and Portugal's African territories, and a statement of consensus expressing gratitude to the host country.[47] The United Kingdom vetoed a draft resolution on Southern Rhodesia, which had been sponsored by Guinea, Somalia, and Yugoslavia.[48]

Opinions about the usefulness of the Addis Ababa meetings varied. Austria, Mongolia, Tunisia, and Yugoslavia (among others) considered that the experiment had been a success, and Secretary-General Waldheim commented that the meetings had been 'a useful and positive experience'.[49] During the course of the meetings, Panama said that the time had come for the Council to meet in Latin America, 'and for this purpose we would offer as a site the capital of Panama'. This enabled the representative of Panama to expatiate on Latin America's important role in securing the decolonization of the African continent, and to complain that Panama was divided into two parts by the Panama Canal, 'a veritable foreign enclave'.[50]

It was to be Panama's turn to preside over the Council in March 1973, and in January Panama issued a formal invitation to the Council to meet in Panama City from 15 to 21 March in order to consider 'measures for the strengthening of international peace and security and the promotion of international co-operation in Latin America, in accordance with the provisions and principles of the Charter and the resolutions relating to the right of self-determination of peoples and strict respect for the sovereignty and independence of States'. The proposal of Panama was formally supported by the Latin American, Arab, and African Groups.[51] On 16 January, the

Council agreed in principle to meet in Panama City at the time suggested and asked a committee of the whole to consider and report on the necessary arrangements (see Chapter 7.1(b)). The committee reported in favour of the Panamanian proposal, but with a shorter agenda, and the committee's report was endorsed by the Council.[52]

Ten meetings were duly held. Twenty-three non-members of the Council and the presiding officers of two UN organs took part, and invitations to participate were also issued to the Secretary-General of the Agency for the Prohibition of Nuclear Weapons in Latin America, the Executive Secretary of the Organization of African Unity in New York, and the Observer of the League of Arab States at the United Nations. At the end of a rather diffuse debate, the United States vetoed a resolution which would have invited the United States and Panama to conclude a new treaty guaranteeing 'full respect for Panama's effective sovereignty over all of its territory', and the Council approved a resolution urging States not to use or encourage coercion against Latin American countries, and a statement of consensus expressing gratitude to the host country.[53]

On 21 May 1990 the representative of Bahrain wrote[54] to the President of the Council asking for an immediate meeting of the Council to discuss 'The situation in the Occupied Arab Territories'. It was known that certain members of the Council wished to invite Yasser Arafat, Chairman of the Executive Committee of the Palestine Liberation Organization, to address the meeting. The United States had made public its intention to refuse Mr Arafat a visa to enter the country to attend a meeting of the Council in New York. The following day the President of the Council issued a statement that 'Following consultations with members of the Security Council . . . the first meeting on the matter will be held at Geneva at the United Nations Office, on Friday 25 May 1990 at 3 p.m.'[55] The 2923rd meeting of the Council was duty held in Geneva, and the Council voted by 11 votes to 1 (USA) with 3 abstentions (Canada, France, and the UK) to allow Mr Arafat to address it.[56] The negative vote by the United States did not constitute a veto because the vote was a procedural one. Unlike the meetings held in 1972 and 1973, listed in Table 18, the Council in 1990 did not hold a formal meeting of the Committee on Council meetings away from Headquarters before taking the decision to meet in Geneva.

2. *The Council Meets*

When the Council holds a formal meeting at UN Headquarters, it meets in a chamber set aside for its use at the south end of the Conference Building, lying between 43rd and 44th Streets in Manhattan, and overlooking the East River. The Security Council chamber was designed by Arenstein Arnenberg of Norway, and the Norwegian Government supplied the marble, inlaid doors, blue and gold tapestry for the walls, curtains, railings, and the main chairs. The outstanding feature of the chamber is a large mural by Per Krogh which, with Nordic allegory, depicts man's struggle to rise from the sinister present to a warless world of freedom and brotherhood.[57]

The President of the Council for the month sits below the mural at the centre of the horseshoe-shaped table, with the Secretary-General or his representative on his right and the secretary of the Council on the left. The other delegates sit in English alphabetical order around the horseshoe, with their deputies and assistants behind them. Verbatim reporters are at tables in the centre of the horseshoe, and booths for interpreters are ranged on either side of the chamber. There are seats for non-members of the Council on the main floor of the chamber, but on important occasions all the seats are soon taken, and some diplomats and officials have to stand. There are seats for the news media, representatives of non-governmental organizations, and members of the public. A few security guards are on hand to deal with possible disturbances and to deter violent assaults on UN diplomats or officials.

The Council Chamber is used primarily for the public exchange of views and the formal voting on proposals discussed in detail in prior informal consultations. The bulk of the Council's work takes place in such consultations and a purpose-built Consultation Room was built in 1978 (see Section 8(1) below) adjacent to the Council Chamber to host consultations of the whole (i.e. those involving all fifteen members of the Council).

5. 'PERIODIC' MEETINGS[58]

Whenever there is a period of special crisis in international politics, ordinary people, and also sometimes diplomats, politicians, and scholars, seek a scapegoat. For most people, a favourite scapegoat is 'the enemy', who (or which) is responsible for the disasters and is almost certainly benefiting from them—the 'conspiracy' explanation of politics. A minority, especially in democratic countries, turn the more usual explanation on its head and consider that their own country is to be blamed for the world's ills—a kind of inverted patriotism which can, none the less, sometimes be put to constructive uses. But there are always a few who blame some aspect of 'the system': the weakness or strength of alliances, the excess or paucity of multilateral aid, the personality (or impersonality) of the Secretary-General, the need to amend the UN Charter, the excessive use of the veto in the Security Council, the failure to add to the number of the Council's members, and so on.

The difficulty about assessing explanations of the latter kind is that it is often not clear whether those who propagate them believe that they are causes or only symptoms of a malady. There is no better illustration of the confusion between cause and effect than some widely held views about the Security Council veto. We review in Chapter 5.3 the way the veto has been used in practice.

Another example of the confusion between cause and effect concerns the holding of what the Charter calls 'periodic' meetings of the Security Council. It was hoped when the Charter was drafted that the United Nations would provide a suitable framework for what has come to be called summit diplomacy, and the Charter provides for periodic meetings 'at which each of its members may, if it so desires, be represented by a member of the Government or by some other specially designated representative' (Article 28(2)). The Rules of Procedure provide that such periodic meetings shall be held 'twice a year, at such times as the Security Council may decide' (Rule 4), a Rule which the Council has cheerfully disregarded. The provisional agenda for a periodic meeting is to be circulated to Council members at least twenty-one days before the opening of a summit meeting (Rule 12).

2. *The Council Meets*

The first four Secretaries-General were in favour of holding periodic high-level Council meetings, and the General Assembly endorsed the idea on a number of occasions.[59] Without express recourse to Article 28(2), members of the Council have from time to time been represented at foreign minister or higher level. In 1965, Pakistan was represented in the Council by its Prime Minister: the provisional record of the meeting quotes the President as calling on 'the Prime Minister of Pakistan', but the official record changes this to 'the representative of Pakistan'.[60] Shortly after this, following the illegal declaration of independence by Southern Rhodesia, Michael Stewart, the British Foreign Secretary, attended a number of meetings of the Council, even though Britain's permanent representative at UN Headquarters, Lord Caradon, was a Minister of State in the British Government.[61] In 1969, the President of Colombia addressed a special meeting of the Council without an agenda, the Council convening for the sole purpose of hearing him.[62] In 1958, the United States, Britain, France, and Canada proposed that the Security Council should be convened under the terms of Article 28(2) to consider the situation in Lebanon and Jordan, but before arrangements for calling a meeting had been completed, the Soviet Government requested that an emergency session of the General Assembly be held.[63] In the circumstances, the proposal for a 'periodic' meeting of the Security Council was dropped.

In 1969, in connection with a proposal to the General Assembly on strengthening international security, the Soviet Union included the convening of 'periodic' meetings of the Council among its specific proposals, and the Assembly, in a preambular paragraph of its subsequent resolution, recalled the terms of Article 28(2).[64] The following year, Finland's permanent representative to the United Nations actively promoted the idea of a 'periodic' meeting of the Council under Article 28(2),[65] with the support or at least acquiescence of a number of countries, including Belgium, Burma, the Republic of China, France, Ireland, Luxembourg, Pakistan, Poland, the Soviet Union, Spain, Syria, the United Kingdom, and the United States.[66] On 12 June 1970, the Security Council approved the following cautious consensus:

> The members of the Security Council have considered the question of initiating periodic meetings in accordance with Article 28(2) of the Charter.

They consider that the holding of periodic meetings, at which each member of the Council would be represented by a member of the Government or by some other specially designated representative, could enhance the authority of the Security Council and make it a more effective instrument for the maintenance of international peace and security.

It is understood that periodic meetings, the purpose of which would be to enable the Security Council to discharge more effectively its responsibilities under the Charter, would provide members with an opportunity for a general exchange of views on the international situation, rather than for dealing with any particular question, and that such meetings would normally be held in private, unless it were otherwise decided.[67]

After further consultation, it was decided to hold the first 'periodic' meeting on 21 October 1970, as part of the twenty-fifth anniversary celebrations of the United Nations, and to direct the discussion to a general review of the international situation.

The Security Council duly convened and, as suggested in the consensus quoted above, decided that its meeting should be private (closed). As a result of this decision, no record of the meeting has been made public. But a *communiqué* was published in accordance with Rule 55, and accounts of the meeting were soon circulating in the corridors. If these are to be relied on, it was not a very inspiring or useful occasion. Speeches were delivered by the eminent statesmen meeting under the presidency of Sr. Lopez-Bravo, the Spanish Foreign Minister, after which a soporific *communiqué* was made public.[68] Four points about the meeting may be noted.

First, if corridor gossip is to be believed, the meeting was not so much 'a general exchange of views' (para. 2 of the *communiqué*) as a series of speeches along much the same lines as those delivered during the General Assembly's annual general debate. Second, the three African members of the Council 'reserved their position' (para. 8 of the *communiqué*) on the platitudes contained in the *communiqué* regarding Southern Africa. Third, the Deputy Foreign Minister of Syria stated that his Government's position was 'reflected in his delegation's statement at the meeting' (para. 8 of the *communiqué*), which hardly enlightened those diplomats who took the trouble to read the *communiqué* precisely because they had not been present at the meeting. Fourth, the members of the Council declared that they would determine the date of the next periodic meeting 'through consultations' (para. 7 of the *communiqué*).

To give the fifteen Council members a measure of encouragement, the other Members of the United Nations proceeded a couple of months later to welcome the decision of the Security Council to hold further 'periodic' meetings in accordance with Article 28(2) of the Charter, and expressed the hope that these meetings would make an important contribution to the strengthening of international security.[69] Secretary-General U Thant also considered that the practice instituted in 1970 'should be continued', but he added

> Such meetings should be more than mere formal occasions and should provide the members of the Council with an opportunity to carry out effectively their responsibilities for the maintenance of international peace and security. In our opinion, these periodic meetings should enable this body to take stock of the international situation and review the achievements made in the implementation of previous decisions. The Council could also take advantage of such meetings, held privately, if need be, to assess potential threats to the peace in areas of instability, make recommendations to the Governments concerned and thus fulfil its role in the prevention of international crises. In cases when, by means of a general consensus or as a result of the position of certain Governments, an important question is withheld from public discussion at the United Nations, I believe that the situation could usefully benefit from consideration by the Council in the course of its periodic meetings.[70]

The Secretary-General stated that the 1970 meeting 'was generally considered to be another step to enhance the authority of the Security Council'. Austria, Finland, Greece, and Sweden were in favour of holding further periodic meetings; Belgium, France, and Iran were also in favour, provided there were adequate preparation; the Netherlands suggested setting target dates for such meetings at the beginning of each year, and Tunisia wanted the General Assembly to set a timetable of six periodic meetings every year.[71]

The lesson of the 1970 experience is not that the United Nations fails to provide a suitable framework for summit diplomacy. It is, first, that the need for summit diplomacy cannot easily be predicted; second, that the participation should be determined by the issues at stake rather than comprise five States designated in a Charter completed in 1945 and ten States elected by the General Assembly to fit a geographical pattern; and third, that summit diplomacy cannot succeed without adequate preparation.

In 1985, in celebration of the fortieth anniversary of the United Nations, the Council decided in informal consultations to hold an open meeting the following month at foreign minister level, to consider the responsibility of the Security Council for world peace and security.[72] The style of debate in 1985 differed little from that in 1970 except that the President (Sir Geoffrey Howe of the United Kingdom), who spoke last, gave the impression of having listened to the other statements, for he commented on several of them. A presidential statement at the end of the meeting was restricted to platitudes, although the members 'resolved to continue the examination of the possibilities for further improvement of the functioning of the Security Council . . . in accordance with the Charter . . . [paying] special attention to the suggestions . . . in the Secretary-General's annual reports'.[73]

The participation of foreign ministers and other government ministers in the work of the Council has increased over the last decade. Foreign Ministers of France, the United Kingdom, and the United States were present at the meeting of the Council on 20 July 1987[74] that passed resolution 598 (1987) on the situation between Iran and Iraq, a vote which marked an important step in the thawing of the Cold War. The Vice-President of the United States, George Bush, attended a meeting[75] of the Council in 1988 following the accidental shooting down of an Iranian civilian aircraft by a US naval ship, with the loss of 290 lives. The foreign ministers from several African countries attended a Council meeting on Angola in 1995, as a ministerial delegation from the Organization of African Unity.[76] Seven foreign ministers (including France, the UK, and the USSR) attended a meeting of the Council on the situation in the Occupied Arab Territories in 1996.[77]

The third and fourth occasions at which all permanent members were represented by their foreign ministers occurred in 1990. Both concerned the situation between Iraq and Kuwait, and at both thirteen Council members were represented at the level of foreign ministers. The first on 25 September[78] adopted resolution 670 (1990), the second on 29 November[79] adopted resolution 678 (1990). The fifth such meeting occurred on 25 September 1991 when the foreign ministers of ten Council members (who were in New York for the opening of the General Assembly) were present when the Council adopted resolution 713 (1991) imposing an arms embargo on Yugoslavia.[80] A meeting was held to commemorate the fiftieth anniversary of the United Nations on 26 September 1995. Called a 'commemorative' meeting by the President and a 'ministerial' meeting by the Secretary-General, it was undoubtably both. Twelve foreign ministers and one deputy foreign minister (including all the permanent members) attended. The occasion was the first time that a woman minister had presided over the body (Mrs Agnelli of Italy).[81] We do not know how many foreign ministers must attend in order that a meeting be designated 'ministerial'.

A meeting of the Council was uniquely held at Head of State or Government level on 31 January 1992, but it was not convened explicitly under Article 28(2) as a 'periodic' meeting. At the conclusion of this meeting the British Prime Minister, as Council President, read out a substantive Presidential statement, which among other things asked the new Secretary-General, Boutros Boutros-Ghali, to prepare an analysis and recommendations on ways for strengthening and making more efficient the capacity of the United Nations for preventive diplomacy, peace-making, and peace-keeping. The Secretary-General's report was duly prepared and published on 17 June 1992. As the Council had expected, the report contained specific recommendations on the role of the United Nations in the new era.[82] Plans were mooted during 1994 for a second meeting of the Security Council at the level of Heads of State or Government, to be held in January 1995, but the meeting never materialized.

6. 'ORIENTATION' AND 'EXCHANGE OF VIEWS' MEETINGS

The response to concerns raised by Member States over the transparency of Council decision-making has been twofold. The first approach has been to 'open up' informal consultations. Some measures to achieve this, such as briefings of non-members by the Presidency, have already been adopted. Others, such as the direct participation of non-members in such consultations, have been resisted by most permanent members and by some other States. France advocated a second approach, which can potentially complement the first, in an *aide-mémoire* (reproduced in Appendix XI) of 11 December 1994 which promoted the greater use of public meetings of the Council. Its aim was to create '. . . a better balance between public and private meetings'. France advocated two new forms of Council meeting that could supplement existing ones in which the Council often met effectively only to formally adopt decisions. The two proposed forms were:

(a) 'Orientation' debates open to all Members of the Organization at a time when the Council is preparing to begin consideration of an important question;
(b) Public exchanges of views between members of the Security Council, where non-members of the Council could attend but not speak.

France requested a meeting of the Council on 16 December 1994 to discuss the *aide-mémoire* and other aspects of the Council's working methods. At this meeting it took the opportunity to explain the *raison d'être* behind its proposals. France argued that making informal consultations more public would paralyse them, and advocated instead restoring 'the balance between official meetings and informal consultations'.[83] France said that a distinction should be made between 'information, consultation and general exchanges of views—which with some exceptions could be the subject of public debate—and, on the other hand, negotiation and the drafting of texts, for which other procedures are preferable'.[84] Some Council representatives have expressed the view that on a number of occasions matters discussed in informal consultations of the whole could have been dealt with in a public Council meeting without any detriment to the functioning of the Council. If this is the case, the French approach of more public meetings appears to be both a feasible and desirable method of enhancing Council transparency. At the end of the debate in December 1994 the President issued a Statement[85] on behalf of the Council stating, rather blandly, that there should be an increased recourse to open meetings of the Council, particularly at an early stage in its consideration of a subject. The Council would decide, on a case-by-case basis, when to schedule public meetings of this sort.

In practice the idea of public exchanges of view contained in the French *aide-mémoire* did not take off. 'Orientation' debates fared better, while few were held in 1995, their use increased in the first few months of 1996. One was held on Liberia on 25 January 1996 under the presidency of Sir John Weston of the United Kingdom. The meeting was widely welcomed by Council members as establishing a good precedent for open Council deliberations.[86] The following month Madeleine Albright of the US took over the presidency and convened an orientation debate on the situation in Angola. New Zealand praised this decision, taking the view that 'all too often in the past, the only chance for public debate has been after the Council has come to its decision'.[87] In March Ambassador Legwaila of Botswana convened an orientation debate on Somalia[88] and this was followed in April by a similar debate on the situation in Afganistan. Orientation debates were also held in the course of 1996 on Burundi, Israel, and UN peace-keeping operations.[89] In spite of these efforts the overall proportion of meetings held in public actually declined slightly between 1994 and 1996 in comparison to informal consultations of the whole, giving rise to complaints in the General Assembly. The annual reports of the Security Council to the General Assembly for the years 1993–4, 1994–5, and 1995–6 give the following statistics:

16 June 1993 to 15 June 1994: 153 Formal meetings 252 Consultations of the Whole
16 June 1994 to 15 June 1995: 152 Formal meetings 274 Consultations of the Whole
16 June 1995 to 15 June 1996: 132 Formal meetings 240 Consultations of the Whole

Percentage of public (formal) meetings: 1993–4: 60.7 %. 1994–5: 55.5% 1995–96: 55%

Vigorous attempts were made by Portugal to encourage the use of orientation debates, proposing a total of six such debates during its Presidency in April 1997. Not all of these debates took place because some Council members considered that it was not the right moment to hold them.

The language of 'orientation meetings' has also been used in other UN contexts, and these should not be confused with meetings of the

Council. On 21 March 1997 the Secretariat of the Iraq Sanctions Committee held 'an orientation meeting on the procedures for implementation of Security Council resolution 986 (1995)'. Despite the similar name this was clearly a general technical briefing rather than a meeting of the Council. The UN *Journal* reported that it was 'aimed at familiarizing participants with the requirements for completing application forms for humanitarian supplies' and that it was 'open to all interested Member and Observer States, United Nations agencies, intergovernmental organization and non-governmental organizations'.[90]

7. PRIVATE (CLOSED) MEETINGS

We have referred in Chapter 1 to the sense of outrage felt by some medium and smaller countries when they discovered that the Security Council might sometimes meet in private. Diplomats were still under the spell of Woodrow Wilson's 'open covenants of peace, openly arrived at', whereas in fact many of the most crucial and lasting covenants of peace have to be arrived at privately. As Paul-Henri Spaak put it:

> Those who are involved [in open diplomacy] are forced to pay more attention to the repercussions of their actions in the outside world than to the goal they are seeking to achieve. They are bent on asserting themselves rather than trying to convince others of the rightness of their cause. They give far more thought to public opinion at home than to the problems which call for a solution.[91]

There are, to be sure, diplomatic activities which ought to be conducted in the full light of day. 'Nobody, however distinguished,' according to Lord Robert Cecil, 'works any worse for knowing that his proceedings will come up later for public discussion before the world'.[92] Certain functions of criticism and debate are suitably undertaken in public: but negotiation is usually best conducted in private.[93]

Under its rules the Security Council should normally meet in public (Rule 48), but there is one matter which, according to the Rules of Procedure, must be conducted in private; discussion and decision of any recommendation to the General Assembly regarding the appointment of the Secretary-General. The Council may decide that, for a private meeting, the record shall be made in a single copy only, to be kept by the Secretary-General (Rule 51). Any UN Member which has taken part in a private meeting has the right to consult the single copy of the record in the Secretary-General's office. Authorized representatives of UN Members which have not taken part in the meeting may, if the Council agrees, be granted similar access at any time (Rule 56). The Council issues a *communiqué* through the Secretary-General after each private meeting (Rule 55), and this is published in the official records in place of a verbatim record.

(a) Private meetings for the purpose of recommendations on the appointment of the Secretary-General

In the case of the *communiqués* issued in connection with the appointment of the Secretary-General, a consistent form of words has not been followed. In two cases, 1953 and 1996, the *communiqués* indicated the results of voting had that taken place in secret ballots on particular candidates. In a number of cases in which the Council has considered candidates, there has been widespread speculation of a veto or vetoes being cast, but no mention of this in Council *communiqués*. Caution needs to be applied here since the balloting performed by the Council in these cases may have been conducted in a way so as to provide an indication of the voting *intention* of Council members if a formal vote were to be held. Thus while we have referred to speculation about vetoes below, it is possible that the negative votes of permanent members in such ballots constituted a sign of 'discouragement' rather than a formal veto.

The first volume of the *Repertoire* of the Security Council covering the period 1946–51 stated that, at a private meeting to recommend a person for appointment as Secretary-General, the Council voted 'in such a manner as to ascertain whether any permanent member had cast a negative vote'.[94] This sentence has not appeared in later volumes of the *Repertoire.* The *communiqué* issued after the private meeting on 12 October 1950 says nothing about voting, but Trygve Lie reported in his memoirs that the Soviet Union vetoed a

Yugoslav proposal that he be reappointed.[95] The *communiqués* of the private Council meetings held on 13 and 14 March 1953 give details of the voting pattern on four candidates; the US proposal of Brigadier-General Carlos P. Romulo (one in favour, 3 against, 7 abstentions),[96] the Soviet proposal of Stanislaw Skrzeszewski (one in favour, three against, and 7 abstentions),[97] the Danish proposal of Lester B. Pearson (9 in favour, one vote against, and one abstention),[98] and Mrs V. L. Pandit (2 in favour, one vote against, with eight abstentions).[99] In the case of Pearson, the *communiqué* added, 'since the negative vote was cast by a permanent member, the proposal was not adopted'.[100] Lie later reported that the Soviet Union had cast the veto concerned.[101] The *communiqués* for the 615th and 616th meetings simply stated that no nominations had been received. Finally on 31 March 1953 a *communiqué* was issued stating that by a vote of ten votes in favour and none against, with one abstention the Council recommended the appointment of Dag Hammarskjold.

In 1961 and 1966, there was general agreement to recommend the appointment of U Thant as Secretary-General. The only reference to voting in the three *communiqués* issued in December 1971, when Kurt Waldheim was recommended for appointment, is that 'having received a number of nominations for the post of Secretary-General, the Council voted by secret ballots on those nominations. As a result of the balloting, the Security Council proceeded to adopt unanimously a resolution recommending the appointment of Kurt Waldheim';[102] but it is known that there were vetoes in 1971. The Council similarly did not refer in its *communiqué* to any vetoes in the reappointment of Waldheim in 1976, in the election of Pérez de Cuéllar in 1981, or in the initial appointment of Boutros-Ghali, although it is widely believed that some were cast in those years. When the Council was considering whether to appoint Boutros Boutros-Ghali for a second term in 1996 it issued a *communiqué* of its 3714th (closed) meeting in which it stated that a vote had been taken on a draft resolution proposing the reappointment of Boutros-Ghali. 'The draft resolution received 14 votes in favour, one vote against and no abstentions. Since the negative vote was cast by a permanent member, the draft resolution was not adopted'.[103] The Council issued another *communiqué* on 13 December 1996, stating that it had decided, 'by acclamation'[104] to recommend the appointment of Mr Kofi Annan as the seventh Secretary-General.

(b) Private meetings for other purposes

(i) Private meetings vs informal consultations of the whole

It is important to distinguish between private meetings and informal consultations of the whole. Private meetings have a clear statutory existence under the Charter and the Rules of Procedure, an official (but private) record is kept (Rule 53), and a *communiqué* is issued through the Secretary-General at the end of each meeting. Informal consultations of the whole have no statutory basis, but have obtained a *de facto* official status (see below). Sometimes in the past, it was apparently not entirely clear to all the members whether the Council is engaged in informal consultations or is holding a private (closed) meeting. On 27 October 1973, the Council was summoned to meet at 10.30 a.m. to consider the situation in the Middle East. Members duly gathered and engaged in informal discussion until 7.45 p.m. One member later described this as 'an informal, closed meeting' (India), another as an 'informal consultative meeting' (Soviet Union), a third as 'our informal discussion' (Sudan), while a fourth member told Sydney Bailey afterwards that, in his opinion, it had been a formal but closed meeting.[105] In fact the records show that what took place were informal consultations of the whole.[106] Such consultations have now become so commonplace that it would be unlikely that confusion of this sort would occur again. Moreover, the availability of full translation and other services in the Consultation Room has reduced the 'practical' need for official private meetings, with the exception of those for the appointment of the Secretary-General, required by Rule 48 of the Rules of Procedure. Private meetings may, nevertheless, be a useful means in the future by which non-members of the Council can be invited to participate in confidential but formal discussions prior to the adoption of a decision. The private meetings held by the Council in the past, other than those specifically for purpose of the appointment of the Secretary-General, can be placed into two categories. Those where only a *communiqué* was issued by the Secretary-General after the meeting, and those in which both a *communiqué* and a public verbatim record were issued.

(ii) Private meetings where only a communiqué *was issued*

From 1950 to 1992 the Council met in private to discuss its draft annual report to the Assembly. On each occasion a *communiqué* was issued after the close of each meeting. Before 1950, practice was not consistent. In 1948 the Council approved the draft report on 19 August 1948 at an open meeting (the 355th), subject to the unanimous agreement of a sub-committee, composed of representatives of France, the Ukrainian Soviet Socialist Republic, the Union of Soviet Socialist Republics, the United Kingdom, and the United States, on the corrections presented to them in the course of the meeting of the Council.[107] In 1993 a decision was taken that the Council should consider its draft report at a public meeting. This has been the case since.

There have been only a handful of other cases where private meetings have been held and only a *communiqué* subsequently issued. Three such meetings[108] took place following a public exchange of views over a dispute relating to the Suez Canal in October 1956. The private meetings were sought 'in order to explore the possibility of a peaceful solution of the problem'.[109] The first 'periodic' meeting of the Council in 1970 was a private meeting of this type,[110] as was a meeting on the situation in Cyprus in 1974.[111] Particularly since the building of the Consultation Room in 1978 it has been easier for Council members confidentially to consider disputes between States through a variety of methods of informal consultation, and the utility of private meetings for this purpose has declined. However, there have been occasions when the Council has seen advantage in a holding a private meeting but subsequently issuing a public record of proceedings. These cases are outlined in the following section.

(iii) Private meetings where both a communiqué *and a public verbatim record were issued*

There have been three occasions when the Council considered that it should hold a meeting in private, but issue a public verbatim record of the proceedings, in addition to a *communiqué*:

Case 1. The first instance was its 1760th meeting on 15 December 1973, when the Council wished to consider the Middle East. The

President (China) had stated the previous day that it would be 'a formal closed meeting'. He began the proceedings by saying that, as a result of consultations, he understood that there was general agreement not to invoke Rule 51. Accordingly, the verbatim record would be circulated in all the working languages as an unrestricted document, but since the meeting was 'private', a *communiqué* would also be issued, as required by Rule 55, at its conclusion.[112]

Case 2. At its 1853rd meeting on 16 November 1975, the Council held a private meeting on the situation concerning Western Sahara 'in order to give the members of the Council an opportunity to question the concerned parties'.[113] It was agreed that a verbatim record of the meeting would be prepared and distributed in the same way as was usual for a public meeting. The Council also adopted a *communiqué* at the end of the meeting. In a Council debate in 1991 Sir David Hannay reflected on the decision in 1975, judging that the Council had chosen this option since 'private meetings would best assist such exploratory discussion designed to clarify ideas and identify possible ways forward'.

Case 3. At its 2977th public meeting on 13 February 1991, in the midst of the Gulf War, the Council convened to discuss the situation between Iraq and Kuwait. After the adoption of the agenda the United Kingdom made a motion under Rule 48 of the Rules of Procedure that the meeting be continued in private, but that a verbatim record of the meeting be circulated in all working languages as an unrestricted document in accordance with Rule 49 of the Rules of Procedure. The arguments used to support and oppose the UK proposal can be found in the verbatim record of the public part of the 2977th meeting.

This last case was also considered in section 1 of this chapter in the context of the requests for the Council to convene from two of its members. We explained that the United Kingdom proposal was a compromise, originally put forward by Austria in informal consultations, between those opposed to any formal meeting of the Council at that time, and those who sought an immediate public debate. Because of the significance of the issue at the time we have included here a detailed analysis of the public vs. private dimension of the debate.

The United Kingdom proposed a private meeting since:

> We should do nothing which could detract from the Council's unity of purpose or blur the signal that is sent to the outside world. In our view we cannot afford to send mixed signals when that might only delay the realization that a peaceful solution to this crisis has to begin with Iraqi withdrawal from Kuwait. This occasion calls for serious and careful consideration of all developments away from the glare of immediate publicity.

Yemen argued that the Council needed to meet in public to give voice to non-violent solutions to the conflict, such as the current mediation effort by Soviet envoy Primakov. Yemen added that the idea that public division in the Council would give Baghdad a 'propaganda' coup presumed that those who were happy with the course of the war were a priori right. Cuba agreed, arguing that the Council had for six and a half months of public debate, met publicly 'on 12 occasions to adopt 12 resolutions in front of television cameras, before live radio microphone, in the presence of dozens of newspapermen'. Resolutions 661 (1990), 665 (1990), and 678 (1990) had aroused very public disagreement in front of the world's media, so why was this different now?

The Soviet Union then spoke deflating much of Yemen and Cuba's case, by arguing that a public meeting might make more difficult the work of the Soviet Union and other countries in their initiatives for an alternative, peaceful solution.

After speeches by seven other Council members the United Kingdom proposal was narrowly adopted by a vote of nine votes in favour to two against (Cuba and Yemen), with four abstentions (China, Ecuador, India, and Zimbabwe).[114] The part of the meeting that took place in private resumed six times, and an official *communiqué* was eventually issued following the final part of the meeting on 2 March 1991.

This case gives us an interesting insight into why it can still be helpful for a meeting to be held in private even if a verbatim record of proceedings is to be published. In this instance the answer lies in the expression of the British ambassador, quoted above, that he wished the Council to avoid 'the glare of *immediate* publicity' (our italics). Since a verbatim record was issued after each resumption of the Council's meetings, it is unlikely that the views expressed within the Council were significantly different in *content* from those that would have been made in a public setting. However, the *impact* of written records a day or two after the speeches were made contrasted enormously from the potential impact of stirring speeches made live by dissenting states on network television. The television cameras had broadcast live in the autumn of 1990, as the Council debated and adopted a number of historic resolutions, and it was frequently quipped that Cable News Network (CNN) had become the sixteenth member of the Security Council.[115] With the Allied land and air offensive under way, and the inevitable unease generated about the consequent loss of civilian and military life, there was concern among the Allies that some members of the Council that had supported the previous 12 resolutions might begin to waiver, and particularly to waiver cogently in front of the television cameras. The 'strategy' of holding a private meeting with verbatim records appears to have been quite successful; events were moving so quickly that by the time the verbatim records of each of the private sessions were issued, the media had lost interest in them.

The other advantage of a private meeting over informal consultations of the whole in this case was the opportunity it gave for non-members of the Council to participate in the meeting and have their views heard by the Council.

8. INFORMAL CONSULTATIONS

The United Nations Charter and the Rules of Procedure of the Security Council do not refer to consultations of Council members, but these have, particularly since the mid-1970s, been an essential component of UN diplomacy. Almost by definition informal consultations are hard to define and precisely categorize. Inconsistent usage in the course of everyday debate, coupled with the inevitable ambiguities resulting from translation and interpretation have produced a plethera of terms to refer to 'meetings' other than those planned for in the Charter: informal consultations, informal meetings of members of the Council, consultations, consultations of the whole, informals, formal informals, informal informals. This has caused considerable confusion amongst both authors and practitioners.

Following Council practice and to simplify matters, we have placed such informal 'meetings' into two categories: (1) *informal consultations (of the whole)*, sometimes also referred to as *informals*; (2) *informal consultations* other than consultations of the whole. This distinction has also been made by authors such as Bruno Simma[116] and Davidson Nicol.[117]

From the official records of the Council it is often difficult to determine which type of consultations are being referred to. At the start of a public meeting the President normally states that

> The Security Council will now begin its consideration of the item on its agenda. The Security Council is meeting *in accordance with the understanding reached in its prior consultations* (our italics).

Similarly when the President reads out a Statement he or she usually notes that

> *following consultations among members of the Council*, I have been authorized to make the following statement on behalf of the Council (our italics).

In both these cases the consultations referred to are invariably informal consultations of the whole, often held in the Consultation Room minutes before the public meeting in the neighbouring Council Chamber. However, often bilateral and multilateral consultations between the President and individual members of the Council will also have taken place. What distinguishes these different forms of consultation is examined below.

(a) 'Consultations of the whole'

Consultations of the whole are private gatherings of all 15 Council members, presided over by the Council President, who notifies each member of the time, place, and programme of work to be discussed. The main differences with Council meetings, public or private, are that no official records of consultations of the whole are kept, and that non-members of the Council cannot attend. Furthermore, consultations of the whole are not held in the Council Chamber. Consultations of the whole are not 'meetings' of the Council under the terms of the Charter or the Rules of Procedure, and this is a distinction that has been rigorously maintained. However, consultations of the whole *have* increasingly formalized in recent years, so that they now have many of the attributes of formal private meetings of the Council. There have been four main stages in this formalization process:

(a) The construction of a purpose-built consultation room. In the early years of the Council, consultations of the whole frequently took place in the cramped office allocated to the President, at the side of the Council Chamber, and when interpretation was desired, in Conference Room 5 at UN Headquarters. In 1978 a new Consultation Room next to the Security Council Chamber was completed, built especially for the purpose of holding such consultations, and providing for interpretation into all official languages of the Orgnization. From one year to the next, from 1977 to 1978, the number of informals jumped three times and the time spent in them more than quadrupled.[118]

(b) The listing of consultations of the whole in the UN *Journal* under the heading of Scheduled Meetings. Other consultations and briefings such as those between members of the Security Council, troop contributors and the Secretariat are listed in the section of the *Journal* headed 'Meetings other than meetings of United Nations bodies'. Consultations of the whole may, however, be held at short notice without being announced in the *Journal*. In 1995 the *Journal* began to include a brief list of subjects to be considered at forthcoming consultations of the whole, including details of briefings to be given to the Council.

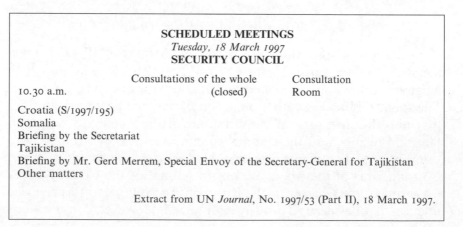

SCHEDULED MEETINGS
Tuesday, 18 March 1997
SECURITY COUNCIL

10.30 a.m.	Consultations of the whole (closed)	Consultation Room

Croatia (S/1997/195)
Somalia
Briefing by the Secretariat
Tajikistan
Briefing by Mr. Gerd Merrem, Special Envoy of the Secretary-General for Tajikistan
Other matters

Extract from UN *Journal*, No. 1997/53 (Part II), 18 March 1997.

(c) The introduction in October 1994 of informal briefings by the Presidency of the Security Council for non-members of the Council on the current work of the Council being undertaken in consultations of the whole. The frequency of such briefings are currently left to the discretion of the President for each month, but they are generally held on a daily basis.

Announcement

As from Wednesday, 5 March 1997, and for the rest of the month, the Presidency of the Security Council will conduct informal briefings on the current work of the Council for Member States of the United Nations which are non-members of the Council daily, except on days on which no informal consultations are scheduled. The briefings will take place at 3 p.m. in the Press Briefing Room (S-226).

Announcement in the UN *Journal*, No. 1997/44, 5 March 1997.

(d) The increasing use of consultations of the whole, to undertake reviews of prior Council decisions and for other matters, without resort to a formal meeting of the Council. They have been used for the following purposes:

(i) The review of sanctions regimes imposed by the Council under Chapter VII of the Charter. The Council conducted reviews of the sanctions it imposed against Iraq (pursuant to paragraph 21 of resolution 678 (1991) and paragraph 6 of resolution 700 (1991)) and Libya (pursuant to paragraph 13 of resolution 748 (1992)) solely through discussion and announcement in the context of consultations of the whole, the outcome being announced through subsequent statements issued by the President. Initially (on three occasions all concerning Iraq)[119] the Council communicated the outcome of its consultations (not to modify the sanctions regimes) through a 'statement to the media on behalf of the members of the Council', made by the President. From March 1992 the statements were issued 'direct': '. . . the President issued the following statement on behalf of the members of the Council . . . '. Twelve such statements were issued after informal consultations held concerning Iraq[120] and four concerning Libya.[121] From 1 January 1994 the Council gave certain statements made by the Council President a special designation as 'Presidential Statements' with their own document symbol series. Of these, one such Presidential Statement concerning sanctions against Iraq was issued[122] and six issued concerning sanctions against Libya[123] as of 31 December 1996.

(ii) The review of the modalities and the question of the continuation or termination of a UN peace-keeping operation. The one example of this practice concerned the United Nations Iraq–Kuwait Observer Mission in 1992. The President informed the Secretary-General that 'the members of the Council have carried out a review, in informal consultations held on 6 April 1992, in accordance with the provisions of resolution 689 (1991) of 9 April [1991], regarding the question of termination or continuation of the Mission as well as its modalities . . .'[124]

(iii) Agreement to support the dispatch of a UN special mission. An example of this practice, again related to Iraq, was a statement issued by the Council President following consultations of the whole on 19 February 1992: 'The members of the Council support the decision of the Secretary-General to dispatch a special mission headed by the Executive Chairman of the Special Commission to visit Iraq immediately . . . the Secretary-General is requested to report on the results of the special mission to the Security Council upon its return'.[125]

(iv) Receiving briefings from Special Representatives and Envoys of the Secretary-General and from members of the Secretariat. A recent example of this frequent occurrence was a briefing given to consultations of the whole in March 1997 by Mr Gerd Merrem, Special Envoy of the Secretary-General for Tajikistan.[126]

The Council has also made use of consultations of the whole for a number of other purposes. Questions related to the status of statements following such consultations have been raised by Argentina in a letter to the President of the Council. This letter is reproduced as Appendix X(d).

Despite this gradual formalization of consultations of the whole, it is clear that they are not meetings of the Council as such, but rather informal meetings of all the members of the Council. Nevertheless, the status of these meetings is still contested. In a debate undertaken by the Council in 1994 on its own working methods and procedures, France stated that

> I should note that informal meetings are not even real Council meetings at all; they have no official existence, and are assigned no number. Yet it is in these meetings that all the Council's work is carried out.[127]

Responding, the ambassador of Brazil agreed that the Rules of Procedure of the Council make no provision for informal consultations, and that they therefore have no legal existence. He proposed that the rules be updated to codify the existence of such consultations. The ambassador of New Zealand took a different approach arguing that UN practice *did* give such meetings an official existence, as proof he cited the fact that consultations of the whole were listed in the *Journal* under the heading entitled 'Scheduled meetings', and that legally mandated 'decisions' such as sanctions reviews (see above) were taken in such informal consultations. On this basis he argued that participation of States that were not members of the Council in decisions taken in consultations of the whole was non-discretionary[128] since Articles 31 and 32 of the Charter should apply equally to such consultations, and Article 32 reads that States '*shall* be invited'[129] (our italics). But, he also agreed with Brazil that the Rules of Procedure should be updated to acknowledge the legal existence of 'informal consultations'.

The most contentious question is whether the review of sanctions regimes and peace-keeping operations in informal consultations of the whole, without recourse to a formal meeting, amounts to the Council taking a decision on such matters, since the taking of decisions in this way could arguably give informal consultations an official legal status. Some Member States believe that a decision is *not* taken in such reviews. First, they argue, the *Council* is not taking a decision, rather the President is summarizing the views of Council *members,* since in recent practice[130] statements by the President are generally issued 'on behalf of the members of the Council' following informal consultations, and 'on behalf of the Council' when read out at a formal meeting. Second, it is argued that a *decision* as such is not being made, rather that 'no decision to change the status quo' is being made. The counter-arguments are first that prior resolutions require the Council to conduct a review at a particular time (e.g. 'to review every 120 days or sooner') on a sanctions regime or peace-keeping operation in the case of UNIKOM, and that this means that a decision, albeit one to change nothing, is implicit in such a review. Second, and linked to the first argument, it is argued that since such a review is required of the Council by prior resolutions, a statement by the President in such circumstances is either being made on behalf of the Council itself, or amounts to a dereliction of duty by the Council in not formally undertaking a review.

We do not find the arguments of either side entirely convincing. States that wish to ensure that an explicit decision is taken for the renewal of a sanctions regime or peace-keeping mandate can seek the insertion in the initial resolution of what David D. Caron describes as a 'sunset clause'.[131] This is the explicit designation of a termination date or terminating event in the resolution. Such a clause is contained in resolutions for most peace-keeping operations. It's absence from resolution 689 (1991) which stated instead that 'the [observer] unit can be terminated only by a further decision of the Council', meant that a review of the modalities and possible termination of the mission was undertaken in informal consultations rather than in a meeting of the Council, as described in section (d) (ii) above. One danger of including such a sunset clause in sanctions regimes is that it could potentially impair the effectiveness of sanctions if dissent over the application of the sanctions regime is voiced at a public Council meeting.

(i) Measures introduced in response to concerns about the transparency of consultations of the whole

Measures preceding consultations. In July 1993 the Council decided to make available to all Member States the tentative forecast of Council work (see Appendices IX and X(b)). The Council began in November 1993 to list the the draft programme of work for consultations of the whole in the UN *Journal*, including details of any planned briefings to the Council. The inclusion of the provisional agenda of formal meetings in the *Journal* had occurred since July 1993 (see Appendix X (a)).

Measures during consultations. From 1 March 1994 the Council began making draft resolutions in blue (i.e. in their provisional form), available to non-members of the Council at the time of consultations of the whole of the Council.[132] This measure was suggested as one which would contribute to Council transparency, and improve the flow of information to non-members of the Council. A draft resolution in 'blue', i.e. printed in blue ink, is regarded as a text that has not been formally tabled. Therefore it remains 'provisional' and can be revised or amended. These revisions or amendments to the provisional text are incorporated in the final version. Once the text is tabled by the sponsor(s), however, further changes are treated as 'revisions' or 'amendments' and so circulated or referred to at the formal meeting of the Council. See the Note on 'Blue draft resolutions' reproduced in Appendix X(g).

Measures following consultations. The introduction of briefings by the President of the Council on the work of the Council, immediately following the consultations. The first such briefing was given by the United Kingdom on 27 October 1994. An invitation was sent out to all permanent missions by the Secretariat to attend the first of 'periodic informal Presidency briefings on the current work of the Security Council'.[133] Such briefings have been continued by subsequent Presidents, and invariably take place on each day for which consultations of the whole occur, and are usually held in the *Briefing Room*. There has been no agreement, however, on the format or frequency of the briefings, and that they occur at all is left to the discretion of the President of the month. The briefings of the President do not contain any attribution of statements to individual representatives. More informally, but in greater detail and with attribution, members of the Council will also brief selected groups (e.g. NAM members) after each consultation of the whole. Such 'group' briefings often take place in the Quiet Room adjacent to the Consultation Room. The Quiet Room no longer lives up to its name, since the addition of a television set with continuous CNN coverage. The larger permanent missions are sometimes able to send diplomats to a number of these simultaneous briefings, thus obtaining a variety of perspectives on what Council members believed transpired. Part of the reluctance on the part of some States in institutionalizing these briefings (for example by making reference to them in the Rules of Procedure) is that this would by inference give a more formalized status to consultations of the whole *per se*.

On 24 January 1996 the Council decided that the Chairman of each of the Council's Sanctions Committees should give an oral briefing to interested Member States after each Committee meeting, in the manner of the briefings given by the Presidency following informal consultations of Council members (see Appendix XIII(c)).

Measures to supplement consultations. We have already described in Section 6 of this chapter, the proposals of France that the Council hold more public meetings to canvass the views of non-members, and to ensure that the views of Council members are publicly aired.

(b) Informal consultations other than consultations of the whole

Almost any informal meeting in connection with the Council's work and involving one or more member of the Council could be classified as an informal consultation. Davidson Nicol has succinctly listed almost every possible permutation:

> Informal consultations involving members of the Security Council can be either bilateral or multilateral. If bilateral they may involve the President and one party who may or may not be a member of the Council; they may involve two members of the Security Council; or they may involve one member of the Security Council and one other party who may or may not be a member of the Security Council. If multilateral, they may involve the President and some other members of the Council; the President and parties to a dispute; the President and representatives of some regional groups; the President and Secretariat officials possibly including the Secretary-General; the President and representatives of liberation movements; or they may involve one or more members of the Security Council and persons in one or more of the above categories with or without inclusion of the President.[134]

From these myriad possibilities for consultation a number of types have become institutionalised, at least to the extent that they have a format and designation recognized by the diplomatic community. At some the attendance of all Council members is expected, such as meetings under the 'Arria formula', at others, such as troop contributor consultations, the participation of all Council members is invited but not always realised. Some forms of consultation, such as 'Groups of Friends', 'Contact Groups' and 'caucuses' within the Council are defined by their limited membership of *ad hoc* or sub-groups of the Council, in certain cases also involving non-members.

(i) The most commonly referred to 'caucus groups' in the Council are the following:[135]

Permanent five ('P5')

Since 1986, at the initiative of the United Kingdom Representative, the permanent members ('P5') began to meet regularly to discuss the work of the Council. Following the end of the Cold War the P5 now meet often. The 'co-ordinator' for these meetings rotates every three months among the permanent members. The working language of meetings of the P5 is English, and meetings take place at one of the five missions, or at a room in the UN building. Each mission is usually represented by the ambassador and the political counsellor of the mission. 'Expert' level meetings of the five are also held at various levels, including Deputy Permanent Representatives, political counsellors, and legal advisers. On occassion the permanent members have issued joint statements reflecting their common position on issues with which the Council is concerned. The 'P5' issue annually a wide-ranging statement following a meeting of the foreign ministers of the five permanent members with the UN Secretary-General.[136] Joint statements of the 'P5' were also issued on the Non-Proliferation Treaty, and on the effects of economic sanctions (reproduced as Appendix XIV).[137]

Western permanent members ('P3')

Britain, France, and the United States meet often to co-ordinate their positions. The three countries have jointly vetoed a Council resolution on thirteen occasions: six times over Namibia; four times on South Africa, twice on attacks against Libya and Libyan aircraft; and once over the invasion of Panama (see Table 8). Such vetoes serve to reinforce the opposition of Western permanent members to a resolution. An individual veto would suffice to defeat a resolution, and a joint veto may either reflect an equal determination to see a resolution defeated, or a gesture of solidarity with the permanent member most affected. The 'P3', being the most directly affected parties, have co-ordinated particularly closely over the imposition, implementation, and review of sanctions against the Libyan Arab Jamahiriya from 1992, imposed following the bombings of Pan Am flight 103 over Lockerbie in Scotland, and UTA flight 772 over the Ténéré desert in the Niger.[138]

Non-aligned

112 of the 185 Members of the United Nations are members of the Movement of Non-Aligned Countries (the NAM).[139] The NAM was originally defined by its independence from both the US and the USSR. In a world with now only one 'superpower' the NAM remains a co-ordinating mechanism for a large number of developing countries. The non-aligned 'caucus' of the Council holds frequent meetings to discuss strategy and has a convenor who changes each month. The group has often formed a powerful bloc on the Council, presenting joint draft resolutions and viewpoints to the Council:

> The caucus of the non-aligned members of the Security Council . . . believe that . . .;[140]
>
> The caucus is firmly opposed to . . .[141]
>
> [Draft resolution] submitted by [Oman] in its capacity as the co-ordinator of the Security Council's Non-Aligned Movement Caucus for this month.[142]

The number of non-aligned members on the Council varies from year to year and is usually five or six, but has been as low as four and as high as seven. This variance occurs for three reasons. The membership of NAM is not synonymous with the combined membership of the African, Asian, and Latin American and Caribbean UN regional groups, or with the G77 group of developing countries. All African States *are* members of NAM, but there are notable omissions from the other two groups. Secondly, Japan, an industrialized country, also competes for one of the two Asian non-permanent seats, and can thus potentially displace a NAM member. Thirdly, Yugoslavia, a member of the East European group was a NAM member and thus could boost the NAM total on the Council when elected. In 1997, the number of NAM members of the Council was down to four, since the non-permanent members included Japan, Costa Rica, and the Republic of Korea, all non-members of NAM although the Republic of Korea nevertheless participated in the NAM caucus as an observer. There would also have been only four NAM members in 1988 if Yugoslavia had not been elected to the Council for the Eastern European group.

Since 1988 the number of NAM members on the Council has been as follows: (The names of the Council members not members of NAM from the Africa, Asia, and Latin American and the Caribbean groupings are given in brackets):

1988 5 Argentina, Brazil, and Japan (but Yugoslavia present)
1989 6 Brazil
1990 7 —
1991 7 —
1992 6 Japan
1993 5 Brazil and Japan
1994 5 Argentina and Brazil
1995 6 Argentina
1996 6 Republic of Korea
1997 4 Costa Rica, Japan, and Republic of Korea

The Non-Aligned Movement as a whole also has a Joint Co-ordinating Committee in conjunction with the 'Group of 77' group of developing countries, to co-ordinate action on specific issues, some of which relate to the positions taken by the Non-Aligned Movement members on the Security Council.[143]

Non-non-aligned

This group, is not as obviously homogeneous as the others, since it is more a collection of States that do not fit into the other groups than a coherent group in itself. Nevertheless, and despite its often diverse membership, the states that constitute this group still meet to co-ordinate their work when this is deemed desirable.

European Union members

The members of the European Union on the Council, both permanent and non-permanent, now often consult on the drafting and amendment of resolutions.[144] On occasion the State holding the Presidency of the Union, whether a Council member or not, will speak on behalf of the European Union.[145]

(ii) 'Friends' and 'Contact' groups

Members undertake consultations in a variety of *ad hoc* Council groups that are established from time to time for specific purposes. *Contact* groups, composed of a few member states, most but not necessarily all of which are Council members, have been established to co-ordinate the resolution of a particular problem. Helen Leigh-Phippard reports that the first such group was the Western Contact Group, set up in April 1977 to facilitate the implementation of resolution 385 (1976) on South African withdrawal from Namibia. It consisted of the then five Western members of the Security Council: Canada, France, the United Kingdom, the United States, and the Federal Republic of Germany. More recently, the Contact Group on Bosnia was set up in April 1994 after negotiations in London, and consisted of France, Germany, Russia, the United Kingdom, and the United States. The Group had a certain independence from the Council, in part since it was attempting to broker a diplomatic solution following the relative stalemate in the Council, and the failure of the Vance–Owen and Owen–Stoltenberg initiatives. It met at various times at the level of Foreign Minister. Though somewhat eclipsed by later US initiatives, the map designed by the Group was to form the basis of the territorial settlement embodied in the Dayton peace agreement.[146] Prior to this, a separate 'Contact Group on Bosnia and Herzegovina of the Organization of the Islamic Conference' was established, and helped draw attention to the plight of Muslims in the region. A number of requests were made on behalf of this group for a formal meeting of the Council in April 1993 so that non-members could voice their concerns, as did the non-aligned caucus on the Council.[147]

There have also been a number of 'groups of friends' established to support the search for a resolution to a particular conflict. 'Friends' groups will often prepare the first draft of a resolution on the conflict with which they are concerned, and will consult other Council members on amendments that would be necessary to achieve a consensus text. The work of 'friends' groups is often acknowledged in Council records, such as those for Haiti,[148] Georgia,[149] El Salvador,[150] and Guatemala.[151] As with 'contact' groups, the meetings of 'friends' are private and informal affairs.

(iii) 'Arria formula' meetings

Named after the Venezuelan ambassador, Diego Arria, who presided over the first meeting in this format, this is 'a very informal consultation process . . . which affords members of the Security Council the opportunity to hear persons [principally visiting dignatories of States not members of the Council] in a confidential, informal setting'.[152] These meetings are held in private with no official records kept. While all Council members normally attend 'Arria formula' meetings, they differ from formal Council meetings in four main respects. First, they are held away from the Council Chamber, usually in Conference Rooms 5, 6, or 7. Secondly, they are generally convened and chaired by a Council member other than the Council President. Thirdly, the convenor notifies the other fourteen Council members of the date and time of an 'Arria formula' meeting by fax from his or her mission, rather than the invitation being issued by the Secretariat. Fourthly, apart from interpreters, the Secretariat is not in attendance. The 'Arria formula' is a meeting of members of the Council, rather than a meeting of the Council, and allows an exchange of views between members of the Council and non-members, which is not the practice in informal consultations of the whole. 'Arria formula' meetings are also a way by which Council members can privately consult non-State parties involved in a dispute. The President of the Palestinian Authority, Yasser Arafat, met with Council members under the format of the 'Arria formula' on 5 March 1997. The holding of an 'Arria formula' meeting can be controversial if it is seen as conferring legitimacy on a non-state party. During a period of civil war in Afghanistan in April 1997 Pakistan suggested that the Council members listen to the Taliban (one of the parties to the conflict in Afghanistan) under the Arria formula. This was strongly resisted by the representative of Afghanistan in the Council chamber.[153]

Opinions differ among non-members seeking greater access to Council decision-making, on whether it would be better to hold 'Arria' meetings with greater frequency, or whether efforts should be focused on obtaining access for non-members to consultations of the whole. In a proposal to the General Assembly Open-ended Working Group in March 1997, Ambassador Razali, President of the General

Assembly, made the former suggestion, but such a development might be a step toward, rather than an alternative to, future access to consultations of the whole.

(iv) Meetings with troop-contributors

Linked to the aforesaid measures have been developments in consultations between the members of the Council, the Secretariat and non-members who are actual or potential troop-contributors to UN peace-keeping operations. The procedures for such meetings were set out in a Presidential statement on 4 November 1994 and further strengthened in a Presidential statement on 28 March 1996 (see Appendices XII (c) and (e)). The wording of these statements made it clear that these are not meetings of the Council itself, but instead are meetings between members of the Council, troop-contributing countries, and the Secretariat jointly chaired by the President of the Council and a representative of the Secretariat

> to facilitate the exchange of information and views in good time before the Council takes decisions on the extension or termination of, or significant changes in, the mandate of a particular peace-keeping operation.[154]

In March 1996 such meetings were extended to include prospective troop contributors and the initial mandates of new operations under consideration by the Council (see Appendix XII (e)). These meetings are described in detail in Chapter 7.

> **Informal Meetings**
>
> Closed consultations among members of the Security Council and troop contributors on the United Nations Support Mission in Haiti (UNSMIH) will be held *today*, 26 November 1996, at 3 p.m. in Conference Room 7.
>
> Closed consultations among members of the Security Council and troop contributors on the United Nations Mission of Observers in Prevlaka (UNMOP) will be held *today*, 26 November 1996, at 4 p.m. in Conference Room 7.
>
> Notice in the UN *Journal*, No. 1996/230, 26 November 1996.

(v) Briefing of Council members by NGOs

On 12 February 1997 Ambassador Juan Somavía of Chile initiated a meeting at which three non-governmental organizations concerned with humanitarian assistance briefed *inter alia* members of the Security Council on the crisis in the Great Lakes region of Africa. In prior consultations a proposal that the Arria formula be adapted for the format of this innovative meeting had been suggested. Instead a format more akin to consultations between members of the Council and troop-contributing States was used, whereby the meeting was convened by the Secretariat (Department of Humanitarian Affairs) and took place in a conference room at UN headquarters. All Council members attended, along with the bureaux of ECOSOC and the Second and Third committees of the General Assembly. In an interview with Agence France Presse after the meeting Ambassador Somavía expressed hopes for further such meetings in the future. The meeting on 12 February 1997 was given little formal recognition in the Council's documentation. Whilst mentioned in a press release produced by the Office of the Spokesman of the Secretary-General, it was not listed in the UN *Journal*. The original proposal that the 'Arria formula' be adapted so that interested members of the Council would have met to hear dispositions by international and non-governmental organizations was to have been called the 'Somavía formula'. Since the meeting in February 1997 was not held under the auspices of the Security Council, a meeting under the 'Somavía formula' has not yet been realized.

9. DURATION OF MEETINGS

In the past when the Security Council met for non-urgent business, it was usually convened for 10.30 a.m. or 11 a.m. and closed at 1 p.m. or soon after, and convened again at 3 p.m. or 3.30 p.m. and closed at around 6 p.m. But the Council is supposed to be 'so organized as to be able to function continuously' (Article 28(1)), and at times of crisis it may be convened at any hour of the day or night and continue in session until its immediate task is completed. In 1956, when the Suez and Hungarian crises erupted simultaneously, the Council was in almost continuous session for several days. On 30 October, for example, the Council met on Suez from 11 a.m. to 1.10 p.m., from 4 p.m. to 7.55 p.m., and from 9 p.m. to 11.05 p.m., and at the beginning of November, it held several long meetings on Hungary, including one called for at 3 a.m. on a Sunday.

Meetings rarely last longer than five hours, but there were several eight-hour meetings in 1971 at the time of the Bangladesh war. Despite some long meetings, notably on the Occupied Territories, in the 1990s the length of meetings grew shorter as the Council often met solely to adopt resolutions and read presidential statements already agreed in informal consultations. These informal consultations, however, grew ever longer in the early 1990s, commensurate with the increase in the Council's workload.

10. THE AGENDA

It is necessary for us to start this section with three definitions.

The *provisional agenda* is the document drawn up by the Secretary-General, and approved by the President of the Council, which is placed before each meeting of the Council; it contains 'the list of matters suggested for the consideration of the Council at a specific meeting' (Rule 7).[155] As noted above the provisional agenda of both Council meetings and the programme for informal consultations is now, whenever possible, listed in advance in the UN *Journal*.

The first item of the provisional agenda is the adoption of the *Agenda* (Rule 9), which is the list of matters which the Council decides should be discussed at a particular meeting.

All items adopted on the agenda and not disposed of or expressly deleted are contained in the *Summary Statement of matters of which the Security Council is seized* (hereafter referred to as the 'Summary Statement'), which the Secretary-General is required to communicate each week to the representatives on the Security Council (Rule 11). One representative defined the expression 'matters of which the Security Council is seized' as meaning 'matters which have been on the agenda of previous meetings and have not been finally disposed of . . .', and the Chairman of the Committee of Experts agreed with this interpretation.[156]

Under Article 12(2) of the Charter, the Secretary-General is also required to notify the General Assembly each year of any matters *relative to the maintenance of international peace and security which are being dealt with by the Security Council.* The purpose of Article 12 was to prevent two of the principal organs of the United Nations from acting simultaneously on the same matter. In 1946 and 1947, the consent of the Council for the notification was given at meetings of the Council;[157] beginning in 1948, consent has been obtained through the circulation by the Secretary-General of a draft notification.[158] This notification, circulated annually, should not be confused with the *Summary Statement* described above.

Certain recurring matters, such as recommendations regarding the appointment of the Secretary-General and the election of judges of the International Court of Justice, are placed on the agenda and Summary Statement only when decisions are needed.

Rule 11 regarding the Summary Statement came into force on 9 April 1946, by which time five matters had been disposed of by the Council. Less than a week was to elapse before the Council was faced with the question of how items in the weekly Summary Statement were to be deleted.

The issue arose when the Soviet Union addressed to the President of the Council a letter in which 'the Government of the USSR insists that the Iranian question should be removed from the agenda of the Security Council'.[159] The complaint of Iran, dated 19 January 1946, had been the first matter brought to the attention of the Security Council. Iran alleged that Soviet officials and armed forces were interfering in the internal affairs of Azerbaijan, causing a situation which might lead to international friction.[160] The matter was considered at three meetings of the Council at the end of January 1946, and the Council adopted a resolution noting the readiness of the parties to seek a solution by negotiation and asking that the Council should be kept informed of the progress of any negotiation. On 4 April, the Council adopted another resolution, 'to defer further proceedings on the Iranian appeal until 6 May, at which time [the parties] are requested to report to the Council whether the withdrawal of all USSR troops from the whole of Iran has been completed'.[161] Two days later, the Soviet Union addressed a letter to the President of the Council, claiming that the Council's second resolution had been 'incorrect and illegal' and asking for the removal of the Iranian question from the agenda. On 9 April, Iran countered by asking that the Iranian complaint should remain on the Council's agenda; but six days later, Iran informed the Council that agreement with the Soviet Union had been reached and that 'the Iranian Government . . . withdraws its complaint'.[162]

When the Council met the next day, there were two documents before it. One was a draft resolution submitted by France, which would have asked the Secretary-General 'to collect the necessary information in order to complete the Security Council's report to the Assembly . . . on [the complaint of Iran] now withdrawn'.[163] The other was a memorandum from Secretary-General Lie on the legal aspects of the question of retaining Iran's complaint on the agenda.[164] Lie later summarized his view as follows:

> The Soviet Union had clearly put itself in a vulnerable position by violating the Tripartite Treaty [of 1942]; it had now given assurance that this violation would be promptly repaired, and Iran had expressed its satisfaction and withdrawn its complaint; in these circumstances I saw no point in keeping the question on the agenda. The United Nations, I felt, should aim to settle disputes, not to inflame them.[165]

Lie and Abe Feller, Lie's Legal Counsel, drew up a memorandum which Lie decided to present to the President of the Council (China). The President, however, took the view that this was a matter for the Council rather than the Secretary-General and did not accept the memorandum; but he did have it read to the Council when it met on 16 April.[166]

Lie's view was essentially a political one, although the memorandum was expressed in legal terms. With the advantage of hindsight, one could conclude that this was not one of Lie's happier efforts.

Lie argued that the Council was acting under Chapter VI of the Charter, under which three courses were open to it:

1. to call on the parties to settle their dispute by peaceful means (Article 33);
2. to undertake an investigation (Article 34);
3. to recommend procedures or terms of settlement (Articles 36–8).

The Council, Lie stated, had not decided on an investigation under Article 34. 'Now that Iran has withdrawn its complaint, the Council can take no action under Articles 33, 36, 37, or 38, since the necessary conditions . . . [namely a dispute . . .] do not exist.' In this situation, 'it may well be that there is no way in which [the Council] can remain seized of the matter'. Lie referred in passing to the argument that the matter 'is no longer a matter solely between the original parties, but one in which the Council collectively has an interest'. This, he thought, 'may well be true', but that did not alter the fact that the Council could act only under the precise terms of the Charter.

On the proposal of the President of the Council, the Secretary-General's memorandum was referred to the Committee of Experts.[167] The Committee duly met the next day and agreed 'in principle that when a matter has been submitted to the Security Council by a party, it cannot be withdrawn from the [Summary Statement] without a decision by the Security Council'. But there agreement ended; and the Committee had no option but to report to its parent body (which had the same membership as itself) that it had not been able to formulate a common opinion.

Three members (France, Poland, and the Soviet Union) had reached the same conclusion as the Secretary-General, though on the basis of different reasoning. They considered that the crucial question was whether the Iranian item was a *dispute* or a *situation.* A *dispute,* they held, was a subjective matter, 'a conflict between two or more States, which exists only by virtue of the opposition between the interested parties'. If the parties to a *dispute* reach agreement, the threat to peace disappears; and if they ask the Security Council to drop the dispute, the Council 'is bound to do so, after having noted that their agreement has put an end to the dispute'.* On the basis of this conclusion, the Iranian complaint should be deleted from the Summary Statement. In the view of the three members, however, a *situation*, unlike a dispute, has 'a clearly objective character', and the Council may remain seized of it even if the State which first brought the matter to the attention of the Council should wish to withdraw it.

The other eight members of the Council (Australia, Brazil, China, Egypt, Mexico, Netherlands, United Kingdom, and United States)

* The International Court of Justice, in its Advisory Opinion on Namibia in 1971, held that, for a matter to be a 'dispute' under Article 27(3) of the Charter, there must have been a 'prior determination *by the Security Council* that a dispute exists' (our italics).[168]

thought that it would be a mistake to regard the problem from a purely legalistic point of view. These members considered ('with variations') that the memorandum of Secretary-General Lie 'had put the problem on too narrow a basis, since it referred only to a dispute and since it treated such a dispute merely as a lawsuit between two parties'. Such a definition implied an 'inexact understanding' of the functions and competence of the Council. Even after the parties to a dispute have reached agreement, 'circumstances may continue to exist . . . which might still leave room for fears regarding the maintenance of peace and which might justify the question's being retained among the matters entrusted to its care'. In particular, the Council might find it necessary to remain seized of a matter 'until the whole or part of the agreement has been executed, or even longer'.[169]

The Council considered the report of its Committee of Experts on 23 April 1946. The Soviet representative reminded the Council that his Government 'insists that the Iranian question should be removed from the agenda'. France reintroduced its earlier proposal requesting the Secretary-General to collect the necessary information, but this was rejected by eight votes to three. The Soviet representative denounced this vote as 'contradictory to the United Nations Charter' and stated that his delegation 'cannot in future take part in discussions of the Iranian question by the Security Council'.[170]

On 8 May, in the absence of the Soviet representative, the Council asked Iran to submit a report by 20 May on the withdrawal of Soviet forces.[171] On 21 May, Iran reported that it did not have sufficient first-hand information as to the true state of affairs in Azerbaijan; but the next day Iran informed the Council that Soviet troops had in fact withdrawn some two weeks earlier.[172] On 22 May, again in the absence of the Soviet representative, the Council decided to adjourn the discussion 'until a date in the near future, the Council to be called at the request of any member'.[173] No meeting was in fact called, and the Iranian item was deleted in 1976.

Matters could in theory be removed from the Summary Statement in one of three ways: by adopting a resolution or taking a decision which disposes of the matter; by the rejection of all proposals submitted; or by explicit decisions to delete, or the rejection of proposals to retain. Requests to delete were usually made by one of the parties, but one item was deleted at the request of the President of the Council.[174] In practice, in the 1980s and early 1990s, the usual method was simply to remove an item from the list of matters of which the Council is seized, by informal agreement. It was regarded as a practical step, taken after the matter had been on the list for several years and undertaken to avoid the appearance of the Council being overloaded with redundant matters which were unlikely to come before the Council for decision. The procedure for removal was for a Member to address the Secretary-General, who then sought consent from Council members by informal communication. In the absence of objection, the item was deleted. Usually, about one item a year was deleted by this procedure. A more radical effort in the 1980s led nowhere. In 1993–4, however, as part of efforts within the Council to improve its working methods, a special effort was made to 'prune' the list, as a result of which 80 items were deleted. A further four items were deleted in January 1996 after 'extensive consideration and appropriate consultation'[175] by the informal working group of the Security Council concerning the Council's documentation and other procedural matters.

In the summer of 1996 a more fundamental change to the deletion of items from the list of matters of which the Security Council is seized (hereafter referred to as 'the list') was attempted. Methods of simplifying the list had first been discussed in the Council's Working Group on Documentation and Other Procedural Matters. Then on 30 July 1996, a Note from the President of the Council was issued.[176] This stated that the Council had decided that, as of 15 September 1996, matters that had not been considered by the Council in the preceding five years would be automatically deleted from the list. Under this proposed arrangement a matter was to be provisionally retained on the list for one year upon the request of a Member State. After this year had elapsed the matter would be automatically deleted if it had not been considered by the Council during the intervening period. Even though the Presidential Note emphasized that the removal of a matter from the list had no implication for the matter's substance, and that it had no effect on the right of members to the Council itself to raise any matter, the Note created a lively response from Member States, in large part because of the failure to consult the wider UN membership before a decision was taken on the proposals. Conceived as a means of reducing the amount of paper that delegates must plough through and simplifying matters; the proposals ended up creating in the short term considerably more paper and a fair amount of confusion. To begin with the Annex of matters seized attached to the Note contained a number of inaccuracies and the Note had to be reissued on 22 August 1996 with these corrected. The responses to the Note from Member States were of three kinds; objections to the substance of the proposals, objections to the way the proposals were agreed by the Council, and objections, following the new proposed procedure, to the deletion of particular items from the list.

Some Member States enumerated all three objections. Pakistan[177] stated that 'the list purports to deal with substantive issues on the Council's list in a procedural manner' and argued that matters on the list require a decision in formal meeting of Council prior to their deletion. Pakistan[178] and Djibouti[179] (the latter speaking on behalf of the Arab Group) called on the Council to rescind its decision and took particular objection to the distinction made in the Note between 'consideration' in formal meetings and informal consultations; since it was proposed that only those matters raised in *formal* meetings would be spared from eventual deletion, ignoring the practice of Council consideration of many important matters through the means of informal consultations. The United Arab Emirates both raised objections to the procedures set forth in the Note, and specifically asked that an item relating to sovereignty over the Greater Tunb, Lesser Tunb, and Abu Musa islands in the Arabian Gulf be retained.[180] In response to the concerns of Member States a new Note was issued by the President of the Council on 29 August 1996[181] stating that after consideration of the views of Member States, no item would be deleted from the list without the prior consent of the Member State concerned, in accordance with the following procedure:

(a) The annual summary statement issued in January of each year by the Secretary-General on matters of which the Council is seized will identify the items to be deleted from the list in the absence of any notification by a Member State by the end of February of the year in question.

(b) If a Member State of the United Nations notifies the Secretary-General that it wishes an item to remain on the list, that item will be retained.

(c) The notification will remain in effect for one year and can be renewed annually.

The new Presidential Note then stated that such notifications received by 15 September 1996 would remain in effect until the issuance of the Secretary-General's annual summary statement of January 1998.

In response to this new Note, Cuba praised the fact that items would no longer be automatically deleted, but regretted that the responsibility for action to prevent deletion still lay with individual Member States.[182] Cuba,[183] Libya,[184] and Tunisia,[185] in separate submissions, were some of the first States to request the retention of items on the list. By the deadline of 15 September 1996 there had been requests for a total of 29 items to be retained of those scheduled for deletion. In the absence of any objections 13 items were removed from the list. This left 126 items of which the Council was seized on 4 January 1997.[186] This list of items is reproduced in Appendix VII.

Over the years, there had been a trend towards vague and general formulations in the titles of items placed on the agenda. After all, purposeful ambiguity has its uses.[187] In the early years, items were generally given titles which indicated their substance: the Egyptian question, the Czechoslovak question, etc. In 1948, however, the item on the situation in Berlin was entitled 'Identical notifications dated 29 September 1948 from the Governments of the French Republic, the United Kingdom, and the United States of America to the Secretary-General'. Since November 1993 (see S/126812 of 29 November 1993) the members of the Security Council have attempted to revert to the use of descriptive formulations of agenda items, whenever possible, at the time of their initial adoption.

If the title indicates the substance of the matter, it is usual for the Council to seek a reasonably objective form of words. In 1950, after the outbreak of the Korean war, the provisional agenda of the Council had as its second item 'Aggression upon the Republic of Korea'.[188] On the proposal of the President (India), the words 'Complaint of . . . ' were inserted.[189] Similarly, in 1952, when the Soviet Union alleged that the United States had resorted to bacteriological warfare in Korea, the provisional agenda of one meeting had as its second item 'Appeal to States to accede to and ratify the Geneva Protocol of 1925 for the prohibition of the use of bacterial weapons'.[190] Even this formulation was thought to be objectionable, and the United States proposed, and the Council agreed, to insert 'Question of an . . .'.[191] On a few occasions, the titles of items have, with the Council's approval, been changed in minor respects after the initial decision to include the item.[192] In 1971, the Council held seven meetings about the war which led to the creation of Bangladesh under such items as 'Letter from . . . ' and 'Report of . . . '. Eventually the title of the item was changed to 'Situation in the India/Pakistan subcontinent'.[193]

The Council has taken what is usually described as a liberal attitude towards requests to place matters on the agenda. At one of the earliest meetings of the Council, the United States representative put the matter like this:

> The position of my Government has, consistently, since the organization of this body, been that the Council cannot deny to a member of the United Nations who states that a condition exists which is likely to threaten international peace and security, the opportunity to present its case . . .
>
> My Government thinks, without prejudice to the merits of the [Ukrainian] complaint [against Greece] or even to the good faith behind the complaint, that the Council should place a minimum of technical requirements in the way of consideration of situations brought to its attention . . .
>
> In my opinion, the Council will be derelict in its duty if it does not examine the complaint and all that may be said and brought to substantiate the complaint, with the most rigid objectivity.[194]

Other members of the Council have expressed similar views.[195]

Procedure can, of course, be used as a diplomatic weapon. A State may, for political reasons, wish to prevent the Council from taking up a matter which it finds embarrassing. There are a number of respectable arguments which can be used in favour of rejecting a proposed item, but the argument which does not now carry much weight in the Council is that the matter is outside the Council's competence. It has become the general view that the Council is not in a position to decide the question of competence until it has placed the matter on its agenda and heard the parties.[196] Here are some typical expressions of that view.

The Council will not prejudice its competence by including the communications addressed to it . . . Once the agenda has been adopted, the members of the Council will have ample opportunity to examine the questions relating to competence.—Belgium.[197]

It may . . . be thought that, in order to discuss its competency in the matter, the Council must first of all have decided to place the item on the agenda. The French delegation has always considered [that] procedure to be the more logical, and the more consistent with the good ordering of the work of the Council.—France.[198]

I should like to make it clear that the adoption of this item on the agenda does not in any way prejudice either the competence of the Security Council in the matter or any of the merits of the case.—Poland (President).[199]

The adoption of the agenda does not decide or affect in any way the question of the Security Council's competence—United Kingdom (President).[200]

The agenda could be adopted without in any way prejudging either the competence of the Security Council or any of the merits of the case.—United States.[201]

The General Assembly has a Rule of Procedure to the effect that any motion calling for a decision on the competence to adopt a proposal shall be put to the vote before a vote on the main proposal. The Security Council has no such rule in express terms, but it would be only common sense to adopt the practice of the Assembly.

Differences of opinion regarding the agenda have to be resolved by voting, but motions regarding the agenda are procedural and thus outside the scope of the veto of the permanent members. In addition to proposals to vary the wording of items, which are usually adopted without a vote, the Council has voted on motions to include an item in, or delete an item from, the agenda; to include an item in the agenda but to postpone consideration; to add an item not included in the provisional agenda; to confirm or change the order of items; to combine two or more items; and to adopt or reject the provisional agenda as a whole. In 1975, the Council twice voted separately on items on the provisional agenda, rejected one item, and then adopted the revised agenda as a whole.[202]

The practice nowadays is to have only one substantive item on the agenda. Often a series of meetings will take place, one after another, each with a new agenda item. This avoids procedural issues or delays caused by one item affecting another.

There is one aspect of the agenda which is sometimes the occasion of political manœuvring. Let us illustrate. Item 57 of the Summary Statement in 1972 was 'The situation in the Middle East'. If one side in the Middle East conflict requests a Council meeting, item 2 of the provisional agenda will be headed 'The situation in the Middle East', and underneath will be listed the letter or letters requesting the meeting. Thus, item 2 of the provisional agenda on 18 July 1972 was as follows,

2. The situation in the Middle East
   (a) Letter dated 5 July 1972 from the Permanent Representative of the Syrian Arab Republic to the United Nations addressed to the President of the Security Council (S/10730)
   (b) Letter dated 5 July 1972 from the Chargé d'affaires, *a.i.*, of the Permanent Mission of Lebanon to the United Nations addressed to the President of the Security Council (S/10731)[203]

These letters from Syria and Lebanon were in virtually identical terms and recalled part of a previous Council resolution calling for 'appropriate steps' which would lead to 'the release in the shortest possible time of all Syrian and Lebanese military and security personnel abducted by Israeli armed forces'.[204]

But there was a further item listed in the provisional agenda. As soon as Israel learned that a Council meeting was to be held to consider the complaints of Syria and Lebanon, it submitted its own letter requesting an urgent meeting of the Council 'to consider the *mutual* release of all prisoners of war' (our italics). The third item of the provisional agenda thus read:

3. The situation in the Middle East
   Letter dated 17 July 1972 from the Permanent Representative of Israel to the United Nations addressed to the President of the Security Council (S/10739)[205]

When the Council met, several representatives pointed out that they had not been consulted by the President about item 3 (China, France, Guinea, India, Japan, Somalia, Soviet Union, Sudan, Yugoslavia) prior to the meeting. The US representative, having 'gone quickly through' the Rules of Procedure, claimed that there was no requirement for prior consultation. The President of the Council (Argentina) then explained the course of events.

On 5 July, the representatives of Syria and Lebanon handed him the two letters requesting a meeting, but after discussion it was agreed to work for implementation of the Council's resolution without an immediate meeting. On 17 July, the representatives of Syria and Lebanon again met the President and expressed the view that it was now necessary to set a date for a meeting of the Council. The President, in response, suggested 3.30 p.m. the following afternoon 'so as to allow a 24-hour period to give both sides time for thought'. After the representative of Israel had been informed that the meeting would be held, he stated his intention of submitting his own letter requesting a meeting of the Council. That letter, dated 17 July, reached the President at about noon on 18 July. The President said that, in accordance with 'unchanging practice', he had included Israel's letter in the provisional agenda. He also said, somewhat less adroitly, that those who complained of lack of consultation were mistaken. 'The President of the Security Council at the beginning of this meeting consulted all members . . . on the adoption of the agenda.'

He then proposed that the Council should vote on whether or not item 3 should be deleted. After a few more interventions, the Council voted by eight votes to none, with seven abstentions, in favour of deleting the item. Eight votes were one short of the number needed to take a decision. The Council thus found itself in an awkward predicament.[206]

The correct procedure, of course, is to put to the vote *the adoption* of the agenda (which is how item 1 of the provisional agenda is invariably worded) and not *the rejection* of the agenda or of any particular item. Usually, if the President proposes that the Council should vote on the *rejection* of an item, an alert member of the Council intervenes in time to prevent the Council from wittingly or unwittingly using faulty procedure.[207]

The situation on 18 July 1972, however, was that a simple majority of the members of the Council favoured the rejection of item 3, but this majority was less than the nine votes needed to take a decision. After further procedural debate, during the course of which the Japanese representative made a sensible but unsuccessful attempt to secure a twenty-minute adjournment for informal consultation, the Council approved item 2 of the provisional agenda on the understanding that item 3 would be dealt with at a separate meeting.[208]

The Council had spent more than two hours deciding what business it should deal with.

Strictly, the Council should discuss only the adoption of the agenda or items of the agenda which the Council itself has approved. Occasionally, however, the Council has found itself listening to speeches concerned neither with the adoption of the agenda nor with items that have been approved. The Council met on 16 June 1969 'for the sole purpose of hearing . . . the views of [the President of Colombia] on certain aspects of the maintenance of international peace and security'.[209] When the Council met in Panama City in March 1972, it had a full discussion on racial discrimination without having approved an agenda. It so happened that, during the period of the Council's meetings in Panama, there occurred the annual International Day for the Elimination of Racial Discrimination (21 March). The Council met and heard statements from the Chairman of the UN Special Committee on Apartheid, the Secretary-General, the Council's President (Panama), and representatives of the Soviet Union and Kenya. It then adopted its agenda (peace and security in Latin America), bade farewell to a senior official in the Secretariat whose term of service had been completed, and at once adjourned. When questioned by the United States about the character of the meeting, the President stated that it had been 'planned and organized in agreement with the Secretary-General and the Chairman of the Special Committee on Apartheid'.[210]

In one respect, the Rules of Procedure are not strictly applied in connection with the agenda. Rule 10 reads

> Any item of the agenda of a meeting of the Security Council, consideration of which has not been completed at that meeting, shall, unless the Security Council otherwise decides, automatically be included in the agenda of the next meeting.

In presenting this Rule to the Council in draft form, the Chairman of the Committee of Experts explained that the term 'agenda' had been used advisedly. 'This rule means that the continued consideration of such business as is left over from one meeting shall constitute part of the agenda of the succeeding meeting.' The Committee of Experts thought that it should be left to the Secretary-General to indicate which items on the provisional agenda were new matters and which items had been held over from previous meetings.[211] The *Repertoire* of Practice of the Security Council commented laconically, however, that 'in practice . . . the provisional agenda has not contained all items of unfinished business'.[212]

The fact that Rule 10 is not strictly applied has been raised in meetings of the Council from time to time. On one such occasion, the initiative for not applying Rule 10 had come from the Secretary-General,[213] but more usually the responsibility has been assumed by the President of the Council for the month, whether acting in the interest of orderly procedure or from more starkly political motives.[214] On more than one occasion, paradoxically, a President has been blamed for applying Rule 10 to the letter.[215] On one famous occasion on which Rule 10 was cited, the President (United States) voted *against* the adoption of the agenda which, in accordance with Rule 7, he had himself approved.[216]

It may be doubted whether Rule 10 serves much useful purpose. The Council is free to take whatever decisions it wishes regarding the agenda, regardless of the precise contents of the provisional agenda. Nowadays it is in any case rare for the agenda to be questioned at a Council meeting since it will invariably have been approved in prior informal consultations.

11. REJECTION OF ITEMS

The Council has been reluctant to reject proposals for including new matters in its agenda, and even when items were rejected, a reasonably full debate took place before it was decided not to admit the matters; indeed, in one case the debate on the adoption of the agenda extended over six meetings (the question of Morocco, 1953).

Four arguments have been used, separately or in combination, why proposed items should not be admitted to the agenda. First, that the proposal was lacking in clarity or that more information was needed before a decision could be taken. This was the view taken by the majority regarding the Soviet proposal in 1946 requesting information on armed forces stationed on non-enemy territories, and also the Arab item in 1957 on Oman.[217]

Secondly, it was argued by France that the proposed item on the

Tunisian question should not be admitted in 1952 because no dispute or threat to peace existed.[218]

A more usual argument, essentially political, is that consideration by the Security Council would have a harmful effect on the situation or dispute, that it will interfere with measures undertaken or contemplated outside the Security Council, or that the timing is inopportune. This argument or a variant of it has been used in almost every case.[219] Finally, it is often possible for States to claim that inscription of the proposed item would represent intervention in matters which are essentially within the domestic jurisdiction of a State.[220] This argument, which was deployed in connection with the item submitted by Ireland in 1969, is not often conclusive when used on its own, as the general view of the Council has been that to include an item in the agenda does not, of itself, constitute intervention.

It has sometimes been argued that a particular matter is being submitted only for propaganda purposes.[221] This argument must always be treated with some reserve. Indeed, David Gilmour has found that the most striking fact about debates in the Security Council on the inscription of items is 'the fact that the arguments used vary according to whose affairs are being brought to the attention of the Security Council'.[222]

Everyone knows that to explain one's own point of view is simply to give the facts, but that when one's adversary does the same, it is propaganda. Most States have at one time or another used the United Nations as a forum for propaganda. This may be a distressing business for those who have to listen; but who would deny that this is preferable to more violent means of struggle? UN deliberative organs serve a necessary function as international safety-valves, allowing the escape of hot air without blowing up the whole machine.

It is noticeable that in the past when developing countries wished to raise non-urgent matters of special concern to them, they often did so when it was the turn of a developing country to preside. In January and February 1972, for example, when Somalia and Sudan presided, the Council held three meetings to discuss a proposal of the Organization for African Unity that the Council should hold a series of meetings in Africa, and held thirteen meetings on African issues in Addis Ababa, plus three meetings in New York on Southern Rhodesia. In May and June 1983, when it was the turn of Zaire and Zimbabwe to preside, the Council held seven meetings on a Nicaraguan complaint, two meetings on the Middle East, twelve meetings on Namibia, and one on South Africa. Nowadays there is no obvious connection between the nationality of the President and the matters raised by States.

12. INTERPRETATION AND TRANSLATION

In UN jargon, 'interpretation' means the rendering into another language of an *oral* statement as it is being delivered (simultaneous) or immediately after its conclusion (consecutive); 'translation' refers to the process of rendering *written* documents into another language. The six languages of the Security Council are now Arabic, Chinese, English, French, Russian, and Spanish. All oral statements given in the Security Council are now interpreted *simultaneously* into the five other languages by the highly skilled interpreters on the UN staff. Representatives who want to hear a speech in an official language other than the one being used by the speaker may use earphones by their seats and a dial to select the language of their choice.

Formerly, the Security Council distinguished between *official* and *working* languages and only English and French were *working* languages. That meant that all speeches were interpreted both *simultaneously* into the other official languages and *consecutively* at the conclusion of each statement into one or both *working* languages.

On 24 January 1969 the Council decided that the work of the United Nations would be enriched and the objectives of the Charter attained by the addition of Russian and Spanish among the *working* languages.[223] The Rules of Procedure were amended accordingly. On 17 January 1974, the Council decided that Chinese should be a *working* as well as an *official* language;[224] the distinction between *official* and *working* languages thus disappeared. On 21 December 1982, Arabic became an official *and* a working language of the Council on the assumption that the Arab States would meet the cost for the first three years; and a month later, a speech of the Jordanian representative was delivered in Arabic and interpreted into the other languages.[225] By resolution 3355 (XXIX) of 18 December 1974, the General Assembly of the United Nations decided that certain United Nations documents should be issued in the German language. A number of Security Council documents, including the provisional rules of procedure, and resolutions and decisions from 1995 onwards, are available in German on the UN World Wide Web Home Page.

Originally, all statements in the Council were interpreted simultaneously *and* consecutively, but in 1948 the Council gave up consecutive interpretation of statements by non-members of the Council. Sometimes the right to *consecutive* interpretation of statements by Council members was waived, but always on the express understanding that this did not constitute a precedent. The combination of *simultaneous* and *consecutive* interpretation was not followed in other UN organs, however, and during the course of 1972, consecutive interpretation was dropped by general consent, so that the Council is now satisfied with *simultaneous* interpretation into the five other languages. If a representative makes a speech in a language other than one of the six languages of the Security Council, 'he shall himself provide for interpretation into one of those languages' (Rule 44). Permanent sound recordings of the proceedings of Council meetings are maintained.

It is interesting how fashions have changed about simultaneous interpretation. Seventy-five years ago, the difficulty of providing diplomats with simultaneous interpretation was regarded as a great boon.

> It is difficult if not impossible [wrote H. A. L. Fisher] to tune an assembly up to a high pitch of excitement if, no matter how fiery and provocative the declamation, the impassive neutrality of the translator is invariably intruded between provocation and reply. Translation therefore tends to keep down the temperature, and in an Assembly dedicated to the promotion of international peace, this adventitious circumstance, so inconvenient, so tedious, so wasteful of time, may not be without its advantages.[226]

There have, indeed, been occasions when the time taken for consecutive interpretation in the Security Council was used for quiet diplomacy, but it was more often the case that consecutive interpretation introduced an annoying element of delay into the proceedings of the Council.

In the early days, there was resistance to the idea of simultaneous interpretation for the United Nations. A committee on the procedure and organization of the General Assembly pointed out in 1947 that, while simultaneous interpretation would contribute greatly to saving time, its use in all circumstances 'is not without serious disadvantages'. The first disadvantage was the sheer technical difficulty of interpretation when the word order of the original language differs from that of the language into which it is to be interpreted. 'In following word for word in a simultaneous interpretation, the interpreter is unable . . . to follow the general line of argument and set it forth clearly for those who are listening.' Secondly, the interpreter will not know in advance what documents will be quoted and is therefore unable to have at hand the official texts cited. Thirdly, the speaker 'does not hear the interpretation and is unable to control its accuracy or correct the errors of the interpreter'. In the case of *consecutive* interpretation, this difficulty did not arise. Indeed, one of us recalls an occasion in the Security Council when the Soviet ambassador, the late Arkady Sobolev (who presumably was without instructions from Moscow) interrupted the consecutive interpreter who had said in English 'the Soviet Government considers' with the words 'No, the Soviet *delegation* considers'.

Finally, according to the 1947 committee, simultaneous interpretation creates a physical and psychological barrier' between the speaker and his colleagues. Representatives 'miss the opportunity of familiarizing themselves with the habits of thought and the languages spoken by the other representatives'. The 1947 committee concluded that simultaneous interpretation 'can be used with advantage' for ordinary debate, but that it is not suitable when detailed negotiations or the reconciliation of various drafts are necessary'.[227]

The difficulties envisaged by the 1947 committee have not, in fact, materialized to any serious extent.

One might expect a representative to use whichever of the six languages comes most easily to him, but one gifted and highly articulate diplomat, the late Victor Andrés Belaúnde of Peru, permitted his mood to determine his choice of language. When he wished to be precise, he used French; when he wished to understate, he used English; when he wished to exaggerate, he used Spanish.

Most of the work of the Secretariat is conducted in English and, to a lesser extent, French. An attempt has been made since 1967 to achieve a better language balance in recruiting new staff. The standard of translation and interpretation in the UN is high, but small mistakes can produce minor diplomatic incidents. In 1991 Iraq made a reference in a Council debate to 'dwarfs' using the Arabic word *gizim.* This was inaccurately translated as 'pygmies', a word that in fact has no Arabic equivalent. The representative of Zaire raised an objection to what he percieved as a pejorative reference which would offend Zaire's 400,000 pygmies. He added that 'the size of a human being has never been a criterion for any scale of values'. Iraq accused him of deflecting debate away from a serious discussion of the situation in Iraq and Kuwait, since the Secretariat had already issued a corrigendum to the verbatim records correcting the offending word.[228]

13. DOCUMENTS AND RECORDS

To those who are not familiar with the documentation of the Security Council, the matter is bound to seem esoteric and perhaps unnecessarily complicated; but there are, in fact, seven main groups of printed documents to which the practitioner or scholar may want to refer.

First, there are the verbatim records of meetings of the Council, the 'Hansard' of the Council, which are issued in separate fascicles, one for each meeting, and which libraries usually bind into annual volumes.

Second, there are letters and reports issued in the S/- series, of which 26,928 had been issued up to the end of 1993; some of these also carry an A/- number if they are for circulation also to members of the General Assembly. Beginning in 1994, the old S/- series was abandoned and replaced by S/- followed by the year of issue, followed by consecutive numbers, such as S/1997/78 relating to former Yugoslavia. All S/- documents of long-term interest are printed in numerical order in quarterly Supplements to the Official Records of the Council or, in the case of certain reports, such as those of *ad hoc* subsidiary bodies, in Special Supplements. The printing of these quarterly supplements became seriously out of date, and in 1995 the

UN Secretariat decided to jump from the last volume issued, covering the period January to March 1987 (S/18553 to S/18771) to a volume covering January to March 1993 (S/24900 to S/24999), with the intention of subsequently plugging the gap created.

Third are the resolutions and decisions of the Council. Individual resolutions of the Security Council were, until 1965, issued in the S/-series and included in the Official Records or Supplements. Beginning in 1965, resolutions have been issued in mimeographed form under the symbol S/RES/-; previous resolutions were assigned numbers 1 to 199. Resolutions are numbered consecutively, the first resolution of 1997 being numbered 1093. The resolutions are also printed annually as volumes of the official records in the series S/INF/-, and in January of the subsequent year concerned as a hefty press release in the series SC/-, to ensure immediate availability. They are classified by subject-matter or item at the front of each volume and listed chronologically at the back. Presidential statements have, since 1 January 1994, been issued under a separate document symbol number, as S/PRST/- followed by their year of issue and then a sequential number, such as S/PRST/1997/3 on Angola (see Appendix X (a)).

Fourth, there has since 1964 been an annual Index to the proceedings of the Security Council (ST/LIB/Ser. B/S/-), indexing both subjects and speeches. This Index is probably of greatest value to those who are already familiar with the Council's system of documentation.

Fifth, there are the annual reports of the Council to the General Assembly, issued under the symbol A/[. . .]/2. These have hitherto been descriptive rather than analytical in nature. Each annual report is issued as a supplement to the Official Records of the General Assembly. Revisions to the format and content of the report were made in 1974, 1985, 1993, 1994, 1995, 1996, and 1997. In 1974, the Council decided to omit the summaries of speeches,[229] and in 1985 the Council decided not to summarize documents of which the complete text is available in some other form.[230] In 1993 the Council decided to add an appendix listing all presidential statements for the period under review and to provide more comprehensive cross-referencing. The Council also agreed that the draft annual report should be made available to all UN Members.[231] The 1994 report contained a more detailed introduction and two new appendicies. These listed communications from the President of the Council and communications and reports from the Secretary-General.[232] In 1995 the introduction was again enhanced and a new appendix listing notes by the President.[233] The report in 1996 contained more introductory material on the Council's Sanctions Committees.[234]

Sixth, there is the *Repertoire of the Practice of the Security Council* (ST/PSCA/1 and Add.-). The original suggestion for the preparation of the *Repertoire* was made by the United Kingdom in the Sixth Committee at the sixth session of the General Assembly. The publication gives an analytical summary of the proceedings of the Council and arranges the material by categories in texts, tables, or in the form of 'cases', organized according to the provisional rules of procedure of the Security Council and by Articles of the Charter of the United Nations.[235] The initial volume of the *Repertoire* was published in 1957 and covered the period 1946–51. Since then ten Supplements have been issued, with the last covering the period 1985–8, being published in 1997. The considerable gap between the period covered by each Supplement and the date of its publication resulted largely from a lack of resources provided to the Security Council Practices and Charter Research Branch of the Security Council Affairs Division, situated within the UN Department of Political Affairs. This was exacerbated by Secretariat cutbacks during a period where Council activity increased significantly. In December 1995, in the light of the problems incurred in the timely publication of the *Repertoire*, the General Assembly requested[236] the Special Committee on the Charter of the United Nations[237] to consider the status of the *Repertoire*, as well as its companion work, the Repertory of Practice of UN Organs. A background note[238] prepared by the Secretariat to assist the Special Committee's work, outlined a number of options for changing the mode of preparation and format of the *Repertoire*. These changes were needed to take account of the significant changes in Council procedure that had occurred over the period that the next Supplement would cover, and to ensure that effective use is made of information technology in both the preparation and dissemination of the *Repertoire*.

Lastly, there are the documents relating to subsidiary organs of the Council. The number of subsidiary organs increased significantly in the 1990s and a list of document symbol numbers for such bodies appears in Table 3.

The records referred to above comprise in the main documents which have been issued provisionally in mimeographed form. Virtually all communications and reports first appear as mimeographed documents with the symbol S/, followed by the document number, and since 1994, the symbol S/[year]/-. Document S/1, issued on 26 January 1946, was a letter from Iran to the President of the Security Council complaining about Soviet interference in the internal affairs of Iran.[239] Document S/1997/138, issued on 18 February 1997, was a letter from Zaire concerning a statement by the spokesman of the Secretary-General on the situation of refugees. Mimeographed documents and resolutions of the Council are issued in six languages (Rule 46). If the Security Council so decides, documents may be published in a language other than one of the six languages of the Council (Rule 47).

A provisional verbatim record of each public meeting of the Council is issued in the series S/PV.-, followed by the number of the meeting. The Rules of Procedure provide that provisional records shall be drawn up in the languages of the Council (Rule 45) and made available to representatives who have participated in a Council meeting by 10 a.m. of the first working day following the meeting (Rule 49),* and that representatives shall inform the Secretary-General of 'any corrections they wish to have made' within two working days of receipt of the provisional record (Rule 50). Corrections which have been requested are approved, unless the President is of the opinion that they are sufficiently important to be submitted to all members of the Security Council. In that event, members must submit any comments they wish to make within two working days. In the absence of such objection, the record is corrected as requested (Rule 52).

To fulfil the requirements of Rules 50 and 52 regarding corrections, the provisional verbatim record (PV) bears a footnote which, in the English language version, states that:

* The Council occasionally agrees to waive the requirement in Rule 49 on the timing of the issuance of the verbatim record. In 1990 when the Council met in Geneva to hear Mr Yasser Arafat speak, it was decided that the verbatim record would be issued in New York subsequently.

This record contains the original text of speeches delivered in English and interpretations of speeches delivered in the other languages. The final text will be printed in the *Official Records of the Security Council.* Corrections should be submitted to original speeches only. They should be incorporated in a copy of the record and be sent under the signature of a member of the delegation concerned, *within one week of the date of publication*, to the Chief of the Verbatim Reporting Section, room C-178.[240]

Corrections should be limited to actual errors and omissions. When a request is submitted for the deletion or addition of a passage, a check is made against the sound recording of the relevant speech. Only in cases of serious errors or omissions affecting the substance of the discussion is a provisional corrigendum, addendum, or revised text prepared and distributed, and then only as an exceptional measure.[241]

Normally, the application of the Rules regarding corrections causes no public difficulty. The only cases we recall of the verbatim record being seriously challenged occurred in 1950 and 1952. The provisional record of the Council meeting held on 16 November 1950 did not contain the text of a statement from the People's Republic of China, which had been read in full to the Council by the Council's secretary. When the Council met the next day, the Soviet Union drew attention to the omission. The President (Yugoslavia) intervened at once to say that the matter would be rectified when the definitive official record was published.[242] On the second occasion, there was some misunderstanding as to whether or not the President had closed the meeting and therefore as to whether certain remarks should or should not form part of the record. Things were put right at the next meeting when a representative read from the sound recording the matter omitted from the provisional record of the previous meeting.[243]

After necessary corrections have been made to the provisional verbatim record, it is supposed to be 'signed by the President' (Rule 53) and 'published . . . as soon as possible' (Rule 54) in the series Security Council Official Records (SCOR),—year,—meeting (date) in the six languages of the Council (Rule 45); but the requirement that the President shall sign the record fell into disuse at an early stage.

In a few cases, written or photographic material referred to or circulated round the table at Council meetings has been incorporated into the Official Records or Supplements.[244] In 1971, a proposal was submitted by Sierra Leone that a film on Namibia (South West Africa) should form part of the Official Records of the Security Council, but the view of members of the Council was that this would constitute a dangerous precedent. The French representative was reluctant to convert the Council into 'a kind of cinema club'. The US representative admitted that he loved to watch movies, but that he was worried about establishing a precedent, and the British representative was afraid that, if films were shown on every matter before the Council, 'we may find ourselves with rather a lot of work'. To the Soviet representative, it was 'a rather clear, simple problem' and his answer was equally clear and simple: 'A film cannot become a document of the Security Council'. The President of the Council (Nicaragua) suggested that to create the precedent requested by Sierra Leone 'would open up a Pandora's box'. He suggested, and Sierra Leone and other Council members agreed, that 'the film be placed in the files of the Secretariat and available to anyone who wished to see it'.[245]

In 1979, Lebanon invited members of the Council to view a documentary film of a village at war in Southern Lebanon, and this was screened the following day in the auditorium of the UN library.[246] In the late 1980s it became more common for non-members as well as members of the Council to request and be granted permission to show audio-visual material in the Council. It is now generally accepted that such material should become part of the Official Records of the Council, but the Council's exact practice in this regard has been inconsistent. In 1983, the United States played a tape-recording from the cockpit of a Korean airliner, and the transcript supplied by the United States was incorporated into the verbatim record.[247] In 1985, at the request of Chad, a videotape was shown in the Council Chamber, and the narration was also incorporated into the official record.[248] In 1989 there was first a 'video presentation' by Panama which had expressed fears of 'imminent war';[249] at a meeting of the Council three months later El Salvador and Nicaragua each presented audio-visual material accusing the other of aggression. El Salvador showed a videotape and Nicaragua a series of slides followed by a videotape.[250] In 1990, a videotape was shown in the Council, and a transcript subsequently included in the official records, both at the request of the Observer of Palestine. The records report that 'The following is the interpretation from Arabic of segments of the audio portions of that tape'.[251] The same wording was used for the showing of a videotape later that month at the request of Kuwait. The videotape was displayed in segments interspersed with purported eyewitness accounts.[252]

The Council may decide that, for a private meeting, a single copy of the verbatim record shall be made and kept by the Secretary-General. In that event, corrections may be submitted within a period of ten days (Rule 51). UN Members which have taken part in a private meeting 'shall at all times have the right to consult the record of that meeting in the office of the Secretary-General'. Other Members may have access to the record of a private meeting but only if the Security Council so authorizes (Rule 56). On three occasions the verbatim record of a private meeting has been issued in addition to a *communiqué*.

The provisional agenda for each meeting of the Security Council is issued in mimeographed form in the series S/Agenda/-, followed by the number of the meeting. The current Provisional Rules of Procedure of the Security Council (dating from 1982) bear the symbol S/96/Rev. 7.

The Secretary-General is supposed to submit to the Council each year a list of records and documents which have been considered confidential, and the Council should decide which of these should be made public and which should remain confidential (Rule 57), but this Rule is not, in fact, consistently applied.

In the early 1990s the UN Secretariat increased its use of electronic media for the dissemination of UN Resolutions and other documents. Security Council resolutions since 1974 and other UN documents were made available to those on the global *Internet* at the site www.un.org.[253] A searchable database of Security Council resolutions since 1994 was established at this site in 1995, and there are plans to extend this further. A full set of searchable UN Security Council and General Assembly resolutions has been published on CD-Rom.

TABLE 3

Symbols of documents of main subsidiary organs of the Security Council

S/AC.4/–	United Nations Commission of Investigation concerning Greek Frontier Incidents, 1947
S/AC.7/–	Conference of the General Assembly and Security Council Committees on Procedure for the Admission of New Members, 1947
S/AC.8/–	Subcommittee on the Greek Question, 1947
S/AC.10/–	United Nations Commission for Indonesia, 1947–51
S/AC.12/–	United Nations Commission for India and Pakistan, 1948–50
S/AC.13/–	Subcommittee [on Laos] established under resolution 132 (S/4216) of 7 September 1959
S/AC.14/–	Expert Committee on South Africa established by resolution 191 (S/5773) of 18 June 1964
S/AC.15/–	Committee established in pursuance of resolution 253 (S/8601) [concerning the question of Southern Rhodesia], 29 May 1968
S/AC.16/–	Committee of Experts [on Mini-States] established at the meeting on 29 August 1969
S/AC.17/–	*Ad Hoc* Subcommittee [on Namibia] established by resolution 276 (S/9620/Rev.1), 30 January 1970
S/AC.18/–	*Ad Hoc* Subcommittee [on Namibia] reestablished by resolution 283 (S/9891), 29 July 1970
S/AC.19/–	Committee on Council Meetings away from Headquarters (Article 28(3) of the Charter), 11 January 1972
S/AC.20/–	Committee established by resolution 421 (1977) concerning the question of South Africa
S/AC.21/–	Commission established under resolution 446 (1979) concerning settlements in the Arab territories occupied since 1967, including Jerusalem
S/AC.22/–	*Ad Hoc* Committee established under resolution 455 (1979) concerning the complaint of Zambia
S/AC.23/–	Commission of Inquiry established under resolution 496 (1981) concerning the situation of Seychelles
S/AC.24/–	*Ad Hoc* Committee established under resolution 507 (1982) concerning the Special Fund for the Republic of Seychelles
S/AC.25/–	Committee concerning the situation between Iraq and Kuwait under resolution 661 (1990)
S/AC.26/–	Governing Council of the Compensation Commission for Kuwait
S/AC.27/–	Committee concerned with the embargo on military deliveries to Yugoslavia established pursuant to resolution 724 (1991)
S/AC.28/–	Committee concerning Libya, resolution 748 (1992)
S/AC.29/–	Committee concerning Somalia, resolution 751 (1992)
S/AC.30/–	Committee concerning Haiti, resolution 841 (1993)
S/AC.31/–	Committee concerning Angola, resolution 864 (1993)
S/AC.32/–	Committee concerning Rwanda, resolution 918 (1994)
S/AC.33/–	Committee concerning Liberia, resolution 985 (1995)
S/C.1/–	Committee of Experts on the Rules of Procedure, 1947–
S/C.2/–	Committee on the Admission of New Members, 1947–
S/C.3/–	Commission for Conventional Armaments, 1947–50
S/CNM/–	Committee on the Admission of New Members, 1946
S/PROCEDURE/–	Committee of Experts on the Rules of Procedure, 1946–7
S/SCS/–	Subcommittee of the Security Council on the Spanish Question, 1946

14. COMMUNICATIONS

The practice regarding the circulation of written communications has provided endless opportunities for UN gamesmanship. When the procedure for circulating communications from non-governmental sources was approved in 1946, there seemed to be general agreement that such communications should be circulated only if they dealt with matters with which the Security Council was seized; that frivolous communications should be ignored; and that the Secretariat, in circulating a list of communications received, should have discretion to indicate the subject-matter of each communication.[254] A list of all communications received from private individuals and non-governmental bodies is therefore circulated under the S/NC document series, and any member of the Council may obtain from the Secretariat a copy of any communication on the list (Appendix to the Rules of Procedure). Minor variations of this procedure occur if a member of the Council or a member of the Organization requests the circulation of a communication from a non-governmental body[255] (or, indeed, from an entity claiming to be a State or States, a regional organization, or agency for collective self-defence, or any other body), regardless of the contents, so long as the communication deals with a matter within the Council's competence.[256] If a member of the Organization transmits a communication and requests that it be circulated as a Council document, both the letter of transmittal and the communication are circulated.

The Secretary-General is required to bring to the Council's attention 'for the consideration of the Security Council in accordance with the provisions of the Charter' all communications from 'States [whether Members of the United Nations or not], organs of the United Nations, or the Secretary-General' (Rule 6). If a State which is not a member of the Council asks to participate in the discussion of some matter, and the Council decides to postpone consideration of the request or to reject it (nowadays a rare proceeding), the Council may invite the State concerned to submit its views in writing for circulation to the Council.[257] The Secretary-General has occasionally circulated documents with a prefatory note to the effect that he is not able to determine whether he is required by the Provisional

Rules of Procedure to circulate the communication, or that the communication is circulated for the convenience of members and the Secretary-General's action is not necessarily an application of Rule 6.[258]

The Secretary-General has also circulated to the Council communications from bodies such as the Organization of American States, the Organization of African Unity, and the North Atlantic Treaty Organization arising from the Charter obligation to keep the Security Council fully informed of activities for the maintenance of international peace and security undertaken or in contemplation under regional arrangements or by regional agencies (Article 54). On three occasions in the period 1946-8, communications concerning aspects of the Trieste question were circulated to the Council at the request of the Council of (four) Foreign Ministers.[259]

Relatively few communications have been circulated expressly to meet the Charter obligation to report immediately to the Council on measures taken in the exercise of the right of individual or collective self-defence after an armed attack has occurred (Article 51). The first was on 13 February 1958, when Tunisia reported on measures taken after France had attacked Sakiet-Sidi-Youssef;[260] another was on 9 May 1972, when the United States reported that, because of North Vietnamese aggression and intransigence, her ports were being mined.[261] In 1975, the Unitcd States reported that it had undertaken 'certain appropriate measures' in response to a Cambodian attack on the US merchant vessel SS *Mayaguez*.[262] In 1986, both Libya and the United States claimed that their actions in the Eastern Mediterranean were taken under or were consistent with Article 51.[263]

States have often claimed to be acting in self-defence—India and Pakistan in Kashmir, Israel and the Arab States in the Middle East, the United States in the Gulf of Tonkin, the Soviet Union in Czechoslovakia. But States have not, as a matter of course, referred to Article 51 to explain the measures they have taken. Egypt cited Article 51 in 1951 to justify restricting shipping through the Suez Canal and in 1967 after the outbreak of the June war;[264] Lebanon in 1958 after asking for help in stopping Egyptian interference in its internal affairs;[265] Israel on the day the Six Day War broke out in 1967, on the ground that there had been an Egyptian attack, as well as in August 1973, to justify the forcible diversion of an Arab passenger aircraft to a military air base in Israel in the mistaken belief that the plane was carrying an important Palestinian leader.[266] Israel has also referred to Article 51 to justify reprisal or punitive action against Arab targets.[267] The United States claimed that it had 'acted in self-defence' after USS *Vincennes* had accidentally shot down an Iranian civilian aircraft with the consequent loss of 290 lives in 1988. The following year the US reported that it had acted in self-defence under the provisions of Article 51 following its shooting down of two Libyan reconnaisance aircraft,[268] and its actions in Panama in 1989[269] although the validity of these claims were disputed by a number of States.[270] In 1993 the US and some members of the Non-Aligned Movement sought to exempt the Government of Bosnia and Herzegovina from the arms embargo imposed on it by resolution 713 (1991) in order that it could exercise its right of self-defence recognized in Article 51, but their draft resolution failed to obtain the required number of votes in the Council.[271]

In June 1993 the United States undertook a military operation against the Iraqi Intelligence Headquarters in Iraq. The US ambassador requested a meeting of the Council to explain that the US had acted in self-defence as recognized in Article 51, following the discovery of a plan to assassinate former President George Bush when he had been on a visit to Kuwait in April 1992. The legitimacy of this claim is questionable since action may only be taken in self-defence under Article 51 'until the Security Council has taken measures necessary to maintain international peace and security'. Given that the assassination plot had occurred more than a year earlier, there appeared to be no need for unilateral action before the Council had considered the facts of the case, and had decided on what action it would take. Nevertheless the actions of the US in this case were supported by many on the Council, and New Zealand expressed gratitude that the US had 'promptly informed the Security Council of the action it has taken'.[272]

At other times the Council itself has authorized States in advance to act in self-defence under the provisions of Article 51. Resolution 661 (1990) explicitly cited the right of individual or collective self-defence in response to Iraq's attack on Kuwait.

One indirect reference to Article 51 took place in 1962, when Cuba complained that its exclusion from the Organization of American

States was contrary to Article 53 of the UN Charter (Regional Arrangements). France suggested that Article 53 did not apply. The OAS action was 'essentially a matter of collective protection which is justified under Article 51'[273]—although nobody claimed that Cuba had engaged in or been subject to 'an armed attack'.

Neither the Charter nor the Provisional Rules of Procedure expressly grant to the Secretary-General discretion regarding the circulation of communications. Secretary-General Hammarskjold stated on one occasion that the only information he had withheld from the Council in the Congo case was 'some information which I have not found it in order to put to the Council, following normal diplomatic rules as regards interests of various Member nations . . . Papers which would never be circulated . . . because of their character, or because of their origin, should not be circulated in this case . . . , unless explicitly requested by members.'[274] On another occasion, after the Soviet Union had refused to have dealings with Hammarskjold, the Soviet representative complained to the President of the Council that 'the United Nations Secretariat' was failing to implement Security Council decisions, and asked for the circulation of a letter from Antoine Gizenga, who was described in the Soviet letter as 'the Head of the Government of the Republic of the Congo', but who had described himself as 'Deputy Prime Minister'. Hammarskjold complied with the Soviet request without demur.[275] Later the same year, shortly after the death of Hammarskjold, the Secretariat was apparently reticent about circulating two communications from Moïse Tshombé, because Katanga was not a separate State but part of the Congo. When the matter was raised in the Security Council, however, U Thant readily agreed to circulate the communications.[276]

What is the Secretary-General to do if he is asked to circulate a document containing disrespectful, offensive, or insulting language? On 11 March 1963, for example, the Revolutionary Government of Cuba asked for the circulation of a document some 6,000 words in length. The strong language used in the document was not qualitatively unprecedented in the annals of United Nations invective; it was, rather, the *quantity* of abusive language which gave the document its distinctive character. A few extracts from the document follow.[277]

. . . lack of respect for the sovereignty of my country, the continual violations of our air space and territorial waters, the organization of a web of espionage and piracy throughout the Caribbean, the infiltration of saboteurs into our territory, and the atmosphere of hysteria which the United States is fostering . . .

. . . a den of spies, saboteurs and counter-revolutionaries and a hotbed of provocation, subversion and aggression.

. . . irresponsible, hypocritical and cynical statements full of rancour and provocations.

. . . stronghold of intervention, subversion, conspiracy and aggression.

Venezuela addressed four letters to the President of the Security Council, and Costa Rica and Paraguay one each, insisting that UN documents intended for circulation 'should be consistent with the importance and dignity of the highest international organization'.[278] The President of the Council (Brazil) could only reply that the language used in communications 'is the responsibility of the Government from which the communication emanates'. The President of the Council had no power 'to modify the language of a communication'.[279]

But the real opportunity for UN gamesmanship for more than five years concerned the circulation of communications from the German Democratic Republic—a matter which had also arisen in other UN organs. The issue was first raised in the context of the Security Council in 1967, in a *note verbale* from the Soviet Union to the Secretary-General. The gist of the Soviet complaint was that communications from the Federal Republic of Germany were circulated by the Secretariat as a matter of course, while communications from the German Democratic Republic were circulated only following a specific request by a member of the Council. As an example of the Secretariat's allegedly discriminatory practice, the Soviet Union cited what had happened about communications received from governments concerning the implementation of the Council's resolutions imposing sanctions against the illegal regime in Southern Rhodesia. Not only had the Secretariat declined 'without any grounds whatsoever' to circulate a communication from the German Democratic Republic until requested to do so by Bulgaria, but the Secretariat had resorted to 'gross distortion' of the State's official name by referring to the State as 'Eastern Germany'. Moreover, at the time of the

Bulgarian request, according to the Soviet Union, Bulgaria had been President of the Security Council.* The practice of the Secretariat, argued the Soviet Union, was 'devoid of any legal foundation' and 'narrowly pro-Western and unobjective'.[280]

The fact that Secretary-General U Thant did not reply until seven weeks later suggests that the matter was sufficiently complicated to necessitate consultations with some of the other States most concerned. The reply, when it appeared, was in two parts. First, on the specific matter of sanctions against Southern Rhodesia, the Security Council had called upon 'States Members of the United Nations or of the specialized agencies' to report to the Secretary-General. Under that formula, the Secretariat had acted properly in circulating the communication from the Federal Republic of Germany. Similarly, the Secretariat had followed the practice of the Council in circulating the communication from the German Democratic Republic as soon as requested to do so by a Council member.

On the wider question of the circulation of documents, the Secretary-General said it was beyond his competence to determine the status of areas in dispute. He could only continue the existing practice until he received from the deliberative organ concerned an explicit directive to the contrary.[281]

There the matter might have rested, had not the Soviet Union soon returned to the attack. It was precisely the practice of the Council which the Soviet Union was challenging; the practice had, moreover, evolved without any express decision of a UN organ. The Soviet Union trusted that the Secretary-General would take steps to discontinue the Secretariat's 'abnormal practice'.[282]

The same problem arose periodically after 1967 in connection with communications from the German Democratic Republic, circulated at the request of a sympathetic President,[283] sometimes leading to a Western protest[284] and an East European riposte,[285] and in one case to an explanation from the Secretary-General about the practice of the Secretariat.[286]

The Western case throughout was simply that only the Federal Republic of Germany was entitled to speak on behalf of Germany in international affairs. The German Democratic Republic was, as the

* This was slightly stretching a point; the Bulgarian request was dated 27 February 1967, while Bulgaria's presidency had been for the month of March.

US representative vividly put it in 1968, 'nothing more than a proxy for the Government of the Soviet Union'.[287] The East European case was that there were in Germany two separate States, a thesis which won increasing acceptance as Chancellor Brandt successfully pursued his *Ostpolitik*. By the end of 1972, the German Democratic Republic had been admitted to the UN Economic Commission for Europe, and on 19 September 1973 both German States were admitted to UN membership. The two Republics were re-unified in 1990.

But even though the problem of circulating communications from the German Democratic Republic had vanished, Rule 6 continued to provide a basis for UN gamesmanship. Indeed, in March 1970, during the presidency of Colombia, Israel requested the circulation of a speech by Abba Eban about the plight of Soviet Jewry, to which the Soviet Union protested, followed by a defence on the part of Israel and a second Soviet protest.[288] The United States took advantage of its presidency during February 1971 to circulate a *note verbale* from the Permanent Observer of the Republic of Vietnam (South);[289] a communication from Bangladesh was circulated in 1971 at the request of India and another one in 1972 at the direction of the President of the Council;[290] in 1974, a communication from Cyprus was circulated at the request of the Secretary-General;[291] the following year, a communication from the Turkish Cypriots was circulated under a covering letter from Turkey;[292] in 1976, a communication from the Palestine Liberation Organization was circulated under a covering letter from Libya;[293] and in 1986, the Soviet Union complained at the circulation by the President of a communication from the Republic of Korea (South).[294] The game is endless, and any number can play.

The general problem of circulating communications eventually caused the Secretary-General to ask for the guidance of the General Assembly. Israel had requested the Secretary-General to circulate an appeal from 239 Jews in the Soviet Union, asking to be allowed 'to reunite with our people in Israel'. The Soviet Union complained that this was 'a typical slanderous letter' circulated with 'the assistance of pro-Israeli members of the staff'. The Secretary-General explained the practice which the Secretariat had followed for many years 'in the absence of guide-lines on the part of the General Assembly'. Israel then complained that 'certain Member States' were using UN organs and facilities 'as mere instruments of their self-centred policies and propaganda'. The Secretary-General circulated the communication 'on the basis of long-standing practice', and he announced his intention of asking the General Assembly to review the current practice regarding the circulation of communications from Member States and to provide him with guidance.[295] But the General Assembly was not able in 1973 to give the guidance for which the Secretary-General had asked and merely took note of a memorandum setting out the existing practice.[296] The problem thereafter got swamped by the wider question of controlling UN documentation.

Problems with nomenclature in documentation also arose following the breakup of the Federal Republic of Yugoslavia. On 19 September 1992,[297] by resolution 777 (1992) the Council considered that the State formerly known as the Socialist Federal Republic of Yugoslavia had ceased to exist and that the Federal Republic of Yugoslavia (Serbia and Montenegro) could not automatically continue as the successor State to that entity, but instead must apply for membership in the United Nations. The resolution also recommended that the General Assembly decide that the Federal Republic of Yugoslavia (Serbia and Montenegro) could not participate in the work of the Assembly. The recommendations in this resolution were accepted by the General Assembly on 22 September.[298] Participation was still permitted in the Security Council and other bodies, and the Council had to decide how to issue an appropriate invitation following a request to participate from the Federal Republic of Yugoslavia. When Mr Jovanovic, the *chargé* of the Federal Republic of Yugoslavia, was invited to participate in Council proceedings on 15 December 1995, he was referred to without a country designation by the President (the Russian Federation) and in the subsequent verbatim records. This is still the current practice at the time of writing. See Chapter 3 for more details.

CHAPTER 3

THE PEOPLE

The Venetian ambassador to Rome was spending the night with the Duke of Tuscany, who complained that Venice had sent to his court as ambassador a man who possessed neither judgment nor knowledge nor even an attractive personality. 'I am not surprised,' said the Venetian ambassador, 'we have many fools in Venice.' 'We also have fools,' replied the Duke, 'but we take care not to export them.'

1. SECRETARY-GENERAL

The responsibilities of the Secretary-General are derived from three main sources: the express and implied provisions of the Charter, the Provisional Rules of Procedure of the Security Council (whether the responsibilities are obligatory or discretionary) and the decisions of the Security Council and other UN organs. In addition to these sources, custom and usage must also be considered.

The first source, the Charter, describes the Secretary-General as 'the chief administrative officer' of the United Nations (Article 97) and states that he shall appoint such staff as the Organization may require, under regulations established by the General Assembly (Article 101(1)). The Secretary-General, 'shall act in that capacity in all meetings . . . of the Security Council' and other deliberative organs, and shall 'perform such other functions as are entrusted to him by these organs' (Article 98). As noted in Chapter 2, the Secretary-General is required by the Charter, 'with the consent of the Security Council', to notify the General Assembly at each session of any matters relative to the maintenance of international peace and security which are being dealt with by the Security Council, and similarly to notify the Assembly (or UN Members if the Assembly is not in session) immediately the Security Council ceases to deal with such matters (Article 12(2)). The Secretary-General and the staff shall not seek or receive instructions from any government or other authority external to the United Nations, and shall refrain from any action which might reflect on their position as international officials responsible only to the Organization (Article 100(1)). UN Members, for their part, undertake to respect the exclusively international character of the responsibilities of the Secretary-General and the staff, and 'not to seek to influence them' in the discharge of their responsibilities (Article 100(2)).

If that were all that the Charter had to say about the duties of the Secretary-General, there would be no need for much further comment. But Article 99 of the Charter confers on the Secretary-General a right which, although at first sight may seem only procedural in character, enables the Secretary-General in practice to undertake a wide range of political and diplomatic activities. Article 99 provides that the Secretary-General may bring to the attention of the Security Council 'any matter which in his opinion may threaten the maintenance of international peace and security'. Furthermore, according to the Rules of Procedure of the Security Council, if the Secretary-General brings a matter to the attention of the Council under Article 99, the President '*shall* call a meeting' (Rule 3, our italics).

The right to bring a matter to the attention of the Security Council under Article 99 has only rarely been expressly invoked. The Security Council met when war broke out in Korea in 1950, its agenda containing both a US communication and a cablegram from the UN Commission on Korea. Secretary-General Lie later claimed that he had invoked Article 99 on that occasion, although his memory in this regard was rather unreliable.[1] Secretary-General Hammarskjold was generally hesitant to invoke Article 99. None the less, on two occasions (the Suez[2] crises and the invasion of Hungary,[3] both in 1956) he told the Security Council that he would have invoked Article 99 had not the matter already been brought to the attention of the Security Council. In bringing the Congo crisis to the attention of the Council in 1960, Hammarskjold used the language of Article 99 without expressly citing it.[4] The result was that he and his colleagues were subject to pressure from those diplomats who believed that resort to

Article 99 would, or at any rate might, lead to the instant liberation of their people from tyrannical rule.

Secretaries-General Thant and Waldheim were similarly conservative in their invocation of Article 99. Thant in fact warned in September 1971 that 'nothing could be more divisive and useless than for the Secretary-General to bring a situation publicly to the Security Council when there is no practical possibility of the Council agreeing on effective or useful action'.[5] Yet both Secretaries-General found cause in the course of their respective terms to use the language of Article 99 to draw the attention of the Security Council to crises, which, in their views, posed a threat to international peace and security. For Thant, it was the situation in 1971 'in East Pakistan *vis-à-vis* the adjoining Indian states'.[6] For Waldheim, it was the 1979 crisis in Iran, where US diplomats were being held hostage.[7]

While Article 99 has only rarely been expressly invoked, it has none the less provided successive Secretaries-General with a convenient hold-all to conduct such activities as each has deemed appropriate to his office, even (or perhaps especially) in the absence of the explicit authority of a policy-making body. Under the implied responsibilities of Article 99, the Secretaries-General have appointed staff, authorized research, made visits, and engaged in diplomatic consultations. The justification for such activities was articulated by Secretary-General Lie when the Security Council was considering the Ukrainian complaint against Greece in 1946. Lie intervened in the discussion 'to make clear my own position as Secretary-General and the rights of this office under the Charter'.

> I hope the Council will understand that the Secretary-General must reserve his right to make such enquiries or investigations as he may think necessary, in order to determine whether or not he should consider bringing any aspect of this matter to the attention of the Council under the provisions of the Charter.[8]

Secretary-General Hammarskjold was equally explicit. Addressing a meeting of a committee of the General Assembly in 1960, Hammarskjold asked how the Secretary-General could draw the attention of the Security Council to threats to peace and security if all he had to rely on were 'reports in the Press or from particular Governments'.

> [The Secretary-General] had to find out for himself, and that could mean that he had to go himself . . . To deny the Secretary-General the right to such personal fact-finding was, in fact, to erase Article 99 from the Charter.

The Secretary-General could not forget 'the responsibilities and needs which flowed from Article 99'.[9] Hammarskjold reinforced this point in 1961 when, having accepted the invitation of President Bourguiba to visit Tunisia, he told the Security Council that it was 'obvious' that he could not discharge his responsibilities 'flowing from' Article 99 unless he could, in case of need, make visits in such a way as to be in a position 'to form a personal opinion about the relevant facts' of a situation which might threaten international peace and security.[10] U Thant made a similar point in 1971.[11] No member of the Council challenged the interpretation of the duties of the Secretary-General stated by Lie in 1946, Hammarskjold in 1960 and 1961, or Thant in 1971.

In addition to the express provisions of the Charter, such as in Article 99 and others mentioned above, the Secretary-General has implied powers arising from Article 33(1), which lists means which may be used to achieve the peaceful settlement of disputes. Among these means are 'other peaceful means of their own choice', which, as noted above, can include States requesting the Secretary-General to use his good offices with a view to seeking a solution.[12] He may also initiate fact-finding missions as a means of probing the opportunities for peace-making, as did U Thant in connection with the Nigerian civil war, Waldheim in connection with the war on the South Asian subcontinent which led to the emergence of Bangladesh, and Pérez de Cuéllar and Boutros-Ghali in more recent operations.[13] In this context, Boutros-Ghali urged on several occasions 'that the Secretary-General be authorized by the General Assembly, pursuant to Article 96 of the Charter, to turn to the [International Court of Justice] for advisory opinions, providing a legal dimension to his diplomatic efforts to resolve disputes'.[14]

The Secretary-General himself, and through the person of the United Nations Legal Counsel—in the exercise of another power implied by the Charter—issues legal opinions upon the request of United Nations organs, some of which are reprinted in the *Juridical Yearbook*. Throughout the term of Boutros-Ghali, whose first three years in office were marked by an enormous increase in the number and scope of United Nations activities in the field of peace and security, the Secretary-General and the Legal Counsel were 'heavily involved in legal work related to the expansion and diversification of the activities of the Security Council', ranging from the establishment of international criminal tribunals as subsidiary bodies of the Security Council, to the establishment of new peace-keeping missions, the conclusion of others, and the implementation of sanctions regimes.[15]

Lastly, the Secretary-General exercises considerable indirect influence by reason of the fact that he supplies documentation for the Security Council and the other organs of the United Nations.

We turn next to the second source of the Secretary-General's functions in regard to the Security Council, to those Rules of Procedure which impose duties, or confer rights, on the Secretary-General. The duties, those functions which the Secretary-General 'shall' perform, are as follows:

1. He gives to representatives on the Security Council notices of meetings of the Council and its subsidiary organs (Rule 25);
2. He draws up the provisional agenda for each meeting of the Council for the approval of the President (Rule 7) and communicates it to representatives on the Council (Rule 8);
3. He provides the Council with the staff that it requires (Rule 24);
4. He examines and reports on the credentials of representatives (Rule 15);
5. He prepares documents required by the Council (Rule 26);
6. He immediatly brings to the attention of all representatives on the Council communications concerning any matter for the consideration of the Council in accordance with the Charter (Rule 6);
7. If the Council decides that, for a private (closed) meeting, the record shall be kept in a single copy only, this record is to be kept by the Secretary-General (Rule 51);
8. Each week he communicates to representatives a summary statement of matters of which the Council is seized and the stage reached in their consideration (Rule 11);
9. Each year, he submits to the Council a list of the records and documents which up to that time have been considered confidential (Rule 57), although this requirement is in practice disregarded;
10. He places before representatives on the Council each application for UN membership (Rule 59).

The third item in particular, the provision of staff by the Secretary-General, would seem to pose some difficulty. In practice, however, that difficulty has proved much less than expected. In 1948, for example, Secretary-General Lie decided solely on his own authority to accede to the request of Count Folke Bernadotte, the UN Mediator in the Middle East, to supply fifty armed guards to exercise control functions in connection with the Palestine truce. The Soviet Union considered Lie's action to be 'incorrect and without legal basis', but a senior official of the Secretariat explained that, before acting on Bernadotte's request, Lie had obtained the advice of the UN Legal Office. The Legal Office had advised that the Secretary-General was empowered to meet the request not only under the terms of a resolution of the General Assembly, which had asked the Secretary-General 'to provide the mediator with the necessary staff to assist in carrying out the functions assigned to [him]', but also in fulfilment of his duties as the chief administrative officer of the United Nations.[16]

In 1958, at the time of the Lebanon crisis, Secretary-General Hammarskjold told the Security Council that he intended to 'use all opportunities offered to the Secretary-General, within the limits set by the Charter and towards developing the United Nations' effort', by strengthening and enlarging the already existing Observation Group in the Lebanon, even though proposals more or less to that effect had already been vetoed.[17]

At the time of the difficulties in the Dominican Republic in 1965, the Council invited Secretary-General U Thant to send a representative to the troubled area for the purpose of reporting to the Council. U Thant informed the Council at another meeting later the same day of the action he was taking, and on a subsequent occasion he assured the Council that the UN staff in the Dominican Republic would be enlarged if that were necessary.[18] In 1973, Secretary-General Waldheim arranged for Major-General Ensio Siilasvuo to be appointed Commander of the UN Emergency Force in the Middle East by an exchange of letters with the President of the Security Council.[19] An exchange of letters of this sort occurs on a frequent and routine basis in the Council for all such appointments.

From these and other cases, it would seem that the usual basis for the appointment of special staff is to be found in Articles 97, 98, and

101(1) and (2) of the Charter, Rule 24 of the Rules of Procedure, and specific decisions of the Security Council. Nevertheless, there have been a number of appointments by the Secretary-General the legal basis for which was more ambiguous. In an address delivered in London in 1970, Secretary-General U Thant said that some situations are so serious that the Secretary-General may decide that his duty requires him to act without the authority of a deliberative organ and sometimes even without a specific request from the parties. Thant then gave a number of examples from his own term of office and that of Dag Hammarskjold. In some of the cases mentioned by Thant, the action taken was the offer of the Secretary-General's good offices, and this may not have required the appointment of special staff. In other cases cited by Thant, it is difficult to assert categorically that the matters fell within the competence of the Security Council. Thant did, however, mention several cases which involved the appointment of special staff in connection with matters of which the Security Council had been seized:[20]

Special Representative of the Secretary-General in Amman, 1958;[21]
Special Consultant to the Secretary-General for co-ordination of UN Activities in Laos, 1959;[22]
Special Representative of the Secretary-General in the Middle East concerning Humanitarian Questions, 1967;[23]
Personal Representative of the Secretary-General in Jerusalem, 1967; [24]
Personal Representative leading the Good Offices Mission to Bahrain, 1970;[25]

Later examples of such appointments included:

Special Representative on the Iraq–Iran frontier, 1974;[26]
Special Representative in Southern Rhodesia, 1977;[27]
Mission to Botswana, 1985;[28]
Special Representative to Western Sahara, 1988;[29]
Special Representative to Angola, 1992;[30]
Special Envoy to Georgia; 1993;[31]

The discretionary rights of the Secretary-General, the functions which under the Rules of Procedure he 'may' perform, include the rights to:

1. Authorize a deputy to act in his place at Council meetings (Rule 21);
2. Make oral or written statements to the Council concerning any question under consideration by it (Rule 22);

3. Propose that the Council should meet at a place other than Headquarters (Rule 5).

With respect to oral statements to the Council by the Secretary-General, an aspect of the second discretionary right, a remarkable change in practice has taken place. In the first decade, during which the Security Council met 709 times, the Secretary-General made only five substantive oral statements to the Council. In the next decade, the Secretary-General made no fewer than fifty-three oral interventions in 561 meetings. Moreover the oral interventions were not necessarily limited to formal matters, such as expressions of condolence on the death of a distinguished Head of State or the transmission of information from UN field missions. Secretary-General Hammarskjold, in particular, increasingly participated in the discussion in the Council as one expression of his concept of the independent and non-partisan Office of Secretary-General and even as the conscience of the Organization, and he responded in blunt terms to Soviet attacks on his conduct of the UN operation in the Congo.

U Thant, Waldheim, Pérez de Cuéllar, Boutros-Ghali, and Annan have all also spoken at Council meetings, often to report on field operations or on how tasks entrusted to them had been discharged, but occasionally to express views on matters before the Council or to suggest courses of action.

Beyond these obligatory and discretionary rights, the Rules of Procedure also describe the Secretary-General as the recipient of credentials (Rules 13–15), of corrections which representatives wish to have made in the verbatim record (Rule 50), and of applications for UN membership (Rule 58). He 'may be appointed . . . as rapporteur for a specified question' (Rule 23). The *communiqué* of a private meeting of the Council is issued through him (Rule 55), and representatives who have taken part in a private meeting for which only a single copy of the record was made may consult the record in the Secretary-General's office (Rule 56). As noted earlier, the President of the Council is required to call a meeting if the Secretary-General brings a matter to the attention of the Council under Article 99 (Rule 3), and Rule 28, taken verbatim from Article 98 of the Charter, requires the Secretary-General to 'act in that capacity in all meetings of the Security Council'.

There are several places in the Rules of Procedure and the Appendix where reference is made, not to the Secretary-General but to the Secretariat. Under the Charter it is the Secretariat, not the Secretary-General, that is a principal organ of the UN. Chapter V (Rules 21–6) is headed 'Secretariat', and Rule 24 provides that the staff required by the Security Council 'shall form part of the Secretariat'. Rule 39 allows the Council to 'invite members of the Secretariat or other persons . . . to supply it with information or to give other assistance'. The Appendix to the Rules deals with the procedure for dealing with those communications from private individuals and non-governmental bodies which relate to matters of which the Council is seized.

The third and final source of obligations entrusted to the Secretary-General in regard to the Security Council are decisions of the Council and other UN organs. Such decisions may or may not specify the Articles of the Charter under which they are taken, but they have all represented applications of Article 98, which empowers the Security Council (as well as the General Assembly, the Economic and Social Council, and the Trusteeship Council) to entrust the Secretary-General with 'functions'.

The number of such resolutions taken by the Security Council has grown as the office of Secretary-General itself has evolved. In the first ten years of the work of the Security Council, 1946–55, 110 resolutions were adopted, of which only three expressly entrusted functions to the Secretary-General. In the ten-year period 1961–70, the Council adopted 131 resolutions, of which no fewer than forty-seven expressly entrusted functions to the Secretary-General. The proportion of such resolutions had risen from 2 per cent in 1946–50 to 39 per cent twenty years later. By 1996 over 75 per cent of resolutions entrusted functions to the Secretary-General, usually to report back to the Council on a specific date with his recommendations.

Alone, however, these figures could create a misleading impression. Many resolutions adopted by the Security Council simply request the Secretary-General to inform the Council about the implementation of the resolution. This, it could be argued, is a normal responsibility of the chief administrative officer of the Organization, which he or she would be expected to discharge whether or not the resolution contained a specific request to that effect.

Nevertheless, not all these resolutions involved requests for routine activities of the Secretary-General. In fact, the Council's resolution 113 (1956) of 4 April 1956 on the Middle East initiated a new era, with a new concept of the role of the Secretary-General. Previous resolutions had asked Secretary-General Lie 'to act as convenor of the Committee'; 'to advise the Security Council of all reports and petitions received from or relating to strategic areas under trusteeship, and to send copies thereof . . . to the Trusteeship Council'; and 'to provide the United Nations representative for India and Pakistan with such services and facilities as may be necessary'. These were functions which the Secretary-General would ordinarily be expected to perform.

Resolution 113 (1956) of 4 April 1956 represented a new departure. On 20 March 1956, the United States had asked for an early meeting of the Council to consider the question of compliance with the Middle East General Armistice Agreements and three unanimous resolutions of the Council. The US letter was circulated the following day, together with a US draft resolution which *inter alia* asked Secretary-General Hammarskjold 'to arrange with the parties for the adoption of any measures which . . . he considers would reduce tensions along the Armistice Demarcation Lines', and to 'report to the Council . . . on the implementation given to this resolution in order to assist the Council in considering what further action may be required'.[32] Six meetings of the Council were held, and all members welcomed the US proposal so long as it was acceptable to the parties. The Soviet delegation considered it appropriate for the Council to invite the Secretary-General to investigate the extent to which the Armistice Agreements and relevant Council resolutions were being carried out, and to explore the possibility of measures to reduce tensions along the Armistice Demarcation Lines.[33] Some minor Soviet amendments were put to the vote and rejected, and the US draft was then adopted unanimously.[34]

This resolution did not entrust the Secretary-General with precisely defined tasks. Rather, the broad mandate relating to the Middle East given to Hammarskjold in 1956—which he used to develop the new instrument of UN peace-keeping—was the first of a series asking the Secretary-General to use his discretion in seeking the fulfilment of the Purposes and Principles of the Charter and previous decisions of the Council. So far has this practice been carried that almost any resolution of the Council which asks for action, whether the resolution be of a binding nature or not, includes as a matter of course a request to the Secretary-General to report on implementation.

To make such a request is usually superfluous: the Secretary-General would report in the normal course of events. It might be preferable to include a specific request addressed to the Secretary-General only if there were something out of the ordinary in the Security Council's wishes. These could include a desire to have a report by a specific date (such as resolution 310 (1972) on Namibia, calling for a report by 31 July 1972); or a request that the Secretary-General should consult a specified person before acting (such as resolutions 294 (1971), 295 (1971), 298 (1971), and 302 (1971), which called for joint action by the Secretary-General and the President of the Security Council); or a resolution expressly conferring unusual discretionary powers on the Secretary-General (such as resolution 169 (1961) on the Congo, which authorized Acting Secretary-General U Thant 'to take vigorous action, including the use of the requisite measure of force, if necessary, for the immediate apprehension, detention pending legal action and/or deportation of all foreign military and para-military personnel and political advisers . . . and mercenaries').

The evolution in the United Nations by which broad responsibilities were conferred on the Secretary-General, by implication under Article 98 of the Charter, was not universally welcomed. This was evident in the Security Council resolutions themselves; the increasing tendency to involve not only the Secretary-General but also the President of the Security Council in following up Council decisions was seen by some people as an effort to reverse or at least halt the expansion of the Secretary-General's role.

The concept of a dynamic and dual role for the Secretary-General, both administrative and political, extolled by Hammarskjold, clashed with the more passive and strictly administrative role favoured by the Soviet Union. The Soviet Union envisaged the Secretary-General as purely the administrative head of the Secretariat, under the strict control of Member States through the UN's policy-making organs, and the Security Council in particular. This clash manifested in the differences of view about the control of UN peace-keeping.

Soviet displeasure with the attitudes as much as the particular actions of Lie and Hammarskjold, resulted in the Soviet *troika* proposal for a three-man board at the head of the UN Secretariat, rather than a single Secretary-General. This would have had the effect of stripping the office of mystique, notably the aura of moral authority achieved by Hammarskjold, and would have turned the Secretary-General into what U Thant was later to call 'a glorified clerk'. Yet it never was adopted, the Security Council evolved practical modalities for handling peace-keeping, and the Soviet Union gradually loosened its strict interpretation of the Secretary-General's role.

The totality of the functions of the Secretary-General under the Charter, under the Rules of Procedure of the Security Council, and under decisions of the political organs, has given rise to the concept of the office of the Secretary-General—not his material office on the 38th floor of the Secretariat building at UN Headquarters, but the sum of the multifarious responsibilities attaching to the position of Secretary-General.

Secretaries-General have on occasion encountered difficulties with Member States in fulfilling their responsibilities. Many of the most notable examples concern responsibilities of the Secretary-General relating to the work of the Security Council. Thant, for example, faced a Soviet Union constantly wary to ensure that he did not interpret his powers too freely. Thant also ran into problems with the United States over his view on the Vietnam War (1965), with Israel over investigations of human rights in the Middle East (1967–8), and with Portugal and South Africa over the implementation of the sanctions regime against Southern Rhodesia (1966). Waldheim likewise encountered difficulties with Portugal and South Africa over Southern Rhodesia (1973), and with various Member States in implementing two major responsibilities entrusted to him during his term, relating to Israel's action in Entebbe, Uganda, and to the Iranian seizure in Teheran of US diplomats as hostages (1979). Pérez de Cuéllar maintained reasonably good relations with all the main groups and blocs of Member States, yet he still ran into some problems in dealing with the investigation of the use of chemical and biological weapons in the Iran–Iraq war. More recently, the tenure of Boutros-Ghali placed the role of the Secretary-General back in the spotlight. As with Hammarskjold, differences in perspective were revealed most vividly in the realm of peace-keeping.

This revival, and indeed extension, of the controversy surrounding the role of the Secretary-General was due in part to the nature and number of situations which confronted the Security Council during Boutros-Ghali's five-year term (January 1992 to December 1996) and the post-Cold War context in which those situations arose, and due in part to the man himself.

While at the start of Boutros-Ghali's term, the members of the Security Council exhibited a new willingness to use the United Nations for peace and security, the traditional instruments at its disposal were not easily applied to new situations. Control over peace-keeping—both political and operational—again became the controversy of the day, particularly as many of those operations were given enforcement responsibilities, some of which were entrusted to the Secretary-General, and some effectively to regional organizations or coalitions of States. The United Nations operations in Somalia and in Bosnia were two of the most prominent examples.

Less publicized but equally controversial was the increasing blurring of the lines between these matters of peace and security, and economic, social, and humanitarian matters, most clearly evident in what Boutros-Ghali described as 'post-conflict peace-building' activities, whether entrusted to UN peace-keepers or other personnel working in the context of peace operations. Traditionally the former matters fell largely within the purview of the Security Council, while the latter fell within the purview of the General Assembly (and through it, to the Economic and Social Council). Thus, during Boutros-Ghali's tenure, not only was the role of the Secretary-General in question, but also the roles of three principal organs of the United Nations—the Secretariat, the Security Council, and the General Assembly—and the relations between them.

Boutros-Ghali was regularly called upon by the Security Council to report on UN peace-keeping operations, on their establishment and feasibility, on their implementation, or on their winding down. Such requests of a Secretary-General were not in themselves unusual; in Hammarskjold's time they had come to be considered routine. What was unusual, however, was what Boutros-Ghali did with them.

The style of Boutros-Ghali's reports was strikingly different from that of his predecessors, and reflected a decidedly analytical bent. He was much more inclined than previous Secretaries-General to put forward definite 'options' (in his words) for dealing with situations and solving problems. Beyond this, Boutros-Ghali frequently gave his own opinion of the situation at hand, attempting to limit the Council's freedom to choose options that may have been politically expedient but were, at least in his view, inadequate to the situation and/or an inappropriate employment of the United Nations and its instruments.[35] On a few occasions, he even went so far as to leave such 'options' out of his reports altogether; the most notable of these omissions was his May 1995 report on the future of the United Nations operation in Bosnia (UNPROFOR), which seemed deliberately to leave out the very option the Security Council later chose, which was to reinforce UNPROFOR—make it more 'robust' was the phrase used by Council members at the time—*without* changing its mandate from peace-keeping to enforcement. Boutros-Ghali thus used his reports to the Security Council as a strategic tool to shape its debates and influence its decisions. Many of his reports were also clearly designed to speak to the relevant parties involved.

More public was Boutros-Ghali's attempt to shape the broader debate on the Security Council and its work, through his report 'An Agenda for Peace'.[36] Following its first-ever summit at the level of Heads of State or Government in January 1992, the Security Council requested the Secretary-General to report and expand upon the analyses and recommendations raised at the summit to strengthen the capacity of the UN for preventive diplomacy, peace-making, and peace-keeping. Boutros-Ghali not only added a fourth concept to this request—that of post-conflict peace-building; he also elevated the status of the entire document from report to *agenda*, launching an ongoing process of internal debate and reflection, rather new to the UN.

As 'An Agenda for Peace' was being discussed, relatively positively but cautiously in both the Security Council and the General Assembly, concern grew particularly among the G-77 and Non-Aligned countries, that the attention given to peace and security was detracting from attention to development. Boutros-Ghali sought and received a request from the General Assembly to prepare a 'Report on An Agenda for Development', which he presented to the

Assembly in May 1994 and followed up in November 1994 with a report containing 'Recommendations' on An Agenda for Development.[37] Then, in January 1995, without any specific request, he issued as a position paper a 'Supplement to An Agenda for Peace', designed to call attention to 'hard decisions' which remained to be taken by Member States.[38] The unorthodox presentation of the Supplement as an unsolicited position paper, and moreover the candid nature of some of its contents, provoked disgruntlement among certain Member States. In December 1996, with barely any mandate, Boutros-Ghali issued 'An Agenda for Democratization' as a supplement to two previous—and minor—reports on operational activities in democratization. This last agenda is by far the most comprehensive and controversial of the three, yet, issued at the close of Boutros-Ghali's term, it has received little public attention.

As if his actions did not speak loudly enough, Boutros-Ghali often referred to Article 100 of the Charter, guaranteeing the independence of the Secretary-General and his staff, as 'Psalm 100 to the Secretary-General'.[39] He was a strong and at times fierce advocate of a dynamic and flexible role of the Secretary-General, implementing the mandates entrusted to him by the Security Council and other UN organs, while at the same time constantly reflecting upon and criticizing those mandates and the Member States which crafted them. Needless to say, this did not always endear him to Member States. His independence and activism likely played a prominent role in the decision of the United States to deny him a second term in office.

At the time of writing, Kofi Annan has focused his energies upon the administration and reform of the United Nations. It remains to be seen, however, how he will come to define his role.

2. PRESIDENT

The Charter allows the Security Council freedom to decide on the method of selecting its President (Article 30). The first draft of the Rules of Procedure provided for the rotation of the presidency in *French* alphabetical order, as had been the practice in the Council of the League of Nations.[40] The Executive Committee of the Preparatory Commission changed this so that the presidency would rotate on a monthly basis in the *English* alphabetical order of the names of the Council's members. The French delegation, not surprisingly, had reservations about this proposal, giving as the reason the fact that it would result in three of the permanent members of the Council serving in succession. France suggested that this difficulty could be avoided if the French alphabetical order were used; alternatively, the order might be determined by drawing lots.[41] The recommendation of the Executive Committee was, however, approved by the Preparatory Commission and later by the Council itself (Rule 18).[42]

The Executive Committee of the Preparatory Commission suggested that, at the Council's first meeting, the representative of the first member of the Council in the English alphabetical order should act as temporary chairman.[43] Accordingly, when the Council met for the first time on 17 January 1946, Norman Makin of Australia acted as temporary chairman. After a provisional rule regarding the presidency had been approved, Australia became President, holding office until 16 February.[44]

After eleven months, all members of the Council had served a one-month term as President. Australia then suggested, and the Council agreed (the United States and the Soviet Union abstaining) to extend the term of office of the United States from 17 December until 31 December 1946, so that thereafter the term of office would correspond to a calendar month. This was done because the General Assembly had decided that the term of non-permanent members of the Council should begin on 1 January. If the change had not been made, a situation would have arisen in which a State might cease being a member of the Council during the term of its presidency.[45]

The presidency attaches to a Member State and not to an individual representative accredited to the Council.[46] The draft rules submitted by the Preparatory Commission contained no procedure for the temporary replacement of the President in case of absence or illness, and in practice no difficulty has arisen on this score.

The Provisional Rules of Procedure allow the President the discretion to cede the presidential chair to the member next in English alphabetical order whenever he 'deems that for the proper fulfilment of the responsibilities of the presidency he should not preside over the Council during consideration of a particular question with which the member he represents is directly connected' (Rule 20).

TABLE 4

Cession of the presidency under Rule 20, 1946–1996

Date	SCOR meeting and page or paragraph no.	Matter under consideration	Member ceding the presidency
A. Cases where the presidency was ceded for one or more meetings			
4 Oct. 1948	361, 1–2	The sitaution in Berlin	United States
10 Jan. 1950	459, 8	Representation of China	Nationalist China
12 Jan.	460, 1–2		
1 Mar. 1951	533, 2	The India–Pakistan question	India
21 Jan. 1954	655, 37	The Palestine question	Lebanon
29 May 1968	1428, 2–4	The situation in Southern Rhodesia	United Kingdom
16 Dec. 1975	1866, 5–8	Letter from Iceland (the Cod War)	United Kingdom
11 Nov. 1983	2495	Situation in the Middle East	Israel
9 Feb. 1990	2907, 6–7	Tension in the Caribbean and Gulf of Mexico	Cuba
10 Nov. 1993	3309, 3	International Court of Justice election	Cape Verde
15 Dec. 1994	3481	The situation concerning Rwanda	Rwanda
B. Cases where the presidency was not ceded			
29 Apr. 1958	814, 2–15	'Urgent measures to put an end to flights by United States military aircrft with atomic and hydrogen bombs in the direction of the frontiers of the Soviet Union'	United States
7 Dec. 1960	912, 3–122	The Congo question	Soviet Union

Some of the cases where Rule 20 has been raised are given in Table 4. Of the cases in group A, the only one calling for comment is the second: it was India which first drew attention to Rule 20, not the President himself (the Republic of China). On a number of other occasions, it was suggested that the representative of the Republic of China could not suitably act as President, but proposals to suspend Rule 18 on the rotation of the presidency or to change the presidency for the month were not adopted.[47]

In the first of the two cases listed in group B, the Council had already held a six-hour meeting under the presidency of the United

States during which the Soviet representative had displayed some annoyance at the way the proceedings were being conducted. At the next meeting, the Soviet Union asked if the President intended to cede the chair, adding that his question was 'prompted by the fact that at the last meeting of the Council, it was sometimes difficult to tell where the statements of the United States representative ended and those of the President of the Council began'. Several members said that the United States had conducted the previous meeting with complete propriety.* The United States representative, Henry Cabot Lodge, a former member of the US Senate, suggested that the spirit of Rule 20 was to be found in the practice of those national parliamentary bodies in which a member disqualifies himself if the matter being considered involves his personal interests. As the Soviet complaint did not involve the selfish national interests of the United States, 'the present occupant of the Chair does not consider that he should vacate it'. The Soviet representative accepted the President's decision, but pointed out that Rule 20 contains 'not a single word . . . about the selfish national interest of any State'.[48]

In the second case listed in group B, the Soviet Union had requested the meeting in a strong statement which attacked Secretary-General Hammarskjold, the UN operation in the Congo, and the United States. When the meeting convened under the presidency of the Soviet Union, the United States suggested that the Soviet representative was 'likely to be too prejudiced to fulfil properly [the] responsibilities as President in this case'. There followed a three-hour procedural debate in which several different questions became inextricably entangled: whether or not the President should cede the chair under Rule 20; whether discussion of the applicability of Rule 20 should precede or follow the adoption of the agenda; whether or not it was appropriate for the Council to list in the agenda a document which was described by France and other members as violent and extremist in tone; and how the agenda should be worded. An amended agenda was finally approved, after which the Soviet representative reminded the Council that France had presided during discussion of the Suez invasion in 1956. If he were to cede the presidency, it would devolve on a member of the British delegation:

* France, no doubt recalling the length of the meeting, pointed out that forced labour was within the competence of the Economic and Social Council rather than of the Security Council.

'could any member of the Security Council assert that the United Kingdom representative is less an interested party in the discussion of the question of the Congo than the Soviet representative—or than any other representative in this chamber?' He concluded by stating firmly that he had no intention of ceding the presidency. The representative of France intervened to say that France had had 'sincere doubts' about presiding during the 1956 Suez debates, but 'nobody had raised any objection or expressed any doubt'. It only remained for the Council to set the time for the next meeting.[49]

The comment of the United States about Soviet handling of the presidency in April 1958 drew attention to the important fact that the President performs a dual role. He is both the representative of a member and the presiding officer of the Council; indeed, he also represents the Council in its capacity as an organ of the United Nations, although always 'under the authority of the Security Council' (Rule 19). But the dual role of the President means that, whenever he speaks at Council meetings, he speaks as President, unless he expressly prefaces his remarks with words to the effect that he is speaking as the representative of Afghanistan, say, or Zimbabwe. When he speaks as national representative, the official UN records still describe him as President.

Considering all the circumstances, it is surprising that this practice so rarely leads to difficulty—although the United States was once driven to remark:

> I believe that Mr Malik's reply was perhaps, at least in part, given as the representative of the USSR rather than as President, but I rather suspect that the President of the Security Council would agree with the representative of the USSR.[50]

Sometimes the presidency has been ceded on the initiative of the representative whose turn had come, sometimes as a result of a hint or demand from another representative. It appears that it is more likely for a President to cede the chair when criticizing than when criticized. Cuba vacated the chair in 1990 when the Council considered a letter from Cuba criticizing US actions in Panama,[51] whereas in 1986 the US did not volunteer (and was not in fact asked) to cede the Presidency when the Council was considering a letter critical of US support for *contra* rebels based in Honduras. In 1994 Rwanda was serving as one of the elected non-permanent members. The situation in Rwanda itself was extremely tense, being marked by grave violations of human rights and international humanitarian law, including acts of genocide. The atrocities in Rwanda reached a peak in July, and there was considerable confusion as to who was entitled to represent Rwanda on the Security Council. There was no Rwandan representative at the sixteen formal meetings of the Council held between 14 July and 7 September, leaving the Council with only fourteen active members. If alphabetical rotation had been strictly followed as required by Rule 18, it would have been Rwanda's turn to preside in September. With Rwanda still unrepresented at Council meetings, the Council decided on 25 August that it would suspend the operation of Rule 18 so that Spain would hold the Presidency for September and Rwanda would take up its Presidency at a later, unspecified date.[52] On 16 September with Rwanda now represented once more on the Council but with a different set of representatives, the Council announced that Rwanda would hold the Presidency in December following the United Kingdom in October, and the United States in November.[53] In December Rwanda duly assumed the Presidency. On 15 December the sole item on the Council's agenda was 'The situation concerning Rwanda'. Taking advantage of Rule 20, and in accordance with a decision reached in prior consultations, the representative of Rwanda ceded the presidential chair for that one meeting to the representative of Argentina. The meeting heard only one speaker, Mr Paul Kagame, the Vice-President and Minister of Defence of Rwanda, and lasted just 15 minutes.[54]

The President as national representative usually speaks last: if he should for some reason wish to speak first, he or she may do so before the adoption of the agenda, as did Nigeria on one occasion.[55] The President represents the Council in its capacity as an organ of the United Nations, and the procedure for the devolution of the presidential chair in particular circumstances does not affect the representative capacity of the President (Rules 19 and 20). The Executive Committee of the Preparatory Commission stated that the provision that the President should represent the Council in its corporate capacity was 'intended to give him the requisite authority to nominate committees and to conclude agreements on behalf of the Council'.[56] In practice, the part of Rule 19 which declares that the

President 'shall represent [the Security Council] in its capacity as an organ of the United Nations' has provided a basis for the President to appeal to the parties in situations of tension or conflict to exercise restraint. It has also enabled the President to submit draft resolutions or decisions, to make oral statements of consensus, or to issue written summaries. [57]

If the President of the Council, advised by the Council's secretary, is not up to the task, difficulties are almost certain to ensue. The President needs 'preparedness, authority and tactical sense'.[58] His duties are stated as follows in the Rules of Procedure:

1. He shall call a meeting of the Council, in circumstances which are set out in section 1 of Chapter 2 of this book (Rules 1–3);
2. He shall approve the provisional agenda for each meeting, which is drawn up by the Secretary-General (the President continues to discharge this duty even when he has ceded the presidency under Rule 20) (Rules 7 and 20);
3. He shall preside over meetings of the Council (Rule 19);
4. He shall call upon representatives in the order in which they have signified their desire to speak (Rule 27);
5. He shall immediately state his ruling if a representative raises a point of order, and if the ruling is challenged, he shall submit the matter to the Council for immediate decision (Rule 30);
6. If two or more amendments to a motion or draft resolution are proposed, he shall rule on the order in which they are to be voted upon (Rule 36);*
7. The Rules note that he shall sign the verbatim record of a meeting of the Council once it has been corrected in accordance with the procedure laid down in Rules 49–51, after which it shall become the official record of the Security Council (Rule 53), though the practice of signing the record was discontinued after the first few meetings;
8. He shall, unless the Security Council decides otherwise, refer each application for UN membership to a committee upon which each member of the Security Council is represented (Rule 59).

The Rules of Procedure specify four matters on which the President acts to some extent on his own discretion:

1. He calls meetings of the Council 'at any time he deems necessary' (Rule 1);

* The application of this Rule is reviewed in Chapter 4.6.

2. He cedes the presidency whenever he deems that he should not preside during the consideration of a particular question with which the member he represents is directly connected (Rule 20);
3. He 'may accord precedence [in debate] to any rapporteur appointed by the Security Council' (Rule 29);
4. If the President is of the opinion that corrections submitted to the verbatim records are sufficiently important to be referred to representatives on the Council, this is done before the verbatim records are approved (Rule 52).

There are other procedural functions which the President performs even though these are not specified in the Provisional Rules of Procedure. The President declares the opening and closing of each meeting, puts the question, announces decisions, and in general is responsible for the maintenance of order and the observance of the Rules of Procedure. When consideration of a matter has been completed, the President may declare that the Council remains seized of the item.[59] If the adoption of a proposal seems to the President to be a matter of great urgency, he or she can try to arrange informally for a limit on the number or length of speeches.[60]

The President performs certain formal tasks. It is now customary at the first meeting each year for the President to welcome the new members of the Council. The President offers condolences on the death of distinguished world figures and, usually, calls for a minute of silence—Mao Tse-tung,[61] Jozip Broz Tito,[62] Sir Seretse Khama,[63] Leonid Ilyich Brezhnev,[64] Indira Gandhi,[65] Olof Palme,[66] Emperor Hirohito,[67] Yitzhak Rabin,[68] François Mitterand,[69] King Moshooshoe II.[70] The President bids farewell to Secretariat officials connected with the work of the Council who have completed their terms of service,[71] and welcomes their successors.[72] Nations are congratulated on scientific or technological achievements,[73] or sympathized with if their country is suffering from human calamity[74] or natural disaster.[75] At the first meeting each month, the President thanks the previous President in fulsome terms for the skilled way the job has been done.

It is also customary for each member of the Council to extend congratulations to the incoming President, and gratitude to the former President, at the first meeting of the month at which the member speaks on an item. This gives representatives the opportunity for some diplomatic word-crafting. At a Council meeting at the end of August 1996 Mr Nsanze of Burundi told the German ambassador:

> Even if a Persian proverb states that politeness benefits more the person who extends it than the person who receives it, your exquisite courtesy and your diplomatic professionalism warrant our admiration.[76]

The absence of greetings or congratulations generally marks a severe animosity between the State represented by the President and another Council member, such as occurs in times of war, and diplomats may apologize if they inadvertently forget them.[77] At the other extreme the delegate of Colombia praised the Yemeni President for being 'an exceptional human being'.[78] Occasionally the President will attempt to dissuade Council members from the 'usual congratulations' to save time. This rarely works. Austria, when President in March 1991, asked fellow Council members to abstain from greetings during that month. Some members acceded to this request, others did not. In April Austria congratulated the new President and then undermined its earlier initiative by thanking 'all those who found kind words to say about the Austrian presidency of the Council in March'.[79]

The President has no express power to call a speaker to order if he or she wanders from the agenda,[80] or indulges in vain repetition,[81] or resorts to abusive language. The President can appeal to representatives to speak briefly[82] and for the avoidance of contentious language (while making it clear that no criticism of previous speakers was intended).[83] On one occasion, the United Kingdom protested that a Cuban speech, in which the United States administration was described as 'the legitimate heirs of the Hitler clique', was a piece of exaggerated and crude rhetoric, deserving contemptuous rejection; and the following day, the President (France) described the language used by Cuba as 'inadmissible'.[84] On another occasion, the President (United Kingdom) said that he had been tempted to rule out of order those delegates who had used 'unhelpfully strong language which went beyond the bounds of civility', and he appealed for the exercise of 'due restraint'.[85] In 1991 following the reversal of Iraq's invasion of Kuwait, Iraq called the Kuwaiti ambassador 'a man with no identity, personal or national'.[86] The Belgium President found this remark 'regrettable'.[87] A Libyan speech attacking the Security

Council as 'only the child of a secret meeting between Roosevelt and Stalin' and now an impotent instrument of US hegemony, led the Western powers to complain at the next meeting about language that exceeded the bounds of propriety.[88]

Israel has sometimes complained when Arab states have called it 'the Israeli entity' or 'the Zionist entity', and Jordan has protested when Israel has called it 'the Palestinian Arab State of Jordan'.[89] The Marxist States of Eastern Europe objected at being called 'satellites' or 'fellow-travellers' of the Soviet Union.[90] When such language was used, the President could only appeal for a correct and unprovocative use of language. The most effective, but most difficult, way to deal with abuse may be to ignore it.

If a meeting is actually in session at midnight on the last day of the month, does the Presidency change? While practice in this matter has not been consistent, it seems that the correct procedure is for the President to adjourn the meeting at midnight or conveniently soon thereafter and for the next President to convene another meeting at once.[91]

Under the terms of a resolution of the Security Council adopted in 1950, which was itself based on a recommendation of the General Assembly of the previous year, the Council decided that 'should an appropriate occasion arise', it would 'base its action upon the principles' contained in a recommendation of the General Assembly. This recommendation, which empowers the President to undertake conciliation, read as follows:

> After a situation or dispute has been brought to the attention of representatives on the Security Council . . . and not later than immediately after the opening statements on behalf of the parties concerned,
>
> (a) The parties shall be invited to meet with the President of the Security Council;
>
> (b) They shall attempt to agree upon a representative on the Security Council to act as rapporteur or conciliator for the case . . .
>
> (c) If a rapporteur or conciliator is appointed, it would be desirable for the Security Council to abstain from further action on the case for a reasonable interval during which actual efforts at conciliation are in progress;
>
> (d) The rapporteur or conciliator so agreed upon and appointed shall attempt to conciliate the situation or dispute, and shall in due course report to the Security Council.[92]

Other tasks have from time to time been laid on the President by decision of the Council: to obtain information;[93] to designate members of a subsidiary organ;[94] to confer with the Secretary-General;[95] to appeal to the parties to a conflict to exercise restraint or respect decisions of the Council;[96] to meet with the parties with a view to easing the tension;[97] to undertake informal consultations;[98] or to follow the implementation of resolutions or decisions of the Council.[99]

On three occasions in 1948, the President felt able to take a diplomatic initiative without consulting the Council in a formal meeting. In January 1948, the President (Belgium) sent identical communications to the Governments of India and Pakistan in connection with the situation in Jammu and Kashmir, appealing to the two States 'to refrain from any step incompatible with the Charter and liable to result in an aggravation of the situation'.[100]

On 1 April 1948, the Council adopted a resolution calling on the Jewish Agency for Palestine and the Arab Higher Committee 'to make representatives available to the Security Council for the purpose of arranging a truce'. When the Council met two weeks later, the President (Colombia) addressed the Council as follows:

> the President was instructed to discuss the possible terms of the truce with the accredited representatives of the two parties. I met with them on two occasions, as I have already informed the Security Council at our informal meetings.

The President, *in his capacity as representative of Colombia*, then introduced a draft resolution pointing out that his proposal was 'the result of the conversations with other members of the Security Council'. After amendment, the draft resolution was adopted.[101]

In connection with the Berlin question in 1948, after the Soviet veto of a six-power proposal, the President of the Council (Argentina), 'in the exercise of his powers', established a Technical Committee on Berlin Currency and Trade from experts nominated by neutral members of the Council. The President for the following month (Belgium) extended the life of the Committee.[102]

These three instances of diplomatic initiative by the President date from 1948. Shortly after this, the role of the Council began to diminish as new functions were assumed by the General Assembly or entrusted to the Secretary-General. By 1959, the Council had so little business that it met only five times during the course of the year (the average number of meetings a year since 1946 has been more than seventy) and adopted only one resolution—and the legality of the proceedings in that one case were challenged by one of the permanent members.[103] Since its enlargement in 1966, and especially since 1990, the Council has gradually resumed its role as an important principal organ. Since 1990, Council members have increasingly prepared statements during informal consultations, and the President of the Council has read out the statements at public meetings at which there was no debate and no voting. From 1 January 1994 such presidential statements were issued with their own document symbol number series. Eighty-two presidential statements were issued in 1994, the largest ever number. This declined in parallel with Council resolutions, falling to sixty-three during the course of 1995 and forty-nine during 1996. In some instances meetings of the Council have been dispensed with altogether and presidential statements have been simply issued 'following consultations'. This procedure appears to be favoured when the Council is conducting periodic reviews of sanctions regimes, and in swiftly responding to acts of terrorism. In the three years from 1994 to 1996 there were a total of 13 presidential statements issued 'following consultations'. These consisted of one sanctions review regarding Iraq[104] and six regarding Libya;[105] two on terrorist attacks in Israel;[106] one on terrorism in Argentina and the United Kingdom;[107] two on the illegal regime in Haiti;[108] and one welcoming the Palestinian elections of 20 January 1996.[109]

Probably the most substantial mandate conferred on the Council's President occurred in 1957 in connection with the India–Pakistan question. A four-power draft resolution was introduced which would have asked the President of the Council, ambassador Gunnar Jarring of Sweden, to visit India and Pakistan to examine with the two Governments proposals likely to contribute towards the settlement of their dispute. The Soviet Union sought to amend the proposal so as to eliminate from it parts unacceptable to India (including, in particular, references to a proposal made by Pakistan 'for the use of a temporary United Nations force' in connection with demilitarization). The proposed amendment was rejected, and the Soviet Union therefore vetoed the main proposal.[110] A new draft resolution was then introduced which omitted the parts unacceptable to India, and this was approved (the Soviet Union abstaining). Ambassador Jarring, in accepting the mission entrusted to him, made it clear that his acceptance was based on the express understanding that the parties were willing to co-operate with him. The result of the mission would largely depend upon the extent of the co-operation he would receive.

In the event, the extent of co-operation from the parties was insufficient, and Jarring reported to the Council in writing that although 'both parties are still desirous of finding a solution', he was unable to suggest 'any concrete proposals which . . . are likely to contribute towards a settlement'.[111]

Five months were to elapse before the Council resumed its consideration of the India–Pakistan question. The debate was then characterized by marathon speeches by representatives of the two parties, but members of the Council vied with one another in showering praise on Jarring—'. . . debt of gratitude . . . cogent and perceptive analysis' (Australia); '. . . deep appreciation for his excellent performance of a very difficult mission' (Republic of China);' . . . skilful handling of the difficult mission' (Cuba); 'warm tribute . . . unanimous in their congratulations and their praise' (France); '. . . congratulate Mr Jarring on the efficient way in which he has executed the mission' (Iraq); '. . . wise and conscientious manner . . . tactful and objective . . . consummate skill' (Philippines); '. . . deep appreciation for the able and conscientious way' (United Kingdom); 'delicate and important task . . . appreciation . . . for the outstanding manner' (United States). [112]

It was partly because Ambassador Jarring had shown such outstanding skill over the India–Pakistan question in 1957 that ten years later he was asked to 'promote agreement' over the even more intractable problems of the Middle East—a task which Jarring again discharged with courage and integrity, but with minimal success.

The President will now often refer to informal consultations, especially when making a statement on behalf of the Council or presenting an agreed proposal. But it can be a lonely and trying job. One President (Kuwait) had this to say:[113]

> I should like to make some observations in my capacity as President. I have seen what is beautiful in the work of the Council and what is not. The presidency of the Council is crippling and restrictive and at times generates

a sense of loneliness and frustration. Some speakers asked why the Council did not act speedily. That is easier said than done. The work of the Council generates its own momentum. It is wise to move when the time is ripe. I have tried to bridge the gap between views that are poles apart . . . I was addressed in language that I would not have accepted had I not been restricted by the presidency. I have seen how the Security Council has been unfairly treated. I might say that it has been abused and misused . . . Nevertheless, I must stress in the positive sense the spirit of co-operation that I have received from all members, particularly those directly involved . . .

I have tried to be fair to every side. I have held consultations with every member. Unfortunately, I was forced to give up because I felt that I was trying to square the circle, to reconcile the irreconcilable.

I see no harm in the fact that I was mildly criticized as President for taking initiatives that did not tally with the views of some members . . . I leave the Council presidency with a clear conscience.

It is important to draw a line between firmness and leniency. It is also important to note that too much patience produces confusion and too much firmness creates antagonism . . . We must strive to place international interests above our narrow national interests if we want to be faithful to the provisions of the Charter . . .

My final observation is that I feel that the presidency of the Council at a time of crisis such as the one we are facing entails being denied basic human rights such as physical comfort and freedom of movement. It is physically restrictive, totally monopolizing and sometimes unbearable.

3. PERMANENT MEMBERS

The Security Council has five permanent members: The [People's] Republic of China, France, the Union of Soviet Socialist Republics (since 24 December 1991 the Russian Federation), the United Kingdom, and the United States of America (Article 23(1)). Since no formal amendment has been made to the wording of Article 23(1) in this regard, the names 'the Republic of China' and 'the USSR' remain in the Charter even though there have been changes to the names of the States involved. These five States have continuous membership of both the Security Council and the Military Staff Committee (Article 47(2)), and also the right to veto non-procedural decisions of the Council and prevent the coming into force of amendments to the Charter (Articles 27(3) and 108). Pending the entry into force of agreements for making armed forces available to the Security Council (Article 43), the Five 'shall consult with one another and . . . with other Members of the United Nations with a view to such joint action . . . as may be necessary for the purpose of maintaining international peace and security' (Article 106).

The major powers among the victorious allies intended to have a predominant role in maintaining international peace and security in the post-war future, and attempts by the medium and smaller countries at San Francisco to curb the primacy of the great powers were of little avail. The Security Council was accorded 'primary responsibility' for maintaining peace, and all UN Members (whether members of the Council or not) were to 'agree to accept and carry out' the Council's decisions (Articles 24(1), 25, and 49). The Council was to be so organized as to be able to function continuously (Article 28(1)), and the five major victors were to have permanent seats.

The delegations of the five permanent members have thus been able to acquire substantial experience of the working of the Council, and this is a considerable but often underestimated benefit of permanent membership. T. F. Tsiang represented the Republic of China on the Council for fifteen years, a longer period than the term of office of any Secretary-General. Yakov Malik was Soviet representative for five of the worst years of the Cold War, and returned in 1968 as an era of *détente* and peaceful coexistence was beginning to unfold. Liu Chieh served for nine years, Henry Cabot Lodge for nearly eight, Armand Bérard for seven (two terms), and Warren Austin, Arkady Sobolev, Sir Pierson Dixon, and Lord Caradon for six years each.

Moreover, the possibility of threatening or exercising the veto on substantive proposals has meant that the permanent members are likely to be consulted during the process of drafting resolutions, except on those rare occasions when a veto is actually desired by the sponsors of a proposal in order to put the vetoing State or States in a bad light or so that the sponsors can claim credit for putting forward militant, even if impractical, proposals. The fact that permanent members are almost always consulted informally before proposals are submitted gives them the opportunity of suggesting changes, backed by the threat of withholding support from or actually voting negatively on unacceptable texts.

Permanent Members

The attempt of the medium and smaller States at San Francisco to curb the powers of the permanent members was ostensibly based on the fear that they would unite in order to impose their will on the rest. Great power unity was feared even more than great power discord. At the Commonwealth Prime Ministers' Conference in 1971, President Nyerere of Tanzania quoted a Swahili proverb to the effect that, when two elephants fight, it is the grass that suffers. Prime Minister Lee Kuan Yew of Singapore capped this by pointing out that, when elephants make love, the grass suffers equally.

The permanent members tried to reassure the others that this possibility did not contain the dangers that had been alleged. In their Yalta statement on the veto, for example, four of the permanent members pointed out that they would not be able to 'act by themselves', since 'any decisions of the Council would have to include the concurring votes of at least two [now four] of the non-permanent members'. Any five (now seven) non-permanent members which found themselves in agreement could prevent the Council from taking a decision and therefore could exercise an *open* or *hidden* veto. But of course, claimed the Five blandly, neither the permanent nor the non-permanent members would use their veto power wilfully to obstruct the operation of the Council.[114] Experience proved this otherwise and the General Assembly has addressed several appeals to the permanent members to seek agreement on limiting the exercise of the veto.[115]

Indeed for forty years the Yalta statement seemed rather out of touch with reality, since the outstanding fact about the Council until the late 1980s was not Great Power unity but Great Power stand-off. The first seven years of the 1990s has witnessed a shift in international power relations, with the end of the Cold War enabling many deadlocked issues to be addressed by the Council.

We review in Section 2 of Chapter 8 some of the proposals that have been made to add to the permanent membership of the Security Council.

A precedent was set in 1946 that the permanent members would almost automatically be elected to many other UN bodies, thereby becoming *de facto* permanent member of UN organs such as the Economic and Social Council. Argentina prepared a preliminary working paper[116] on this subject in 1995. Argentina referred to the phenomena of *de facto* permanent membership as 'the cascade effect', while others preferred to call it the 'permanent member convention'. Under this informal agreement, the permanent members are always appointed to UN bodies of restricted membership, both elected and selected. The permanent members in turn do not stand for positions on the bureau (i.e. Chairman, Vice-Chairman, or Rapporteur) of such bodies. A number of exceptions to this informal agreement have arisen in recent years. In its paper presented to a General Assembly Working Group,[117] Argentina pondered whether new permanent members in an expansion of the Council would also receive such privileges.

The General Assembly has on several occasions expressed the view that the permanent members have a special responsibility for contributing to the financing of peace and security operations.[118] This led to the Assembly agreeing that the permanent members should pay a premium of 20 per cent above their assessed contribution to the UN regular budget, when they pay for peace-keeping operations. There was general assent among permanent members to this effective 'tax' on permanent membership until 1995 when the US Congress announced that contrary to the wishes of the US administration, it would not release funds to pay for more than 25 per cent of the budget for peace-keeping operations, this being the percentage that the US is assessed to pay towards the UN regular budget. This announcement drew widespread international condemnation, not because the US desired to reduce its contributions to the UN, but because it sought to do so unilaterally, rather than through negotiation, in breach of its legal obligations under the Charter. The financial problems that beset the Organization in the 1990s led to some observers suggesting that new permanent members might ease the funding crisis by taking a greater share of contributions. Indeed in 1997 Germany announced that if granted a permanent seat it would be willing to pay 'the same percentage rate of premium surcharge' as the existing permanent members, and argued that equally it should be granted the same power of veto.[119]

The permanent members, as nuclear weapons powers, also have particular responsibilities under the Treaty on the Non-Proliferation of Nuclear Weapons (NPT). Prior to the indefinite renewal of the NPT on 11 May 1995 the permanent members took a number of steps to reassure non-nuclear-weapon States that are Parties to the NPT. Each permanent member made individual assurances concerning their use of nuclear weapons,[120] and the Security Council unanimously passed resolution 984 (1995) on 11 April 1995 (reproduced as Appendix XVII) stating that the Council, and in particular its permanent members, would act immediately if Parties to the NPT were victim of an act, or threat, of aggression, involving nuclear weapons.

The representatives of the permanent members are not necessarily more influential than those who represent non-permanent members. It is true, nevertheless, that those who represent the permanent members wield more *power*, partly because of the threat of the veto, and partly because their periods of service have not been limited to two-year terms. At the same time, we would stress that non-permanent members have sometimes played a decisive role, and their representatives have won high esteem because of personal qualities of courtesy, persistence, and integrity.

4. NON-PERMANENT MEMBERS

The Charter contains a number of seemingly negative concepts: non-self-governing territories, non-procedural decisions, non-governmental organizations, non-permanent members of the Security Council. This is, indeed, a common feature of texts drafted by collective bodies. Someone prepares a first draft, such as: 'All pigs are equal.' Some visionary proposes that the wording be amended to read: 'All *animals* are equal.' This is too much for a traditionalist, who wishes to reinstate the original text and add a new sentence: 'Non-pigs are almost as equal as pigs.'

All Members of the United Nations are declared to be sovereign and equal (Article 2(1)). This, according to the Charter, is one of the Principles according to which 'the Organization and its Members' shall act. But in reality all Members are *not* equal. The permanent members of the Security Council possess veto rights specified in the Charter. Other UN Members do not possess such rights; they have the right of *access* to the Security Council, a right which is virtually unfettered, and the right to declare themselves candidates for one of the elective seats on the Council, a right which is now governed formally by decisions of the General Assembly on the distribution of elective seats,[121] and informally by the system of regional groups and caucuses.

The non-permanent members of the Security Council are elected by the General Assembly for terms of two years. Retiring members are not eligible for immediate re-election (Article 23(2)). The election of non-permanent members is one of the 'important' questions for which a two-thirds majority of the Members of the General Assembly present and voting is required (Article 18(2) of the Charter and Rule 85 of the General Assembly's Rules of Procedure). It is stated in the General Assembly's Rules of Procedure that all elections shall be held by secret ballot and that there shall be no nominations (Rule 94). The ballot is undoubtedly secret, but aspirants for elective seats on the Council have usually been candid about their availability.

The Charter states that in the election of non-permanent members, due regard shall be specially paid

> in the first instance to the contribution of Members of the United Nations to the maintenance of international peace and security and to the other purposes of the Organization, and also to equitable geographical distribution (Article 23(1)).

The British delegation at the Dumbarton Oaks Conference suggested that the Charter should specify that, in the election of non-permanent members of the Security Council, due regard should be paid to the *military* contributions of States to the maintenance of international peace and security. Both the United States and the Soviet Union had reservations about the proposal in this form, and the British delegate[122] therefore agreed to the omission of 'military'. The idea of linking the election of non-permanent members of the Council to contributions to peace and security was revived at San Francisco. Britain suggested adding 'equitable geographical distribution' as another criterion, and the reference to 'the other purposes of the Organization' was inserted because of the difficulties the League of Nations had experienced in collecting financial contributions.[123]

Non-permanent Members

During the first session of the General Assembly, all six elective seats had to be filled.[124] On the first ballot, *five* States received more than the required majority: Brazil, Egypt, Mexico, the Netherlands, and Poland; Australia and Canada were runners-up. Canada withdrew after the third ballot, and Australia was accordingly elected.[125] The pattern of election at the first session was thus as follows:

Latin America	2
Middle East	1
Eastern Europe	1
Western Europe	1
Commonwealth	1

This was not fortuitous; the pattern was based on an informal understanding among the Council's permanent members. The precise content of the agreement has not, to our knowledge, been published, although several US officials were under the impression that there had been a moral commitment to the Soviet Union to ensure 'the continuous presence of two East European countries';[126] but those official spokesmen who have referred to the agreement, and those scholars who have written about it, have tended to use inconsistent language.

The Soviet Union always maintained that the permanent members reached a gentlemen's agreement in 1946 on the distribution of the elective seats. The Five, in the Soviet view,

> undertook to support the election to the Council of candidates nominated by the countries of the five main regions of the world. In accordance with that plan it was agreed that in the election of non-permanent members support would be given to two countries from the Latin-American region . . . while one seat would be allotted to the British Commonwealth, one to the Middle East, one to Western Europe, and one to Eastern Europe.[127]

The Soviet Union maintained for many years that the General Assembly should, as a matter of course, endorse the choices already made informally and privately by regional or ideological groups.

The United States, for its part, has claimed that the 1946 agreement was intended to apply to the first election only; that the only factors to be taken into account in connection with subsequent elections are those specified in Article 23(1) of the Charter; that the States of the Soviet bloc had failed to contribute to the maintenance of international peace and security; that the Charter refers to equitable geographical *distribution* and not *representation*, and that this principle was maintained, at any rate until 1962, by the election for the East European seat of such States as Greece, Turkey, and Yugoslavia.

Some States which were not parties to the 1946 understanding have not felt bound by it. The Indian representative stated this explicitly during the second session of the General Assembly (1947), after reluctantly withdrawing from the contest to permit the election of Ukraine.[128]

> We have been told that the allocation of seats on the Council is based in some arrangement privately arrived at among some of the Powers. But the distribution of Council seats by secret diplomacy to which the members of the General Assembly are not a party cannot, I am sure, find any support in this august body.
>
> Without in any way desiring to offend any of the Powers concerned, the delegation of India must challenge this arrangement.[129]

The Charter requirement that a two-thirds majority of the members present and voting is required for the election of non-permanent members of the Security Council means that, if a seat is contested, balloting can be a tedious and lengthy process. Indeed, a determined minority of one-third of the Members plus one has the possibility of compelling the General Assembly to engage in inconclusive ballots for an indefinite period and, in case of extreme intransigence, could render the Security Council inoperative.

During the second session of the Assembly (1947), there were eleven inconclusive ballots for one of the seats before, as noted above, India withdrew in favour of the Ukrainian SSR. There were thirteen inconclusive ballots during the fifth session (1950) before the Lebanon withdrew in favour of Turkey. It was not until the nineteenth ballot during the sixth session (1951) that Greece received a two-thirds majority.

During the tenth session (1955), with three seats to be filled, no fewer than thirty-six ballots were necessary. On the first ballot, thirty-nine votes were needed for election, and Cuba and Australia obtained the required majority; Poland and the Philippines had thirty-four and thirty-three votes respectively. After four ballots, Poland withdrew in the hope that Yugoslavia might be acceptable as a compromise candidate. Twenty-five further inconclusive ballots were held, with Yugoslavia varying between twenty-five and thirty-three votes; on all these ballots, except the nineteenth, the Philippines was in the lead, but was always at least seven votes short of the required majority.

After the twenty-ninth inconclusive ballot had taken place, the President of the Assembly drew the attention of hungry and weary delegates to the serious situation.

> If no agreement is reached, I for my part am ready to assist the Assembly [the verb was nicely chosen] in reaching a decision by calling a meeting which would not rise until the vacant seat has been filled.[130]

The session of the Assembly was due to close on 10 December, but two days before this the closing date was changed to 16 December. The admission of sixteen new Members on 14 December introduced a new element into the situation. For the next five ballots, which were held on the morning of 16 December, the required two-thirds majority fluctuated between forty-four and forty-six votes. On the thirty-second ballot, the Philippines obtained forty votes, its highest, but still six short of two-thirds.

At 9 o'clock on the evening of 16 December (the revised date for the closing of the session), after all other business had been disposed of, the General Assembly returned to the election. Thirty-four ballots had been held without the third vacancy on the Council being filled. The President announced that there had been consultations with a number of delegations, including the two rivals for the seat, with the object of finding an acceptable solution.

> It was felt that this purpose would be achieved if lots were drawn in the President's office between the two candidates I have already mentioned to decide which should withdraw from the present elections. After completing the first year of the term, the other candidate would offer its resignation from the Security Council. The agreement is that the vacant seat would then be filled for the remainder of the term by the election of the other candidate at the eleventh [1956] session.
>
> The spirit of this compromise solution, for which I do not hesitate to

assume a moral responsibility that will certainly be shared by the other representatives, must ensure that the agreement will be faithfully observed.

In accordance with the procedure I have outlined, lots were drawn in the President's office; as a result the Philippines has withdrawn its candidature at this time in favour of Yugoslavia.

I am sure that the Assembly, in approving this procedure, will recognize that it does not set a precedent and will further agree that, in view of the unusual circumstances, the arrangement should be accepted and carried out.[131]

Following the President's statement, several representatives expressed reservations about the procedure which had been outlined. A few stated flatly that it was illegal; others announced that they had no instructions in connection with such an unexpected development; others expressly said that they could not at that time commit their governments regarding the future, and in particular as to how they would vote in 1956 if Yugoslavia should resign the seat after one year. After an inconclusive debate, the Philippines suggested that a further ballot be held. This time Yugoslavia received thirty-four votes and the Philippines nineteen (forty votes required for election). The President thereupon declared that he released the two parties from the agreement. The Assembly, having at 10.30 p.m. rejected a motion to suspend the meeting and resume it one hour later, decided to extend the session until 20 December.[132]

On the morning of 20 December, the Assembly returned to the question, and on the thirty-sixth ballot Yugoslavia received forty-three votes, five more than the required majority. The three-month session closed, as is the custom, with one minute of silent prayer or meditation.

Having served on the Council during 1956, Yugoslavia informed the Secretary-General that it would not be in a position to serve in 1957.[133] A by-election to fill the vacancy was therefore held in accordance with Rule 141 of the Assembly's Rules of Procedure, and the Philippines was elected, obtaining one vote more than the required majority. Following the election, the Soviet representative stated that there has been a flagrant violation of the rights of the Eastern European Members, adding that the decision illustrated the fact that the United Nations was dwindling in importance.[134]

A similar situation developed during the fourteenth session of the

Assembly in 1959. The terms of office of Canada, Japan, and Panama were due to expire at the end of the year. After a certain amount of preliminary manœuvring, it was agreed informally that Ceylon (Sri Lanka) and Ecuador should succeed Canada and Panama respectively, and they were duly elected on the first ballot. Poland and Turkey were candidates for the third vacancy.

Poland's candidature was announced in July, though for some months before that, Polish diplomats in New York and elsewhere had been preparing the ground. At one time it seemed likely that Greece would be Poland's rival for the seat, but at the last moment Greece withdrew and Turkey was substituted. It was the view of Turkey's supporters that the seat for which it was a candidate should, if possible, be filled by an Eastern European country. One difficulty was that Turkey had, for a time in 1959, been a candidate for one of the Vice-Presidencies of the General Assembly intended for 'Western European and other States', but at the last moment had switched its candidature to one of the Afro-Asian vacancies. By contesting an East European vacancy on the Security Council, Turkey was in effect claiming to belong to three different regions at once. Moreover, the announcement of Turkey's candidature was not made until after the session had begun, by which time some States had already made commitments to Poland.

Fifty-two ballots were needed to resolve the question. The two-thirds majority required for election varied between fifty and fifty-four votes, which meant that a State with at least twenty-eight supporters in every ballot could prevent any other State from being elected. In the event, Poland's vote never fell below thirty-six, and—until the last ballot—Turkey's vote never fell below thirty-three.

Balloting began on 12 October. Thirty-one ballots were held during that month, twelve more during November, and six more on 1 December. The Assembly was due to close on 5 December, though the session was later extended. Turkey let it be known in mid-November that it would consider 'splitting the term' with Poland, and discussions about this took place during the last few days of the session. At the night meeting at the end of the session, 12/13 December, the General Assembly was able to endorse an agreement which had been negotiated in private. The President stated that consultations had taken place between the two candidates and their supporters, as a result of which it had been agreed that Poland was the only candidate but would resign after one year. Turkey would then be the only candidate for the vacancy thus created. 'In the vote, it is understood that the members of the Assembly will confirm that agreement.'[135] At 2.30 a.m. the Assembly proceeded to the election by secret ballot. Poland obtained seventy-one votes, thus being elected on the fifty-second ballot. Three diehards maintained their support for Turkey; Greece and Yemen obtained one vote each; four members abstained, and two (understandably) were absent.

The decision to split the 1956–7 term between Yugoslavia and the Philippines had been reluctantly accepted by the General Assembly as an exceptional measure and on the understanding, as the President put it, 'that it does not set a precedent'. The adoption of the same expedient in 1959 soon came to be regarded as a normal arrangement. In 1960, after thirteen inconclusive ballots, it was announced that Liberia and Ireland would split the 1961–2 term. The following year, after nine inconclusive ballots, Romania and the Philippines agreed to split the 1962–3 term, and the 1964–5 term was split between Czechoslovakia and Malaysia.

As will be explained in Chapter 6.2, the election of Malaysia to serve during 1965 was the occasion for Indonesia's temporary withdrawal from the United Nations.

TABLE 5

Non-permanent members of the Security Council, 1946–1997

	Africa and Asia	Latin America	Eastern Europe	Western Europe	Older Commonwealth States
1946	Egypt	Brazil Mexico	Poland	Netherlands	Australia
1947	Syria	Brazil Colombia	Poland	Belgium	Australia
1948	Syria	Argentina Colombia	Ukrainian SSR	Belgium	Canada
1949	Egypt	Argentina Cuba	Ukrainian SSR	Norway	Canada
1950	Egypt India	Cuba Ecuador	Yugoslavia	Norway	
1951	India	Brazil Ecuador	Yugoslavia	Netherlands Turkey	

Non-permanent Members

	Africa and Asia	Latin America	Eastern Europe	Western Europe	Older Commonwealth States
1952	Pakistan	Brazil		Greece	
		Chile		Netherlands	
				Turkey	
1953	Lebanon	Chile		Denmark	
	Pakistan	Colombia		Greece	
1954	Lebanon	Brazil		Denmark	New Zealand
		Colombia		Turkey	
1955	Iran	Brazil		Belgium	New Zealand
		Peru		Turkey	
1956	Iran	Cuba	Yugoslavia	Belgium	Australia
		Peru	(resigned)		
1957	Iraq	Colombia		Sweden	Australia
	Philippines	Cuba			
1958	Iraq	Colombia		Sweden	Canada
	Japan	Panama			
1959	Japan	Argentina		Italy	Canada
	Tunisia	Panama			
1960	Ceylon	Argentina	Poland	Italy	
	(Sri Lanka)	Ecuador	(resigned)		
	Tunisia				
1961	Ceylon	Chile		Turkey	
	(Sri Lanka)				
	Liberia	Ecuador			
	(resigned)				
	United Arab				
	Republic				
	(Egypt)				
1962	Ghana	Chile			
	United Arab	Venezuela	Romania	Ireland	
	Republic		(resigned)		
	(Egypt)				
1963	Ghana	Brazil		Norway	
	Morocco	Venezuela			
	Philippines				
1964	Ivory Coast	Bolivia			
	Morocco	Brazil	Czecho-	Norway	
			slovakia		
			(resigned)		
1965	Ivory Coast	Bolivia		Netherlands	
	Jordan	Uruguay			
	Malaysia				

cont.

TABLE 5 *cont.*

	Africa	Asia	Latin America	Eastern Europe	Western Europe and Other States
1966	Mali Nigeria Uganda	Japan Jordan	Argentina Uruguay	Bulgaria	Netherlands New Zealand
1967	Ethiopia Mali Nigeria	India Japan	Argentina Brazil	Bulgaria	Canada Denmark
1968	Algeria Ethiopia Senegal	India Pakistan	Brazil Paraguay	Hungary	Canada Denmark
1969	Algeria Senegal Zambia	Nepal Pakistan	Colombia Paraguay	Hungary	Finland Spain
1970	Burundi Sierra Leone Zambia	Nepal Syria	Colombia Nicaragua	Poland	Finland Spain
1971	Burundi Sierra Leone Somalia	Japan Syria	Argentina Nicaragua	Poland	Belgium Italy
1972	Guinea Somalia Sudan	India Japan	Argentina Panama	Yugoslavia	Belgium Italy
1973	Guinea Kenya Sudan	India Indonesia	Panama Peru	Yugoslavia	Australia Austria
1974	Cameroon Mauritania Kenya	Indonesia Iraq	Costa Rica Peru	Byelorussian SSR	Australia Austria
1975	Cameroon Mauritania Tanzania	Japan Iraq	Costa Rica Guyana	Byelorussian SSR	Italy Sweden
1976	Benin Libya Tanzania	Japan Pakistan	Guyana Panama	Romania	Italy Sweden
1977	Benin Libya Mauritania	India Pakistan	Panama Venezuela	Romania	Canada German Federal Republic
1978	Gabon Mauritania Nigeria	India Kuwait	Bolivia Venezuela	Czecho-slovakia	Canada German Federal Republic
1979	Gabon Nigeria Zambia	Bangladesh Kuwait	Bolivia Jamaica	Czecho-slovakia	Norway Portugal
1980	Niger Tunisia Zambia	Bangladesh Philippines	Jamaica Mexico	German Democratic Republic	Norway Portugal
1981	Niger Tunisia Uganda	Japan Philippines	Mexico Panama	German Democratic Republic	Ireland Spain

	Africa	Asia	Latin America	Eastern Europe	Western Europe and Other States
1982	Togo Uganda Zaire	Japan Jordan	Guyana Panama	Poland	Ireland Spain
1983	Togo Zaire Zimbabwe	Jordan Pakistan	Guyana Nicaragua	Poland	Malta Netherlands
1984	Egypt Upper Volta/ Burkina Faso Zimbabwe	India Pakistan	Nicaragua Peru	Ukrainian SSR	Malta Netherlands
1985	Burkina Faso Egypt Madagascar	India Thailand	Peru Trinidad and Tobago	Ukrainian SSR	Australia Denmark
1986	Congo Ghana Madagascar	Thailand United Arab Emirates	Trinidad and Tobago Venezuela	Bulgaria	Australia Denmark
1987	Congo Ghana Zambia	Japan United Arab Emirates	Argentina Venezuela	Bulgaria	Federal Republic of Germany Italy
1988	Algeria Senegal Zambia	Japan Nepal	Argentina Brazil	Yugoslavia	Federal Republic of Germany Italy
1989	Algeria Ethiopia Senegal	Malaysia Nepal	Brazil Colombia	Yugoslavia	Canada Finland
1990	Cote d'Ivoire Ethiopia Zaire	Democratic Yemen Malaysia	Colombia Cuba	Romania	Canada Finland
1991	Cote d'Ivoire Zaire Zimbabwe	India Yemen	Cuba Ecuador	Romania	Austria Belgium
1992	Cape Verde Morocco Zimbabwe	India Japan	Ecuador Venezuela	Hungary	Austria Belgium
1993	Cape Verde Djibouti Morocco	Japan Pakistan	Brazil Venezuela	Hungary	New Zealand Spain
1994	Djibouti Nigeria Rwanda	Oman Pakistan	Argentina Brazil	Czech Republic	New Zealand Spain
1995	Botswana Nigeria Rwanda	Indonesia Oman	Argentina Honduras	Czech Republic	Germany Italy
1996	Botswana Egypt Guinea-Bissau	Indonesia Republic of Korea	Chile Honduras	Poland	Germany Italy
1997	Egypt Guinea-Bissau Kenya	Japan Republic of Korea	Chile Costa Rica	Poland	Portugal Sweden

There have been two distinct but related difficulties over the distribution of elective seats. From 1950 onwards, there was disagreement over the seat originally earmarked for Eastern Europe. This difficulty was aggravated by the growth in the total UN membership, especially in 1955 and 1960, so that it was increasingly difficult to achieve 'equitable geographical distribution' with only six seats to be filled by General Assembly election. To make matters worse, the requirement of a two-thirds majority for election meant that a determined minority of UN Members (one-third plus one) could, theoretically, prevent a vacancy on the Council from being filled and thus make it impossible for the Council to function, 'continuously' or otherwise.

The obvious solution, to enlarge the Council, presented two problems. The first was a straightforward matter of mechanics: the larger the Council, the easier it would be to achieve 'equitable geographical distribution'; but beyond a certain point, bigness would constitute an obstacle to effective working. In due course, it became apparent in the 1960s that an increase from 11 to 15 would provide the optimum size—enough to ensure more equitable distribution, but not so much that size *per se* would add materially to the difficulties already faced by the Council.

The other difficulty was that enlargement could be achieved only by amending the Charter, a matter subject to veto by any of the permanent members, and the Soviet Union had taken the position that no Charter amendments were acceptable until the question of Chinese representation had been rectified. For the Soviet Union to have persisted with this position might have been logical, but it would have been imprudent, for it would have alienated Third World opinion which the Soviet Union was assiduously cultivating.

In 1963, on the initiative of a group of forty-four African and Asian States, the General Assembly decided to enlarge the Security Council to fifteen members (and the Economic and Social Council from eighteen to twenty-seven members) and to allocate the ten elective seats on the Council as follows:[136]

African States	3
Asian States	2
Eastern European States	1

Non-permanent Members

Latin American States	2
Western European and other States	2

The Communist countries and France opposed the enlargement of the Security Council, and the abstainers comprised Portugal, South Africa, the United Kingdom, and the United States.

In a letter sent to Secretary-General Thant after the 1963 session of the General Assembly had concluded, the Soviet Government pointed out that it had repeatedly drawn the attention of African and Asian delegations to the obstacles in the way of enlarging the two Councils while the People's Republic of China was deprived of its rights in the United Nations. As an exceptional measure, the Soviet Government would have agreed to enlargement of the Councils 'provided the Government of the People's Republic of China explicitly declared its consent'. On 8 December 1963, however, the Chinese Government had informed the Soviet Government that it approved of solving the problem not by enlarging the Councils but 'by means of a just distribution of the seats now available'.[137]

In spite of initial opposition to enlargement, Secretary-General Thant was able to report on 27 September 1965 that sufficient ratifications had been received, including those of the permanent members of the Security Council, for the Charter amendments to have entered into force,[138] and elections for the enlarged Council were held during the course of the 1965 session of the General Assembly.

The membership of the Organization continued to grow after the expansion of the Council in the mid-1960s, and it was not long before reform was again on the agenda. The total membership grew steadily from 115 in 1964 to 160 in 1990, and then, partly as a result of the break-up of the Soviet Union and Yugoslavia and the admission to UN membership of the newly-independent units, UN membership reached 185 in 1994. There were thus 180 candidates to share the 10 elective seats on the Security Council.

5. OTHER PARTICIPANTS

(a) Member States that are non-members of the Council

If the Security Council is to fulfil its primary responsibility for the maintenance of international peace and security, non-members of the Council must have access to it; and this right of access is laid down in the Charter and the Rules of Procedure—though in a somewhat complicated manner.

(i). UN Members which are not members of the Security Council

(a) '*shall be invited* to participate, without vote, in the discussion' relating to a dispute *to which it is a party* (Article 32, our italics);

(b) '*may be invited*, as the result of *a decision of the Security Council,* to participate, without vote, in the discussion of 'any situation which might lead to international friction or give rise to a dispute' or 'any dispute' which the Member has brought to the attention of the Council (Articles 34 and 35(1), and Rule 37, our italics);

(c) '*may* participate, without vote, in the discussion of any question brought before the Security Council *whenever the Security Council* considers that *the interests of that Member are specially affected*' (Article 31 and Rule 37, our italics);

(d) when the Council has decided to use force it *shall* before calling upon a Member not represented on the Council to provide armed forces in fulfilment of obligations under Article 43, *invite* that member to participate, *if it so desires, in the decisions* (not simply in the discussions) concerning the employment of contingents of that Member's armed forces (Article 44, our italics).

(ii). A non-Member of the United Nations may bring to the attention of the Council (or, indeed, the General Assembly) '*any dispute to which it is a party* if it accepts in advance, for the purposes of the dispute, the obligations of pacific settlement provided in the . . . Charter' (Article 35(2)). Such a non-Member '*shall be invited* to participate, without vote, in the discussion [in the Security Council] relating to the dispute. The Security Council shall lay down such conditions as it deems just' for the participation of non-Members of the United Nations (Article 32, our italics). Representatives of non-UN Members which are not parties to a dispute could presumably be invited to participate under Rule 39 if the

Council considered them competent to supply information or give other assistance.

(iii). Members of the Secretariat whom the Council considers competent for the purpose may be invited by the Council to supply it with information or to give other assistance in examining matters within the Council's competence (Rule 39).

(iv). 'Other persons' may be similarly invited by the Council to supply information or give other assistance (Rule 39).

Requests to participate steadily increased after 1960, and no fewer than thirty-two UN Members which were not members of the Security Council took part in the debates on the Congo question in the period 1960–4, when the Council itself had only eleven members; and, on one occasion, four African foreign ministers participated 'on behalf of all African States'.[139] Debates on Namibia often attracted a substantial number of non-members of the Council. In 1985, fifty-nine non-members took part in the debate, and in 1983, no fewer than sixty-three, many of them foreign ministers.[140] In 1991 57 non-members plus 2 Observers participated in a private meeting of the Council on 'The situation between Iraq and Kuwait'.[141]

States invited to participate in the discussion of an item on the Council's agenda are seated at the Council table throughout the discussion or are called to the Council table in order to address the Council and then return to their reserved seats at the side of the Council Chamber. The determination as to whether an invited State shall be allowed to sit at the table throughout the discussion is based on the Council's practice in the matter, according to which the party requesting the Council meeting and those directly involved are generally invited, at their request (usually made orally), to be seated at the table throughout the discussion. Such invited States have at times specifically indicated their wish not to be seated permanently at the table. In cases where the treatment of seating would not be routine, the President of the Council gives specific instructions in the matter.

On occasion there are not enough seats at the Council table for all those who had requested to be seated at the table through the discussion. In those instances an understanding is reached, on the basis of consultations, as to who would sit at the Council table throughout the discussion or whether it would be necessary for one of the parties seated permanently at the table to yield its seat temporarily in order to enable a speaker seated at the side of the Council Chamber to address the Council.[142] Requests to participate from officers of subsidiary organs of the General Assembly are granted as a matter of course. Other requests to take part were usually granted without a written proposal and without a vote. In 1971, India and Pakistan were invited to take part in the Council's deliberations on the situation in the India/Pakistan subcontinent though neither had formally asked to do so.[143]

The *Repertoire of Practice of the Security Council* states that 'material relevant to participation . . . cannot . . . be satisfactorily arranged within a classification derived directly from [the] texts', since on many occasions the Council has extended invitations 'in circumstances the correspondence of which to those envisaged in [the] texts has been the subject of no definite pronouncement by the Council.'[144] Under Article 30 of the Charter the Council is the master of its own procedure and so has the freedom to initiate invitations in any manner that it desires.

Requests by UN Members to participate in the discussion are rarely rejected. Cases of the rejection of requests from UN Members have included that of the Philippines to participate in the discussion of the second phase of the Indonesian question (7 August 1947), a decision which was soon reversed; eleven Members in connection with Tunisia (14 April 1952); and thirteen Members in connection with Morocco (3 September 1953). Other proposals which have been rejected were by Belgium that East Indonesia and Borneo be invited to participate in the discussion of the second phase of the Indonesian question (14 August and 22 August 1947), a proposal by Pakistan that Sheikh Abdullah be invited to participate in the debate on the India–Pakistan question (12 May 1964), and a request from a representative of the illegal regime in Southern Rhodesia (18 May 1966). The Council had requests from the Republic of Croatia, Bosnia and Herzegovina and the Federal Republic of Yugoslavia to participate in its 3189th meeting, held on 30 March 1993 to discuss the extension of the UNPROFOR mandate on the territory of the Republic of Croatia. The Council decided, after prior consultations of the whole, to invite only the representative of Croatia to participate in the discussion.

In a few cases, Members which have asked to participate in the discussion have been invited to submit their views in writing.

In the few cases in which requests to participate have been rejected, the issue which carried most weight was not simply whether the non-member was or was not a party to a dispute or whether its representative was or was not competent to supply the Council with information, but whether an invitation to participate in the proceedings of the Security Council would confer unwarranted legitimacy on the applicant. On a number of occasions in 1980, Western States agreed to the participation of Afghanistan (a UN Member) on the understanding that this did not represent recognition of the new regime.[145]

There are two express limitations to the participation of non-members of the Council. First, the Charter states that the participation of non-members is 'without vote' (Articles 31 and 32). Second, UN Members may submit proposals and draft resolutions, but these will be put to a vote 'only at the request of a representative on the Security Council' (Rule 38). Thus Tunisia, a non-member of the Council in 1971, tried to co-sponsor a proposal on the situation in the India/Pakistan subcontinent but withdrew the request after an objection had been voiced.[146] In 1980, a proposal on Jerusalem was submitted by 39 Islamic States, put to the vote at the request of three Council members, and adopted as resolution 476 (1980).[147] In 1983, a proposal of the Arab League on the territories occupied by Israel was put to the vote at the request of Jordan and vetoed by the United States (see Table 8, veto 159).[148] In 1985, a Nicaraguan proposal was put to the vote at the request of India: three paragraphs were vetoed by the United States (see Table 8, vetoes 166–8) and the truncated proposal was then adopted as resolution 562 (1985).[149]

Sometimes, but not very often, a UN Member with the right to be heard decides not to participate, as with Israel in December 1975, presumably because the Council invited also the Palestine Liberation Organization.[150]

The normal practice of the Council is to hear first the Member State or States submitting the matter, and then any other States directly concerned; this is sometimes followed by statements of reply. The Council then proceeds to a general debate. On one occasion, the South African representative protested that the Council had been unwilling to hear him until after the resolution had been adopted,[151] but this was by no means an uncommon occurrence.[152]

When a representative is invited to participate, he or she may do so until that particular phase of the discussion of the matter is completed. If, after one phase is completed, the Council later resumes discussion of the same item, a new invitation is sought. Sometimes requests to participate are received after the initial phase of the Council's consideration of a question, and such requests are not denied solely because of the lateness in applying. In the case of States not Members of the United Nations, the usual practice about speaking first cannot always be followed. If a State invited to participate has to send a special delegation, the Council may be unwilling to suspend all consideration of the matter pending the arrival of its representative.[153]

On a number of occasions, proposals have been made that representatives of States not members of the Council should be invited to take part in the discussion regarding the adoption of the agenda, but the Council has rejected such proposals, or allowed non-members to comment on the agenda only after the vote on it has been taken. Only rare exceptions to this practice have occurred, and the circumstances were unusual. On 6 January 1948, the Council began discussing the situation in Jammu and Kashmir; discussion on the item continued at four further meetings. On 22 January, however, in the provisional agenda for the meeting, the item was entitled 'India–Pakistan question'. The President explained that this change had been made on his own responsibility 'in consequence of a letter . . . addressed to me by the Pakistan Minister for Foreign Affairs'. He suggested that the Council should make an exception to its usual practice and allow the Indian representative to speak. A long discussion ensued, in which India took part, and in the end the Council adopted the provisional agenda with the item in its amended form.[154]

Another example was on 20 August 1969. Ireland had requested an urgent meeting to consider 'the situation in the six counties of Northern Ireland'. Britain asked the Council to reject the provisional agenda on the ground that the matter was one of domestic jurisdiction and therefore beyond the Council's competence. Almost certainly by pre-arrangement, and without any objection from the United Kingdom, Ireland's Foreign Minister was invited to address the Council. The British representative replied in conciliatory terms.

Zambia then proposed that, without taking a decision on the provisional agenda, the Council should adjourn, and the motion was adopted unanimously. The honour of all concerned was satisfied.[155]

It is the orthodox view that an invited representative does not have the right to raise points of order or take part in procedural discussions.[156] When the issue first arose in 1947, the President (Syria) stated: 'I am sorry but the raising of points of order is limited to members of the Council.'[157] On a very few occasions, however, invited representatives have succeeded in overcoming the obstacles.[158] Once an interruption occurs, even if improperly, it is difficult to proceed with the discussion until the President has disposed of the question which has been raised.

This section would not be complete without mentioning one non-member of the Council who rarely failed to participate in the debates, whatever the subject, until his death in 1979. This was Jamil Baroody, a Lebanese Christian, who represented Saudi Arabia. Baroody's interventions were always wide-ranging, often entertaining; but he tended to speak at inconvenient times and at excessive length. One of us recalls his characteristic contribution to a debate on the Middle East in 1976 in which Baroody brought in Abraham and his wives and concubines, King David, Alexander the Great, the Seleucids, the Romans, the Byzantines, the Mongols, the Khazars, the Caliphs, Theodore Herzl and the Zionist movement, European empires, and Irgun and the Stern Gang. Suddenly he realized the time, and he brought his oration to a quick end.

And let God be my witness: if at any time the Jews, as a minority, become the scapegoat in any country and I am alive, I shall be among the first to defend them as human beings . . .

I think I must go to the Tunisian reception tonight, otherwise I would keep you until 10 o'clock [it was then 7.45 p.m.]. I have a lot of material I have not used. But in the event of the gentleman from Israel asking for the floor, please list my name immediately after his, Mr President, and I shall refute what he says . . . And then, as he hopes, Christian, Gentile and Moslem can live in peace and harmony with the Jews, who are our brothers in humanity.[159]

(b) The participation of the PLO/the Permanent Observer of Palestine

On 14 October 1974, the General Assembly invited the Palestine Liberation Organization (PLO) to participate in its deliberations on the question of Palestine, and a month later Yasser Arafat addressed the Assembly.[160] A year after this, Egypt asked that the PLO should be invited to participate in a Security Council debate on the Middle East. When the Council met, the President (United Kingdom) reported that there had been informal discussions and it had been agreed that, should the Egyptian proposal be approved (which was a foregone conclusion), the invitation would confer on the PLO 'the same rights of participation as are conferred when a Member State is invited'. This and subsequent invitations to the PLO (and since January 1989 to the Permanent Observer for Palestine) were granted neither under Rule 37, nor under Rule 39 of the Council's rules of procedure, but with the same rights of participation as under Rule 37. All such invitations were opposed by the United States until a compromise was reached on 28 February 1994.[161] The Council was considering 'The situation in the Occupied Arab Territories' and an invitation was issued to the Permanent Observer of Palestine 'in accordance with the rules of procedure and the previous practice in this regard'[162] to participate in the debate. The United States raised no objection and Mr Al-Kidwa, the representative of Palestine, expressed appreciation for the positive change in the American position. This formula has been used in subsequent invitations to the Permanent Observer of Palestine.

(c) The participation of the Federal Republic of Yugoslavia in meetings of the Council

The Council was faced with a unique dilemma in September 1992 over how to treat requests for participation from the Federal Republic of Yugoslavia. The General Assembly, following a recommendation from the Security Council,[163] had decided by resolution 47/1 on 22 September 1992 that the Federal Republic of Yugoslavia 'should apply for membership in the United Nations, and that it shall not participate in the work of the General Assembly'. This did not, however, preclude its continued participation in meetings of the Security Council. In response to enquiries from States as to the exact consequences of this decision, the UN Legal Counsel clarified that the Assembly resolution did not amount to suspension under Article 5 of the Charter or expulsion under Article 6, and that its only effect was to prevent participation of the Federal Republic of Yugoslavia in the work of the General Assembly.[164]

In response to this unique situation, the Security Council adopted, from 22 September 1992, a special form of invitation when faced with a request for participation from the Federal Republic of Yugoslavia. According to this formula, the President of the Council, in response to a written request from the representative of the Federal Republic of Yugoslavia, invited that representative, by name (His Excellency Foreign Minister Ilija Djukic; Ambassador Dragomir Djokic; His Excellency Foreign Minister Vladislav Jovanovic) with the consent of the Council, to address the Council in the course of the discussion of the item before it.[165] While seated at the Council table, that representative sat behind the nameplate 'Yugoslavia'.

(d) The participation of Member States that are not members of the Council in informal consultations of the whole

There are no provisions in the Council's rules of procedure concerning informal 'consultations of the whole'. The proliferation of such consultations in the 1990s, at times becoming substitutes for formal meetings of the Council and the place where substantive decisions are made, resulted in calls for a mechanism by which Articles 31 and 32 of the Charter could be applied to such informal consultations. In January 1996 Ambassador Kovanda of the Czech Republic made a detailed proposal along these lines.[166] Kovanda posed the dilemma of a non-member of the Council being present in informal consultations when the Council discussed a question that concerned that State. He acknowledged that Council members might feel discomfort and constrained in freely expressing themselves, thus undermining the *raison d'être* of informal consultations. However, he argued, the Council had actually experienced an analogous situation when Rwanda was a member of the Council, and the outcome had had positive as well as negative dimensions. Kovanda pointed to the lessons he believed can be learnt from the example of Rwanda.

In 1994 and 1995 the Security Council adopted more than 30 resolutions and presidential statements concerning various aspects of the situation in Rwanda. Rwanda itself was a member from 1994 to 1995 and so attended most of the informal consultations that preceded these resolutions and statements. Rwanda's attendance occurred despite the fact that it was represented during this period by permanent representatives of two diametrically different governments, with the exception of a few weeks when the country was not represented at all. The postponement of Rwanda's turn as Council President from September to December 1994, and its decision to cede the Presidential chair for one meeting to Argentina when it did assume the Presidency, did not affect its presence in both Council meetings and informal consultations during this period. Kovanda argued that Rwanda's presence at times made the Council's work more difficult, but that Rwanda's participation in informal consultations had the positive dimension that the Council had an immediate understanding of the thinking of the Rwandan authorities. Kovanda concluded that despite the potential drawbacks of extending Article 31 to informal consultations of the Council, doing so would outweigh these and represent a positive contribution to transparency.

We are not convinced by this argument. Such a development could serve to drive confidential exchanges of view, essential to reaching political agreement, into more secretive fora. Such calls for participation by non-members can most effectively be countered by ensuring that exchanges of view that can be aired publicly are made at a public Council meeting.

(e) The participation of troop-contributing States

The proliferation of peace-keeping operations in the early 1990s also brought with it increased requests for attendance at Council meetings from non-member troop-contributors. Article 44 of the UN Charter raises interesting questions in this regard. The Article states that

> When the Security Council has decided to use force it shall, before calling upon a Member not represented on it to provide armed forces in fulfilment

of the obligations assumed under Article 43, invite that Member, if the Member so desires, to participate in the decisions of the Security Council concerning the employment of contingents of that Member's armed forces.

It has commonly been assumed that this Article has no practical significance since there have been no special agreements concluded under Article 43 that would place obligations on Member States to provide armed forces.[167] In the case of peace-keeping, forces are provided on a voluntary basis, and Member States retain almost total control over the use to which their forces are put. Nevertheless the tendency of the Council during the 1990s to establish peace-keeping mandates under Chapter VII of the Charter, has brought such operations closer to the role envisaged in Articles 43 and 44, and has given rise to claims by some States that they have a right to participate in Council decisions on changes to the mandates of such operations. Such requests are problematic since negotiations on the formulation of the mandate of an operation, its modification, extension or termination, frequently now take place in informal consultations, which non-members cannot attend.

After considerable debate on the subject, the Council in 1994 decided to address these concerns without bringing non-members into informal consultations. Instead the Council issued a presidential statement which instituted meetings, *as a matter of course*, between members of the Council, troop-contributing countries, and the Secretariat to facilitate the exchange of information and views. These views would then be reported by the President of the Council in the course of informal consultations (see Appendix XII(c)). After considerable further debate in 1995 under the agenda item 'An Agenda for Peace: Peace-keeping', the Council extended these arrangements to include consultations with prospective troop-contributors when the Council is considering establishing a new peace-keeping operation (see Appendix XII(e).[168] The developments in consultations with troop-contributors are considered further in Chapter 7.

(f) Participation of individuals

Rule 39 permits the Council to invite members of the Secretariat or other persons, whom it considers competent for the purpose, to supply it with information or to give other assistance. This rule has been used to secure the participation of the presiding officers of UN organs dealing with matters within the Council's competence, as well as private individuals having duties within the Council's sphere of responsibility. When beginning the consideration of its draft annual report to the General Assembly the Council by custom invites the Director of the Secretariat Security Council Affairs Division to make a brief explanatory statement on the preparation, format, and circulation of the report.[169] Members of the Secretariat are also frequently requested to brief the Council in the course of informal consultations of the whole.

More controversial have been requests to participate from individuals claiming to represent substantial bodies of opinion, such as the Jewish Agency for Palestine before the creation of the State of Israel, the Arab Higher Committee, spokesmen for the Turkish-speaking community in Cyprus, and representatives of liberation movements. In the first twenty-five years, only nine persons (other than officers of UN bodies) were invited to participate in the deliberations of the Council, and in each case the Council acted hesitantly. Beginning in 1971, however, liberation movements were invited to participate in debates on issues with which they were directly concerned. In 1972, this concept was widened when Abdul Minty of the Anti-Apartheid Movement and Canon Burgess Carr of the All-Africa Conference of Churches were invited to speak on general questions relating to Africa. Soon the Council was inviting anyone whom the majority of members wished to hear: Ken Fry, a member of the Australian House of Representatives, on Timor (1976); Olof Palme of Sweden, a representative of the World Council of Churches, and the Christian Institute of South Africa on South Africa (1977); a former South African newspaper editor, Donald Woods, also on South Africa (1978); two mayors and an Islamic judge from the territories occupied by Israel, on the Middle East (1980); Bishop Desmond Tutu again on South Africa (1984); and seven 'witnesses' of the Iraqi occupation of Kuwait (1991). Sometimes persons whose participation was invited never spoke, as with the Islamic judge in 1980.[170]

An unusual procedure was followed in November 1990 when the representative of Kuwait announced that

. . . my Country's delegation has the honour to be joined now by some brothers and sisters who will speak before the Council of their experiences under the occupation and its effects on individuals, the economy and virtually everything in Kuwait. I have pleasure in introducing to the Council the following witnesses: Mrs Fatima Fahed, Mrs Iman Adnan, Dr Issah Ibrahim, Mr Mukarji, Mr Shamma, and Mr Fawzi Badr.[171]

It appears from the verbatim records that these individuals were deemed to be members of the Kuwaiti delegation, and thus did not require a decision of the Council to be invited to speak. There appears to have been a small discrepancy in that the verbatim records list a total of seven witnesses (by number rather than name), whilst only six were introduced by name by the representative of Kuwait.[172]

On occasion, objections have been raised to the participation of individuals when it has been felt that such participation might legitimize Council involvement in matters considered to be outside its jurisdiction. On 11 August 1992 Belgium, France, the UK, and the US requested that the Council should meet on an urgent basis to hear Mr Max van der Stoel speak on the situation in Iraq. Mr van der Stoel was to be invited to speak in his personal capacity, under Rule 39 of the Provisional Rules of Procedure. China, Ecuador, India, and Zimbabwe objected to this invitation on the basis that Mr van der Stoel had been appointed as Special Rapporteur on the human rights situation in Iraq, and that his appointment had been made by the Commission on Human Rights, a subsidiary body of the Economic and Social Council. It was argued that the Security Council was not the appropriate body to discuss human rights issues, and pointed out that Mr van der Stoel's report on human rights in Iraq had not yet been considered by the Commission. China, speaking this time as Council President, stated that these objections would be noted in the official records.[173] Following this, no objections were raised to Mr van der Stoel's participation at the meeting. A similar situation occurred three months later with China and Zimbabwe objecting to 'personal' invitations to Mr Mazowiecki (also a Special Rapporteur appointed by the Commission) on 13 November,[174] and to a further invitation to Mr van der Stoel, on 23 November.[175] In both cases they were permitted to participate following the noting of objections.

(g) Participation of regional organizations

Regional agencies are supposed to keep the Security Council informed of activities undertaken or contemplated for the maintenance of international peace and security (Article 54), but in fact representatives of regional agencies have usually participated to present a point of view rather than to report on activities: the Organization of African Unity, for example, first invited in 1971; the League of Arab States, first invited in 1973; the Organization of the Islamic Conference in 1985; the Russian Federation for the CIS operation in Georgia in 1995. Representatives of specialized agencies and the International Atomic Energy Agency have also been invited when this has been deemed relevant. The concept of regionalism under the Charter is considered below in Section 8 of this chapter.

6. PERMANENT MISSIONS*[176]

The Charter makes no specific provision for permanent missions of Member States. They were established, in the first instance, by members of the three Councils provided for in the Charter (Security, Economic and Social, Trusteeship) and, as UN organs meeting between sessions of the General Assembly proliferated, were found to be necessary by almost all UN Members. In 1948, the General Assembly gave its blessing to the idea of permanent missions on the grounds that they 'assist in the realization of the purposes and principles of the United Nations and, in particular, [help] to keep the necessary liaison between Member States and the Secretariat'.[177] Specific provisions regarding the status of permanent representatives are contained in the Convention on the Privileges and Immunities of the United Nations and the Headquarters Agreement with the United States.[178] While the establishment of permanent missions at UN Headquarters is not obligatory, Members have found it essential to

* The word *mission* sometimes causes confusion in UN circles. Permanent missions accredited to the United Nations are distinct from Visiting Missions set up by the Trusteeship Council (Article 87). Needless to say, members of these two kinds of mission are never called 'missionaries'.

have them. In January 1997 the UN publication *Permanent Missions to the United Nations*[179] indicated that only one Member (Palau) had not established a permanent mission in New York.

The normal diplomatic practice of obtaining prior agreement that a diplomatic agent is acceptable to the State to which he or she is accredited is not followed at the United Nations.

In 1949, Secretary-General Lie suggested a standard form of credentials, but there is no question of the Secretary-General granting or withholding recognition. The head of a permanent mission presents his credentials to the Secretary-General on assuming his post, but there is nothing like the traditional ceremonial which is used at the Court of St James's and in some other capitals.

Secretary-General Hammarskjold greatly valued the system of permanent representation.

> Over the years, the diplomatic representatives accredited to the United Nations have developed a co-operation and built mutual contacts in dealing with problems they have in common, which in reality makes them members of a kind of continuous diplomatic conference, in which they are informally following and able to discuss, on a personal basis, all political questions which are important for the work of the Organization. These continuous informal deliberations do not lend themselves to publicity, and they receive none. But it would be a grave mistake to conclude from this that they are unimportant. On the contrary, the flexible and confidential forms in which these discussions can be pursued have given them a particular value as a complement to other diplomatic contacts and to all the various conferences and public exchanges . . . which constitute the normal operating procedures in a more traditional diplomacy.

The permanent delegations, wrote Hammarskjold, are 'pioneers in the development of international co-operation'. The system of permanent representation 'may well come to be regarded as the most important 'common law' development which has taken place so far within the constitutional framework of the Charter'.[180]

The individuals who have represented the Council's members have represented States, and the policies they have promoted have been the policies of governments. At a time when the United States and Britain were pursuing different policies in the UN Atomic Energy Commission, an American official reported to Washington as follows:

I said that any government which wished to could, of course, lean heavily on the fiction that their representatives were speaking only for themselves, but that this should be recognized to be, in reality, a fiction.[181]

The best ambassadors undoubtedly find opportunities of influencing policy. They may not necessarily write their own briefs, but the effective ones are those who can ensure that the instructions they receive from their capitals can be followed without violation of conscience, and who are able to present unpalatable policies in a way which will arouse least opposition. Some representatives on the Security Council have sometimes found it hard to conceal how disagreeable has been the task of promoting obnoxious policies, but this is exceptional. Most representatives most of the time have given the impression of enjoying the diplomacy of the Security Council and of believing wholeheartedly in the instructions they receive from their national capitals. Some, no doubt, are actors, enjoying their role on a world stage, participating in what Conor Cruise O'Brien has called a Sacred Drama.

Although the Charter states optimistically that the United Nations shall place no restriction on the eligibility of men and women to participate 'in any capacity and under conditions of equality' in its work (Article 8), it was not until 1972 that a member of the Security Council was represented by a woman. The honour fell to Africa, the country was Guinea, a non-permanent member of the Council, and the representative was a highly skilled diplomat, Jeanne Martin Cisse. Since then a number of women have reached the rank of Permanent Representative to the United Nations. Madeleine Albright, who became the first female US Ambassador to the UN in 1993, went on to become US Secretary of State in 1996.

7. GROUPS

If the development of permanent missions can be thought of as pioneering, even more so can the evolution of a rudimentary party system at the United Nations. The groups, to paraphrase Edmund Burke, are bodies of UN Members, united 'for promoting by their joint endeavours' certain regional or ideological interests, sometimes upon 'some particular principle in which they are all agreed'.

Groups

The system of blocs, groups, and caucuses in the General Assembly has by now been much studied by scholars: it hardly needs saying that the system also operates in the Security Council, although in a somewhat different manner. The emergence of groups was a natural corollary of the fact that like-minded Members tended to desire the same outcome at the conclusion of a UN debate, and it was therefore prudent to concert tactics in advance. The twenty Latin American Republics engaged in this practice at the San Francisco Conference.

TABLE 6

UN Members by region, 1 January 1997[a]

Eastern Europe (21)		
Albania	Georgia	Slovak Republic
Armenia	Hungary	Slovenia
Azebaijan	Latvia	The former Yugoslav Republic of Macedonia
Belarus	Lithuania	Ukraine
Bosnia and Herzegovina	Moldova	Yugoslavia (some rights of membership in suspense)
Bulgaria	Poland	
Croatia	Romania	
Czech Republic	Russian Federation	
Western Europe and other States (27)		
Andorra	Greece	New Zealand
Australia	Iceland	Norway
Austria	Ireland	Portugal
Belgium	Italy	San Marino
Canada	Liechtenstein	Spain
Denmark	Luxembourg	Sweden
Finland	Malta	Turkey
France	Monaco	United Kingdom
Germany	Netherlands	United States
Latin America and Caribbean (33)		
Antigua and Barbuda	Dominican Republic	Paraguay
Argentina	Ecuador	Peru
Bahamas	El Salvador	Saint Christopher and Nevis
Barbados	Grenada	Saint Lucia
Belize	Guatemala	Saint Vincent and the Grenadines
Bolivia	Guyana	Suriname
Brazil	Haiti	Trinidad and Tobago
Chile	Honduras	Uruguay
Colombia	Jamaica	Venezuela
Costa Rica	Mexico	
Cuba	Nicaragua	
Dominica	Panama	

cont.

TABLE 6 *cont.*

Asia (49)

Afghanistan	Kazakhstan	Qatar
Bahrain	Kuwait	Republic of Korea
Bangladesh	Kyrgyzstan	Samoa
Bhutan	Laos	Saudi Arabia
Brunei-Darassalam	Lebanon	Singapore
Cambodia	Malaysia	Solomon Islands
China	Maldives	Sri Lanka
Cyprus	Marshall Islands	Syria
Democratic People's Republic of Korea	Micronesia	Tajikistan
Fiji	Mongolia	Thailand
India	Myanmar	Turkmenistan
Indonesia	Nepal	United Arab Emirates
Iran	Oman	Uzbekistan
Iraq	Pakistan	Vanuatu
Japan	Palau	Viet Nam
Jordan	Papua New Guinea	Yemen
	Philippines	

Africa (53)

Algeria	Gabon	Nigeria
Angola	Gambia	Rwanda
Benin	Ghana	Sao Tome and Principe
Botswana	Guinea	Senegal
Burkina Faso	Guinea-Bissau	Seychelles
Burundi	Kenya	Sierra Leone
Cameroon	Lesotho	Somalia
Cape Verde	Liberia	South Africa
Central African Republic	Libya	Sudan
Chad	Madagascar	Swaziland
Comoros	Malawi	Tanzania
Congo	Mali	Togo
Cote d'Ivoire	Mauritania	Tunisia
Djibouti	Mauritius	Uganda
Egypt	Morocco	Zaire (DRC)
Equitorial Guinea	Mozambique	Zambia
Eritrea	Namibia	Zimbabwe
Ethiopia	Niger	

States not currently members of a UN regional group (2)

Estonia	Israel

[a] Based on UN Groupings used for electoral purposes.

In the early days, it soon became apparent that the East European Members (after 1948, including Czechoslovakia, but not Yugoslavia) pursued a common line, with the Soviet Union playing a dominant role. Opposed to the Soviet bloc on many issues was a less cohesive body of Members under US leadership, comprising Northern, Western, and Southern Europe, Latin America, and the older Commonwealth States. Ten States from Africa, the Middle East, and Asia were relatively uncommitted. By 1950, an Arab–Asian Group had come into existence, and after the Bandung Conference of 1955, this was transformed into an Afro-Asian Group. It was this Group which benefited from the new admissions in and after 1955, and by 1970 it had for many purposes separated into an Asian Group and an African Group, with an Arab Group comprising both Asian and African States.

Three developments served to crystallize the group system. First, the so-called Gentleman's Agreement of 1946 about the distribution of elective seats on the Security Council was based more on ideas of ideological or regional solidarity than on 'contribution . . . to the maintenance of international peace and security and . . . the other purposes of the Organization' (Article 23(1)). Second, the General Assembly decided in 1963 on geographical patterns for the non-permanent membership of the Security Council (and for the Economic and Social Council), and for the distribution of chairmanships and vice-presidencies in the General Assembly.[182] Third, in July 1971, the UN *Journal* began publishing monthly information regarding the current chairmanship of regional groups.[183]

The group system is of primary relevance in the General Assembly, but it manifests itself in the Security Council in the form of documents and statements on behalf of 'The African-Asian Group Members of the United Nations',[184] 'in accordance with the mandate given to me by the representatives of Non-Aligned Countries',[185] 'on behalf of the front-line countries',[186] 'the twenty-first Islamic Conference of Foreign Ministers',[187] 'Chairman of the Group of Asian States',[188] 'as Chairman of the Latin American Group',[189] 'as Chairman of the Group of East European States'.[190] 'Draft resolutions have been submitted on behalf of such groups.'[191]

It is sometimes not entirely clear for whom these representatives are speaking, but it is possible to discover the regional distribution of UN Members by reference to the elections by the General Assembly to the Council since a formal geographical pattern came into effect, supplemented by the information about the monthly chairmanship of regional groups which is given in the UN *Journal*, and from occasional (but not always accurate) information in the UN *Chronicle*.[192] Member States may be a member of one group for electoral purposes and another for certain political purposes. Turkey, for example, for electoral purposes is a member of the group 'Western Europe and other States' which it chairs roughly once every two or three years,[193] but for political purposes is also a member of the Asian Group,[194] and on at least one occasion was a candidate for an office reserved for Eastern Europe. One State, Israel, has been denied its request to join the Asian group to which it geographically belongs, and it has since been campaigning to be accepted by the Western Europe and other States Group (WEOG) on a temporary basis. The geographical distribution of UN Members for electoral purposes, as of 1 January 1997, is shown in Table 6 on pp. 169–70. Apart from these five electoral groups to which all UN members except Israel (denied) and Estonia (attempting to join WEOG) belong, there are a number of groupings to which States belong for political purposes. As of 1 January 1997, one hundred and twelve UN Members were members of the Non-Aligned Movement and fifty-three UN Members were members of the Commonwealth. Other sub-groups include the Arab League (twenty-one); the Gulf Co-operation Council (six); the Association of South-East Asian Nations (ASEAN) (seven); the Group of 77 (one hundred and thirty UN Members); the European Union (fifteen); the North Atlantic Treaty Organization (NATO) (sixteen); the Organization of American States (OAS) (thirty-five); the Organization of African Unity (fifty-three); the Organization of the Islamic Conference (fifty-three); the Organization for Security and Co-operation in Europe (OSCE) (fifty-five); and the South Pacific Forum (fifteen).[195] The UN has also received official communications from Conferences of Countries having French or Portugese as a Common Language.[196]

These overt manifestations are, of course, only the tip of the iceberg. The groups represent forums for a great deal of private multilateral diplomacy. Because the United Nations has become a somewhat unwieldy body, the group system facilitates its working in some respects, and the groups are undoubtedly valued by representatives with only minimal instructions from their capitals. Groupings can help prevent a State from being isolated, and have become increasingly important in the late 1980s and 1990s as the number of informal consultations and subsequent resolutions and decisions passed can place considerable burdens on members of the Council with small permanent missions.

The case against the groups is much like that often made against the party system at the national level: that the practice of caucusing before discussion and debate tends to make debate meaningless and diplomacy impossible, since members of groups may have already made commitments to their partners from which they cannot later disengage. Adlai Stevenson took a strong line in 1946 against full United States participation in the Latin American or any other regional group.[197]

8. REGIONALISM

Not all the world's regions had established regional organizations when the Charter was completed in 1945. Winston Churchill had wanted the Charter to include a section on the crucial role of regional bodies for dealing with threats to peace and acts of aggression. Churchill's British colleagues thought that his initial ideas were too far-fetched, and he was persuaded to develop a more modest proposal.

US leaders did not greatly mind what the Europeans did, but thcy were aware of the strong support for regionalism among the twenty republics of Latin America. At a regional conference held in the castle of Chapultepec in Mexico City, agreement was reached on a resolution (later known as the Act of Chapultepec) calling for joint action in repelling aggression against any of the Latin American Republics.

At the same time, on the initiative of Anthony Eden, seven Arab countries joined together to form the League of Arab States to facilitate co-operation on non-military matters (22 March 1945).

When it came to drafting the UN Charter, a distinction was made between military alliances for collective self-defence (Article 51) and agencies for regional co-operation on civil matters (Articles 52–4).

The part of the Charter immediately following Article 51, which is in Chapter VII and concerns the inherent right of self-defence, comprises a chapter on Regional Arrangements (Chapter VIII). Article

33 on the means for the pacific settlement of disputes includes 'resort to regional arrangements or agencies'. The initiative for regional action at the UN may be taken by the Security Council or the States concerned. The first Article specifically devoted to regionalism asserts that nothing in the Charter precludes the use of regional arrangements provided that the arrangements 'are consistent with the Purposes and Principles of the United Nations', that the disputes are local in character, are suitable and appropriate for pacific settlement through regional arrangements or by regional agencies, and that the Security Council is kept fully informed of activities undertaken 'or in contemplation . . . But no enforcement action shall be undertaken without the authorization of the Security Council, with the exception of measures against any enemy state . . .' Self-defence measures taken with reference to Article 51 are to be immediately reported to the Security Council and shall not affect the authority and responsibility of the Council; the Council shall be informed of regional action 'undertaken *or in contemplation*' (our italics).

Before the 1990s Chapter VIII had been useful mainly for debating purposes, to argue that some matter should *not* be placed on the agenda of the Security Council because it had been or was being or should be dealt with by the appropriate regional agency. That argument was raised in connection with Guatemala (June 1954), Lebanon (February 1958), Cuba (July 1960), the Dominican Republic (September 1960 and May 1965), Panama (January 1964), and Cyprus (March 1964).

The Security Council rarely included a reference to Chapter VIII in its resolutions before 1991, but there were thirteen such references in resolutions and one in a presidential statement in 1992. The summit meeting of the Security Council in January 1992 gave the first indication that the Council wished to see a greater role for regional organizations under Chapter VIII. The presidential statement issued at the conclusion of that meeting asked Boutros-Ghali to prepare recommendations on ways of strengthening the capacity of the United Nations for preventive diplomacy, peace-making and peace-keeping, and suggested that the Secretary-General could cover . . . *the contribution to be made by regional organizations in accordance with Chapter VIII of the Charter of the United Nations in helping the work of the Council* (our italics).[198] The resulting report, *An Agenda for Peace*, contained an optimistic section explaining that regional organizations had a new contribution to make, after being impaired by the Cold War. The experience of regional organizations in Somalia (OAU, Arab League, and the Organization of the Islamic Conference) and the former Yugoslavia (European Union and the Conference on Security and Co-operation in Europe (CSCE later OSCE)), indicated many of the problems as well as the benefits of the use of regional entities.[199] Nevertheless, Boutros-Ghali, who wrote his doctoral thesis on regional organizations, continued to support the concept of an enlarged role for such bodies. On 1 August 1994 the Secretary-General convened a meeting with the heads of regional organizations that have co-operated in peace-keeping activities, in order to assess that co-operation, with a view to augmenting it in the future. Also in 1994, the General Assembly adopted a resolution approving a Declaration on the Enhancement of Co-operation between the United Nations and Regional Arrangements or Agencies in the Maintenance of International Peace and Security.[200] The second meeting between the United Nations and regional organizations on co-operation in peace-making, peace-keeping, and other fields took place at UN Headquarters on 15 and 16 February 1996. This meeting reflected the increased co-operation between the United Nations and regional organizations in a wide variety of activities. These ranged from diplomatic support, such as co-operation between the United Nations and OSCE in Georgia/Abkhazia and in Nagorny Karabakh; operational support, such as that of NATO for the UN Protection Force (UNPROFOR) during United Nations operations in Bosnia and Herzegovina; co-deployment, such as with the CIS in Georgia and Tajikistan and with ECOWAS in Liberia; and joint operations, as with the OAS in the human rights mission in Haiti.

9. CREDENTIALS

The draft rules of procedure recommended by the Preparatory Commission contained no provisions for the examination of credentials in the Security Council. The Committee of Experts, in a report dated 5 February 1946, proposed rules to the effect that each member of the Council should be represented at meetings by an accredited representative; that the credentials of representatives should be examined by the President and two other members of the Council, who would report their findings to the Council for approval;* that, pending the approval of the credentials of representatives, they should be seated provisionally with the same rights as other representatives; and that any representative to whose credentials there had been objection should have the same rights as other representatives until the matter had been decided.[201]

In a revised draft submitted later in 1946, there were a number of additions and changes. Credentials were to be submitted to the Secretary-General 'not less than twenty-four hours' before a representative took his seat; a Prime Minister or Minister of Foreign Affairs of a member of the Council should be entitled to sit on the Council without submitting credentials; a UN Member not a member of the Council, if invited to participate in the Council's deliberations, should submit credentials in the same manner as for members of the Council; and credentials should be examined by the Secretary-General rather than by the President, and two other members of the Council: nothing was said about the person authorized to issue credentials. The changes were approved by the Council, except that 'Head of Government' was substituted for 'Prime Minister'.[202]

A further change in the Rules of Procedure relating to credentials was made in 1950, arising out of discussion of the question of Chinese representation. India suggested that the Rules should state that credentials should be issued either by the Head of the State or of the Government, or by the Minister for Foreign Affairs. The Committee of Experts, and later the Council, approved the proposal.[203] This change was to acquire special significance a decade later when the President of the Congo (Leopoldville), Joseph Kasavubu, and the former Prime Minister, Patrice Lumumba, designated different people to represent the Congo in the Security Council. The Council escaped from this predicament by not inviting *either* to participate in its proceedings (14 September 1960).

In the early years, the practice was to include in the provisional agenda the report of the Secretary-General regarding his examina-

* This was similar to the procedure adopted by the Economic and Social Council.

tion of credentials and, after the adoption of the agenda, to approve the credentials if there had been no objection. Since 1948, reports of the Secretary-General on credentials have not been included in the provisional agenda but are circulated to members of the Council. The reports are regarded as having been approved unless there is a specific request that they be considered.

In practice, credentials are submitted to and reported on by the Secretary-General only when changes are made in the representation of members of the Council, and when elected members are newly appointed. In the case of non-members of the Council, the strict requirements of the Rules of Procedure have not always been enforced.[204]

The legal situation about representation and credentials was described as follows by the UN Legal Counsel (29 April 1977):[205]

1. Permanent missions of Member States are established to ensure the proper representation of States to the Organization with a view to keeping the necessary liaison with the Secretariat in periods between sessions of the different organs of the United Nations [General Assembly resolution 257 (III)].
2. Since the creation of the United Nations, a practice has developed that the head of a permanent mission, designated by his Government, present[s] to the Secretary-General, who is the chief administrative officer of the Organization, his letter of accreditation or appointment—so-called credentials—issued either by the Head of State or Government or by the Minister for Foreign Affairs.
3. The practice in the United Nations has always been that, unless the credentials provide otherwise, the permanent representative is authorized to act before all organs of the Organization for which there are no special requirements as regards representation. Since, however, the rules of procedure of the principal organs of the United Nations (General Assembly, Security Council, Economic and Social Council, Trusteeship Council) require full powers to be communicated to the Secretary-General, the General Assembly in resolution 257 A (III) has recommended that Member States desiring their permanent representative to represent them on one or more of the organs of the United Nations should specify the organs in the credentials.
4. In the report 'Permanent Missions to the United Nations' submitted by the Secretary-General at each regular session of the General Assembly, Member States which have authorized their permanent representative to

represent them in all organs of the United Nations are marked with an asterisk and when the authorization relates to certain organs, with two asterisks. Full powers before all organs sometimes use the phrase: '*any organs, commissions or other bodies of the United Nations other than specialized agencies*', or '*all principal and subsidiary organs*', or '*all matters brought before the United Nations*'. As to full powers for certain organs, it will be noted that the organ generally specified in the credentials is the Security Council. However, States which are members of the Security Council generally submit full powers to this effect in a separate instrument. No mention to that effect appears in the report of the Secretary-General referred to above.

Apart from the question of the representation of China, which is reviewed below (Section 10), difficulties regarding credentials have not been frequent. They have arisen either following sudden and fundamental changes of government after which the status of the diplomatic staff in New York was for a time uncertain (as in the cases of Hungary in 1956,[206] Iraq in 1958,[207] Cyprus in 1974,[208] Democratic Kampuchea in 1979, Grenada in 1983, and Rwanda in 1994), or where competing authorities in a country have purported to issue credentials in respect of different people (as in the case of the Congo (Leopoldville) in 1960,[209] the Dominican Republic in 1965),[210] and Panama in 1989). In such cases, the main issue has not been the validity of the credentials but the legitimacy of the issuing authority. While these situations provide opportunities for members of the Council to make political points in the guise of discussing credentials, the Council has been content to evade the issue until the picture has become clear. Secretary-General Thant expressed the view that the 'clearest' of these cases was in connection with the representation of Iraq in 1958. In that instance, the President interpreted Rule 17 as indicating that the representative of Iraq, who had been occupying the seat of Iraq, should continue to sit in that seat with the same rights as other representatives, until the Council arrived at another conclusion. Following the receipt of further documentation, a new representative of Iraq took his place in the Council on 7 August 1958.[211] In other words, a decision on disputed credentials after a change of government is deferred until it has become clear that a successor government has established its authority.

At the first meeting of the Council held in 1968, Algeria asked whether Rule 15* meant that the Council should give 'tacit' approval to the Secretary-General's report on credentials, or whether it was 'necessary for these reports to be approved explicitly'. The President (Pakistan) stated what had been the Council's practice. This, however, did not clear up the point raised by Algeria. If objection had been raised to the credentials of one or several representatives, said Algeria, 'it becomes necessary . . . for the report to be approved explicitly'. France and the Soviet Union supported the Algerian interpretation, and the President disposed of the matter by suggesting that the Secretary-General should present to the Council 'some information in regard to the recent practice'. This was duly done, and the information provided by the Secretary-General was that 'in the absence of any request that [the reports of the Secretary-General] be considered by the Council, [they] have been approved without objection'.[212]

During the debate on a complaint by Chad on Libyan interference in 1983, Libya commented that the United States and France were trying to make Chad into their stooge. At the end of the speech, the President (Luc de la Barre de Nanteuil of France) commented tartly that Libya had 'once again trampled on the authority of the [Security] Council', which had recognized the legitimacy of the Government of Chad several months previously.[213] This presidential comment, even if true, had little bearing on Chad's complaint or Libya's riposte.

10. REPRESENTATION OF CHINA[214]

The Central People's Government of the People's Republic of China had been established in Beijing (Peking) on 1 October 1949. On 18 November, Foreign Minister Zhou Enlai (Chou En-lai) sent statements to the President of the General Assembly and to Secretary-General Lie stating that the delegation appointed by the Nationalist Government had no authority to speak for the Chinese people.[215] The General Assembly was in session at the time but the

* Rule 15 reads in part: 'The credentials of representatives on the Security Council . . . shall be examined by the Secretary-General who shall submit a report to the Security Council *for approval*' (our italics).

credentials of the Nationalist Chinese representatives had already been approved, and no action was taken.[216]

After the conclusion of the session, the Soviet Union raised the question of Chinese representation at a meeting of the Security Council held on 29 December 1949 to consider the Kashmir question. The Soviet representative said he supported the Chinese communication and that the Soviet Government would not regard 'the Kuomintang representative . . . as being empowered to represent the Chinese people'. He did not, however, submit a formal proposal of his own. The representative of Nationalist China declared that he represented the legitimate government of China. The President (Canada) pointed out that the matter was not on the Council's provisional agenda and suggested that the Council, having heard the statements, should pass to other business. The Soviet representative raised no objection, and the Council proceeded with its work.[217]

On 8 January 1950, Zhou Enlai sent another note to Secretary-General Lie as well as one to the members of the Security Council, protesting at the Council's failure 'to expel the illegitimate representative of the Chinese Kuomintang reactionary clique'. At the next meeting of the Council on 10 January 1950, with the representative of Nationalist China in the chair, the Soviet representative repeated his opposition to the presence in the Council of a representative of Nationalist China, and formally proposed that his credentials be not recognized and that he be excluded from the Council. The Nationalist Chinese President stated that the Soviet proposal would be printed and distributed, whereupon the Soviet representative objected to a ruling from 'a person who does not represent anyone'. The President put his ruling to the vote, and it was upheld by eight votes to two (Soviet Union and Yugoslavia), India abstaining. The Soviet representative then declared that he could not participate in the work of the Council 'or take part in this meeting . . . until the Kuomintang representative has been excluded', whereupon he left the Council chamber.[218]

When the Council met two days later, the Soviet representative was in his place, and the first item was the Soviet proposal from the previous meeting. On this occasion Nationalist China ceded the presidency to Cuba. After a debate extending over two meetings, the Soviet draft resolution was rejected by six votes to three, with two abstentions. The Soviet representative then declared that he could not sit in the Council 'until the representative of the Kuomintang group . . . has been removed' and that he would not 'recognize as legal any decision of the Security Council adopted with the participation of the representative of the Kuomintang group'. The Soviet representative then left the chamber,[219] and he did not return until the following August, when it was his turn to preside. It was in the absence of the Soviet Union that the Council authorized UN military action to support South Korea.

On 19/20 January 1950, Zhou Enlai sent a further communication to Secretary-General Lie and members of the Security Council, announcing that Chang Wen-t'ien* had been appointed Chairman of the delegation of the People's Republic of China to attend the meetings and to participate in the work of the United Nations'.[220] Secretary-General Lie summarized his views at the time as follows.

> I did not feel that approval or disapproval of a régime was in question: it was a matter of recognizing the facts of international life . . . It was *China*, not Chiang Kai-shek, that belonged to the United Nations . . . How could Chiang Kai-shek speak for China?[221]

Lie entered into informal conversations, first with four of the permanent members of the Security Council, then with the non-permanent members, and finally with the representative of Nationalist China. Sir Alexander Cadogan of the United Kingdom surprised Lie by suggesting that the Soviet attitude might be based on 'a calculated policy of discouraging rather than encouraging recognition of the new Chinese government by either the United States or France. China, he pointed out, could thereby be kept more effectively in isolation from the West'. T. F. Tsiang, the representative of Nationalist China, was 'highly excited during most of the conversation', which was 'unlike his normal placid self'. He stated several times that the Beijing government 'would never survive the two to three months famine period'.[222]

Lie had asked Abe Feller and Ivan Kerno, legal experts in the Secretariat, to prepare a memorandum on the legal aspects of UN representation, and had given copies of the memorandum to

* Also known by his *nom de plume* as Chang Lo-fu or simply Lo Fu. Chinese Ambassador to the Soviet Union, 1951–5; Vice Minister for Foreign Affairs, 1954–9; Acting Foreign Minister during the absence abroad of Zhou Enlai, April 1955 and November 1956 to February 1957; not active in public life after September 1959.

members of the Security Council on a confidential basis. The press got wind of this, so on 8 March 1950 Lie sent a copy to the President of the Security Council (Ecuador) for publication.[223]

It was stated in the legal memorandum that the primary difficulty was that the question of the representation of China had been linked to the question of recognition by Member States. This linkage was unfortunate from the practical standpoint because it made representation dependent entirely on a numerical count of the number of Members in a particular organ which recognized one government or another. It was also wrong from the standpoint of legal theory, since recognition of a State is a unilateral act which is decided by each State in accordance with its own free appreciation of the situation. Until the Chinese question arose, the practice in organs of the United Nations had been consistently to distinguish between representation and recognition. 'The United Nations is not an association limited to like-minded States and governments of similar ideological persuasion . . . It must of necessity include States of varying and even conflicting ideologies.' The Chinese case was unique not because it involved a revolutionary change of government but because it was the first in which two rival governments existed. Where a revolutionary government presented itself as representing a State, in rivalry to another government, the question should be which of the two was in a position to employ the resources and direct the people of the State in fulfilment of the obligations of Membership. This meant an inquiry as to whether the new government exercised effective authority within the territory of the State and was habitually obeyed by the bulk of the population.[224]

The representative of Nationalist China immediately protested at Secretary-General Lie's action.

> Your memorandum is . . . an attack on the cause of freedom . . . If it is too much to expect you to use your influence against Communism, it is certainly not too much to expect you to remain at least neutral . . . In the present instance you have supplied argument against my delegation and in favour of the Soviet Union delegation. You have destroyed public confidence in the impartiality of the Secretariat.[225]

Thereafter, the Chinese Nationalists treated Secretary-General Lie with considerable reserve and abstained in both the Security Council and the General Assembly later in the year when the extension of Lie's term of office was put to the vote.

During the course of the Security Council meetings in 1950, India suggested that the Council's Rules of Procedure were defective in not stating who may issue credentials. India proposed that credentials should be issued by either the Head of the State or the Government concerned or by its Minister for Foreign Affairs, and that a decision to change the representation of a State in the Council should not be made until all Member States had had the opportunity of expressing their views on the matter. These proposals were referred to the Committee of Experts, which approved the first concerning the issuance of credentials. As to the second, there was general agreement in the Committee that it would be desirable to establish some uniform procedure which could be adopted by all organs of the United Nations, but the majority considered that this was not a matter for the Security Council but for the General Assembly. The Committee believed that the Council should not, for the time being, take a decision on the second proposal. These recommendations of the Committee were approved by the Council.[226]

In August 1950 it was the turn of the Soviet representative to preside over meetings of the Security Council. The Council met on the first day of the month, and the Soviet President at once ruled that 'the representative of the Kuomintang group' did not represent China and therefore could not take part in meetings of the Council. This decision was put to the vote and overruled. The Council then took up a Soviet proposal to include in the agenda an item entitled 'Recognition of the representative of the Central People's Government of the People's Republic of China as the representative of China', and eventually decided by five votes to five with one abstention to reject the Soviet proposal.[227]

The question of Chinese representation was raised by the Soviet Union on four subsequent occasions: 1951, 1955 (twice), and 1967. In 1955, the Council agreed to a US proposal 'not to consider any proposals to exclude the representative of the Government of the Republic of China, or to seat representatives of the Central People's Government of the People's Republic of China'.[228] The matter was also raised by Somalia in 1971, but the Council took no action.[229]

CHART I

General Assembly voting on the representation of China, 1961–1971

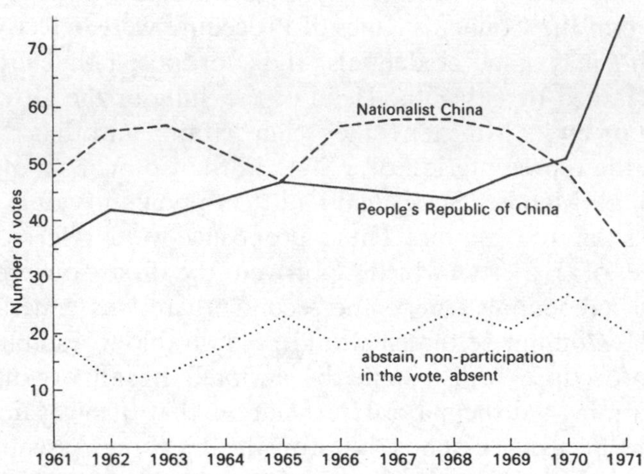

Between 1951 and 1971, the General Assembly decided either to postpone consideration of the matter or not to consider it, but when neither of these ploys would work, the issue was put to the vote but failed to secure a two-thirds majority. Finally, at a marathon meeting lasting from 5 p.m. to 11.25 p.m. on 25 October 1971, during the course of which a Swedish diplomat allegedly made a rude remark about Saudi Arabian ambassador Baroody and a Tanzanian diplomat reportedly expressed his glee by dancing in one of the aisles,[230] the Assembly voted by seventy-six votes to thirty-five, with twenty States abstaining or absent, 'to restore all its rights to the People's Republic of China . . . and to expel forthwith the representatives of Chiang Kai-shek from the place which they unlawfully occupy'.[231] The Chinese delegation formally took its seat in the Assembly three weeks later and, after some embarrassed speeches of welcome, a reasonably soothing statement was made by China's Deputy Minister of Foreign Affairs, Ch'iao Kuan-hua.[232]

It was almost exactly twenty-one years since a representative of the People's Republic, Wu Hsiu-ch'uan,* had taken part in the proceedings

* Vice-Minister for Foreign Affairs, 1951–5; Ambassador to Yugoslavia, 1955–8; severely criticized in 1967 for ideological deviations.

of the Security Council, during discussion of complaints of aggression upon the Republic of Korea and of armed invasion of Taiwan.[233] Few people remembered, however, that, on the urging of the United States, the Chinese delegation at San Francisco had not been exclusively Kuomintang but had included Communist and other Chinese political elements. Among those who signed the UN Charter was Tung Pi-wu, who eventually became President of the People's Republic of China. On 2 November, U Thant informed the Security Council that China had appointed Huang Hua and Chen Chu as representative and deputy representative respectively on the Council. The Secretary-General reported that the credentials of Messrs. Huang and Chen were in order, and when the Council met, members of the Council were eager to express their welcome to the Chinese.[234] *

For twenty years, the General Assembly had approved US-sponsored draft resolutions to postpone consideration of proposals on Chinese representation (1951–3), or not to consider such proposals (1954–60), or that proposals to that effect were 'important' within the meaning of Article 18 of the Charter (1961–70) and so requiring a two-thirds majority. The effect of these gimmicks was to prevent a straightforward vote on whether the Beijing Government or the Kuomintang regime on Taiwan had a better claim to represent China.

During this period, when China's UN seat was occupied by a representative of the rump Kuomintang government which had taken refuge on Taiwan, the situation had become increasingly anomalous. Security Council diplomacy on matters relating to China was more and more unreal. When it was China's month to preside, the normal arrangements for informal consultations under the auspices of the President could not be relied on, and members of the Council would solemnly thank the representative of Nationalist China the following month for his consideration in not calling any meetings. Occasionally a discordant note was introduced into the proceedings of the Council when the Soviet representative would address the representative of Nationalist China as plain 'Mr Liu'.[235] The change of representation in 1971 injected the bitter Sino-Soviet dispute into the proceedings of

* The Soviet representative was, however, careful to call Mr Huang of China 'colleague', while Mr Kulaga of Poland was addressed as 'comrade'.

the Council, usually initiated by China. But these polemics gradually subsided. China began the practice of not participating in certain votes, and there were other procedural difficulties for a time.

By the mid-1980s China had become a normal UN Member, but the issue of Chinese representation was not to completely leave the UN stage. On 6 August 1993 Nicaragua and six other Central American States requested, in a letter to the Secretary-General,[236] that the General Assembly at its forty-eighth session undertake 'Consideration of the exceptional situation of the Republic of China in Taiwan in its international context, based on the Principle of Universality and in accordance with the established model of parallel representation of divided countries at the United Nations'. The seven States attached to their letter a draft resolution that would have established an *ad hoc* committee to study the issue, and an explanatory memorandum in which they argued that General Assembly resolution 2758 (XXVI) (1971) had not succeeded in fully resolving the problems arising from the division of China. The inclusion of this item was strongly opposed by the People's Republic of China, and was not included in the agenda of the Assembly. A similar attempt to place this item on the Assembly's agenda failed at the forty-ninth, fiftieth, and fifty-first General Assembly sessions. However, the number of co-sponsors grew from 7 in 1993 to 12 in 1994; 15 in 1995 and 16 in 1996.

An opportunity for the People's Republic of China to express its anger at the attempts of some States to give greater international recognition to Taiwan arose on 10 January 1997. That evening the Council voted on a draft resolution[237] to send a group of military observers to Guatemala, following the historic signing of a Peace Agreement between the Government of Guatemala and the URNG[238] on 29 December 1996. Whilst fully supporting its provisions China vetoed the resolution explaining that it had done so because 'the Government of Guatemala has, for four consecutive years, unscrupulously supported activities aimed at splitting China at the United Nations . . . it was furthermore bent on inviting . . . the authorities of Taiwan to the signing ceremony of the peace Agreement in Guatemala . . . .'[239] Ten days later China voted in favour of an almost identical resolution,[240] and circulated at that meeting a 'position paper' stating that China had reached agreement with the Government of Guatemala, through joint efforts, on the obstacles to China's support.[241]

On 16 July 1997 nine states (of which Guatemala was not one) attempted to place a new agenda item on the Provisional Agenda of the fifty-second session of the General Assembly, this time with the title 'Need to Review General Assembly Resolution 2758 (XXVI) of 25 October 1971 owing to the fundamental change in the international situation and to the coexistence of two Governments across the Taiwan Strait'.[242] The attempt failed.

II. PRECEDENCE

The niceties of ordinary diplomatic precedence are resolved by reference to the Vienna Convention on Diplomatic Relations, buttressed by custom and tradition. The situation regarding precedence at the United Nations is extremely complicated, but the Chief of Protocol doubtless has his or her own detailed guide-lines. The order of precedence for the Security Council is as follows:[243]

1. Heads of State
2. President of the General Assembly when the General Assembly is in session
3. Secretary-General
4. Heads of Government
5. President of the Security Council
6. Ministers of Foreign Affairs

It is interesting to note that the President of the Assembly takes precedence over the Secretary-General while the Assembly is in session.

When Heads of State or Government, or other representatives of special distinction appear in the Security Council, they are, if they so wish, escorted to and from the Chamber.

CHAPTER 4

DIPLOMACY AND DEBATE

> Thus the great secret of negotiation is to bring out prominently the common advantage to both parties of any proposal.

DEBATE and decisions are the visible parts of diplomacy. Debate can serve several purposes: to get certain facts or points of view on the record, to satisfy public opinion at home, to please friends or annoy adversaries, sometimes even to influence the outcome. But debate is only a part, and often only a minor part, of the process by which the Security Council tries to achieve its purposes.

Public debate on controversial questions may be useful, but usually only if it is accompanied by private discussion and negotiation. Indeed, occasions occur when debate is unnecessary or even harmful. When the Security Council decided by consensus in April 1972 to increase the number of UN observers on the Lebanese side of the frontier between Lebanon and Israel, 'a formal meeting of the Security Council was not considered necessary'. The President of the Council, Sir Colin Crowe of the United Kingdom, said he had consulted members of the Council informally and evidently discovered that public debate would reveal differences which would hamper agreement. Indeed, the President issued a note expressing China's reservations, although the reservations were evidently not substantial enough to lead to a Chinese veto.[1] As is made clear in Chapter 2, there has been an increasing tendency to reach agreement in informal negotiations and for the Council's conclusions to be read out by the President as a statement.

Diplomacy is governed by custom and etiquette, but debate takes place in accordance with both written and unwritten procedures. The written procedures are contained in Chapter VI of the Council's Provisional Rules of Procedure entitled 'Conduct of Business'.

The Charter states that the Council shall adopt its own rules of procedure (Article 30), but the present Rules are only provisional. The President, declares Rule 19 tautologically, shall preside over the meetings of the Council. The President declares the opening and closing of each meeting, calls upon speakers, puts questions, announces decisions, and maintains order.

Knowledge of the Council's procedure and practice is a great diplomatic asset: 'there are many delegates [wrote John Humphrey] who owe their reputations and influence to their knowledge of and experience with the rules of procedure', though he adds that 'these delegates are not necessarily the most productive'.[2]

1. ORDER OF SPEAKERS

The order of speakers is governed by two Rules. Rule 27 states that the President *shall* call upon representatives in the order in which they signify their desire to speak. For this purpose, the secretary of the Council, sitting on the President's left during meetings, maintains a list of speakers. But Rule 27 is qualified by Rule 29, which designates certain people who *may* be accorded precedence: any rapporteur appointed by the Council, the chairman of a commission or committee for the purpose of explaining its report, or the rapporteur appointed by a commission or committee to present its report.

As a result of presidential rulings which have been confirmed or which have not been challenged or overruled, one can reach the following conclusions about the practice of the Council:

1. The word *representative* used in Rule 27 applies not only to members of the Council, but also to UN Members which are not members of the Council, and to States which are not members of the United Nations but which have been invited to participate without vote under Rules 37–9.[3]
2. Representatives who wish to inscribe their names on the list of speakers should inform the secretary of the Council rather than the President. To keep two separate lists, as has sometimes been done, makes for confusion.[4]
3. Representatives may place their names on the list of speakers even before the agenda is adopted.[5]

4. Members of the Council are called to speak before non-members.[6]
5. A representative whose name is on the list of speakers cannot normally yield his place to another representative; to suspend Rule 27 and change the order of speakers requires an express decision of the Council.[7] Very occasionally, the normal practice is relaxed. In October 1973, for example, the President (Australia), 'with the consent of the representative of Indonesia' who was next on the speaker's list, himself suspended Rule 27 to allow representatives to express condolences regarding those diplomats and UN officials and their families who had been killed during an air attack on Damascus.[8]
6. A Member of the United Nations which calls for a meeting of the Security Council may speak first. In November 1950, for example, the United States called for a meeting of the Council to discuss the Korean question. Soviet Ambassador Malik objected to the adoption of the agenda, but found himself in a minority of one when the matter was put to the vote. He then proposed that China be invited to participate, adding that the Soviet delegation 'insists' that his proposal be considered before the Council discussed the substance of the Korean question. The President (Yugoslavia) then stated that

   > it is the established practice in the Security Council—a practice confirmed by a series of precedents—that the delegation requesting a meeting of the Council should be called upon to speak first.[9]

7. In the case of non-UN Members, the precedents are inconclusive. When the Hyderabad question was considered in 1948, the representative of Hyderabad spoke first.[10] In November 1950, however, a meeting of the Council was called by the Soviet Union, 'which took into account the request of the delegation of the People's Republic of China'. The practice of the Council, said Soviet Ambassador Malik, was that, when a State placed an item on the Council's agenda, its representative should be the first to outline his position. 'First the accuser [said Malik], and then the accused'. The matter was not that simple, however, as the United States had already placed its name at the head of the speakers' list. After a lengthy discussion, the President (Yugoslavia) put the Soviet proposal to the vote, and it was rejected.[11]
8. Parties to a situation or dispute, whether or not Council members,

almost always speak immediately after the Member which called for the meeting. There have, it is true, been a few occasions when this practice was not followed. At one meeting, called jointly by the United Kingdom and Cyprus to discuss the Cyprus question, the United Kingdom spoke first.[12] When the Council met on 9 November 1967 at the request of Egypt to consider the Middle East question, the speakers' list was headed by Egypt, with Israel seventh on the list. US Ambassador Goldberg proposed that Israel should be allowed to speak second. After some discussion, the US proposal was put to the vote but failed to obtain the affirmative vote of nine members.[13] The circumstances in these two cases were to some extent unusual, and they may be regarded as exceptions to established custom.

9. The President usually speaks last as his country's representative, but on one occasion the President (John Garba of Nigeria) spoke substantively as the first speaker.[14]

The order of speakers, unless changed by express decision of the Council, is thus usually as follows:

Member requesting the meeting
Others directly involved in the question or dispute
Members of the Council
President of the Council, in his capacity as representative
Non-members of the Council

On one occasion, during the Cuban missile crisis of 1962, US Ambassador Adlai Stevenson addressed a direct question to Soviet Ambassador Valerian Zorin and demanded an immediate answer.[15] This was, in effect, an informal proposal to change the order of speakers, and a President would be fully within his rights in refusing such a request or insisting that it be put to the vote.[16] Similarly, representatives who have asked to make a further statement must wait their turn, unless the President obtains the agreement of the Council to vary the order of speakers.[17]

Express requests to change the order of speakers, especially those which are politically motivated (and which of them are not?), are likely to be rejected if put to the vote, although changes which have been informally agreed among the representatives usually cause no difficulty.[18]

2. INTERRUPTING THE SPEAKER

The purpose of the Rules of Procedure is to enable the work of the Council to proceed smoothly and within predictable limits. It is, nevertheless, necessary to have an emergency procedure for interrupting the debate if a breach of the Rules or other abnormal development occurs. Any procedure which permits a representative other than the President to interrupt a speaker is open to abuse, and many so-called points of order are nothing of the kind: they are matters of substance in disguise.

Nowhere in the Rules of Procedure is a point of order defined, and this lacuna provides endless scope for confusion (or, indeed, deliberate obfuscation). The point of order is believed to have been a British invention, and is defined as follows in the standard work on British parliamentary procedure:*

> Although it is the duty of the President to interfere in the first instance for the preservation of order when, in his judgment, the occasion demands his interference, it is also the right of any member of the Council who conceives that a breach of order has been committed, if the President refrains from interfering (either because he does not consider it necessary to do so, or because he does not perceive that a breach of order has been committed), to rise in his place, interrupting any representative who may be speaking, and direct the attention of the Chair to the matter, provided he does so the moment the alleged breach of order occurs.[19]

A committee on rationalizing the procedures of the UN General Assembly defined a point of order as follows (1971):

> A point of order is basically an intervention directed to the presiding officer, requesting him to make use of some power inherent in his office or specifically given him under the rules of procedure. It may, for example, relate to the manner in which the debate is conducted, to the maintenance of order, to the observance of the rules of procedure or to the way in which presiding officers exercise the powers conferred upon them by the rules.[20] Under a point of order, a representative may request the presiding officer

* We have adapted the quotation to the terminology of the Security Council by changing 'Speaker' to 'President', and 'Member' to 'member of the Council' on the first occasion and 'representative' on the second.

to apply a certain rule of procedure or he may question the way in which the [presiding] officer applies the rule. Thus, within the scope of the rules of procedure, representatives are enabled to direct the attention of the presiding officer to violations or misapplications of the rules by other representatives or by the presiding officer himself . . .

Points of order . . . involve questions necessitating a ruling by the presiding officer, subject to possible appeal. They are therefore distinct from procedural motions provided for in [Rule 33], which can be decided only by a vote and on which more than one motion may be entertained at the same time, rule [33] laying down the precedence of such motions. They are also distinct from requests for information or clarification, or from remarks relating to the material arrangements (seating, interpretation system, temperature of the room), documents, translations etc., which—while they may have to be dealt with by the presiding officer—do not require rulings from him.[21]

The only proper way by which a representative other than the President may interrupt another representative while he is speaking is by raising a point of order. If a representative raises a point of order, the President shall immediately state his ruling. If the ruling is challenged, the President shall submit the matter to the Council for immediate decision, and it shall stand unless overruled (Rule 30).

The method of raising and disposing of points of order is stated in Rule 30 of the Council's Rules of Procedure, but one must take account also of the established practice of the Council. It is useful, in addition, to bear in mind Rules 73, 90, 115, and 130 of the General Assembly's Rules of Procedure and the 1971 report of the Committee on rationalizing the procedures of the General Assembly. From these sources, the following conclusions emerge.

1. A point of order, being a matter to be decided by the President, should not deal with any matter outside the President's competence. In particular, a point of order should not concern the substance of the matter under discussion. The purely procedural nature of points of order calls for brevity.[22] When a President of the Security Council (Piero Vinci of Italy) was once asked to define a point of order, he replied: 'The only thing I can do is to read out rule 30 of the provisional rules of procedure which says . . .'.[23] We need hardly add that Rule 30 contains no definition of a point of order!

The only circumstances in which the President may refuse to

entertain a point of order raised by a member of the Council is if an earlier point of order has not been resolved. As Dr Lange of Poland put it when he was President of the Council in 1946,

any representative can raise a point of order at any time, and it is a matter for his own judgment at what moment to do so.[24]

2. A point of order raised while voting is in progress should concern only the actual conduct of the voting.[25]

3. A point of order must be immediately decided by the President in accordance with the Rules of Procedure, taking precedence over any other matter, including procedural motions.[26] If the Rules of Procedure are correctly followed, no point of order on the same or a different subject may be entertained until the initial point of order and any challenge thereto have been disposed of.* [27]

In 1973, during the October War in the Middle East, the President (Sir Laurence McIntyre of Australia) was confronted with a number of simultaneous points of order raised by representatives who had not been given the floor. Faced with such an unusual situation, the President decided to suspend the proceedings for a few minutes so that tempers might cool.[28]

4. It is for the President to rule on a point of order. Nevertheless, both the President and representatives may request information or clarification regarding a point of order. The President may, if he considers it necessary, request an expression of views from representatives before giving his ruling; but the President should terminate an exchange of views and give his ruling as soon as he is ready to announce it.[29] There is no provision in the Rules of Procedure for submitting a point of order for the decision of the Council—although Sir Pierson Dixon of the United Kingdom was once able to secure a vote on whether the Yugoslav proposal to convene the General Assembly in an emergency special session over Suez in 1956 was or was not in order.[30]

5. According to Rule 30, if a representative challenges the President's ruling, he shall 'submit his ruling to the Security Council for immediate decision and it shall stand unless overruled.'

The first volume of the *Repertoire* states that, beginning with the meeting of the Council held on 1 August 1950, 'all votes resulting

* A Committee of the General Assembly once managed to accumulate 84 unresolved points of order!

from challenges to Presidential rulings have been entered in the Official Records as votes on proposals to overrule.'[31] Subsequently the challenge to a ruling has usually been put to a vote.[32]

6. Any challenge to the President's ruling shall be decided by the Council immediately. A point of order or any challenge to a ruling thereon is not debatable.[33] Needless to say, this is easier said than done. During the debate on the Bangladesh war in 1971, the Soviet Union proposed that a representative of Bangladesh be invited to participate in the proceedings. The President (J. B. Taylor-Kamara of Sierra Leone) asked that the matter be deferred until a document had been circulated, and he later interpreted the Soviet request as a point of order and his own response as a Presidential ruling. India, a non-member of the Council, then intervened in the discussion, which was a dual breach of procedure: that non-members had no rights regarding the Council's procedure, and that a challenge to a Presidential ruling should be put to the vote at once without debate. After two further interventions, the President announced that he would put his ruling to a vote. After three more speakers had participated in the debate, the Council decided to support the President's ruling.[34] A few days later, a similar issue arose when the Soviet Union proposed that the Council should hear from representatives of 'those who have lived through the serious political crisis and suffered all the conditions of hardship created in East Pakistan'. The President again interpreted the Soviet proposal as a point of order and ruled that he could not allow the participation of representatives of a State which failed to meet the recognized criteria of international law. India again intervened, as did Pakistan (three times), another non-member. After considerable debate, during which the President repeated his ruling, the Soviet representative stated that he did not wish his challenge to be put to the vote.[35]

7. A representative may interrupt the speech of another representative to raise a point of order; but unless a grave breach of order is alleged to be occurring, a point of order should, if possible, be delayed until the end of a speech.[36]

8. In spite of a few breaches in the past, it is not proper for non-members of the Council to raise points of order.[37]

9. In no circumstances should a motion or proposal made by the President, or by any other representative, be converted into a

'ruling'. In October 1947, when Sir Alexander Cadogan of the United Kingdom was President, he proposed that the Security Council should meet again in two days' time, but when this proposal was put to the vote, it was found to be unacceptable. When questioned by Soviet Ambassador Gromyko about the procedural situation, Sir Alexander replied uncertainly: 'I might be held to have given a ruling, and the vote might have had the effect of reversing my ruling. I am not sure.' He then proceeded to 'rule' that the Council should meet the following week, twice repeating that this was the President's 'ruling'. Colonel Hodgson of Australia then intervened to say, 'The President can rule only when a point of order has been raised.'[38]

A similar confusion arose in 1948. The Council had been discussing a proposal that it should request information from the Committee of Good Offices in Indonesia. Towards the end of the meeting, the President (the Ukrainian SSR) tried to sum up the situation with the words, 'The President has made a ruling . . . that a telegram should be sent to the Committee of Good Offices.' This led the United Kingdom to complain about the 'extraordinary procedure' by which, if a procedural proposal were made, the President could apparently simply rule on it. 'There is a great deal of difference between a question of procedure and a point of order.'[39]

The practice just described continued to trouble the Council in the 1960s but has not caused confusion in recent times since such matters are invariably sorted out in informal consultations.[40] A procedural motion may be submitted to and adopted by the Council with or without a vote; but a motion or proposal should never be disguised as a ruling.

Our impression is that the Council is considerably less troubled than formerly with needless or bogus points of order or other unwarranted interruptions, except in the now rare cases of deliberate filibustering.[41]

3. RIGHT OF REPLY

There is no express provision in the Council's Rules of Procedure for the right of reply. This differs from the Rules of the General Assembly which provide that a presiding officer may accord the right of reply if a speech delivered after the list of speakers has been closed makes this desirable.[42] Presidents of the Council have usually tried to maintain an analogous practice[43] whilst using different terminology. In the case of the Council, upon request, the President will usually invite a representative 'to make a further statement'. There has not always been agreement on this practice. In December 1987 in a debate on the Situation in the Occupied Arab Territories, the Council President (Soviet Union) invited India 'to speak in excercise of his right of reply'. At this point Sir Crispin Tickell of the United Kingdom intervened with a point of order: 'I understand that in fact there are no rights of reply in the Security Council . . . although we welcome statements'. The President replied: 'I am obliged to beg to differ with the statement made by the representative of the United Kingdom. We have, with the consent of the Council, invited the representative of India to make a statement. According to established practice in the Council he has the right to exercise his right of reply, and I now call upon him.'[44] 'Rights of reply' by India, Israel, India (again), and the Palestine Liberation Organization followed. Both representatives were partially right. Whilst there is no express provision for the right to reply in the Council's Rules of Procedure, the phrase has often been used by Council Presidents in the past.[45] Since Sir Crispin Tickell's intervention in 1987, Council Presidents have preferred the formulation 'further statement'. The present practice is to ask the Council members whether they agree to a further statement being made.

4. MOTIONS, PROPOSALS, SUGGESTIONS

To avoid confusion later, we must start with attempted definitions of expressions used in the Rules of Procedure or in the customary language of the Security Council. The expressions to be defined are:

1. Motion (Rules 34–6), motion of order;
2. Proposal, draft resolution, proposed resolution (Rules 31–6, 38);
3. Substantive motion (Rule 31);
4. Original proposal (Rule 36);
5. Principal motion (Rules 32, 33);
6. Suggestion.

1. Procedural proposals were sometimes called *motions of order* by the Committee of Experts. The chairman reported that the Committee thought that the Rules of Procedure dealing with the conduct of business should contain some detailed provisions concerning 'points and motions of order'. It is safe to assume that motions of order were procedural motions, because it was while discussing them that the question of closure of debate was raised.[46] In the Rules of Procedure, the expression 'motions of order' is not used, but Rules 34–6 use the word *motion*. A motion, if approved, becomes a decision, the several meanings of which in UN parlance are discussed in Chapter 5.1 below.

2. A *proposal* (Rule 38), also called a *draft resolution* (Rules 32–6 and 38) or *proposed resolution* (Rule 31), is submitted in express terms and is usually concerned with substance rather than procedure. When a proposal is approved by the Council, it becomes a decision or a resolution; a draft or proposed resolution, when approved, becomes a resolution.

3. When the relevant Rules were first considered by the Council, Australia suggested that *substantive motions* (Rule 31) are 'motions which deal with matters of substance in contrast with proposed resolutions which might deal with any question'—a definition which was not challenged.[47] If this interpretation is correct, a substantive motion is synonymous with what would now be called a substantive proposal or draft resolution, that is to say, a proposal or draft resolution or proposed resolution on a matter of substance.

4. The *original proposal* is a proposal to which amendments have been offered, and it is not put to the vote until all amendments and sub-amendments thereto have been disposed of (Rule 36).[48]

5. When we come to *principal motions* (Rules 32 and 33), we encounter nothing but obscurity. In reply to a question raised by the United Kingdom, the chairman of the Committee of Experts said that the term 'principal motions' covered 'both substantive motions *and amendments*'; the term had been used to enable 'a distinction to be made between principal motions and draft resolutions, on the one hand, and motions on points of order proper, on the other hand'. That, one might have thought, was reasonably clear. A principal motion, according to that interpretation, is a proposal or amendment on the substance of a matter, what in Rule 31 is called a substantive

motion, while a plain motion concerns procedure. But an intervention a few minutes later by Australia, assuredly meant to be helpful, had the effect of causing utter confusion. In the opinion of the Australian representative, a principal motion was a motion or draft resolution 'moved originally *before any amendment is offered*', in other words, 'the original proposal' as used in Rule 36 and defined in paragraph 4 above. The intention, thought the Australian representative, had been to distinguish between 'principal motions *in contrast to amendments* . . .'

Sir Alexander Cadogan, the British representative, almost certainly with his tongue in his cheek, expressed his gratitude to the Australian representative.

I confess that I had not understood the thing. I think I do now . . . This discussion will be on the record, and I think that will explain the apparent conflict of terminology in the future.[49]

All one can say with certainty is that a principal motion is either a substantive proposal (chairman of the Committee of Experts) or an original proposal (Australia).

Principal motions, however defined, and draft resolutions, are put to the vote in the order of their submission unless the Council decides to the contrary.[50] Draft resolutions are voted on in parts only if the sponsors agree.[51]

6. A *suggestion* is less formal than a motion or a proposal. It is a trial balloon floated by a representative during the course of a meeting, sometimes without much premeditation, and not necessarily in very precise language. If the response to a suggestion is favourable, it may be converted into a formal motion or proposal. A suggestion *per se* is not put to the vote.

At a very early meeting of the Council, the President (Australia) asked whether a Soviet 'suggestion' had a seconder. Brazil said that, as a matter of courtesy, *any* proposal should be discussed: 'I do not think that a proposal by one member of the Council should be disposed of because there is no supporter.' As no opposing view was put forward, the President expressed the wishes of the Council 'that we should not seek a seconder to a resolution'.[52] The Council later adopted a Rule to the effect that it was unnecessary for a motion or draft resolution to be seconded before being put to the vote (Rule 34).

According to Rule 31, proposed resolutions, proposed amendments, and proposed substantive motions 'shall normally be placed before the representatives in writing'. The Council has, wisely, paid full regard to the adverb 'normally' in Rule 31 and has not insisted that *all* proposals and amendments be circulated in written form.[53] Occasionally there has been some minor bickering as to whether a particular proposal fell within one of the precise categories contained in Rule 31, but the skill of the President or the common sense of representatives has made it possible for the Council to overcome such obstacles expeditiously.[54] When the Council was considering Cyprus in 1974, the Soviet Union wanted to suspend the meeting, but a motion to that effect was defeated. The Soviet Union then introduced an amendment to the proposal under discussion and insisted that it be circulated in writing in all official languages. This was clearly a manœuvre to filibuster, and a considerable debate ensued. Finally, the Soviet request was put to the vote and defeated.[55]

Rule 32 provides that principal motions and draft resolutions shall have precedence in the order of their submission. The Council may, if it so wishes, suspend this Rule by a procedural vote and afford priority to a particular draft resolution. Even when circumstances have been abnormal, the Council has tended to vote on draft resolutions in the order of their submission.[56] But on a few occasions the Council has voted to consider proposals in a different order.[57]

On one occasion, uncertainty arose as to whether a draft resolution, submitted by a non-member and put to the vote in amended form at the request of a member in accordance with Rule 38, should have precedence over proposals submitted by members of the Council. On 22 December 1955, Syria, a non-member of the Council, had submitted a draft resolution. On 9 January 1956, the Soviet Union submitted an amended version of it and asked that the amended proposal be put to the vote. Other proposals were submitted later by other delegations, and the Council voted to grant priority to one of these.[58]

When the Council was considering peace and security in South East Asia in 1979, the President of the Council (Abdalla Yaccoub Bishara of Kuwait) persuaded China to submit a draft resolution through him, thus saving time and avoiding 'unnecessary acrimony'.[59]

5. 'PRECEDENCE MOTIONS' (RULE 33)

A Security Council debate may have clearly defined phases: the opening statements by the parties and other interested States, a general debate, a debate on proposals and amendments. Often the phases will not be sharply differentiated and the Council will move imperceptibly from one phase to the next.

For an ingenious representative, there is a whole range of filibustering techniques which can be used to prevent the Council from passing to the next phase or from coming to a decision. If armed conflict is taking place, the friends of the State or States which expect to win may want to prolong debate in the Security Council and prevent the early adoption of a resolution calling for a cease-fire. The friends of the losing side, on the contrary, will want to hurry the debate or even skip it, and proceed to a cease-fire call as soon as possible. These tendencies were evident at times during the Korean War between 1 August and 8 November 1950, for example, during the Suez fiasco at the end of October 1956, during the Six Day War in 1967, during the October War in 1973, and at the end of the Gulf War in 1991, to cite only five examples.

Filibustering, as a form of deliberate obstruction, is a negative phenomenon. There can, on the other hand, be positive reasons for discontinuing debate: to obtain certain facts from impartial observers, to enable representatives to receive advice or instructions from their capitals, to explore informally the possibilities of agreement, and so on. For this reason, the Council has at its disposal a variety of techniques by which debate can be suspended or terminated, either to facilitate positive purposes or to frustrate negative ones. These techniques are listed in Rule 33:

1. Suspension of the meeting;
2. Adjournment of the meeting;
3. Adjournment of the meeting to a certain day or hour;
4. Reference of any matter to a committee, the Secretary-General, or a rapporteur;
5. Postponement of the discussion of a question to a certain day, or indefinitely;
6. Introduction of an amendment.

All the motions listed in Rule 33 'shall have precedence in the order named over all principal motions and draft resolutions relative to the subject before the meeting'. Rule 33 further stipulates that any motion for the suspension (1 above) or for the simple adjournment of a meeting (2 above) shall be decided without debate. All 'precedence motions', as they may be called, are beyond the scope of the veto. If a 'precedence motion' is moved by a non-member of the Council, it may be put to the vote only at the request of a Council member.[60]

How should a representative move a 'precedence motion' if the only means by which he may jump the queue of representatives awaiting their turn to speak is by raising a point of order, which is by definition a matter subject to presidential ruling? Strictly speaking, the representative should ask for the floor on a point of order. When he has the floor, he should ask for the President's agreement to his moving a 'precedence motion', and this agreement should be granted automatically. The representative is then free to move one of the motions listed in Rule 33.* In practice, the stages of the correct procedure are nearly always conflated.[62]

The Committee of Experts considered whether provision should be made for the closure of debate (which was desired by the United States),[63] but in the end no recommendation to provide expressly in the Rules of Procedure for the closure was made.

Although there is no provision in the Rules for making a clear separation between the general debate of an item and the discussion of proposals, Presidents have generally followed, as one President (Poland) put it, 'a good and normal practice that the general debate should come to an end at some time, and then the concrete [draft] resolutions can be taken up'.[64]

(a) Suspension of meeting

The first kind of motion listed under the first paragraph of Rule 33 is for the suspension of the meeting. This means that the meeting is stopped for an agreed period of time (which is almost always exceeded); when the Council resumes, it is still the same meeting so

* The same procedure should be followed if a representative seeks information or clarification.[61]

that it is not necessary to readopt the agenda or reinvite the participation of non-members. Suspensions have varied in length between ten or fifteen minutes[65] and a number of days.[66] The usual reason for a suspension is to allow informal consultations among Council members, but the Council has been suspended so that a key representative may take a phone call, to allow representatives to consult their capitals, to give time for the translation and circulation of documents, to enable a representative to lobby for his or her preferred solution, or even for a bomb scare.[67]

Meetings were not often suspended in the early years, and we recall few meetings with suspensions before 1964. The first case we recall was at the Council's eighth meeting on 5 February 1946. At the next meeting, held on 6 February 1946 to elect members of the International Court of Justice, there were six suspensions totalling more than six hours.[68] There was another suspension in 1946, which was called 'a recess', which lasted thirty-seven minutes.[69] We recall a meeting on the admission of new Members being suspended in 1952, a suspension in 1953 during consideration of the Palestine question, one in 1955 on the admission of new Members, and two suspensions during one meeting in 1957 on the Palestine question.[70] There was also a fifteen-minute suspension on 24 November 1961 following the Soviet veto of a US amendment to a proposal of Egypt, Ceylon, and Liberia relating to the Congo.[71] A meeting of the Council in 1964 was distinguished by three suspensions.[72] Meetings to elect members of the International Court of Justice, such as those in 1987, 1993, and 1996 have frequently been suspended while the Council waits for the General Assembly to ballot. Suspensions were used more frequently in the 1990s when delegates strove for consensus texts on contentious issues, and so suspended meetings briefly for recourse to informal consultations. During negotiations on a resolution on the Situation in the Occupied Arab Territories the Council was suspended twice at a meeting on 26 May 1990[73] and then once more on 31 May 1990 in an attempt to broker an agreement. Delegates failed to reach a consensus and the United States subsequently vetoed a resolution proposing to send a three-member Council commission to the Occupied Territories.[74] In a related debate later that year, on the treatment of Palestinians, both suspensions and adjournments occurred at meetings on 10 and 17 December before a consensus resolution and presidential statement were arrived at on 20 December.[75]

The use of multiple suspensions marked the exceptional meeting held during the 1990–1 Gulf War which, after meeting once in public on 13 February 1991,[76] was suspended and began meeting in private (but with a public verbatim record) the following day. This meeting then suspended and resumed a further five times between 14 February and 2 March.[77] Through this procedure the Council was able to maintain the particular formula that was tortuously arrived at after lengthy negotiations (see Chapter 2), and allowed the one meeting to last more than two weeks.

Suspensions appeared to come into vogue in 1992 with the Council frequently suspending meetings on occasions when individuals addressed the Council. The Council suspended three times on 11 March 1992 with Mr Rolf Ekeus and Mr Hans Blix, once on 16 July 1992 with Mr Mangosuthu G. Buthelezi, and four times at a meeting on 23–4 November 1992 attended by Mr van der Stoel and the Deputy Prime Minister of Iraq, Mr Tariq Aziz. The suspensions employed between 1993 and 1997 appeared to be mainly to allow Council members to break for lunch,[78] an exception being a contentious meeting held on the Occupied Arab Territories from 12 to 15 May 1995[79] which was suspended twice while negotiations continued on a draft resolution. As in May 1990 the consultations failed to bring about a consensus and on 17 May the United States vetoed a resolution on Israeli expropriation of land in East Jerusalem.[80]

(b) *Adjournment of meeting*

There are two kinds of adjournment provided for in Rule 33, an adjournment *sine die* (in the second paragraph of the rule called 'the simple adjournment') or an adjournment to a certain day or hour. In deciding which form of adjournment to move, a representative will be guided by the fact that any motion for the simple adjournment 'shall be decided without debate', whereas adjournment to a named hour or day can be debated before being put to the vote (Rule 33).

(i) Adjournment sine die

The Council has only rarely resorted to the simple adjournment. We believe that on the first occasion on which it did so, the Council immediately thereafter proceeded to fix the day and time of its next meeting![81] On another occasion, the Council decided upon the simple adjournment, whereupon the President (Denmark) said:

The motion is adopted. The meeting will be adjourned until tomorrow. I take it that it should be tomorrow morning.[82]

On 30 January 1962, immediately after the adoption of an agenda concerned with the Congo question, Ambassador Adlai Stevenson of the United States moved the simple adjournment, adding that the motion 'is not debatable, and I request that it be put immediately to the vote'. It took the President, Sir Patrick Dean of the United Kingdom, an hour and a half before he managed to put the US motion to the vote, because of bogus points of order raised by Soviet Ambassador Zorin.[83]

Example cases of simple adjournment, with the date of the next meeting on the same item, are given in Table 7. It will be seen that Case 1 was a reasonable adjournment to enable China to respond to an invitation to participate in the discussion. In Case 2, the item was submerged by more serious and pressing Middle East questions following the Suez episode. In Cases 3, 6, and 7, meetings were convened quite soon after the adjournment. The Congo question (Case 4) was allowed to lapse by general consent, and was not discussed by the Security Council after January 1962. Benedetto Conforti considered that the decision in this case was 'illegal' because 'the dissenting minority was deprived even of the possibility of expressing its opinion on the adoption of the agenda'.[84] The Cuban complaint (Case 12) was similarly allowed to lapse. Case 8 allowed Ireland to state its anxieties about the situation in Northern Ireland without pressing to a vote a question involving the issue of domestic jurisdiction.

The one curiosity in Table 7 is Case 5 on Kashmir. After debate extending over six meetings, Pakistan had on 17 February 1964 requested 'a few days' postponement'. Morocco had then proposed a simple adjournment, to which the Council had agreed. A fortnight

TABLE 7

Some cases of simple adjournment under Rule 33, 1946–1996

Case no.	Date	Meeting and para. no.	Subject (short title)	Date of next meeting on same item
1	31 Jan. 1955	690, 148–9[a]	Hostilities in the area of certain islands off the coast of China	14 Feb. 1955
2	29 Oct. 1956	747, 11[b]	French complaint concerning military assistance tendered by the Egyptian Government to the rebels in Algeria	—
3	12 Sept. 1960	898, 8–14	The Congo question	14 Sept. 1960
4	30 Jan. 1962	989, 30–75	The Congo question	—
5	17 Feb. 1964	1093, 4–22	The India–Pakistan question	17 Mar. 1964
6	7 June 1967	1350, 85–105	The situation in the Middle East	8 June 1967
7	13 June 1967	1358, 329–34	The situation in the Middle East	13 June 1967
8	20 Aug. 1969	1503, 68–70	Complaint of Ireland	—
9	20 July 1972	1652, 57	Middle East	21 July 1972
10	24 Aug. 1972	1659, 188	UN Membership	25 Aug. 1972
11	20 April 1973	1710, 74 and 82	Middle East	21 April 1973
12	18 Sept. 1973	1742, 215	Complaint of Cuba	—
13	31 March 1976	1906, 217–18	Aggression by South Africa	—
14	31 Oct. 1977	2045, 70–5 and 78–9	South Africa	4 Nov. 1977
15	3 April 1982	2350, 136–45	Falklands (Malvinas)	—
16	3 June 1982	2372, 10–31	Falklands (Malvinas)	4 June 1982
17	1 March 1994	3341	The Situation in the Occupied Arab territories	

[a] Meeting adjourned following an invitation to the People's Republic of China to participate in the debate.

[b] Meeting adjourned 'to give the Egyptian delegation time to make its preparations'.

later, on 4 March, Pakistan had requested the President to convene a meeting. On 8 March, India had objected to an early meeting. Faced with irreconcilable requests from Pakistan and India, the President (Nationalist China) convened the Council on 17 March so that it could consider how to resolve the matter. India and Pakistan participated fully in the procedural debate, and in the end the Council adjourned for three more days, 'at which time [stated the President] the Council will proceed at once with a discussion, if necessary, to decide whether to resume consideration of this item.' The Council duly met on 20 March and decided to adjourn until 5 May, when it at last turned its attention to the substance of the problem.[85] Once a motion for the simple adjournment has been adopted, no other motion is in order.[86]

(ii) Adjournment to a particular date and time

Each motion to adjourn to a fixed time is a motion in its own right and not an amendment to a previous adjournment motion. On one occasion, disagreement had arisen in the Council between Soviet ambassador Sobolev and US Ambassador Lodge about the time of the next meeting, and both had made proposals. In an attempt to be helpful, Yugoslavia suggested a compromise, which the President (Peru) surprisingly treated as an amendment to one of the proposals. Both the Soviet and the US motions were put to the vote and both failed to secure sufficient affirmative votes. In the circumstances, the President wisely changed his mind and treated the Yugoslav suggestion as a formal proposal which would be adopted in the absence of alternatives, and the Council raised no objection.[87]

On 8 December 1990 the Council convened,[88] with Yemen as President, following a request[89] from Colombia, Cuba, Malaysia, and Yemen that it should meet to consider a draft resolution[90] on the safety and protection of Palestinians under Israeli occupation. Certain permanent members, however, wanted more time in informal consultations to further amend the draft resolution to produce a consensus text, and so did not want an immediate vote. Before the agenda was adopted the representative of the USSR formally moved 'under rule 33.3 of the provisional rules of procedure of the Security Council, that we adjourn the meeting and meet again at 3 p.m. on Monday 10 December'.[91] Debate was permitted on this motion since it was made under Rule 33.3 rather than 33.1 or 33.2, and Malaysia spoke to oppose the USSR expressing the view that any further informal consultations 'would dilute the draft resolution'.[92] Malaysia was backed by Colombia and Cuba. Yemen as President then put the USSR's proposal to a vote, securing nine in favour, four against and two abstentions, and the meeting adjourned following a statement of explanation of vote from the President in his national capacity, with additional comments from Cuba, Ethiopia, and the United States. The meeting was called to order on Monday 10 December and was immediately suspended by the President, pending consultations.[93] The meeting resumed at 7.40 p.m. with the USSR immediately formally moving to adjourn the meeting under Rule 33.3. The President reminded delegates of the rule that he himself had forgotten two days earlier—that explanations of vote may only be given before the vote on a motion to adjourn. Cuba and Malaysia again opposed the motion, managing to raise a number of their substantive objections in what was essentially a procedural debate, and it was defeated again by the same voting pattern. The Council was convened a third time on 12 December,[94] and this time without discussion, but by the same voting pattern, adopted an identical proposal from the USSR under Rule 33.3 to adjourn the meeting until 3 p.m. on Monday 17 December. After a further meeting was suspended after the adoption of the agenda the Council finally reached a consensus and unanimously adopted resolution 681 (1990) and an associated presidential statement.[95]

A request by Cuba in 1990 that a meeting on Palau's status be deferred, was interpreted by the President to be a proposal of adjournment under Rule 33.3. After a brief debate the motion was defeated by two votes to nine, with four abstentions.[96]

(c) *'Shall be decided without debate'*

Rule 33 states that motions for the suspension or simple adjournment of meetings shall be decided without debate.

The sole exception to this Rule is the general practice about points of order, namely, that these may be raised at any time, that the President shall rule immediately, and that if the President's ruling is challenged, the matter shall be submitted to the Council for immediate decision (Rule 30).

A variety of circumstances have made it impossible to apply consistently the Rule about deciding on the suspension or simple adjournment without debate: an ingenious or unscrupulous representative, a weak or inexperienced President, insistence on explaining a vote, the raising of a second point of order before the first one has been disposed of, discussion of whether a motion for adjournment or postponement phrased in an unusual way is for indefinite adjournment or postponement, or to a certain day—all these are among the means by which representatives have managed to engage in debate contrary to the Rules of Procedure.[97]

Much trouble would be saved if representatives would use the precise language of Rule 33 rather than such expressions as 'take a recess' (a great favourite with American representatives, this),[98] 'defer consideration',[99] 'defer action',[100] postpone voting',[101] or 'postpone a decision'[102] which are not to be found in the Rules of Procedure and have no formally agreed and precise meanings. The consistent use of the language of Rule 33 would avoid the misfortune which overtook Soviet Ambassador Sobolev at the time of the Hungarian revolt in 1956. Sobolev moved the postponement of discussion for three or four days to enable the Council to obtain information. The President, Ambassador Cornut-Gentille of France, interpreted Sobolev as moving not postponement of the discussion but the simple adjournment of the meeting. He therefore ruled that no discussion was permissible and quickly put the motion to the vote.* [103]

(d) Reference to a committee, the Secretary-General, or a rapporteur

Motions to refer any matter to one of the agencies cited in Rule 33 have rarely given rise to difficulty. It is true that in 1947 a proposal was made by Poland to submit Hungary's application for UN membership to the Committee on Admission of New Members. Colombia, somewhat hesitantly, asked whether this motion should not have precedence under Rule 33. The President, Ambassador Quo of China, who was at times brusque and indeed arbitrary, ruled that another proposal had priority 'because it was submitted even before the meeting began'. Ambassador Quo must have forgotten that Rule 33 has precedence over Rule 32; in the absence of a decision to the contrary by the Council, the Polish motion should have been put to the vote first.

* In mitigation of Cornut-Gentille's venial mistake, it should be added that the coincidence of the Suez and Hungarian crises with his presidency of the Security Council had imposed a considerable strain on him. He collapsed two days later.

There is the possibility of confusion over the precise meaning of 'a rapporteur'. This has been interpreted to include any individual to whom the Council has entrusted responsibilities. Thus, when in 1957 the Council wanted information on two incidents in the Middle East, the President (Cuba) stated:

I considered, as I still do, that the representative of the Philippines proposed something for which provision is made in Rule 33 (point 4) . . . that is, that we ask a rapporteur—in this instance the Chief of Staff [of UNTSO] . . . to submit two reports.[104]

It should be noted that 'a committee' is not limited to a subsidiary organ of the Council. After the allegation that the United States had resorted to germ warfare in Korea, the Soviet Union proposed that the Council should appeal to States to ratify the Geneva Protocol of 1925, which bans the use in war of chemical and bacteriological weapons. The United States moved that, 'pursuant to rule 33, paragraph 4 . . . the Soviet Union draft resolution be referred to the Disarmament Commission' which had been established by the General Assembly, not the Security Council. Soviet Ambassador Malik pointed out that the Disarmament Commission was 'not a commission or a committee set up by the Security Council. Consequently rule 33 . . . does not apply'. No representative supported the Soviet Union on this point. Nevertheless, Malik, who was presiding, insisted that the matter be put to the vote. This was duly done, but his position secured only one affirmative vote, with ten abstentions.[105]

(e) Postponement

As motions to postpone discussion have so often led to confusion, it may be as well to look first at the precise wording of Rule 33, to see in particular what the differences are between postponement and adjournment. Rule 33 deals in one clause with postponement 'to a certain day' as well as postponement 'indefinitely'. Postponement relates to 'discussion of the question', whereas adjournment relates to 'the meeting'.

If it is decided to resume consideration on a particular day, the distinction between adjournment and postponement is almost always a distinction without a difference. There is, however, a discernible difference between 'the simple adjournment' and postponement 'indefinitely': the former implies that the Council will resume consideration after an undetermined lapse of time, whereas indefinite postponement has no such implication.

The question of postponement first arose before the Council had adopted Rule 33. The Council had just begun its consideration of the complaints of Syria and Lebanon about the presence of British and French troops in their countries. The question had been raised whether the matter was a situation or a dispute, an issue which could have had a bearing on whether the United Kingdom and France would have had to abstain from voting on any substantive proposal on the matter. China suggested that the Council should delay taking a decision until the parties had been heard, a suggestion supported by the Netherlands. 'This is a new body', said the Dutch ambassador; 'We must work very guardedly in these matters.' The Council agreed to the Chinese proposal.[106]

Rule 33 was adopted on 16 May 1946, and the question of postponement next arose the following August, when the United States urged the Council to 'take no action' or 'postpone consideration' of the applications for UN membership of Albania and Mongolia, so that he could avoid 'the painful necessity of casting a negative vote [veto] at this time'. The Netherlands pointed out that a motion for postponement had precedence under Rule 33, and the President (Poland) agreed that this was 'logical'. Secretary-General Lie was asked for his opinion, but it is clear from his answer that he had misunderstood the question. The US motion was then put to the vote and defeated, whereupon proposals to admit Albania and Mongolia were also defeated.[107] Most subsequent decisions to postpone have been 'to a certain date',[108] but two cases of what were, in effect, indefinite postponements are worthy of note.

On 9 January 1947, at the suggestion of the President (Australia), the Council 'deferred until a later meeting' a letter transmitting the first report of the Atomic Energy Commission. The matter was taken up by the Council again on 13 February 1947.[109]

The other case is of greater interest. When the Council met on 31 January 1955 to consider the hostilities between China and the rump Kuomintang regime based on Taiwan, Soviet Ambassador Sobolev questioned the right of 'the bankrupt Chiang Kai-shek group' to represent China. US Ambassador Lodge then moved that the Council should decide 'not to consider' proposals to exclude the Chinese Nationalists or to seat representatives of the People's Republic of China—a proposal which Lodge had successfully moved during the previous session of the General Assembly. Lodge was supported by Sir Pierson Dixon of the United Kingdom and Ambassador Henri Hoppenot of France as well as by Turkey, and the US motion was quickly adopted by ten votes to one.[110]

(f) Introduction of an amendment

We review in the next section the means by which the Council determines the order in which amendments shall be voted on, and it is only necessary to note here that the introduction of an amendment is the last form of 'precedence motion': that is to say, in the absence of a motion to suspend or adjourn the meeting, or to refer any matter to a committee, the Secretary-General, or a rapporteur, or to postpone discussion of a question, the introduction of an amendment has precedence over all motions and draft resolutions relative to the subject before the meeting (Rule 33).

6. AMENDMENTS

If two or more amendments to a motion or draft resolution are proposed, the President shall rule on the order in which they are to be voted upon. Ordinarily, the Security Council shall first vote on the amendment furthest removed in substance from the original proposal and then on the amendment next furthest removed until all amendments have been put to the vote, but when an amendment adds to or deletes from the text of a motion or draft resolution, that amendment shall be voted on first. (Rule 36)

At first sight, this Rule raises almost as many questions as it answers. What is the relationship between the first and the second sentences? Is it intended that the procedures outlined in the second sentence should apply in ordinary circumstances and that the President should be required to rule only when the circumstances are extraordinary? Or does the second sentence represent guidance to the

President as to how he should ordinarily rule? Is a presidential ruling open to challenge, and if so, is it the ruling or the challenge which is put to the vote? Why is the second part of the second sentence (beginning 'but when an amendment adds to . . .') placed at the end rather than at the beginning of the sentence?

Before these questions can be answered, some further explanation is needed about presidential rulings. The President is required by the Provisional Rules of Procedure to rule on points of order (Rule 30) and on the order in which amendments shall be put to the vote (Rule 36). We have suggested earlier that in no circumstances should a motion or proposal, whether submitted by the President or by another member of the Council, be converted into a ruling. We suggest elsewhere that, in spite of one unfortunate precedent to the contrary, the President should not attempt to settle whether a motion or proposal is procedural or substantive (and therefore whether or not it is subject to veto) by a 'ruling'. The permanent members of the Council clearly intended at San Francisco that the so-called preliminary question should be settled by a vote of the Council—in other words, that the preliminary question would be as much subject to veto as the main question, what is often called the double veto.[111]

Are there any circumstances, then, in which the President may be asked or required to make a ruling other than those arising from Rules 30 (points of order) and 36 (order of voting on amendments)?

The answer is unquestionably 'yes'. In enforcing the Provisional Rules of Procedure, or reminding members of the customary practice of the Council, or in dealing with issues of procedure not expressly covered by the Rules or by precedent, the President cannot avoid offering interpretations or expressing opinions. Sometimes one or more members of the Council will ask the President to go further and 'rule' on a question of procedure, or even insist that he do so.

No President can be compelled to give a ruling if he is adamant in his refusal to do so, as was Soviet Ambassador Malik at five successive meetings of the Council in 1950. Nationalist China had asked: 'Does the President consider it obligatory upon him to carry out the decision of the Security Council of 25 June [1950] by inviting the representative of the Republic of [South] Korea to take his place at the Council table?' This point of order, as it was termed by Nationalist China, was repeated in identical or similar terms by six other representatives. Fourteen times the President refused to rule. The question raised by Nationalist China, said the President, was not a point of order but a proposal. In the President's view, the matter should not be the subject of a presidential ruling but should be discussed until the Council was ready to decide the matter.[112] Even if the question raised by Nationalist China was hardly a genuine point of order, the President's conduct was, in the circumstances, a scarcely concealed filibuster.

Usually, however, the President will prefer to interpret the Rules and practice of the Council for the guidance of representatives, or express an opinion, or give a ruling. In spite of the clear provision in the Rules of Procedure on the order in which motions and proposals shall be put to the vote ('the order of their submission', Rule 32), the President may be asked whether a different order would not be more logical or more fair. The President rules on such a question by reference to the appropriate Rule of Procedure or precedent.[113] If he gives a ruling, it can be challenged, and the challenge can be put to the vote in accordance with the text of Rule 30.[114] If, on the other hand, the President wishes to deal with a situation not covered by the Provisional Rules of Procedure, or for which the Council has no agreed practice, by offering a motion or proposal of his own rather than by giving a ruling, as was the wish of Ambassador Malik in connection with the participation of North Korea and China in the work of the Council in August 1950,[115] and if one or more members object to the President's motion or proposal, then it can be submitted to the Council for decision.

There have, to be sure, been occasions when it has not been entirely clear which course the President was adopting. How is one to understand a situation in which the President, when asked whether a particular text was a proposal or an amendment, replies: 'I have decided it is an amendment . . . but I do not want to impose my own personal opinion . . . I am now going to ask the Council whether it considers the majority proposal [of the drafting committee] to be an amendment'?[116] Perhaps it is best to regard occasions of this kind as aberrations from the norm rather than helpful precedents.

Amendments

We can now return to the questions posed at the beginning, which fortunately can be answered relatively briefly. Rule 36 about the order of voting on amendments was approved on 16 May 1946. Six weeks later, the question arose as to its meaning, and Soviet Ambassador Gromyko asked if the Assistant Secretary-General in charge of Security Council affairs could elucidate the matter, which he did in the following terms.

> If there are two or more amendments, the President shall rule [in French, *déterminera*] the order in which these amendments should be put to the vote. If there are disagreements with the ruling [*la décision*] of the President, the Council shall decide which amendment . . . shall be put to the vote first.[117]

As nobody challenged this interpretation, it can be assumed to have represented the view of the Council at the time. A contemporary example indicates the continued validity of this approach. On 3 March 1991[118] the Security Council had before it a draft resolution on the situation between Iraq and Kuwait.[119] Cuba had submitted no less than 18 amendments to it. The President, after quoting Rule 36, proposed an ordering of the amendments. There was no objection to the ordering that he proposed and the amendments were voted on in turn, all failing to obtain the required number of votes.

One can, then, answer the questions posed earlier as follows. First, both parts of the second sentence are intended to guide the President in making a ruling. Second, if a ruling is challenged, the challenge should be put to the vote. Third, regarding the two parts of the second sentence, there seems no reason why they should not be reversed.

If this interpretation is correct, one might paraphrase Rule 36 as follows.

> If two or more amendments to a motion or proposal are submitted, the President shall rule on the order in which they are to be voted upon. If the ruling is challenged, the President shall submit the challenge to the Security Council for its decision.
>
> In making his ruling, the President shall bear in mind that ordinarily when an amendment adds to or deletes from the text of a motion or proposal, that amendment shall be voted on first, and that in other cases, the

Council shall first vote on the amendment furthest removed in substance from the original proposal, and then on the amendment next furthest removed, until all amendments have been put to the vote.

It is easy to conceive of situations in which it is by no means clear whether a particular text is an amendment or a separate proposal disguised as an amendment in order to gain a procedural advantage. On one early occasion, following the submission of a US proposal, various alternative suggestions were made in the course of the debate. The question then arose whether these suggestions represented amendments to the US proposal and therefore should be put to the vote first, or were separate proposals to be voted on in the order of their submission in accordance with Rule 32. The debate on this question was somewhat confused, but the President (Poland) finally ruled that suggestions, if not accepted by the sponsor of the original proposal, had to be put in the form of amendments and be formally introduced if they were to take precedence over the original US proposal. This was a sound ruling and was accepted by the Council.[120]

But consider a more complicated case in which it is proposed that the Council recommend to the General Assembly that a mixed bag of States be admitted into UN membership. Imagine a further text which proposes to add a couple more States to the list, or to delete some. Is that a bona fide amendment, or a separate proposal?

This is not, as it happens, a hypothetical example: it is precisely what happened in December 1955. Brazil and New Zealand had proposed that the Council, having considered separately a list of eighteen applications for UN membership in the order of their submission, should recommend the admission of all of them. Nationalist China submitted an amendment to add the Republic of (South) Korea and the Republic of (South) Vietnam.[121] It was taken for granted that the Soviet Union would accept the admission of both South and North Korea, and both South and North Vietnam, but that, if only the two southern Republics were being proposed for admission, the Soviet veto would operate, as it had previously. How would Soviet Ambassador Sobolev play this, we wondered, and how would the President deal with whatever procedural tangle would inevitably arise?

Ambassador Sobolev began by describing the action of Nationalist China as deliberate obstruction (which was not very wide of the mark). The text was, in Sobolev's view, not an amendment but a completely new proposal.

The President (New Zealand) then stated how he intended to proceed. He would first put to the vote the first preambular paragraph of the original proposal, then the introductory words of the second preambular paragraph ('Having considered . . .'), then in separate votes the two countries named in the Nationalist Chinese text, then the eighteen countries named in the original proposal, and then the final operative paragraph. This, it seemed at the time, was to treat the text of Nationalist China as an amendment rather than a separate proposal, but not to apply to the full the last part of Rule 36, which declares that, when an amendment adds to the text of a draft resolution, the amendment shall be voted on first.

Sobolev, whose experience of the Security Council spanned a decade, was quick to react to the statement of the President's intentions. The procedure suggested by the President was, he said, 'incomprehensible and inexplicable'. The amendment added to the original proposal and should be put to the vote first, as indicated in Rule 36. But then Sobolev must have realized that he might be setting a trap for himself, for if the procedure he had just suggested were to be followed, he would be forced to veto South Korea and South Vietnam early in the proceedings, with the risk that this would wreck the 'package deal' on which informal agreement had been reached. If the Council were to encounter two vetoes before it reached the main business, the informal agreement might collapse and the Soviet Union would incur the odium. So Sobolev went quickly into reverse and, forgetting all about Rule 36, suggested that the 'normal and logical and . . . correct' procedure would be to vote first on the eighteen applicants named in the original proposal, and then on 'those new States' mentioned by Nationalist China. And as if to emphasize the confusion which threatened, Sobolev asked plaintively: 'What is happening here? Could we not have an explanation?'

The procedural debate which ensued did nothing to dispel the confusion. The President asserted that he was following normal practice. Sobolev proposed that all the applications for membership should be taken in the chronological order of their submission. The President reiterated his intention; Sobolev reiterated his new proposal; the President put the Soviet proposal to the vote; to nobody's surprise, it was defeated.

The Council then proceeded as the President had all along intended,[122] but who could be sure at the end of the day whether the text submitted by Nationalist China was an amendment or a separate proposal?

In the instance described, a reasonable case could be made for treating Nationalist China's text either as a proposal or as an amendment. Often it will be a matter of no great importance which way the decision goes. In the case just described, the Soviet Union vetoed South Korea and South Vietnam; Albania's application was approved; Mongolia came next and was vetoed by Nationalist China; of the remaining sixteen applicants, the Soviet Union vetoed all which had non-Communist governments: the package deal seemed in danger of collapse. Two days later, however, a smaller package deal went through, but two of the original eighteen, Japan and Mongolia, had their applications deferred.

The situation in 1955 was without precedent. Normally, each application for membership comes before the Council as a separate proposal. In 1955, what was being sought was a 'package' of admissions. Some minor tinkering with previous practice was unavoidable, and attention was being focused on the 'package deal' aspect to such an extent that representatives had little time for the precise status of the text submitted by Nationalist China.

There had, indeed, been earlier cases in which representatives had tried to convert a proposal into an amendment, in order to have it put to the vote before a proposal submitted earlier by another representative. Quite properly, the Presidents had refused to countenance such manœuvres.[123]

7. STATEMENTS BEFORE OR AFTER THE VOTE

When the general debate is completed, and also the debate on proposals and amendments, and either before or after the voting, members of the Council may make statements in explanation of their votes or otherwise. This is not intended to allow a repetition of what has already been said but provides an opportunity to explain why a member has voted in favour of a proposal on general grounds in spite of reservations about one or more aspects, or why a member would have voted in favour of certain paragraphs if the sponsor(s) had agreed to a vote in parts, or to clarify some other aspect of the voting. On one occasion the President (Sir Harold E. Walter of Mauritius) suggested that explanations of vote should be submitted in writing, but the idea did not find favour.[124] Now Council members almost invariably use statements before or after the vote rather than taking part in the debate.

The opportunity for an explanation of vote can be a valuable means by which a permanent member can express dissatisfaction with parts of a resolution without vetoing a resolution through the casting of a negative vote. The Council held a politically charged meeting on 18 March 1994, following the killing by a Jewish settler of Palestinians at prayer in the Al Ibrahimi mosque in Hebron. The United States had asked for a paragraph-by-paragraph vote on the draft resolution under consideration, and abstained on two of the preambular paragraphs, before abstaining on the resolution as a whole. In a subsequent statement after the vote the US raised objections to the context of references to 'Jerusalem' and to 'occupied Palestinian territory', and stated that

> had this language been in the operative paragraphs, we would have vetoed the resolution . . . the US Government chose instead to disavow this language and express our opposition by abstaining on the second and sixth preambular paragraphs.[125]

When a permanent member does feel the necessity to cast a negative vote, a statement is usually made to explain the circumstances behind the decision. Following its warning (above) in respect to references to Jerusalem in operative paragraphs of resolutions, the United States vetoed in May 1995 a text on the Occupied Arab Territories which it believed could prejudge and prejudice the outcome of a sensitive negotiation process. A statement after the resolution had been voted on was used to remind others of the consistency of the US position.

In January 1997 China vetoed a resolution on the authorization of a military component to the UN Human Rights Verification Mission in Guatemala.[126] In its statement China used diplomatic language to convey the message that it actually had no problem with the provisions of the resolution, but had vetoed it because of its anger at the recognition given to the authorities of Taiwan by the Guatemalan government.[127]

CHAPTER 5

VOTING

> Make each proposition which you put forward appear as a statement of the interests of those with whom you are negotiating.

A PROPOSAL (or draft resolution) may be submitted by any member of the Council, and that member is known as the sponsor of the proposal; if more than one member, they are the co-sponsors. A Member of the United Nations which is not a Council member may also submit a proposal, but it is put to the vote only at the request of a Council member (Rule 38).

A procedural motion or draft resolution may be withdrawn at any time 'so long as no vote has been taken with respect to it'. If a procedural motion or draft resolution has more than one sponsor ('has been seconded', as the Rules of Procedure put it) and the first sponsor decides to withdraw it, the other sponsor or sponsors may require that it be put to the vote with the same 'right of precedence as if the original sponsor had not withdrawn it' (Rule 35). What Rule 35 says about the withdrawal of a motion or draft resolution is generally taken to apply to an amendment or sub-amendment, although there is no express provision to this effect in the Provisional Rules of Procedure. A distinction is made in practice between the decision of a sponsor not to press to a vote a motion, draft resolution, or amendment, and a decision formally to withdraw such a text.[1]

In one early case, a Council President (Ambassador Quo of China) refused to allow the sponsor of an amendment to change it into a draft resolution, maintaining that the amendment, 'having been submitted to the Council, has become the property of the Council'.[2] This would now seem rather a severe practice, but the idea that a proposal can become 'the property' of the Council was reinforced by an incident which occurred in 1962. Cuba, not a member of the Council, had submitted a draft resolution, which was being put to the vote at the request of the Soviet Union. A separate vote was requested on one paragraph, which was then defeated. From the Cuban point of view, the deletion of this paragraph emasculated the proposal, so the Soviet Union, with Cuba's agreement, stated that Cuba 'does not insist on a vote on the remaining parts of the resolution'. The President (Venezuela) did not take the narrow or harsh view that the amended proposal was now the property of the Council, but he cited the first sentence of Rule 35, to the effect that a motion or draft resolution can be withdrawn at any time so long as no vote has been taken with respect to it. As a vote had already been taken on the third paragraph, the President ruled that 'no one is entitled to withdraw the draft resolution'. The Soviet Union challenged the ruling, but it was upheld. The Council then rejected the amended Cuban proposal.

The Soviet Union objected strongly to the way the matter was handled. 'Against the will of the sponsor of the draft resolution and after certain provisions by which the sponsor sets great store have been rejected, an attempt is still being made to have the remaining part of the draft resolution put to the vote, in a form which is unacceptable to the sponsor.'[3] We have some sympathy with the Soviet point of view in this case. Even if the Rules of Procedure, strictly interpreted, were on the side of the President, common sense was surely on the side of the Soviet Union and Cuba.

A motion or draft resolution almost always consists of several parts, which are put to the vote separately at the request of any representative, except when the original sponsor objects (Rule 32). Sponsors have freely exercised their right to object to parts of a draft resolution being voted on separately, usually on the ground that the text as a whole represented a delicate balance which would be upset by the deletion of certain parts.[4]

The question has sometimes arisen whether a proposal, having been put to the vote in parts and all parts having been approved, should then be put to the vote as a whole. Although there have been some exceptions,[5] members of the Council have usually considered that approval of the separate parts is insufficient and that the proposal as a whole should also be put to the vote.[6] Sir Alexander Cadogan of the United Kingdom expressed clearly the reasons for this course,

There may be certain paragraphs of the resolution of which I entirely approve, but which I do not accept in the context in which they stand.

Similarly, one may vote against a particular paragraph because one sees some objection to it, and yet, because of the context and because of the importance of getting the whole resolution, one may vote for the whole resolution.[7]

Curious as it may perhaps seem, it follows from Sir Alexander Cadogan's remarks that, even if all the parts of a draft resolution have been *rejected*, there might still be a case for putting the proposal as a whole to a vote. This has, indeed, happened on at least one occasion—perhaps unnecessarily, as all the parts had been vetoed, as was the fate of the proposal as a whole.[8]

In applying the Rules of Procedure about voting separately on parts of a proposal, the question has arisen as to who is 'the original mover' (Rule 32) in cases where the author of a proposal is not a member of the Council but where the proposal is being put to the vote at the request of a Council member (Rule 38). The question can be illustrated by reference to an incident in 1962. Cuba had called for the convening of the Security Council after the Organization of American States had suspended Cuba's membership at a meeting of Foreign Ministers held at Punta del Este in Uruguay. Cuba proposed, in particular, that the Security Council should ask the International Court of Justice for an Advisory Opinion on certain legal questions related to the Punta del Este decisions, and should also, as a provisional measure under Article 40 of the UN Charter, call for the suspension of the decisions. Ghana asked for a separate vote on one paragraph, and this required the consent of 'the original mover'. Egypt stated that this was the first occasion on which a non-member of the Council had submitted a proposal under Rule 38, and that it was being put to the vote at the request of the Soviet Union. 'There seems to be some doubt about who is the author of such a draft resolution.' After considerable discussion, the Council wisely agreed that out of courtesy to Cuba, and as an exception, not setting a precedent, Cuba should be asked whether it objected to having a separate vote on the paragraph in question—to which Cuba agreed in a statement precisely thirteen words in length.[9]

The Egyptian representative may have been factually correct in stating that the 1962 incident was the first time that a proposal submitted by a non-member was being put to the vote under Rule 38, but the situation was not completely unprecedented. The question had first arisen in 1946, but before the adoption of Rule 38. The Council was considering the situation in Indonesia at the request of the Ukrainian SSR, a non-member of the Council. During the course of the debate, the Ukrainian SSR submitted a draft resolution, and the President (Australia) immediately consulted the Council as to whether the Ukrainian SSR was entitled to submit a proposal. China, Egypt, France, the Netherlands, Poland, and the Soviet Union favoured allowing the Ukrainian SSR to submit a proposal 'without prejudice and . . . not . . . a precedent'. US Ambassador Stettinius at first expressed reservations, but later withdrew them. The Ukrainian proposal was duly put to the vote but was rejected.[10]

We have referred in Chapter 4 to the difficulty of distinguishing between a proposal and an amendment when the Council is dealing with a 'package' of applications for UN membership. The question of voting on proposals in parts has arisen at least twice in the same context. In 1947, the Soviet Union favoured the admission of five applicants, but the West insisted on having them considered individually, with the result that applications supported by the Soviet Union (Hungary, Romania, Bulgaria) failed to obtain sufficient affirmative votes, while applications supported by the West (Finland, Italy) ran into Soviet vetoes.[11]

In 1955 there was agreement in the Council on recommending the admission of sixteen applicants, but as Nationalist China had vetoed Mongolia, the Soviet Union retaliated by vetoing Japan. The Soviet Union then submitted a proposal recommending the admission of both Mongolia and Japan. France expressed the view that there should be two separate votes, to which the Soviet Union objected. The President (New Zealand), correctly interpreting the political situation in the Council, but disregarding the strict requirement of Rule 32, put the Soviet proposal to the vote as a whole, and it secured only one vote.[12]

As noted in Chapter 4.4, principal motions and draft resolutions are put to the vote in the order of their submission unless the Council decides otherwise.[13]

On one occasion, a non-member of the Council asked for a vote on an urgent proposal before rather than at the end of the debate.

The President (Ivor Richard of the United Kingdom) said that there were thirteen names on the list of speakers, but all had agreed to defer their speeches until after the vote. After five brief explanations of vote, the Council approved the urgent proposal.[14]

It should be borne in mind that when the debate on a particular phase of an item is concluded, there is no requirement on the Council to adopt a resolution or make a statement. Debate itself with no decision may bring about the desired change.

I. PROCEDURAL MOTIONS

The provisions of Article 27 of the Charter relating to voting in the Security Council were, in their essentials, worked out at the summit meeting of the United States, United Kingdom, and Soviet Union held in the Crimea in February 1945, and are usually known as the Yalta formula. Before examining Article 27, however, it may be as well to refer to decisions of two kinds which are not covered by this formula.

First, in the election of judges of the International Court of Justice, 'an absolute majority of votes' is required in the Security Council (Statute of the Court, Article 10). It has always been accepted without question that this means an absolute majority of the members of the Council and not simply an absolute majority of those members participating in the vote—that is to say, six votes out of a Council of eleven members or eight votes out of a Council of fifteen.

Second, Article 109 of the Charter provides that certain decisions regarding conferences to review the Charter should be taken by 'a vote of any seven members' of the Council in conjunction with a decision of the General Assembly (Charter, Article 109). Following the enlargement of the Security Council, the General Assembly decided that a vote of nine members of the Council would be needed to fix the date and place of a conference to review the Charter, and an amendment to this effect was submitted for ratification by Member States.[15]

As for other decisions of the Council, the Yalta formula distinguished between 'procedural' and 'all other' matters. Decisions of the Council on procedural matters were to require 'an affirmative vote of seven members' out of a Council of eleven—changed to nine members when the Council was enlarged to fifteen. The Council has treated the following matters as procedural:

Inclusion of items in the agenda
Order of items
Deferment of consideration of items
Removal of an item from the list of matters of which the Council is seized
Rulings of the President
Suspension of a meeting
Adjournment of a meeting
Invitations to participate
Conduct of business
Convocation of an emergency special session of the General Assembly

2. SUBSTANTIVE DECISIONS

Decisions on non-procedural (substantive) matters are made by an affirmative vote of nine (originally seven) members, including the concurring votes of the five permanent members (Article 27(3)). It is not necessary to repeat here the arguments which were used in 1945 to justify or oppose the Yalta formula. Unanimity had been a normal requirement in traditional diplomacy, and the sponsoring powers at the San Francisco Conference stated blandly that the Yalta formula represented a significant advance.

> The Yalta voting formula substitutes for the rule of complete unanimity of the League [of Nations] Council a system of qualified majority voting in the Security Council . . . As regards the permanent members, there is no question under the Yalta formula of investing them with a new right . . . It should also be remembered that under the Yalta formula the five major powers could not act by themselves, since even under the unanimity requirement any decisions of the Council would have to include the concurring votes of at least two of the non-permanent members.[16]

The sponsoring powers evidently wished it to be thought that objection to the veto was based on the fear that the five big powers would gang up on the medium and smaller powers; this notion persisted even after the Council had got into its stride. In fact, of course, the problem in the Council for four and a half decades had not been to prevent great power domination but to bring about great power agreement.

The situation at San Francisco was that the medium and smaller countries considered that to give the five major powers permanent membership of the Security Council, and the right to block substantive action, was incompatible with the principle of the sovereign equality of States, which had been included in the Dumbarton Oaks proposals. A good many of the States participating in the San Francisco Conference wished to get rid of the veto entirely; but once they realized that without the veto there would be no United Nations, attention was directed to a less ambitious aim. Under Australian leadership, an attempt was made to limit the veto to decisions taken under what became Chapter VII of the Charter (threats to peace, breaches of the peace, and acts of aggression), while leaving free of great power veto decisions falling under what became Chapter VI (pacific settlement of disputes). Similar proposals have again been made in the 1990s in the context of the General Assembly *Open-ended Working Group on the Question of Equitable Representation On and Increase in the Membership of the Security Council* (see Chapter 8.2).

The five major powers were at one in their determination to have the right of veto as regards both the pacific settlement of disputes and enforcement measures. However, it was with difficulty, and only after the matter had been taken up in Moscow with Stalin personally, that the Soviet Union would agree to exclude from the scope of the veto a decision merely to consider and discuss a dispute or situation.

The Provisional Rules of Procedure are singularly unhelpful about the conduct of voting. As is made clear in Chapter 1.3, the Rules simply state that voting shall be in accordance with the Charter and the Statute of the International Court of Justice (Rule 40).

3. THE VETO

Article 27 of the Charter states that decisions on non-procedural matters in the Council 'shall be made by an affirmative vote of nine members including the concurring votes of the permanent members'. Thus a veto can be described as the failure of the Council to adopt a resolution due to the negative vote of one or more permanent members, during a vote in which nine or more members of the Council have voted in favour.

Until recent years, it was more usual to find the veto denounced or defended than its use analysed, for there are difficulties in the way of objective analysis. A permanent member of the Council does not have to explain why the veto has been exercised; all that is necessary is to cast a negative vote. On the other hand, a permanent member who gives half a dozen reasons for a veto when one would suffice is protesting too much. Moreover, a public explanation is not necessarily the real reason: any diplomatic decision is likely to be based on a complex of motives which do not necessarily sound plausible or respectable when paraded in public.

For the first two decades, the veto was thought of in the West as almost synonymous with Soviet foreign policy. With the expansion of the Council to 15 members in 1966, the dominance of Western powers in the Council was gone, and 86 per cent of the vetoes cast in public meetings since 1 January 1966 have been by Western permanent members (see Table 8). The expansion of the Council also marked a shift in Council practice towards the search for consensus texts. The search for consensus during informal consultations has led to fewer vetoes being cast, since resolutions which lack the backing of the permanent members are seldom brought to a formal vote in the Council. The *threat* of the use of the veto during informal consultations, while infrequent, has thus become as or more important than its actual use in formal meetings. Hiscocks noted in 1973 that opinions are divided over 'whether or not the development of consensus procedure since 1965 represents an improvement in the Security Council's practice'.[17] The search for agreement might lead to the watering down of resolutions and statements until they had beccome ambiguous or even meaningless but alternatively could create a more positive climate for possible joint action on major issues.

When vetoes have occurred in recent cases it has usually been as a result of a miscalculation that a permanent member would not carry through its threat of a negative vote, or because the other members felt that it was more important for them to be seen to publicly support a particular position, than it was for them to avoid a veto occurring. Examples of the former include the Russian veto of a proposal on the funding of the UN peace-keeping operation in Cyprus in 1993 (Table 8, veto no. 195), and the Chinese veto of the sending of military observers to Guatemala in 1997 (veto no. 198). Both countries subsequently agreed to support almost identical resolutions to the ones that they had vetoed. In the case of the Chinese veto, the representative of the Russian Federation regretted that the draft resolution 'was put to a vote with such haste, at a time when consultations on the issue could have continued'. Examples of the latter were US vetoes of draft resolutions on Israeli expropriation of land in East Jerusalem in 1995,[18] and the re-appointment of Boutros Boutros-Ghali in 1996.[19] In both these cases the resolutions were supported by the other 14 members of the Council, and the US had given prior notice that it would exercise its power of veto if the text was put to the vote.

In the early years, the United States was eager to find ways of short-circuiting the veto by such means as the *Uniting for Peace* resolution, which includes a provision whereby 'if the Security Council, because of lack of unanimity of the permanent members, fails to exercise its primary responsibility for the maintenance of international peace and security in any case where there appears to be a threat to the peace, breach of the peace, or act of aggression, the General Assembly shall consider the matter immediately . . .'[20] It is clear from the published volumes on US foreign relations that one motive for passing the *Uniting for Peace* resolution in November 1950 was the realization that action in North Korea earlier in the year had been possible only because the Soviet Union was boycotting the Security Council when the Korean War broke out, so that the Security Council could take decisions without the interposition of a Soviet veto.

There was no reason why the General Assembly should not amend its Rules of Procedure so that it could meet at short notice, but it was of doubtful legality for the Assembly to purport to apply enforcement measures whether or not the Security Council was deadlocked by the veto. Most of the friends of the United States were unenthusiastic about the proposed change, and in Britain the matter went to the cabinet. Foreign Office officials told the US ambassador (Lewis Douglas) that the United Kingdom wanted to avoid the 'bluntness' of the US approach. It was all very well to devise means of avoiding the veto, but there might come a time when the UK might need the veto. If, for reasons of relations with the US, Britain would have to vote for the resolution, it wanted to put on record its doubts as to the legality of the procedure envisaged.[21]

The *Uniting for Peace* resolution also provided for a Peace Observation Commission of fourteen members 'to observe and report on the situation in any area where there exists international tension the continuance of which is likely to endanger the maintenance of international peace and security'. In that event the Security Council was authorized to utilize the Peace Observation Commission.

The General Assembly asked several times in the early years that the permanent members should limit or renounce the veto.[22] The United States was for a time in favour of an agreement not to use the veto on specified matters, such as the admission of new Members. When the United States first cast a veto on applications for membership, the US ambassador went out of his way to explain that, while US tactics had changed, US principles remained inviolate, for the United States still favoured the principle of universality of UN membership.[23] Six months later, after vetoing a substantive proposal on the Middle East, the US ambassador said that his country's negative vote arose from its commitment to the peace process.[24]

The vetoes cast from 1946 to the middle of 1997 are shown in Table 8. Up to 1 August 1997, 202 proposals had been vetoed, 200 at public meetings and 2 at private meetings. Since some proposals had attracted more than one negative vote from a permanent member, the 202 vetoed proposals represented 242 actual vetoes (see Table 9). This total does not include the 31 vetoes said to have been cast in connection with 25 draft resolutions at private meetings of the Council, but which were not reported in official *communiqués*. These are listed in Table 8 part (*c*).

Table 9 presents a summary of vetoes cast by decade. It reflects the changes in international politics since the Second World War. Of 110 vetoes in the first two post-war decades, no fewer than 101 vetoes were cast by the Soviet Union. Of 91 vetoes in the next twenty years, 2 were by China, 11 by France, 13 by the Soviet Union, 19 by the United Kingdom, and 46 by the United States. Of 37 vetoes in the fifth decade, 24 were cast by the United States and 8 by the United Kingdom.

TABLE 8

Vetoes cast in the Security Council, 16 February 1946–1 August 1997
Total of 202 official vetoed resolutions—200 public and 2 private
(a) Vetoes cast at public meetings of the Council, reported in Official Records

No.	Date	Meeting and page or paragraph no(s).	Subject	Text of vetoed proposal (meeting and page no. or S/no. until 1948, S/no. thereafter)	Permanent member(s) voting negatively
1	16 Feb. 1946	23, pp. 367–8	Syrian and Lebanese question	22nd mtg. pp. 332–3	USSR
2	18 June 1946	47, pp. 378–80	Spanish question	45th mtg. p. 326	USSR
3	26 June 1946	49, p. 413	Spanish question	40th mtg. p. 401	USSR
4	26 June 1946	49, pp. 421–2	Spanish question	49th mtg. p. 421	France, USSR
5	26 June 1946	49, p. 446	Spanish question	49th mtg. p. 444	USSR
6–8	29 Aug. 1946	57, p. 139	Applications for Membership	57th mtg. pp. 138–9	USSR
9	20 Sept. 1946	70, p. 412	Ukrainian complaint against Greece	70th mtg. p. 412	USSR
10	25 Mar. 1947	122, p. 609	Incidents in the Corfu Channel	122nd mtg. pp. 608–9	USSR
11	29 July 1947	170, p. 1612	Greek frontier incidents	170th mtg. pp. 1602–11	USSR
12–14	18 Aug. 1947	186, pp. 2041–2, 2045	Applications for Membership	186th mtg. pp. 2041–5	USSR
15–16	19 Aug. 1947	188, pp. 2093–4, 2098–9	Greek frontier incidents	S/471 and Add. 1, S/486	USSR
17–18	21 Aug. 1947	190, pp. 2127, 2130–1	Applications for Membership	190th mtg. pp. 2127, 2130–1	USSR
19	25 Aug. 1947	194, pp. 2199–200	Indonesian question	194th mtg. p. 2199	France
20–1	15 Sept. 1947	202, pp. 2399–2400	Greek frontier incidents	202nd mtg. pp. 2369, 2399–400	USSR
22–3	1 Oct. 1947	206, p. 2476	Applications for Membership	206th mtg. p. 2476	USSR

TABLE 8 *cont.*

No.	Date	Meeting and page or paragraph no(s).	Subject	Text of vetoed proposal (meeting and page no. or S/no. until 1948, S/no. thereafter)	Permanent member(s) voting negatively
24	10 Apr. 1948	279, pp. 15–16	Applications for Membership	279th mtg. pp. 15–16	USSR
25–6	24 May 1948	303, pp. 19, 28–9	Czechoslovak question	303rd mtg. pp. 19, 28	USSR
27	22 June 1948	325, p. 12	International control of atomic energy	S/836	USSR
28	18 Aug. 1948	351, p. 22	Application for Membership	351st mtg. p. 22	USSR
29	25 Oct. 1948	372, p. 14	Berlin	S/1048	USSR
30	15 Dec. 1948	384, p. 39	Application for Membership	384th mtg. p. 39	USSR
31	8 Apr. 1949	423, p. 15	Application for Membership	S/1305	USSR
32	7 Sept. 1949	439, p. 16	Application for Membership	S/1385	USSR
33–9	13 Sept. 1949	443, pp. 28–33	Application for Membership	S/1331	USSR
40	11 Oct. 1949	450, p. 14	Disarmament	S/1398	USSR
41–2	18 Oct. 1949	452, pp. 21–3	Disarmament	S/1399/Rev. 1, S/1408/ Rev. 1	USSR
43–4	13 Dec. 1949	456, pp. 33–4	Indonesian question	S/1431	USSR
45	6 Sept. 1950	496, pp. 18–19	Complaint of aggression upon the Republic of Korea	S/1653	USSR
46	12 Sept. 1950	501, p. 28	Complaint of bombing of China	S/1752	USSR
47	30 Nov. 1950	530, p. 28	Complaint of aggression upon the Republic of Korea	S/1894	USSR
48	6 Feb. 1952	573, para. 105	Application for Membership	S/2443	USSR
49	3 July 1952	587, para. 16	Request for investigation of alleged bacterial warfare	S/2671	USSR
50	9 July 1952	590, para. 17	Request for investigation of alleged bacterial warfare	S/2688	USSR
51	16 Sept. 1952	600, para. 97	Application for Membership	S/2483	USSR
52	18 Sept. 1952	602, para. 73	Application for Membership	S/2754	USSR
53–5	19 Sept. 1952	603, para. 64–6	Application for Membership	S/2758–60	USSR

56	22 Jan. 1954	656, para. 135	Palestine question	S/3151/Rev. 2	USSR
57	29 Mar. 1954	664, para. 69	Palestine question	S/3188 and Corr. 1	USSR
58	18 June 1954	674, para. 71	Thailand question	S/3229	USSR
59	20 June 1954	675, paras. 194–5	Guatemalan question	S/3236/Rev. 1	USSR
60–74	13 Dec. 1955	704, paras. 51–2, 57–9, 61–2, 65–72	Applications for Membership	S/3502, S/3506	USSR
75	13 Dec. 1955	704, para. 54	Applications for Membership	S/3502	China
76	14 Dec. 1955	705, para. 28	Applications for Membership	Amendment to S/3509	USSR
77	15 Dec. 1955	706, para. 116	Applications for Membership	S/3510	USSR
78	13 Oct. 1956	743, para. 106	Complaint by France and the UK against Egypt (Suez Canal)	S/3671, as amended	USSR
79	30 Oct. 1956	749, para. 186	Palestine question	S/3710, as amended	France, UK
80	30 Oct. 1956	750, para. 23	Palestine question (Egyptian complaint against France and UK)	S/3713/Rev. 1, as amended	France, UK
81	4 Nov. 1956	754, para. 68	Hungary	S/3730/Rev. 1	USSR
82	20 Feb. 1957	773, para. 126	India–Pakistan question	S/3787	USSR
83–4	9 Sept. 1957	790, paras. 9, 56	Applications for Membership	S/3884–5	USSR
85	2 May 1958	817, para. 3	Soviet complaint of flights by US aircraft	S/3995, as amended	USSR
86	18 July 1958	834, para. 68	Complaint by Lebanon of UAR interference	S/4050/Rev. 1	USSR
87	22 July 1958	837, para. 9	Complaint by Lebanon of UAR interference	S/4055/Rev. 1	USSR
88–9	9 Dec. 1958	843, paras. 35, 48	Applications for Membership	S/4129 and Rev. 1; S/4130 and Rev. 1	USSR
90–1	26 July 1960	883, paras. 188, 189	RB-47 incident	S/4409/Rev. 1, S/4411	USSR
92	17 Sept. 1960	906, para. 157	Congo question	S/4523	USSR
93	4 Dec. 1960	911, para. 246	Application for Membership	S/4567/Rev. 1	USSR
94	13 Dec. 1960	920, para. 156	Congo question	S/4578/Rev. 1	USSR

Table 8 *cont.*

No.	Date	Meeting and page or paragraph no(s).	Subject	Text of vetoed proposal (meeting and page no. or S/no. until 1948, S/no. thereafter)	Permanent member(s) voting negatively
95–6	20–1 Feb. 1961	942, paras. 139, 175	Congo question	S/4733, as amended	USSR
97	7 July 1961	960, para. 44	Kuwait	S/4855	USSR
98–9	24 Nov. 1961	982, paras. 81, 84	Congo question	S/4989/Revs. 1 and 2	USSR
100	30 Nov. 1961	985, para. 44	Application for Membership	S/5006	USSR
101	18 Dec. 1961	988, para. 129	Goa	S/5033	USSR
102	22 June 1962	1016, para. 92	India–Pakistan question	S/5134	USSR
103	3 Sept. 1963	1063, para. 64	Palestine question	S/5407	USSR
104	13 Sept. 1963	1069, para. 64	Southern Rhodesia	S/5425/Rev. 1	UK
105	17 Sept. 1964	1152, para. 64	Relations between Malaysia and Indonesia	S/5973	USSR
106	21 Dec. 1964	1182, para. 41	Palestine question	S/6113, as amended, S/6116	USSR
107	4 Nov. 1966	1319, para. 55	Palestine question	S/7575/Rev. 1	USSR
108	23 Aug. 1968	1443, para. 284	Czechoslovakia	S/8761 and Add. 1	USSR
109	17 Mar. 1970	1534, para. 207	Southern Rhodesia	S/9696, as amended	UK, USA
110	10 Nov. 1970	1556, para. 212	Southern Rhodesia	S/9976	UK
111	4 Dec. 1971	1606, para. 371	India/Pakistan subcontinent	S/10416	USSR
112	5 Dec. 1971	1607, para. 240	India/Pakistan subcontinent	S/10423	USSR
113	13 Dec. 1971	1613, para. 231	India/Pakistan subcontinent	S/10446/Rev. 1	USSR
114	30 Dec. 1971	1623, para. 272	Southern Rhodesia	S/10489	UK
115	4 Feb. 1972	1639, para. 48	Southern Rhodesia	S/10606	UK
116	25 Aug. 1972	1660, para. 85	Admission of new Members	S/10771	China
117	10 Sept. 1972	1662, para. 72	Middle East	S/10784	China, USSR
118	10 Sept. 1972	1662, para. 74	Middle East	S/10786	USA
119	29 Sept. 1972	1666, paras. 119–21	Southern Rhodesia	S/10805/Rev. 1	UK
120	21 Mar. 1973	1704, para. 66	Panama Canal	S/10931/Rev. 1	USA
121	22 May 1973	1716, para. 48	Southern Rhodesia	S/10928	UK, USA
122	26 July 1973	1735, para. 97	Middle East	S/10974	USA
123	31 July 1974	1788, para. 237	Cyprus	S/11400, as amended	USSR

124	30 Oct. 1974	1808, para. 155	UN and South Africa	S/11543	France, UK, USA
125	6 June 1975	1829, para. 160	Namibia	S/11713	France, UK, USA
126–7	11 Aug. 1975	1836, paras. 105–6	Admission of new Members	S/11795, S/11796	USA
128–9	30 Sept. 1975	1846, paras. 41–2	Admission of new Members	S/11832–3	USA
130	8 Dec. 1975	11862, para. 118	Middle East	S/11898	USA
131	26 Jan. 1976	1879, para. 67	Middle East, including Palestine question	S/11940	USA
132	6 Feb. 1976	1888, para. 247	Comoros	S/11967	France
133	25 Mar. 1976	1899, para. 106	Occupied Arab territories	S/12022	USA
134	23 June 1976	1932, para. 208	Admission of new Members	S/12110	USA
135	29 June 1976	1938, para. 119	Palestinian rights	S/12119	USA
136	19 Oct. 1976	1963, para. 121	Namibia	S/12211	France, UK, USA
137	15 Nov. 1976	1972, para. 119	Admission of new Members	S/12226	USA
138–40	31 Oct. 1977	2045, paras. 53–5	South Africa	S/12310/Rev. 1, S/12311 Rev. 1, S/12312/Rev. 1	France 3, UK 3, USA 3
141	15 Jan. 1979	2112, para. 4	Complaint of Kampuchea against Vietnam	S/13027	USSR
142	16 Mar. 1979	2129, para. 72	South East Asia	S/13162	USSR
143	7 Jan. 1980	2190, para. 140	Afghanistan	S/13729	USSR
144	13 Jan. 1980	2191/Add. 1	US hostages in Iran	S/13735	USSR
145	30 Apr. 1980	2220, pp. 67–70	Palestinian rights	S/13911	USA
146–9	30 Apr. 1981	2277, pp. 8–12	Namibia	S/14459, S/14460/Rev. 1, S/14461–2	France 4, UK 4, USA 4
150	31 Aug. 1981	2300, p. 17	Complaint of Angola against South Africa	S/14664/Rev. 2	USA
151	20 Jan. 1982	2329, p. 52	Occupied Arab territories	S/14832/Rev. 1	USA
152	2 Apr. 1982	2347, p. 61	Complaint of Nicaragua against the USA	S/14941	USA
153	2 Apr. 1982	2348, p. 4	Occupied Arab territories	S/14943	USA
154	20 Apr. 1982	2357, p. 38	Occupied Arab territories	S/14985	USA
155	4 June 1982	2373, p. 16	Falklands (Malvinas)	S/15156/Rev. 2	UK, USA
156	8 June 1982	2377, pp. 8–10	Middle East	S/15185	USA
157	26 June 1982	2381, pp. 8–10	Middle East	S/15255/Rev. 2	USA
158	6 Aug. 1982	2391, p. 13	Middle East	S/15347/Rev. 1	USA
159	2 Aug. 1983	2461, pp. 103–5	Occupied Arab territories	S/15895	USA

TABLE 8 *cont.*

No.	Date	Meeting and page or paragraph no(s).	Subject	Text of vetoed proposal (meeting and page no. or S/no. until 1948, S/no. thereafter)	Permanent member(s) voting negatively
160	12 Sept. 1983	2476, pp. 53–5	Shooting down of Korean airliner	S/15966/Rev. 1	USSR
161	27 Oct. 1983	2491, p. 197	Grenada	S/16077/Rev. 1	USA
162	29 Feb. 1984	2519, p. 36	Middle East	S/16351/Rev. 2	USSR
163	4 Apr. 1984	2529, p. 111	Complaint of Nicaragua against the USA	S/16463	USA
164	6 Sept. 1984	2556, pp. 19–20	Middle East	S/16732	USA
165	12 Mar. 1985	2573, p. 83	Middle East	S/17000	USA
166–8	10 May 1985	2580, pp. 123–4	Complaint of Nicaragua against the USA	S/17172, 8th preambular and first two operative paras.	USA
169	26 July 1985	2602, pp. 42–5	South Africa	S/17363	UK, USA
170	13 Sept. 1985	2605, p. 81	Occupied Arab territories	S/17459	USA
171	15 Nov. 1985	2629, p. 28	Namibia	S/17633	UK, USA
172	17 Jan. 1986	2642, p. 38	Middle East	S/17330/Rev. 2	USA
173	30 Jan. 1986	2650, p. 31	Occupied Arab territories	S/17769/Rev. 1	USA
174	6 Feb. 1986	2655, pp. 114–15	Syrian complaint against Israel	S/17796/Rev. 1	USA
175	21 Apr. 1986	2682, p. 43	US attacks on Libya	S/18016/Rev. 1	France, UK, USA
176	23 May 1986	2686, pp. 128–30	South Africa	S/18087/Rev. 1	UK, USA
177	18 June 1986	2693, p. 48	Complaint of Angola against South Africa	S/18163	UK, USA
178	31 July 1986	2704, pp. 54–5	Complaint of Nicaragua against the USA	S/18250	USA
179	28 Oct. 1986	2718, p. 51	Complaint of Nicaragua against the USA	S/18428	USA
180	20 Feb. 1987	2738, p. 67	South Africa	S/18705	UK, USA
181	9 Apr. 1987	2747, p. 21	Namibia	S/18785	UK, USA
182	18 Jan. 1988	2784, pp. 49–50	Lebanon	S/19434	USA

183	1 Feb. 1988	2790, p. 42	Occupied Arab territories	S/19466	USA
184	8 Mar. 1988	2797, p. 19	Sanctions against South Africa	S/19585	USA, UK
185	15 Apr. 1988	2806, p. 53	Occupied Arab territories	S/19780	USA
186	10 May 1988	2814, p. 58	Invasion of Lebanon	S/19868	USA
187	14 Dec. 1988	S/2832, p. 28	Israeli raid on Lebanon	S/20322	USA
188	11 Jan. 1989	2841, p. 48	Shooting down of Libyan aircraft	S/20378	France, UK, USA
189	17 Feb. 1989	2850, p. 34	Occupied Arab territories	S/20463	USA
190	9 June 1989	2867, p. 31	Occupied Arab territories	S/20677	USA
191	7 Nov. 1989	2889, p. 42	Occupied Arab territories	S/20945/Rev. 1	USA
192	23 Dec. 1989	2902, pp. 18–20	Invasion of Panama	S/21048	France, UK, USA
193	17 Jan. 1990	2905, p. 36	Violation of diplomatic immunities in Panama	S/21084	USA
194	31 May 1990	2926, p. 36	Occupied Arab territories	S/21326	USA
195	11 May 1993	3211, p. 6	Cyprus (finances)	S/25693	Russian Federation
196	2 Dec. 1994	3475, p. 11	Bosnia and Herzegovina	S/1994/1358	Russian Federation
197	17 May 1995	3538	Occupied Arab territories	S/1995/394	USA
198	10 Jan. 1997	3730, p. 17	Guatemala	S/1997/18	China
199	7 Mar. 1997	3746	Occupied Arab territories	S/1997/199	USA
200	21 Mar. 1997	3756, p. 6	Occupied Arab territories	S/1997/241	USA

(b) Vetoes cast at private meetings of the Council, reported in official communiqués

No.	Date	Meeting no.	Subject	Text of vetoed proposal S/no.	Permanent member [acknowledged] to have voted negatively
201	13 Mar. 1953	613, p. 1	Appointment of Secretary-General	S/PV. 613	Not stated [USSR]
202	19 Nov. 1996	3714	Appointment of Secretary-General	S/1996/952	Not stated [USA]

TABLE 8 *cont.*

(c) Unofficial vetoed resolutions, vetoes said *to have been cast in formal ballots at private meetings of the Security Council,* not *reported in official* communiqués[a]

No.	Date	Meeting no.	Subject	Source of information	Permanent member said to have voted negatively
1	12 Oct. 1950	510	Appointment of Secretary-General	Lie, p. 376–7: Schwebel, p. 189–90	USSR
2–7	17, 20, and 21 Dec. 1971	1618–20	Appointment of Secretary-General	Thant, p. 438	USSR 4, China 2, UK 1
8	7 Dec. 1976	1978	Appointment of Secretary-General	Urquhart, p. 268	China
9–25	27, 28 Oct.; 4, 17 Nov. 1981	2303–5, 2310	Appointment of Secretary-General	Waldheim, p. 233–5; Romulo, p. 154–5	China 16, USA 5, USSR 1

[a] This list does not include 'straw polls' which took place during Council deliberations prior to the appointments of Pérez de Cuéllar, Boutros-Ghali, and Kofi Annan.

Table 9

Summary of vetoes in the Security Council[a], *16 February 1946–1 August 1997*

Member	1946–55	1956–65	1966–75	1976–85	1986–95	1996–1 August 1997	Total
China	1	0	2	0	0	1	4
France	2	2	2	9	3	0	18
Soviet Union/ Russian Federation	75	26	7	6	2	0	116
UK	0	3	8	11	8	0	30
USA	0	0	12	34	24	2	72
Official veto cast in a private meeting[b]	1	0	0	0	0	1	2

[a] The total number of vetoes cast during this period (242) is greater than the number of vetoed resolutions (202) since some resolutions were vetoed by more than one permanent member.

[b] This table includes only those vetoes reported in official Council verbatim records or official *communiqués*. 31 other vetoes are said to have been cast in private meetings of the Council, in the course of voting on 25 draft resolutions. See Table 8 section (c).

4. THE DOUBLE VETO

Having addressed the veto, it is now necessary to define the double veto and the way it has been used and misused. To understand this procedure, we must start with two definitions.

The main or substantive question is the matter that is submitted to the Security Council for decision. If it is approved by the Security Council, whether by the requisite majority or unanimously or without a vote, it becomes a decision. All resolutions of the Council are now numbered, beginning with no. 1 on 25 January 1946, which entrusted the Military Staff Committee with certain specified tasks; the last resolution in 1996 was approved on 26 December 1996, was numbered 1092 (1996), and concerned the UN peace-keeping force in Cyprus.

It is open to any member of the Council to insist that a particular proposal is non-procedural rather than procedural. If this is accepted, the original proposal is liable to veto. In the early days (1946–9), several attempts were made to veto the preliminary question; for that to be done, the Council must decide first that the preliminary question was substantive.

The sponsoring powers at San Francisco took their stand on a formula that had been agreed at the Yalta summit meeting the previous February, and the Yalta formula (as it came to be called) was made public at San Francisco on 8 June 1945 (see Appendix III). Part of the difficulty of applying the Yalta formula lay in the so-called chain of events theory. It is possible to envisage a chain of events which would begin with a decision simply to call a meeting of the Security Council to consider whether or not a particular matter should be included in the matters of which the Security Council is seized, but which might lead in the end to a proposal for enforcement action. At what point in such a chain of events would the matter cease to be merely procedural and become substantive and therefore liable to veto? Moreover, as the Council approaches the frontier between procedure and substance (wherever that frontier might be) was it not likely that members of the Council, including the permanent members, might find it impossible to agree on the preliminary question of whether a particular proposal was procedural or non-procedural? In other words, if a decision of the Council would be needed on the nature of the preliminary question (procedural or non-procedural), would such a decision require a vote of any seven (now nine) members of the Council or would it have to include the concurring votes of the permanent members?

In paragraph 2 of Part 1 of the Yalta formula are to be found illustrations of matters that were regarded by the sponsoring powers as procedural. The Yalta statement then indicated in paragraph 3 that no member would be able to prevent the Council from considering and discussing a dispute or situation brought to the Council's attention under what is now Article 35 of the Charter, that parties to a dispute could not be prevented from being heard by the Council, and that the veto could not be used to prevent 'any member of the Council from reminding UN Members of their general obligations assumed under the Charter as regards peaceful settlement of international disputes'. Beyond that point, decisions and actions of the Council 'may even initiate a chain of events which might in the end require the Council . . . to invoke measures of enforcement'. Under the Yalta formula, the sponsoring powers 'could not act by themselves' since decisions of the Council would have to include the concurring votes of at least two of the non-permanent members.

Clearly the Yalta formula bristles with difficulties: it begs important questions; and it was surely disingenuous in asserting that differences of view on the preliminary question were 'unlikely' to arise. Moreover, the substance of the statement was not approved by the San Francisco Conference but was simply a declaration of intent on the part of the sponsoring powers; its precise legal status has been a matter of dispute.

Should a decision to establish a subsidiary organ charged with the task of elucidating the facts be regarded as merely procedural, or could a decision to establish such an organ initiate a chain of events which might, in the end, require the Council to invoke measures of enforcement, in which case the decision would be deemed substantive? If the President of the Council should rule that a particular proposal is procedural and if the ruling should be challenged, should the matter be resolved by taking a vote on the preliminary question—which according to the Yalta formula would be subject to veto—or by submitting either the President's ruling or the challenge to his ruling to a decision of the Council—which would not be subject to veto? Should the preliminary question be settled before the main question, on the ground that a vote cannot usefully be taken on the main proposal without first knowing whether it is a matter of procedure or substance? Or, on the contrary, should the main question be settled first on the ground that it cannot be known if it will be necessary to determine the preliminary question until after the main question has been voted on?

The question of the double veto arose several times in the early years. The proceedings were often confused and inconclusive, but it is possible to deduce from these eight cases a number of principles.

(a) Case 1: The Spanish question, 1946

Australia and the United Kingdom had proposed that, without prejudice to the rights of the General Assembly, the Security Council should keep the Spanish question under continuous review and maintain it on the list of matters of which the Council was seized. This proposal was put to the vote and received nine votes in favour, the Soviet Union and Poland voting against. The President (Castillo Nájera of Mexico) then declared that the resolution had been carried, because he 'thought it was a matter of procedure'. The Soviet Union disputed the President's conclusion and said that if any member of the Council disagreed with the Soviet interpretation, he would ask for a vote on the preliminary question. The President declared that the observations of the Soviet representative 'would have been timely' before the vote; nevertheless, he put to the vote his ruling that the question had been procedural. Eight members voted that the proposal of Australia and the United Kingdom had indeed been procedural, while France and the Soviet Union voted in the negative. The President then stated that the proposal was one of substance and had been defeated.[25]

(b) Case 2: Membership, 1946

The United States had proposed a postponement of voting on the applications of Albania and Mongolia for admission to the United Nations. The President (Dr Oscar Lange of Poland) ruled that the

US proposal was procedural; but there was some dissent, and he therefore announced that he would put the question to the vote. What was voted on, however, was not the President's ruling, but the preliminary question: 'I would like all those who believe that it is a matter of procedure to raise their hands.' The result was that the United States, Poland, and three other members voted in favour; Nationalist China, France, the Soviet Union, and the United Kingdom voted against; and two members abstained. The President then interpreted the result of the vote in the following terms:

> The question which the Council was asked was whether it supports my ruling that this is a matter of procedure. There were five votes in favour, and four against. These four against are all permanent members. Under that condition, it seems clear that my ruling has not been supported . . . Consequently, I regret the ruling has not been adopted by the Council, and we shall have to treat the resolution asking to postpone voting on Albania as a matter of substance.

This interpretation of the situation was questioned, so the President offered to 'formulate it in the form of a ruling and ask for challenges and a vote'. He then said that he interpreted the vote which had taken place as meaning that the US proposal was 'not to be considered a matter of procedure'. The United States accepted this formulation, and the proposal to postpone consideration of Albania's application was rejected. Only six votes were cast in favour; France, Poland, and the Soviet Union voted against; and there were two abstentions.[26]

(c) Case 3: Ukrainian complaint against Greece, 1946

The United States had proposed the establishment of a commission under Article 34 of the Charter, to investigate the facts, examine statements, and report to the Council on the Ukrainian complaint against Greece. The President (Andrei Gromyko of the Soviet Union) ruled that the proposal related to the substance of the matter. This was challenged by France and Australia, but the United States agreed with the President. The representative of France intimated that he did not insist that a vote be taken on the question of whether or not the matter was procedural, and the US proposal was then put to the vote and vetoed.[27]

(d) Case 4: Incidents in the Corfu Channel, 1947

Australia had proposed that a subcommittee be appointed to examine all available evidence relating to the Corfu Channel case and to make a report on the facts as disclosed by such evidence. The British representative said he wished to raise two questions.

> As a party to this dispute, I am deprived of my vote under Article 27, paragraph 3, of the Charter when it is a matter of decision under Chapter VI. I presume, though, that the vote which we are going to take is a purely procedural one and that I can exercise my vote.

The United Kingdom was raising two quite separate issues. Was it the case that the United Kingdom was a party to a dispute and, under paragraph 27(3) of the Charter, would have to abstain from voting? Secondly, was the issue a matter of procedure rather than substance so that the other four permanent members would have no right of veto?

The President of the Council (Fernand van Langehove of Belgium) ruled that the proposed study was not covered by Chapter VI.

> Chapter VI does not mention decisions of the kind which we have now to take . . . The sole function of the future subcommittee will be to facilitate the Council's work by classifying information submitted to the Council; there is no question in this case of undertaking an investigation.

The Soviet Union disputed the President's view, and also held that the President was not entitled to settle a question of this kind on his own authority; but he did not ask that the Council take a decision on the preliminary question, nor did he formally challenge the President's ruling. In the event, the United Kingdom voted in favour of the Australian proposal and the Soviet Union abstained.[28]

(e) Case 5: Greek frontier incidents, 1947

The United States had proposed that the General Assembly be requested, pursuant to Article 12 of the Charter, to consider and make recommendations with regard to the incidents on the Greek frontier. The question of whether or not the US proposal was procedural was raised; and after rejection of proposals to adjourn the meeting and postpone voting, Belgium suggested that the Council should vote first on the main question. The President (Soviet Ambassador Gromyko) ruled, however, that the preliminary question should be decided first. The ruling was challenged, put to the vote, and overruled. The United States proposal was then put to the vote and received nine affirmative votes, with Poland and the Soviet Union opposing. The President then declared that the US proposal had been rejected, but this interpretation was challenged, whereupon the President put to the vote, not his ruling, but the motion that the United States proposal had been procedural. There were eight votes in favour, with the Soviet Union and Poland against, and Syria abstaining. The President then declared that, as a permanent member of the Council had voted against the proposal, it had to be regarded as procedural. This interpretation was not challenged.[29]

(f) Case 6: Czechoslovak question, 1948

After the coup in Czechoslovakia in 1948, it was alleged that the political independence of Czechoslovakia had been violated by a Soviet threat to use force, and that the new situation endangered world peace. The Soviet representative vehemently opposed United Nations consideration of the situation in Czechoslovakia as a violation of Article 2(7) of the Charter forbidding intervention in internal affairs, and as calculated to increase international tension. The Soviet Union maintained that the allegation that events within Czechoslovakia had been instigated by the Soviet Union was absurd. He said that the changes in Czechoslovakia had been effected by strictly constitutional means, and that there were no grounds for any investigation by the United Nations.

Chile and Argentina submitted a draft resolution which, 'without prejudice of [*sic*] any decisions which may be taken in accordance with Article 34 of the Charter', would have appointed a subcommittee of three members to receive or to hear 'evidence, statements and testimonies and to report to the Security Council'. The Soviet representative took the view that the proposal was 'not of a procedural nature, but concerns the substance of the question', and he therefore proposed that a vote be taken on the preliminary question. The United States and other representatives disputed this view: the proposal before the Council was clearly procedural, and no vote on the preliminary question was necessary. The President (Alexandre Parodi of France) declared, however, that a vote should be taken on the preliminary question, and that this should precede the vote on the main question. The Soviet Union and the Ukrainian SSR voted against treating the proposal of Chile and Argentina as procedural, France abstained, and the other eight members of the Council voted in favour.

The President then interpreted the vote as a decision to regard the main proposal as substantive, but this interpretation was challenged. The challenge was put to the vote in the following terms: 'Will those who object to my interpretation raise their hands?' Six members voted to reject the President's ruling; the Soviet Union and the Ukraine voted to uphold the ruling; and France, the United Kingdom, and the United States abstained. Since the proposal to reject the President's interpretation failed to receive seven votes, the interpretation stood. The proposal of Chile and Argentina was then put to the vote and was vetoed by the Soviet Union. Explaining his vote, the Soviet representative said he had used the veto 'in order to prevent the United States or the Security Council . . . from interfering in the internal affairs of the sovereign State of Czechoslovakia. That is our right.'[30]

(g) Case 7: Complaint of armed invasion of Taiwan, 1950

The Council was considering the complaint of armed invasion of Taiwan, and it was proposed that a representative of the People's Republic of China should be invited to participate in the discussion. Nationalist China took the view that such a proposal was substantive, but the President (Sir Gladwyn Jebb of the United Kingdom) ruled that the Council should vote first on the main question; 'after we have taken it, we can argue this question out as to whether the vote is valid or not'. There followed the usual discussion about the Yalta formula. The United States representative said that if the main question were put to the vote first, he would regard the question as a procedural one and vote in the negative. If the Council should then take a vote on the preliminary question and decide that the main question was 'substantive rather than procedural and that, hence, my negative vote constituted a veto, I would reserve the right to change my negative vote to an abstention'.

Two separate proposals to invite the People's Republic of China to participate were put to the vote, but failed to secure the necessary seven votes. One of the resolutions was resubmitted the next day, receiving seven votes in favour, three against (Nationalist China, Cuba, and the United States), and one abstention. The President declared that in his opinion the resolution had been adopted, but this was challenged by Nationalist China. After discussion extending over parts of two meetings, the President asked the Council to vote on whether or not the main question had been procedural. There were nine votes in favour, Nationalist China against, and one abstention (Cuba). The President then declared that the proposal had been adopted. Nationalist China protested against this and suggested that an advisory opinion of the International Court of Justice should be sought. The President of the Council regarded this as challenging his ruling and asked the Council to vote on the challenge. When the challenge was put to the vote, however, the surprising result was that there were no votes in favour, none against, and no abstentions! The President regarded this as approving his ruling, and the issue lapsed.[31]

(h) Case 8: The question of Laos, 1959

France, the United Kingdom, and the United States had proposed that the Council appoint a subcommittee on the question of Laos 'to examine the statements made before the Security Council . . . to receive further statements and documents and to conduct such inquiries as it may determine necessary'. The Soviet Union held that the proposal was substantive, and the President of the Council (Egidio Ortona of Italy) put the question to the vote. All members of the Council except the Soviet Union voted that the proposal was procedural; the Soviet representative, by no means unexpectedly, voted in the negative. Following the vote, the President declared that the proposal was procedural. The Soviet representative protested at this interpretation, but the main proposal was put to the vote and, in spite of the negative Soviet vote, declared by the President to have been adopted.[32]

On the basis of the eight cases, we believe that the following considerations should be borne in mind if the question of the double veto should recur.

First, it hardly needs stressing that the double veto is not a device to enable a permanent member of the Council to block a procedural decision. The Yalta formula listed certain decisions which were to be regarded as procedural, and the double veto could arise in connection with such matters only if it could be reasonably argued that the 'chain of events' idea was applicable. In practice, the problem has arisen mainly in connection with proposals to establish subsidiary organs for making studies or investigations, when it was or could have been contended that a decision to establish a subsidiary organ could conceivably initiate a chain of events which might, in the end, require the Council to take enforcement action (Cases 3, 4, 6, and 8). The proposal to invite a representative of the People's Republic of China to take part in the discussion of the complaint of armed invasion of Taiwan (Case 7) was outside the scope of the double veto, since the Yalta formula specifically mentioned invitations to participate as procedural.

Secondly, if there is doubt whether a proposal submitted to the Council is procedural or substantive, the Council should not proceed to vote on the main question until after the preliminary question has been settled. The practice of the Council has not been consistent on this point, but the fact is that the way a member of the Council will vote may well depend on whether the main question is regarded as a matter of procedure or a matter of substance. It is an absurd situation when, as in Case 7, a member of the Council has to reserve the right to change his vote on the main question if, after it has been settled, the preliminary question should be decided in a way contrary to his own views. In Case 1, the President (the representative of Mexico) indicated that it would have been better had the preliminary question been raised earlier, and in Case 5 the President (the Soviet representative) ruled that the preliminary question should be settled before the main question—though he was challenged and overruled on this point.

Thirdly, the Yalta formula declares that if it should be necessary to decide whether a procedural or a substantive vote is to apply, the decision on the preliminary question is to be made by a vote of the Council. Neither inadvertently nor by design should the President attempt to settle the question by a 'ruling'. It would seem in Case 2 that the President (the representative of Poland) was not correct in attempting to rule that the US proposal was procedural. Once the issue had been posed, however, it was appropriate to resolve it by voting on the preliminary question, although the President caused unnecessary confusion by interpreting the result of the vote as a rejection of his ruling.

5. THE 'HIDDEN VETO'

A permanent member can pursue one of two courses if it wishes to defeat a substantive proposal: to cast a negative vote, or to persuade enough members of the Council to vote in the negative or to abstain so that the proposal fails to secure the requisite number of affirmative votes. This proceeding was called by the Soviet Union 'the hidden veto' or 'the indirect veto'.[33] The matter was expressed like this:

> I think that all or almost all of us here . . . know quite well that, given the existence in the Security Council of a firm majority prepared at all times to defend and support certain views of the Western Powers [1961], there is no need for the representatives of those powers to cast a negative vote.[34]

It has never been the case that there has been a majority prepared 'at all times' to defend and support Western policies, though it is true that until the enlargement of the Council in 1966, the Council was so composed that anti-Western policies could usually be defeated without the use of the veto. That is no longer the case.

The use of the word 'veto' in relation to the failure of the Council to adopt a proposal because of insufficient affirmative votes is perhaps misleading. It is important, however, to be reminded that the non-permanent members, acting in concert, with or without the abstention or non-participation of permanent members, do have the power to block decisions of the Council. This in practice happens rarely. Examples include the Israeli rescue of the passengers of a hijacked aircraft at Entebbe. A United Kingdom proposal to condem aerial hijacking was put to the vote, and two members abstained while the Soviet Union and six others declined to participate in the vote. The British proposal was therefore defeated.[35]

More recently in an example in which a policy rift between the US and Europeans over Bosnia was brought to the fore, occurred in

1993. A draft resolution[36] was proposed by the non-aligned caucus on the Council, with the support of the US, aiming to exempt the Government of Bosnia and Herzegovina from the arms embargo imposed by resolution 713 (1991). The voting on the draft resolution was 6 in favour (NAM members plus the US), none against and nine abstentions.[37]

6. ABSTENTIONS

There are two kinds of abstention from voting in the Security Council. First, parties to a dispute 'shall' abstain from voting on substantive proposals for pacific settlement (Articles 27(3) and 52(3) of the Charter). This is known in UN jargon as an obligatory abstention. Secondly, members who have no wish to vote either for or against a substantive proposal may abstain from voting. This is known as a voluntary abstention.[38]

In Article 27(3) of the Charter, two qualifying words are used to describe votes of approval: 'an *affirmative* vote of nine [originally seven] members including the *concurring* votes of the permanent members' (our italics). Do these two italicized words have identical meanings, or was it intended that an abstention, though not an affirmative vote, should be regarded as a form of concurrence?

At San Francisco, the sponsoring powers gave the impression that substantive decisions would require the unanimity of the five permanent members plus the concurring votes of at least two others.[39] This interpretation was quite clear as far as it went, though it did not deal with a situation in which a permanent member was a party to a dispute and was required to abstain from voting. Under pressure from some of the medium and smaller powers, the sponsoring powers held a closed meeting to review the question of abstentions and accepted the US view that a permanent member could not abstain from voting unless it was a party to a dispute. To use subsequent jargon, permanent members would be required to cast obligatory abstentions in the prescribed circumstances but would not be able to cast voluntary abstentions. The five permanent members kept this interpretation to themselves.[40]

Washington soon had second thoughts about this understanding, and a rule of procedure was drafted by the United States to the effect that a permanent member could indicate whether an abstention was to be deemed a veto or a form of concurrence. This draft was shown to the other four permanent members: the Soviet Union did not want any express rule on the matter; the other three, while not enthusiastic, said they would not oppose the US proposal.[41] Before the matter could be resolved, however, a situation arose in which the Soviet Union wished to abstain but not to veto, and the other permanent members raised no objection.[42] The other permanent members soon followed suit,[43] and in 1971 the International Court of Justice stated that this procedure had been 'generally accepted' and was evidence of 'a general practice'.[44] Between 1946 and 1996, the permanent members had together cast some three hundred voluntary abstentions.

Obligatory abstentions are those by parties to proposals for pacific settlement of a dispute.[45] The question whether a member should be required to abstain has arisen on thirteen occasions.

Case 1: Syrian and Lebanese question, 1946

In their submission to the Council, Syria and Lebanon maintained that the presence of British and French troops in their countries might give rise to 'serious disputes'. This allegation was supported by the Soviet Union but denied by France.

One proposal was submitted to the Council but later was withdrawn. Two proposals were put to the vote and defeated, each receiving four affirmative votes; the States casting the votes are not identified in the official records. A fourth proposal was vetoed by the Soviet Union (the first use of the veto power); the seven affirmative votes are not identified in the official records, and abstentions were not counted.[46]

Case 2: Iranian question, 1946

The Iranian question, in its second phase, was described by Iran as a dispute between Iran and the Soviet Union. A Soviet proposal that consideration of the communication of Iran should be postponed was rejected on 27 March 1946, whereupon the Soviet representative stated that he was not in a position to take a further part in a discussion of the Iranian question and left the Council chamber. Three decisions were taken in the absence of the Soviet representative: an invitation to the representative of Iran to state his point of view concerning the question of postponement, a request to the Secretary-General to report on the status of negotiations, and a decision to defer proceedings and request the two governments to report.

The Soviet representative resumed participation in the discussion of the Iranian question on 4 April 1946 and took part on 23 April in the voting on a French proposal (which was rejected) which would have taken note of a letter from Iran withdrawing the complaint, have noted that agreement had been reached between the two governments, and have requested the Secretary-General to collect the necessary information in order to complete the report of the Security Council to the General Assembly. The French proposal was rejected, whereupon the Soviet Union again withdrew and did not attend subsequent meetings at which the Iranian question was discussed.[47]

Case 3: Relations between Siam (Thailand) and France, 1946

On 25 May 1946, Siam (Thailand) informed the United Nations of tension on the frontiers between French Indo-China and Siam. Siam was not at that time a Member of the United Nations, and the question was not placed on the agenda. On 28 November 1946, the representative of Siam withdrew the complaint, and on 12 December, the Security Council recommended that Siam be admitted to UN membership.[48]

Case 4: Incidents in the Corfu Channel, 1947

The Corfu Channel question was submitted to the Security Council by the United Kingdom under Article 35 of the Charter; but on 18 February 1946, the British representative asked the Council, taking into account the failure of attempts at settlement through diplomatic correspondence, to recommend settlement of the dispute by direct negotiation between the two governments under Article 36 of the Charter. Article 36 concerns 'a dispute' or 'a situation of like nature'.

On 27 February, the Council was asked to vote on a proposal submitted by Australia, and amended in accordance with a suggestion of Nationalist China, to appoint a subcommittee to report on the facts. Before the vote was taken, the British representative stated that he assumed the Australian proposal was procedural and that therefore he was not required to abstain. The Soviet representative disputed the British case, but he said that he would not vote against a motion to consider the matter procedural as he did not wish to hinder the setting up of the subcommittee. The President (Fernand van Langenhove of Belgium) said that the establishment of a subcommittee was not concerned with the pacific settlement of disputes since 'Chapter VI does not mention decisions of the kind which we have now to take', and he was supported by Colombia, Syria, and the United States. The United Kingdom voted in favour of the proposal but did not take part in the voting on the proposal of the President about the composition of the subcommittee.[49]

On 25 March 1947, the Soviet Union vetoed an amended British proposal which would have found that the mines could not have been laid without the knowledge of the Albanian authorities and would have recommended that the two governments settle the dispute on the basis of the Council's finding; the British representative declared he was 'not voting'.

In a subsequent decision to recommend the reference of the dispute to the International Court of Justice, the United Kingdom again did not participate in the vote.[50]

Case 5: Egyptian question, 1947

Egypt had stated that the presence of British troops in Egypt and the Sudan had 'given rise to a dispute', and Poland and the Soviet Union also expressed the view that a dispute existed. Several proposals and amendments were submitted, and the United Kingdom abstained from voting.[51]

Case 6: India–Pakistan question, 1948

The question of relations between India and Pakistan was first submitted to the Security Council by India on 1 January 1948, and Pakistan submitted a counter-complaint two weeks later, alleging that the situation had 'given rise to disputes'.

India was a member of the Security Council during 1950–1 and Pakistan was a member during 1952–3.

During 1950–1, the Council adopted three resolutions on the India–Pakistan question (resolution 80, 14 March 1950; resolution 91, 30 March 1951; and resolution 96, 19 November 1951) and took three other decisions. India abstained on each occasion.

During 1952 and 1953, one decision was taken on the India–Pakistan question without a vote, and one resolution was adopted (resolution 98, 23 December 1952). Pakistan did not participate in the voting.[52]

The India–Pakistan question has not been considered by the Council since 1965.

Case 7: Hyderabad question, 1948

The Hyderabad question came to the attention of the Security Council as a result of a communication from the Hyderabad Government of 21 August 1948, claiming that there was a 'grave dispute' between Hyderabad and India, which was likely to endanger international peace and security.[53] No substantive decisions have been taken by the Council.

Case 8: Palestine question, 1951

In 1951, Israel asked the Council to consider the restrictions which Egypt had imposed on the passage of ships through the Suez Canal, maintaining that the actions of Egypt were endangering the peace and security of the Middle East. Egypt contended that Israel had no right to bring the matter before the Council. Nevertheless, Egypt held that the matter was without doubt a dispute and that if the Council should proceed to a vote, those States which had protested to the Egyptian Government about the restrictions should be regarded as parties to the dispute and therefore required to abstain from voting. At a later stage in the debate, Egypt submitted to the Council a draft resolution which sought to request from the International Court of Justice an advisory opinion on the following question:

In the light of the Charter of the United Nations, particularly paragraph 3 of Article 27, and in view of the debate in the Security Council, are France, the Netherlands, Turkey, the United Kingdom and the United States of America obliged to abstain from voting on the question of the restrictions imposed by Egypt in relation to the passage through the Suez Canal of some war materials to Israel?

The five States whose right to vote had been questioned held that to accept Egypt's contention would lead to 'quite incongruous results' and would 'paralyse the Security Council'. They could see 'no reason why they should be debarred from voting'.

Egypt decided not to press to the vote its own proposed request for an advisory opinion 'since it obviously would not be approved by the requisite majority'. A proposal calling on Egypt to terminate restrictions on the passage of shipping through the Canal was put to the vote and became resolution 95 (1951), the five States which had protested to Egypt voting affirmatively.[54]

Case 9: Adolf Eichmann, 1960

Argentina, then a member of the Security Council, complained that Israel's capture of Adolf Eichmann from Argentine territory was a violation of sovereign rights and, if repeated, would endanger international peace and security. Argentina submitted a draft resolution to that effect and accepted two amendments proposed by the United States. Before the vote was taken, the Argentine representative stated that, without going into a legal or procedural analysis, Argentina did not intend to participate in the vote. The resolution was, however, adopted by eight votes, with two abstentions.[55]

Case 10: South Africa, 1974

When the Council was considering African questions in 1974, Madagascar suggested that States which had given substantial support to South Africa might be considered to be parties to a dispute and thus required to abstain from voting.[56] The matter was not pursued.

Case 11: The Comoros, 1976

The Comoros (formerly a French protectorate) had complained of French aggression, and a draft resolution critical of French policy had been vetoed by France. Benin then raised the question whether France, as a party to a dispute, should not have been required to abstain from voting. A considerable discussion ensued. The President (Daniel P. Moynihan of the United States) said that it would have been timely to have raised the issue before the vote. He had studied the Council's *Repertoire* and believed that it was right and proper for France to have taken part in the voting.[57]

Case 12: Falklands (Malvinas), 1982

After Argentine forces had landed in the Falklands (Malvinas), the Council was debating a British proposal for an immediate cessation of hostilities and withdrawal of Argentine forces. Panama asked the President of the Council (Kamanda wa Kamanda of Zaire) to rule on whether the United Kingdom had the right to vote on its own proposal. The British representative said that his proposal was not one for peaceful settlement but was a provisional measure under Article 40 of the Charter. After Spain had supported the British interpretation, the President said that if there were no further comments, the Council would proceed to the vote. The vote was unanimous.[58]

Case 13: Chad–Libya, 1983

The Council, under the Presidency of de la Barre de Nanteuil of France, was considering complaints from Chad and Libya. Iran maintained that France was interfering in Chad's internal affairs and so should not be allowed to vote. The President reproved Iran for making false accusations, and the matter was allowed to drop.[59] No draft resolution was submitted.

When States submit matters to the Council, they are now very cautious about complaining that a dispute exists lest they and their friends should be required to abstain from voting. The practice of the Council in the above thirteen cases was as follows. In Case 3, the item was not inscribed. In Case 1, the official records indicate total votes only. In Case 2, the Soviet Union was absent when the crucial vote took place. As regards Case 7, no substantive proposal was put to the vote: the same was true of Case 13, but there is no reason to think that France would have abstained had there been a vote. As for the remaining cases, States either abstained or did not participate in the vote in Cases 4, 5, 6, and 9, but took part in the voting in Cases 8, 10, 11, and 12.

Two firm conclusions can be drawn about the correct practice of the Council. First, it is the Council itself rather than the parties that determines whether a dispute exists. Second, if there is any question about an obligatory abstention under Article 27(3), the matter should be settled before the voting takes place.

7. ABSENCE

Absences from meetings of the Security Council may occur either because a representative fails to reach the place where the Council is meeting in time (involuntary absence) or because a representative deliberately stays away (boycott), either as a form of protest and/or so as to be able to allege later that the proceedings were illegal. Involuntary absence has been rare, though the Ukrainian SSR failed to reach Paris in time for an unexpected meeting of the Council after the second Dutch 'police action' in Indonesia.[60] The Soviet Union boycotted five meetings of the Council on the Iranian complaint in 1946, during which the Council took several decisions.[61] A more fateful boycott took place in 1950 when the Soviet Union was absent from 13 January until 1 August because of the Council's failure to expel Nationalist China.[62] It was during the Soviet absence that the Council took its first four decisions on Korea. The general view has been that a boycott is tantamount to voluntary abstention, and that the proceedings in the absence of one or more members are valid.[63]

During the situation of civil war in Rwanda in the summer of 1994, it was unclear who was entitled to represent the country on the Security Council. As a result there was no Rwandese representative on the Council from 14 July to 7 September 1994, and the Council passed four resolutions with only 14 members during that period.[64]

TABLE 10

Absence from the Council when a resolution has been voted on, 1946–1996

No.	Resolution	Date	State absent
1.	3 (1946)	4 April 1946	USSR
2.	5 (1946)	8 May 1946	USSR
3.	79 (1950)	17 January 1950	USSR
4.	80 (1950)	14 March 1950	USSR
5.	81 (1950)	24 May 1950	USSR
6.	82 (1950)	25 June 1950	USSR
7.	83 (1950)	27 June 1950	USSR
8.	84 (1950)	7 July 1950	USSR
9.	85 (1950)	31 July 1950	USSR
10.	937 (1994)	21 July 1994	Rwanda
11.	938 (1994)	28 July 1994	Rwanda
12.	939 (1994)	29 July 1994	Rwanda
13.	940 (1994)	31 July 1994	Rwanda

8. NON-PARTICIPATION IN THE VOTE

There were nine cases of non-participation in the vote before 1971, either as a form of protest against the wisdom or legality of the proceedings,[65] or as a substitute for an obligatory abstention.[66] After China took its seat in the Security Council, it began to refrain from participating in the vote on matters arising from decisions taken when Nationalist China occupied the Chinese seat, and this continued for almost a decade. Soon other countries followed suit, though usually from less obvious motives. China did not participate in seventy-three votes during the period 1971–81, eighteen relating to Cyprus (mainly peace-keeping), forty-four to the Middle East (mainly peace-keeping), five to Southern Africa, and five to other issues. Iraq did not participate in thirteen votes, Libya in eight, Benin in seven, and the Byelorussian SSR in four. France did not participate in the vote on the application of the Comoros for UN membership, and Uganda did not participate in a procedural motion during the Falklands (Malvinas) conflict. Britain did not participate in one vote on Southern Rhodesia in 1980, and the United States in one vote relating to Lebanon in 1982. Since 1982 there has been only one case of non-participation in a vote, this was Yemen's decision not to participate in voting on resolution 660 (1990) concerning Iraq's invasion of

Kuwait.* When non-participation in the vote in the case of resolutions alone is considered, we arrive at the distribution given in Table 11.

TABLE 11

Non-participation in votes on resolutions, 1946–1996

	1946–55	1956–65	1966–75	1976–85	1986–96	Total
China		1	26	40		67
Iraq			10			10
Benin				6		6
Libya				6		6
France		1	1			2
UK	1			1		2
Argentina		1				1
Australia	1					1
Egypt	1					1
India	1					1
Pakistan	1					1
USA				1		1
Yemen					1	1
Yugoslavia	1					1

9. CONSENSUS AND UNANIMITY[67]

Many procedural motions are now approved without a vote: questions relating to the agenda, the suspension or adjournment of meetings, invitations to participate, reference of matters to subsidiary organs, the composition of such organs, requests for information, decisions that consideration of a particular stage of a matter has been completed.

Draft resolutions or other decisions of substance may be approved at meetings of the Council by vote, whether by the requisite majority or unanimously. Decisions may also be made by consensus or without a vote, as shown in the case of resolutions, in Table 12 below. In such cases, the text is usually worked out in informal consultations and then circulated as a written document or declared by the President in open meeting to have been approved.[68]

In the first two years, such decisions always took the form of resolutions in express terms. Beginning in 1948, however, such decisions

* The figures in this section relate to the non-participation of States in votes at Council meetings at which they are *present*, as opposed to the circumstances in which States are *absent* from the Council as described in Section 7 of this chapter.

sometimes took the form of impartial summaries by the President. If no member dissociated itself from the statement or asked that it be approved by vote, it began to be assumed that the statement represented the consensus of the Council. In the aftermath of the Middle East war of 1967, decisions of the Council were sometimes made by written documents only. It is almost certain that this procedure was resorted to in order to avoid having open meetings of the Council at which one or more of the parties would insist on engaging in angry polemics. In recent years it has been rare that votes are taken on statements by the President on behalf of the Council, or on behalf of the members of the Council. These are agreed beforehand in the course of informal consultations. From 1991 to 1996 it was common that statements by the President on behalf of the members of the Council concerning reviews of sanctions imposed against Iraq and Libya were not announced at a formal meeting of the Council, but instead were read out to the press or simply issued in written form.

TABLE 12

Security Council resolutions adopted 'without a vote' or 'by consensus', 1946–1996

Date	Subject	Res. or decision
25 Jan. 1946	Military Staff Committee	Res. 1
26 June 1946#	Spain	Res. 7
15 Nov. 1946	International Court of Justice	Res. 11 (S/191)
10 Dec. 1946#	Greece	Res. 12
1 Aug. 1947#	Indonesia	Res. 27 (S/459)
9 Dec. 1947	Palestine	Res. 37 (S/612)
21 Apr. 1948#	India–Pakistan	Res. 47 (S/726)
29 May 1948#	Palestine	Res. 50 (S/801)
19 Aug. 1948#	Palestine	Res. 56 (S/983)
28 Sept. 1948*	International Court of Justice	Res. 58 (S/969)
19 Oct.1948*	Palestine	Res. 59
29 Oct. 1948	Palestine	Res. 60 (S/1062)
16 Nov. 1948#	Palestine	Res. 62 (S/1080)
28 Jan. 1949#	Indonesia	Res. 67 (S/1234)
11 Aug. 1949	Palestine	Res. 72 (S/1376)
28 July 1954	International Court of Justice	Res. 105 (S/3274)
6 Sept. 1956	International Court of Justice	Res. 117
25 Nov. 1958	International Court of Justice	Res. 130 (S/4118)
31 May 1960	International Court of Justice	Res. 137 (S/4331)
10 Aug. 1965	International Court of Justice	Res. 208
27 Sept. 1965	India–Pakistan	Res. 214 (S/6720)
15 Nov. 1967	Congo (Zaire)	Res. 241

Date	Subject	Res. or decision
24 Jan. 1969	Official languages of SC	Res. 263
26 Aug. 1969	Middle East	Res. 270 (S/9410)
23 Oct. 1969	International Court of Justice	Res. 272
9 Sept. 1970	Aerial hijacking	Res. 286 (S/9933/Rev. 1 and Corr. 1)
26 Jan. 1973*	Meeting outside Headquarters	Res. 325
22 June 1973	UN Membership (German Democratic Republic and Federal Republic of Germany)	Res. 335
17 Jan. 1974	Chinese as SC language	Res. 345 (S/11192)
10 June 1974	UN Membership (Bangladesh)	Res. 351
13 Dec. 1974+	Cyprus	Res. 365 (S/11574)
12 Mar. 1975	Cyprus	Res. 367 (S/11657)
22 Oct. 1975+	Western Sahara	Res. 377 (S/11858)
2 Nov. 1975+	Western Sahara	Res. 379 (S/11865)
6 Nov. 1975+	Western Sahara	Res. 380 (S/11870)
19 June 1976+	South Africa	Res. 392 (S/12103)
25 Aug. 1976+	Greece and Turkey	Res. 395 (S/12187)
22 Dec. 1976+	South Africa	Res. 402 (S/12260)
8 Feb. 1977+	Benin	Res. 404 (S/12282/Rev. 1)
14 Apr. 1977+	Benin	Res. 405 (S/12322)
25 May 1977	Botswana	Res. 406 (S/12334)
25 May 1977	Lesotho	Res. 407 (S/12335)
27 May 1977	Southern Rhodesia	Res. 409 (S/12339)
20 July 1977+	UN Membership (Vietnam)	Res. 413 (S/12366)
15 Sept. 1977	Cyprus	Res. 414 (S/12394)
24 Nov. 1977	Benin	Res. 419 (S/12454/Rev. 1)
27 Nov. 1978+	Cyprus	Res. 440 (S/12940)
23 Nov. 1979+	Zambia	Res. 455 (S/13645)
30 Apr. 1982+	Chad	Res. 504 (S/15013)
21 Dec. 1982+	Arabic as SC language	Res. 528 (S/15531)
28 Nov. 1986+	South Africa	Res. 591 (S/18474)
8 Aug. 1991	UN Membership (Democratic People's Republic of Korea, and Republic of Korea)	Res. 702
9 Aug. 1991	UN Membership (Micronesia)	Res. 703 (S/22896)
9 Aug. 1991	UN Membership (Marshall Islands)	Res. 704
12 Sept. 1991	UN Membership (Estonia)	Res. 709 (S/23021)
12 Sept. 1991	UN Membership (Latvia)	Res. 710 (S/23021)
12 Sept. 1991	UN Membership (Lithuania)	Res. 711 (S/23021)
21 Nov. 1991+	Secretary-General	Res. 720
12 Dec. 1991+	Cyprus	Res. 723
23 Jan. 1992	UN Membership (Kazakhstan)	Res. 732
29 Jan. 1992	UN Membership (Armenia, Krygystan, Uzbekistan, Tajikistan)	Res. 735–8
5 Feb. 1992	UN Membership (Moldova)	Res. 739
7 Feb. 1992	UN Membership (Turkmenistan)	Res. 741 (S/23523)
14 Feb. 1992	UN Membership (Azerbaijan)	Res. 742 (S/23569)
25 Feb 1992	UN Membership (San Marino)	Res. 744 (S/23634)

TABLE 12 *cont.*

Date	Subject	Res. or decision
18 May 1992	UN Membership (Croatia and Slovenia)	Res. 753–4
20 May 1992	UN Membership (Bosnia and Herzegovena)	Res. 755 (S/23974)
6 July 1992	UN Membership (Georgia)	Res. 763 (S/24231)
8 Jan. 1993	UN Membership (Slovak Republic, Czech Republic)	Res. 800, 801
7 Apr. 1993	UN Membership (the former Yugoslav Republic of Macedonia)	Res. 817
18 May 1992	UN Membership (Croatia and Slovenia)	Res. 753–4
26 May 1993	UN Membership (Eritrea and Monaco)	Res. 828, 829
8 July 1993	UN Membership (Andorra)	Res. 848
21 Oct. 1993	Appointment of Ramon Escovar-Salom	Res. 877
18 Mar. 1994#	Occupied Arab Territories	Res. 904
8 July 1994	Appointment of Richard Goldstone	Res. 936
21 Oct. 1994	International Court of Justice	Res. 951
15 Dec. 1994	UN Membership (Palau)	Res. 963[a]
9 Mar. 1995	International Court of Justice	Res. 979
22 Mar. 1995	International Court of Justice	Res. 980
7 Nov. 1995	International Court of Justice	Res. 1018

No resolutions were adopted by consensus or without a vote in the course of 1996, but forty-three out of a total of 50 resolutions were passed unanimously.

* Indicates adopted 'unanimously in the absence of objections'.

+ Indicates adopted 'by consensus'.

# Indicates resolutions adopted without a vote, when taken as a whole, but where separate votes have been taken on parts of the resolution.

[a] Note by the President: 'I would point out that, when adopting the aforementioned resolution, the Security Council decided to have recourse to the provisions of the last paragraph of rule 60 of its provisional rules of procedure in order to submit its recommendation to the General Assembly at its forty-ninth session. In accordance with rule 60, paragraph 2, of the provisional rules of procedure of the Security Council, I also request you to transmit to the General Assembly at its forty-ninth session, for its information, the verbatim records of the 3468th and 3469th meetings of the Council, at which the application of the Republic of Palau was considered.'

Whether a particular decision should be included in Table 12 or not depends on whether or not the text was put to the vote. Thus on 26 August 1969, the President of the Council (Jaime de Pinies of Spain) introduced a proposal on the Middle East which, he said, represented 'a consensus of opinion among the members of the Council'.

Without putting the proposal to a vote, he declared that the draft resolution had been adopted unanimously.[69] As there was no vote, the decision has been included in Table 12. The following year, however, a different President (George J. Tomeh of Syria) presented a text which also had 'the support of all members of the Council' and represented 'the consensus which has emerged'. The President of the Council then put the text to the vote by show of hands and it was approved *nem. con.*[70] As it was put to the vote, it is *not* included in Table 12, even though there were no negative votes.

To assess the degree of unanimity in the Council over time it is necessary to include also those resolutions where a vote *was* taken, but where it secured unanimous support (11 in favour until 1966 and 15 thereafter). Chart 2 below attempts to portray this graphically.

10. WHEN ARE DECISIONS BINDING?

The word *decision* is used in several different senses in the parlance of the Security Council, and this has occasionally made for confusion. There is, in the first place, its use in Article 27 of the Charter: 'Decisions of the Security Council . . . shall be made by an affirmative vote of seven [now nine] members.' Article 27 does not use the word in the same sense as in other Articles of the Charter which refer to decisions of the Security Council (Articles 25, 44, 48) or to the Council's power to decide (Articles 37(2), 39, 40, 41, 49). According to a report prepared in 1950,

> the term 'decisions of the Security Council' in Article 27 of the Charter refers to all types of action which the Security Council may take, whether it does so under Chapter V on procedure and organization, or under Chapter VI in relation to the pacific settlement of disputes, or whether it makes 'recommendations' or 'decisions' under Chapter VII.
>
> These observations show that the term 'decisions' *in the Charter Articles relating to voting* is used in a broad sense to cover all types of action by United Nations organs.[71]

In the *Repertoire* of Security Council practice, the word *decision* is defined as follows:

CHART 2

Council resolutions: degree of unanimity
summary chart of voting on resolutions passed in the years 1946–1996

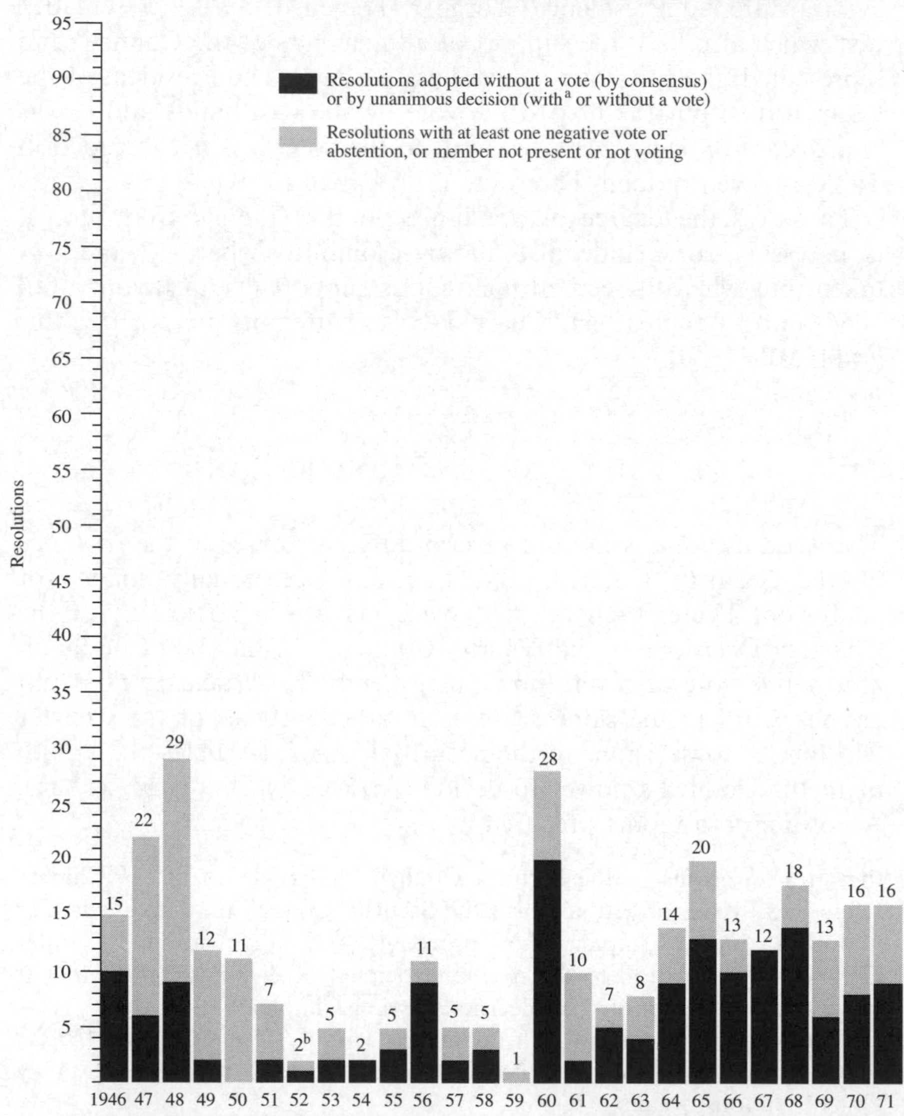

[a] With all members present and voting.
[b] No vote is recorded in the Official Records for one of these resolutions, but it has been assumed here that the vote was by consensus or adopted without a vote.

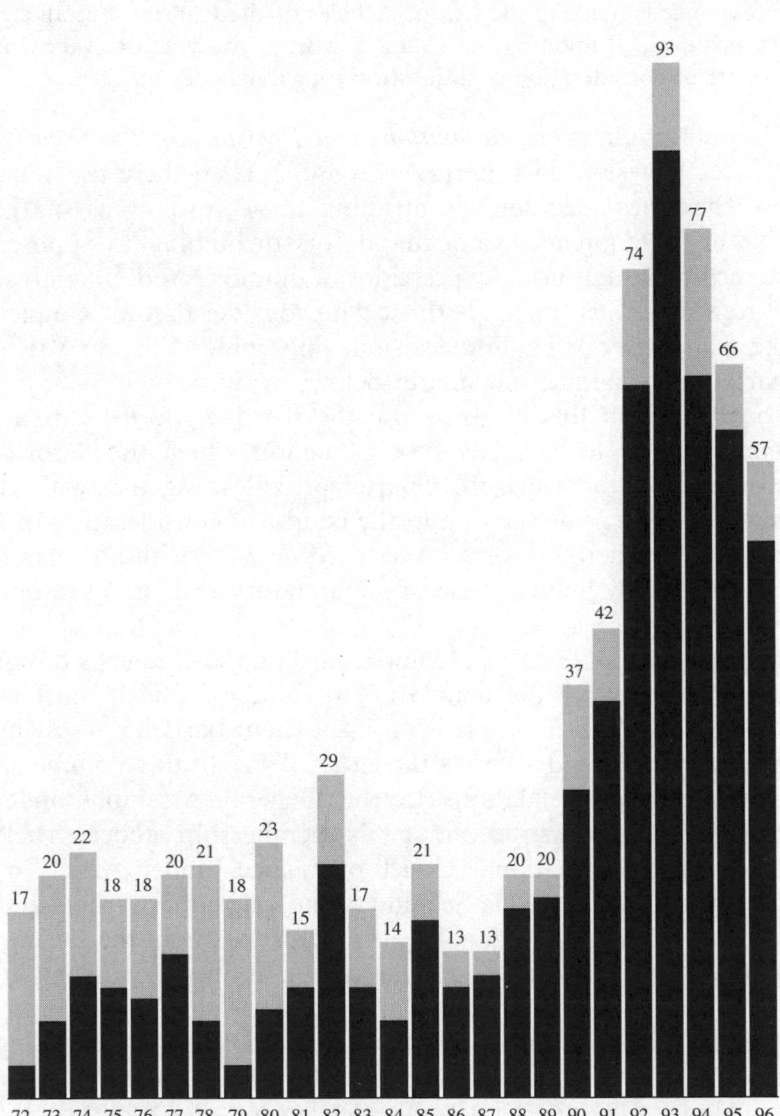
17 20 22 18 18 20 21 18 23 15 29 17 14 21 13 13 20 20 37 42 74 93 77 66 57
72 73 74 75 76 77 78 79 80 81 82 83 84 85 86 87 88 89 90 91 92 93 94 95 96

The term 'decision' has necessarily been used . . . as a technical term . . . and should be understood solely in this sense, and *not in the sense of its usage in the Charter*. These decisions include not only 'decisions' to which specific reference is made in the text of Articles of the Charter, but all significant steps decided upon by the Council, whether by vote or otherwise, in the course of consideration of a question (our italics).[72]

The annual publication, *Resolutions and Decisions of the Security Council* uses 'decision' in a narrower sense.[73] Then there are some who use the word 'decision' as meaning those resolutions of the Council which are intended to be mandatory or binding, as opposed to mere recommendations or expressions of opinion. And, to confuse the picture still further, there are those who consider that the Council can take mandatory or binding decisions only under Chapter VII of the Charter. We examine this matter below.

We have tried in this book to use the word *decision* as in the *Repertoire*, that is to say, any type of action which the Security Council may take for which the Charter provides, together with all other significant steps decided on in the course of consideration of a question; but nowhere do we use the word *decision* without qualification in the strictly limited sense of a mandatory or binding resolution.

There have been differences of view regarding the Council's power to take decisions which are mandatory or binding, and it must be admitted that the Charter alone is an insufficient basis for resolving these differences. Nobody doubts the Council's right to recommend. It may make recommendations to the General Assembly under Articles 4 to 6 of the Charter about UN membership, under Article 94(2) about the International Court of Justice, under Article 97 about the appointment of the Secretary-General, under Article 4(3) of the Statute of the International Court of Justice about the election of judges, and under Article 69 of the Statute about amendments to the Statute.

The Security Council may also make recommendations regarding a system for the regulation of armaments under Article 26 of the Charter. Under Chapter VI (Pacific Settlement of Disputes), the Council may call upon the parties to a dispute to settle it by peaceful means (Article 33(2)), recommend appropriate procedures or methods of adjustment of a dispute or a situation of like nature

(Article 36(1)), recommend such terms of settlement as it may consider appropriate if the Council deems it likely that the continuance of a dispute will endanger peace and security (Article 37(2)) or make other recommendations with a view to pacific settlement if all the parties so request (Article 38).

Under Chapter VII (Action with respect to Threats to the Peace, Breaches of the Peace, and Acts of Aggression), the Council may call upon the parties to comply with such provisional measures as it deems necessary or desirable (Article 40), make recommendations to maintain or restore international peace and security (Article 39), or call upon Members to apply non-military enforcement measures (Article 41). Under Chapter VIII, the Council may encourage the development of pacific settlement of local disputes through regional arrangements or agencies (Article 52(3)).

It is also beyond question that the Council can take internal organizational and procedural decisions under Chapter V which bind the Council itself, and has the power under Chapters VII and VIII to take decisions which are binding on non-members. Indeed, the Council has in practice taken such decisions—even though it may have lacked the means to enforce them fully. Moreover, the International Court of Justice has advised that 'it is the Security Council which, exclusively, may order coercive action'.[74] Articles 39, 41, 42, and 53(1) empower the Council to decide on measures to maintain or restore peace, and Article 49 states that Members 'shall' join in affording mutual assistance in carrying out the measures decided upon by the Council. This obligation is reinforced by the general principle stated in Article 2(5), that Members shall give every assistance in any action the United Nations takes in accordance with the Charter; and by the more specific commitment of Article 25, by which UN Members agree to accept and carry out the Security Council's decisions in accordance with the UN Charter. But it should be stressed that the absence of a specific reference to Articles 2(5), 25, or 49 does not necessarily mean that a resolution is not mandatory or binding: the Council's decision of 14 March 1968 regarding Namibia 'might be considered as containing an implied reference to Article 49', as the *Repertoire* so delicately puts it.[75] And whether or not the Council cites Articles 2(5), 25, or 49, UN Members have by Article 24 conferred on the Security Council the primary responsibility for maintaining peace, irrespective of the specific powers laid down in other parts of the Charter, and the Council has from time to time cited Article 24 or used its language to emphasize its general responsibilities.[76]

The question remains whether the Security Council can take mandatory or binding decisions under Chapter VI. In its Advisory Opinion on Namibia (1971), the International Court of Justice noted that the reference in Article 24(2) of the Charter to specific powers of the Council 'does not exclude the existence of general powers to discharge the responsibilities conferred in [Article 24(1)]'. The Court rejected the view that Article 25 of the Charter applies only to enforcement measures adopted under Chapter VII.

> Article 25 is not confined to decisions in regard to enforcement action but applies to 'the decisions of the Security Council' adopted in accordance with the Charter.*

When the Security Council adopts a decision under Article 25 in accordance with the Charter, said the Court, it is for UN Members to comply with that decision, including those members of the Council which voted against it and those UN Members which are not members of the Council. Whether the powers under Article 25 were exercised in any particular case had to be determined by reference to 'the terms of the resolution to be interpreted, the discussions leading to it, the Charter provisions invoked and, in general, all circumstances that might assist in determining the legal consequences of the resolution . . .' The Court advised that specified decisions of the Council on Namibia are 'binding on all States Members of the United Nations, which are thus under obligation to accept and carry them out'.[77]

Reflecting in 1993 on the applicability of the Advisory Opinion on Namibia to recent examples concerning Iraq and Kuwait, former Yugoslavia, Libya, Somalia, Liberia, and Haiti, Helmut Freudenschuß concludes that 'up to a point' recent practice supports the view that

> neither Article 25 nor Chapter VII as such but the will or the intention of the Security Council to take a binding decision is the decisive yardstick with which a solution has to be judged.[78]

* We wonder why the Court did not add a reference to enforcement action under Article 53(1) of Chapter VIII.

The ICJ Advisory Opinion answered part of the question posed earlier: the Council can invoke Article 25 when taking decisions under Chapter VI. But can the Council take binding decisions under Chapter VI if Article 25 is not invoked? In particular, are decisions to investigate under Article 34 'binding' on UN Members, which are thus under obligation 'to accept and carry them out'?

This question was much debated in the early days, when Western powers wished to investigate charges of Communist subversion directed against Greece. The Western view then was that UN Members were under an obligation to accept UN investigating bodies.[79] The Communist States, on the other hand, held that all decisions under Chapter VI, including decisions to investigate, are recommendations only, and that Article 25 does not apply to recommendations.[80]

When the Palestine question came before the Security Council the following year, there had been a slight but perceptible shift of emphasis on the part of Western States. The question in 1948 was not whether to investigate, because everyone knew that Palestine was aflame with fighting: the question was whether the Council should seek to restore peace by acting under Chapter VI or Chapter VII of the Charter. The United States submitted a proposal which included a determination that the situation in Palestine constituted a threat to and breach of the peace under Article 39 of Chapter VII. Argentina, Belgium, Canada, China, and the United Kingdom immediately expressed a preference for a Chapter VI resolution, since the Council had neither the will nor the means to impose a solution. But the interesting thing about the 1948 debates is that speakers took it for granted that a decision under Chapter VI would be in the nature of a recommendation while a decision under Chapter VII would be 'coercive', to use the language of the time.[81]

This interpretation was strengthened during the Kashmir debates in 1957. Krishna Menon of India repeatedly said that Chapter VI resolutions are only recommendations, and that India was bound only by those resolutions to which it had consented. If the Security Council wished to enforce its decisions, according to Menon, it must first make a determination under Article 39 in Chapter VII.[82]

Secretary-General Hammarskjold tried to stem the tide when dealing with the Congo question in 1960 and 1961. In one of its early decisions, the Security Council requested States to refrain from any action which might impede the restoration of law and order in the Congo, or the exercise by the Government of its authority, or which might undermine the country's territorial integrity and political independence. Later, the Council called upon UN Members to carry out its (the Council's) Congo decisions 'in accordance with Articles 25 and 49 of the Charter'. Hammarskjold pointed out on several occasions that the Council's decisions were 'binding', 'obligatory', and 'mandatory'.[83]

The reference to Article 49 in the second resolution cited by Hammarskjold provided a basis for claiming that the Council had acted under Chapter VII. On 21 February 1961, the Council reaffirmed previous decisions and authorized 'the use of force, if necessary, in the last resort'. Hammarskjold thereafter regarded this resolution, 'like the early resolutions on the Congo . . . as a mandatory decision . . . in accordance with Article 25 . . .' and 'binding on all Member States'; and he repeatedly stressed the resolution's 'peremptory and unconditional nature' which demanded 'prompt and unconditional implementation'.[84]

Hammarskjold put the matter in a broader context in the Introduction to his last Annual Report. Article 25, he wrote, had the effect of making decisions of the Security Council mandatory, 'except, of course, when such decisions take the form of 'recommendations' within the terms of Chapter VI or certain other articles of the Charter'. There had, however, been a tendency to regard the Council's decisions, even when taken under Chapter VII, as recommendations, binding only to the extent that the party concerned had freely committed itself to carry them out. Here was a clear dichotomy between the aims of the Charter and general political practice, he wrote. If the co-operation needed to make the Charter a living reality were not to be achieved, and if respect for the obligations of Article 25 were allowed to diminish, 'this would spell the end of the possibilities of the Organization to grow into what the Charter indicates as the clear intentions of the founders . . .'[85] But in spite of Hammarskjold's stand, it was increasingly taken for granted that the Council could take decisions binding on others only under Chapter VII. It is true that the Arab countries and the States of the Soviet bloc tried from time to time to have the famous resolution 242 on the Middle East regarded as binding. A Soviet statement in 1968 maintained that resolution 242 is not a recommendation or an opinion that Governments are free to follow or ignore. In joining the United Nations, every State has undertaken to fulfil unconditionally the decisions of the Security Council taken in accordance with the United Nations Charter.[86]

This was not the position which the Soviet Union had taken in the early post-war years. Moreover, the Western countries had also changed their minds, but in the opposite direction. Indeed, when the Council came to debate the 1971 Advisory Opinion of the International Court of Justice on Namibia, Italy took the line that it was for the Council itself to decide when its resolutions have a binding character,[87] while Britain and France took the view that the Council can take binding decisions only under Chapter VII and after an express determination under Article 39.[88]

While it had become generally accepted until a few years ago, the idea that such an express determination under Article 39 was necessary before a binding decision could be taken under Chapter VII is now under question. Helmut Freudenschuß has pointed out that in at least eight cases in the 1990s (SCR 687, 724, 771, 819, 820, 824, 833, and 844) the Council did not make such a prior determination. All of these resolutions *were* a follow-up to previous resolutions which *did* contain determination of a threat; however, Freudenschuß rejects the argument that such a prior reference makes a further determination unnecessary, and points to the lack of relevance of the sequential links between a number of the resolutions.[89]

The exponential increase in the use of Chapter VII in Council resolutions from 1990, particularly for peace-keeping operations and the imposition of sanctions, has led to shifts in the nature of the debate about Chapter VII decisions. Concerns arose from some quarters that Chapter VII was being used to take mandatory decisions on matters outside the traditional jurisdiction of the Council.

Beginning in 1990, the Council also increasingly imposed non-military sanctions against States, and even non-State entities, citing Chapter VII of the Charter or using its precise language. The end of the Cold War gave the Council greater scope to apply sanctions against violators of its decisions or challengers to its authority. Sanctions were applied against Iraq, Yugoslavia, Somalia, Libya, Liberia, UNITA in Angola, Haiti, Mozambique, Rwanda, Burundi, and Sierra Leone.

TABLE 13

Five decades of Chapter VII resolutions, 1946–31 December 1995

1946–55
54 (1948), *62 (1948), #82 (1950), #83 (1950), #84 (1950)

1956–65
*146 (1960), 161 (1961), 169 (1961), #217 (1965)

1966–75
#221 (1966), 232 (1966), 253 (1968), 277 (1968), 288 (1970), 314 (1972)

1976–85
*386 (1976), 388 (1976), 409 (1977), 418 (1977), #421 (1977), 502 (1982)

1986–95
598 (1987), 660 (1990), 661 (1990), 664 (1990), +665 (1990), 666 (1990), 667 (1990), *669 (1990), 670 (1990), 674 (1990), 677 (1990), 678 (1990), 686 (1991), 687 (1991), 689 (1991), 692 (1991), 699 (1991), 700 (1991), 705 (1991), 706 (1991), 707 (1991), 712 (1991), 713 (1991), 715 (1991), 724 (1991), 733 (1992), 743 (1992), 748 (1992), 757 (1992), 760 (1992), 770 (1992), 771 (1992), 778 (1992), 787 (1992), 788 (1992), 794 (1992), 806 (1993), 807 (1993), 813 (1993), 814 (1993), 815 (1993), 816 (1993), 819 (1993), 820 (1993), 824 (1993), 827 (1993), 833 (1993), 836 (1993), 837 (1993), 841 (1993), 844 (1993), 847 (1993), 859 (1993), 861 (1993), 864 (1993), 869 (1993), 870 (1993), 871 (1993), 873 (1993), 875 (1993), 878 (1993), 883 (1993), 886 (1993), 897 (1994), 899 (1994), 900 (1994), 908 (1994), 910 (1994), 913 (1994), 914 (1994), 915 (1994), 917 (1994), 918 (1994), 919 (1994), 923 (1994), 929 (1994), 940 (1994), 941 (1994), 942 (1994), 943 (1994), 944 (1994), 947 (1994), 949 (1994), 954 (1994), 955 (1994), 958 (1994), 967 (1994), 970 (1995), 981 (1995), 982 (1995), 986 (1995), 987 (1995), 988 (1995), 990 (1995), 992 (1995), 994 (1995), 998 (1995), 1003 (1995), 1004 (1995), 1005 (1995), 1009 (1995), 1011 (1995), 1015 (1995), 1021 (1995), 1022 (1995), 1025 (1995), 1026 (1995), 1031 (1995).

# Indicates that the resolution uses wording which contains only an implicit reference to Chapter VII.
* Indicates that the resolution refers to a specific article under Chapter VII of the Charter, but not explicitly to Chapter VII itself.
+ Recalls a previous Chapter VII resolution in its second preambular paragraph.

When are Decisions Binding?

In the first 44 years, the Security Council adopted 22 resolutions which cited Chapter VII of the Charter, or used its wording: in the next six years, 1990 to 1996, the Council adopted 107 resolutions under Chapter VII.

CHAPTER 6

RELATIONS WITH OTHER ORGANS

> An ambassador's speeches should contain more sense than words . . . He should therefore at the outset think rather of what is in their minds than of immediately expressing what is in his own.

I. MILITARY STAFF COMMITTEE

Every other Thursday or occasionally Friday, the United Nations *Journal* announces that a meeting (closed) of the Military Staff Committee (MSC) will take place that morning in Conference Room E; the 1356th such meeting was held on 3 July 1997. We may be sure that what happens at a closed meeting of a UN organ is known only to the members of the organ and the very discreet officials designated to service it, but it is no secret that meetings of the MSC now last only a few minutes, and that the only business transacted is to approve the provisional agenda and to confirm that another meeting will be held after an interval of fourteen days. If the published records are to be believed, the MSC has done little substantive work since 2 July 1948 when it informed the Council that it was unable to fulfil the mandate which the Council had entrusted to it two years previously.[1]

The functions of the MSC are laid down in the Charter as being to advise and assist the Security Council on all questions relating to the Council's military requirements for the maintenance of international peace and security; to advise and assist the Council on the employment and command of armed forces placed at its disposal, and to be responsible for the strategic direction of such forces; to assist the Council with plans for the application of armed force; to assist the Council to establish limits regarding the strength and degree of readiness of, and plans for the combined action of, national air-force contingents to be made available for urgent international enforcement action; to advise and assist the Council on all questions relating to the regulation of armaments, 'and possible disarmament'; and the MSC may, with the authorization of the Council and after consultation with appropriate regional agencies, establish such regional subcommittees as may be needed (Articles 26, 45–7).

The MSC is composed of the five permanent members of the Security Council—or, to be precise, 'the Chiefs of Staff of the permanent members . . . or their representatives'. Any UN Member which is not a member of the MSC 'shall be invited . . . to be associated with it when the efficient discharge of the Committee's responsibilities requires the participation of that member in its work' (Article 47(2)).

The Preparatory Commission evidently regarded the work of the MSC as of great importance and recommended that the provisional agenda for the first meeting of the Security Council should include an item 'Adoption of a directive to the Military Staff Committee to meet at a given place and date' and, further, that the directive should instruct the MSC 'as its first task, to draw up proposals for its organization (including the appropriate secretarial staff) and procedure, and to submit these proposals to the Security Council'. Accordingly, on 25 January 1946, the Security Council, after some mild banter initiated by Andrei Vyshinsky about the fog in London ('political and otherwise', interjected Ernest Bevin) adopted its first resolution without a vote, instructing the MSC to begin its work in London on 1 February 1946. The Council also had on its agenda an item 'Discussion of the best means of arriving at the conclusion of the special agreements [for the provision of armed forces and related facilities] referred to in the Charter (Article 43)'; but consideration of this item was in fact deferred.[2]

The MSC was not established until 4 February 1946, but it was quickly able to prepare a draft statute and draft rules of procedure. On 14 February, the MSC adjourned pending the move of the Security Council from London to New York, and the chairman transmitted to the President of the Council the two drafts.[3]

On 16 February, the Security Council took three decisions about the work of the MSC. First, it instructed the Committee of Experts to examine the MSC report (containing the draft statute and draft rules of procedure, together with a detailed commentary thereon prepared by the Secretariat). Second, it authorized the MSC to operate provisionally along the lines of its own proposals for procedure, pending the approval by the Security Council of the two drafts. Third, it requested the MSC 'as its first task, to examine from the military point of view the provisions contained in Article 43 of the Charter' (special agreements for making armed forces, assistance, and facilities available to the Security Council).[4]

The MSC resumed its work on 25 March 1946 at the Henry Hudson Hotel in New York, and a subcommittee was set up to advise on the basic principles which should govern the organization of United Nations forces; this subcommittee met for the first time on 28 March, and the five members agreed to submit in writing by 3 April 'a statement of the principles which shall govern the organization of United Nations forces . . . ' The three Western members and China met the deadline, but the Soviet Union was silent.[5] In desperation, the four other members proposed that another subcommittee should be established, and on 5 June the MSC set up a new subcommittee to study the question of preparing a draft form of special agreement concerning the provision of forces between the United Nations and Member States.

Meanwhile, the chairman of the MSC and Secretary-General Lie had engaged in a lengthy correspondence. Apparently Lie considered that the MSC, in its draft statute and rules of procedure, had not given sufficient recognition to the important responsibilities and prerogatives of the Secretary-General under the Charter.[6] The difficulties were eventually ironed out, and the MSC issued revised texts on 1 August 1946.[7] But the MSC had not come to the end of its troubles, for the Committee of Experts poured out a stream of requests for elucidation.[8] On 17 July 1947, however, the Committee of Experts issued its report on the two MSC drafts, which the Security Council had requested seventeen months earlier.[9]

On 13 February 1947, the Security Council had adopted a resolution on disarmament (the Soviet Union abstaining), to give effect to two resolutions of the General Assembly. The decision of the Security Council included a request to the MSC to submit 'as soon as possible and as a matter of urgency' the recommendations which the Council had asked for a year earlier 'and, as a first step, to submit . . . not later than 30 April 1947, its recommendations with regard to the basic principles which should govern the organization of the United Nations armed force'. The Security Council, by the same decision, set up a Commission for Conventional Armaments and asked it, *inter alia,* to 'make such proposals as it may deem desirable concerning the studies which the Military Staff Committee . . . might be asked to undertake'.[10]

As a result of the renewed request of the Security Council, the MSC issued a report on 30 April 1947, consisting of forty-one draft articles, some with alternative texts reflecting disagreements within the Committee.[11] Twenty-five articles were approved by the Security Council on a provisional basis, most of them unanimously, although a few were adopted with abstentions. But on the remainder, which concerned the most important questions, agreement was impossible, and the debate simply petered out and was never resumed. Of the sixteen articles on which agreement had not been reached, the Soviet Union was in the minority in fourteen cases, France in five, China and the United Kingdom in one each, and the United States not at all. The United States was determined to show that the Soviet Union bore the responsibility for the failure to agree, but the British Foreign Office had urged the press to take the line that the MSC report represented progress, and not to stress the failure to reach full agreement.[12]

The MSC's report was considered inconclusively during all or part of eleven meetings of the Security Council in June and July 1947. At one point, the Council decided by ten votes, with one abstention, to invite the representative of the chairman of the MSC to sit at the Council table to interpret the recommendations of the MSC. In the event the interpretation of the MSC's recommendations was undertaken in writing.[13] Meanwhile, the MSC on 16 May 1947 decided on a four-point programme of work and set up a subcommittee to examine informally the first item in the programme, namely, to establish a preliminary estimate of the overall strength and composition of the armed forces to be made available to the Security Council. On 16 June 1947, the Security Council formally asked the MSC to continue its work concurrently with the Council's consideration of the MSC report.[14] The MSC subcommittee submitted progress

6. *Relations with Other Organs*

TABLE 14

Military Staff Committee: chronology, 1946–1996

		Doc. ref.
1946		
25 Jan.	Security Council (SC) directs MSC to draw up proposals for its organization and procedure.	2nd mtg., pp. 12–14; SC res. I
4–14 Feb.	MSC meets in London	
14 Feb.	MSC transmits to SC draft statute and and draft rules of procedure.	S/10 (restricted)
16 Feb.	SC authorizes MSC to operate provisionally in accordance with its own proposals for procedure and directs it to examine Article 43 from the military point of view; sends draft statute and draft rules of procedure to Committee of Experts.	23rd mtg., p. 369
25 Mar.	MSC resumes work in New York and establishes subcommittee to consider basic principles which should govern the use of UN forces.	
9 Apr. to 24 July	Exchange of communications with Secretary-General.	
5 June	MSC establishes subcommittee to consider standard form of agreement for the provision of military forces.	
1 Aug.	MSC issues revised statute and rules of procedure.	S/115 (restricted)
1947		
13 Feb.	SC asks MSC to hasten reply to its directive of 16 Feb. 1946 and, as a first step, to report on the basic principles which should govern the organization of UN armed forces.	S/268/Rev. I/Corr. I
30 Apr.	MSC issues study of general principles governing the organization of the UN armed force.	Special supplement no. I, S/336
16 May	MSC agrees on future programme of work and establishes subcommittee to discuss informally the overall strength and composition of armed forces to be made available to the SC.	
4 June to 15 July	SC considers work of MSC	138th mtg., pp. 952–62; 139th mtg., pp. 963–87; 140th mtg., pp. 989–1002; 141st mtg., pp. 1005–20; 142nd mtg., pp. 1023–41; 143rd mtg. pp. 1053–64; 145th mtg., pp. 1066–91; 146th mtg.,

		Doc. ref.
		pp. 1094–113; 149th mtg., pp. 1157–79; 154th mtg., pp. 1266–76; 157th mtg., pp. 1294–312
16 June	SC asks MSC to continue work concurrently with SC.	141st mtg., pp. 1018–20
18–20 June	MSC clarifies Articles 5 and 6 of its report.	142nd mtg., pp. 1027, 1029–31, 1034–7; 143rd mtg., pp. 1053–4 (S/380) and 1061–2 [China, France, United Kingdom, and United States]
24 and 27 June	MSC clarifies Article 18 of its report.	145th mtg., pp. 1078, 1082–91; 148th mtg., p. 1158
25, 26, and 30 June	MSC provides estimate of overall strength of armed forces needed by SC.	146th mtg., pp. 1104, 1107–13; Supplement no. 13, pp. 133–40, S/394
30 June	Subcommittee appointed 16 May transmits progress report to MSC.	
30 June and 7 July	MSC supplies provisional estimate of forces to be supplied by permanent members of SC.	149th mtg., pp. 1175, 1178–9; 154th mtg., p. 1267
15 July	Subcommittee appointed 16 May transmits further progress report to MSC.	
17 July	Committee of Experts reports on draft statute and rules of procedure.	S/421 (restricted)
23 Dec.	Subcommittee reports to MSC on strength and composition of armed forces needed by SC.	
1948		
2 July	MSC informs SC that its deadlocked.	S/879 (mimeo.)
6 Aug.	Views of four permanent members [China, France, United Kingdom, and United States] as to reasons for deadlock.	MS/417 (mimeo.)
16 Aug.	Soviet views as to reasons for deadlock.	MS/420 (mimeo.)
1950		
19 Jan. to 26 Oct.	Soviet Union boycotts meetings of MSC.	GAOR, 5th Session Supplement no. 2, A/1361, p. 62 (MS 513); 6th session, Supplement no. 2, A/1873, pp. 98–9 (MS 556)
1990		
25 Aug.	To use, as appropriate, mechanisms of MSC to facilitate the monitoring of the implementation of UN Sanctions against Iraq.	SC res. 665 (S/21640)

reports on 30 June and 15 July 1947, and on 23 December 1947 the subcommittee returned to the MSC the task which had been entrusted to it. On 23 June 1948, the MSC completed consideration of the subcommittee's report without reaching agreement, and on 2 July the chairman of the MSC informed the President of the Security Council that the MSC was deadlocked.[15] The divergent views of the members of the MSC were expressed in two letters to the Security Council in August 1948.[16]

The MSC has continued to meet briefly every other week, although even these meetings were boycotted by the Soviet Union from 19 January to 26 October 1950, when its representatives were boycotting the Security Council because of the failure to expel Nationalist China.[17]

Proposals to resuscitate the MSC have been made from time to time,[18] but so far without much concrete result. However, in 1990 the crisis in the Gulf erupted and it appeared that the MSC might be entrusted with serious work. On 25 August 1990, during the critical period following Iraq's invasion and purported annexation of Kuwait, the Security Council held a late night meeting beginning at 3.15 a.m. The meeting passed resolution 665 (1990) which asked the MSC to co-ordinate a naval 'interdiction' against Iraq.[19] Although the resolution was supported by 13 States with only two abstentions, a number of States[20] asked to make statements before or after the vote expressing concern that the exact role of the Council and the MSC in co-ordinating the naval 'interdiction' had not been made clear in the resolution. The Soviet Union, in a more positive statement, was 'prepared to make full use of the opportunities afforded by the machinery of the Military Staff Committee'.[21]

Francis Delon reports that at the end of 1990 two or three informal meetings of the Military Staff Committee were held for the purpose of exchanging information on implementation of the provisions of Security Council resolutions 661 (1990), 665 (1990), and 670 (1990). Because of the informal character of these meetings, they were held at the Permanent Mission of France (the co-ordinator of the P5 at that time), rather than at UN Headquarters.[22] The MSC was not formally activated at this time and the command and control of operations in the Gulf remained in national hands.

The MSC can also, in theory, play an important role regarding disarmament. It is supposed to advise and assist the Security Council on all questions relating to 'the regulation of armaments, and possible disarmament' (Article 47). There are three references in the Charter to disarmament, but all three are expressed in very modest terms. The first is in the section defining the functions of the Security Council. As far as the General Assembly is concerned, it may 'consider' the general principle of co-operation in the maintenance of international peace and security, including the principles governing disarmament and the regulation of armaments' (Article 11(1)). The Security Council, with the assistance of the Military Staff Committee, shall be responsible for formulating plans for the establishment of a system for the regulation of armaments (Article 26).

2. GENERAL ASSEMBLY

The relationship between the Security Council and the General Assembly is intricate and fluid. The Council consists of a limited number of States (originally eleven, now fifteen). The Council has primary responsibility for a specific task, the maintenance of international peace and security, and Members have agreed that the Council acts on their behalf, while the Assembly has broad responsibilities and may discuss any matter within the scope of the UN Charter. Non-procedural decisions of the Council are susceptible to veto by any of the permanent members, whereas the Assembly decides important questions by a two-thirds vote without any veto. The Council may take *decisions* regarding peace and security which are binding on all UN Members; the Assembly may make *recommendations* on such matters. The Council is supposed to be so organized as to be able to function continuously, meeting when there is work to be done, whereas the Assembly convenes for a routine three-month session in September. Nowadays, in fact, the Assembly effectively remains in session throughout the year and may be reconvened at any time.

To be sure, the Assembly has some influence on the Security Council. It elects the non-permanent members of the Council (Article

23(2)), and receives from the Council annual and special reports (Articles 15(1)) and 24(3)). The Assembly may call the attention of the Council to situations which are likely to endanger international peace and security (Article 11(3)), thus paralleling the responsibilities of the Secretary-General under Article 99, and it may also make recommendations to the Council with regard to the general principles of co-operation in the maintenance of international peace and security (Article 11(1)). If any question relating to the maintenance of international peace and security is brought before the Assembly by the Council, the Assembly may discuss it and may make recommendations, except that the Charter states that the Assembly may not make recommendations with regard to a dispute or situation if the Council is exercising the functions assigned to it in the Charter in respect of that dispute or situation (Article 11(2) and 12(1)). Any question 'on which action is necessary' shall be referred by the Assembly to the Council, either before or after discussion (Article 11(2)).

The Secretary-General notifies the Assembly of matters relating to the maintenance of international peace which are being dealt with by the Council, and when the Council ceases to deal with such matters (Article 12(2)). The Assembly may meet in special session at the request of the Council (Article 20).

Significant power of the Council is derived from the fact that it addresses recommendations on specified matters to the Assembly, and in the absence of such recommendations, the Assembly is powerless to act. The Council makes recommendations to the Assembly regarding the admission, suspension, or expulsion of Members (Articles 4(2), 5, and 6), the appointment of the Secretary-General (Article 97), the conditions under which a State which is not a UN Member may become a party to the Statute of the International Court of Justice (Article 93(2)), and the conditions under which a State which is a party to the Statute of the International Court of Justice but is not a Member of the United Nations may participate in electing members of the Court and in making amendments to the Statute (Articles 4(3) and 69 of the Statute). The Security Council and the General Assembly proceed independently of one another to elect members of the Court (Article 8 of the Statute, also Articles 10–12).

(a) Elections and appointments

When it comes to those elections and appointments that are made jointly with the General Assembly, the Security Council is clearly the senior partner. It is inconceivable that the recommendations of the Council would be rejected by the General Assembly, whereas the Council has had no hesitation in disregarding recommendations of the General Assembly—concerning the veto, for example. In the early years an attempt was made by some Members to operate the United Nations along the lines envisaged by the founders, but the frequent use of the veto by the Soviet Union led to various attempts to increase the authority of the General Assembly.[23] The Assembly played a leading role from 1950 to 1955, but there then followed a period lasting until 1961 in which Secretary-General Hammarskjold was entrusted with or assumed major diplomatic and operational responsibilities. With the enlargement of the Security Council from eleven to fifteen members, which came into force on 31 August 1965, there was 'a gradual return to Charter fundamentals', as Secretary-General U Thant put it, and the Security Council in particular began 'to return to something like the original Charter concept'.[24] U Thant considered, nevertheless, that the General Assembly might regain a crucial role. In the Introduction to his final Annual Report, Thant wrote:

> The General Assembly . . . could become increasingly effective over the whole field of United Nations operations, including the maintenance of international peace and security, primary responsibility for which is vested in the Security Council . . . Any balanced and sober recommendations which it can adopt [added Thant optimistically] will surely not go unheeded even in the most powerful nations in the world.[25]

Unfortunately, powerful nations seem to find little difficulty in disregarding the General Assembly, even when the Assembly's resolutions are balanced and sober.

In the US drafts for an international organization in the early 1940s, the body which later became the Security Council was called the Executive Committee,[26] suggesting that the Security Council–Executive Committee was to *execute* policy laid down by the Assembly. Indeed, there was a tendency at one time to think of the Security Council as a kind of UN cabinet and the Assembly as a kind of legislature. Such analogies can be highly misleading, and it is probably best to think of the Security Council as *sui generis*.

(b) Annual and special reports

The draft Charter at San Francisco included an Article to the effect that the Security Council should issue annual reports, and special reports as needed. The delegates were generally in favour of this, but questions were raised as to the destination of such reports and, consequently, what form they should take. It was quickly agreed that the reports, both annual and special, should go directly to the General Assembly. Some delegations thought that the purpose of sending reports to the Assembly was simply 'for information', while others thought that they were for action in support of the Security Council and especially in support of what became Articles 41 and 42 on enforcement measures. This was part of the general conflict between those who wanted to reduce the role of the Security Council and those, particularly the permanent members, who believed that such a policy would render the UN impotent and ineffective. Eventually it was decided that the reports were 'for its [the General Assembly's] consideration' (Article 24(3)). There was then inserted in the Chapter dealing with the General Assembly a linking Article to the effect that the Assembly would 'receive and consider' reports of both kinds (annual and special), and the reports would include 'an account of the measures that the Security Council had decided upon or taken to maintain international peace and security'. From the beginning, the title of the report has included the words 'to the General Assembly' and it is issued as Supplement no. 2 of the Assembly's official records (Article 15(1)). The procedure for handling the reports in the General Assembly has to be understood in light of the fact that the Security Council acts on behalf of all UN Members (Article 24(1) and that Members have agreed to accept and carry out the decisions of the Security Council in accordance with the Charter (Article 25).

The basic format of the report has remained unaltered. Part 1 provides a summary of the proceedings of the Security Council concerning its responsibilites for maintaining international peace and security. Part 2 deals with 'other matters', such as UN membership, the appointment of the Secretary-General, and the Council's responsibilities regarding the election of members of the International Court of Justice. Part 3, merely six lines in length, states blandly that the Military Staff Committee has functioned continuously under its draft rules of procedure, held a total of 'x' meetings (27 in 1995–6) and remains prepared to carry out the functions assigned to it under the terms of Article 47. Part 4 deals with matters brought to the attention of the Council but not discussed. The report's appendices now include listings of the members of the Council, the names of accredited representatives and alternates, the President of the month, meetings of the Council and subsidiary organs, resolutions adopted, Council statements and communications, and the list of matters of which the Council is seized. Originally speeches delivered in the Council were summarized, but in December 1974 the Council decided to make its report shorter and more concise, so that the names of representatives are now simply listed. The Council reaffirmed in 1985 that the report should be shortened, but with little immediate success. The report's size grew steadily during the early 1990s, from 176 pages in 1990 to 552 pages in 1994, only to finally come down in size in 1995 (337 pages) and 1996 (303 pages), in large part due to changes in the font and formatting of the report. The details of the revisions made to the report have been previously described in Chapter 2 Section 13.

The annual report of the Security Council to the General Assembly is drafted by the Secretariat and circulated in draft form to Council members. Proposed amendments to the report are usually raised in informal consultations prior to the formal adoption of the report at (since 1993) a public meeting of the Council. Until recently, the Council's report was usually placed on the General Assembly's agenda as a matter of routine, and the Assembly took note of it without discussion. An earlier exception to this was at the Assembly's twenty-sixth and twenty-seventh sessions, in 1971 and 1972, when the Assembly sought the views of Member States on ways of enhancing the effectiveness of the Council.[27] The assembled views were relayed to the Council at the Assembly's twenty-eight session.[28]

The rapid growth in Council activity from 1989 to 1993 (from 20 resolutions in 1989 to 74 in 1992 and 93 in 1993) was coupled with an increased reliance on informal consultations, to which non-members of the Council were not admitted. Non-members felt excluded at a time when Council decisions, such as the economic effects of Council mandated sanctions,[29] were affecting many States. The report of the Council to the Assembly soon became a suitable occasion for this frustration felt by States to be expressed. Matters were made worse when the report covering the period 16 June 1991 to 15 June 1992 was not prepared in time for consideration by the Assembly during the main part of its regular session. This delay infuriated a number of delegations and after finally debating the report in June of 1993, the Assembly agreed to have a substantive debate on annual reports to the Assembly by the other principal organs.[30] From 1993 onwards the occasion of the presentation of the report of the Council became an important opportunity for Members to raise issues concerning the respective competencies and responsibilities of these two principal organs. The ensuing annual debates raised two sets of issues, those related directly to the format, content, and timing of the report, and those related more broadly to recent developments in the procedure and practice of the Council. We examine briefly below the four most recent annual reports, and the thematic issues of the report's format and Council transparency that permeated the General Assembly debates.

(i) The annual report for 1992–3

The report of the Council for the period 16 June 1992 to 15 June 1993 *was* prepared on time for the main part of the forty-eighth session of the General Assembly, and in a new innovation was introduced orally by the Council President Ambassador Sardenberg of Brazil. Ambassador Sardenberg began by describing the recommendations recently implemented by the Council following the recommendations of its informal working group on documentation, established in June 1993. These included the fact that the draft report of the Council would no longer be issued as a confidential document, and would be adopted at a public meeting; inclusion of the provisional agendas of meetings of the Council in the *Journal*; and the distribution of the informal monthly forecast of the Council's programme of work to all Member States.

(ii) The annual report for 1993–4

The report for 1993–4 contained a seven-page introduction and a four-page summary dealing with steps taken by the Council on documentation and related matters. The report itself, 552 pages in length, became available on 24 October 1994[31] only two days before the matter was scheduled for consideration by the Assembly. Informal representations were made to the Assembly's President by the non-aligned group, leading to a re-scheduling of the Assembly's programme of work, and following the precedent set by Ambassador Sardenberg, the report was introduced by the Council President, Sir David Hannay of the United Kingdom, on 31 October.

Sir David introduced the report with a review of steps the Council had recently taken to improve communication with non-members. Since March 1994, draft resolutions in their 'blue' form were made immediately available for non-members; the first informal presidency briefing for non-members on the current work of the Council took place on 27 October 1994; and steps had been taken to enhance consultations with troop-contributing countries regarding peace-keeping operations.

The report's reception was similar to that of the previous year on the subject of its format and contents, but more upbeat on wider procedural developments. Many more Western States contributed to the debate than in 1993, particularly on peace-keeping consultations. Concerns were raised by some States over the way in which they saw the Council 'broaden, arbitrarily, the definition of what constitutes a threat to international peace and security'.[32] Whereas the 'constant recourse to Chapter VII of the Charter' was seen as 'excessive and disproportionate'.[33]

(iii) The annual report for 1994–5

Ambassador Salim Bin Mohammed Al-Khussaiby of Oman introduced the Council's report for the period 1994–5. He enumerated five developments in Council practice that had arisen during that period. First, the Council had acknowledged that it would have increased recourse to open meetings at which to hear the views of all UN Members on important matters. The first such meeting was held in

January 1995 on the report of the Secretary-General, 'Supplement to An Agenda for Peace'. Second, briefings on the work of the Council to non-members by the Presidency following informal consultations had now become established practice. Third, in March 1995 the Council had agreed a number of measures to increase the transparency of the Sanctions Committees. Fourth, the Council had introduced new procedures for consultation with troop-contributing countries, following an initiative by Argentina and New Zealand. Fifth, the Council had continued to review and remove items from the list of matters of which the Council is seized.

While positive about many of initiatives taken to improve Council transparency and working methods, there were numerous calls for the extension and institutionalization of these measures. It was argued that orientation meetings had not become the established part of Council practice as envisaged in presidential statement S/PRST/1994/81, and that meetings with troop-contributors were 'consultative only in name'.[34]

(iv) The annual report for 1995–6

The report was introduced by Ambassador Wisnumurti of Indonesia. Rather confusingly he combined speaking both as President, and in the capacity of his delegation, expressing satisfaction with the increased use of orientation debates by the Council, and his delegation's hopes for the introduction of the 'long-awaited practice of allowing interested States that are not members of the Council to participate in informal consultations'.[35]

The reactions of a number of States to the report, especially those of the Non-Aligned Movement, focused on the issues of transparency, principally for informal consultations of the whole, and for the meetings of Sanctions Committees. In particular a number of delegations gave support to a Czech proposal for a new interpretation of Article 31 of the Charter to allow for the participation of non-members of the Council in informal consultations when questions affecting them were being considered by the Council.

Issues relating to the format of the report and the transparency of Council decision-making have appeared consistently each year that the Assembly has had an opportunity to debate the annual report of the Security Council. We outline below some of the arguments expressed, and potential difficulties arising in their implementation.

(v) Reflections on the format of the report

As might be expected Member States viewed the occasion of the annual presentation of the report as a means of increasing Council 'accountability' to the Assembly, under the provisions of Articles 15 and 24 of the Charter. Each year a number of States called for fundamental changes to the format and content of the report. Malaysia and others[36] took issue with the description of the purpose of the report contained in its introduction:

> [the Report] is intended not as a substitute for the records of the Security Council, which constitute the only comprehensive and authoritative account of its deliberations, but as a guide to the activities of the Security Council during the period covered.[37]

The function of the report as 'a mere diary'[38] of the Council's activities and decisions was rejected; instead it should 'provide the means for Member States to assess its actions and, where necessary, respond or make appropriate recommendations'.[39] A number of specific suggestions were made to make the report more analytical and less purely enumerative. The report should include an analytical summary of discussions on each substantive issue considered by the Council, embracing both Council meetings and informal consultations of the whole.[40] It should reflect the information conveyed orally by Secretariat officials to the Council, and the text of letters between the President of the Council and the Secretary-General, when these are not published as official UN documents.[41] The report could be modelled on the report of the Secretary-General on the work of the Organization, contain explanations of its decisions, and account for its actions or inaction.[42] The report should be supplemented by the monthly issuance of special reports during the year,[43] it should account for the experiences of UN operations in Bosnia, Somalia, Rwanda, and elsewhere,[44] it should also address the work of the Council's ten subsidiary bodies.[45]

A brief reference to Sanctions Committees in the introduction to the report was a small contribution to the last of these requests, but the fundamental demand for more analysis has continued to go unrequited. Anticipating criticism in 1996 the Indonesian ambassador on introducing that year's report expressed the view of his delegation that the lack of analysis was an inherent feature of such a report. He added that 'It is hard to believe that 15 members of the Security Council would agree a common understanding and interpretation of the Council's endeavours'.[46] Indeed there is the fundamental practical problem of *whose* analysis would be used. Members of the Secretariat currently prepare the draft annual report, and are able to do so because the report is almost entirely a compilation of existing public documents. Attempting an analysis of, for example, why the Council used particular language in a specific resolution, is likely to face enormous hurdles. Council resolutions and other decisions are frequently the fruits of laboured negotiations, with the resultant text reflecting numerous political trade-offs and nuances. There is no simple method of introducing 'neutral' analysis of State motivations into the report. The consequence of this is that while the report in its present form provides an *occasion* for UN Members to raise concerns about the work of the Council over the previous 12 months, it does very little to *facilitate* the raising of such concerns.

On 12 June 1997 a Presidential Note was issued following a further review of the format of the annual report of the Council to the General Assembly, by the members of the Council. This Note is reproduced as Appendix X (f).

The Note reported that members were agreed upon a number of changes that would take effect in the report covering the period 16 June 1997 to 15 June 1998. Future reports would include appendices containing the full text of resolutions, decisions, and presidential statements adopted or voted upon by the Council, and information about meetings with troop-contributors. They would also contain factual data, including the dates of formal meetings and informal consultations at which a subject was discussed. The most significant innovation was that there would be attached, as an addendum to the report, brief assessments on the work of the Security Council, which representatives who had completed their functions as President of the Security Council might wish to prepare. Such assessments would carry a disclaimer that they should not necessarily be considered as representing the views of the Security Council.

(vi) Reflections on Council transparency

Each year that the report of the Council has been publicly considered by the Assembly, concerns have been raised by non-members over the extent to which discussion and decision-making has mainly taken place in closed informal consultations, leaving formal meetings as short *pro forma* occasions. Algeria commented that 'a balance must be found between the use of informal consultations, the usefulness of which cannot be questioned, and the duty adequately to inform the international community in whose name the Council acts'.[47] Problems arise, however, not just over what sort of balance should be struck, but also which measures would really improve Council transparency. To begin with, the meaning of transparency is unclear. The representative of Djibouti commented that 'In one sense, perhaps, that which is least transparent is the meaning to be attached to transparency itself. There may be as many meanings of transparency as there are Members of the United Nations.'[48] Moreover, measures intended to improve transparency may not produce the intended results. One frequently cited proposal is for non-members to be given greater access to attend consultations of the whole. The danger of this proposal is that discussion of confidential matters would be driven into more secretive and informal fora. On the positive side, non-members may glean more information on less confidential matters through attending such consultations than at present. On the other hand such a development would further institutionalize consultations of the whole, and make it likely that Council deliberations would more routinely take place in consultations rather than formal meetings. This would in turn reduce the scrutiny that could be placed on Council decision-making by the public, the media, and scholars. From this perspective there would be a reduction in transparency. Moreover, while certain non-members may gain more information from consultations, this information would not be public, and therefore of little use to those States who seek to increase the 'accountability' of the Council to the General Assembly through a more public airing of the arguments of Council members for and against particular decisions of the Council.

(c) Threats to peace and security

Article 11(3) of the Charter empowers the Assembly to call the attention of the Security Council to situations which are likely to endanger international peace and security. If the Assembly refers a matter to the Council, it need not expressly invoke Article 11(3).

A significant implied use of Article 11(3) was the Assembly's decision of 29 November 1947 on the Palestine question.[49] The Assembly directed three matters to the Council:

(a) to take the necessary measures for implementing the plan for the future government of Palestine;
(b) to consider whether the situation in Palestine constituted a threat to the peace;
(c) to determine that any attempt to alter by force the settlement envisaged in the Assembly's decision would constitute a threat to the peace, breach of the peace, or act of aggression.

Under Article 11(1), the Assembly may make recommendations to the Security Council (or to UN Members, or to both) with regard to 'the general principles of co-operation in the maintenance of international peace and security, including the principles governing disarmament and the regulation of armaments'. An example of a recommendation with regard to the general principles of co-operation directed by the Assembly to the Security Council is to be found in part of a resolution of 28 April 1949 recommending the appointment of a rapporteur or conciliator when a situation or dispute is brought before the Council. The Security Council noted the Assembly's decision and decided to base its action upon the principles contained in it, should an appropriate occasion arise.[50] Recommendations of the Assembly bearing upon the principles governing disarmament and the regulation of armaments were addressed to the Council in the early years,[51] but would now be addressed to the disarmament negotiating body in Geneva.

Article 11(2), which has to be read in conjunction with Articles 10 and 12(1), empowers the Assembly to make recommendations to the Council (or to the State or States concerned, or to both) with regard to any questions relating to the maintenance of international peace and security. 'Any such question on which action is necessary shall be referred to the Security Council by the General Assembly either before or after discussion.' Article 10 empowers the Assembly to make recommendations to the Council (or to UN Members, or to both) on any questions or matters within the scope of the Charter or relating to the powers and functions of any organ provided for in the Charter.

On the face of it, Article 12(1) states a limitation on the Assembly's right to recommend, in that while the Security Council is 'exercising in respect of any dispute or situation the functions assigned to it in the . . . Charter', the Assembly shall not make any recommendation with regard to that dispute or situation unless the Council so requests. This raises questions about the meaning of such phrases as 'while the Security Council is exercising . . . the functions assigned to it' and 'on which action is necessary', as well as the more general question of the relationship between the extensive responsibilities of the Assembly and the 'primary' responsibility of the Council concerning the maintenance of international peace and security. Let us examine some of the Charter expressions.

The Secretary-General, with the consent of the Security Council, shall notify the General Assembly at each session of any matters relative to the maintenance of international peace and security which are being dealt with by the Security Council and shall similarly notify the General Assembly . . . immediately the Security Council ceases to deal with such matters (Article 12(2)).

The intention at San Francisco was to give a role concerning world peace to both the Council and the Assembly, though the Council's responsibility was to be 'primary', and the duties carried out under that responsibility were to be undertaken on behalf of all UN Members. Both the Security Council and the Assembly were given broad powers of discussion; both organs were given the right to make recommendations; but when it came to taking binding decisions in order to maintain or restore world peace, the task was laid squarely on the Council.

In order to avoid a situation in which both organs might act simultaneously but inconsistently on the same matter, the Secretary-General was to notify the Assembly of matters 'being dealt with' by the Council. This Notification is in practice based on the Summary Statement prepared by the Secretary-General under Rule 11, but some items are excluded from the Notification as they are not considered to relate directly to the maintenance of international peace and security. The Notification has correspondingly been reduced in size as the Council has introduced procedures to cut down on the list of items in the Statement prepared under Rule 11.

In 1946 and 1947, the consent of the Council required by Article 12(2) was given at formal meetings. Since 1947, the consent has been obtained through the circulation by the Secretary-General of a draft. Since 1951, the Notification has had two main categories: matters discussed by the Council since the previous Notification, and other matters of which the Council remains seized. The Notification also contains a note of any items which have been deleted from the list of matters of which the Council was seized during the period under review. Although Article 12(2) requires the Secretary-General to inform the General Assembly or UN Members 'immediately' the Council ceases to deal with a matter relating to peace and security, this is done through circulation of Addenda to the Notification, as required.

The General Assembly may discuss any questions or any matters . . . (Article 10). The General Assembly may discuss any questions . . . (Article 11(2)).

The Assembly clearly has very wide powers of discussion. When the Council was discussing China's complaint that the United States was preventing the liberation of Taiwan in September 1950, the Republic of China opposed discussion on the ground that much the same item was on the agenda of the General Assembly. The Soviet Union argued (quite correctly) that nothing in the Charter was designed to forbid *discussion* of the same question simultaneously in the Council and the Assembly. The United States admitted that the situation was complicated, promising nothing but confusion; but as to the procedure to be followed, the United States was willing to have the charges against it heard in either or both organs. The Council then twice rejected a paragraph in draft resolutions submitted by Ecuador which would have noted that a similar complaint was being considered by the Assembly.[52] It is a fair deduction from the language of the Charter, from opinions of the UN Legal Counsel,[53] and from practice by the Council and the Assembly, that the simultaneous *discussion* of the same matter by the Council and the Assembly is not forbidden, even if it may sometimes be imprudent.

General Assembly

The General Assembly . . . may make recommendations with regard to [questions relating to the maintenance of international peace and security] . . . to the Security Council . . . While the Security Council is exercising in respect of any dispute or situation the functions assigned to it in the . . . Charter, the General Assembly shall not make any recommendation with regard to that dispute or situation unless the Security Council so requests (Articles 11(2) and 12(1)).

We must first examine the words 'while the Security Council is exercising . . . the functions assigned to it . . . ' If the Council deletes an item from the list of matters of which it is seized, or decides to defer consideration of a question, then the Council is not exercising the functions assigned to it. A similar situation arises if the Security Council expressly asks the Assembly to take up a matter. But what is to be done if the Council neither deletes an item from the list of matters with which it is seized, nor defers consideration, nor expressly brings a matter to the attention of the Assembly?

A sensible interpretation of the Charter was expressed by Mexico as long ago as 1946:

> If [an] item is kept on the agenda, and if the Security Council is to exercise the functions assigned to it, some kind of action will be necessary; but merely to keep something . . . on the agenda is not to take action, and therefore not to exercise a function.[54]
>
> It seems to us that when the Security Council is not engaged in the study of a problem or in its solution, when it has not taken any interim measures . . . but is merely leaving the matter on its agenda . . ., then . . . it is not fitting to regard such procedure as constituting the continuous exercise of the Council's functions within the meaning of Article 12.[55]

This common-sense interpretation of Article 12(1) has allowed the Assembly to make recommendations regarding such matters as Tunisia, South Africa, Angola, and other Portuguese territories in Africa, Southern Rhodesia, and Namibia (South West Africa). Indeed, the UN Legal Counsel noted in 1964 that 'the General Assembly, beginning in 1960, adopted several resolutions clearly containing recommendations in cases of which the Security Council was then seized and . . . in none of these cases . . . did a member object to the recommendation on the ground of Article 12. Nevertheless, [continued the Legal Counsel], it would be difficult to maintain that it [Article 12] is legally no longer in effect'.[56] And in 1968, the Legal Counsel advised:

The General Assembly has interpreted the words 'is exercising' as meaning 'is exercising at this moment'; consequently, it has made recommendations on . . . matters which the Security Council was also considering.[57]

Any . . . question [relating to the maintenance of international peace and security] on which action is necessary shall be referred to the Security Council by the General Assembly (Article 11(2)).

This expression inevitably led to a good deal of contention during the period when the Security Council, hindered by the threat or use of the veto, was eclipsed by the Assembly. The problem was epitomized in part of the 'Uniting for Peace' resolution of 1950.[58] Much that was in that resolution should have raised no difficulty: the Assembly is fully within its rights in establishing procedures for meeting at short notice, for example, or in recommending that the permanent members of the Security Council should discuss problems likely to threaten world peace. But it was the intention of the sponsors of the 'Uniting for Peace' resolution that, if the Security Council should be unable to fulfil its primary responsibility for world peace, the Assembly should be entitled to recommend enforcement measures.

Our understanding of the Charter and of UN practice is that, while the responsibility of the Council is primary, it is not exclusive: the Assembly has a residual or secondary concern for world peace. If peace is imperilled, and if the Council should fail to act, the Assembly is entitled both to discuss the matter and to *recommend* enforcement measures 'to the Members . . . or to the Security Council or to both', as Article 10 has it, but not to *order* them.

From the beginning, the United Kingdom and the United States have regarded 'action' in Article 11(2) as meaning enforcement action. In 1962, the International Court of Justice advised that 'action' refers to 'coercive or enforcement action'; the word 'action' must mean 'such action as is solely within the province of the Security Council'.[59]

(d) Special sessions of the General Assembly

Under Article 20, the Security Council may convoke special sessions of the General Assembly. According to Rule 8 of the Assembly's

Rules of Procedure, special sessions of the Assembly convoked by the Council (or by UN Members) shall be convened within fifteen days, emergency special sessions within twenty-four hours.

When the Security Council, by procedural vote, refers a matter to the General Assembly, it is implicitly admitting its failure to discharge fully its primary responsibility for world peace, and acknowledging that the Assembly should now exercise its secondary role. But the fact that a matter has been referred by the Council to the Assembly does not of itself eliminate the constitutional constraints under which the Assembly has to operate and, in particular, the fact that the Assembly cannot take *binding* decisions to maintain world peace.

(e) Subsidiary organs established by the General Assembly

Certain subsidiary organs established by the Assembly have played a part in the work of the Council, either because they have been placed by the Assembly in a special relation to the Council or because the Council has made use of the services of a subsidiary organ or invited its officers to participate in debates.

Some of these subsidiary organs are still active (Relief and Works Agency for Palestine Refugees in the near East, the Committee on the peaceful uses of outer space, Committee on the exercise of the inalienable rights of the Palestinian people).

(f) Action relating to UN membership

The admission, suspension, or expulsion of Members is effected by 'the General Assembly upon the recommendation of the Security Council' (Articles 4(2), 5, and 6). The Assembly has always taken a 'liberal' attitude to applications for membership and has periodically chided the Council for failing to recommend the admission of applicants.[60]

Under Rule 60, the Council is to transmit to the Assembly within specified time limits a record of its discussion of each application. If the Council does not recommend admission, or postpones consideration, it is to transmit also 'a special report'. In practice, a favourable recommendation is accompanied by any report of the Council's

Committee on the Admission of New Members; in case of a failure to recommend admission, the Council's special report lists the applicants, how they were included in the agenda of the Council, an indication of the position of members of the Council, and the Council's decision on each application.

In no case has the Council discussed or recommended the suspension of any Member from the exercise of the rights and privileges of membership after preventive or enforcement action has been taken against the Member, or the expulsion of any Member for persistently violating Charter principles. In the case of the Federal Republic of Yugoslavia the Council recommended that it should apply for membership in the United Nations and that it should not participate in the work of the General Assembly. The UN Legal Counsel clarified that this did not amount to suspension under Article 5 or expulsion under Article 6 (see Chapter 3). Withdrawal from the United Nations is not provided for in the Charter, but Indonesia decided to discontinue active participation in the work of the United Nations during 1965 and part of 1966, and in 1965 Pakistan warned the Security Council that if it failed to secure an equitable and honourable settlement in Jammu and Kashmir, 'Pakistan will have to leave the United Nations.'[61]

Indonesia's withdrawal from active participation in the work of the United Nations was ostensibly caused by the election of Malaysia as a non-permanent member of the Security Council on 29 December 1964, to serve a one-year term in place of Czechoslovakia. President Sukarno had accused Malaysia of neo-colonialism, and Indonesia stated that it was taking the 'revolutionary' step of withdrawing because of the fact that Malaysia ('this feeble and highly controversial new 'State') had been elected to the Security Council was a violation of the Charter, and also in the hope that the act of withdrawal would become 'the catalyst to reform and retool the United Nations'.[62]

Secretary-General Thant held private consultations with members of the Security Council and 'heads of regional groups', and then circulated an informal *aide-mémoire* about 'some practical effects of the Indonesian letter' (e.g. removal of the Indonesian flag from outside the Headquarters building). Thant sent a letter to Indonesia expressing 'profound regret' at Indonesia's action and looking forward to a resumption of co-operation by Indonesia; Malaysia claimed that its election to the Security Council was neither illegal nor improper nor in any other way questionable; the United Kingdom insisted that Indonesia's withdrawal was not justified and did not relieve it from honouring 'the fundamental principles embodied in Article 2 of the Charter relative to the maintenance of international peace and security'; while Italy pointed out that the Charter made no provision for withdrawal.[63] Czechoslovakia and the Soviet Union used the occasion to point out that splitting the two-year term for membership of the Security Council between Czechoslovakia and Malaysia had 'unlawfully' deprived Eastern Europe of the place in the Security Council 'which by right belongs to the socialist countries'.[64]

Sukarno lost effective power in Indonesia in 1965, and on 19 September 1966, Indonesia decided 'to resume full co-operation with the United Nations'. The Office of Legal Affairs in the UN Secretariat advised Thant that if UN Members were in general willing to interpret Indonesia's action as a cessation of co-operation rather than withdrawal from the United Nations, the Secretary-General could take the necessary administrative action for Indonesia to participate again in UN proceedings. Indonesia's Foreign Minister conferred with the Secretary-General and the President of the General Assembly on 22 September, and on 28 September the General Assembly agreed without objection to Indonesia's return to the fold.[65]

(g) Financing peace-keeping operations

The question of financing peace-keeping operations which have been launched by the Security Council would require a book in itself if it were to receive thorough treatment. In Sydney Bailey's book on the General Assembly, he reviewed the difficulties over paying for the first UN Emergency Force in the Middle East and for the Congo operation.[66] The problem of paying for UN peace-keeping has arisen mainly from the unwillingness of some States to pay for operations to which they have had a political objection. When the Yemen Observation Mission was being discussed, the Soviet Union maintained that the financial aspects were the responsibility of the Security

Council, even though the parties themselves were meeting the expenses; and the Soviet Union abstained when the Council voted to establish the Mission. When the Council established the Force in Cyprus, the Soviet Union expressly pointed out that the resolution 'imposes no financial obligations on Members of the United Nations who contribute no contingents to those forces'. When the Observer Mission for India and Pakistan was created, the Soviet Union again emphasized that 'only the Security Council' was competent to decide on financing.[67]

Thus when the Council came to re-establish a UN Emergency Force for the Middle East in 1973, it was clear that difficulties would be avoided only if the Security Council were to play a crucial role in decisions about financing. Ambassador Yakov Malik repeated the Soviet position of principle about the authority of the Security Council, and when it was suggested that the entire cost of the Force should be borne by the two superpowers, he remarked acidly that, on the contrary, the aggressor should pay. In spite of the fact that the authorizing resolution contained no reference to finance, the Soviet Union voted in favour 'by way of an exception and in this particular instance' out of respect for the Non-Aligned Members of the Council and Egypt. China did not participate in this or several other votes on the Middle East.[68] Reflecting the earlier concerns of the Soviet Union over peace-keeping financing, on 11 May 1993 the Russian Federation vetoed a draft resolution on financing peace-keeping in Cyprus: sixteen days later, the Russian Federation cast a favourable vote on a draft resolution much like the one that had failed on the previous occasion.[69]

The issue of financing is complicated because of the different UN organs which have established field missions and the different systems for meeting the expenses of them. Observer groups have been established by internal decisions of the UN Secretariat. The first major peace-keeping operation was launched by decision of the General Assembly (the UN Emergency Force in Sinai, 1956). The standard practice now, however, is for the Security Council to initiate peace-keeping operations.

The expenses of observer missions have been met by assessed contributions from the regular UN budget. One peace-keeping operation (Yemen, 1963–4) was paid for by the parties. Part of the cost of two other operations (UNFICYP in Cyprus (all until 15 June 1993), and UNIKOM in Iraq/Kuwait) are currently financed by special contributions.

(h) Election of non-permanent members of the Security Council

The General Assembly is entrusted with the responsibility of electing the non-permanent members of the Security Council. Could the Assembly bring the work of the Council to a halt simply by refusing to elect, so that the Council would not be properly constituted?

The UN Office of Legal Affairs has advised that the General Assembly should continue balloting until the result required by the Charter is achieved: 'the obligation of the Assembly in this regard is absolute and mandatory.' A Security Council of less than fifteen members would not be legally constituted, but this would not affect the functioning of the Council. The failure of the General Assembly to fulfil its constitutional obligations cannot be held to produce legal consequences so fundamental to the United Nations as the paralysis of a principal organ. The Council should continue to function notwithstanding the fact that it would not be legally constituted.[70]

3. ECONOMIC AND SOCIAL COUNCIL

Although Article 65 of the Charter provides that the Economic and Social Council (ECOSOC) may furnish the Security Council with information and shall assist the Security Council upon its request, there is little direct connection between the two bodies. Both organs may deal with self-determination and other aspects of human rights, ECOSOC being required by the Charter to promote these goals because they are necessary for peaceful and friendly relations, the Security Council being called on to deal with situations in which their denial leads to friction or endangers world peace. ECOSOC may also consider problems relating to refugees or war victims arising from matters which are within the competence of the Security Council.[71] In 1972, the President of the Economic and Social Council, after consulting the Vice-Presidents, sent a *note verbale* to the

Secretary-General stressing the 'close connection and a positive interrelationship' between matters within the purview of the Security Council on the one hand and economic and social development on the other.[72] There was some slight overlap between the two bodies in implementing the Security Council's policy of sanctions against the illegal regime in Southern Rhodesia. In 1973, the Security Council asked the Economic and Social Council 'to consider periodically the question of economic assistance to Zambia'.[73] When the Security Council met in Panama City later in 1973, it adopted a resolution urging States 'to adopt appropriate measures to impede the activities of those enterprises which deliberately attempt to coerce the Latin American countries'.[74] The 1992 report of Boutros-Ghali to the Security Council, 'An Agenda for Peace', highlighted the concept of post-conflict peace-building and emphasized the need to 'address the deepest causes of conflict: economic despair, social injustice and political oppression',[75] and throughout his term of office he reiterated the importance of the relationship between peace and development. In 1995 Boutros-Ghali attempted to breathe life into the use of Article 65 and suggested that the Economic and Social Council 'might introduce a flexible high-level inter-sessional mechanism in order to facilitate a timely response to evolving socio-economic realities'. Such a mechanism could provide the Security Council with 'reports on situations in the economic and social areas, which, in its opinion, constitute threats to international peace and security'.[76]

There have been a number of proposals from independent observers of the UN system for the establishment of an Economic and Social Security Council to review the threats to global economic security and agree on necessary action.[77] Many States, however, oppose the diminution of the role of the Bretton Woods institutions that such a proposal would entail.

In the 1990s the Security Council became involved in various matters which had a bearing on the work of ECOSOC, and in particular one of its subsidiary bodies, the Commission on Human Rights. The Centre for Human Rights provided secretariat assistance to a number of electoral assistance missions established by the Security Council, and certain peace-keeping operations were given a human rights monitoring role as part of their mandate. The perceived 'encroachment' of the Security Council into these areas was not welcomed by all States, and we have already described in Chapter 3 how objections were raised to formal presentations being made to the Council by UN Human Rights rapporteurs appointed by the Commission on Human Rights.

4. TRUSTEESHIP COUNCIL

Although the Trusteeship Council has been suspended, we nevertheless include a historical section on the past relationship between the Trusteeship Council and the Security Council here, if for no other reason than that in theory territories may in the future be voluntarily placed under the trusteeship system, as envisaged in Article 77(1)(c) of the Charter.

When the United Nations was established there were intended to be two links between the Security Council and the Trusteeship Council, one relating to trust territories designated as or including strategic areas and the other arising from the fact that permanent members of the Security Council were also permanent members of the Trusteeship Council. The Security Council also had to deal with the fact that one territory formerly held under the mandate system of the League of Nations (Namibia) had not been placed under UN trusteeship.

1. Article 77 of the Charter lists categories of territories which 'may be placed' under trusteeship, and Article 82 provides that any trust territory may be designated 'a strategic area or areas'. The approval of the terms of trusteeship agreements for strategic trust territories, as well as their alteration or amendment, was the responsibility of the Security Council, whereas for ordinary trust territories, this responsibility was to be exercised by the General Assembly assisted by the Trusteeship Council. The Security Council, rather than the General Assembly assisted by the Trusteeship Council, was supposed to exercise 'all functions of the United Nations' relating to strategic trust territories.

Only one administering authority designated a trust territory as a strategic area: the United States so designated the Pacific Islands,[78] formerly administered by Japan under League of Nations mandate and taken by the United States during and after the Second World War. In February 1947, the United States submitted to the Security Council a draft trusteeship agreement for the Pacific Islands which, after amendment, was unanimously approved by the Council.[79] On 15 November 1947, the Security Council asked the Committee of Experts to advise how the Council should exercise its functions regarding strategic trust territories.[80] On 7 March 1949, the Security Council approved a proposal by which the Trusteeship Council was asked to exercise the supervisory functions specified in Articles 87 and 88 of the Charter relating to the political, economic, social, and educational advancement of the inhabitants of strategic trust territories, and to submit to the Security Council its reports and recommendations thereon. The Secretary-General was asked to advise the Security Council of all reports and petitions.[81]

The first report of the Trusteeship Council on the Pacific Islands was submitted to the Security Council on 22 July 1949, and annually thereafter, until the territory achieved the objectives of the trusteeship system.

2. The question of the composition of the Trusteeship Council arose from two provisions of the Charter which eventually proved incompatible: that the membership of the Trusteeship Council should be equally divided between Members administering trust territories and Members which do not, and that the five permanent members of the Security Council should also be permanent members of the Trusteeship Council (Article 86(1)(b) and (c)).[82] The first provision had been proposed at San Francisco by the United States, the second by the Soviet Union.[83] The balance of membership between administering and non-administering members was to be maintained by elections by the General Assembly.

It does not seem to have occurred to anyone at San Francisco that the objective of 'self-government or independence' might eventually be achieved for some territories and that this would complicate the problem of constituting the Trusteeship Council, but this possibility was raised by the United Kingdom later in 1945. If a State ceased to be an administering authority, commented the United Kingdom, it would lose its membership of the Trusteeship Council and, in order to maintain parity of membership, the result would be to displace one of the members elected by the General Assembly. If, however, the administering authority happened to be also a permanent member of the Security Council, the effect would be to displace *two* elected members.[84]

France and Italy ceased to be administering members in 1960, Belgium in 1962, and New Zealand and the United Kingdom in 1968. This left the Trusteeship Council composed of two administering members (Australia and the United States), four permanent members of the Security Council not administering Trust Territories (China, France, the Soviet Union, and the United Kingdom), and no members elected by the General Assembly. Parity of membership had vanished.

3. The only territory under League of Nations mandate which was not brought within the UN trusteeship system was South West Africa (Namibia). South Africa, the administering authority, informed the General Assembly in 1946 that a majority of the inhabitants of the territory desired its incorporation into South Africa. Thus began a conflict between South Africa and UN organs about the present and future status of the territory. Initially, the problem concerned the General Assembly and the International Court of Justice, but in 1968, the question of South Africa's 'continuing defiance . . . of the authority of the United Nations and its complete disregard for world opinion' was referred to the Security Council.[85]

Two years earlier, the General Assembly had decided to terminate South Africa's mandate over South West Africa,[86] but the States with the will to expel South Africa from the territory did not have the means to do so. In 1968, the Security Council condemned South Africa for refusing to comply with the General Assembly's decision, and later in the year censured South Africa for its defiance of the United Nations by disregarding the earlier resolution of condemnation.[87] The following year, the Security Council went a stage further by formally recognizing that the General Assembly had terminated the mandate of South Africa over the territory. The Council continued to concern itself with the matter,[88] until 1989 when the territory achieved the goal of the trusteeship system and, in 1990, UN membership.

All the territories placed under trusteeship had achieved independence by 1976 except for the Pacific Islands administered by the United States. The Marshall Islands and the Micronesian Federation (the Caroline Islands other than Palau) attained independence in 1991. The mandate entrusted to the United States of America as the Administering Power for the last trust territory, Palau, came to an end with the entry into force of a Compact of Free Association between Palau and the United States. Palau became a Member of the United Nations shortly afterwards in 1994.[89] With Palau's accession to independence, the Trusteeship Council had successfully completed the task entrusted to it under the Charter with respect to those territories placed under the Trusteeship Council following the Second World War. The founders of the Charter appear not to have contemplated that the trusteeship system would eventually discharge its responsibilities, and thus it did not automatically cease to exist in 1994. Instead, in anticipation of Palau's independence, the Trusteeship Council decided to adopt a number of amendments to its Rules of Procedures so that it no longer needed to meet regularly.[90] France, as President of the Trusteeship Council in November 1994, pointed out that these procedural modifications would allow the Trusteeship Council to continue operating with very little cost to the Organization, whilst avoiding changes to its statute that might close doors in the future.[91]

In 1995 Malta put forward a proposal to the General Assembly to 'transform the Trusteeship Council into a body that safeguards the interests of future generations by enhancing its mandate to include the common heritage of mankind'.[92] Malta advocated 'granting to the [Trusteeship] Council a role in . . . promoting human rights and safeguarding peoples in situations of complete breakdown of the State'[93] as well as addressing environmental issues. After consideration the General Assembly called for States to submit written comments on the future of the Trusteeship Council by 30 June 1996.[94] There was no unanimity in the views submitted by States. Lesotho and Sweden advocated variants of Malta's proposal, suggesting that the Trusteeship Council be given a mandate over the global commons. The United States suggested that the Council be eliminated using the same procedure as that adopted for the deletion of the Charter's 'enemy States' clauses. Jamaica, Malaysia, the United Arab Emirates, and Zimbabwe agreed with the US that the Council should be abolished. Pakistan wanted to retain the Council, as did Norway which saw little 'to gain from abolishing the Council through a formal amendment of the Charter. Rather a rationalization of administrative procedures may be considered in order to avoid unnecessary meetings and reports.'[95]

5. INTERNATIONAL COURT OF JUSTICE

The Security Council is involved in six functions relating to the International Court of Justice, three of them in conjunction with the General Assembly.

1. The Security Council and the General Assembly together elect the judges (Article 8 of the Statute of the Court);
2. The Council lays down the conditions under which the Court shall be open to States which are not parties to the Statute (Article 35(2) of the Statute);
3. The Council makes recommendations to the General Assembly regarding the conditions under which each State which is not a Member of the United Nations may become a party to the Statute of the Court (Article 93(2));
4. The Council makes recommendations to the General Assembly regarding the conditions under which a party to the Statute which is not a Member of the United Nations may participate in electing the members of the Court and in making amendments to the Statute (Articles 4(3) and 69 of the Statute);
5. The Council may request the Court to give an advisory opinion on any legal question (Article 96(1));
6. The Council may recommend that the parties to a legal dispute should refer it to the International Court of Justice (implied in Articles 33 and 36).

The qualifications of the judges are set out in Articles 2, 3, and 9 of the Statute of the Court; the method of nomination in Articles 4(1) and (2), and 5 to 7; and the procedure for election in Articles 4(3), 8, and 10 to 14, supplemented by Rules 40 and 61 of the Provisional Rules of Procedure of the Security Council and Rules 151 and 152 of the Rules of Procedure of the General Assembly. The judges are elected by both the Security Council and the General Assembly, but the two organs 'proceed independently of one another'. It is laid down in the Statute that 'an absolute majority of votes' is required in both organs, and the practice has always been to interpret the words 'absolute majority' as meaning a majority of the qualified electors, whether or not they vote.[96] In the election of members of the Court a majority of the members of the Security Council is sufficient to take a decision. No distinction is made between permanent and non-permanent members, so there is no veto.

There is a procedure set out in the Statute for a joint conference of members appointed by the Security Council and the General Assembly if 'after the third meeting' one or more seats still remain unfilled.[97] When the Council came to hold the first election in 1946, there was some uncertainty as to the precise meaning of 'meeting'. The United Kingdom and China considered that 'at each meeting it is the duty of the electing board to produce a complete list'. The Soviet Union, the Netherlands, Mexico, and France held that a meeting meant simply a ballot or vote; and this was also the view of the President of the Assembly, who had been invited to address the Security Council. In a 'meeting' which began at 10.30 a.m. and lasted, with suspensions, until 11.38 p.m., the Council held four ballots, although making it clear that this should not be regarded as a precedent. The meaning of 'meeting' was resolved the following year when the Council approved a new rule to the effect that a meeting should 'continue until as many candidates as are required for all the seats to be filled have obtained in one or more ballots an absolute majority of votes'.[98]

The procedure of election is complicated, and often lengthy. Judges are to be elected regardless of their nationality, from among persons of high moral character who possess the qualifications required in their respective countries for appointment to the highest judicial offices or are juriconsults of recognized competence in international law. The electors are to bear in mind not only that the persons to be elected should individually possess the qualifications required, but also (the somewhat archaic language of the Charter states) that in the body as a whole the representation of the main forms of civilization and of the principal legal systems of the world should be assured. The Court consists of fifteen members, no two of whom may be nationals of the same State. Judges serve for nine years, the term of five judges expiring every three years,[99] except where a judge is elected to replace a member whose term of office has not expired. In this situation a judge shall serve for the remainder of his or her predecessor's term. This was the case in the election of the first female judge elected to the Court, Rosalyn Higgins (United Kingdom). Judge Higgins was elected on 12 July 1995 to serve until 5 February 2000, that period being the remainder of the term left vacant by the resignation of Judge Sir Robert Yewdall Jennings.[100]

When the Security Council comes to elect judges, the members indicate the candidates for whom they wish to vote by placing crosses on the left-hand side of the ballot papers. Each member of the Council may vote for not more than five candidates on the first ballot, and on later ballots for five minus the number who have already received absolute majorities. Except in the case of a deadlock, when a special procedure applies, the only candidates eligible for election are those whose names appear in the list of candidates prepared by the Secretary-General. The General Assembly decided in 1960 that its general rule providing that ballots be restricted to the candidates who obtain the greatest number of votes in unrestricted ballots did not apply to elections to the Court.[101]

If, in the first ballot, less than five candidates receive an absolute majority, a second ballot is held, and balloting continues in the same meeting until five candidates receive the required majority. When this occurs but not until this time, the President of the Security Council notifies the President of the General Assembly of the names of the five candidates who have received an absolute majority. Such notification is not, however, communicated to the Assembly until the Assembly has itself given five candidates an absolute majority of votes. If, upon comparison of the two lists, less than five candidates have received an absolute majority of votes in both bodies, the Council and the Assembly proceed, again independently of each other, in a second meeting, and if necessary a third meeting, to elect candidates by further ballots for the remaining vacancies, the procedure continuing until both organs have elected five candidates.[102]

If, after the third meeting, one or more seats are still unfilled, the Council and the Assembly may at any time, at the request of either body, form a joint conference consisting of six members, three appointed by each body. This joint conference may, by an absolute majority, agree upon a candidate for each seat still vacant and submit the name for the approval of the Council and the Assembly. A joint conference may, if the decision is unanimous, submit the name of a candidate not included in the list of nominations, provided the candidate fulfils the required conditions. If a joint conference is satisfied that it will not be able to procure an election, those members of the Court already elected proceed, within a period fixed by the Security Council, to fill any vacancies by selection from among those candidates who have obtained votes in the Council or in the Assembly. In the event of a tied vote, the eldest judge has a casting vote.[103]

This is complicated enough, but there is one further difficulty; imagine a situation in which more candidates receive 'an absolute majority of votes' in the Security Council than there are seats to be filled. If there are five vacancies, the members of the Council can between them cast seventy-five votes, and thus nine candidates can secure eight votes each, more than an absolute majority.

This is not just a theoretical possibility. In 1951, at a time when the Security Council was composed of 11 members and an absolute majority constituted six or more votes, five judges had to be elected. The first six candidates in the first ballot, with the number of votes they obtained, were as follows:

G. H. Hackworth (United States)	11
S. A. Golunsky (Soviet Union)	9
H. Klaestad (Norway)	8
Enrique Armand Ugon (Uruguay)	7
Benegal Rau (India)	7
Charles de Visscher (Belgium)	7

The President evidently realized in advance that difficulties might arise, and before the ballot was taken, he stated: 'If more than five candidates obtain an absolute majority, the President will decide upon the procedure to be followed.' When it became apparent that this had indeed occurred, the President suggested that there were four possible courses:

1. The Council might simply communicate to the General Assembly the names of the six candidates obtaining an absolute majority of votes;
2. The Council might consider as elected the three top candidates with 11, 9, and 8 votes respectively and ballot again for the other two places, voting being restricted to the next three candidates, who had received seven votes each;

3. The Council might consider the three top candidates elected and ballot again for the other two places, *all persons nominated being eligible* except the three already elected;
4. The Council might start again by conducting a completely new vote on all the candidates.

After some discussion and a short suspension of the meeting, the President ruled that course 1 was incompatible with the Statute, and this ruling was not challenged. The Council next considered a proposal formally submitted by India 'that the Security Council awaits the receipt of the result of the ballot in the General Assembly before it takes a vote again on this matter'. This proposal was rejected, two votes being cast in favour, four against, with five abstentions. Further discussion ensued, and then the Council decided by nine votes to one, with one abstention, to adopt the last of the President's four proposals. The Council accordingly conducted a new ballot, and only five candidates secured the required majority:[104]

Enrique Armand Ugon	9
G. H. Hackworth	9
H. Klaestad	9
Benegal Rau	8
S. A. Golunsky	7

A similar situation arose in 1954, and the Council followed the precedent of 1951. Three ballots produced absolute majorities for six candidates, and so were of no effect; the fourth ballot produced an absolute majority for only four candidates, who were declared elected; a fifth ballot produced an absolute majority for one more candidate.[105]

In 1963, the problem arose once again, but this time there was an added element, as one of the candidates eliminated (Fouad Ammoun of Lebanon) had, on the first ballot, received more votes than two of the candidates finally elected.[106]

Messrs. Forster, Gros, and Padilla Nervo had the same support throughout; Zafrulla Khan increased his vote by one on the second ballot; and Sir Gerald Fitzmaurice did the same on the third. Although Fouad Ammoun had received the third highest vote on the first ballot, he lost ground on each subsequent ballot.

TABLE 15

Voting on six of the ten candidates for the International Court of Justice, 1963

	Votes obtained on ballot no.				
	1	2	3	4	
Fouad Ammoun (Lebanon)	7	6	5	3	
Sir Gerald Fitzmaurice (United Kingdom)	7	7	8		elected on 3rd ballot
Isaac Forster (Senegal)	6	6	6	6	elected on 4th ballot
André Gros (France)	8	8	8		elected on 3rd ballot
Luis Padilla Nervo (Mexico)	9	9	9		elected on 3rd ballot
Muhammad Zafrulla Khan (Pakistan)	6	7	7		elected on 3rd ballot

Lebanon was considerably put out by the whole affair. It described the procedure followed in 1963 as incorrect, unjust, undemocratic, and illogical; and it not unnaturally commented that it had led to 'a surprising result'. Lebanon asked whether a revision of the procedure might not be the subject of an item for the following session of the General Assembly, and suggested also that the conformity of the procedure with the Statute of the Court might have to be determined by an advisory opinion of the Court. No formal proposal was submitted, however.[107]

In 1965, the Egyptian judge, Abdel Hamid Badawi, died before his term of office was completed and Fouad Ammoun was elected in his place.[108] In 1966, twenty ballots were needed in the Security Council before five candidates received sufficient votes. There then followed a complicated discussion as to whether the meeting should be suspended or adjourned while the General Assembly completed its task. The Council was first suspended for an hour and then, after further debate, adjourned. The following day, three more ballots were needed before five candidates had been elected by both the Security Council and the General Assembly, one candidate who had received a majority on the first ballot in the Council being eliminated.[109]

No special difficulties arose in 1969, 1972, or 1975, but fourteen ballots were needed in 1978. In 1981, there was some confusion because the votes of three candidates were miscounted on the first ballot, and more than six weeks were to elapse before the record was set right. Fortunately, this muddle did not affect the result.[110] In 1981–2 the Security Council, after receiving advice from the Legal Counsel, left a casual vacancy unfilled beyond the time limit specified in Article 5(1) of the Statute.[111] In 1982, when filling another casual vacancy, the Council decided not to count the votes until balloting had been completed in both the Council and the General Assembly.[112] In 1984, five candidates were elected by simultaneous votes in the Security Council and the General Assembly; in the subsequent election, 1987, four candidates were elected on the first ballot, and one more on the second ballot, in 1990 the election was straightforward but required three rounds of voting.

The election in 1993 was exceptional in two respects. First, the President of the Council for the month in which the election took place was also a candidate for election to the Court. Mr José Luis Jesus (Cape Verde) announced that 'after fully considering the exceptional circumstances of this case' he would cede the Presidential Chair under Rule 20 of the Provisional Rules of Procedure, for the duration of the election.[113] Second, the voting in the Council and the Assembly produced different results. The first ballot in the Council produced five candidates with the required majority of votes:

Carl-August Fleischhauer (Germany)	15
Shigeru Oda (Japan)	15
Jiuyong Shi (China)	15
Geza Herczegh (Hungary)	13
José Luis Jesus (Cape Verde)	9

Abdul G. Koroma (Sierra Leone)	3
Samuel K. B. Asante (Ghana)	2
Alexander Yankov (Bulgaria)	2
Rodger M. A. Chongwe (Zimbabwe)	1

The result of the ballot was forwarded to the General Assembly and after almost four hours of consideration the Assembly announced the result of its own balloting. Five candidates had received an absolute majority of votes in the Assembly: Messrs Fleischhauer, Herczegh, Oda, Shi, and Koroma who had only obtained 3 votes in the first round of Council balloting. After announcing the election of the four candidates on which the Council and the Assembly were both agreed, the Security Council voted again on just Mr Jesus and Mr Koroma (the other remaining candidates having withdrawn). In the ballot Mr Jesus received 9 votes and Mr Koroma 6 votes. The Assembly took another ballot and reported again that Mr Koroma had received 'an absolute majority of votes in the General Assembly'. The President of the Council then announced that 'the balloting in the Security Council and the General Assembly has yielded different results',[114] and that the Council would proceed to a third meeting on the item. After a five-minute adjournment the President announced that Mr Jesus had withdrawn from the election and Abdul G. Koroma was elected unanimously by the Council, and subsequently by an absolute majority in the Assembly, to the remaining vacant seat on the Court.[115]

In 1995 the Council took four rounds of voting to fill a casual vacancy. In round one Mr Luigi Ferrari Bravo (Italy) topped the list with six votes, with Mr Pieter Hendrik Kooijmans (Netherlands) second with five. The order was reversed in round two with Mr Kooijmans obtaining 7 votes to Mr Ferrari Bravo's 6. Mr Ferrari Bravo went back into poll position with seven votes to Mr Kooijmans's six in round three, and went on to obtain the required eight votes in a fourth round of voting.

In 1996 the UN secretary General circulated a version of his standard memorandum[116] setting out the procedure to be followed in the conduct of the election, and the relevant part of this memorandum is reproduced as Appendix V of this book. The 1996 election resulted in 4 candidates being elected on the first ballot, no candidate obtaining the required eight votes in the second ballot and one candidate obtaining exactly eight votes in a third ballot.[117]

Under Articles 36 to 38 of the Charter, the Security Council may make recommendations regarding the pacific settlement of disputes. Article 33(1) mentions judicial settlement as one of the means open to the parties, and Article 36(3) states that legal disputes should 'as a general rule' be referred by the parties to the International Court of Justice. From time to time, members of the Security Council have suggested that a matter be referred to the Court,[118] but only in two cases has the Security Council expressly recommended that a dispute should be referred to the International Court of Justice.

Two British naval vessels had been damaged by mines in the Corfu

Channel on 22 October 1946, and forty-four sailors had been killed and forty-two injured. The United Kingdom held Albania responsible and requested an apology and compensation. As Albania's response was unsatisfactory, the United Kingdom took the matter to the Security Council.

A British proposal to find that Albania had laid an unnotified minefield in the Corfu Strait was vetoed by the Soviet Union, whereupon the United Kingdom proposed that the Council should recommend that the parties should refer the dispute to the International Court of Justice. The second British proposal was approved by the Council, Poland and the Soviet Union abstaining and the United Kingdom, as a party to the dispute, not participating in the vote. The President of the Council pointed out that, although Albania was not at that time a Member of the United Nations, it had accepted the obligations of membership as contained in the Council's invitation to Albania to participate in the discussion of the case, and that consequently Albania was 'obliged to comply with the provisions of both the Charter and of the Statute of the International Court of Justice.'[119]

In its judgment of 9 April 1949, the Court found that Albania was responsible under international law for the explosions which had occurred in Albanian waters and for the consequent damage and loss of life, and was under a duty to pay compensation. The Court found that the United Kingdom had not violated Albanian sovereignty by sending ships through the Strait, but that the subsequent minesweeping operation by the United Kingdom was a violation of Albanian sovereignty. On 15 December 1949, the Court found that compensation was due to the United Kingdom. In this case Article 94(1) of the Charter required compliance with the Court's decision.

The second case in which the Security Council recommended that a matter be referred to the Court concerned the cluster of issues between Greece and Turkey, including Cyprus. The Council invited the two governments 'to continue to take into account the contribution that appropriate judicial means, in particular the International Court of Justice, are qualified to make to the settlement of any remaining legal differences'.[120] The parties did not, in the event, take up the suggestion.

If a party to a case fails to perform the obligations incumbent upon it under a judgment, Article 94(2) of the Charter permits the other party to have recourse to the Security Council. The Council, if it deems necessary, may 'make recommendations or decide upon measures to be taken to give effect to the [Court's] judgment'.

The United Kingdom did not invoke Article 94(2) in the Corfu Channel case; but in the Anglo-Iranian Oil Company case in 1951, the United Kingdom implicitly invoked Article 94(2) of the Charter as well as Article 41(2) of the Statute of the Court, under which the parties and the Security Council are to be given notice of any provisional measures which ought to be taken to preserve the respective rights of either party, pending 'the final decision'.

On 20 March 1951, the Iranian Parliament had nationalized the oil industry. As a consequence of this action, the United Kingdom instituted proceedings against Iran in the International Court of Justice, requesting the Court to indicate interim measures of protection. This the Court did on 5 July 1951 by an Order indicating measures which were to be reciprocally observed.[121] The United Kingdom maintained that by this Order the Court had implicitly recognized the accuracy of the British contention that the actions of the Iranian authorities threatened to bring the production and refining of oil to a standstill, endangering life and property. Iran, however, declared that the Court lacked competence and that its Order was invalid. Iran then ordered the expulsion of the remaining staff of the Anglo-Iranian Oil Company, whereupon the United Kingdom asked the Security Council to consider the matter 'as one of extreme urgency'.[122]

The matter was debated in six meetings of the Security Council in October 1951 and then adjourned pending a decision of the Court on its own competence.[123] On 22 July 1952, the Court declared that it lacked jurisdiction, the British judge (Sir Arnold McNair) concurring.

Several contentious cases before the Court have related to issues with which the Security Council was seized. In 1973, Pakistan instituted proceedings against India regarding 195 Pakistani prisoners of war whom India proposed to hand over to Bangladesh for trial as war criminals. India held that the Court had no jurisdiction in the matter. Pakistan eventually asked the Court to discontinue proceedings.

In the Fisheries Jurisdiction cases between Britain and Iceland and the Federal Republic of Germany and Iceland, the Court made

Orders on 17 August 1972 indicating interim measures of protection to prevent an aggravation or extension of the disputes pending the Court's final decisions. In the Nuclear Tests cases between Australia and France and New Zealand and France, the Court similarly made Orders on 22 June 1973 indicating interim measures of protection. Iceland and France failed to comply with these Orders. Neither the United Kingdom nor the Federal Republic of Germany in the Fisheries Jurisdiction cases, and neither Australia nor New Zealand in the Nuclear Tests cases, complained to the Security Council that Iceland and France respectively had failed to comply with the provisional measures of protection indicated by the Court.

In the case of the US diplomatic hostages in Iran, the Court held that diplomatic immunity was an essential prerequisite for relations between States. Iran was in violation of the rules of general international law, should release the hostages, restore the embassy premises to the United States, and make reparation. The case was finally resolved as a result of Algerian mediation.

In 1984, Nicaragua instituted proceedings against the United States regarding alleged US responsibility for military and paramilitary activities against Nicaragua. The United States held that the Court lacked jurisdiction and, on 18 January 1985, announced that it would not participate in further proceedings. The Court delivered its judgment on 27 June 1986, largely supporting the Nicaraguan case. Nicaragua then called for an emergency meeting of the Security Council to consider US aggression, and a non-aligned draft resolution ran into a US veto on 31 July. On 17 October, Nicaragua asked the Council to consider US non-compliance with the judgment of the Court. A draft resolution calling for full compliance with the Court's judgment was vetoed by the United States on 28 October 1986.[124]

The most contentious recent case involving the Court was what is now referred to as 'the *Lockerbie* case'. The case had its origins in the bombing of a US civilian aeroplane (Pan Am flight 103) over Lockerbie in Scotland in 1988. After a number of investigations the Lord Advocate of Scotland and a Grand Jury of the United States charged and indicted two Libyan nationals, Abdelbaset Ali Mohamed Al Megrahi and Al Amin Khalifa, of complicity in the bombing. Libya then went to the ICJ arguing that the acts alleged constituted an offence under the 1971 Montreal Convention, and that the UK and US were in breach of the convention by virtue of the pressure they were placing on Libya to surrender the two Libyan nationals for trial. On this premiss Libya asked the Court on 3 March 1992 to indicate provisional measures that the UK and US should cease and desist from threats and further action against Libya.

The Court opened its hearings on the request for the indication of provisional measures on 26 March 1992, with the President of the case declining to use his discretionary powers under Article 74(4) of the Rules of the Court to call upon the parties to the dispute to act in a way which would not prejudice any future Order on provisional measures. Five public sittings of the Court followed on 26, 27, and 28 March with both parties presenting oral arguments on the request for the indication of provisional measures.

On 31 March 1992 the Security Council adopted resolution 748 (1992) under Chapter VII of the Charter, imposing aviation, diplomatic, and military sanctions on Libya, on the basis of Libya's failure to co-operate over the implementation of resolution 731 (1992) of 21 January 1992. Libya had questioned the legality of this original resolution on the grounds that it was acting in full compliance with the requirements of the Montreal Convention (to which Libya, the UK, and US were all parties). In response to resolution 748 (1992) the Court invited the parties to submit their views on the legal implications of the resolution for the case before the Court. After receiving these views the Court emphasized that it was not called upon to give a definitive judgment of the legality of resolution 748 (1992), but that nevertheless 'whatever the situation previous to the adoption of that resolution, the rights claimed by Libya under the Montreal Convention cannot now be regarded as appropriate for protection by the indication of provisional measures'.[125] The Court also found that the obligations of States under Article 103 of the UN Charter prevailed over their obligations under any other international agreement, including the Montreal Convention, and that all States were obliged to accept and carry out the decision contained in resolution 748 (1992) in accordance with Article 25 of the Charter.[126] The Court thus 'found that the circumstances of the case were not such as to require the exercise of its powers under Article 41 of the Statute to indicate provisional measures'.[127] We support the view expressed by Vaughan Lowe (in the *Cambridge Law Journal*) that the Court acted correctly in coming to this conclusion since a mere application to the Court should not be enough to prevent the Security Council from exercising its proper functions. Lowe further argued that the Council was at fault in this case since resolution 748 (1992) 'changed the rules in the middle of the game'[128] by disregarding the provisions of the Montreal Convention, and that it was 'not self-evident that the Security Council was right in determining that there was a threat to international peace and security at the time of the adoption of resolution 748 (1992)'.[129]

The 'intervention' of the Council in this case raises issues of the respective roles of Council and Court, and in particular the perennial issue of 'quis custodiet ipsos custodes?' in relation to Security Council action. If the Council is the final arbiter of what is defined as a threat to international peace, and it can make mandatory demands of UN Members to take action it deems necessary to address breaches of the peace, is there any means by which a State might challenge the legality of a Council decision? Furthermore, if there *is* to be the facility of appeal to international legal processes, can this be designed so that it does not prevent the Council from carrying out its functions?

Much has been written on the lessons from *Lockerbie* for the question of judicial review,[130] and more generally about the desirability and feasibility of a mechanism of judicial review *per se*.[131] We will not repeat these writings here, save to say that despite the practical obstacles to its realization, we believe that a form of judicial review could and should be introduced, and that this could bolster rather than diminish the authority of the Council. While Council resolutions must enjoy at least a presumption of validity so that an application to the Council cannot automatically paralyse the work of the Council, there is still room for a review of the constitutional validity of a resolution in certain circumstances.[132] This viewpoint has been espoused by Mohammed Bedjaoui, a former President of the ICJ, who has argued that a form of judicial review of Council acts, whilst presently at a rudimentary stage in both concept and implementation, would provide a firmer foundation for the full exercise of the responsibilities of the Security Council under the Charter:

> Nobody should deny the right of international political organs, especially the Security Council, to the full exercise of their individual powers to interpret the Charter in their activities from day to day, and to take their

decisions in the light of their own interpretation. Nobody should deny, on the other hand, that a member State has a right to challenge a decision and to have its reservations duly recorded. *It is merely hoped that, where questions arise which are deemed important on account of their repercussions for peace, that very importance will not be seized upon as a reason for forgetting that what it calls for is not so much a release form the bondage of rules as a firmer anchorage in law.* Such situations call for an agreed effort to make room for a judicial verification of legality. (Italics in original)[133]

Boutros-Ghali saw the General Assembly playing a key role in this regard. In his often overlooked report, 'An Agenda for Democratization', presented to the General Assembly on 20 December 1996, and effectively his last major conceptual contribution before leaving office, he reflects that:

The General Assembly should not hesitate to draw upon [Article 96] in referring to the Court questions concerning the consistency of resolutions adopted by United Nations bodies with the Charter of the United Nations.[134]

6. NON-GOVERNMENTAL ORGANIZATIONS

When the Council had completed the third reading of the Provisional Rules of Procedure, an Appendix was approved for dealing with communications from private individuals and non-governmental bodies. A list of communications relating to matters of which the Security Council is seized was to be circulated to all representatives on the Security Council, and a copy of any communication on the list should be given to any representative on the Council at his request.[135] Rule 39 states that the Council may invite a member of the Secretariat, or any other person whom it considers competent for the purpose, to supply it with information or give other assistance in examining matters within its competence. The Council thus has a recognized procedure for dealing with written or oral communications. No difficulties have arisen about this matter at public meetings of the Council.

It will be seen from Appendix VIII, listing the communications received by the Security Council between 1 November 1996 and 31 December 1996, that the communications in a typical sample related to a variety of issues (13) and that three of them carried more than one signature.[136]

At a meeting convened by the Secretariat, three international NGOs briefed, *inter alia,* members of the Council on the humanitarian situation in the Great Lakes Region of Africa in February 1997 at the initiative of Ambassador Somavía of Chile. (See Chapter 2.8). There may be other ways in the future by which the Council could benefit from the expertise of NGOs.

7. APPOINTMENT OF THE SECRETARY-GENERAL

The procedure for appointing the Secretary-General is based on Article 97 of the Charter, which states that the Secretary-General shall be 'appointed by the General Assembly upon the recommendation of the Security Council', supplemented by Rule 48 of the Rules of Procedure of the Security Council and Rule 142 of the Rules of Procedure of the General Assembly. In theory, the Security Council might interpret the Charter as permitting the recommendation of *several* candidates for the post, leaving the final choice to the General Assembly. The General Assembly, at one of its earliest meetings, approved a recommendation of the Preparatory Commission to the effect that it would be 'desirable for the Security Council to proffer one candidate only', and the Security Council has followed that practice.[137] No candidate recommended by the Security Council has been rejected by the General Assembly.

The Preparatory Commission also proposed that any recommendation to the General Assembly regarding the appointment of the Secretary-General should be discussed and decided at a private meeting, and this was approved by both the Security Council and the General Assembly.[138] After a private meeting of the Security Council, a *communiqué* is issued giving information as to the stage reached in considering the recommendation to be made to the Assembly.[139] The Assembly has recorded the view that any vote in the Security Council recommending a candidate to the General Assembly should be by secret ballot, and the Council has followed this practice.[140]

The names of a number of possible candidates for first Secretary-General were discussed informally in January 1946, and it soon became apparent that the only name which was acceptable to both the United States and the Soviet Union was Trygve Lie of Norway, who had just been defeated by Paul-Henri Spaak of Belgium for the Presidency of the first session of the General Assembly. On 29 January, the Security Council unanimously endorsed a US proposal that Lie should be recommended for appointment, and this recommendation was approved by the Assembly.[141] The General Assembly accepted a suggestion from its President that the ballot should be in public meeting rather than in private; and all subsequent appointments have been made in public meetings. Members of the Assembly conduct the ballot by voting either in favour of or against the recommendation of the Security Council. Decisions are by simple majority of the Members present and voting, unless the Assembly determines otherwise.

After the Assembly has appointed the Secretary-General, a formal ceremony of installation takes place. The Secretary-General takes the oath of office and immediately assumes his title and functions.

Trygve Lie's five-year term of office was due to expire on 1 February 1951, and his initial intention was to 'honestly oppose any plan for continuing . . . in office'. Accordingly, he announced on 16 December 1949 that he was not a candidate for reappointment. By then, he had received informal intimations that the Soviet Union wished him to serve a second term, and later he received similar assurances from the United States. It was Lie's support for vigorous United Nations action in Korea that led the Soviet Union to withdraw its support, and this led Lie to (as he put it) 'secretly change my position under pressure while continuing in public to say "no"'.[142] When the Security Council began to consider its recommendation, seven of the eleven members favoured Lie's reappointment. The Soviet Union was by now resolutely opposed to Lie. Nationalist China, a permanent member of the Security Council with the right of veto, had broken with Lie because of his attitude towards Chinese representation, but was prepared to support almost any other non-Communist candidate. India and Egypt were not definitely committed, being willing to support any candidate with general support.

For three weeks, the Security Council canvassed a number of names and a variety of procedures, but deadlock was complete. Then on 1 November 1950, the General Assembly decided that Trygve Lie should continue in office for a period of three years from 1 February 1951.[143]

There was, in fact, no way of complying literally with the provisions of the Charter. In spite of repeated efforts, the Security Council had been unable to agree on a candidate to be recommended to the General Assembly, yet the United Nations had to have a Secretary-General if it were to continue as an effective instrument. Probably a vote of the General Assembly asking Lie to continue in office was the best that could be managed in the circumstances.

Lie's announcement that he would resign was made public 'suddenly and without warning' on 10 November 1952,[144] but it was not until the following March that the Security Council took up once again the matter of recommending a successor. Four names were considered and voted on at meetings on 11, 13, and 19 March. For the first time the official *communiqués* of these meetings revealed the names of the candidates and the results of the secret balloting undertaken. On 13 March the US proposal of Brigadier-General Carlos P. Rómulo and the Soviet proposal of Stanislaw Skrzeszewski each identically received one vote in favour, three against and 7 abstentions.[145] Both candidates therefore failed to obtain the required seven affirmative votes. The Council then considered a third candidate, Lester B. Pearson, a Canadian national proposed by Denmark. He received nine votes in favour, one against, and one abstention. The *communiqué* reported that 'since the negative vote was cast by a permanent member, the proposal was not adopted'.[146] Lie later reported that the Soviet Union had cast the veto concerned. The Council met again on 19 March to consider one candidate, V. L. Pandit, proposed by the Soviet Union. Mrs Pandit received 2 votes in favour, one vote against, with eight abstentions, and therefore failed to obtain the required number of affirmative votes.[147] It has frequently been overlooked by contemporary commentators that one of the five candidates formally voted on by the Security Council in 1953 was a woman. The *communiqués* for the 615th and 616th meetings simply stated that no new nominations had been received. Finally on 31 March, the Council was able to agree to recommend the appointment of Dag Hammarskjold. The nomination was made by France, and the voting was ten in favour, with one abstention. The recommendation was endorsed by the General Assembly a week later.[148]

On 26 September 1957, the Security Council unanimously decided to recommend the reappointment of Hammarskjold for a further term of five years, and this was approved later the same day by the General Assembly.[149]

Hammarskjold was killed in an air crash on 18 September 1961, and at one stage it seemed likely that the Soviet Union would use the occasion of Hammarskjold's death to resurrect the troika proposal for a three-man directorate for the United Nations Secretariat. It soon became apparent, however, that there was little support for the Soviet idea, and the search began for a new candidate—if possible, from a neutral state, and preferably from the Afro-Asian area. The interregnum was reasonably short, and on 3 November 1961 the Security Council adopted a draft resolution submitted by Ceylon, Liberia, and the United Arab Republic recommending that U Thant of Burma (Myanmar) be appointed acting Secretary-General for the unexpired portion of Hammarskjold's term of office. This was subsequently agreed by the General Assembly. A year later, the Security Council recommended that U Thant be appointed Secretary-General for a term expiring five years from the date of his original appointment, and this was approved by the General Assembly.[150]

The appointment of U Thant for a second term came in December 1966, after an uneasy period of uncertainty in which Thant had been increasingly outspoken in criticizing aspects of US policy in Vietnam which seemed to him to violate Charter principles. Nobody was sure whether or not he wished or could be persuaded to serve a second term, but on 1 September he addressed to all UN Members a letter outlining 'some of the problems which the Organization has had to face'. He stated that he had decided not to offer himself for a second term and was as a consequence leaving the Security Council 'unfettered in its recommendation'. His reasons were 'personal, official and political'. He said he had been experiencing 'increasing restrictions on the legitimate prerogatives' of the Secretary-General. 'I do not subscribe to the view . . . that the Secretary-General should be a glorified clerk.' The Secretary-General 'must take the necessary initiatives in the political and diplomatic fields'. But Thant said that if it should prove impossible to find an acceptable successor by the expiry of his term of office on 3 November 1966, he might consider serving until the end of the

TABLE 16

Appointment of the Secretary-General, 1946–1996

	Date of Security Council meeting	Date of plenary meeting of the General Assembly
Appointment of Trygve Lie	30 Jan. 1946	1 Feb. 1946
Continuation in office of Trygve Lie	—	1 Nov. 1950
Appointment of Dag Hammarskjold	31 Mar. 1953	7 Apr. 1953
Reappointment of Dag Hammarskjold	26 Sept. 1957	26 Sept. 1957
Appointment of U Thant as Acting Secretary-General	3 Nov. 1961	3 Nov. 1961
Appointment of U Thant as Secretary-General	30 Nov. 1962	30 Nov. 1962
Consensus of the members of the Security Council welcoming U Thant's readiness to 'consider serving until the end of the present twenty-first session of the 'General Assembly'	29 Sept. 1966	—
Extension of U Thant's appointment 'until the end of the twenty-first regular session of the General Assembly	28 Oct. 1966	1 Nov. 1966
Reappointment of U Thant 'for another term of office'	2 Dec. 1966	2 Dec. 1966
Appointment of Kurt Waldheim	21 Dec. 1971	22 Dec. 1971
Reappointment of Kurt Waldheim	7 Dec. 1976	8 Dec. 1976
Appointment of Javier Pérez de Cuéllar	11 Dec. 1981	15 Dec. 1981
Reappointment of Javier Pérez de Cuéllar	10 Oct. 1986	10 Oct 1986
Appointment of Boutros Boutros-Ghali	21 Nov. 1991	13 Dec. 1991
Appointment of Kofi Annan	13 Dec. 1996	18 Dec. 1996

twenty-first session of the General Assembly, that is to say, until the end of 1966.[151]

To some observers, U Thant's remarks seemed a clear indication of his wishes, but on 29 September 1966, in a statement of consensus, the Security Council welcomed U Thant's readiness to consider serving until the end of the session of the General Assembly and stated that if Thant should be willing to serve another term, 'it would fully meet the desires of the members of this Security Council'. On 28 October, the Security Council formally recommended the extension of his appointment until the end of the session of the General Assembly, and this was approved by the Assembly.[152]

On 2 December 1966, the matter was finally resolved. The President of the Security Council, speaking on behalf of the Council, stated that 'the higher interests of the Organization would be best served if U Thant continues in the post of Secretary-General'; and the Council had 'unanimously decided to appeal to U Thant's dedication . . . and to ask him to continue'. The President said that members of the Council 'fully respect his position and his action in bringing basic issues . . . to their notice'. For his part, U Thant expressed appreciation for what had been said, and agreed to serve a further term. The decision was unanimous in both the Security Council and the General Assembly.[153]

For the circumstances of U Thant's retirement in 1971, we have only the uninformative published records of UN organs and the scanty accounts in Thant's and Kurt Waldheim's memoirs. Britain is believed to have favoured the appointment of Max Jakobson of Finland and, according to Thant, joined with China in vetoing Waldheim on 17 December: none of the other candidates received sufficient votes that day. There were ten more ballots on 20 December, with the Soviet Union vetoing Jakobson and Carlos Ortiz de Rozas of Argentina, and China vetoing Waldheim. The Soviet Union repeated the vetoes of Jakobson and Ortiz de Rozas on 21 December, and Waldheim was elected.[154] China again vetoed Waldheim on the first ballot in 1976 but then allowed the recommendation to go through.[155] If corridor gossip is to be believed, in 1981 China vetoed Waldheim sixteen times and the United States cast fifteen[156] negative votes against Salim Ahmed Salim of Tanzania before the appointment of Javier Pérez de Cuéllar was approved. Only five of the US negative votes amounted to vetoes since on ten occasions Salim received less than nine affirmative votes. By December Olara Otunnu, the Ugandan ambassador, assumed the Council Presidency. He persuaded Salim and Waldheim to 'suspend' their candidacies while other names were considered. Otunnu suggested that a series of 'straw polls' be taken whereby Council members indicate their 'encouragement' or 'discouragement' of the six candidates then put forward. This would indicate where vetoes might lie if a formal vote were to be taken. After the elimination of four of the candidates a straw poll indicated that Prince Sadruddin Aga Khan had received 10 votes, but 'discouragement' from a permanent member (apparently the Soviet Union). Pérez de Cuéllar had received 7 encouragements and no discouragements. A formal vote was taken before lunch on 11 December 1981. Both candidates received 9 or 10 votes but with one veto for Sadruddin. Pérez de Cuéllar was subsequently appointed. There were apparently no vetoes when Pérez de Cuéllar's reappointment was approved in 1986.[157]

In 1991 the search for a successor for Pérez de Cuéllar got underway. On 21 October 1991, the Security Council undertook two 'straw polls' to assess the level of support for nine candidates, eight of them from Africa. Bernard Chidzero of Zimbabwe and Boutros-Ghali of Egypt topped the poll with 10 votes each. A second staw poll was taken of proposals by Western Council members. China and the Non-Aligned members did not vote in this poll and the results were: Hans Van den Broek of the Netherlands (7), Sadruddin Aga Khan of Iran (6), Brian Mulrooney of Canada (5), Gro Harlem Brundland of Norway (2), and Thorvald Stoltenberg of Norway (2). A third poll was taken containing all candidates from the first two polls. The two Africans remained favourites and on 11 and 12 November the Council held two more polls, this time colour coding the ballot papers to indicate opposition, abstention, and, on 12 November, vetoes. The two front-runners did not receive indications of a veto and the Council took its first formal vote on 21 November. Mr Chidzero, who had led in the final staw poll, got only 7 votes; Mr Boutros-Ghali received a winning majority.[158] The Security Council met to recommend Boutros-Ghali to the Assembly unanimously by secret ballot on 21 November 1991[159] and he was formally appointed by the Assembly on 3 December 1991.[160]

Boutros-Ghali's attempt to be reappointed for a second term in office did not run as smoothly. We have here included a detailed but tentative account, derived from a number of sources,[161] of the events that led up to his replacement by Kofi Annan in 1996. In June 1995 Boutros-Ghali floated the idea that he might be interested in standing for a second term in office as UN Secretary-General. Like Pérez de Cuéllar before him, Boutros-Ghali had previously stated that he wished to serve for one term only. As noted in Chapter 3, tensions had been gradually growing between the Secretary-General and the US administration since he came to office. These tensions increased in the course of 1996. On 11 January 1996 Boutros-Ghali, speaking in London, described States as 'dishonest' when they mandated new tasks for the UN, whilst denying it the resources needed to undertake them. This drew a rebuke from the US ambassador that 'he should be a little concerned with his choice of words'. In an article in the March–April edition of *Foreign Affairs* entitled 'Global Leadership After the Cold War' Boutros-Ghali emphasized that 'independence' is 'the one word above all to characterize the role of the Secretary-General' hinting at an intention to continue as a forthright Secretary-General in a second term. He grew more outspoken in the spring of 1996, visibly irritated by some of the criticism of his first term of office. In a speech in Paris on 20 March he stated that 'In recent years I have often witnessed or been subjected to harsh judgements, including by those very people who were the main obstacles to the efficiency of the United Nations. I have also seen the Secretary-General take the blame for things that were due to the hesitations and contradictions of States—and, strangely enough, the most powerful States'. By April 1996, and with the Presidential election looming, the US Administration appears to have decided that it would not support Boutros-Ghali for a second term, and there are reports that the US attempted to broker a deal under which Boutros-Ghali would be offered a one-year extension if he agreed to step down. Following the Secretary-General's refusal to contemplate this 'package', relations declined further with the Americans angered by the publication of a UN report[162] casting as deliberate the Israeli army shelling of a UN post at Qana in Southern Lebanon. On 13 May 1996 US Secretary of State Warren Christopher met Boutros-Ghali to inform him of the definite US decision that it would veto a second term. Certain leaders in the Republican Party had long caricatured Boutros-Ghali as the epitome of everything wrong with the United Nations, and this was accentuated as the US Presidential election got under way. Against this background the Clinton Administration let it be known publicly on 19 June, through the *New York Times*, that if necessary it would use its veto to block a second term for Boutros-Ghali and that its opposition was 'irrevocable'. Boutros-Ghali, backed by France, announced that he nevertheless intended to stand, subsequently receiving the endorsement of an Organization of African Unity meeting in July. At the start of November Security Council members met informally to agree procedures for the selection of the Secretary-General. It was agreed that there would be an initial formal private meeting of the Council on 19 November 1996 at which only one name, that of Boutros-Ghali, would be put forward for consideration. At that meeting the Council had before it a draft resolution[163] submitted by ten Council members, including three permanent members (Botswana, Chile, China, Egypt, France, Germany, Guinea-Bissau, Honduras, Indonesia, and the Russian Federation). The members that did not sponsor the resolution were: Italy, Poland, the Republic of Korea, the United Kingdom, and the United States. The official *communiqué* issued by Council through the Secretary-General after the meeting, in accordance with Rule 55 of the provisional rules of procedure, recorded that 'In a vote taken by secret ballot, the draft resolution received 14 votes in favour, one vote against and no abstentions. Since the negative vote was cast by a permanent member, the draft resolution was not adopted'.[164] The United States subsequently stated that it had cast the veto concerned. The vote was principally a means by which Council members could express their irritation with the manner in which the US had approached this appointment. Following the vote Boutros-Ghali announced that he was not withdrawing his candidacy. After further consultations both inside and outside the Council the Ambassador of Botswana re-affirmed on 25 November that the OAU still backed Boutros-Ghali. This produced speculation that there might be a stand-off in the Council similar to that which occurred when the Soviet Union repeatedly vetoed the re-election of Trygve Lie in 1950–1. In the case of Lie the General Assembly intervened and exercised its right to extend Lie's term of office, rather than re-elect him. This was only possible because the original recommendation from the Security Council to the Assembly to appoint Lie[165] contained no mention of the length of the term of office for which it was valid. In the case of all subsequent appointments and reappointments, the Council has specified a finite term of office, and presumably the General Assembly could not have unilaterally extended the term, even if it had desired to do so.[166] By 29 November OAU members were growing fearful that unless they swiftly produced alternative names, the field might be opened up to non-African candidates. In a letter from the Chairman of the OAU, Paul Biya of Cameroon, African governments were encouraged to make their nominations known to the Security Council. On 4 December Boutros-Ghali declared that he had temporarily 'suspended' his candidacy, presumably with the intention of coming back into the race if there were a deadlock over the choice of a replacement. Diplomats pointed to the parallel with Council voting in 1981 when Tanzanian front-runner Salim A. Salim suspended his candidacy in the face of a US veto. The Council at that time proceeded to elect Pérez de Cuéllar as Secretary-General.[167] With the field now opened up the Council considered the nominations of four African governments. Côte D'Ivoire nominated its Foreign Minister, Amara Essy;[168] Ghana the UN Under-Secretary-General for Peace-Keeping, Kofi Annan;[169] Mauritania, Ambassador Ahmedou Ould-Abdallah;[170] and Niger, Hamid Algabid, the Secretary-General of the Organization of the Islamic Conference.[171] The Council was told that further names were due to be submitted and decided to wait. On Monday, 9 December no further names had been submitted and the Council began consideration of those nominations received. The Council President, Ambassador Paolo Fulci of Italy, then announced that Council members would meet in consultations the next day to conduct 'straw polls' on the four candidates. The polls the following day, which took about 45 minutes, were held in private, but the results of the deliberations were soon widely known. Polls were taken with coloured paper (red for permanent members, white for non-permanent) to indicate where vetoes might lie. The slips were designated as either 'encourage' or 'discourage'. In the first round Kofi Annan received twelve votes of encouragement, and only two discouragements, one of which was red. Amara Essy received eleven encouragements and four discouragements, two of which were red. The other two candidates received seven encouragements and two red slips each. In the second round Annan attracted ten encouragements but three against, including one red; Essy seven encouragement slips and two reds. Hamid Algabid received five encouragements and Ould-Abdallah just three, putting them both out of the running. Council members, stalemated for the time being, decided to resume their discussions on the appointment of the Secretary-General the next day. Emerging from the closed deliberations, Council President Fulci jested that the secretive and drawn-out process is like choosing the Pope, except that the Security Council consultation room could hardly match the Sistine Chapel. 'If you stare at the ceiling, there are no frescoes by Michaelangelo to inspire you' he said. One well-informed observer reported that France was 'discouraging' Annan, while the US and UK were 'discouraging' the other three candidates.

Council members began their deliberations again the following morning (11 December) at 11.30 a.m. Three polls were held. Annan received 12 encouragement slips in the first and 11 in the second and third, with a single red slip of discouragement. Essy received seven encouragements on the first two polls and then dropped to six, with two red slips against. Ould-Abdallah drew only four supporters in round one and three on the next two, while Algabid dropped from four encouragements in the first round to two in the subsequent two rounds. Both Ould-Abdallah and Algabid continued to attract two red slips of discouragement during all three rounds.

Resuming its meeting on 12 December Council members polled again. Annan received 13 encouragements on the first and 14 on the second, with still one red slip of discouragement. Pressure began to mount on France from African countries fearful that continued deadlock would lead to invitations for candidates from other regions to come forward, and ideas surfaced among some of the permanent members about the possible composition of the UN Secretariat under Annan.[172] The next day, a rainy Friday 13th saw a reverse in the French position on Annan, and the other candidates withdrew from the race. The Council members held an informal vote unanimously endorsing Annan, followed by a formal private meeting. At that meeting the Council adopted by acclamation two resolutions, one recommending to the General Assembly Annan's appointment as UN Secretary-General for a term of office from 1 January 1997 to 31 December 2001,[173] and the other, in a new precedent, commending Boutros-Ghali's initiation of UN reform and expressing its deep appreciation for his dedication to the purposes and principles of the UN Charter.[174] The resolution of recommendation was then forwarded the same day to the General Assembly.[175] In a statement[176] issued on the evening of 13 December the General Assembly President, Razali Ismail of Malaysia welcomed the Council's recommendation. His statement reflected the extent to which the Assembly's appointment of the Secretary-General was a formality. He stated that 'As President of the General Assembly, I promise to work closely with him [Annan] in our common efforts' and that 'Permanent Representatives will meet with the incoming Secretary-General before they appoint him . . . ' Nevertheless the statement also stated that to provide delegations with sufficient time to consult their capitals on the Council's recommendation, the Assembly's meeting would not be held until the afternoon of Tuesday, 17 December. At the meeting on 17 December the Assembly duly appointed Kofi Annan as the UN's seventh Secretary-General, by acclamation.

The highly political and mainly secretive nature of the process of selecting a new UN Secretary-General has led to calls for a more public and systematic search procedure. Sir Brian Urquhart and Erskine Childers have proposed[177] that all Secretaries-General should be appointed for a single seven-year term, that there should be a formal search committee, accountable to the Security Council, a timetable for the submission of nominations, a check on the background and qualifications of short-listed candidates, and complete transparency in both informal and formal voting by the Council when a decision is made. Critics argue that it is not possible to 'institutionalize' in this way what by its nature will be a political negotiation among States. Besides, it is argued, this method of selection can produce candidates who are both suitably qualified and who will have the support and confidence of the Member States that constitute the Organization. We agree that excellent candidates can emerge in this way, but that the probability of this occurring would be increased if some of the measures suggested above were adopted.

CHAPTER 7

SUBSIDIARY ORGANS

> There is all the difference between the attempt to debauch the subjects of a sovereign prince in order to ensnare them into conspiracy against him, and the legitimate endeavour to use every opportunity for acquiring information. The latter practice has always been permissible, and indeed is a necessary part of diplomacy.

ARTICLE 29 of the Charter empowers the Council to establish 'such subsidiary organs as it deems necessary for the performance of its functions'. Some of these have been given tasks related to one issue and are terminated when the mandate has been fulfilled: others have a long-term existence and are activated when there is work to be done. A subsidiary organ may be one person or a committee, a peace-keeping force or a tribunal; it can be established either by the Security Council or by the President of the Council and/or the Secretary-General pursuant to a decision of the Council; it can conduct its operations at UN Headquarters or in the field; it can be given an *ad hoc* assignment or a continuing responsibility. The only Rule of Procedure governing the appointment of subsidiary organs is Rule 28, which simply states that the Council may appoint a commission or committee or a rapporteur for a specified question.

No fewer than twenty-four subsidiary organs were established during the first three years, 1946–8, partly because standing committees were needed for certain procedural or constitutional matters, but mainly because drafting or negotiating groups were set up to deal with matters which nowadays would be the subject of informal negotiations. During the next fourteen years 1949–62, when the Council was often in the doldrums, only six subsidiary organs were created: a Commission for Indonesia (1949), Representatives for India and Pakistan (1950 and 1951), the Observer Group in Lebanon (1958), a Subcommittee on Laos (1959), and the operation in the Congo

(1960). In the 1990s there has been an explosion of subsidiary organs, eight sanctions committees and 26 peace-keeping operations have been established since 1989, along with various commissions of inquiry and *ad hoc* criminal tribunals, and a number of individuals appointed as Special Representatives of the Secretary-General.

Placing subsidiary organs into groups is an arbitrary task, and in this chapter we have divided organs into four categories, reflecting the main function of the organ. These four are Procedure, Membership, Peace and Security, and Miscellaneous.

1. ORGANS CONCERNED WITH COUNCIL PROCEDURE

(a) *Committee of Experts*

The Committee of Experts consists of all the members of the Security Council. It was established at the first meeting of the Council, to examine and report on the provisional rules of procedure drafted by the Preparatory Commission.[1] Its responsibilities have always been in the procedural and constitutional field, and it has been thought of primarily as a working body in which argument and debate has played a less important role than when the same representatives meet as the Security Council. The specific tasks which have been entrusted to the Committee of Experts are set out in Table 17. Two proposals to refer matters to the Committee of Experts have been made in the Security Council but not pressed to a vote.[2]

On ten occasions, the chairman of the Committee of Experts was invited to sit at the Council table in order to introduce and interpret the Committee's report.[3] This was a somewhat curious procedure, as the membership of the Committee and the Council were identical. There was a thirty-four year gap in the work of the Committee between the task entrusted to it in November 1953 to study and report on the conditions on which Japan and San Marino might become parties to the Statute of the International Court of Justice, and a similar task in October 1987 regarding the Republic of Nauru (see Table 17). The tasks undertaken by the Committee in the past are now more likely to be dealt with in informal consultations of

Council members, and through informal bodies such as the Council's informal working group concerning documentation and other procedural questions.

(b) Committee on Council meetings away from Headquarters

The Security Council normally meets at Headquarters (Rule 5), but meetings were held in London (January and February 1946) and Paris (September to December 1948 and November 1951 to February 1952) where the General Assembly was meeting, to suit the convenience of Council members. Suggestions for meetings away from Headquarters for political or symbolic purposes were made in connection with the Congo in 1960 and 1961, and the Dominican Republic in 1965, but were not acted on.[4] It was not until 1972 and 1973 that the Council decided to hold a series of meetings away from Headquarters expressly to demonstrate concern for the problems of a particular region, and then again in 1990 to hear Mr Yasser Arafat. We reviewed these decisions of the Council in Chapter 2.4.

It was to prepare for the decision to meet in Addis Ababa in 1972 that the Security Council created a committee of the whole to examine the financial, legal, and other problems involved. The Committee met eight times in 1972 and six times in 1973. Apart from the considerable expense of meeting away from Headquarters, and the often inadequate facilities there was uneasiness on the part of some States that if the staff and members of the Council were to be absent from New York for any considerable time, the Council would not be able to 'function continuously' as required by Article 28(1) of the Charter. The Committee decided that this objection was not insuperable, and recommended that the Secretary-General should negotiate with the host government an agreement on legal aspects along the lines set out in a Secretariat working paper in 1972.[5] When the Council decided to meet in Geneva in 1990 so that Mr Yasser Arafat would be able to address the Council, it did not refer the matter to the Committee.

TABLE 17

Tasks entrusted to the Committee of Experts and Reports of the Committee, 1946–1996

Date		Meeting and page or para. no.	Date(s) of reports(s)	SCOR
17 Jan. 1946 16 Feb. 1946	To consider the Provisional Rules of Procedure recommended by the Preparatory Commission	1, p. 1111 23, p. 368	5 Feb., 13 and 31 May, 17 June 1946	1st year, 1st series, Supplement no. 2, pp. 1–8, 20–30, 39–40, 41–3, S/6, S/57, S/71, S/88
1 Feb. 1946	To indicate how communications from non-governmental bodies and persons should be dealt with	6, p. 72	5 Apr. 1946	31st meeting, p. 117 S/29
16 Feb. 1946	To examine the draft statute and draft rules of procedure submitted by the Military Staff Committee	23, p. 369	17 July 1947	S/421 (restricted)
16 Apr. 1946	To examine and report on a memorandum from the Secretary-General concerning the retention of the Iranian question on the agenda	33, p. 145	18 Apr. 1946	1st year, 1st series, Supplement no. 2, pp. 47–50, S/42
10 July 1946	To examine and report on the conditions under which the International Court of Justice should be open to States not parties to the Statute	50, pp. 7–8	24 Sept. 1946	1st year, 2nd series, Supplement no. 6, pp. 153–6, S/169
30 Oct. 1946	To examine and report on the conditions on which Switzerland might become a party to the Statute of the International Court of Justice	78, pp. 486–7	12 Nov. 1946	1st year, 2nd series, Supplement no. 8, pp. 159–61, S/191
29 Nov. 1946	To appoint a subcommittee to confer with a committee of the General Assembly with a view to preparing rules governing the admission of new Members	81, pp. 504–5	25 Aug. 1947	2nd year, Supplement no. 19, pp. 157–65, S/520 and Add. 1.

27 Aug. 1947	To consider and report on the recommendations of the General Assembly of 13 Dec. 1946 (GA res. 40(1)) regarding the voting procedure in the Security Council	197, pp. 2267–81	—	—
15 Nov. 1947 19 Dec. 1947	To report on the respective functions of the Security Council and the Trusteeship Council with regard to strategic trust territories	220, pp. 2756–63 224, pp. 2812–17	12 June 1948	3rd year, Supplement for June 1948, pp. 1–10, S/642
8 Apr. 1949	To report on the request of Liechtenstein to become a party to the Statute of the International Court of Justice	423, pp. 16–17	23 June 1949	4th year, Supplement for July 1949, pp. 2–3, S/1342
17 Jan. 1950	To consider Indian draft amendments to the Provisional Rules of Procedure of the Security Council concerning representation and credentials	462, pp. 10–13	14 Feb. 1950	5th year, Supplement for January to May 1950, pp. 16–18, S/1457 and Corr. 1
23 Nov. 1953	To study and report on the conditions on which Japan and San Marino might become parties to the Statute of the International Court of Justice	641, paras. 1–3	1 and 2 Dec. 1953	8th year, Supplement for October to December 1953, pp. 72–3, S/3146, S/3147
15 Oct. 1987	Conditions on which the Republic of Nauru may become a party to the Statute of the International Court of Justice	2753, pp. 2–3	16 Oct. 1987	S/129213, S/PV.2754

TABLE 18

Work of the Committee on Council meetings away from Headquarters, 1972–1996

Request	Date of Security Council reference to Committee	No. of meetings held	Report of Committee SCOR	Security Council decision	Places and dates of meetings
GA res. 2863 (XXVI), 20 Dec. 1971: S/10480, 29 Dec. 1971	11 Jan. 1972	8	27th year, Supplement for Jan. to Mar. 1972, pp. 20–7, S/10514	SC res. 308, 19 Jan. 1972	Addis Ababa, 28 Jan.–4 Feb. 1972
SCOR, 28th year, Supplement for Jan. to Mar. 1973, p. 27, S/10858	16 Jan. 1973	6	28th year, Supplement for Jan. to Mar. 1973, pp. 32–8, S/10868	SC res. 325, 26 Jan. 1973	Panama City 15–21 Mar. 1973

• The decision of the Council to hold its 2923rd meeting in Geneva on 25 May 1990 was taken without recourse to the Committee.

2. ORGANS CONCERNED WITH MEMBERSHIP

(a) Committee on Admission of New Members

The work of the Committee on Admission of New Members may be considered in three phases. During the first phase (1946–9), applications for membership were, with four exceptions to be noted below, referred to the Committee as a matter of course and examined by the Committee with some care. After 1949, applications were dealt with by the Security Council without the help of a committee. Indonesia was admitted in 1950, and after the package deal of twelve admissions in 1955, applications were accepted by the Security Council without much question, until 1971, when the practice was resumed of referring all applications to the Committee.

TABLE 19

Applications for UN membership referred to the Committee on Admission of New Members, 1946–9, 1971–84, and 1990–6

Applicant	Date of application	Referred to Committee: S/COR meeting and page or para. no.	Report of Committee SCOR	Date Security Council recommended admission	Date General Assembly decided on admission
A. 1946–9					
Afghanistan	2 July 1946	42, pp. 278–85	1st year, 2nd series, Supplement no. 4, p. 67, S/133	29 Aug. 1946	19 Nov. 1946
Albania	undated*	342, pp. 278–85	1st year, 2nd series, Supplement no. 4, pp. 56–64, S/133	14 Dec. 1955	14 Dec. 1955
		152, pp. 1229–31	2nd year, Special Supplement no. 3, pp. 4–8, S/479 and Corr. 1	14 Dec. 1955	14 Dec. 1955
Austria	2 July 1947	154, pp. 1260–6	2nd year, Special Supplement no. 3, S/479 and Corr. 1, p. 24	14 Dec. 1955	14 Dec. 1955
Bulgaria	26 July 1947	178, pp. 1826–8	2nd year, Special Supplement no. 3, S/479 and Corr. 1, pp. 25–6	14 Dec. 1955	14 Dec. 1955
Burma	27 Feb. 1948	261, p. 2	3rd year, Supplement for Apr. 1948, pp. 1–3, S/706	10 Apr. 1948	19 Apr. 1948
Ceylon	25 May 1948	318, p. 2	3rd year, Supplement for Aug. 1948, p. 78, S/859	14 Dec. 1955	14 Dec. 1955
Hungary	22 Apr. 1947	132, pp. 820–1	2nd year, Special Supplement no. 3, pp. 21–2, S/479 and Corr. 1	14 Dec. 1955	14 Dec. 1955
Iceland	2 Aug. 1946	51, pp. 14–16	1st year, 2nd series, Supplement no. 4, pp. 74–5, S/133	29 Aug. 1946	19 Nov. 1946
Ireland	2 Aug. 1946	51, pp. 14–16	1st year, 2nd series, Supplement no. 4, p. 72, S/133		
		152, pp. 1229–31	2nd year, Special Supplement no. 3, pp. 15–16, S/479 and Corr. 1	14 Dec. 1955	14 Dec. 1955
Israel	29 Nov. 1948	383, pp. 7–25	3rd year, Supplement for Dec. 1948, pp. 119–20, S/1110 and Corr. 1	4 Mar. 1949	11 May 1949

TABLE 19 *cont.*

Applicant	Date of application	Referred to Committee: S/COR meeting and page or para. no.	Report of Committee SCOR	Date Security Council recommended admission	Date General Assembly decided on admission
Italy	7 May 1947	137, pp. 945–6	2nd year, Special Supplement no. 3, pp. 22–4, S/479 and Corr. 1	14 Dec. 1955	14 Dec. 1955
Korea, Republic of	19 Jan. 1949	409, pp. 3–12	4th year, Supplement for Apr. 1949, pp. 1–5, S/1281	—	—
Mongolia	24 June 1946	42, pp. 278–85	1st year, 2nd series, Supplement no. 4, pp. 64–7, S/133		
		152, pp. 1229–31	2nd year, Special Supplement no. 3, pp. 8–13, S/479 and Corr. 1	27 Oct. 1961	27 Oct. 1961
Nepal	13 Feb. 1949	423, p. 16	4th year, Supplement for Sept. to Dec. 1949, pp. 10–12, S/1382	14 Dec. 1955	14 Dec. 1955
Portugal	2 Aug. 1946	51, pp. 14–16	1st year, 2nd series, Supplement no. 4, pp. 72–4, S/133		
		152, pp. 1229–31	2nd year, Special Supplement no. 3, pp. 16–17, S/479 and Corr. 1	14 Dec. 1955	14 Dec. 1955
Romania	10 July 1947	161, pp. 1389–91	2nd year, Special Supplement no. 3, pp. 24–5, S/479 and Corr. 1	14 Dec. 1955	14 Dec. 1955
Siam (Thailand)	20 May 1946†	51, pp. 14–16	1st year, 2nd series, Supplement no. 4, pp. 75–7, S/133	12 Dec. 1946	16 Dec. 1946
Sweden	9 Aug. 1946	51, pp. 14–16	1st year, 2nd series, Supplement no. 4, pp. 77–8, S/133	29 Aug. 1946	19 Nov. 1946
Transjordan (Jordan)	26 June 1946	42, pp. 278–85	1st year, 2nd series, Supplement no. 4, pp. 68–72, S/133		
		152, pp. 1229–31	2nd year, Special Supplement no. 3, pp. 14–15, S/479 and Corr. 1	14 Dec. 1955	14 Dec. 1955
Yemen	21 July 1947	168, pp. 1549–50	2nd year, Special Supplement no. 3, p. 25, S/479 and Corr. 1	18 Aug. 1947	30 Sept. 1947

B. 1971–84					
Angola	22 Apr. 1976	1931, para. 2	31st year, Supplement for Apr. to June 1976, p. 21, S/12110	—	—
			31st year, Supplement for Oct. to Dec. 1976, p. 25, S/12234	22 Nov. 1976	1 Dec. 1976
Antigua and Barbuda	1 Nov. 1981	2307, p. 2	36th year, Supplement for Oct. to Dec. 1981, p. 21, S/14748	10 Nov. 1981	11 Nov. 1981
Bahamas	10 July 1973	1731, para. 6	28th year, Supplement for July to Sept. 1973, p. 16, S/10968	18 July 1973	18 Sept. 1973
Bahrain	15 Aug. 1971	1574, para. 2	26th year, Supplement for July to Sept. 1971, p. 54, S/10294, paras. 3–4	18 Sept. 1971	21 Sept. 1971
Bangladesh, People's Republic of	8 Aug. 1972	1658, para. 107	27th year, Supplement for July to Sept. 1972, pp. 93–4, S/10773	—	—
			29th year, Supplement for Apr. to June 1974, p. 154, S/11316	10 June 1974	17 Sept. 1974
Belize	21 Sept. 1981	2301, p. 3	36th year, Supplement for July to Sept. 1981, pp. 81–2, S/14703	23 Sept. 1981	25 Sept. 1981
Bhutan	22 Dec. 1970	1565, para. 126	26th year, Supplement for Jan. to Mar. 1971, p. 65, S/10109	10 Feb. 1971	21 Sept. 1971
Brunei Darussalam	8 Feb. 1984	2517, p. 2	39th year, Supplement for Jan. to Mar. 1984, p. 72, S/16367	24 Feb. 1984	21 Sept. 1984
Cape Verde	21 July 1975	1837, para. 2	30th year, Supplement for July to Sept. 1975, p. 46, S/11800	18 Aug. 1975	16 Sept. 1975
Comoros	29 Sept. 1975	1847, paras. 4–5	30th year, Supplement for Oct. to Dec. 1975, p. 16, S/11850	17 Oct. 1975	12 Nov. 1975
Djibouti, Republic of	6 July 1977	2020, paras. 12–13	32nd year, Supplement for July to Sept. 1977, p. 44, S/12359	7 July 1977	20 Sept. 1977
Dominica	21 Nov. 1978	2104, paras. 3–4	33rd year, Supplement for Oct. to Dec. 1978, p. 90, S/12956	6 Dec. 1978	18 Dec. 1978
German Democratic Republic	12 June 1973	1729, para. 1	28th year, Supplement for Apr. to June 1973, pp. 77–8, S/10957	22 June 1973	18 Sept. 1973
Germany, Federal Republic of	13 June 1973				

TABLE 19 *cont.*

Applicant	Date of application	Referred to Committee: S/COR meeting and page or para. no.	Report of Committee SCOR	Date Security Council recommended admission	Date General Assembly decided on admission
Grenada	30 May 1974	1777, paras. 1–3	29th year, Supplement for Apr. to June 1974, p. 158, S/11322	21 June 1974	17 Sept. 1974
Guinea Bissau	16 July 1974	1790, para. 2	29th year, Supplement for July to Sept. 1974, p. 100, S/11437	12 Aug. 1974	17 Sept. 1974
Mozambique	31 July 1975	1837, para. 4	30th year, Supplement for July to Sept. 1975, p. 47, S/11805	18 Aug. 1975	16 Sept. 1975
Oman	24 May 1971	1574, para. 2	26th year, Supplement for June to Aug. 1971, p. 54, S/10294, para. 2; Supplement for Sept. to Dec. 1971, p. 69, S/10345	30 Sept. 1971	7 Oct. 1971
Papua New Guinea	16 Sept. 1975	1839, para. 9	30th year, Supplement for July to Sept. 1975, p. 65, S/11829	22 Sept. 1975	10 Oct. 1975
Qatar	4 Sept. 1971	1577, para. 3	26th year, Supplement for Sept. to Dec. 1971, p. 63, S/10318	15 Sept. 1971	21 Sept. 1971
Saint Christopher and Nevis	19 Sept. 1983	2478, p. 2	38th year, Supplement for July to Sept. 1983, p. 98, S/15997	22 Sept. 1984	23 Sept. 1983
Saint Lucia	28 Aug. 1979	2166, paras. 11–12	34th year, Supplement for July to Sept. 1979, p. 134, S/13535	12 Sept. 1979	18 Sept. 1979
Saint Vincent and the Grenadines	8 Jan. 1980	2197, para. 2	35th year, Supplement for Jan. to Mar. 1980, p. 23, S/13814	19 Feb. 1980	16 Sept. 1980
São Tomé and Principé	13 Aug. 1975	1837, para. 3	30th year, Supplement for July to Sept. 1975, pp. 47–8, S/11806	18 Aug. 1975	16 Sept. 1975
Solomon Islands	24 July 1978	2083, paras. 4–5	33rd year, Supplement for July to Sept. 1978, p. 50, S/12801	17 Aug. 1978	19 Sept. 1978
Surinam	25 Nov. 1975	1857, paras. 3–4	30th year, Supplement for Oct. to Dec. 1975, p. 47, S/11884	1 Dec. 1975	4 Dec. 1975

United Arab Emirates	2 Dec. 1971	1608, paras. 5–9	26th year, Supplement for Sept. to Dec. 1971, p. 96, S/10430	8 Dec. 1971	9 Dec. 1971
Vanuatu	22 May 1981	2290, p. 3	36th year, Supplement for July to Sept. 1981, pp. 8–9, S/14580	8 July 1981	15 Sept. 1981
Vietnam, Provisional Revolutionary Government of	15 July 1975	1834, para. 139	30th year, Supplement for July to Sept. 1975, p. 43 S/11794	—	—
South Vietnam, Socialist Republic of	10 Aug. 1976	1955, para. 66	31st year, Supplement for Oct. to Dec. 1976, p. 21, S/12225	—	—
	10 July 1977	2022, para. 2	32nd year, Supplement for July to Sept. 1977, p. 450 (S/12367)	20 July 1977	20 Sept. 1977
Western Samoa	29 Nov. 1976	1976, para. 5	31st year, Supplement for Oct. to Dec. 1976, p. 37, S/12249	1 Dec. 1976	15 Dec. 1976
Zimbabwe	17 July 1980	2243, para. 5	35th year, Supplement for July to Sept. 1980, p. 20, S/14076	30 July 1980	25 Aug. 1980
C. 1990–6					
Andorra	9 June 1993	3250	S/26051	8 July 1993	28 July 1993
Armenia	21 Dec. 1991	3035	S/23475	29 Jan. 1992	2 Mar. 1992
Azerbaijan	14 Jan. 1992	3051	S/23569	14 Feb. 1992	2 Mar. 1992
Bosnia and Herzegovina	8 May 1992	3078	S/23974	20 May 1992	22 May 1992
Croatia	11 Feb. 1992	3073	S/23935	18 May 1992	22 May 1992
Czech Republic	4 Jan. 1993	3156	S/25067	8 Jan. 1993	19 Jan. 1993
Eritrea	12 May 1993	3215	S/25841	26 May 1993	28 May 1993
Estonia	30 Aug. 1991	3006	S/23002	12 Sept. 1991	17 Sept. 1991
The former Yugoslav Republic of Macedonia	30 July 1992	3195	S/25544	7 Apr. 1993	8 Apr. 1993
Georgia	6 May 1992	3090	S/24231	6 July 1992	31 July 1992
Kazakhistan	31 Dec. 1991	3032	S/23456	23 Jan. 1992	2 Mar. 1992
Kyrgyzstan	6 Jan. 1992	3036	S/23476	29 Jan. 1992	2 Mar. 1992

TABLE 19 *cont.*

Applicant	Date of application	Referred to Committee: S/COR meeting and page or para. no.	Report of Committee SCOR	Date Security Council recommended admission	Date General Assembly decided on admission
Korea, Democratic People's Republic of	2 July 1991	2998	S/22895	8 Aug. 1991	17 Sept. 1991
Korea, Republic of	19 July 1991	2998	S/22895	8 Aug. 1991	17 Sept. 1991
Latvia	30 Aug. 1991	3006	S/23003	12 Sept. 1991	17 Sept. 1991
Liechtenstein	10 Aug. 1990	2935	S/21506	14 Aug. 1990	18 Sept. 1990
Lithuania	29 Aug. 1991	3006	S/23004	12 Sept. 1991	17 Sept. 1991
Marshall Islands	25 July 1991	3000	S/22897	9 Aug. 1991	17 Sept. 1991
Micronesia, Federated States of	17 July 1991	2999	S/22896	9 Aug. 1991	17 Sept. 1991
Moldova, Republic of	17 Jan. 1992	3045	S/23511	5 Feb. 1992	2 Mar. 1992
Monaco, Principality of	14 May 1993	3216	S/25842	26 May 1993	28 May 1993
Namibia	6 April 1990	2917	S/21251	17 Apr. 1990	23 Apr. 1990
Palau	14 Nov. 1994	3468	S/1994/1356	29 Nov. 1994	15 Dec. 1994
San Marino	19 Feb. 1992	3054	S/23634	25 Feb. 1992	2 Mar. 1992
Slovak Republic	1 Jan. 1993	3155	S/25066	8 Jan. 1993	19 Jan. 1993
Slovenia	5 May 1992	3074	S/23936	18 May 1992	22 May 1992
Tajikistan	16 Jan. 1992	3038	S/23478	29 Jan. 1992	2 Mar. 1992
Turkmenistan	20 Jan. 1992	3048	S/23523	7 Feb. 1992	2 Mar. 1992
Uzbekistan	6 Jan. 1992	3037	S/23477	29 Jan. 1992	2 Mar. 1992

* Application received by Secretariat on 25 Jan. 1946.
† Application received by Secretariat on 3 Aug. 1946.

The Committee was established on 17 May 1946. The draft rules of procedure prepared by the Preparatory Commission had provided that a State desiring to become a Member of the United Nations should submit to the Secretary-General an application, accompanied by a declaration of its readiness to accept the obligations contained in the Charter; that the application should be placed before the Security Council, which would decide whether the applicant was peace-loving, and able and willing to carry out the obligations of the Charter; and that, should the Security Council decide to recommend an applicant for admission, the recommendation would be placed before the General Assembly.[6] The Committee of Experts recommended two changes to this procedure. First, the Committee proposed that 'unless the Security Council decides otherwise, the application shall be referred by the President to a committee of the Security Council upon which each member of the . . . Council shall be represented . . . [and the] committee shall examine any application . . . and report its conclusions'. Second, the Committee of Experts 'thought it useful to lay down time limits'.[7]

Australia, at that time spearheading the campaign to increase the rights of the medium and smaller UN Members, was opposed to the proposal of the Committee of Experts that applications should go to the Security Council before going to the General Assembly. Australia held that the Security Council 'was not in any sense the executive committee of the Organization' but 'a body with defined powers . . .' The General Assembly was 'the only organ entitled to speak on this matter for all Members' and 'the only body which . . . can make the final and binding decision on the subject of admission'. Nor was the Security Council empowered to establish the route along which an application for membership should travel. Indeed, the correct procedure was that each application should go first to the General Assembly, which would decide whether the application should be entertained, after which it should be remitted to the Security Council. Australia urged the Council to defer a decision pending consultation with the General Assembly.[8] Australia was in a minority of one, however, and the Council approved the procedure recommended by the Committee of Experts.[9]

Australia raised the matter again the following year and again proposed that the General Assembly should consider applications for membership before remitting them to the Security Council. The proposal was submitted first to a joint meeting of a body appointed by the General Assembly and a subcommittee of the Security Council's Committee of Experts, and then to the Council itself, but again Australia was without success. In 1950, the International Court of Justice made it clear in an Advisory Opinion that, irrespective of which UN organ considers an application first, the admission of a State 'cannot be effected by a decision of the General Assembly when the Security Council has made no recommendation for admission'.[10]

The Council's rules for dealing with applications for membership were revised in 1947, as follows:[11]

1. Formerly an application had to be accompanied by a declaration of the applicant's readiness to accept the obligations contained in the Charter. This was changed to provide that each application should contain a declaration 'made in a formal instrument' that the applicant accepts the Charter obligations.
2. New provisions were inserted to require the Security Council to forward to the General Assembly with each positive recommendation 'a complete record of the discussion'.
3. In the event that the Security Council should not recommend an applicant for admission or should postpone consideration, the Council was required to submit to the Assembly 'a special report . . . with a complete record of the discussion'.

The Council's Rules of Procedure regarding the admission of new Members have never required that each application should necessarily be submitted to the Committee on Admission of New Members, but that this should be done 'unless the Security Council decides otherwise' (Rule 59). During the period 1946–9, the Security Council referred to the Committee twenty-five applications or re-applications from twenty states (see Table 19, part A).[12] The President of the Council referred to the Committee applications from Austria, Bulgaria, Burma, Ceylon, Israel, Nepal, Romania, and Yemen: the Security Council itself decided to refer to the Committee applications from Afghanistan, Albania, Hungary, Iceland, Ireland, Italy, Jordan (Transjordan), Republic of Korea, Mongolia, Portugal, Sweden, and Thailand (Siam). During the same period (1946–9), the Council considered the application of Finland without referring it to the Committee (although the proposal to admit Finland was vetoed by the Soviet Union);[13] after the partition of India, recommended the admission of Pakistan without first referring the application to the Committee;[14] decided not to refer to the Committee the application from the Democratic People's Republic of Korea;[15] and took no action on the application of the Democratic Republic of (North) Vietnam.

It was intended that the Committee on Admission of New Members should obtain the information necessary to judge whether each applicant satisfied the requirements of Article 4(1) of the Charter, namely, whether the applicant was a State, peace-loving,* accepted the obligations of the Charter, was able to carry out the obligations, and was willing to do so.

In some cases, the Committee has had before it summaries of information prepared by the Secretariat concerning the applicant State. On occasion, the Committee has seen fit to draw up and communicate to the applicant for reply a questionnaire concerning various matters on which the Committee wished to be informed.[16]

In one case, the application of Israel, the Committee reported on 7 December 1948 that it was 'not . . . in possession of the requisite information to enable it to come to any decision'.[17] In another case, the application of Nepal, the Committee decided to transmit to the Government of Nepal the Secretariat working paper and the summary records of its own discussion of the application, with a request that the Government of Nepal provide 'additional information . . . particularly concerning its sovereignty and . . . independence'.[18]

During the late 1960s, a number of the major powers had become uneasy at the rather casual way some applications for membership were being dealt with by the Security Council, and in 1970 France suggested the reactivation of the Council's Committee on Admission of New Members. Informal consultations among Council members followed. On 10 October 1970, when Fiji's application for membership was being considered, the Council decided to reinstate the former practice, but not to apply it in Fiji's case;[19] and on 9 February

* There was a certain irony in the fact that, to demonstrate its peace-loving nature and thus qualify for original membership, a State had to declare war on the Axis powers. Colombia proposed in 1972 that the 'peace-loving' requirement should be dropped in order to 'open the doors of the Organization to all States' willing to accept and fulfil the obligations of Membership. UN wits allege that 'loving' has only carnal connotations in Spanish.

1971, the Council referred Bhutan's application to the Committee on Admission of New Members, the first such referral for more than two decades.[20]

The Committee met thirty-four times between 31 July 1946 and 22 August 1949, and sixty-one times between 9 February 1971 and 31 December 1996.* In the case of the Committee's first four reports (1946–8), the chairman of the Committee was invited to sit at the Council table to introduce and interpret them.[21]

Of the cases since 1970 in which there was delay, one concerned Oman. This was initially delayed on a technicality, and when the Committee's favourable recommendation eventually reached the Council, Democratic Yemen opposed admission on the ground that Oman was still a British colony.[22] The proposal to recommend admitting Oman was, nevertheless, unanimously approved by the Council on 30 September 1971, and the General Assembly decided on admission a week later—by 117 votes to one (Democratic Yemen), with twelve Members abstaining or absent.[23]

China opposed the admission of Bangladesh in 1972 'pending the full implementation of the relevant United Nations resolutions and a reasonable settlement of [other] issues . . .' Eleven members of the Committee favoured admission, and three expressed a wish to have the matter postponed. The Committee duly reported to that effect to the Security Council, and on 25 August 1972, a proposal by India, the Soviet Union, the United Kingdom, and Yugoslavia that Bangladesh be recommended for admission was vetoed by China. The General Assembly later went on record as considering Bangladesh to be 'eligible for membership' and as desiring its admission 'at an early date'. Bangladesh was finally admitted in 1974. [24]

In the case of Zimbabwe's application in 1980, the Security Council asked that its recommendation be placed on the supplementary list of items for the agenda of a special session of the General Assembly.[25] Zimbabwe was admitted on 25 August 1980.

* According to the UN *Journal* of 26 June 1968, the Committee on Admission of New Members was due to meet the following day. According to the Security Council's annual reports, however, the Committee did not meet between 22 August 1949 and 9 Feb. 1971.[26] If a meeting was, indeed, held in 1968, whether formal or informal, it was no doubt concerned with the mini-State problem.

CHART 3

UN membership, 1946–1996

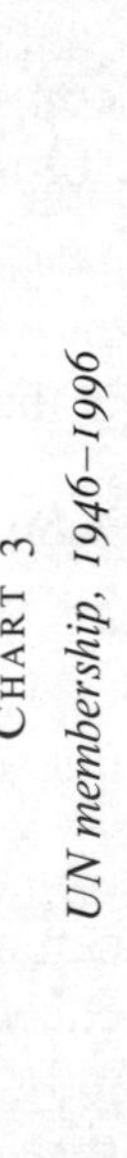
Czechoslovakia separated to form Czech Republic and Slovakia (1993)
Two Germanys united. Two Yemens united
People's Republic of China seated
Indonesia resumes membership
Union of Tanganyika and Zanzibar to form Tanzania
Syria resumes separate membership
Indonesia suspends membership
Egypt and Syria unite to form United Arab Republic
Number of Members
190
180
170
160
150
140
130
120
110
100
90
80
70
60
50
40
30
20
10
1946
48
50
52
54
56
58
60
62
64
66
68
70
72
74
76
78
80
82
84
86
88
90
92
94
96

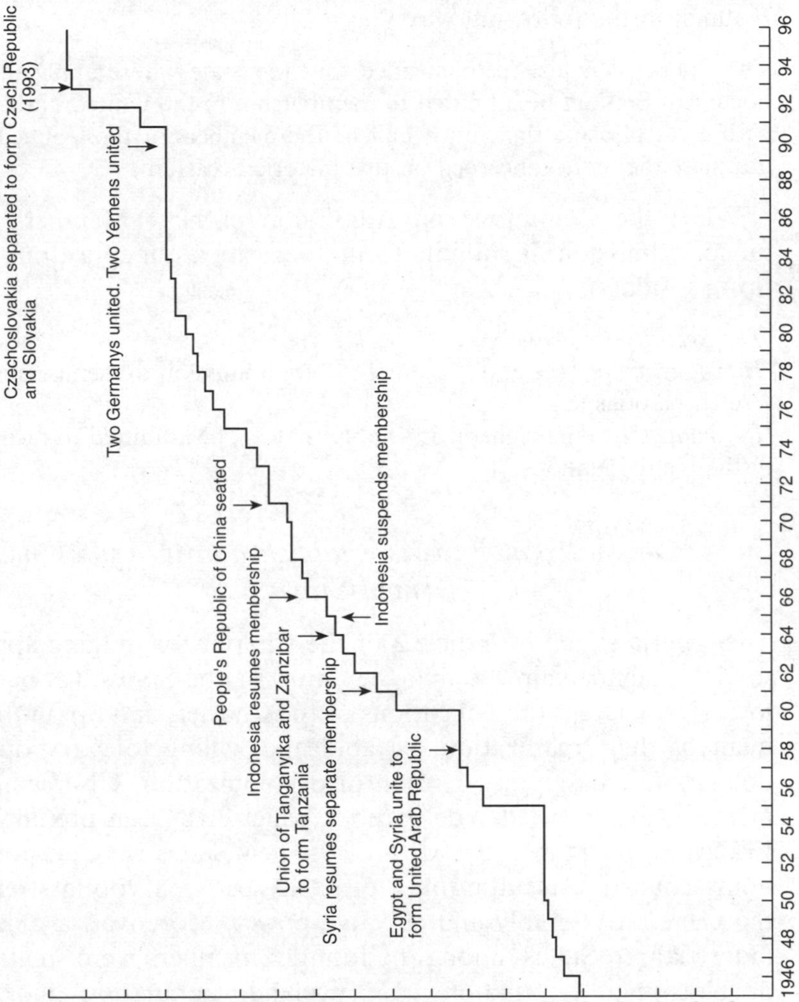

In 1993 the Committee recommended to the Council that it accept into membership a State whose name was a matter of dispute. Because of objections from Greece to the name Republic of *Macedonia*, the former Yugoslav Republic of Macedonia was recommended for membership as a State by the Committee and the Council in the following way:

The Council has just recommended that the State whose application is in document S/25147 be admitted to membership in the United Nations. It is with great pleasure that, on behalf of the members of the Council, I congratulate the State concerned on this historic occasion . . .[27]

When the Committee on Admission of New Members recommends admission, it submits to the Security Council a draft resolution as follows:

'*The Security Council*,
'*Having examined* the application of . . . for admission to membership in the United Nations (S/ . . .),
'*Recommends* to the General Assembly that . . . be admitted to membership in the United Nations.'

(b) Committee of Experts established at its 1506th meeting (mini-States)

The criteria stated in Article 4 of the Charter for judging applicants for UN membership are that they must (1) be States, (2) be 'peace-loving', (3) accept the obligations of the Charter, and (4) 'in the judgment of the Organization, be able and willing to carry out these obligations'. Largely as a result of decolonization, UN membership increased from the fifty delegations which had been present at San Francisco to 123 in 1967. Most of the new States were poorer developing countries, resulting in a disparity between voting strength in the General Assembly and effective power. Moreover, a number of industrialized States among the founder members were small in size or had small populations (e.g. Iceland—population 200,000, or Luxembourg—population 300,000) making it potentially difficult for them to find the resources to meet all the obligations of UN membership. Of the newly admitted States about twenty (in 1967) had populations of less than a quarter of a million.

Secretary-General Thant drew attention to aspects of the mini-State problem in the introduction to his annual report in 1967. Even the smallest colony had the right to determine its own future, he wrote, but UN membership imposes onerous obligations. A distinction should therefore be made between the right to independence and the question of full UN membership. He suggested that the competent organs should study the criteria for UN membership as well as other forms of association for those micro-States (or Lilliputian States, as they had been called in the League of Nations) which would not qualify for full membership.[28]

The United States had been concerned about other aspects of the problem, believing that the future admission of a large number of mini-States might distort the voting process in the General Assembly; but to raise the matter was almost always tactless, since the move might be interpreted as a slight by countries or territories awaiting admission. In 1967, however, there were no pending applications for membership from newly independent States, and the United States suggested that the Security Council should seek advice and assistance on the matter from the Council's Committee on New Members, which had been inactive for some twenty years.[29]

For eighteen months nothing much happened, although on four occasions the Council's President for the month reported that more urgent matters had prevented him from engaging in the necessary informal consultations.[30] Finally, in July and August 1969, US Ambassador Yost raised the matter formally with Secretary-General Thant and with the President of the Security Council, and at the end of August, the Security Council met twice to consider a US proposal that the Secretary-General should be urged to raise the matter in the General Assembly.[31]

The US proposal was no doubt a ploy to force a reluctant Security Council to take some action. The United States had originally suggested that the matter be referred to a Security Council committee. Month after month had gone by, and no Council meeting had been held to consider the US proposal: the President for the month had been either too busy to engage in consultations, or had consulted the other Council members and made little or no progress. The United States had then discussed the matter with the Secretary-General, who evidently was willing to review the mini-State question in the introductions to his annual reports, but not to force the issue. From the debate in the Council in August 1969, it is clear that the only matter on which there was agreement in the Council was to shunt the problem on to a siding, in the form of a committee of experts consisting of all the members of the Security Council.[32]

This Committee of Experts held eight closed meetings between 12 September 1969 and 10 June 1970, and then issued an interim report; three more meetings were held in 1971.[33] The United States proposed the establishment of a new class of Associate Members for exceptionally small new States. The United Kingdom suggested that very small States should enjoy the benefits of UN membership but should be allowed to renounce voluntarily certain rights—in particular the right to vote and the right to be a candidate for membership of certain UN organs. Colombia later proposed a modified form of association for mini-States 'fundamentally different from the proposal made [in 1969] by one of the super-Powers [the United States]': the form of association proposed by Colombia was, in fact, similar to the proposal of the United Kingdom in 1970. It was reported on good authority that the UN Legal Counsel advised that neither the US nor the UK proposal was consonant with the Charter.[34]

In the early 1990s, a number of States with very small populations were admitted into membership.[35] This again brought to the fore the 'mini-States' question. A former legal adviser to the Bahamas Ministry of Foreign Affairs, Dr Peter D. Maynard, has pointed to the advantages of welcoming small States into full membership of the United Nations.[36] Despite their small populations, small island States have jurisdiction over vast areas of ocean space. Kiribati, which has not decided to become a UN Member, has a surface area of 726 sq. km., while its exclusive economic zone covers an area of 3.5 million sq. km. Equally many small states play an important role in maintaining global biological diversity. Small States such as Fiji have made valuable contributions to UN peace-keeping operations.

3. ORGANS CONCERNED WITH THE MAINTENANCE OF INTERNATIONAL PEACE AND SECURITY

(a) Fact-finding missions

An important function of the Council's authority to appoint subsidiary organs is the investigation of any dispute or situation which might threaten world peace. This should be distinguished from inquiry which, in the language of the UN Charter, is one method for the peaceful settlement of disputes (Articles 33 and 34). The two procedures are sometimes lumped together as fact-finding.

In an article reviewing the experience of the United Nations in the collection of facts, one of us recalled an experience of President Kennedy in September 1963. Feeling the need to take a fresh look at the situation in South Vietnam, Kennedy sent an experienced diplomat who had previously served as political counsellor in the Saigon embassy together with the Pentagon's senior expert in counter-insurgency, to see things at first-hand. Their assessments of conditions in South Vietnam were so diametrically opposed that Kennedy was moved to ask, 'You two did visit the same country, didn't you?' [37]

The trouble with facts is not that they are in short supply but that there is a superabundance of them. Any diplomat worth his salt knows how to select facts in order to support a weak case. Fact-finding in the UN context may consist of the painstaking collection of information using the most rigorous rules of evidence, or it may be the amassing of reports in order to bolster a predetermined political position.

It is not surprising, therefore, that there should have been different views in the Security Council on whether proposals to set up subsidiary organs with fact-finding responsibilities should be subject to veto. As Articles 28 to 32 come in part of the Charter with the sub-heading *Procedure*, it has been argued that all decisions taken on the basis of these articles are procedural and therefore outside the scope of the veto. According to this view, a decision to establish a subsidiary organ under Article 29 is a procedural matter, whatever the organ's mandate. The Soviet Union, on the other hand, argued that an investigating body must be seen within the context of the 'chain of events' theory which the five major powers adumbrated at San Francisco.

The San Francisco statement on voting, which does not have the same legal authority as the Charter but expressed the views which the major powers held in 1945,[38] makes it clear that the setting up of such bodies or agencies as the Council deems necessary for the performance of its functions should be governed by a procedural vote. The statement goes on, however, to elaborate a 'chain of events' theory by which any proposal which initiates a chain of events which might, in the end, require the Council to invoke enforcement measures under Chapter VII of the Charter is therefore subject to veto. This chain of events could be initiated at an early stage—for example, by a decision to make an investigation. 'It is to such decisions and actions that unanimity of the permanent members [the veto] applies.'[39]

This problem arose in the very early days. The Council was discussing the Spanish question, and Australia proposed

> in accordance with Article 34 of the Charter, to make further inquiries in order to determine whether or not . . . a situation [leading to international friction and endangering international peace and security] exists.

Discussion of the Spanish question was adjourned, but when it was resumed a week later, the Australian representative submitted a revised proposal.

> I have cut out the idea of a formal investigation under Article 34 so as to enable the proposed body to be brought in under Article 29 as a subsidiary organ; and I call it a subcommittee instead of a committee.

The published records do not indicate why the change was made, although we assume that the revised wording was more acceptable to the Soviet Union. The resolution finally decided

> to make further studies in order to determine whether the situation in Spain has led to international friction and does endanger international peace and security . . . [and] *appoints* a subcommittee . . . to examine the statements made . . . to receive further statements and documents, and to conduct such inquiries as it may deem necessary.[40]

The same issue arose later in 1946 in connection with the Ukrainian complaint against Greece. The United States submitted a proposal to establish a commission of investigation 'acting under Article 34 of the Charter'. The President (the Soviet Union) stated that the US proposal 'relates to the substance of the matter' and was accordingly within the scope of the veto. France suggested that, on the contrary, the US proposal 'comes under the provision of Article 29 of the Charter'. The Soviet Union insisted that, in accordance with the San Francisco statement, the US proposal was a question of substance, and the United States agreed. The US proposal was put to the vote, and the negative Soviet vote was regarded as a veto.[41]

In 1947, the issue arose in connection with the Corfu Channel incident, but it became entangled with a different question, whether the United Kingdom was a party to a dispute and therefore required to abstain from voting. The President (Belgium), supported by the United Kingdom, Colombia, Syria, and the United States, took the view that a proposal to appoint a subcommittee 'to examine all the available evidence . . . [and] to request further information' was procedural. The Soviet Union took a contrary stand but, as it was not opposed to the setting up of a subcommittee, abstained when the proposal was put to a vote.[42]

In connection with the Czechoslovak question in 1948, Chile (a non-member of the Council) proposed that a subcommittee should be set up

> in accordance with Article 34 of the Charter . . . to receive or to hear . . . evidence, statements and testimonies.

The United States held that the proposal was 'clearly a procedural decision . . . The use of such a subsidiary organ to assist the Security Council . . . is expressly provided for in Article 29 . . .' This view was supported by Canada and Syria. The Soviet Union, however, considered the proposal substantive, and cast a double veto.[43]

One more example may be cited. When Laos sought UN assistance in 1959, three Western members of the Council proposed that a subcommittee should be appointed 'to examine the statements made before the Security Council . . . to receive further statements and documents and to conduct such inquiries as it may determine necessary'. In the Western view, this was simply the establishing of a subsidiary organ for which a procedural vote was sufficient, but for the Soviet Union this was or might be the first step in a chain of events which might lead to goodness knows what. A Soviet attempt to exercise the double veto was frustrated by a Presidential ruling.[44] It is not surprising that the authors of a standard work on the UN Charter should write that the practice of the Council regarding proposals for investigation or inquiry 'has not been consistent'.[45]

This issue of the application of the veto to subsidiary organs appears to have subsided since the enlargement of the Security Council in 1965.

(b) Peace-keeping operations

Peace-keeping is not referred to in the United Nations Charter, but in the absence of agreements to make armed forces available to the Security Council, peace-keeping has become an important means by which the Council can contribute to the maintenance of international peace and security. As of 30 June 1996 there had been 41 UN peace-keeping operations. Fifteen were established in the forty years between 1948 and 1988; the other 26 have all been set up since 1989. A description of each operation, including authorizing resolutions, function, location and duration, is contained in Appendix VI.

(i) Authorization

The first operation, the United Nations Truce Supervision Organization (UNTSO), was established by the Security Council in the Middle East in 1948. All these operations, save two, have been authorized by the Security Council. The first peace-keeping force *per se*, the United Nations Emergency Force (UNEF 1) was in fact established by the General Assembly, in the wake of paralysis in the Security Council. The Assembly also authorized the United Nations Security Force in West New Guinea (West Irian) (UNSF) established on 21 September 1962. Of the operations authorized by the Council, all except one were authorized by an explicit resolution of the Council. The exception being the United Nations Good Offices Mission in Afghanistan and Pakistan (UNGOMAP) which was authorized by a letter dated 25 April 1988 from the President of the Security Council addressed to the Secretary-General,[46] and later endorsed by two Council resolutions.[47]

(ii) Mandate

The nature of peace-keeping has changed significantly from the time of UNEF 1. This operation had provided the model for Cold War operations: it was impartial, there with the consent of the protagonists, and would resort to the use of force only in self-defence. The only Cold War operation that employed a significant amount of force was the United Nations Operation in the Congo (ONUC) from 1960 to 1961. To permit this the Council passed resolutions containing the following operative paragraphs:

Urges that the United Nations take immediately all appropriate measures to prevent the occurrence of civil war in the Congo, including . . . the use of force, if necessary, in the last resort.[48]

Authorizes the Secretary-General to take vigorous action, including the use of the requisite measure of force, if necessary, for the immediate apprehension . . . of all foreign military and paramilitary personnel and political advisors . . . [49]

In the 1980s and early 1990s UN peace-keeping operations grew more complex and multifunctional, with political, humanitarian, social, and economic components requiring civilian experts and staff to work in parallel with soldiers. Operations from El Salvador to Cambodia maintained the principles of consent and impartiality but embodied a wide variety of functions from election and human rights monitoring to mine-clearing and troop demobilization. The period from 1993 to 1997 witnessed a further development in UN peace-keeping. Operations maintained the multifunctional complexity of the early 1990s but a majority of operations were now deployed with mandates under Chapter VII of the Charter, and deployed in situations where fighting was still ongoing. This inevitably placed UN personnel in situations where they were likely to come under attack, as had also occurred in the Congo. A typical resolution, in this case for the UN Protection Force in former Yugoslavia, contained the following wording:

Acting under Chapter VII of the Charter

Authorizes UNPROFOR . . . acting in self-defence, to take the necessary measures, including the use of force, in reply to bombardments against the safe areas by any of the parties or to armed incursion into them or in the event of any deliberate obstruction in or around those areas to the freedom of movement of the Force or of protected humanitarian convoys.[50]

The experience of attacks on peace-keepers in Bosnia, Somalia, and Rwanda has led to a renewed stress on peace-keeping as an impartial, consensual activity, and instead employing *ad hoc* authorization where greater force is deemed to be required. It has thus become more common for the Council to *authorize* Member States to act to use 'all necessary means' to achieve specific objectives, with the possibility of significantly greater military force than would be politically feasible under direct UN command. The distinction between peace-keeping operations acting under Chapter VII, but still under the operational control of the Security Council and the Secretary-General, on the one hand, and authorization for Member States to take action under Chapter VII on behalf of the Council on the other, is an important one. Nevertheless Member States *are* required to report to the Council on the action that they have taken in implementing Council resolutions. These operations are listed in Table 21 and considered further, later in this chapter.

In addition to changes in the authorization and mandate of operations there have been a number of other procedural developments in peace-keeping operations the 1990s. The process of recent reflection on peace-keeping began with the publication of *An Agenda for Peace*, the report produced by the Secretary-General in response to the request made by the Council at its Summit level meeting in January 1992. The report led to debate in both the Assembly and the Council and a number of Council statements relating to peace-keeping. These included a statement on 29 October 1992 regarding the readiness of States to provide the UN with forces or capabilities; on 26 February 1993 regarding problems relating to humanitarian assistance; on 31 March 1993 relating to the safety of UN personnel (followed by resolution 686 (1993) on the same issue on 29 September 1993); and on 28 May 1993 relating to peace-keeping operational budgets.

(iii) Improving UN peace-keeping capacity

At the request of the General Assembly, the Secretary-General produced on 14 March 1994 a follow-up to *An Agenda for Peace* entitled 'Improving the capacity of the United Nations for peace-keeping'. This report led to further debate both in the Council and in the General Assembly's Special Committee on Peace-keeping Operations. The Special Committee held six meetings between 28 March and 29 April to discuss the report and associated proposals from Member States. Following the recommendations of the Committee, the Assembly adopted resolution 49/37[51] on a 'Comprehensive review of the whole question of peace-keeping operations in all their aspects'. This resolution amounted to a thorough summary of the views of the general membership on the dilemmas facing UN peace-keeping. Meanwhile the Council took a number of initiatives, formally in response to the Secretary-General's report, but equally influenced by fast-moving developments in current peace-keeping operations. On 3 May 1994 the Council issued a statement that the following factors needed to be taken into account when the establishment of a new peace-keeping operation was under consideration:

– whether a situation exists the continuation of which is likely to endanger or constitute a threat to international peace and security;
– whether regional or subregional organizations and arrangements exist and are ready and able to assist in resolving the situation;
– whether a cease-fire exists and whether the parties have committed themselves to a peace process intended to reach a political settlement;
– whether a clear political goal exists and whether it can be reflected in the mandate;
– whether a precise mandate for a United Nations operation can be formulated;
– whether the safety and security of United Nations personnel can be reasonably ensured.

The statement (reproduced as Appendix XII (a)) also addressed communication with non-members of the Council, stand-by arrangements, command and control, and a number of other issues.

(iv) Stand-by arrangements

The Security Council, in a statement by its President on 27 July 1994 (reproduced as Appendix XII (f)), reiterated the importance it attaches to improving the capacity of the United Nations for rapid deployment and reinforcement of peace-keeping operations. The

Secretary-General had already taken steps to encourage States to make offers of resources—such as military and civilian personnel, specialized services and equipment—that they might be prepared to make available for use by the UN for specific peace-keeping operations at short notice. Stand-by arrangements have proved valuable in the planning of operations such as the UN Angola Verification Mission III and the United Nations Mission in Haiti. However, such arrangements address only logistics and not political will. Member States will still be reluctant to respond to requests for participation in operations where the risks to their own personnel outweigh the perceived benefits of participation. A further statement by the President of the Security Council was issued on 19 December 1995 (reproduced as Appendix XII (g)) encouraging States that had not done so to participate in the stand-by arrangements.

(v) Consultations with troop-contributors

The significant increase in the cost of peace-keeping operations in the early 1990s, for which all Member States were liable, coupled with the transition in some operations from peace-keeping to peace enforcement, with attendant greater risk for peace-keeping participants, led to calls from non-members of the Council for a greater input into decision-making on peace-keeping. In May 1993, at the initiative of the Secretary-General, the 'first meeting of troop-contributors'[52] took place, in connection with the United Nations Protection Force. Such meetings increased in frequency, but did not satisfy all the concerns of non-members.[53] In May 1994 the Council acknowledged 'the need for enhanced consultations and exchange of information with troop-contributing countries regarding peace-keeping operations, including their planning, management and co-ordination'.[54] Following this statement the Council made some contentious decisions on changes to the mandates of ongoing peace-keeping operations. Many troop-contributors felt that this showed that existing methods of consultation were fine for information sharing but inadequate when a question of change to an operation's mandate was involved. Specific criticisms were that consultations had not been held 'in good time', that inadequate background information had been supplied, and that there was little indication that anything said by non-members would influence subsequent decisions of the Council.

Reflecting these concerns, Argentina and New Zealand requested that the President of the Council call a meeting to consider procedural questions concerning the operation of the Council in this area.[55] The two countries believed that an institutionalization of consultation mechanisms was desirable and suggested the convening of a standing committee of the Council to review regularly reports on peace-keeping missions and to provide for consultations with non-members. A number of other States wrote letters to the President endorsing the concerns of Argentina and New Zealand.[56] Egypt pointed out that the overwhelming majority of UN peace-keeping forces and observers came from States not members of the Council. Egypt endorsed the proposal that the Council establish a subsidiary organ for the purpose of consultations, under the provisions of Article 29 of the Charter. It also argued that the Council should apply the spirit* of Article 44 of the UN Charter, which reads:

> When the Security Council has decided to use force it shall, before calling upon a Member not represented on it to provide armed forces in fulfilment of the obligations assumed under Article 43, invite that Member, if the Member so desires, to participate in the decisions of the Security Council concerning the employment of contingents of that Member's armed forces.

Austria supported efforts to include potential as well as actual troop-contributors in consultations between the Secretariat and the Council prior to the deployment of a new operation.

The Council duly met on 4 November 1994 and issued a presidential statement (reproduced as Appendix XII(c)) setting out procedures for consultations between members of the Security Council, troop-contributing countries, and the Secretariat. It stated that such consultations should be held 'in good time' with an informal background paper circulated well in advance; that they would be chaired jointly by the Presidency of the Council and a Secretariat representative; and would be listed in the UN *Journal* and the monthly forecast of Council work. A number of Council members felt that setting

* Most commentators would reject the direct applicability of Article 44 to peace-keeping operations, not least because contributions to such operations are made on a voluntary basis.

up a subsidiary organ for the purpose of undertaking consultations would reduce Council efficiency, and such a proposal was not included in the statement.

In the debate following the adoption of the statement there was widespread support for the measures introduced. Welcoming the statement the representative of China quoted an ancient Chinese saying:

> One will be enlightened by listening to various views, and benighted by heeding only a one-sided view.[57]

Some delegations, however, argued that further steps needed to be taken. Malaysia referred to a paper entitled 'Political Direction and Support'[58] produced by non-permanent members and troop-contributors. These States presented a detailed list of situations for which consultations should be called:

> . . . when the mandate of a new peace-keeping operation was being formulated; when the concept and/or plan of operation of a peace-keeping operation was being considered; when the extension of the mandate of a peace-keeping operation was being considered; when a substantive modification of the mandate of an existing peace-keeping operation, including the broadening or narrowing of its geographical scope, changes in rules of engagement, introduction of new functions or components and so forth, was being considered; when significant developments occurred which, in the opinion of the Secretary-General, of members of the Security Council or of troop-contributors, were likely to affect materially the functioning of the operation or its ability to fulfil its mandate; or when the withdrawal of the operation in whole or in part was being considered.[59]

In 1995 a new report by the Secretary-General 'Supplement to an Agenda for Peace: Position Paper of the Secretary-General on the Occasion of the Fiftieth Anniversary of the United Nations' was published.[60] On 22 February 1995 the members of the Council issued a statement (reproduced as Appendix XII (b)) in response to 'the Supplement' addressing issues such as conflict prevention, the economic and social roots of conflict, peace-keeping, disarmament, economic sanctions, and the role of regional organizations. The debate following the issuing of 'the Supplement' also brought more widespread calls from States for the 'institutionalization' of consultations, and a subsidiary organ to include troop-contributing nations.[61] These calls were repeated in a Council meeting on 20 December 1995 called explicitly to consider improvements to such consultations. The meeting demonstrated a clear division between four of the permanent members (France, Russian Federation, United Kingdom, and the United States) who recognized failings in the present arrangements but who sought 'pragmatic' changes as a remedy, and thirty-six troop-contributing States who had been meeting informally, and who proposed the formal establishment of a subsidiary body. China's statement was neutral. As a result of this debate, and considerable further negotiation informally, the Council in a further presidential statement on 28 March 1996 (reproduced as Appendix XII(e)) set out further measures to strengthen consultations. The measures adopted were closer to those suggested by the permanent members than by other troop-contributors, in that they did not go much further toward the institutionalization of such meetings. The statement announced that meetings with troop-contributing States would be chaired primarily by the Presidency of the Council, with support from a Secretariat representative, rather than jointly as before; that meetings would be held with prospective contributors before the establishment of a new peace-keeping operation, and that information about meetings with troop-contributors would be appended to the Council's annual report to the General Assembly. Some Council members notified the President of the Council that they had refrained from breaking the consensus necessary for the adoption of a presidential statement, but that they wished the Council to revisit the matter so that the *de jure* as well as the *de facto* right of troop contributors to express their views could be recognized by the Council.[62]

(c) International tribunals

The Security Council has established two international tribunals in response to violations of international humanitarian law. The first concerned the former Yugoslavia. Following reports of widespread violations of international humanitarian law within the territory of former Yugoslavia, and especially in Bosnia and Herzegovina, the Council established a Commission of Experts to examine such reports.[63] The Commission was to present its findings to the Secretary-General, who would then report to the Security Council.

The atrocities reported were so extreme that on 22 February 1993[64] the Council took the unprecedented step of deciding to establish an international tribunal 'for the prosecution of persons responsible for serious violations of international humanitarian law committed in the territory of the former Yugoslavia since 1991'. The Council formally established the International Tribunal by resolution 827 (1993) on 25 May 1993.

A similar international tribunal was established in the light of atrocities committed in Rwanda. As with the case of the former Yugoslavia the Council first established a Commission of Experts to report on violations of international humanitarian law in Rwanda, on 1 July 1994. The Council proceeded on 8 November 1994 to establish, by resolution 955 (1994), 'an international tribunal for prosecuting those responsible for genocide and other serious violations of humanitarian law committed in Rwanda, and Rwandans responsible for such violations committed in neighbouring States between 1 January and 31 December 1994'.[65] The Statute of the International Tribunal for Rwanda, which was annexed to resolution 955 (1994), set out the competence of the Tribunal for Rwanda (its subject-matter, territorial and temporal jurisdiction) principles of individual criminal responsibility, the organization and structure of the Tribunal and the procedure for pre-trial, trial, and post-trial proceedings, including the principle of due process of law and the rights of the accused. The absence of the death penalty from the list of penalties which the Tribunal was empowered to impose was one of the reasons why Rwanda voted against the resolution, although Rwanda's Permanent Representative to the United Nations declared his country's readiness to co-operate and work with the Tribunal.[66] The Statutes of the two International Tribunals were almost identical. We have therefore reproduced only one, the Statute of the International Tribunal for Rwanda, as Appendix XVIII.

The tribunals for the former Yugoslavia and Rwanda share a common Appeals Chamber and a common Prosecutor. The respective establishing resolutions (827 (1993) and 955 (1994)) also both contained a determination that the respective situations constituted 'a threat to international peace and security', and stated that the Council was '*Acting* under Chapter VII of the Charter . . .' Secretary-General Boutros-Ghali argued, in the case of Rwanda, that the establishment of the International Tribunal under Chapter VII of the Charter was necessary to ensure not only the cooperation of Rwanda throughout the lifespan of the Tribunal, but the cooperation of all States in whose territory persons alleged to have committed serious violations of international humanitarian law and acts of genocide might be situated. The recourse to Chapter VII was also necessary to ensure a speedy and expeditious method of establishing the Tribunal.[67]

(d) Sanctions Committees

The Security Council passed resolutions to apply sanctions in 11 cases between 1946 and 1996. In the four cases marked with an asterisk, sanctions had been lifted as of 1 January 1997: Angola, Haiti*, Iraq, Liberia, Libya, Rwanda, South Africa*, Southern Rhodesia*, Somalia, Sudan, and the former Yugoslavia*. The severest economic embargo is currently faced by Iraq, but Iraq has recently begun trading oil for humanitarian supplies, under a UN agreement. The União Nacional para a Independência Total de Angola (UNITA) is facing an oil and arms embargo, while military embargoes apply to Somalia, Liberia, and Rwanda. Lesser diplomatic sanctions apply to Sudan.

It is now standard procedure for the Security Council to establish a sanctions committee as a subsidiary organ for each sanctions regime that it imposes. The only present exception to this rule is that no committee has been established in relation to the sanctions imposed against Sudan. Nowadays sanctions committees are 'committees of the whole' of the Council, and meet in private. A record of their discussions is issued with a 'Limited' document distribution designation, currently one or two months after a meeting has taken place. As can be seen from the list of sanctions committees contained in Table 20, eight out of ten sanctions committees have been established since 1990. The principal purposes of these sanctions committees are to examine reports from States on how they are implementing sanctions and, where necessary, to seek further details from them; to consider information about possible violations; and to make recommendations to the Council on ways of increasing the effectiveness of sanctions.[68] The sanctions committees for Iraq, Libya, and Yugoslavia had the additional task of giving approval to certain transactions and flights for humanitarian purposes, and the committees faced a particularly heavy work load in this respect. Secretary-General Boutros-Ghali reported in November 1995 that the backlog in processing humanitarian applications submitted to the relevant sanctions committees had been eliminated.[69]

UN mandated sanctions on a country can have an enormous impact on the lives of its citizens, and thus the sanctions committees have become a prominent focus of international debate. One consequence of this has been attempts to produce greater transparency in the operation of sanctions committees. Three Presidential Notes relating to the workings of the sanctions committees were issued in 1995 and 1996. The first on 29 March 1995 included six measures: increasing the number of press releases issued after meetings; the status of communications lists under the 'No objection' procedure to be made available to any delegation that wishes to have a copy; a list of all other decisions by each active committee to be prepared by the Secretariat, on a regular basis, and made available to any delegation that requests it; the annual report of the Security Council to the General Assembly to contain more information about each committee, and individual annual reports to be prepared by each committee, providing a concise indication of the committee's activities; and an effort to be made to expedite the preparation of the summary records of each committee. On 31 May 1995 the Council agreed to continue the practice of hearing comments by States and organizations concerned during closed meetings of the sanctions committees on issues arising from implementation of sanctions regimes imposed by the Security Council; and on 24 January 1996 the Council agreed that the chairman of each committee should give an oral briefing to UN Members following each committee meeting. These Presidential Notes are reproduced as Appendix XIII (a–c).

The proliferation of UN sanctions regimes in the 1990s has brought to the fore the dilemmas involved in applying sanctions as a political tool. Sanctions often appear to harm the poor in a particular State, rather than affect the well-being or political stance of those in government. Boutros-Ghali cautioned that

> Action taken by the international community to end oppression or bring about change by non-military means can have major ramifications for those who are already victimized by inequitable political and economic structures.

TABLE 20

Meetings of Security Council sanctions committees

Committee	Authorizing resolution	Number of meetings																	
		1968	69	70	71	72	73	74	75	76	77	78	79	80	81	82	83	84	85
Southern Rhodesia	253 (1968)	3	22	11	27	53	66	45	38	20	19[a]	19	31	0	0	0	0	0	0
South Africa	421 (1977)										0	6	16	23	9	0	4	5	3

Committee	Authorizing resolution	Number of meetings									
		1986	87	88	89	90	91	92	93	94	95
South Africa	421 (1977)	10	3	4	7[b]	8	3	6	4	1	
Iraq	661 (1990)					22	37	24	22	13	11
Yugoslavia	724 (1991)						1	47	46	22	23
Libya	748 (1992)							14	19	14	16
Somalia	751 (1992)							4	3	2	1
Haiti	841 (1993)								6	5	—
Angola	864 (1993)								4	3	1
Rwanda	918 (1994)									1	3
Liberia	985 (1995)										2

[a] The 284th meeting of the Committee held on 21 December 1976 was resumed on 14 March 1977. Meeting record (S/AC.15/SR.284) was reissued containing both parts of the meeting.

[b] The *Index to the Proceedings of the Security Council* fails to record a 90th meeting of this Committee, and it is therefore not included in these figures.

SCHEDULED MEETINGS

Monday, 17 March 1997

SECURITY COUNCIL

SECURITY COUNCIL COMMITTEE ESTABLISHED BY RESOLUTION 661 (1990) CONCERNING THE SITUATION BETWEEN IRAQ AND KUWAIT

3.30 p.m.	151st meeting* (closed)	Conference Room 7

* The Chairman of the Committee will give an oral briefing to interested members of the United Nations in the same conference room, immediately after the meeting. Following the oral briefing to members, the Chairman will give a briefing to the Press in the Press Room.

Extract from UN *Journal*, No. 1997/52 (Part II), 15 March 1997.

Economic sanctions hit the poor hardest and can have a deleterious impact on the work of humanitarian organizations.[70]

The importance of objectively assessing the short- and long-term humanitarian consequences of sanctions was emphasized by the permanent members in a joint non-paper in April 1995 (reproduced as Appendix XIV).

During the nuclear era, considerable intellectual effort was devoted to the circumstances in which nuclear weapons might have to be used, against which type of target, and such related matters as the accuracy of the weapon in particular situations, the amount of yield, etc. It would be of value if similar intellectual efforts could now be deployed on the wider issues of non-military and (non-nuclear) military coercion. One might start by looking at the coercive measures that have actually been used under Chapter VII of the Charter from sanctions to military enforcement, noting particularly the extent to which they satisfy the two aspects of the Just War doctrine, (*jus ad bellum* and *jus in bello*). This will not be easy in many cases, since the wording of Security Council resolutions may not tell one much about what actually happened on the ground ('all necessary means'). One should also look at where is the point of decision-making: the Secretary-General, a named State or States, a sanctions committee, a military commander, and so on.

States have a right under the Charter to consult the Security Council with regard to solving economic problems that affect them arising out of the indirect effects of UN enforcement measures taken against other States (Article 50). In the 1990s many more 'third States' have been affected in this way as a result of the imposition of sanctions. The General Assembly's *Special Committee on the Charter of the United Nations and on the Strengthening of the Role of the Organization* has been an important forum for calls for the effective implementation of the provisions for consultation under the Charter in this regard.[71] Adequate compensation for affected States is likely to result in a more comprehensive and effective application of a sanctions regime.

The following sanctions committees have been established by the Council:

(i) Security Council Committee established by resolution 253 (1968) concerning the question of Southern Rhodesia

The first 'sanctions' committee to be established by the Security Council in accordance with Rule 28 of the Provisional Rules of Procedure, was in relation to Southern Rhodesia in 1968. Following the Unilateral Declaration of Independence by Smith, the Council mandated an arms and oil embargo against Southern Rhodesia on 20 November 1965 (resolution 217 (1965)). These measures were strengthened a year later on 16 December by further sanctions on commodities (resolution 232 (1966)). Since these measures had 'so far failed to bring the rebellion in Southern Rhodesia to an end', the Council, on 29 May 1968, and acting under Chapter VII of the Charter, adopted resolution 253 (1968)). This resolution introduced tightened sanctions, and established a committee to (*a*) examine and report on the implementation of the resolution, and (*b*) to seek further information from Member States and specialized agencies as to any potential breach of the sanctions. The committee held a total of 354 meetings, before the lifting of sanctions by resolution 460 (1979) on 21 December 1979.

(ii) Security Council Committee established by resolution 421 (1977) on the question of South Africa

Acting under Chapter VII of the Charter, the Security Council adopted resolution 418 (1977) of 4 November 1977 imposing an arms embargo against South Africa. Avoiding the two and a half year gap between the initiation of sanctions and the establishment of a sanctions committee that occurred in the case of Southern Rhodesia, the Council moved quickly to establish a committee to oversee sanctions against South Africa on 9 December 1977 (resolution 421 (1977)). The committee held a total of 112 meetings, until it was dissolved upon the termination of the arms embargo and other restrictions on 25 May 1994, by resolution 919 (1994).

(iii) Security Council Committee established by resolution 661 (1990) concerning the situation between Iraq and Kuwait

This Committee was established under Chapter VII of the Charter to ensure the effective implementation of sanctions against Iraq, following its invasion and purported annexation of Kuwait. The Committee's mandate, outlined in resolution 661 (1990) of 6 August 1990, was to examine reports of the Secretary-General on progress in implementing the resolution, and to seek information from all States on action taken by them in this regard. Resolution 687 (1991) of 3 April 1991, the cease-fire resolution, declared that the full trade embargo against Iraq would remain in place, and that there would be periodic reviews every 60 days (para. 21) and every 120 days (para. 28) of Iraqi compliance with the obligations imposed under resolution 687. Resolution 712 of 19 September 1991, the terms of which were rejected by the Government of Iraq, would have allowed a partial lifting of the embargo, enabling Iraq to sell some of its oil and use the proceeds for humanitarian purposes, under strict UN monitoring. Nearly four years later the Government of Iraq and the UN concluded a Memorandum of Understanding, under which Iraq agreed to the provisions of resolution 986 of 14 April 1995 whereby Iraq could sell up to $1 billion of oil every 90 days and use the proceeds for humanitarian supplies to the country. The Committee adopted on 8 August 1996 the procedures for the implementation of resolution 986.

Setting the pattern for subsequent committees of this type, the Security Council elected an individual permanent representative as its Chairman in his personal capacity for the calendar year, while two delegations were elected to provide the Vice-Chairmen for the year.

At its meeting on 17 August 1990 the Committee agreed that all its decisions were to be taken by consensus. The Committee had held 142 meetings as of 8 August 1996.

(iv) Security Council Committee established pursuant to resolution 724 (1991) concerning Yugoslavia

This Committee was established by resolution 724 (1991) to monitor the implementation of the arms embargo against 'Yugoslavia' imposed by resolution 713 (1991). This applied a 'general and complete embargo on all deliveries of weapons and military equipment to Yugoslavia'; which, as was confirmed by resolution 727 (1992) of 8 January 1992, applied to all areas that had been part of Yugoslavia. The mandate of the Committee grew as further resolutions in the course of 1992–3 imposed economic and other sanctions on the Federal Republic of Yugoslavia (Serbia and Montenegro). Following the agreement of the Federal Republic of Yugoslavia to close its borders to the Bosnian Serbs, certain sanctions against the Federal Republic were suspended on 5 October 1994.[72] New sanctions were simultaneously imposed on the Bosnian Serbs.[73] Following the initialling on 21 November 1995 near Dayton, Ohio, of the General Framework Agreement for Peace in Bosnia and Herzegovina, the Council by resolution 1022 (1995),[74] suspended indefinitely, the sanctions against the Federal Republic of Yugoslavia (Serbia and Montenegro). By resolution 1021 (1995) a date was set (13 March 1996) for the termination of most aspects of the arms embargo. The remaining sanctions were terminated by resolution 1074 (1996) of 1 October 1996. The Committee held 141 meetings before it was wound up on 15 November 1996.

(v) Security Council Committee established pursuant to resolution 748 (1992) concerning the Libyan Arab Jamahiriya

This Committee was established by resolution 748 (1992) adopted on 31 March 1992 under Chapter VII of the UN Charter. The resolution determined that Libya had failed to demonstrate its renunciation of terrorism through insufficient co-operation in establishing the responsibility for the destruction of Pan Am flight 103 and Union de transports aériens flight 772, as specified in resolution 731 (1992) of 21

January 1992. The Committee, established under Rule 28 of the Council's Provisional Rules of Procedure, had responsibility for the implementation of sanctions against Libya, including the decisions of the Council to ban any aircraft taking off from, or landing in Libya, the supply of military equipment, aircraft or aircraft components to Libya, and the significant reduction in staff at Libyan diplomatic missions and consular posts. The Committee had the tasks of examining reports of the Secretary-General and Member States on sanctions implementation, considering expeditiously applications for the approval of flights on humanitarian grounds, and giving special attention to any communications from States under Article 50 of the Charter pertaining to special economic problems that might arise for other States through the implementation of the measures contained in the resolution. On 11 November 1993 the Council tightened sanctions on Libya, approving the freezing of Libyan funds in other countries, and banning the provision to Libya of equipment for oil refining and transportation. Considerable efforts were made during 1994 and 1995 by the Council of the League of Arab States, the Movement of Non-Aligned States, and the Organization of African Unity, to have the Council reconsider the imposition of sanctions. The Committee undertook regular reviews of the sanctions regime, but on each occasion did not find that conditions existed for any modification. The Committee had held 73 meetings as of 3 February 1997.

(vi) Security Council Committee established pursuant to resolution 751 (1992) concerning Somalia

This Committee was established by resolution 751 (1992) of 24 April 1992 to ensure the effective implementation of the embargo, imposed by resolution 733 (1992) of 23 January 1992 on all deliveries of weapons and military equipment to Somalia. On the basis of the guidelines adopted on 8 May 1992, decisions of the Committee were to be taken by consensus. As of 31 July 1996 the Committee had held 11 meetings.

(vii) Security Council Committee established pursuant to resolution 864 (1993) concerning the situation in Angola

This Committee was established by resolution 864 (1994) on 15 September 1994 to supervise the imposition of an oil and arms embargo on the União Nacional para a Independência Total de Angola (UNITA). This was an interesting departure since it imposed sanctions on a non-state entity. This set a precedent for the imposition of sanctions in Europe against another non-state entity, the Bosnian Serbs, eight days later. Additional sanctions were imposed against UNITA by resolution 1127 of 28 August 1997. The Committee had held 10 meetings as of 31 July 1996.

(viii) Security Council Committee established pursuant to resolution 918 (1994) concerning Rwanda

This Committee was established by resolution 918 (1994) of 17 May 1994 to ensure the effective implementation of an arms embargo imposed, under Chapter VII of the UN Charter, on Rwanda. The arms embargo was suspended by the Council, and terminated on 1 September 1996. In September 1995, by paragraph 3 of resolution 1013 (1995),[75] the Committee was given a new task of providing the International Commission of Inquiry with information relating to the sale and supply of arms to former Rwandese government forces in the Great Lakes region. The Committee had held 5 meetings as of 31 July 1996.

(ix) Security Council Committee established pursuant to resolution 985 (1995) concerning Liberia

This Committee was established by resolution 985 (1995) to ensure the effective implementation of the general and complete embargo imposed by resolution 788 (1992) on all deliveries of weapons and military equipment to Liberia. On the basis of the guidelines issued for the conduct of its work, adopted on 25 May 1995, as is standard for sanctions committees, all decisions of the Committee have been taken by consensus. The Committee had held 3 meetings as of 31 July 1996.

(x) Security Council Committee established pursuant to resolution 841 (1993) concerning Haiti

Following recommendations from the Organization of American States, the Security Council established by resolution 841 (1993) of 16 June 1993 a trade embargo against Haiti concerning the sale of petroleum products and arms. By this resolution the Council also established a Committee to oversee the implementation of the sanctions. The Council reaffirmed on 15 November 1993 that the sanctions imposed against Haiti would remain in force until the objectives of the Governor's Island Agreement had been fulfilled, including the departure of the Commander-in-Chief of the Haitian Armed Forces, the creation of a new police force permitting the restoration of constitutional order to Haiti, and the return of the democratically elected President.[76] Further sanctions were imposed on 6 May 1994.[77] Finally, with the return of President Aristide imminent, the Council decided under resolution 944 (1994) of 29 September 1994, to terminate the sanctions measures and dissolve the Committee established under resolution 841 (1993) 'with effect from 0001 hours Eastern Standard Time on the day after the return to Haiti of President Jean-Bertrand Aristide'. The confirmation of the return of President Aristide and the lifting of sanctions was made in resolution 948 (1994).

(e) UN peace-enforcement

As outlined above, peace-keeping operations in the 1990s were frequently given mandates under Chapter VII of the Charter, allowing for limited force to be used in particular circumstances. At other times the Council has chosen to authorize States or coalitions of States to take enforcement action in implementation of Council decisions. In the case of Korea in 1950 the Council only *recommended* action, in the case of Southern Rhodesia it *called upon* the United Kingdom to act. Subsequently it has *authorized* States to act in the following situations: in Iraq in 1990–1, in Somalia in 1992, in Rwanda and Haiti in 1994, in Bosnia in 1995–6, and in Zaire (DRC) in 1996. The wording used in each authorization is given in Table 21.

The advantages and potential dangers of this method of enforcement were summed up by Boutros-Ghali in his introduction to the 1996 third edition of the UN publication 'Blue Helmets':

> Enforcement action, duly authorized by the Security Council, is greatly preferable to the unilateral use of force. Such action is, however, a double-edged sword. It offers the Organization a capacity not otherwise available but carries with it the risk of potential damage to the credibility and stature of the United Nations. Once the Security Council authorizes such interventions,

TABLE 21

Enforcement Action by Member States authorized by the Security Council, 1946–1996

Unified Command in Korea:
Authorizing resolutions: 83 (1950) and 84 (1950)
Date: 27 June and 10 July 1950
Wording of authorization:*

Having determined that the armed attack upon the Republic of Korea . . . constitutes a breach of the peace . . .

Recommends that the Members of the United Nations furnish such assistance to the Republic of Korea as may be necessary to repel the armed attack . . .

Recommends that all Members providing military forces and other assistance . . . make such forces and other assistance available to a unified command under the United States of America.

Southern Rhodesia:
Authorizing resolution: 221 (1966)
Date: 9 April 1966
Wording of authorization:

Determines that the . . . situation constitutes a threat to the peace . . .

Calls upon the Government of the United Kingdom . . . to prevent, by the use of force if necessary, the arrival at Beira of vessels reasonably believed to be carrying oil destined for Southern Rhodesia . . .

Coalition Force Against Iraq:
Authorizing resolution: 678 (1990)
Date: 29 November 1990
Wording of authorization:

Acting under Chapter VII of the Charter . . .

Authorizes Member States co-operating with the Government of Kuwait . . . to use all necessary means to uphold and implement resolution 660 (1990) and all subsequent relevant resolutions to restore international peace and security in the area.

United Task Force (UNITAF) (Somalia):
Authorizing resolution: 794 (1992)
Date: 3 December 1992
Wording of authorization:

Acting under Chapter VII of the Charter of the United Nations, *authorizes* the Secretary-General and Member States . . . to use all necessary means to establish as soon as possible a secure environment for humanitarian relief operations in Somalia.

Temporary International Presence in Rwanda (Operation Turquoise):
Authorizing resolution: 929 (1994)
Date: 22 June 1994
Wording of authorization:

Acting under Chapter VII of the Charter of the United Nations, *authorizes* the Member States co-operating with the Secretary-General to conduct [a temporary operation under national command and control] . . . using all necessary means to achieve the humanitarian objectives set out in . . . resolution 925 (1994).

Multinational Force in Haiti (MNF)
Authorizing resolution: 940 (1994)
Date: 31 July 1994
Wording of authorization:

Acting under Chapter VII of the Charter of the United Nations, *authorizes* Member States to form a multinational force under unified command and control and, in this framework, to use all necessary means to . . . establish and maintain a secure and stable environment that will permit implementation of the Governors Island Agreement . . .

Implementation Force in Bosnia and Herzegovina (IFOR):
Authorizing resolution: 1031 (1995)
Date: 15 December 1995
Wording of authorization:

Acting under Chapter VII of the Charter of the United Nations . . .

Authorizes Member States to establish a multinational implementation force (IFOR) under unified command and control . . . [and to] take all necessary measures to effect the implementation of and ensure compliance with . . . the Peace Agreement . . .

Authorizes the Member States . . . to take all necessary measures to ensure compliance with the rules and procedures . . . governing command and control of airspace over Bosnia and Herzegovina with respect to all civilian and military air traffic . . .

Authorizes Member States to take all necessary measures, at the request of IFOR, either in defence of IFOR or to assist the force in carrying out its mission, and recognizes the right of the force to take all necessary measures to defend itself from attack or threat of attack . . .

Multinational Force in Eastern Zaire
Authorizing resolution: 1080 (1996)
Date: 15 November 1996
Wording of authorization:

Acting under Chapter VII of the Charter of the United Nations . . .

Authorizes the Member States co-operating with the Secretary-General to conduct the operation [to facilitate the immediate return of humanitarian organizations and the effective delivery by civilian relief organizations of humanitarian aid . . .] . . . to achieve, by using all necessary means, the humanitarian objectives set . . .

Stabilization Force in Bosnia and Herzegovina (SFOR):
Authorizing resolution: 1088 (1996)
Date: 12 December 1996
Wording of authorization:

SFOR was the legal successor to IFOR, and the authorizing provisions in resolution 1088 (1996) closely mirror those of resolution 1031 (1995) for IFOR, including:

Acting under Chapter VII of the Charter of the United Nations . . .

Authorizes Member States to take all necessary measures, at the request of IFOR, either in defence of IFOR or to assist the force in carrying out its mission, and recognizes the right of the force to take all necessary measures to defend itself from attack or threat of attack . . .

* In each case the authorization is preceded by the words: *The Security Council.*

States may claim international legitimacy and approval for measures not initially envisaged by the Council.[78]

(f) Other miscellaneous organs for the maintenance of international peace and security

(i) United Nations Compensation Commission

This Commission was established by resolution 692 (1991) of 20 May 1991, to implement certain provisions of resolution 687 (1991). The Commission, based in Geneva, has had the responsibility of determining the amount of compensation that Iraq is liable to pay to the Government of Kuwait and private persons, as a consequence of its invasion.

(ii) UN Special Commission (UNSCOM) established pursuant to resolution 687 (1991)

The Special Commission was established pursuant to paragraph 9(b) of resolution 687 (1991), and was mandated to supervise the destruction, removal, or rendering harmless of all Iraqi chemical and biological weapons. This embraced stocks of agents, related subsystems and components, all research, development, support, and manufacturing facilities, as well as all ballistic missiles with a range greater than 150 kilometres and related major parts, and repair and production facilities. Under resolution 1051 of 27 March 1996 an export/import monitoring system was established for Iraq, under which countries exporting to Iraq had to notify the UN Special Commission and the International Atomic Energy Agency regarding the supply of 'dual-use' items to Iraq. Resolution 687 (1991) also led to the establishment of the Iraq–Kuwait Boundary Demarcation Commission. This has now concluded its work.

4. OTHER SUBSIDIARY BODIES

(a) Informal Working Group of the Security Council concerning the Council's documentation and other procedural questions

As its name might suggest this informal group is not a subsidiary organ of the Council, but (like drafting groups) is an outgrowth of informal consultations, to which it is subordinate and reports. Its meetings are not recorded in the *Index to Proceedings of the Security Council*, and no summary records are published. In many other respects it resembles the Committee of Experts (see above) in that it is a working rather than a debating body, was established to assist Council members with procedural matters, and its composition is identical to that of the Council. The *Working Group* was established by Council members following discussions in informal consultations.

The Group was established in 1993, and meets as and when necessary. The main purpose of the Group has been to study and make recommendations on proposals for changes to the Council's procedures and documentation. Such proposals have to a degree arisen in response to demands for more transparency in the work of the Council. Almost all the developments in the Council's working methods since 1993 that have been included in presidential statements, had their origins in meetings of the *Working Group*. A number of these statements are reproduced as Appendices to this book.

CHAPTER 8

NEW CHARTER, NEW MEMBERS, NEW RULES, NEW WORKING PRACTICES, OR NEW NATIONAL POLICIES?

> While the final responsibility for all success or failure in diplomacy would seem to rest upon the . . . ministers at home, it is none the less true that since these ministers can only act upon information from abroad, the influence which an enlightened diplomat can exercise upon the actions and designs of the home government is very large.

I. NEW CHARTER?

We have nowhere in this book expressed the view that improvements in the working of the Security Council depend upon changes in the Charter. To be sure, many of the provisions of the Charter are unsatisfactory diplomatic compromises, but we are lucky to have a United Nations. The process by which the Organization was constructed was painful, and it is astonishing that the United Nations has survived the stresses of five difficult decades. The provisions in the Charter which are most criticized—the veto, for example—are precisely the matters on which one or more of the five permanent members would be most unyielding, and no amendment can take effect if it is not ratified by all of the permanent members.

This is not to say that there will be no amendments to the Charter. Both the Security Council and the Economic and Social Council have already been enlarged, and further enlargement of the former is likely, potentially involving the addition of new permanent members (see 'New Members?' below). But the broad structure of the United Nations, the principles on which it is based, the purposes to which it is directed, are likely to remain unaltered. The principal challenge is not to draft a better Charter: it is to make better use of the Charter we have.

There are, of course, ideas and phrases in the Charter that are now redundant. Articles 53 and 107 refer to any State which, during the Second World War, had been an enemy of any signatory of the Charter. The implication of these two Articles is that ex-enemy States are of lesser status than the rest of the membership, as enforcement measures may be taken against them without the authority of the Security Council, whereas the Council's authority is needed for normal enforcement. Japan in particular has campaigned for the deletion of these Articles, for primarily symbolic reasons since in practice the references in the Charter would not now be invoked. On 15 December 1995 the General Assembly accepted a recommendation from the Special Committee on the Charter to delete the 'enemy State clauses' at its earliest appropriate future session. This is likely to occur in a package with other changes requiring Charter amendment, such as an expansion of the membership of the Security Council. This would simplify the ratification process for Member States.

There are other parts of the Charter that have not been implemented, but are disregarded. The Military Staff Committee continues to meet every two weeks, but with the exception of some informal meetings at the end of 1990 (see Chapter 6.1) it has not fulfilled the functions envisaged for it in the Charter. This has not prevented the Security Council from launching over 40 peace-keeping operations in the last 51 years, many authorized under Chapter VII of the Charter (even though the concept of and the word 'peace-keeping' does not appear in the Charter), nor has it prevented the Council from authorizing Member States to take enforcement action in implementation of its decisions (see Chapter 7 Table 21).

There have also been other *de facto* changes when there is general agreement. Article 27 (3) of the Charter states that decisions by the Security Council on non-procedural matters shall be made by an 'affirmative vote' of nine (originally seven) members of the Council, including 'the concurring votes' of the permanent members. Did the drafters of the Charter intend that 'affirmative' and 'concurring' should have the same meaning, corresponding to a Yes vote? If the same meaning was intended, why was different language used? This issue came up during the early months, when the Soviet Union was unwilling to vote Yes but did not wish to veto. The other four permanent members raised no objection, and by the end of 1948, all four had taken advantage of the procedure pioneered by the Soviet Union.[1]

When the Soviet Union broke up in 1991, Boris Yeltsin, the President of the Russian Federation, addressed a letter to the Secretary-General informing him that 'the membership of the Union of Soviet Socialist Republics in the United Nations, including the Security Council . . . is continued, with the support of the states of the Commonwealth of Independent States, by the Russian Federation'.[2] The Secretary-General then forwarded the letter to the President of the Security Council, who happened at the time to be the Permanent Representative of the Russian Federation, and asked him to circulate it. At the next meeting of the Security Council, the USSR placard was replaced by one that read 'Russian Federation'.[3] Some commentators have suggested that this amounted to a *de facto* amendment to Article 23(1), which lists the Union of Soviet Socialist Republics as a permanent member of the Council. It does not, however, since the legal position is that the Russian Federation is simply the continuation of the USSR with a different name and with reduced territory. Thus the position with regard to the Charter is analogous to that of the earlier name change of the Republic of China to the People's Republic of China. The Charter wording referring to the Republic of China in Article 23(1) has remained unchanged.

The Charter should not be treated as if it were holy writ. It was devised during the Second World War in a situation very different from the present. Decolonization was but a dream. The preamble to the Charter affirmed 'faith in fundamental human rights, in the dignity and worth of the human person, in the equal rights of men and women and of nations large and small . . .' UN organs have set standards to achieve these goals, but the States of which the UN is composed have made minimal progress in changing aspirations into reality. The fault is not in the Charter, but in ourselves.

2. NEW MEMBERS?

Now, during the UN's sixth decade, there is growing pressure for an enlargement in the membership of the Security Council, and at the time of writing (August 1997) the General Assembly's working group on this issue is continuing its search for a solution acceptable to sufficient Member States. The difficulty in writing a book about Council procedure is that one is always aiming at a moving target—new, albeit usually minor, procedural measures are adopted almost every month. There is perhaps even greater danger in attempting to describe the present negotiations on possible changes to the membership, voting procedures, and other aspects of the Council's work. There is only space here to make some cursory observations on the highly complex issues involved, and any subsequent agreement by States could make such observations appear out of date. Nevertheless we believe that it is valuable to include here a brief outline of the background and issues involved.

(a) The background to the establishment of the General Assembly Working Group

The enlargement of the Council from eleven to fifteen members entered into force on 31 August 1965 and took effect on 1 January 1966. Since that time there have been a number of proposals for a further expansion in the Council's membership. In 1979 a proposal was made to increase the number of non-permanent members to fourteen. The following year, at the thirty-fifth session of the General Assembly, a group of African, Asian, and Latin American States put forward a resolution proposing the addition of six non-permanent members, to give a total Council size of 21, with a majority of 14 members required for a resolution to be passed. The proposed geographical distribution of non-permanent seats was:*

* The sixteenth seat was to alternate between Latin America (half the time) and Africa, WEOG and Eastern Europe (each one-sixth of the time).

Africa	5⅙
Asia	4
Latin America and the Caribbean	3½
Western Europe and other States	2⅙
Eastern Europe	1⅙

On 14 December 1979 ten developing countries requested the inclusion of a new item on the agenda of the General Assembly, the *question of equitable representation on and increase in the membership of the Security Council.* An explanatory memorandum that accompanied the request, in accordance with Rule 20 of the Assembly's Rules of Procedure, outlined the arguments for the item's inclusion. The memorandum noted that the membership of the United Nations had increased from 113 at the time of the enlargement of the Council to 152 in 1979, whilst the membership of the Council had remained at 15. It also noted that there was one non-permanent seat for 18.5 Asian States, one for 16.3 African States, one for 14 Latin American States, one for 11 Western European and other States, and one for 10 Eastern European States. The item was included on the agenda in 1979 and each year subsequently, but it was not until 1992 that the Assembly successfully adopted a resolution on the subject.

Following support for 'more balanced representation' in UN bodies at the Tenth Conference of Heads of State or Government of Non-Aligned Countries, held in Jakarta in September 1992,[4] the UN General Assembly adopted by consensus on 11 December a resolution inviting Member States to submit written comments on a possible review of the membership of the Council.[5] The resolution was proposed by thirty-six developing States and one State from Eastern Europe.[6] At this time the membership of the Organization had increased to 179 and there was now one non-permanent seat for 22 Asian States; 17 for both African and Latin American States; 12 for Western Europe and other States; and 10 for Eastern Europe.

Following an examination of the comments submitted by Member States during the course of the year the General Assembly on 10 December 1993 adopted a resolution establishing an *Open-ended Working Group* 'to consider all aspects of the question of increase in the membership of the Security Council'.[7] The carefully negotiated preambular paragraph of the resolution recognized the need to review the membership of the Security Council and related matters in view of the substantial increase in the membership of the United Nations, especially of developing countries, as well as the changes in international relations.[8]

It is interesting that in 1992 the Assembly choose to take up the matter of Council expansion, having deferred it annually for thirteen years. There is no doubt that the 'activism' of the United Nations stemming from the newly found consensus among the permanent members in the early 1990s, had placed the Security Council in the public spotlight, and this possibly made it a more appealing prospect for potential new permanent members. The motivation for reform of some other States can perhaps also be accounted for in terms of the new co-operation in the Council, but in their case out of a desire for 'damage limitation' rather than an attempt to share the limelight. Many States, particularly from developing countries, witnessed that the UN was intervening more readily than in the past, and in some situations hitherto considered to be within the domestic jurisdiction of the State concerned. Many of these interventions were welcomed, but the declining ability of non-members to influence Council decisions reminded such States that they themselves might become subject to unwelcome intervention at a future time. The shift towards permanent member co-operation, with many substantive decisions now being taken in private during consultations of the whole, also hastened the pursuit of Council enlargement, being seen by non-members as a possible means by which to regain access and influence. Conversely, as the *Open-ended Working Group* proceeded with its work the Council continued to undertake a number of procedural changes aimed at increasing Council transparency and encouraging the participation of non-members. To an extent these measures 'took some of the wind out of the sails' of the momentum toward Council reform. Likewise the damage to the image of the Organization resulting from UN peace-keeping operations in Bosnia and Somalia both made the 'prize' of permanent membership less glittering, as well as decreasing the will of the permanent members of the Council to launch and fund new, and potentially interventionist, operations. The prospect of a less interventionist Council might, temporarily, have reduced the pressure of developing countries for an immediate expansion of the Council, but their underlying desire for an expansion, expressed since 1979, remained. This does not deny that the minor influence of external events can have a substantial impact on the perceived advantages of a swift but concrete compromise agreement set against the advantages of spending time in negotiations attempting to maximize national gain. For potential new permanent members such as Japan and Germany, external considerations can change the perceived worth of such membership and thus affect the extent to which sacrifices are willing to be made to obtain the goal.

(b) The Open-ended Working Group: A summary of progress

The *Working Group* met for the first time in January 1994 and had 21 further meetings before the submission of its first report to the Assembly in September. This report noted that there had been 'a convergence of views that the membership of the Council should be enlarged'.[9] The 49th session of the General Assembly approved the continuation of the Group's work and it met 33 times (11 times formally and 21 times informally) from January to September 1995. In 1995 the Group produced, as in 1994, a brief formal report,[10] but also circulated to the General Assembly a number of the Group's 'non-papers' including a detailed set of observations and assessment by the two Vice-Chairmen, the Permanent Representatives of Finland and Thailand. This pattern was repeated in 1996 with a short formal report complemented by a substantial compendium of proposals from Member States. A total of 56 meetings (39 formal and 17 informal) were held in the course of the year. In the first two and a half months of 1997 the Vice-Presidents of the Working Group carried out bilateral consultations, in turn, with 165 countries.[11] They apparently reported to the Working Group that 'a very large majority expressed a preference for an increase in both permanent and non-permanent seats',[12] but this conclusion was objected to by some States. On 20 March 1997 the President of the General Assembly proposed, in the form of a draft resolution, a package solution to the Working Group. His proposals included the enlargement of the Council through the addition of 5 permanent and 4 non-permanent members. The new permanent members would not be granted the power of veto and an affirmative vote of 15 out of the

24 members of the Council would be required for a Council decision. A review conference would be held after 10 years.

(c) The Open-ended Working Group: A review of some of the main issues

(i) Size and composition of the Council

Permanent Membership

(a) Changes affecting the existing permanent members. The permanent five have strongly resisted attempts to question their continued right to occupy permanent seats, and attempts to modify the associated rights that accrue from this category of membership. Questioning of the existing members *per se* has arisen largely in the context of proposals that would add Germany to the permanent membership, with the result of a Council with three permanent members from Western Europe. This has led to some developing countries, and the Committee on Foreign Affairs and Security of the European Parliament,[13] to call for a single European Union permanent seat on the Council. The existing members that would be affected by this change, France and the United Kingdom, have unsurprisingly rejected any such proposal. First, they have argued that Title V of the Maastricht Treaty, on a common foreign and security policy for the Union, does not envisage such collective permanent membership. Second that granting membership to regional *organizations* would not strengthen the Council. In the course of the Working Group's deliberations there was an unstated convergence of views that it would be politically unfeasible to entertain any changes to the membership of the existing permanent members at this stage, in no small part because the existing permanent members would have to vote for their own abolition. There have, however, been a number of calls for modifications to the privileges accruing to permanent membership, such as the *permanent members' convention* and the power of veto. Suggestions from members of the Non-Aligned Movement have included restricting the use of the veto to Chapter VII of the Charter, and requiring at least two vetoes to be cast for a resolution to be defeated. A former British ambassador to the UN, Sir David Hannay,[14] has suggested that the veto should not be used

in votes on the appointment of the UN Secretary-General. Others have suggested that it should not be applicable to the admission of new Member States. The key question remains whether such restrictions would be voluntarily imposed or mandatory. Such modifications need not necessitate a Charter amendment, since a formal or informal agreement to designate certain decisions as procedural, thus placing them outside the scope of the veto under Article 27 of the Charter, could be arrived at. A similar exercise was carried out in the late 1940s under the Interim Committee of the General Assembly, at the instigation of the United States.[15] Its recommendations were not subsequently adopted.

(b) Candidates for new permanent members. When the composition of the Council was agreed at San Francisco in 1945 there was much debate on the criteria for non-permanent members, however, the selection of permanent members was seen as a political decision. Whilst commentators have suggested assorted criteria for the selection of new permanent members, the ultimate choice is likely to remain primarily a political excercise.

Japan and Germany, currently the second and third largest contributors to the UN regular budget, have had the support of many States in their quest for permanent membership. The challenge facing the Working Group has been to represent adequately in an enlarged Council both the industrialized North and the three main developing country regions (Africa, Asia, and Latin America and the Caribbean). A number of proposals have been made suggesting the creation of shared or rotating permanent seats. The extension or not of the veto to new permanent members has also been the subject of much debate.

Non-permanent members: modalities for election

States have raised three principal sets of proposals regarding non-permanent members. The first would be to have no new permanent members, and an increase in the non-permanent category only, with the modalities and criteria for election remaining the same. The second would again be to enlarge the Council solely by adding more non-permanent members, but with different modalities and criteria for their election. The third would entail an expansion of both permanent and non-permanent categories, with the non-permanent members either retaining existing modalities and criteria for election, or all or some being subject to new modalities and criteria. Exactly what is entailed by the proposals for new modalities or criteria has been a subject of much debate.

Currently, regional electoral groups annually recommend candidates for election by the General Assembly to the vacant non-permanent Security Council seats. The distribution of non-permanent seats by which this takes place is based on an agreement made in 1963 when the Council was expanded from 11 to 15 members. The issue of the geographical distribution of new non-permanent seats, as well as the overall geographical distribution of both permanent and non-permanent seats is likely to be fundamental to an agreed package on Council enlargement.

Council size

Under Article 24 of the Charter the Council must ensure prompt and effective action for the maintenance of international peace and security, and do so on behalf of the wider UN membership. It would be easy to conclude from these functions that Council size should be determined by the needs of representation on the one hand and efficiency and effectiveness on the other. That is, that it must be sufficiently large to adequately represent the membership, while remaining small enough to operate efficiently. In practice perceptions of whether the Council is acting in a representative manner are based more on the perceived legitimacy of the content of Council *actions* than on the size and composition of its membership. The need to ensure prompt action *does* require an efficient Council, and a small membership undoubtably contributes to this goal, but efficiency is determined as much by a willingness of members to co-operate in the smooth running of Council decision-making. Moreover, effectiveness, as opposed to efficiency, may be aided by a larger Council membership which brings more political, financial, or military resources to the Council's work.

(ii) Working methods and transparency of the Council

We described above how positions on Council enlargement could be influenced by procedural developments in the Council's day-to-day operations. In its September 1996 report the *Open-ended Working Group* reaffirmed that final agreement on the Council's composition and size; decision-making; working methods and transparency; and other matters, 'should comprise a comprehensive package'. During 1996 the Council deepened its consideration of working methods of the Council, as well as the relationship between the Council and the general membership, and other principal organs of the UN. The issues discussed are addressed in detail elsewhere in this book, and so will be only briefly highlighted here. In its report, the Group noted the steps that had been taken to enhance transparency and improve working methods, but there was disagreement as to whether further formalization and institutionalization of these measures was desirable. Discussion in the Group focused on a number of specific proposals including those by the Movement of Non-aligned Countries,[16] the Czech Republic,[17] and by Argentina and New Zealand.[18] The particular issues given prominence in the Group's work were: the reports of the Council to the General Assembly; briefings to non-members of the Council; consultations with present and potential troop-contributing countries; the work of the sanctions committees; effective flow of information and exchange of views between the Council and the Assembly; and the participation of non-members of the Council in its discussions (Articles 31 and 32). In fact the *Open-ended Working Group* has acted in parallel with the *Working Group of the Security Council concerning the Council's documentation and other procedural questions*, the former providing a forum for General Assembly debate, the latter Council debate, of frequently the same issues.

(iii) Voting

The issues of the extension of the veto to new permanent members, and of limiting the veto power of existing members, has already been touched upon on pages 386–7 above. The Working Group also gave consideration to the question of the number of affirmative votes required for Council decisions on both substantive and procedural matters (known as the 'voting majority' or the 'action threshold'). The larger the ratio of non-permanent to permanent members in an expanded Council, the easier it becomes for non-permanent members to exercise an effective veto by acting collectively. At present since nine or more affirmative votes are required for a Council decision, seven or more non-permanent members possess a 'hidden veto' since by voting against, abstaining from, or not participating in a decision, they can defeat it. Taking Ambassador Razali's proposal as an example, if 15 affirmative votes out of 24 are required for a decision, ten or more non-permanent members can defeat any proposal. Moreover, since ten of the non-permanent members in the expanded Council outlined in his proposal would be from developing countries, non-permanent States from the South would for the first time be able to exercise a collective veto, assuming sufficient voting discipline. Boutros-Ghali had referred to the importance of this voting threshold in a speech to the Ministry for Foreign Affairs in Mexico in March 1996:

> In this way, an effective 'group veto' might be created for the developing world—without placing that veto into the hands of any single state. By greatly enhancing the strength and importance of the new non-permanent members, raising the threshold for Council action is seen by some as a key element of a new framework balancing the possible addition of Germany and Japan as permanent members with the imperative of making the Council more representative by strengthening the voice of the developing world.[19]

(iv) Periodic review

States are divided as to whether periodic review would help or hinder a solution. One argument often made in favour is that it would make an immediate expansion of the Council appear less irrevocable. The key issues in any review clause would be its timing, and the extent and limits of the review, especially in relation to current and possible new permanent members.

3. NEW RULES?

Since the last edition of this book went to press a decade ago, the day-to-day operation of the Council has changed significantly. Nowadays, agreement on the substance of decisions that will be taken, along with the procedure to be followed, is almost always reached in the course of informal consultations prior to a public meeting of the Council. One consequence of this has been that while there have been major developments in the procedure of the Council over the last decade, there have been less explicit references to the Rules of Procedure at public meetings of the Council. In the mid-1990s possible amendments to the Rules of Procedure, and the removal of their 'Provisional' designation were often mentioned in the Open-ended Working Group and during the General Assembly's debate on the annual report of the Security Council. The most common calls were for a recognition of the existence of informal consultations in the Rules of Procedure, and what was often referred to as the 'institutionalization' of recent changes in the working practices of the Council, through amendments to the Rules, or through the addition of Presidential Statements as new Appendices to the Rules.

Certain provisions in the Rules are clearly redundant or unnecessary (the last ten words of Rule 1, Rules 4 and 10, the second paragraph of Rule 12, the first sentence of Rule 21, Rules 23, 24, 28, and 40, the last sentence of Rule 53, and Rule 57); three Rules contain expressions which are both ambiguous and unnecessary (Rules 31–3); one Rule could with advantage be clarified (Rule 36); and there is a lack of consistency in referring to 'member(s) of' and 'representative(s) on' the Council. In the pages that follow, we review the Provisional Rules of Procedure and the Appendix, using roughly the order of subjects indicated by the section headings of the Rules.

(a) Meetings

The President of the Council can call a meeting in many circumstances: at the request of any member of the Council; if the General Assembly addresses to the Council a recommendation or refers to it a question or situation; if the Secretary-General expressly invokes Article 99 regarding any matter which in his opinion may threaten the maintenance of international peace and security; or if a State draws the Council's attention to a dispute or situation. The President consults Council members informally and arranges the meeting to suit the wishes or convenience of the members (Rules 1–3). This procedure has worked satisfactorily most of the time, and no change in the Rules would be likely to improve things.

The phrase 'but the interval between meetings shall not exceed fourteen days', which was inserted in Rule 1 by the Committee of Experts in 1946 'to stress . . . the permanent nature of the Security Council',[20] is now redundant.

The Charter provides in Article 28(2) for 'periodic meetings at which each of [the Council's] members may, if it so desires, be represented by a member of the government or by some other specially designated representative'; Rule 4, stipulating that such 'periodic' meetings shall be held twice a year, was approved by the Security Council on 9 April 1946.[21]

This Rule has been generally ignored, and no advantage would be lost if Rule 4 (and possibly also Rule 12 about the provisional agenda for a 'periodic' meeting) were now dropped.

The Council 'normally' meets at UN Headquarters, but in accordance with Article 28(3) and Rule 5, the Council may decide to meet elsewhere if it judges that this would facilitate its work. The meetings held in London and in Paris where the General Assembly was in session were to the convenience of all and thus facilitated the Council's work; but it is unclear whether the meetings held away from Headquarters in the past were of sufficient benefit to justify the disruption and expense involved in the Council moving temporarily from New York (see Chapters 2.4 and 7.1).

Under Rule 48 of the Rules of Procedure, in the absence of a decision to the contrary, the Council should meet in public. The prevalence of informal consultations of Council members has tended to undermine this rule, leaving public meetings as short formalized events.

Following a recommendation of the Executive Committee of the Preparatory Commission, the Rules of Procedure require the Council to meet in private when making recommendations to the General Assembly regarding the appointment of the Secretary-General. At the end of a private meeting, a *communiqué* may be issued through the Secretary-General in place of, or in addition to, a verbatim record. The Council may decide to keep a record of a private meeting in a single copy only, and any such record is kept by the Secretary-General. Representatives of UN Members who have taken part in a private meeting have access to the record kept by the Secretary-General, and the Council may grant access to this record to the authorized representatives of other Members (Rules 48, 51, 55, and 56). Australia assumed in 1946, when these Rules were adopted, that the decision to meet in private would be taken at a public meeting, and nobody challenged this assumption.[22] One result of the increased reliance on informal consultations prior to a public meeting of the Council, has been that the desire among members of the Council to hold private Council meetings, excluding those mandatory for the appointment of the Secretary-General, appears to have diminished.

As the Council acts on behalf of the whole membership, it has a special obligation to act as transparently as possible, so long as this does not interfere with its primary responsibility for maintaining international peace and security. As was discussed in Chapter 2, non-members of the Council cannot attend informal consultations of Council members, whilst they can, if agreed by the Council, attend private meetings of the Council. Indeed, informal consultations are presently nowhere mentioned in the Rules of Procedure. Council members developed the format of 'Arria formula' meetings in which they could meet informally with visiting dignitaries to discuss issues with which they were concerned. There have been calls both for more 'Arria formula' meetings to allow consultation with affected non-members, and for incorporation of a provision in the Rules of Procedure that non-members can request to attend informal consultations of Council members on subjects that directly affect them. Such proposals raise a number of dilemmas.* The problem lies not so much with the holding of informal consultations *per se*, since these are an essential part of diplomacy and the negotiation process, but rather that in the post Cold War era, the Council has been taking decisions, on the imposition of sanctions and other matters, that can have far-reaching consequences for non-members. The measures undertaken so far by the Council to increase the transparency of its decision-making have not entirely satisfied non-members, but this may be as much a consequence of the substance of its decisions, than of the procedures adopted for the decision-making process. Some of

* An excellent review of the benefits and disadvantages of informal consultations is to be found in Loie Feuerle 'Informal Consultation: A Mechanism in Security Council Decision-Making', *New York Journal of International Law and Politics* (fall 1985), pp. 267–308. Whilst written in 1985 it remains highly relevant to the current debate in the late 1990s.

the remedies suggested by some non-members, such as admitting non-members into informal consultations, could potentially inhibit a frank exchange of views, leading more to set-piece speeches. Real negotiation and the honest exchange of views could then be driven into more secretive fora such as meetings at Permanent Missions. An alternative approach, suggested by France, is to acknowledge that some Council discussions that in earlier decades would have been aired publicly are now held in the course of informal consultations. Increasing the number of public meetings, coupled with genuine consultation with concerned non-members at early stages in the deliberations of Council members, may be a more effective way of addressing the concerns of non-members than amending the Rules of Procedure to admit non-members to informal consultations. A large proviso is that the success of this approach rests on the willingness of members of the Council to carry out genuine consultations with concerned States; and this is clearly something that is impossible to enforce. However, if adequate consultation does not take place in the future, it is likely that pressure for more formal changes to the Rules of Procedure will grow.

Another option to enhance Council transparency (albeit enhanced for non-members but not the media or the public) is for the Security Council to hold more formal private meetings in place of informal consultations of the whole. Such meetings would be appropriate when the Council members wish to meet away from the glare of publicity but are happy for non-members to be present. Such a format was successfully adopted in 1991 during the Gulf War.

Before we move beyond the subject of meetings, it is convenient to mention here Rule 61, which was added in 1947 after a tiresome difference of opinion about the meaning of the Statute of the International Court of Justice. The Statute refers to 'meetings' of the Security Council and the General Assembly for the election of judges (Articles 11 and 12 of the Statute). When the first election took place in 1946, the President of the Security Council (Australia), supported by Britain and China, took the view that a meeting of the Security Council was a sitting of the Council at which one or more votes would take place. But the majority of members of the Council, or a majority of those who spoke, supported by the President of the General Assembly (Paul-Henri Spaak), interpreted meeting to mean a vote or ballot. An *ad hoc* arrangement was resorted to in 1946, and the General Assembly and the Security Council later agreed unanimously that a 'meeting' of either organ for the election of judges 'shall continue until as many candidates as are required for all the seats to be filled have obtained in one or more ballots an absolute majority of votes'.[23] It would make for greater clarity if Rule 61 were to read 'Any meetings of the Security Council . . .' It would then be clear that 'Any meeting' does not mean 'Any vote' or 'Any ballot'.

(b) Agenda

The provisional agenda for each ordinary meeting of the Council is officially drawn up by the Secretary-General (in practice other members of the Secretariat), approved by the President, and communicated to members at least three days before the meeting; but in urgent circumstances (which is now usually the case), the provisional agenda may be communicated simultaneously with the notice of the meeting. In practice the provisional agenda is nowadays invariably approved in advance in informal consultations, and then formally adopted at the Council meeting. The provisional agenda for a 'periodic' meeting is to be circulated at least twenty-one days before the meeting, and subsequent changes or additions are to be brought to the notice of members at least five days before the meeting; in urgent circumstances, the Council may add to its agenda at any time during a 'periodic' meeting. The first item of the provisional agenda is the adoption of the agenda (Rules 7–9 and 12). Current practice has been to have only one substantial agenda item per meeting of the Council, in part to simplify the procedural aspects.

Since 30 June 1993 the provisional agenda for meetings of the Council has been included in the *Journal*, providing that it has been approved in informal consultations in good time. The draft programme of work for informal consultations has also been listed in the *Journal* since November 1993. Calls have been made for an extension of these practices, *inter alia,* to include an annotated agenda in the *Journal* for both meetings and informal consultations, to include the type of action (e.g. decision on a draft resolution, reports, exchange of views, etc.) expected to be taken at the meeting.[24]

The Secretary-General brings to the attention of the Council communications from named sources 'concerning any matter for the consideration of the Security Council in accordance with the provisions of the Charter' (Rule 6). The provisional agenda is composed of those items which have been brought to the Council's attention under Rule 6, or items, consideration of which was not completed at a previous meeting, or matters which the Council has previously decided to defer (Rules 7 and 10).

Under Rule 11, the Secretary-General communicates to the members of the Council a weekly summary statement of matters of which the Council is seized and of the stage reached in their consideration. A notification to the General Assembly of matters relative to the maintenance of international peace and security which are being dealt with by the Security Council, is also circulated. This notification, which is required by Article 12(2) of the Charter, is based on the summary statement. The Committee of Experts proposed Rule 11 'for the convenience of the members of the Security Council'.[25]

Since 22 August 1972, the Secretary-General economized by reproducing the full up-to-date summary statement only once a year and issuing each week an addendum to the basic list, indicating any items on which action has been taken by the Council during the period covered.[26] Special efforts were made in the 1990s to reduce the number of obsolete items on the list of matters of which the Council is seized. The members of the Council introduced in 1996 a new procedure for deleting items from the list. Now States must notify the Secretary-General that they wish an item to remain in the summary statement, or it will be automatically deleted (see Chapter 2.10).

Rule 10 provides that any item, consideration of which has not been completed at a meeting of the Council, shall, unless the Council decides to the contrary, 'automatically be included in the agenda of the next meeting'. This text was proposed by the Committee of Experts in 1946 to ensure that 'the continued consideration of such business as is left over from one meeting shall constitute part of the agenda of the next meeting'. The use of the word *agenda* was, according to the chairman of the Committee of Experts, used advisedly.[27] In practice, the Council has correctly interpreted *agenda* in Rule 10 to mean the list of things to be done.

If ever this interpretation were to give rise to misunderstanding, it would be possible to amend Rule 10 to read:

Any item of the agenda of a meeting of the Security Council, consideration of which has not been completed at that meeting, shall, unless the Security Council decides otherwise, be automatically included in the list of matters of which the Security Council is seized.

(c) Representation and credentials

A Head of Government or Minister of Foreign Affairs of a Member is entitled to sit on the Security Council without submitting credentials. The credentials of other representatives, issued by the Head of the State or of the Government or the Minister of Foreign Affairs, are to be communicated to the Secretary-General not less than twenty-four hours before they are seated or attend, and the Secretary-General examines the credentials and submits a written report on them to the Council for approval. Pending the approval of the credentials, a representative on the Council is seated provisionally with the same rights as other representatives; any representative on the Council to whose credentials objection has been made 'within the Council' continues to sit with the same rights as other representatives until the Council has decided the matter (Rules 13–17). There is no indication in the Provisional Rules of Procedure as to the course to be followed if objection is made to the credentials of a non-member of the Council, but it would be logical to apply the procedure outlined in Rule 17, which deals with objections to the credentials of representatives on the Council.

Since 1948, the reports of the Secretary-General on credentials have been circulated to Council members and, in the absence of any request that they be considered by the Council, are regarded as approved without objection. In practice, credentials are submitted and reported on only when changes in representation are made and when non-permanent members have been newly elected.

When the question of the representation of China was being considered in 1950, India drew attention to the fact that none of the Rules of Procedure indicates what is to be done when questions arise as to which is the recognized government of a particular State. In order to obviate a situation in which different UN organs might 'by their own majorities' reach different decisions, India favoured some uniform procedure which could be adopted by all the organs. In order to 'set the ball rolling', India submitted a draft new Rule to the effect that, where the right of a person to represent a State on the Security Council is called into question on the ground that he or she does not represent the recognized government of that State, the President of the Council should, before submitting the question to the Council, ascertain 'by telegraph if necessary', and place before the Council the views of the governments of all other UN Members on the matter.[28] The Indian proposal was remitted to the Committee of Experts, which praised India's laudable initiative but thought that the matter should go to the General Assembly for study.[29]

It was Cuba which took the matter to the General Assembly where, after a period of confused and unsatisfactory debate and diplomacy, a resolution was adopted which, in its first operative paragraph, recommended that whenever more than one authority claims to be the government entitled to represent a Member State in the United Nations, and this becomes the subject of controversy, the question should be considered 'in the light of the purposes and principles of the Charter and the circumstances of each case'.[30] This platitudinous advice was regularly recalled by the United States and its partners in connection with the representation of China, but it may be doubted whether it throws significant light on the problem of governmental legitimacy.

(d) Presidency

The presidency rotates on a monthly basis in the English alphabetical order of the members of the Security Council (Rule 18). In Chapter 3.2 we examined the unusual circumstances in which Rule 18 was suspended in August 1994 by a decision of Council members, since it was felt the question of the representation of Rwanda on the Council would not have been resolved by September 1994 so as to allow that State to assume the presidency.

The President represents the Council in its capacity as an organ of the United Nations, and it is said that this gives him 'the requisite authority to nominate committees and to conclude agreements on behalf of the Council'.[31] He is given precedence after the President of the General Assembly, in accordance with the order of principal organs named in Article 7 of the Charter.[32] The presidency is 'deemed to attach to the member State concerned and not to the person of its representative',[33] and if the President is unable to preside because of illness or for personal reasons, 'the presidency . . . [is] assumed by an accredited representative of the same State'.[34] This happened in October 1956, for example, when Louis de Guiringaud took over the presidency after Bernard Cornut-Gentille's collapse.

The President presides over Council meetings (Rule 19). He performs tasks specified in the Rules of Procedure (Rules 1, 2, 3, 7, 27, 30, 36, 53, and 59) and acts in his discretion over four matters mentioned in the Rules (Rules 1, 20, 29, and 52).

The Secretariat stressed at an early stage that it would not be possible to elaborate the Rules so as to provide for 'the multitudinous variety of procedural problems that may arise'. The Secretariat suggested that, 'at least as regards the regulation of debate, certain powers [should] inhere in the office of President as such, and that he should advance rulings which shall be valid in the absence of objection'.[35] The President is guided by certain customary practices of the presiding officers of intergovernmental organs.

No Rule governs the fact that, unlike the President of the General Assembly, the President of the Security Council also acts as the representative of a Council member. This can lead to confusion, as happened in Panama City on 21 March 1973, and it has been suggested that this might be minimized or eliminated if a new Rule were adopted to the effect that, whenever the President speaks in his capacity as representative of a member of the Council rather than as President, he shall preface his remarks with an indication to that effect. This is, in fact, now done regularly, and it is doubtful whether difficulties on this score have been sufficiently frequent or grave to require a new Rule.

Rule 20 provides for the devolution of the presidential chair whenever the President deems that, for the proper fulfilment of the responsibilities of the presidency, he should not preside during consideration of a particular question with which the member he represents is 'directly connected'. All members of the Council are *concerned* about any matter which the Council decides to consider, but not all members are '*directly* connected' with every such matter.

The initiative for invoking Rule 20 is to be taken by the President himself. The Committee of Experts was unanimous that the obligation to leave the chair 'was essentially a moral one', and that to leave the matter to the President's discretion 'was alone suitable for the conception which the representatives on the Security Council have of their duties'.[36] It is, of course, open to any other member of the Council, under Rule 30, to ask the President whether or not he intends to cede the presidency during the consideration of any particular question.

(e) Secretariat

Chapter V of the Rules of Procedure is headed 'Secretariat', which is named in Article 7 of the Charter as one of the six principal organs of the United Nations. The staff who comprise the Secretariat are appointed by the Secretary-General, who is the Organization's chief administrative officer (Articles 97 and 101(1)). The Rules in the Chapter headed 'Secretariat' specify tasks which are to be performed under the authority of the Secretary-General.

In addition to the other rights and duties of the Secretary-General arising from the Charter, the Rules of Procedure require the Secretary-General to 'act in that capacity' in all meetings of the Security Council (Article 98 and Rule 21) and to provide the staff required by the Security Council (Rule 24). The Secretary-General may authorize a deputy to act in his place (second sentence of Rule 21). This deputy is not the deputy Secretary-General but the Secretary-General's personal representative at those meetings of the Security Council from which he is unavoidably absent. The Committee of Experts agreed unanimously in 1946 that the Secretary-General or his deputy 'should have the same power in relation to [committees, commissions, or other subsidiary organs of the Council] unless the Council should decide otherwise'.[37] The Secretary-General or his deputy may make oral or written statements concerning any question under consideration by the Council (Rule 22). The Council may also invite any member of the Secretariat 'to supply it with information or to give other assistance' (Rule 39).

Other duties of the Secretary-General are specified in Rules 6–8, 11, 13–15, 25, 26, 50, 51, and 55–9, as are three matters on which the Secretary-General acts at his own discretion (Rules 5, 21, and 22).

Rule 23, which is probably unnecessary but harmless, states that the Secretary-General 'may be appointed . . . as rapporteur for a specified question'. The crucial aspect, on which the Committee of Experts made a unanimous comment in its report in 1946 but did not translate into a Rule, is that 'such an appointment should clearly be subject to the consent of the Secretary-General in each case'.[38]

The Appendix to the Rules of Procedure provides that the Secretariat shall, if requested, give to any representative on the Council a copy of any communication from a private individual or a non-governmental body relating to a matter of which the Council is seized.

(f) Conduct of business

Thirteen Rules deal with the conduct of the Council's business. Three are concerned with the participation of non-members (37 to 39), two with the order of speakers (27 and 29), one with points of order (30), five with procedural motions and draft resolutions (31 to 35), one with amendments (36), one with certain subsidiary organs (28), and several indirectly with voting (32 to 38).

The Charter and the Provisional Rules of Procedure provide in specified circumstances for the participation of UN Members which are not members of the Security Council, of non-Members of the United Nations, of members of the Secretariat, and of 'other persons' competent to give information or other assistance. Under Articles 31 and 35(1) of the Charter and Rule 37, UN Members which are not members of the Council may be invited to participate without vote whenever the Council considers that the interests of that Member are specially affected or when that Member has brought to the attention of the Council a dispute or a situation which might lead to international friction or give rise to a dispute.

So far so good. But in two circumstances the Charter provides that a State not a member of the Council shall be invited to participate although there is no Rule of Procedure which expressly gives effect to the Charter provisions: 'in the discussion' relating to any dispute to which the Member is a party (Article 32), and 'in the decisions' if the Council calls upon a Member to provide armed forces (Article 44). In the case of a party to a dispute (Article 32), the Committee of Experts reported in 1946 that it 'did not consider it advisable to provide [in Rule 37] for Members invited in accordance with Article 32 of the Charter because the invitation to a Member under this Article is mandatory.'[39] The Council thus obtains the participation of parties to a dispute under Article 32 by regarding a party to a dispute as a Member whose interests are specially affected and thus covered by Rule 37, or by regarding the representative of a party to a dispute as a person competent to supply information or give other assistance and thus covered by Rule 39. By the 1990s the participation of non-members in public meetings of the Council had become routine and almost automatic. Instead the debate had turned to the question of possible participation of non-members in 'informal consultations of the whole' (see above).

There is no Rule of Procedure providing for the participation of non-UN Members who are parties to a dispute, as required by Articles 32 and 35(2) of the Charter, or of non-UN Members who bring a question or situation which is not a dispute to the Council's attention, analogous to the procedure for UN Members under Articles 31 and 35(1) of the Charter.[40] Presumably the Council would regard the representatives of such States as persons competent to supply information or to give other assistance, and therefore within the scope of Rule 39.

Rule 39, which was inserted by the Preparatory Commission in face of US opposition,[41] provides for the participation of members of the Secretariat and other persons considered competent to supply information or give other assistance 'in examining matters within [the Council's] competence'.

Neither the Charter nor the Rules make express provision for the participation in the Council's debates of representatives of liberation movements, ethnic or religious communities, or political parties. In the absence of such provision, the Council had been generous in granting requests to participate, though the United States, until 1994, consistently objected to the formulation adopted by the Council regarding the invitation to participate of the Palestine Liberation Organization.

There has been no resort to Article 44 of the Charter concerning participation in the Council's decisions on the employment of national military contingents, as the Council has not expressly implemented the provision in Article 43 for making such forces available to the Council for enforcement action.

The order of speakers in Council debates is governed by Rule 27, which states that the President shall call upon representatives in the order in which they signify their desire to speak, and by Rule 29, which allows the President to accord precedence to any rapporteur appointed by the Council or to the chairman of a commission or committee who has to explain a report to the Council. These two Rules have to be applied in the light of the customary practice of the Council, which is that, in the absence of a decision to the contrary, the usual order of speakers in a debate is: Member(s) requesting the meeting; other parties to the question, situation, or dispute; members of the Council; non-members of the Council; and the President (in his capacity as national representative). Sometimes, however, Council members speak before or after the vote, that is as part of the voting process and after all the speeches.

Rule 30 provides for the raising of points of order, for immediate presidential rulings, and for decisions by the Council in the event of challenges to presidential rulings: UN procedural committees have found it impossible to devise comprehensive definitions of what constitute legitimate points of order, although the General Assembly has provided in paragraph 79 of Annex V to its Rule of Procedure some recommendations about the raising of points of order, drafted by a committee on rationalizing the Assembly's procedures and organization. But however carefully or rigidly a point of order is defined, representatives will find ways of making substantive comments in the guise of raising points of order.

Ambiguity in the wording of Rule 30 has caused much confusion. Some sources, including the second edition of this book, suggested that differences in the application of Rule 30 had arisen from differences in the original language versions of the Rules. In fact the six official language versions are similar in meaning; it is the actual wording of Rule 30 that is ambiguous.

> Rule 30 states that: 'If a representative raises a point of order, the President shall immediately state his ruling. If it is challenged, the President shall submit his ruling to the Security Council for immediate decision and it shall stand unless overruled.'

In reaching a 'decision' on a challenge to a ruling, it is not clear from the wording of Rule 30 whether the ruling or the challenge should be put to the vote. In practice both procedures have been followed, and both are permissible under the Rules of Procedure. The presence of the final words 'shall stand unless overruled' means that whether the challenge or the ruling is put to the vote, there must be at least nine out of fifteen (originally seven out of eleven) members voting in favour of the challenge or against the ruling, for the ruling to fail. Whilst putting the challenge to the vote has the most precedents,[42] an intelligent President will choose which voting procedure to propose on the basis of the political context of each ruling and challenge.

In 1962 the Soviet Union argued that members of the Council should be able to discuss a ruling before a challenge to it is put to the vote, on the premiss that the Russian translation of Rule 30 states that 'the President shall submit his ruling for *consideration* by the Security Council for immediate decision'[43] (our italics). The President stated simply that the English version governed their present discussion, that the French version accorded with it, and he then proceeded to put the challenge to the vote.

Procedure for dealing with motions and proposals is provided for in Rules 31 to 35. Rule 31 requires that motions and proposals (and amendments) shall 'normally' be submitted in writing; Rule 34 states that motions and proposals do not need to be seconded before being put to the vote; Rule 35 provides for the withdrawal of motions and proposals; the first sentence of Rule 32 and Rule 33 deals with the order of voting on motions and proposals (and the introduction of amendments); and the second sentence of Rule 32 provides for voting separately on parts of a motion or proposal.

The main defect of these Rules is the inconsistency of the language and the uncertainty as to the meaning of 'substantive motions' in Rule 31 and of 'principal motions' in Rules 32 and 33. Motions deal with procedure, proposals (proposed or draft resolutions) with other matters; the original proposal is a proposal to which amendments have been submitted.

The expressions 'substantive motions' used in Rule 31 and 'principal motions' used in Rules 32 and 33 only cause confusion; if these Rules cannot be amended, the doubtful expressions are best forgotten.

An amendment is 'normally' to be placed before members of the Council in writing (Rule 31), and its introduction takes precedence in accordance with the order stated in Rule 33. If more than one amendment is submitted, the order of voting is governed by Rule 36. To the extent that differences of view about the order of voting on amendments can be resolved by reference to a Rule of Procedure, Rule 36 has served a useful purpose.

We suggest, nevertheless, for the reasons indicated in Chapter 4.6, that this Rule would be clearer if it were to read as follows:

If two or more amendments to a motion or proposal are submitted, the President shall rule on the order in which they are to be voted upon. [If the ruling is challenged, the President shall submit the challenge to the Security Council for its decision.]

In making his ruling, the President shall bear in mind that ordinarily, when an amendment adds to or deletes from the text of a motion or proposal, that amendment shall be voted on first, and that in other cases the Council shall first vote on the amendment furthest removed in substance from the original proposal, and then on the amendment next furthest removed, until all amendments have been put to the vote.

The first version of Rule 28, as drafted by the Committee of Experts, read platitudinously: 'The Security Council may appoint a rapporteur for a specified question.'[44] When this draft came before the Council, Sir Alexander Cadogan of the United Kingdom raised the question whether the rule was really necessary, but he thought that, if it were being retained, it should be made consistent with the second paragraph of the next rule.[45] It was therefore amended to read: 'The Security Council may appoint a commission or committee or rapporteur for a specified question.' This is a partial application of Article 29 of the Charter, which authorizes the Security Council to establish such subsidiary organs as it deems necessary for the performance of its functions. In 1950, the Council approved the basic principles of a proposal of the General Assembly, which had originated with the British delegation after study of the experience of the League of Nations, for the appointment of a rapporteur or conciliator for a situation or dispute brought to the Council's attention. According to Ambassador Chauvel of France, at that time President of the Council, the rapporteur or conciliator might be the President himself or any other member of the Council. Once appointed, he should carry out his work 'independently of his office, if he is

President, and . . . even independently of his membership of the Council' (see Chapter 3.2).[46]

The Committee of Experts was of the opinion in 1946 that, in principle, only a representative on the Council or the Secretary-General was likely to be appointed rapporteur, but the Committee did not want to exclude the possibility that, in exceptional circumstances, the Council might appoint some other specially qualified person as rapporteur.[47]

(g) Voting

Rule 40 is perhaps the most unnecessary Rule of them all. Although it consists of only twenty-six words, it comprises the whole of Chapter VII of the Provisional Rules of Procedure. It was first drafted by the Executive Committee of the Preparatory Commission, with the comment that certain delegations were doubtful 'whether the provisions of the Charter relating to voting would by themselves prove adequate'. The prevailing view, however, was that it was undesirable to elaborate additional rules regarding voting at that time (November 1945).[48] The draft rule was approved by the Preparatory Commission itself in December 1945 and by the Committee of Experts in February 1946. There then ensued a titanic struggle between the United States and the Soviet Union.

The Soviet Union wanted to entrench both the veto and the double veto in the Rules of Procedure, whereas at the time the United States would have liked to get rid of the double veto altogether, even though its 'legitimacy' had been recognized in the San Francisco Statement of the five permanent members of the Council on 8 June 1945.[49] In the end, the Committee of Experts submitted a revised version of the Rules of Procedure on 13 May 1946 with this rule unaltered 'for the time being' pending further study. The Committee reported that there had been 'a full and free exchange of views on this subject' (which evidently meant that things had got pretty difficult) and that some members had taken the view that the Rules 'should contain detailed provisions covering the mechanics of the vote and the majorities by which various decisions . . . should be taken'.[50] Three days later, the Council approved the text without debate.

Rule 40 can thus be regarded as not only the most unnecessary of all the Rules, but also as the most provisional. Neither the Committee of Experts nor the Security Council has yet resumed the 'further study' which the Committee of Experts decided 'to postpone' forty-nine years ago, other than in the context of inconclusive exchanges of view concerning the veto.

(h) Languages and records

Now that the distinction between official and working languages has disappeared, Rules 41 to 47 are much simpler. The six languages of the Security Council are Arabic, Chinese, English, French, Russian, and Spanish. Speeches made in any of the six languages are interpreted into the other five languages, and verbatim records, resolutions, and other documents are issued in the six languages (Rules 41, 42, 45, and 46). Rule 43, which was only necessary when the Council distinguished between official and working languages, has been deleted. A representative speaking in a language other than one of the six language of the Council shall provide interpretation into one of those languages (Rule 44). The working languages of the UN Secretariat continue to be English and French, and when Council members meet in small informal drafting groups, only English is generally employed, with interpretation into French on occasion. The Council can decide to publish any of its documents in a language other than one of the languages of the Council (Rule 47). In particular, a German Translation Section of the Office of Conference and Support Services in the UN Department of Administration and Management[51] has been established, funded entirely by extrabudgetary resources, mainly provided by the German Government. This section undertakes the translation of Security Council and other UN documents into German and had an estimated budget of $US 1,860,000 for 1998–9.[52]

A verbatim record of each Council meeting is available in provisional form by 10 a.m. of the first working day following the meeting. Representatives who have taken part in the meeting may suggest corrections which they wish to have made, within a week if the meeting was held in public and within ten days if the meeting was in private. The longer period allowed for suggesting corrections to the record of a private meeting is because of 'the difficulty of consulting the record in those instances when the Council has decided that only a single copy . . . shall be kept'.[53] The Committee of Experts took the view in 1946 'that . . . in principle, the formal approval of records is the prerogative of the Security Council itself, but that it would be appropriate to delegate this power to the President except when a major difficulty necessitates an exchange of views within the Council'.[54] The Rules therefore, provide that the President may refer 'sufficiently important' corrections to representatives on the Council, who then have the right to submit any comments they wish to make (Rules 49 to 52).

If no corrections have been requested, or if the President is of the opinion that corrections are not 'sufficiently important' to be referred to the Council, or if corrections are referred to the Council but do not give rise to comments, or when agreement is reached after the submission of comments, the provisional record is considered as approved and thereupon becomes 'the official record'. The official record is then published in the six languages 'as soon as possible' (Rules 52 to 54).

From the earliest days, the President has not signed the corrected record, as required by the last sentence of Rule 53, and nothing would be lost if this sentence were deleted.

The Secretary-General brings to the attention of the Council communications 'concerning any matter for the consideration of the Security Council in accordance with . . . the Charter', if the communication is from a State, a UN organ, or from the Secretary-General himself (Rule 6). In the case of communications from private individuals or non-governmental bodies relating to matters of which the Council is seized, a list of communications is circulated to members of the Council, and the Secretariat gives a copy of any particular communication to a member of the Council who so requests (Appendix to the Provisional Rules of Procedure). When presenting the text of this Appendix, the chairman of the Committee of Experts said that the intention was to exclude frivolous communications.[55] The Secretariat suggested in 1946 that 'the standard practice should be for communications to be addressed to the Secretary-General',[56] but this advice has not been consistently followed.

Each year, the Secretary-General notifies members of the Council of records and documents which up to that time have been considered confidential, and the Council decides which shall be made public, which shall be available on a limited or restricted basis to UN Members only, and which shall remain confidential (Rule 57).

(i) Admission of new Members

The Executive Committee of the Preparatory Commission drafted three simple rules relating to applications for UN membership. A State wishing to become a Member was to submit to the Secretary-General an application, together with a declaration of its readiness to accept the obligations contained in the Charter. This application would be placed before the Security Council, which would decide whether the applicant was a peace-loving State and was able and willing to carry out the Charter obligations. If the Security Council should make a favourable recommendation, this should be placed before the General Assembly. These rules were approved by the Preparatory Commission in December 1945 and by the Committee of Experts in February 1946.

In a revision submitted by the Committee of Experts in May 1946, two additions were made. First, unless the Security Council should decide otherwise, the President should refer each application to a committee composed of all the members of the Security Council. Secondly, the Council should in normal circumstances transmit its recommendations to the General Assembly not less than twenty-five days before a regular session or four days before a special session; but in 'special circumstances', the Council might disregard the time limits.[57] The amended rules were duly approved by the Council.

Australia reserved its position on these rules in the Committee of Experts on the ground that the procedure failed to accord a proper role to the General Assembly in dealing with applications for membership, but a proposal to defer approval of the draft rules until after consultation with the General Assembly secured only the Australian vote in the Council.[58]

Two changes to the Rules of Procedure were made in 1947, following consultations between the General Assembly and the Security Council. First, Rule 58 was amended to provide that an applicant's acceptance of the obligations of the Charter should be 'made in a formal instrument'. Second, two new paragraphs were inserted in Rule 60 to the effect that the Council should submit to the General Assembly with its recommendation 'a complete record of the discussion'; in cases where the Council did not make a favourable recommendation, it should also submit 'a special report'. The opportunity was taken to make a minor verbal correction to the English text of what is now paragraph 4 of Rule 60.[59]

The procedure for dealing with applications for membership has been satisfactory since the revival of the Council's Committee on Admission of New Members.

Two other procedural matters have been considered by the Committee of Experts without a rule being recommended. The first was the question of a quorum. Some members thought that the adoption of a special rule on this subject 'might raise difficulties', and so the Committee of Experts took no decision.[60]

The other matter was the closure of debates, to which the United States attached special importance. The Committee of Experts reported that this matter involved 'the very important problem of the limitation of the right of each representative to give full expression to his point of view', and the question was postponed to a later date. US Ambassador Stettinius raised the matter again in the Security Council. He believed that it would be possible to devise a rule which, while not preventing freedom of expression, would contribute to orderly procedure, and he expressed the hope that the Committee of Experts would take the matter up again 'at an early date'. The Committee of Experts did not take the hint, however, presumably because of a general view that the provisions in Rule 33 for adjourning the meeting or postponing discussion were sufficient for terminating debate.[61]

4. NEW WORKING PRACTICES?

As we have shown, the Council made a number of changes to its working practices in the 1990s, without amending the Charter, or its Rules of Procedure. The decision to make many of these changes was taken on the recommendation of the Council's informal working group concerning the Council's documentation and other procedural questions, sometimes through the adoption of proposals raised in the General Assembly's Open-ended Working Group. The decisions were announced in a series of statements by the President of the Council, many of which are reproduced as appendices to this book. This approach has the benefit of being incremental and easy to undertake, and allows the Council flexibilty in adapting its methods of work to changing situations. Many non-members of the Council, whilst welcoming the changes in working practices that have taken place, see value in greater codification of procedural developments, as they view this as more likely to ensure that they are routinely and fully informed and consulted on matters that concern them.

5. NEW NATIONAL POLICIES?

If the Charter is to remain substantially unamended, and if only marginal improvements in the working of the Security Council are likely to follow from changes in the Provisional Rules of Procedure or the established practices of the Council, in which direction should we look for a remedy to improve the effectiveness of the Security Council in its primary task of maintaining world peace? Is there a panacea if only we were to look with sufficient care and perseverance?

Alas, we have concluded that there is no panacea, nor ever likely to be one; but we can, nevertheless, work for a more effective Security Council through changes in national attitudes and national policies, as States review their perceptions of national interest in the light of the national interests of others. All States and all regions stand to gain from a firmer and more humane international order in which short-term national advantage is not pursued to the limit if to do so frustrates the universal common good. The obligation to relate short-term to long-term considerations, the national interest to the global, is needed for prudential as well as for ethical reasons. Most governments recognize these inter-relationships part of the time; but at moments of crisis, the short term and national tends to swamp the long term and universal.

When in 1693 William Penn, the Anglo-American Quaker wrote a pamphlet advocating an international parliament for keeping the peace, he considered the objection that the strongest and richest sovereigns would never agree. Penn's comment was that no sovereign was stronger than all the rest. 'And if this be called a lessening of their power, it must be only because the great fish can no longer eat up the little ones.'[62]

APPENDIX I (a)

EXTRACTS FROM THE UN CHARTER

WE THE PEOPLES
OF THE UNITED NATIONS
DETERMINED

to save succeeding generations from the scourge of war, which twice in our lifetime has brought untold sorrow to mankind, and

to reaffirm faith in fundamental human rights, in the dignity and worth of the human person, in the equal rights of men and women and of nations large and small, and

to establish conditions under which justice and respect for the obligations arising from treaties and other sources of international law can be maintained, and

to promote social progress and better standards of life in larger freedom,

AND FOR THESE ENDS

to practise tolerance and live together in peace with one another as good neighbours, and

to unite our strength to maintain international peace and security, and

to ensure, by the acceptance of principles and the institution of methods, that armed force shall not be used, save in the common interest, and

to employ international machinery for the promotion of the economic and social advancement of all peoples,

HAVE RESOLVED TO
COMBINE OUR EFFORTS TO
ACCOMPLISH THESE AIMS

Accordingly, our respective Governments, through representatives assembled in the city of San Francisco, who have exhibited their full powers found to be in good and due form, have agreed to the present Charter of the United Nations and do hereby establish an international organization to be known as the United Nations.

Appendix I

CHAPTER I

PURPOSES AND PRINCIPLES

Article 1

The purposes of the United Nations are:

1. To maintain international peace and security, and to that end: to take effective collective measures for the prevention and removal of threats to the peace, and for the suppression of acts of aggression or other breaches of the peace, and to bring about by peaceful means, and in conformity with the principles of justice and international law, adjustment or settlement of international disputes or situations which might lead to a breach of the peace;

2. To develop friendly relations among nations based on respect for the principle of equal rights and self-determination of peoples, and to take other appropriate measures to strengthen universal peace;

3. To achieve international co-operation in solving international problems of an economic, social, cultural or humanitarian character, and in promoting and encouraging respect for human rights and for fundamental freedoms for all without distinction as to race, sex, language, or religion; and

4. To be a centre for harmonizing the actions of nations in the attainment of these common ends.

Article 2

The Organization and its Members, in pursuit of the Purposes stated in Article 1, shall act in accordance with the following Principles.

1. The Organization is based on the principle of the sovereign equality of all its Members.

2. All Members, in order to ensure to all of them the rights and benefits resulting from membership, shall fulfil in good faith the obligations assumed by them in accordance with the present Charter.

3. All Members shall settle their international disputes by peaceful means in such a manner that international peace and security, and justice, are not endangered.

4. All Members shall refrain in their international relations from the threat or use of force against the territorial integrity or political independence of any state, or in any other manner inconsistent with the Purposes of the United Nations.

5. All Members shall give the United Nations every assistance in any action it takes in accordance with the present Charter, and shall refrain from giving assistance to any state against which the United Nations is taking preventive or enforcement action.

6. The Organization shall ensure that states which are not Members of the United Nations act in accordance with these Principles so far as may be necessary for the maintenance of international peace and security.

7. Nothing contained in the present Charter shall authorize the United Nations to intervene in matters which are essentially within the domestic jurisdiction of any state or shall require the Members to submit such matters to settlement under the present Charter; but this principle shall not prejudice the application of enforcement measures under Chapter VII.

CHAPTER II

MEMBERSHIP

. . .

Article 4

1. Membership in the United Nations is open to all . . . peace-loving states which accept the obligations contained in the present Charter and, in the judgment of the Organization, are able and willing to carry out these obligations.

2. The admission of any such state to membership in the United Nations will be effected by a decision of the General Assembly upon the recommendation of the Security Council.

Article 5

A Member of the United Nations against which preventive or enforcement action has been taken by the Security Council may be suspended from the exercise of the rights and privileges of membership by the General Assembly upon the recommendation of the Security Council. The exercise of these rights and privileges may be restored by the Security Council.

Article 6

A Member of the United Nations which has persistently violated the Principles contained in the present Charter may be expelled from the

Organization by the General Assembly upon the recommendation of the Security Council.

CHAPTER III

ORGANS

Article 7

1. There are established as the principal organs of the United Nations: a General Assembly, a Security Council, and Economic and Social Council, a Trusteeship Council, an International Court of Justice, and a Secretariat.
2. Such subsidiary organs as may be found necessary may be established in accordance with the present Charter.

Article 8

The United Nations shall place no restrictions on the eligibility of men and women to participate in any capacity and under conditions of equality in its principal and subsidiary organs.

CHAPTER IV

THE GENERAL ASSEMBLY

. . .

Functions and Powers

Article 10

The General Assembly may discuss any questions or any matters within the scope of the present Charter or relating to the powers and functions of any organs provided for in the present Charter, and, except as provided in Article 12, may make recommendations to the Members of the United Nations or to the Security Council or to both on any such questions or matters.

Article 11

1. The General Assembly may consider the general principles of co-operation in the maintenance of international peace and security, including the principles governing disarmament and the regulation of armaments, and may make recommendations with regard to such principles to the Members or to the Security Council or to both.

2. The General Assembly may discuss any questions relating to the maintenance of international peace and security brought before it by any Member of the United Nations, or by the Security Council, or by a state which is not a Member of the United Nations in accordance with Article 35, paragraph 2, and, except as provided in Article 12, may make recommendations with regard to any such questions to the state or states concerned or to the Security Council or to both. Any such question on which action is necessary shall be referred to the Security Council by the General Assembly either before or after discussion.

3. The General Assembly may call the attention of the Security Council to situations which are likely to endanger international peace and security.

4. The powers of the General Assembly set forth in this Article shall not limit the general scope of Article 10.

Article 12

1. While the Security Council is exercising in respect of any dispute or situation the functions assigned to it in the present Charter, the General Assembly shall not make any recommendation with regard to that dispute or situation unless the Security Council so requests.

2. The Secretary-General, with the consent of the Security Council, shall notify the General Assembly at each session of any matters relative to the maintenance of international peace and security which are being dealt with by the Security Council and shall similarly notify the General Assembly, or the Members of the United Nations if the General Assembly is not in session, immediately the Security Council ceases to deal with such matters.

Article 13

1. The General Assembly shall initiate studies and make recommendations for the purpose of:

a. promoting international co-operation in the political field and encouraging the progressive development of international law and its codification;

b. promoting international co-operation in the economic, social, cultural, educational, and health fields, and assisting in the realization of human rights and fundamental freedoms for all without distinction as to race, sex, language, or religion.

2. The further responsibilities, functions and powers of the General Assembly with respect to matters mentioned in paragraph 1(b) above are set forth in Chapters IX and X.

Article 14

Subject to the provisions of Article 12, the General Assembly may recommend measures for the peaceful adjustment of any situation, regardless of origin, which it deems likely to impair the general welfare or friendly relations among nations, including situations resulting from a violation of the provisions of the present Charter setting forth the Purposes and Principles of the United Nations.

Article 15

1. The General Assembly shall receive and consider annual and special reports from the Security Council; these reports shall include an account of the measures that the Security Council has decided upon or taken to maintain international peace and security.

. . .

Article 17

1. The General Assembly shall consider and approve the budget of the Organization.

2. The expenses of the Organization shall be borne by the Members as apportioned by the General Assembly.

. . .

Article 18

Voting

1. Each member of the General Assembly shall have one vote.

2. Decisions of the General Assembly on important questions shall be

made by a two-thirds majority of the members present and voting. These questions shall include: recommendations with respect to the maintenance of international peace and security, the election of the non-permanent members of the Security Council, the election of the members of the Economic and Social Council, the election of members of the Trusteeship Council in accordance with paragraph 1(c) of Article 86, the admission of new Members to the United Nations, the suspension of the rights and privileges of membership, the expulsion of Members, questions relating to the operation of the trusteeship system, and budgetary questions.

3. Decisions on other questions, including the determination of additional categories of questions to be decided by a two-thirds majority, shall be made by a majority of the members present and voting.

Article 19

A Member of the United Nations which is in arrears in the payment of its financial contributions to the Organization shall have no vote in the General Assembly if the amount of its arrears equals or exceeds the amount of the contributions due from it for the preceding two full years. The General Assembly may, nevertheless, permit such a Member to vote if it is satisfied that the failure to pay is due to conditions beyond the control of the Member.

Procedure

Article 20

The General Assembly shall meet in regular annual sessions and in such special sessions as occasion may require. Special sessions shall be convoked by the Secretary-General at the request of the Security Council or of a majority of the Members of the United Nations.

. . .

Appendix I

Chapter V
THE SECURITY COUNCIL

Composition

Article 23

1. The Security Council shall consist of fifteen Members of the United Nations. The Republic of China, France, the Union of Soviet Socialist Republics, the United Kingdom of Great Britain and Northern Ireland, and the United States of America shall be permanent members of the Security Council. The General Assembly shall elect ten other Members of the United Nations to be non-permanent members of the Security Council, due regard being specially paid, in the first instance to the contribution of Members of the United Nations to the maintenance of international peace and security and to the other purposes of the Organization, and also to equitable geographical distribution.

2. The non-permanent members of the Security Council shall be elected for a term of two years . . . A retiring member shall not be eligible for immediate re-election.

3. Each member of the Security Council shall have one representative.

Functions and Powers

Article 24

1. In order to ensure prompt and effective action by the United Nations, its Members confer on the Security Council primary responsibility for the maintenance of international peace and security, and agree that in carrying out its duties under this responsibility the Security Council acts on their behalf.

2. In discharging these duties the Security Council shall act in accordance with the Purposes and Principles of the United Nations. The specific powers granted to the Security Council for the discharge of these duties are laid down in Chapters VI, VII, VIII, and XII.

3. The Security Council shall submit annual and, when necessary, special reports to the General Assembly for its consideration.

Article 25

The Members of the United Nations agree to accept and carry out the decisions of the Security Council in accordance with the present Charter.

Article 26

In order to promote the establishment and maintenance of international peace and security with the least diversion for armaments of the world's human and economic resources, the Security Council shall be responsible for formulating, with the assistance of the Military Staff Committee referred to in Article 47, plans to be submitted to the Members of the United Nations for the establishment of a system for the regulation of armaments.

Voting

Article 27

1. Each member of the Security Council shall have one vote.
2. Decisions of the Security Council on procedural matters shall be made by an affirmative vote of nine members.
3. Decisions of the Security Council on all other matters shall be made by an affirmative vote of nine members including the concurring votes of the permanent members; provided that, in decisions under Chapter VI, and under paragraph 3 of Article 52, a party to a dispute shall abstain from voting.

Procedure

Article 28

1. The Security Council shall be so organized as to be able to function continuously. Each member of the Security Council shall for this purpose be represented at all times at the seat of the Organization.
2. The Security Council shall hold periodic meetings at which each of its members may, if it so desires, be represented by a member of the government or by some other specially designated representative.
3. The Security Council may hold meetings at such places other than the seat of the Organization as in its judgment will best facilitate its work.

Article 29

The Security Council may establish such subsidiary organs as it deems necessary for the performance of its functions.

Article 30

The Security Council shall adopt its own rules of procedure, including the method of selecting its President.

Article 31

Any Member of the United Nations which is not a member of the Security Council may participate, without vote, in the discussion of any question brought before the Security Council whenever the latter considers that the interests of that Member are specially affected.

Article 32

Any Member of the United Nations which is not a member of the Security Council or any state which is not a Member of the United Nations, if it is a party to a dispute under consideration by the Security Council, shall be invited to participate, without vote, in the discussion relating to the dispute. The Security Council shall lay down such conditions as it deems just for the participation of a state which is not a Member of the United Nations.

CHAPTER VI

PACIFIC SETTLEMENT OF DISPUTES

Article 33

1. The parties to any dispute, the continuance of which is likely to endanger the maintenance of international peace and security, shall, first of all, seek a solution by negotiation, enquiry, mediation, conciliation, arbitration, judicial settlement, resort to regional agencies or arrangements, or other peaceful means of their own choice.
2. The Security Council shall, when it deems necessary, call upon the parties to settle their dispute by such means.

Article 34

The Security Council may investigate any dispute, or any situation which might lead to international friction or give rise to a dispute, in order to determine whether the continuance of the dispute or situation is likely to endanger the maintenance of international peace and security.

Article 35

1. Any Member of the United Nations may bring any dispute, or any situation of the nature referred to in Article 34, to the attention of the Security Council or of the General Assembly.

2.. A state which is not a Member of the United Nations may bring to the attention of the Security Council or of the General Assembly any dispute to which it is a party if it accepts in advance, for the purposes of the dispute, the obligations of pacific settlement provided in the present Charter.

3. The proceedings of the General Assembly in respect of matters brought to its attention under this Article will be subject to the provisions of Articles 11 and 12.

Article 36

1. The Security Council may, at any stage of a dispute of the nature referred to in Article 33 or of a situation of like nature, recommend appropriate procedures or methods of adjustment.

2. The Security Council should take into consideration any procedures for the settlement of the dispute which have already been adopted by the parties.

3. In making recommendations under this Article the Security Council should also take into consideration that legal disputes should as a general rule be referred by the parties to the International Court of Justice in accordance with the provisions of the Statute of the Court.

Article 37

1. Should the parties to a dispute of the nature referred to in Article 33 fail to settle it by the means indicated in that Article, they shall refer it to the Security Council.

2. If the Security Council deems that the continuance of the dispute is in fact likely to endanger the maintenance of international peace and security,

it shall decide whether to take action under Article 36 or to recommend such terms of settlement as it may consider appropriate.

Article 38

Without prejudice to the provision of Articles 33 to 37, the Security Council may, if all the parties to any dispute so request, make recommendations to the parties with a view to a pacific settlement of the dispute.

CHAPTER VII

ACTION WITH RESPECT TO THREATS TO THE PEACE, BREACHES OF THE PEACE, AND ACTS OF AGGRESSION

Article 39

The Security Council shall determine the existence of any threat to the peace, breach of the peace, or act of aggression and shall make recommendations, or decide what measure shall be taken in accordance with Articles 41 and 42, to maintain or restore international peace and security.

Article 40

In order to prevent an aggravation of the situation, the Security Council may, before making the recommendations or deciding upon the measures provided for in Article 39, call upon the parties concerned to comply with such provisional measures as it deems necessary or desirable. Such provisional measures shall be without prejudice to the rights, claims, or position of the parties concerned. The Security Council shall duly take account of failure to comply with such provisional measures.

Article 41

The Security Council may decide what measures not involving the use of armed force are to be employed to give effect to its decisions, and it may call upon the Members of the United Nations to apply such measures. These may include complete or partial interruption of economic relations and of rail, sea, air, postal, telegraphic, radio, and other means of communication, and the severance of diplomatic relations.

Article 42

Should the Security Council consider what measures provided for in Article 41 would be inadequate or have proved to be inadequate, it may take such action by air, sea, or land forces as may be necessary to maintain or restore international peace and security. Such action may include demonstrations, blockade, and other operations by air, sea, or land forces of Members of the United Nations.

Article 43

1. All Members of the United Nations, in order to contribute to the maintenance of international peace and security, undertake to make available to the Security Council, on its call and in accordance with a special agreement or agreements, armed forces, assistance, and facilities, including rights of passage, necessary for the purpose of maintaining international peace and security.

2. Such agreement or agreements shall govern the numbers and types of forces, their degree of readiness and general location, and the nature of the facilities and assistance to be provided.

3. The agreement or agreements shall be negotiated as soon as possible on the initiative of the Security Council. They shall be concluded between the Security Council and Members or between the Security Council and groups of Members and shall be subject to ratification by the signatory states in accordance with their respective constitutional processes.

Article 44

When the Security Council has decided to use force it shall, before calling upon a Member not represented on it to provide armed forces in fulfilment of the obligations assumed under Article 43, invite that Member, if the Member so desires, to participate in the decisions of the Security Council concerning the employment of contingents of that Member's armed forces.

Article 45

In order to enable the United Nations to take urgent military measures, Members shall hold immediately available national air-force contingents for combined international enforcement action. The strength and degree of readiness of these contingents and plans for their combined action shall be determined, within the limits laid down in the special agreement or agreements referred to in Article 43, by the Security Council with the assistance of the Military Staff Committee.

Article 46

Plans for the application of armed force shall be made by the Security Council with the assistance of the Military Staff Committee.

Article 47

1. There shall be established a Military Staff Committee to advise and assist the Security Council on all questions relating to the Security Council's military requirements for the maintenance of international peace and security, the employment and command of forces placed at its disposal, the regulation of armaments, and possible disarmament.

2. The Military Staff Committee shall consist of the Chiefs of Staff of the permanent members of the Security Council or their representatives. Any Member of the United Nations not permanently represented on the Committee shall be invited by the Committee to be associated with it when the efficient discharge of the Committee's responsibilities requires the participation of that Member in its work.

3. The Military Staff Committee shall be responsible under the Security Council for the strategic direction of any armed forces placed at the disposal of the Security Council. Questions relating to the command of such forces shall be worked out subsequently.

4. The Military Staff Committee, with the authorization of the Security Council and after consultation with appropriate regional agencies, may establish regional subcommittees.

Article 48

1. The action required to carry out the decisions of the Security Council for the maintenance of international peace and security shall be taken by all the Members of the United Nations or by some of them, as the Security Council may determine.

2. Such decisions shall be carried out by the Members of the United Nations directly and through their action in the appropriate international agencies of which they are members.

Article 49

The Members of the United Nations shall join in affording mutual assistance in carrying out the measures decided upon by the Security Council.

Article 50

If preventive or enforcement measures against any state are taken by the Security Council, any other state, whether a Member of the United Nations or not, which finds itself confronted with special economic problems arising from the carrying out of those measures shall have the right to consult the Security Council with regard to a solution of those problems.

Article 51

Nothing in the present Charter shall impair the inherent right of individual or collective self-defence if an armed attack occurs against a Member of the United Nations, until the Security Council has taken measures necessary to maintain international peace and security. Measures taken by Members in the exercise of this right of self-defence shall be immediately reported to the Security Council and shall not in any way affect the authority and responsibility of the Security Council under the present Charter to take at any time such action as it deems necessary in order to maintain or restore international peace and security.

Chapter VIII

REGIONAL ARRANGEMENTS

Article 52

1. Nothing in the present Charter precludes the existence of regional arrangements or agencies for dealing with such matters relating to the maintenance of international peace and security as are appropriate for regional action, provided that such arrangements or agencies and their activities are consistent with the Purposes and Principles of the United Nations.
2. The Members of the United Nations entering into such arrangements or constituting such agencies shall make every effort to achieve pacific settlement of local disputes through such regional arrangements or by such regional agencies before referring them to the Security Council.

3. The Security Council shall encourage the development of pacific settlement of local disputes through such regional arrangements or by such regional agencies either on the initiative of the states concerned or by reference from the Security Council.

4. This Article in no way impairs the application of Articles 34 and 35.

Article 53

1. The Security Council shall, where appropriate, utilize such regional arrangements or agencies for enforcement action under its authority. But no enforcement action shall be taken under regional arrangements or by regional agencies without the authorization of the Security Council, with the exception of measures against any enemy state, as defined in paragraph 2 of this Article, provided for pursuant to Article 107 or in regional arrangements directed against renewal of aggressive policy on the part of any such state, until such time as the Organization may, on request of the Governments concerned, be charged with the responsibility for preventing further aggression by such a state.

2. The term enemy state as used in paragraph 1 of this Article applies to any state which during the Second World War has been an enemy of any signatory of the present Charter.

Article 54

The Security Council shall at all times be kept fully informed of activities undertaken or in contemplation under regional arrangements or by regional agencies for the maintenance of international peace and security.

CHAPTER IX

INTERNATIONAL ECONOMIC AND SOCIAL CO-OPERATION

Article 55

With a view to the creation of conditions of stability and well-being which are necessary for peaceful and friendly relations among nations based on respect for the principle of equal rights and self-determination of peoples, the United Nations shall promote:

a. higher standards of living, full employment, and conditions of economic and social progress and development;

b. solutions of international economic, social, health, and related problems; and international cultural and educational co-operation; and

c. universal respect for, and observance of, human rights and fundamental freedoms for all without distinction as to race, sex, language, or religion.

Article 56

All Members pledge themselves to take joint and separate action in co-operation with the Organization for the achievement of the purposes set forth in Article 55.

. . .

CHAPTER X

THE ECONOMIC AND SOCIAL COUNCIL

Article 65

The Economic and Social Council may furnish information to the Security Council and shall assist the Security Council upon its request.

. . .

CHAPTER XI

DECLARATION REGARDING NON-SELF-GOVERNING TERRITORIES

Article 73

Members of the United Nations which have or assume responsibilities for the administration of territories whose peoples have not yet attained a full measure of self-government recognize the principle that the interests of the inhabitants of these territories are paramount, and accept as a sacred trust the obligation to promote to the utmost, within the system of international peace and security established by the present Charter, the well-being of the inhabitants of these territories, and, to this end:

. . .

c. to further international peace and security;

. . .

Chapter XII

INTERNATIONAL TRUSTEESHIP SYSTEM

Article 76

The basic objectives of the trusteeship system, in accordance with the Purposes of the United Nations laid down in Article 1 of the present Charter, shall be:

a. to further international peace and security;

. . .

Article 77

1. The trusteeship system shall apply to such territories in the following categories as may be placed thereunder by means of trusteeship agreements:

a. territories now held under mandate;

b. territories which may be detached from enemy states as a result of the Second World War; and

c. territories voluntarily placed under the system by states responsible for their administration.

2. It will be a matter for subsequent agreement as to which territories in the foregoing categories will be brought under the trusteeship system and upon what terms.

. . .

Article 82

There may be designated, in any trusteeship agreement, a strategic area or areas which may include part or all of the trust territory to which the agreement applies, without prejudice to any special agreement or agreements made under Article 43.

Article 83

1. All functions of the United Nations relating to strategic areas, including the approval of the terms of the trusteeship agreements and of their alteration or amendment, shall be exercised by the Security Council.

. . .

3. The Security Council shall, subject to the provisions of the trusteeship agreements and without prejudice to security considerations, avail itself of the assistance of the Trusteeship Council to perform those functions of the United Nations under the trusteeship system relating to political, economic, social, and educational matters in the strategic areas.

Article 84

It shall be the duty of the administering authority to ensure that the trust territory shall play its part in the maintenance of international peace and security. To this end the administering authority may make use of volunteer forces, facilities, and assistance from the trust territory in carrying out the obligations towards the Security Council undertaken in this regard by the administering authority, as well as for local defence and the maintenance of law and order within the trust territory.

. . .

Chapter XIII
THE TRUSTEESHIP COUNCIL

Composition

Article 86

1. The Trusteeship Council shall consist of the following Members of the United Nations:

a. those Members administering trust territories;

b. such of those Members mentioned by name in Article 23 as are not administering trust territories; and

c. as many other Members elected for three-year terms by the General Assembly as may be necessary to ensure that the total number of members of the Trusteeship Council is equally divided between those Members of the United Nations which administer trust territories and those which do not.

. . .

Chapter XIV
THE INTERNATIONAL COURT OF JUSTICE

Article 92

The International Court of Justice shall be the principal judicial organ of the United Nations. It shall function in accordance with the annexed Statute, which is based upon the Statute of the Permanent Court of International Justice and forms an integral part of the present Charter.

Article 93

1. All Members of the United Nations are *ipso facto* parties to the Statute of the International Court of Justice.

2. A state which is not a Member of the United Nations may become a party to the Statute of the International Court of Justice on conditions to

be determined in each case by the General Assembly upon the recommendation of the Security Council.

Article 94

1. Each Member of the United Nations undertakes to comply with the decision of the International Court of Justice in any case to which it is a party.

2. If any party to a case fails to perform the obligations incumbent upon it under a judgment rendered by the Court, the other party may have recourse to the Security Council, which may, if it deems necessary, make recommendations or decide upon measures to be taken to give effect to the judgment.

Article 95

Nothing in the present Charter shall prevent Members of the United Nations from entrusting the solution of their differences to other tribunals by virtue of agreements already in existence or which may be concluded in the future.

Article 96

1. The General Assembly or the Security Council may request the International Court of Justice to give an advisory opinion on any legal question.

. . .

Chapter XV

THE SECRETARIAT

Article 97

The Secretariat shall comprise a Secretary-General and such staff as the Organization may require. The Secretary-General shall be appointed by the General Assembly upon the recommendation of the Security Council. He shall be the chief administrative officer of the Organization.

Appendix I

Article 98

The Secretary-General shall act in that capacity in all meetings of the General Assembly, of the Security Council, of the Economic and Social Council, and of the Trusteeship Council, and shall perform such other functions as are entrusted to him by these organs. The Secretary-General shall make an annual report to the General Assembly on the work of the Organization.

Article 99

The Secretary-General may bring to the attention of the Security Council any matter which in his opinion may threaten the maintenance of international peace and security.

Article 100

1. In the performance of their duties the Secretary-General and the staff shall not seek or receive instructions from any government or from any other authority external to the Organization. They shall refrain from any action which might reflect on their position as international officials responsible only to the Organization.

2. Each Member of the United Nations undertakes to respect the exclusively international character of the responsibilities of the Secretary-General and the staff and not to seek to influence them in the discharge of their responsibilities.

Article 101

1. The staff shall be appointed by the Secretary-General under regulations established by the General Assembly.

2. Appropriate staffs shall be permanently assigned to the Economic and Social Council, the Trusteeship Council, and, as required, to other organs of the United Nations. These staffs shall form a part of the Secretariat.

3. The paramount consideration in the employment of the staff and in the determination of the conditions of service shall be the necessity of securing the highest standards of efficiency, competence, and integrity. Due regard shall be paid to the importance of recruiting the staff on as wide a geographical basis as possible.

CHAPTER XVI

MISCELLANEOUS PROVISIONS

. . .

Article 103

In the event of a conflict between the obligations of the Members of the United Nations under the present Charter and their obligations under any other international agreement, their obligations under the present Charter shall prevail.

. . .

CHAPTER XVII

TRANSITIONAL SECURITY ARRANGEMENTS

Article 106

Pending the coming into force of such special agreements referred to in Article 43 as in the opinion of the Security Council enable it to begin the exercise of its responsibilities under Article 42, the parties to the Four-Nation Declaration, signed at Moscow, October 30, 1943, and France, shall, in accordance with the provisions of paragraph 5 of that Declaration, consult with one another and as occasion requires with other Members of the United Nations with a view to such joint action on behalf of the Organization as may be necessary for the purpose of maintaining international peace and security.

Article 107

Nothing in the present Charter shall invalidate or preclude action, in relation to any state which during the Second World War has been an enemy of any signatory to the present Charter, taken or authorized as a result of that war by the Governments having responsibility for such action.

CHAPTER XVIII

AMENDMENTS

Article 108

Amendments to the present Charter shall come into force for all Members of the United Nations when they have been adopted by a vote of two-thirds of the members of the General Assembly and ratified in accordance with their respective constitutional processes by two-thirds of the Members of the United Nations, including all the permanent members of the Security Council.

Article 109

1. A General Conference of the Members of the United Nations for the purpose of reviewing the present Charter may be held at a date and place to be fixed by a two-thirds vote of the members of the General Assembly and by a vote of any nine members of the Security Council. Each Member of the United Nations shall have one vote in the conference.

2. Any alteration of the present Charter recommended by a two-thirds vote of the conference shall take effect when ratified in accordance with their respective constitutional processes by two-thirds of the Members of the United Nations including all the permanent members of the Security Council.

. . .

APPENDIX I (b)

EXTRACTS FROM THE STATUTE OF THE INTERNATIONAL COURT OF JUSTICE

Article 1

The International Court of Justice established by the Charter of the United Nations as the principal judicial organ of the United Nations shall be constituted and shall function in accordance with the provisions of the present Statute.

. . .

Article 2

The Court shall be composed of a body of independent judges, elected regardless of their nationality from among persons of high moral character, who possess the qualifications required in their respective countries for appointment to the highest judicial offices, or are jurisconsults of recognized competence in international law.

Article 3

1. The Court shall consist of fifteen members, no two of whom may be nationals of the same state.

. . .

Article 4

1. The members of the Court shall be elected by the General Assembly and by the Security Council from a list of persons nominated by the national groups in the Permanent Court of Arbitration, in accordance with the following provisions.

. . .

3. The conditions under which a state which is a party to the present Statute but is not a Member of the United Nations may participate in electing the members of the Court shall, in the absence of a special agreement, be laid down by the General Assembly upon recommendation of the Security Council.

. . .

Article 8

The General Assembly and the Security Council shall proceed independently of one another to elect the members of the Court.

Article 9

At every election, the electors shall bear in mind not only that the persons to be elected should individually possess the qualifications required, but also that in the body as a whole the representation of the main forms of civilization and of the principal legal systems of the world should be assured.

Article 10

1. Those candidates who obtain an absolute majority of votes in the General Assembly and in the Security Council shall be considered as elected.
2. Any vote of the Security Council, whether for the election of judges or for the appointment of members of the conference envisaged in Article 12, shall be taken without any distinction between permanent and non-permanent members of the Security Council.
3. In the event of more than one national of the same state obtaining an absolute majority of the votes both of the General Assembly and of the Security Council, the eldest of these only shall be considered as elected.

Article 11

If, after the first meeting held for the purpose of the election, one or more seats remain to be filled, a second and, if necessary, a third meeting shall take place.

Article 12

1. If, after the third meeting, one or more seats still remain unfilled, a joint conference consisting of six members, three appointed by the General Assembly and three by the Security Council, may be formed at any time at the request of either the General Assembly or the Security Council, for the purpose of choosing by the vote of an absolute majority one name for each seat still vacant, to submit to the General Assembly and the Security Council for their respective acceptance.

2. If the joint conference is unanimously agreed upon any person who fulfils the required conditions, he may be included in its list, even though he was not included in the list of nominations . . .

3. If the joint conference is satisfied that it will not be successful in procuring an election, those members of the Court who have already been elected shall, within a period to be fixed by the Security Council, proceed to fill the vacant seats by selection from among those candidates who have obtained votes either in the General Assembly or in the Security Council.

4. In the event of an equality of votes among the judges, the eldest judge shall have a casting vote.

. . .

Article 35

1. The Court shall be open to the states parties to the present Statute.

2. The conditions under which the Court shall be open to other states shall, subject to the special provisions contained in treaties in force, be laid down by the Security Council, but in no case shall such conditions place the parties in a position of inequality before the Court.

3. When a state which is not a Member of the United Nations is a party to a case, the Court shall fix the amount which that party is to contribute towards the expenses of the Court. The provision shall not apply if such state is bearing a share of the expenses of the Court.

. . .

Article 41

1. The Court shall have the power to indicate, if it considers that circumstances so require, any provisional measures which ought to be taken to preserve the respective rights of either party.

2. Pending the final decision, notice of the measures suggested shall forthwith be given to the parties and to the Security Council.

. . .

Article 65

1. The Court may give an advisory opinion on any legal question at the request of whatever body may be authorized by or in accordance with the Charter of the United Nations to make such a request.

. . .

Article 69

Amendments to the present Statute shall be effected by the same procedure as is provided by the Charter of the United Nations for amendments to that Charter, subject however to any provisions which the General Assembly upon recommendation of the Security Council may adopt concerning the participation of states which are parties to the present Statute but are not Members of the United Nations.

. . .

APPENDIX II

PROVISIONAL RULES OF PROCEDURE OF THE SECURITY COUNCIL, AS AMENDED 21 DEC. 1982*

CHAPTER I

MEETINGS

Rule 1

Meetings of the Security Council shall, with the exception of the periodic meetings referred to in rule 4, be held at the call of the President at any time he deems necessary, but the interval between meetings shall not exceed fourteen days.

Rule 2

The President shall call a meeting of the Security Council at the request of any member of the Security Council.

Rule 3

The President shall call a meeting of the Security Council if a dispute or situation is brought to the attention of the Security Council under Article 35 or under Article 11 (3) of the Charter, or if the General Assembly makes recommendations or refers any question to the Security Council under Article 11 (2), or if the Secretary-General brings to the attention of the Security Council any matter under Article 99.

Rule 4

Periodic meetings of the Security Council called for in Article 28 (2) of the Charter shall be held twice a year, at such times as the Security Council may decide.

* UN doc. S/96/Rev. 7.

Rule 5

Meetings of the Security Council shall normally be held at the seat of the United Nations.

Any member of the Security Council or the Secretary-General may propose that the Security Council should meet at another place. Should the Security Council accept any such proposal, it shall decide upon the place, and the period during which the Council shall meet at such place.

CHAPTER II

AGENDA

Rule 6

The Secretary-General shall immediately bring to the attention of all representatives on the Security Council all communications from States, organs of the United Nations, or the Secretary-General concerning any matter for the consideration of the Security Council in accordance with the provisions of the Charter.

Rule 7

The provisional agenda for each meeting of the Security Council shall be drawn up by the Secretary-General and approved by the President of the Security Council.

Only items which have been brought to the attention of the representatives on the Security Council in accordance with rule 6, items covered by rule 10, or matters which the Security Council had previously decided to defer, may be included in the provisional agenda.

Rule 8

The provisional agenda for a meeting shall be communicated by the Secretary-General to the representatives on the Security Council at least three days before the meeting, but in urgent circumstances it may be communicated simultaneously with the notice of the meeting.

Rule 9

The first item of the provisional agenda for each meeting of the Security Council shall be the adoption of the agenda.

Rule 10

Any item of the agenda of a meeting of the Security Council, consideration of which has not been completed at that meeting, shall, unless the Security Council otherwise decides, automatically be included in the agenda of the next meeting.

Rule 11

The Secretary-General shall communicate each week to the representatives on the Security Council a summary statement of matters of which the Security Council is seized and of the stage reached in their consideration.

Rule 12

The provisional agenda for each periodic meeting shall be circulated to the members of the Security Council at least twenty-one days before the opening of the meeting. Any subsequent change in or addition to the provisional agenda shall be brought to the notice of the members at least five days before the meeting. The Security Council may, however, in urgent circumstances, make additions to the agenda at any time during a periodic meeting.

The provisions of rule 7, paragraph 1, and of rule 9, shall apply also to periodic meetings.

Chapter III

REPRESENTATION AND CREDENTIALS

Rule 13

Each member of the Security Council shall be represented at the meetings of the Security Council by an accredited representative. The credentials of a representative on the Security Council shall be communicated to the Secretary-General not less than twenty-four hours before he takes his seat on the Security Council. The credentials shall be issued either by the Head of the State or of the Government concerned or by its Minister of Foreign Affairs. The Head of Government or Minister of Foreign Affairs of each member of the Security Council shall be entitled to sit on the Security Council without submitting credentials.

Rule 14

Any Member of the United Nations not a member of the Security Council and any State not a Member of the United Nations, if invited to participate in a meeting or meetings of the Security Council, shall submit credentials for the representative appointed by it for this purpose. The credentials of such a representative shall be communicated to the Secretary-General not less than twenty-four hours before the first meeting which he is invited to attend.

Rule 15

The credentials of representatives on the Security Council and of any representative appointed in accordance with rule 14 shall be examined by the Secretary-General who shall submit a report to the Security Council for approval.

Rule 16

Pending the approval of the credentials of a representative on the Security Council in accordance with rule 15, such representative shall be seated provisionally with the same rights as other representatives.

Rule 17

Any representative on the Security Council, to whose credentials objection has been made within the Security Council, shall continue to sit with the same rights as other representatives until the Security Council has decided the matter.

CHAPTER IV

PRESIDENCY

Rule 18

The presidency of the Security Council shall be held in turn by the members of the Security Council in the English alphabetical order of their names. Each President shall hold office for one calendar month.

Rule 19

The President shall preside over the meetings of the Security Council and, under the authority of the Security Council, shall represent it in its capacity as an organ of the United Nations.

Rule 20

Whenever the President of the Security Council deems that for the proper fulfilment of the responsibilities of the presidency he should not preside over the Council during the consideration of a particular question with which the member he represents is directly connected, he shall indicate his decision to the Council. The presidential chair shall then devolve, for the purpose of the consideration of that question, on the representative of the member next in English alphabetical order, it being understood that the provisions of this rule shall apply to the representatives on the Security Council called upon successively to preside. This rule shall not affect the representative capacity of the President as stated in rule 19, or his duties under rule 7.

CHAPTER V

SECRETARIAT

Rule 21

The Secretary-General shall act in that capacity in all meetings of the Security Council. The Secretary-General may authorize a deputy to act in his place at meetings of the Security Council.

Rule 22

The Secretary-General, or his deputy acting on his behalf, may make either oral or written statements to the Security Council concerning any question under consideration by it.

Rule 23

The Secretary-General may be appointed by the Security Council, in accordance with rule 28, as rapporteur for a specified question.

Rule 24

The Secretary-General shall provide the staff required by the Security Council. This staff shall form a part of the Secretariat.

Rule 25

The Secretary-General shall give to representatives on the Security Council notice of meetings of the Security Council and of its commissions and committees.

Rule 26

The Secretary-General shall be responsible for the preparation of documents required by the Security Council and shall, except in urgent circumstances, distribute them at least forty-eight hours in advance of the meeting at which they are to be considered.

CHAPTER VI

CONDUCT OF BUSINESS

Rule 27

The President shall call upon representatives in the order in which they signify their desire to speak.

Rule 28

The Security Council may appoint a commission or committee or a rapporteur for a specified question.

Rule 29

The President may accord precedence to any rapporteur appointed by the Security Council.

The Chairman of a commission or committee, or the rapporteur appointed by the commission or committee to present its report, may be accorded precedence for the purpose of explaining the report.

Rule 30

If a representative raises a point of order, the President shall immediately state his ruling. If it is challenged, the President shall submit his ruling to the Security Council for immediate decision and it shall stand unless overruled.

Rule 31

Proposed resolutions, amendments and substantive motions shall normally be placed before the representatives in writing.

Rule 32

Principal motions and draft resolutions shall have precedence in the order of their submission.

Parts of a motion or of a draft resolution shall be voted on separately at the request of any representative, unless the original mover objects.

Rule 33

The following motions shall have precedence in the order named over all principal motions and draft resolutions relative to the subject before the meeting:

1. To suspend the meeting;
2. To adjourn the meeting;
3. To adjourn the meeting to a certain day or hour;

4. To refer any matter to a committee, to the Secretary-General or to a rapporteur;
5. To postpone discussion of the question to a certain day or indefinitely; or
6. To introduce an amendment.

Any motion for the suspension or for the simple adjournment of the meeting shall be decided without debate.

Rule 34

It shall not be necessary for any motion or draft resolution proposed by a representative on the Security Council to be seconded before being put to a vote.

Rule 35

A motion or draft resolution can at any time be withdrawn so long as no vote has been taken with respect to it.

If the motion or draft resolution has been seconded, the representative on the Security Council who has seconded it may require that it be put to the vote as his motion or draft resolution with the same right of precedence as if the original mover had not withdrawn it.

Rule 36

If two or more amendments to a motion or draft resolution are proposed, the President shall rule on the order in which they are to be voted upon. Ordinarily, the Security Council shall first vote on the amendment furthest removed in substance from the original proposal and then on the amendment next furthest removed until all amendments have been put to the vote, but when an amendment adds to or deletes from the text of a motion or draft resolution, that amendment shall be voted on first.

Rule 37

Any Member of the United Nations which is not a member of the Security Council may be invited, as the result of a decision of the Security Council to participate, without vote, in the discussion of any question brought before the Security Council when the Security Council considers that the interests of that Member are specially affected, or when a Member brings a matter to the attention of the Security Council in accordance with Article 35 (1) of the Charter.

Rule 38

Any Member of the United Nations invited in accordance with the preceding rule, or in application of Article 32 of the Charter, to participate in the discussions of the Security Council may submit proposals and draft resolutions. These proposals and draft resolutions may be put to a vote only at the request of a representative on the Security Council.

Rule 39

The Security Council may invite members of the Secretariat or other persons, whom it considers competent for the purpose, to supply it with information or to give other assistance in examining matters within its competence.

Chapter VII

VOTING

Rule 40

Voting in the Security Council shall be in accordance with the relevant Articles of the Charter and of the Statute of the International Court of Justice.

Chapter VIII

LANGUAGES

Rule 41

Arabic, Chinese, English, French, Russian and Spanish shall be both the official and the working languages of the Security Council.

Rule 42

Speeches made in any of the six languages of the Security Council shall be interpreted into the other five languages.

Rule 43

[Deleted]

Rule 44

Any representative may make a speech in a language other than the languages of the Security Council. In this case, he shall himself provide for interpretation into one of those languages. Interpretation into the other languages of the Security Council by the interpreters of the Secretariat may be based on the interpretation given in the first such language.

Rule 45

Verbatim records of meetings of the Security Council shall be drawn up in the languages of the Council.

Rule 46

All resolutions and other documents shall be published in the languages of the Security Council.

Rule 47

Documents of the Security Council shall, if the Security Council so decides, be published in any language other than the languages of the Council.

Chapter IX

PUBLICITY OF MEETINGS, RECORDS

Rule 48

Unless it decides otherwise, the Security Council shall meet in public. Any recommendation to the General Assembly regarding the appointment of the Secretary-General shall be discussed and decided at a private meeting.

Rule 49

Subject to the provisions of rule 51, the verbatim record of each meeting of the Security Council shall be made available to the representatives on the Security Council and to the representatives of any other States which have participated in the meeting not later than 10 a.m. of the first working day following the meeting.

Rule 50

The representatives of the States which have participated in the meeting shall, within two working days after the time indicated in rule 49, inform the Secretary-General of any corrections they wish to have made in the verbatim record.

Rule 51

The Security Council may decide that for a private meeting the record shall be made in a single copy alone. This record shall be kept by the Secretary-General. The representatives of the States which have participated in the meeting shall, within a period of ten days, inform the Secretary-General of any corrections they wish to have made in this record.

Rule 52

Corrections that have been requested shall be considered approved unless the President is of the opinion that they are sufficiently important to be submitted to the representatives on the Security Council. In the latter case, the representatives on the Security Council shall submit within two working days any comments they may wish to make. In the absence of objections in this period of time, the record shall be corrected as requested.

Rule 53

The verbatim record referred to in rule 49 or the record referred to in rule 51, in which no corrections have been requested in the period of time required by rules 50 and 51, respectively, or which has been corrected in accordance with the provisions of rule 52, shall be considered as approved. It shall be signed by the President and shall become the official record of the Security Council.

Rule 54

The official record of public meetings of the Security Council, as well as the documents annexed thereto, shall be published in the official languages as soon as possible.

Rule 55

At the close of each private meeting the Security Council shall issue a *communiqué* through the Secretary-General.

Rule 56

The representatives of the Members of the United Nations which have taken part in a private meeting shall at all times have the right to consult the record of that meeting in the office of the Secretary-General. The Security Council may at any time grant access to this record to authorized representatives of other Members of the United Nations.

Rule 57

The Secretary-General shall, once each year, submit to the Security Council a list of the records and documents which up to that time have been considered confidential. The Security Council shall decide which of these shall be made available to other Members of the United Nations, which shall be made public, and which shall continue to remain confidential.

Chapter X

ADMISSION OF NEW MEMBERS

Rule 58

Any State which desires to become a Member of the United Nations shall submit an application to the Secretary-General. This application shall contain a declaration made in a formal instrument that it accepts the obligations contained in the Charter.

Rule 59

The Secretary-General shall immediately place the application for membership before the representatives on the Security Council. Unless the Security Council decides otherwise, the application shall be referred by the President to a committee of the Security Council upon which each member of the Security Council shall be represented. The committee shall examine any application referred to it and report its conclusions thereon to the Council not less than thirty-five days in advance of a regular session of the General Assembly or, if a special session of the General Assembly is called, not less than fourteen days in advance of such session.

Rule 60

The Security Council shall decide whether in its judgment the applicant is a peace-loving State and is able and willing to carry out the obligations contained in the Charter and, accordingly, whether to recommend the applicant State for membership.

If the Security Council recommends the applicant State for membership, it shall forward to the General Assembly the recommendation with a complete record of the discussion.

If the Security Council does not recommend the applicant State for membership or postpones the consideration of the application, it shall submit a special report to the General Assembly with a complete record of the discussion.

In order to ensure the consideration of its recommendation at the next session of the General Assembly following the receipt of the application, the Security Council shall make its recommendation not less than twenty-five days in advance of a regular session of the General Assembly, nor less than four days in advance of a special session.

In special circumstances, the Security Council may decide to make a recommendation to the General Assembly concerning an application for membership subsequent to the expiration of the time limits set forth in the preceding paragraph.

Chapter XI

RELATIONS WITH OTHER UNITED NATIONS ORGANS

Rule 61

Any meeting of the Security Council held in pursuance of the Statute of the International Court of Justice for the purpose of the election of members of the Court shall continue until as many candidates as are required for all the seats to be filled have obtained in one or more ballots an absolute majority of votes.

APPENDIX

PROVISIONAL PROCEDURE FOR DEALING WITH COMMUNICATIONS FROM PRIVATE INDIVIDUALS AND NON-GOVERNMENTAL BODIES

A. A list of all communications from private individuals and non-governmental bodies relating to matters of which the Security Council is seized shall be circulated to all representatives on the Security Council.

B. A copy of any communication on the list shall be given by the Secretariat to any representative on the Security Council at his request.

APPENDIX III

THE YALTA FORMULA ON VOTING IN THE SECURITY COUNCIL, 8 JUNE 1945*

Statement by the delegations of the four sponsoring Governments, to which the delegation of France also subscribed. The references are to the Dumbarton Oaks Proposals for the establishment of a General International Organization; references in square brackets are to the Charter as finally adopted.

Specific questions covering the voting procedure in the Security Council have been submitted by a Subcommittee of the Conference Committee on Structure and Procedures of the Security Council to the Delegations of the four Governments sponsoring the Conference—the United States of America, the United Kingdom of Great Britain and Northern Ireland, the Union of Soviet Socialist Republics, and the Republic of China. In dealing with these questions, the four Delegations desire to make the following statement of their general attitude towards the whole question of unanimity of permanent members in the decisions of the Security Council.

I

1. The Yalta voting formula recognizes that the Security Council, in discharging its responsibilities for the maintenance of international peace and security, will have two broad groups of functions. Under Chapter VIII [of the Dumbarton Oaks proposals, which became Chapters VI, VII, and VIII of the Charter], the Council will have to make decisions which involve its taking direct measures in connection with settlement of disputes, adjustment of situations likely to lead to disputes, determination of threats to the peace, and suppression of breaches of the peace. It will also have to make decisions which do not involve the taking of such measures. The Yalta formula provides that the second of these two groups of decisions will be governed by a procedural vote—that is, the vote of any seven members. The first group of decisions will be governed by a qualified vote—that is, the vote of seven members, including the concurring votes of the five permanent

* UNCIO, 1945, Vol. XI, pp. 710–14.

members, subject to the proviso that in decisions under Section A [Chapter VI] and a part of Section C of Chapter VIII [Article 52(3)] parties to a dispute shall abstain from voting.

2. For example, under the Yalta formula a procedural vote will govern the decisions made under the entire Section D of Chapter VI [Articles 28–32]. This means that the Council will, by a vote of any seven of its members, adopt or alter its rules of procedure; determine the method of selecting its President; organize itself in such a way as to be able to function continuously; select the times and places of its regular and special meetings; establish such bodies or agencies as it may deem necessary for the performance of its functions; invite a member of the Organization not represented on the Council to participate in its discussions when that Member's interests are specially affected; and invite any State when it is a party to a dispute being considered by the Council to participate in the discussion relating to that dispute.

3. Further, no individual member of the Council can alone prevent consideration and discussion by the Council of a dispute or situation brought to its attention under paragraph 2, Section A, Chapter VIII [Article 35]. Nor can parties to such dispute be prevented by these means from being heard by the Council. Likewise, the requirement for unanimity of the permanent members cannot prevent any member of the Council from reminding the Members of the Organization of their general obligations assumed under the Charter as regards peaceful settlement of international disputes.

4. Beyond this point, decisions and actions by the Security Council may well have major political consequences and may even initiate a chain of events which might, in the end, require the Council under its responsibilities to invoke measures of enforcement under Section B, Chapter VIII [Chapter VII]. This chain of events begins when the Council decides to make an investigation, or determines that the time has come to call upon States to settle their difference, or makes recommendations to the parties. It is to such decisions and actions that unanimity of the permanent members applies, with the important proviso, referred to above, for abstention from voting by parties to a dispute.

5. To illustrate: in ordering an investigation, the Council has to consider whether the investigation—which may involve calling for reports, hearing witnesses, dispatching a commission of inquiry, or other means—might not further aggravate the situation. After investigation, the Council must determine whether the continuance of the situation or dispute would be likely to endanger international peace and security. If it so determines, the Council would be under obligation to take further steps. Similarly, the decision to make recommendations, even when all parties request it to do so, or to call

upon parties to a dispute to fulfil their obligations under the Charter, might be the first step on a course of action from which the Security Council could withdraw only at the risk of failing to discharge its responsibilities.

6. In appraising the significance of the vote required to take such decisions or actions, it is useful to make comparison with the requirements of the League Covenant with reference to decisions of the League Council. Substantive decisions of the League of Nations Council could be taken only by the unanimous vote of all its members, whether permanent or not, with the exception of parties to a dispute under Article XV of the League Covenant. Under Article XI, under which most of the disputes brought before the League were dealt with and decisions to make investigations taken, the unanimity rule was invariably interpreted to include even the votes of the parties to a dispute.

7. The Yalta voting formula substitutes for the rule of complete unanimity of the League Council a system of qualified majority voting in the Security Council. Under this system non-permanent members of the Security Council individually would have no 'veto'. As regards the permanent members, there is no question under the Yalta formula of investing them with a new right, namely, the right to veto, a right which the permanent members of the League Council always had. The formula proposed for the taking of action in the Security Council by a majority of seven would make the operation of the Council less subject to obstruction than was the case under the League of Nations rule of complete unanimity.

8. It should also be remembered that under the Yalta formula the five major powers could not act by themselves, since even under the unanimity requirement any decisions of the Council would have to include the concurring votes of at least two of the non-permanent members. In other words, it would be possible for five non-permanent members as a group to exercise a 'veto'. It is not to be assumed, however, that the permanent members, any more than the non-permanent members, would use their 'veto' power wilfully to obstruct the operation of the Council.

9. In view of the primary responsibilities of the permanent members, they could not be expected, in the present condition of the world, to assume the obligation to act in so serious a matter as the maintenance of international peace and security in consequence of a decision in which they had not concurred. Therefore, if a majority voting in the Security Council is to be made possible, the only practicable method is to provide, in respect of non-procedural decisions, for unanimity of the permanent members plus the concurring votes of at least two of the non-permanent members.

10. For all these reasons, the four sponsoring Governments agreed on the Yalta formula and have presented it to this Conference as essential if an

international organization is to be created through which all peace-loving nations can effectively discharge their common responsibilities for the maintenance of international peace and security.

II

In the light of the considerations set forth in Part I of this statement, it is clear what the answers to the questions submitted by the Subcommittee should be, with the exception of Question 19. [Question 19 reads: 'In case a decision has to be taken as to whether a certain point is a procedural matter, is that preliminary question to be considered in itself as a procedural matter or is the veto applicable to such preliminary question?'] The answer to that question is as follows:

1. In the opinion of the Delegations of the sponsoring Governments, the Draft Charter itself contains an indication of the application of the voting procedures to the various functions of the Council.

2. In this case, it will be unlikely that there will arise in the future any matters of great importance on which a decision will have to be made as to whether a procedural vote would apply. Should, however, such a matter arise, the decision regarding the preliminary question as to whether or not such a matter is procedural must be taken by a vote of seven members of the Security Council, including the concurring votes of the permanent members.

APPENDIX IV (a)

OPINION OF THE LEGAL COUNSEL ON RELATIONS BETWEEN THE GENERAL ASSEMBLY AND THE SECURITY COUNCIL, 10 SEPT. 1964*

(A) Relevant provisions of the charter

1. The following provisions of the Charter are relevant to the question of simultaneous consideration by the General Assembly and the Security Council of the same agenda item:

'Article 12

'1. While the Security Council is exercising in respect of any dispute or situation the functions assigned to it in the present Charter, the General Assembly shall not make any recommendation with regard to that dispute or situation unless the Security Council so requests.

'2. The Secretary-General, with the consent of the Security Council, shall notify the General Assembly at each session of any matters relative to the maintenance of international peace and security which are being dealt with by the Security Council and shall similarly notify the General Assembly, or the Members of the United Nations if the General Assembly is not in session, immediately the Security Council ceases to deal with such matters.'

'Article 10

'The General Assembly may discuss any questions or any matters within the scope of the present Charter or relating to the powers and functions of any organs provided for in the present Charter, and, except as provided in Article 12, may make recommendations to the Members of the United Nations or to the Security Council or to both on any such questions or matters.'

* *Juridical Yearbook 1964*, pp. 228–37.

'*Article 11*

'2. The General Assembly may discuss any questions relating to the maintenance of international peace and security brought before it by any Member of the United Nations, or by the Security Council, or by a state which is not a Member of the United Nations in accordance with Article 35, paragraph 2, and, except as provided in Article 12, may make recommendations with regard to any such questions to the state or states concerned or to the Security Council or to both. Any such question on which action is necessary shall be referred to the Security Council by the General Assembly either before or after discussion.'

'*Article 35*

'1. Any Member of the United Nations may bring any dispute, or any situation of the nature referred to in Article 34, to the attention of the Security Council or of the General Assembly.

. . .

'3. The proceedings of the General Assembly in respect of matters brought to its attention under this Article will be subject to the provisions of Articles 11 and 12.'

(B) Practice of the United Nations

2. Since the inception of the United Nations, there have been many occasions on which a question was considered both by the General Assembly and by the Security Council. These instances may be grouped for the purpose of presentation into two general categories: questions which were first considered by the Security Council and then by the General Assembly and questions which were first considered by the General Assembly and then by the Security Council.

(i) Items originally submitted to the Security Council and later considered by the General Assembly

(1) *Consideration by the General Assembly at the request of the Security Council*

3. The Security Council had requested the convening of *emergency special sessions* of the General Assembly in accordance with rule 8(*b*) of the rules of procedure of the Assembly pursuant to Assembly resolution 377 A

(V) ('Uniting for Peace') in the following cases: (1) the question of the invasion of Egypt; (2) the question of Hungary; (3) the question of Lebanon and Jordan and (4) the situation in the Congo.* In each of these cases, the request was made in the form of a resolution adopted by the Security Council on the ground that the Security Council was unable to exercise its primary responsibility for the maintenance of international peace and security because of the lack of unanimity among its permanent members.

4. The Security Council has also requested the convening of a *special session* of the General Assembly in accordance with rule 8(*a*) of the Assembly's rules of procedure. Thus, on 1 April 1948, the Council adopted a resolution requesting the Secretary-General to convoke a special session of the General Assembly 'to consider further the question of the future government of Palestine'.†

5. The Security Council had also sent to the General Assembly questions which were considered at *regular sessions* of the Assembly. This was done by removal of the question from the list of matters of which the Security Council was seized. For example, on 4 November 1946, the Security Council resolved 'that the situation in Spain is to be taken off the list of matters of which the Council is seized, and that all records and documents of the case be put at the disposal of the General Assembly'. The Council requested 'the Secretary-General to notify the General Assembly of this decision.' In the case of the Greek frontier incidents question, the Security Council, on 15 September 1947, '(*a*) [*resolved*] that the dispute between Greece, on the one hand, and Albania, Yugoslavia and Bulgaria, on the other, be taken off the list of matters of which the Council is seized; and (*b*) [*requested*] that the Secretary-General be instructed to place all records and documents in the case at the disposal of the Assembly General.' In another case, a proposal to defer consideration of an item (Complaint of armed invasion of Taiwan (Formosa), 1950) before the Council when a similar item was to be discussed by the General Assembly was adopted by the Council.

6. Although no decision had been taken by the Security Council to request the General Assembly to make recommendations in respect of a matter of which the Council remained seized, the possibility for the Council

* There was an emergency special session of the General Assembly on the Middle East in 1967 convered at the request of the Soviet Union. S.D.B.

† It may be noted that the Palestine question was first submitted to the General Assembly which referred certain aspects falling within the scope of Chapter VII of the Charter to the Security Council for consideration. It may also be noted that in the course of the discussion which led to the adoption of the above-mentioned resolution, the representative of Belgium expressed the following opinion: '. . . the convoking of the General Assembly would not prevent the Council from considering, in the meantime, any substantive proposals which it might be in a position to submit to the General Assembly.'

to make such a request is clearly set forth in Article 12, paragraph 1, of the Charter. On several occasions, a request of this nature had been formulated in draft resolutions submitted to the Security Council. Thus, in connection with the Greek frontier incidents question considered by the Council in September 1947, a draft resolution was proposed by the United States which read as follows:

> '*The Security Council*, pursuant to Article 12 of the Charter,
>
> '(*a*) *Requests* the General Assembly to consider the dispute between Greece on the one hand and Albania, Yugoslavia and Bulgaria on the other, and to make any recommendations with regard to that dispute which it deems appropriate under the circumstances;
>
> '(*b*) *Instructs* the Secretary-General to place all records and documents in the case at the disposal of the General Assembly.'

In connexion with the question of South Rhodesia, considered by the Council in September 1963, a three-power draft resolution was submitted which, after inviting the United Kingdom Government to take certain actions, would request 'the General Assembly to continue its examination of the question . . .. with a view to securing a just and lasting settlement.' Both draft resolutions referred to above failed of adoption owing to the negative vote of a permanent member. In the first case, the objection was made on the ground that a request to the Assembly for recommendation would mean an abdication by the Council of its primary responsibility for the maintenance of international peace and security under the Charter. In the second case, the objection was made to the effect that the question was one of domestic jurisdiction and neither the Security Council nor the General Assembly was competent to deal with it. The rejection of the draft resolution is, therefore, not to be construed as a denial of the power of the Security Council to request the General Assembly for recommendations as provided for in Article 12, paragraph 1, of the Charter.

(2) *Consideration by the General Assembly at the request of Member States*

The Indonesian question

7. The Indonesian question as submitted by Australia in July 1947 was considered by the Security Council in the years 1947, 1948 and 1949. By a letter dated 30 and 31 March 1949, the delegations of India and Australia requested that the Indonesian question be placed on the agenda of the second part of the third regular session of the General Assembly. On 12 April, during the consideration by the General Assembly of adoption of this agenda item, the representative of the Netherlands, supported by the representatives of Norway and Belgium, invoked Article 12, paragraph 1 of the

Charter as a ground for objecting to the inclusion of the item in the agenda. They stated that the General Assembly could not make recommendations on the subject unless it was so requested by the Security Council and that a discussion in the General Assembly could in no way lead to any conclusion. On the other hand, the representative of Iraq, while recognizing the existence of procedural difficulties, considered that as long as paragraph 2 of Article 11 of the Charter remained in effect, the General Assembly had a right to discuss any question and any dispute which was before the Security Council.* After the General Assembly had voted in favour of inclusion of the item on its agenda, a resolution was adopted to defer further consideration of the item to the fourth regular session of the Assembly (resolution 274 (III)).

8. At the Assembly's fourth session, two draft resolutions were submitted in the *ad hoc* Political Committee. The first draft resolution provided that the General Assembly should 'welcome' the announcement that an agreement had been reached at the Round-Table Conference, 'commend' the parties concerned and the United Nations Commission for Indonesia for their contributions thereto and 'welcome' the forthcoming establishment of the Republic of the United States of Indonesia as an independent sovereign State. The second draft resolution contained provisions for the withdrawal of the Netherlands forces, the establishment of a United Nations commission to observe the implementation of such measures and to investigate the activities of the Netherlands authorities, as well as instructions to the commission regarding its work. During the discussion, the Chairman drew the attention of the Committee to the provisions of Article 12, paragraph 1, of the Charter. Pointing out that the Security Council was still seized of the question, he stated that, before putting each of the draft resolutions to the vote, he would ask the Committee to pronounce itself on whether its terms constituted a recommendation within the meaning of Article 12, paragraph 1. The *ad hoc* Political Committee decided by 42 votes to one with 6 abstentions, that the first draft resolution did not constitute a recommendation within the meaning of Article 12, paragraph 1, and by 42 votes to 5 with 4 abstentions, that the second draft resolution did constitute a

* In this connection, the representative of Iraq stated at the 190th plenary meeting that 'The right of the General Assembly to discuss any situation or dispute already before the Security Council had been thoroughly considered at the San Francisco Conference. Some delegations had thought that the General Assembly should have the right to discuss questions of any kind, even if they were before the Security Council, and to make recommendations with regard to them. Other delegations had opposed the granting of such a right to the General Assembly. A compromise had finally been reached whereby the General Assembly could consider a question which was on the agenda of the Security Council but could not make recommendations upon it.'

recommendation. The first draft resolution was then adopted and the second rejected.*

The Tunisian question

9. On 20 July 1961, Tunisia requested a meeting of the Security Council as a matter of extreme urgency to consider its complaint against France 'for acts of aggression infringing the sovereignty and security of Tunisia and threatening international peace and security.' On 22 July, the Council adopted a resolution which (1) called for an immediate cease-fire and a return of all armed forces to their original position and (2) decided to continue the debate. On 29 July, three draft resolutions dealing with implementation of the earlier resolution were rejected by the Council.

10. On 7 August, a number of delegations requested the convening of a special session of the General Assembly 'to consider the grave situation in Tunisia obtaining since 19 July 1961, in view of the failure of the Security Council to take appropriate action'. On the receipt of the concurrence of a majority of the Members on 10 August, the Secretary-General summoned, in accordance with rule 8(*a*) of the Assembly's rules of procedure, the third special session of the General Assembly to meet on 21 August. In its resolution 1622 (S–III) adopted on 25 August, the Assembly, while noting that the Security Council had failed to take further appropriate action, reaffirmed the Security Council's interim resolution, urged the Government of France to implement fully the provisions of the operative paragraph I of that resolution, recognized the sovereign right of Tunisia to call for the withdrawal of all French armed forces present on its territory without its consent, and called upon the Governments of France and Tunisia to enter into immediate negotiations to devise peaceful and agreed measures for the withdrawal of French armed forces from Tunisian territory.

The situation in Angola

11. The question of Angola was first submitted to the Security Council in February 1961. On 15 March, the Council failed to adopt a draft reso-

* A similar situation arose at the first emergency special session of the General Assembly in connexion with two draft resolutions, submitted by the United States. Objection to those draft resolutions were raised on the ground that the first draft resolution which dealt with the Palestine question in general and the second which dealt with the Suez Canal question were matters of which the Security Council was actually seized. The emergency session had been convened to consider the situation arisen from the invasion of Egypt and not another question. The two draft resolution were subsequently withdrawn.

lution which would call upon Portugal to implement General Assembly resolution 1514 (XV) (containing the declaration on ending colonialism) and propose to establish a sub-committee to examine the question and report to the Council. On 20 March, 39 delegations requested the inclusion of the question in the Assembly's agenda. Opposition to consideration of the question by the Assembly was based on Article 2, paragraph 7, of the Charter. During the discussion, a number of delegations proposing the item stated that because of the failure of the Security Council to take action, it had become necessary to refer the question to the General Assembly, which should take immediate measures to bring about a solution of the problem. A draft resolution identical in terms with that submitted to the Security Council, except that the proposed sub-committee would examine statements before the Assembly (rather than the Council) and report to the Assembly, was adopted as resolution 1603 (XV) on 20 April 1961.

(ii) Items submitted to the General Assembly and later also considered by the Security Council

(1) *By decision of the General Assembly*

12. The Palestine question was originally submitted to the General Assembly. In its resolution 181 (II), the Assembly recommended to Members the adoption and implementation of a plan of partition with economic union and *requested the Security Council* to take the necessary measures provided for in the plan and to consider, if circumstances during the transitional period required such consideration, whether the situation in Palestine constituted a threat to the peace. Since then the Palestine question had continued to be on the agenda of both the General Assembly and the Security Council, with the latter dealing generally with security and military aspects of the question and the former with political, economic and social aspects.

(2) *At the request of Member States*

13. Only in one case had the Security Council rejected the request by a Member State for inclusion in its agenda of an item which was before the General Assembly and in respect of which arguments based on Article 12, paragraph 1, of the Charter were advanced. This was the case of a USSR request dated 5 November 1956 for consideration by the Council of an item entitled 'Non-compliance by the United Kingdom, France and Israel with the decision of the emergency special session of the General Assembly of the United Nations of 2 November 1956 and immediate steps to halt the aggression of the aforesaid States against Egypt.' On the one hand it was argued that just as the General Assembly could not consider a question of which

the Security Council was seized, so the Security Council could not logically consider a question pending before the General Assembly, particularly one referred to the Assembly by the Council itself. On the other hand it was contended that the fact that the General Assembly was taking action on a question did not relieve the Security Council of the obligation to act if the circumstances demanded it. The USSR request was rejected by 3 votes in favour, 4 against with 4 abstentions.

14. In the more recent cases dealt with below, whether the questions were originally submitted to the General Assembly or the Security Council, concurrent consideration by the two organs of those questions took place and in most cases both organs adopted substantive resolutions without reference to Article 12, paragraph 1, of the Charter.

The situation in the Congo, 1960–1961

15. At its fourth emergency special session convened at the request of the Security Council (resolution adopted on 16/17 September 1960) to consider the situation in the Congo, the General Assembly adopted, on 20 September 1960, resolution 1474 (ES–IV) which took note of the resolutions previously adopted by the Security Council and requested Member States to take certain actions. By a letter dated 16 September 1960, the USSR requested the inclusion of the Congo question as an additional item in the agenda of the fifteenth regular session of the General Assembly. On 28 September, the General Committee decided to include the item in the agenda of the Assembly. On 6 December 1960, the USSR proposed that the question of the situation in the Congo and the steps to be taken on the matter should be examined at the earliest possible date by the Security Council and the General Assembly. The Council met from 7 to 14 December but failed to adopt three draft resolutions before it. On 16 December, the General Assembly resumed consideration of the situation in the Congo and had before it two draft resolutions (one submitted by 7 Afro-Asian States and Yugoslavia, and the other by the United States and the United Kingdom), both containing provisions requiring specific action. The two draft resolutions were rejected by vote, but Article 12, paragraph 1, of the Charter was not referred to during the discussion. On 20 December, the Assembly adopted resolution 1592 (XV) to keep the item on the agenda of its resumed fifteenth session.

16. The Security Council met again from 12 to 14 January and from 1 to 21 February 1961 to consider the Congo question at the request of the USSR. These meetings resulted in the adoption by the Council, on 21 February, of a resolution dealing with the situation. Consideration of the

Congo question by the General Assembly at its resumed fifteenth session resulted in the adoption, on 15 April 1961, of resolutions 1599 (XV) calling upon States to take certain action and 'deciding' on the complete withdrawal and evacuation of military personnel and political advisers not under the United Nations Command, 1600 (XV) establishing a Commission of Conciliation and 1601 (XV) establishing a Commission of Investigation. At no time was Article 12, paragraph 1, of the Charter invoked as a limitation of the competence of the Assembly to make recommendations.

The situation in Angola, 1961–1962

17. After the General Assembly adopted on 20 April 1961 resolution 1603 (XV) to establish a sub-committee (*see* paragraph 11 above), a group of States, by a letter dated 26 May 1961, requested consideration by the Security Council of the Angolan question. On 9 June, the Council adopted a resolution reaffirming the Assembly resolution, calling upon Portugal to desist from repressive measures and requesting the sub-committee to report both to the Security Council and to the Assembly.

18. By a letter dated 19 July 1961 addressed to the Secretary-General, a group of States considered the situation in Angola as endangering international peace and security and reserved the right to ask for 'effective remedial action to be taken either by the Security Council or by the General Assembly.' The item entitled 'The situation in Angola: report of the Sub-committee established by General Assembly resolution 1603 (XV)' was placed on the provisional agenda of the sixteenth session of the Assembly. Portugal objected to the inclusion of this agenda item on ground of Article 2, paragraph 7, of the Charter. On 30 January 1962, the Assembly adopted resolution 1742 (XVI) by which it decided to continue the Sub-Committee, requested Member States to take certain actions and recommended 'the Security Council, in the light of the Council's resolution of 9 June 1961 and of the present resolution, to keep the matter under constant review.'

The apartheid *question, 1960–1963*

19. Beginning with its twelfth session, the General Assembly has adopted at each regular session a resolution on the question of race conflict in South Africa resulting from the policies of *apartheid* of the Government of South Africa. Resolution 1375 (XIV) on this question was adopted by the Assembly on 17 November 1959. On 25 March 1960, 29 Asian-African States requested an urgent meeting of the Security Council to consider the situation arising out of the large-scale killings of unarmed and peaceful

demonstrators against racial discrimination and segregation in the Union of South Africa. They considered that the situation endangered international peace and security. The question was taken up by the Council on 30 March. On 1 April, the Council adopted a resolution calling upon the Union Government to initiate measures to bring about racial harmony and to abandon its policies of *apartheid* and racial discrimination. Subsequently, the Assembly adopted the following resolutions on the *apartheid* question: 1598 (XV) of 13 April 1961, 1663 (XVI) of 28 November 1961, and 1761 (XVII) of 6 November 1962. In the last-mentioned resolution, the Assembly decided to establish a Special Committee on *apartheid*, invited Member States to inform the General Assembly at its eighteenth session regarding actions taken, separately or collectively, in dissuading the Government of South Africa from pursuing its policies of *apartheid*, and requested 'the Security Council to take appropriate measures, including sanctions, to secure South Africa's compliance with the resolutions of the General Assembly and of the Security Council on this subject and, if necessary, to consider action under Article 6 of the Charter.'

20. On 11 July 1963, 32 African States requested a meeting of the Security Council to consider the explosive situation in South Africa which constituted a serious threat to international peace and security. Meanwhile, the Special Committee on *apartheid* had submitted its reports both to the General Assembly and to the Security Council. On 7 August, the Council adopted a resolution calling upon the Government of South Africa to abandon its policies of *apartheid* and to liberate prisoners, calling upon all States to cease forthwith the sale and shipment of arms and ammunition of all types and requesting the Secretary-General to keep the situation in South Africa under observation and to report to the Security Council by 30 October 1963.

21. In accordance with Assembly resolution 1761 (XVII) (*see* paragraph 19 above), the item 'The policies of *apartheid* of the Government of the Republic of South Africa: reports of the Special Committee . . . and replies by Member States under General Assembly resolution 1761 (XVII)' was included in the agenda of the Assembly's eighteenth session. On 11 October 1963, the Assembly adopted resolution 1881 (XVIII) requesting once more the Government of South Africa to release political prisoners, requesting all Member States to make all necessary efforts to ensure compliance by the Government of South Africa with the Assembly's request, and requesting the Secretary-General 'to report to the General Assembly and the Security Council, as soon as possible during the eighteenth session', on the implementation of the resolution.

22. On 23 October, 32 States requested a meeting of the Security Council

to consider the report submitted by the Secretary-General pursuant to Council resolution of 7 August. On 4 December, the Council adopted a resolution which reaffirmed in essence the provisions of its previous resolution and requested the Secretary-General to establish a group of experts to examine methods of resolving the situation.

23. Meanwhile, a report of the Secretary-General pursuant to Assembly resolution 1881 (XVIII) of 11 October (*see* paragraph 21 above) was circulated to the General Assembly on 19 November. After consideration, the Assembly adopted, on 16 December 1963, resolution 1978 (XVIII) appealing again to all States to take appropriate measures and requesting the Special Committee to continue its work and submit reports to the General Assembly and to the Security Council whenever appropriate. In the same resolution the Assembly further requested the Secretary-General to provide relief and assistance, through appropriate international agencies, to the families of all persons persecuted by the Government of South Africa and to report thereon to the Assembly at its nineteenth session.

24. In the course of the practically simultaneous consideration of the *apartheid* question in the Security Council and in the General Assembly, no reference was made to Article 12, paragraph 1 of the Charter.

The question relating to Territories under Portuguese Administration, 1962–1963

25. By resolution 1699 (XVI) of 19 December 1961, the General Assembly established a Special Committee on Territories under Portuguese Administration to report on the question. In its resolution 1807 (XVII) of 14 December 1962, the Assembly, noting the opinion of the Special Committee concerning the implications of the supply of military equipment to the Portuguese Government, urged Portugal to give effect to the recommendations of the Special Committee, requested the Special Committee on the Situation with regard to the Implementation of the Declaration on the Granting of Independence to Colonial Countries and Peoples to examine the situation, called upon Member States to use their influence to induce Portugal to carry out its obligations under Chapter XI of the Charter, requested all States to refrain from offering Portugal assistance and to prevent the sale and supply of arms and military equipment to the Portuguese Government, and requested 'the Security Council, in case the Portuguese Government should refuse to comply with the present resolution and previous General Assembly resolutions on this question, to take all appropriate measures to secure the compliance of Portugal with its obligations as a Member State.'

26. On 4 April 1963, the Special Committee on the Situation with regard to the Implementation of the Declaration on the Granting of Independence to Colonial Countries and Peoples adopted a resolution drawing the immediate attention of the Security Council to the situation in the Territories under Portuguese administration, with a view to the Council taking appropriate measures, including sanctions, to secure the compliance by Portugal of the relevant resolutions of the General Assembly and of the Security Council. The text of this resolution and the report of the Special Committee were transmitted to the Council.

27. On 11 July 1963, the President of the Security Council received a request from 32 African States to convene a meeting of the Council. On 31 July, the Council adopted a resolution by which it called upon Portugal to take certain action, requested all States to prevent sale and supply of arms and military equipment to the Portuguese Government and requested the Secretary-General to report to the Country by 31 October.

28. On 3 December, the General Assembly adopted resolution 1913 (XVIII) by which the Assembly, recalling the resolutions previously adopted by the Assembly and the Council on the question and in particular the provisions of Council resolution of 31 July, and noting with regret and concern the continued refusal of the Portuguese Government to implement those resolutions, requested 'the Security Council to consider immediately the question of Territories under Portuguese administration and to adopt necessary measures to give effect to its own decisions, particularly those contained in the resolution of 31 July 1963' and decided to maintain the question on the agenda of its eighteenth session.

29. Prior to the adoption by the General Assembly of resolution 1913 (XVIII), 29 African States requested the convening of the Security Council to consider the report of the Secretary-General submitted in pursuance of Council resolution of 31 July 1963. The Council began consideration of the question on 6 December. On 11 December, the Council adopted a resolution which, *inter alia*, called upon all States to comply with Council resolution of 31 July and requested the Secretary-General to continue his efforts and report to the Council not later than 1 June 1964.

30. During the discussion of the question in the Assembly and the Council the provisions of Article 12, paragraph 1, of the Charter were not mentioned. Objection to the competence of the two organs to deal with the question was raised by Portugal on ground of Article 2, paragraph 7.

The question of Southern Rhodesia, 1962–1963

31. By resolution 1755 (XVII) of 12 October 1962, the General Assembly urged the Government of the United Kingdom to take measures to secure

the release of political prisoners and to lift the ban on the Zimbabwe African Peoples Union. In its resolution 1760 (XVII) of 31 October, the Assembly, *inter alia*, requested the Government of the United Kingdom to take certain measures including the convening of a constitutional conference on Southern Rhodesia, requested the Acting Secretary-General to lend his good offices to promote conciliation and decided to keep the question on the agenda of its seventeenth session.

32. On 2 and 30 August 1963, requests were made by a number of African States for a meeting of the Security Council to consider the question of Southern Rhodesia. The Council met from 9 to 13 September but failed to adopt a draft resolution submitted by Ghana, Morocco and the Philippines, owing to the negative vote of a permanent member.

33. On 18 July 1963, a group of States requested the inclusion of the question of Southern Rhodesia in the agenda of the eighteenth session of the General Assembly. After consideration of the question, the Assembly adopted two resolutions. By resolution 1883 (XVIII) of 14 October, the Assembly invited the Government of the United Kingdom not to take certain actions relating to the status of Southern Rhodesia, on the one hand, and to put into effect the previous Assembly resolutions concerning the question, on the other. By resolution 1889 (XVIII) of 6 November, the Assembly, *inter alia*, invited once more the United Kingdom to hold a constitutional conference, urged all Member States to use their influence with a view to ensuring the realization of the legitimate aspirations of the people of Southern Rhodesia, requested the Secretary General to continue to use his good offices and decided to keep the question on the agenda of its eighteenth session.

(C) Conclusions

34. Without a detailed legal analysis being undertaken, the following brief observations may be made on the basis of the text of the Charter provisions and of the survey of the past practice of the General Assembly and the Security Council as summarized in this note.

(*i*) A request by the Government of a Member State to have a question of which the Security Council is seized placed on the provisional agenda or the supplementary list of items for a regular session of the General Assembly would have to be complied with by the Secretary-General. The General Assembly itself, acting on the basis of a recommendation by the General Committee, would decide whether it wishes to include the item in the agenda of the session.

(*ii*) In the event the Security Council removes the question from the list of matters of which is seized or in the event the Security Council specifically requests the General Assembly to consider the question, the Assembly could perform in regard to that question its functions under the Charter without any special limitations as to the nature and scope of its recommendations.

(*iii*) Even if the Security Council remains seized of the question, Article 12 of the Charter would not bar the General Assembly from considering and discussing the question as it is only 'recommendations' which are prohibited by the Article.

(*iv*) The above summary of the practice contains instances in which the General Assembly recognized the distinction for purposes of Article 12 between 'recommendations' and resolutions which were not recommendatory. In the latter category, for example, were resolutions welcoming steps taken by the parties to the dispute and commending Member States or United Nations organs for their contributions to the settlement.

(*v*) The most interesting feature of the practice is that the General Assembly, beginning in 1960, adopted several resolutions clearly containing recommendations in cases of which the Security Council was then seized and could reasonably be regarded as exercising its functions in regard to that question. Six such cases have been found in which the General Assembly appears to have departed from the actual text of Article 12. In none of these cases, however, did a Member object to the recommendation on the ground of Article 12.

(*vi*) Although Article 12 has not been invoked in these cases, it would be difficult to maintain that it is legally no longer in effect. A Member may therefore argue in the General Assembly that Article 12 forbids the adoption of a recommendation in the case, and the point, if pressed, may have to be decided by the General Assembly.

(*vii*) Finally, it is to be noted that Governments may argue that the phrase 'recommendation with regard to that dispute or situation', used in Article 12, is not applicable to certain types of resolutions, such as a confirmation by the General Assembly of a Security Council resolution, or a resolution reminding Member States to comply with certain Charter principles. There may, of course, be disagreement as to whether such resolutions contain implied recommendations and, if raised, this issue would have to be determined by the General Assembly, either by explicit decision or implicitly in its action on the proposed resolution.

APPENDIX IV (b)

OPINION OF THE LEGAL COUNSEL ON RELATIONS BETWEEN THE GENERAL ASSEMBLY AND THE SECURITY COUNCIL, 12 DEC. 1968*

The Legal Counsel replied to [a] question put by the representative of Peru who had asked whether the adoption of measures of the kind provided for in operative paragraph 7 of . . . draft resolution [A/C.3/L.1637/Rev. 2] [by which the General Assembly would call upon all States to sever all relations with South Africa, Portugal and the illegal minority regime in Southern Rhodesia and to scrupulously refrain from giving any military or economic assistance to these regimes] was within the competence of the Third Committee. Article 10 of the United Nations Charter stated that the General Assembly might discuss any question or any matter within the scope of the Charter or relating to the powers and functions of any organs provided for in the Charter, and, except as provided in Article 12, might make recommendations to the Members of the United Nations or to the Security Council. Article 12 provided that, while the Security Council was exercising in respect of any dispute or situation the functions assigned to it in the Charter, the General Assembly should not make any recommendation with regard to that dispute or situation unless the Security Council so requested. The matters relating to South Africa, Southern Rhodesia and the Territories under Portuguese rule were on the agenda of the Security Council and, in principle, the General Assembly could not make any recommendations. However, the Assembly had interpreted the words 'is exercising' as meaning 'is exercising at this moment'; consequently, it had made recommendations on other matters which the Security Council was also considering. Thus, in accordance with that practice followed by the General Assembly, there were no obstacles to the recommending of measures of the kind provided for in draft resolution A/C.3/L.1637/Rev. 2.

* *Juridical Yearbook 1968*, p. 185 (footnote omitted).

APPENDIX V

MEMORANDUM BY THE SECRETARY-GENERAL ON THE PROCEDURE TO BE FOLLOWED IN THE ELECTION OF A MEMBER OF THE INTERNATIONAL COURT OF JUSTICE, 24 JANUARY 1996, S/1997/40.

EXTRACT

III. PROCEDURE IN THE GENERAL ASSEMBLY AND IN THE SECURITY COUNCIL

7. The election will take place in accordance with the following provisions:

(a) The Statute of the Court, in particular Articles 2 to 4, 7 to 12 and 14;

(b) Rules 150 and 151 of the rules of procedure of the General Assembly;

(c) Rules 40 and 61 of the provisional rules of procedure of the Security Council.

8. In accordance with General Assembly resolution 264 (III) of 8 October 1948, Nauru and Switzerland, which are parties to the Statute of the Court but not Members of the United Nations, have been invited to participate in the General Assembly in electing members of the Court in the same manner as the States Members of the United Nations.

9. On the date of the election, the General Assembly and the Security Council will proceed, independently of one another, to elect a member of the Court to fill the vacancy (Article 8 of the Statute).

10. According to Article 2 of the Statute, judges are to be elected, regardless of their nationality, from among persons of high moral character, who possess the qualifications required in their respective countries for appointment to the highest judicial offices, or are jurisconsults of recognized competence in international law. Article 9 requires electors to bear in mind not

only that the person to be elected should individually possess the qualifications required, but also that in the body as a whole the representation of the main forms of civilization and of the principal legal systems of the world should be assured.

11. The candidate who obtains an absolute majority of votes both in the General Assembly and in the Security Council will be considered as elected (Article 10, paragraph 1, of the Statute).

12. The consistent practice of the United Nations has been to interpret the words 'absolute majority' as meaning a majority of all electors. The electors in the General Assembly are all 185 Member States, together with the two non-member States mentioned in paragraph 8 above that are parties to the Statute of the Court. Accordingly, as at the date of the present memorandum, 94 votes constitutes an absolute majority in the Assembly for the purpose of the Court election.

13. In the Security Council, eight votes constitutes an absolute majority and no distinction is made between permanent and non-permanent members of the Council (Article 10, paragraph 2, of the Statute).

14. Only those candidates whose names appear on the ballot papers are eligible for election. The electors in the General Assembly and in the Security Council will indicate the candidate for whom they wish to vote by placing a cross against the name on the ballot paper. Each elector may vote for only one candidate.

15. At the 915th plenary meeting of the General Assembly, on 16 November 1960, a procedural discussion took place as to whether rule 94 (then rule 96) of the rules of procedure of the Assembly should be applied in elections to the International Court of Justice. That rule lays down a procedure for restricted ballots in the event that, after the first ballot, the requisite number of candidates have not obtained the required majority. The Assembly decided that the rule did not apply to elections to the Court and it proceeded to elect the requisite number of candidates by a series of unrestricted ballots. That decision has been followed consistently.

16. If in the first ballot in either the General Assembly or the Security Council no candidate receives an absolute majority, a second ballot will be held and balloting will continue in the same meeting until a candidate has obtained the required majority (rule 151 of the rules of procedure of the Assembly and rule 61 of the provisional rules of procedure of the Council).

17. Cases have arisen in the Security Council in which more than the required number of candidates have obtained an absolute majority on the same ballot. The practice followed by the Council has been to hold a new vote on all the candidates, and for the President of the Council to make no notification to the President of the General Assembly until only the required

number of candidates, and no more, have obtained an absolute majority in the Council.

18. When a candidate has obtained the required majority in one of the organs, the President of that organ will notify the President of the other organ of the name of that candidate. Such notification is not communicated by the President of the second organ to the members until that organ has itself given a candidate the required majority of votes.

19. If, upon comparison of the name of the candidate so selected by the General Assembly and by the Security Council, it is found that the result is different, the Assembly and the Council will proceed, again independently of each other, in a second meeting and, if necessary, a third meeting, to elect one candidate by further ballots, the results again being compared after one candidate has obtained an absolute majority in each organ. If necessary, the above procedure will be repeated until the General Assembly and the Security Council have given an absolute majority of votes to the same candidate.

20. If, however, after the third meeting the vacancy still remains unfilled, the special procedure set out in Article 12 of the Statute of the Court may be resorted to at the request of either the General Assembly or the Security Council.

APPENDIX VI

UNITED NATIONS PEACE-KEEPING OPERATIONS 1948–96. DETAILS OF AUTHORIZING RESOLUTIONS, FUNCTION, LOCATION AND DURATION.*

Information valid as of 30 June 1996*.

UNITED NATIONS TRUCE SUPERVISION ORGANIZATION (UNTSO)

Authorization: Security Council resolutions:
50 (1948) of 29 May 1948
54 (1948) of 15 July 1948
73 (1949) of 11 August 1949
101 (1953) of 24 November 1953
114 (1956) of 4 June 1956
236 (1967) of 11 June 1967
Consensus of 9/10 July 1967 (S/8047)
Consensus of 19 April 1972 (S/10611)
339 (1973) of 23 October 1973

Function: Established to assist the Mediator and the Truce Commission in supervising the observance of the truce in Palestine. Since then, UNTSO has performed various tasks entrusted to it by the Security Council, including the supervision of the General Armistice Agreements of 1949 and the observation of the cease-fire in the Suez Canal area and the Golan Heights following the Arab-Israeli war of June 1967. At present, UNTSO assists and cooperates with UNDOF on the Golan Heights in the Israel-Syria sector, and UNIFIL in the Israel-Lebanon sector. UNTSO also has a presence in the Egypt-Israel sector in the Sinai. In addition, UNTSO maintains offices in Beirut and Damascus

* Information for this Appendix is derived from the 3rd edition of the United Nations publication 'Blue Helmets' 1996.

Headquarters: Government House, Jerusalem

Duration: 11 June 1948 to date

First United Nations Emergency Force (UNEF I)

Authorization: General Assembly resolutions:
998 (ES-I) of 4 November 1956
1000 (ES-I) of 5 November 1956
1001 (ES-I) of 7 November 1956
1125 (XI) of 2 February 1957

Function: Established to secure and supervise the cessation of hostilities, including the withdrawal of the armed forces of France, Israel and the United kingdom from Egyptian territory, and, after the withdrawal, to serve as a buffer between the Egyptian and Israeli forces. In May 1967, Egypt compels UNEF I to withdraw

Location: First the Suez Canal sector and the Sinai peninsula. Later along the Armistice Demarcation Line in the Gaza area and the international frontier in the Sinai peninsula (on the Egyptian side)

Headquarters: Gaza

Duration: November 1956–June 1967

Second United Nations Emergency Force (UNEF II)

Authorization: Security Council resolutions:
340 (1973) of 25 October 1973
341 (1973) of 27 October 1973
346 (1974) of 8 April 1974
362 (1974) of 23 October 1974
368 (1975) of 17 April 1975
371 (1975) of 24 July 1975
378 (1975) of 23 October 1975
396 (1976) of 22 October 1976
416 (1977) of 21 October 1977
438 (1978) of 23 October 1978

Function: Established to supervise the cease-fire between Egyptian and Israeli forces and, following the conclusion of the agreements of 18 January 1974 and 4 September 1975, to supervise the redeployment of Egyptian and Israeli forces and to man and control the buffer zones established under those agreements

Location: Suez Canal sector and later the Sinai peninsula

Headquarters: Ismailia

Duration: 25 October 1973–24 July 1979

United Nations Disengagement Observer Force (UNDOF)

Authorization: Security Council resolutions:

350 (1974) of 31 May 1974
363 (1974) of 29 November 1974
369 (1975) of 28 May 1975
381 (1975) of 30 November 1975
390 (1976) of 28 May 1976
398 (1976) of 30 November 1976
408 (1977) of 26 May 1977
420 (1977) of 30 November 1977
429 (1978) of 31 May 1978
441 (1978) of 30 November 1978
449 (1979) of 30 May 1979
456 (1979) of 30 November 1979
470 (1980) of 30 May 1980
481 (1980) of 26 November 1980
485 (1981) of 22 May 1981
493 (1981) of 23 November 1981
506 (1982) of 26 May 1982
524 (1982) of 29 November 1982
531 (1983) of 26 May 1983
543 (1983) of 29 November 1983
551 (1984) of 30 May 1984
557 (1984) of 28 November 1984
563 (1985) of 21 May 1985
576 (1985) of 21 November 1985
584 (1986) of 29 May 1986

590 (1986) of 26 November 1986
596 (1987) of 29 May 1987
603 (1987) of 25 November 1987
613 (1988) of 31 May 1988
624 (1988) of 30 November 1988
633 (1989) of 30 May 1989
645 (1989) of 29 November 1989
655 (1990) of 31 May 1990
679 (1990) of 30 November 1990
695 (1991) of 30 May 1991
722 (1991) of 29 November 1991
756 (1992) of 29 May 1992
790 (1992) of 25 November 1992
830 (1993) of 26 May 1993
887 (1993) of 29 November 1993
921 (1994) of 26 May 1994
962 (1994) of 29 November 1994
996 (1995) of 30 May 1995
1024 (1995) of 28 November 1995
1057 (1996) of 30 May 1996

Function: Established after the 1973 Middle East war to maintain the cease-fire between Israel and Syria, to supervise the disengagement of Israeli and Syrian forces, and to supervise the areas of separation and limitation, as provided in the Agreement on Disengagement of 31 May 1974. Since its establishment, UNDOF has continued to perform its functions effectively with the cooperation of the parties. The situation in the Israeli-Syria sector has remained quiet, and there have been no serious incidents

Location: Syrian Golan Heights

Headquarters: Camp Faouar

Duration: 3 June 1974 to date

United Nations Interim Force in Lebanon (UNIFIL)

Authorization: Security Council resolutions:

425 (1978) of 19 March 1978
426 (1978) of 19 March 1978

427 (1978) of 3 May 1978
434 (1978) of 18 September 1978
444 (1979) of 19 January 1979
450 (1979) of 14 June 1979
459 (1979) of 19 December 1979
474 (1980) of 17 June 1980
483 (1980) of 17 December 1980
488 (1981) of 19 June 1981
498 (1981) of 18 December 1981
501 (1982) of 25 February 1982
511 (1982) of 18 June 1982
519 (1982) of 17 August 1982
523 (1982) of 18 October 1982
529 (1983) of 18 January 1983
536 (1983) of 18 July 1983
538 (1983) of 18 October 1983
549 (1984) of 19 April 1984
555 (1984) of 12 October 1984
561 (1985) of 17 April 1985
575 (1985) of 17 October 1985
583 (1986) of 18 April 1986
586 (1986) of 18 July 1986
594 (1987) of 15 January 1987
599 (1987) of 31 July 1987
609 (1988) of 29 January 1988
617 (1988) of 29 July 1988
630 (1989) of 30 January 1989
639 (1989) of 31 July 1989
648 (1990) of 31 January 1990
659 (1990) of 31 July 1990
684 (1991) of 30 January 1991
701 (1991) of 31 July 1991
734 (1992) of 29 January 1992
768 (1992) of 30 July 1992
803 (1993) of 28 January 1993
852 (1993) of 28 July 1993
895 (1994) of 28 January 1994
938 (1994) of 28 July 1994
974 (1995) of 30 January 1995
1006 (1995) of 28 July 1995
1039 (1996) of 29 January 1996

Function: Established to confirm the withdrawal of Israeli forces from southern Lebanon, to restore international peace and security and to assist the Government of Lebanon in ensuring the return of its effective authority in the area. UNIFIL has, however, been prevented from fully implementing its mandate. Israel has maintained its occupation of parts of south Lebanon, where the Israeli forces and their local auxiliary continue to be targets of attacks by groups that have proclaimed their resistance to the occupation. UNIFIL does its best to limit the conflict and protect the inhabitants from the fighting. In doing so, it contributes to stability in the area

Location: Southern Lebanon

Headquarters: Naqoura

Duration: 19 March 1978 to date

United Nations Observation Group in Lebanon (UNOGIL)

Authorization: Security Council resolution 128 (1958) of 11 June 1958

Function: Established to ensure that there was no illegal infiltration of personnel or supply of arms or other *matériel* across the Lebanese borders. After the conflict had been settled, tensions eased and UNOGIL was withdrawn

Location: Lebanese-Syrian border areas and vicinity of zones held by opposing forces

Headquarters: Beirut

Duration: 12 June–9 December 1958

United Nations Yemen Observation Mission (UNYOM)

Authorization: Security Council resolution 179 (1963) of 11 June 1963

Function: Established to observe and certify the implementation of the disengagement agreement between Saudi Arabia and the United Arab Republic

Location: Yemen

Headquarters: Sana'a

Duration: 4 July 1963–4 September 1964

United Nations Military Observer Group in India and Pakistan (UNMOGIP)

Authorization: Security Council resolutions:
47 (1948) of 21 April 1948
91 (1951) of 30 March 1951
201 (1965) of 6 September 1965

Function: Established to supervise, in the State of Jammu and Kashmir, the cease-fire between India and Pakistan. Following the 1972 India-Pakistan agreement defining a Line of Control in Kashmir, India took the position that the mandate of UNMOGIP had lapsed. Pakistan, however, did not accept this position. Given that disagreement, the Secretary-General's position has been that UNMOGIP can be terminated only by a decision of the Security Council. In the absence of such a decision, UNMOGIP has been maintained with the same mandate and functions

Location: The cease-fire line between India and Pakistan in the State of Jammu and Kashmir

Headquarters: Rawalpindi (November–April)
Srinagar (May–October)

Duration: 24 January 1949 to date

United Nations India-Pakistan Observation Mission (UNIPOM)

Authorization: Security Council resolution 211 (1965) of 20 September 1965

Function: Established to supervise the cease-fire along the India-Pakistan border except in the State of Jammu and Kashmir, where UNMOGIP operated, and the withdrawal of all armed personnel to the positions held by them before 5 August 1965. After the withdrawal of the troops by India and Pakistan had been completed on schedule, UNIPOM was terminated

Location: Along the India-Pakistan border between Kashmir and the Arabian Sea

Headquarters: Lahore (Pakistan)/Amritsar (India)

Duration: 23 September 1965–22 March 1966

United Nations Peace-keeping Force in Cyprus (UNFICYP)

Authorization: Security Council resolutions:
186 (1964) of 4 March 1964
187 (1964) of 13 March 1964
192 (1964) of 20 June 1964
Consensus of 11 August 1964
194 (1964) of 25 September 1964
198 (1964) of 18 December 1964
201 (1965) of 19 March 1965
206 (1965) of 16 June 1965
219 (1965) of 17 December 1965
220 (1966) of 16 March 1966
222 (1966) of 16 June 1966
231 (1966) of 15 December 1966
238 (1967) of 19 June 1967
244 (1967) of 22 December 1967
247 (1968) of 18 March 1968
254 (1968) of 18 June 1968
261 (1968) of 10 December 1968
266 (1969) of 10 June 1969
274 (1969) of 11 December 1969
281 (1970) of 9 June 1970
291 (1970) of 10 December 1970
293 (1971) of 26 May 1971
305 (1971) of 13 December 1971
315 (1972) of 15 June 1972
324 (1972) of 12 December 1972

334 (1973) of 5 June 1973
343 (1973) of 14 December 1973
349 (1974) of 29 May 1974
364 (1974) of 13 December 1974
370 (1975) of 13 June 1975
383 (1975) of 13 December 1975
391 (1976) of 15 June 1976
401 (1976) of 14 December 1976
410 (1977) of 15 June 1977
422 (1977) of 15 December 1977
430 (1978) of 16 June 1978
443 (1978) of 14 December 1978
451 (1979) of 15 June 1979
458 (1979) of 14 December 1979
472 (1980) of 13 June 1980
482 (1980) of 11 December 1980
486 (1981) of 4 June 1981
495 (1981) of 14 December 1981
510 (1982) of 15 June 1982
526 (1982) of 14 December 1982
534 (1983) of 15 June 1983
541 (1983) of 18 November 1983
544 (1983) of 15 December 1983
553 (1984) of 15 June 1984
559 (1984) of 14 December 1984
565 (1985) of 14 June 1985
578 (1985) of 12 December 1985
585 (1986) of 13 June 1986
593 (1986) of 11 December 1986
597 (1987) of 12 June 1987
604 (1987) of 14 December 1987
614 (1988) of 15 June 1988
625 (1988) of 15 December 1988
634 (1989) of 9 June 1989
646 (1989) of 14 December 1989
657 (1990) of 15 June 1990
680 (1990) of 14 December 1990
697 (1991) of 14 June 1991
723 (1991) of 12 December 1991
759 (1992) of 12 June 1992
789 (1992) of 25 November 1992

796 (1992) of 14 December 1992
831 (1993) of 27 May 1993
839 (1993) of 11 June 1993
889 (1993) of 15 December 1993
927 (1994) of 15 June 1994
969 (1994) of 21 December 1994
1000 (1995) of 23 June 1995
1032 (1995) of 19 December 1995
1062 (1996) of 28 June 1996

Function: Established to prevent a recurrence of fighting between the Greek Cypriot and Turkish Cypriot communities and to contribute to the maintenance and restoration of law and order and a return to normal conditions. After the hostilities of 1974, UNFICYP's mandate was expanded. Following a de facto cease-fire, which came into effect on 16 August 1974, UNFICYP has supervised the cease-fire and maintained a buffer zone between the lines of the Cyprus National Guard and of the Turkish and Turkish Cypriot forces. In the absence of a political settlement to the Cyprus problem, UNFICYP continues its presence on the island

Location: Cyprus

Headquarters: Nicosia

Duration: 27 March 1964 to date

United Nations Operation in the Congo (ONUC)

Authorization: Security Council resolutions:

143 (1960) of 14 July 1960
145 (1960) of 22 July 1960
146 (1960) of 9 August 1960
161 (1961) of 21 February 1961
169 (1961) of 24 November 1961

Function: Initially established to ensure the withdrawal of Belgian forces, to assist the Government in maintaining law and order and to provide technical assistance. The function of ONUC was subsequently modified to include maintaining the territorial integrity and political independence of the Congo, preventing the occurrence of civil war and securing the removal from the Congo of all foreign military, para-military and advisory personnel not under the United Nations Command, and all mercenaries

Location: Republic of the Congo (now Zaire)

Headquarters: Leopoldville

Duration: 15 July 1960–30 June 1964

United Nations Transition Assistance Group (UNTAG)

Authorization: Security Council resolutions:
435 (1978) of 29 September 1978
632 (1989) of 16 February 1989

Function: Established to assist the Special Representative of the Secretary-General to ensure the early independence of Namibia through free and fair elections under the supervision and control of the United Nations. UNTAG was also to help the Special Representative to ensure that: all hostile acts were ended; troops were confined to base, and, in the case of the South Africans, ultimately withdrawn from Namibia; all discriminatory laws were repealed, political prisoners were released, Namibian refugees were permitted to return, intimidation of any kind was prevented, law and order were impartially maintained. Independent Namibia joined the United Nations in April 1990

Location: Namibia and Angola

Headquarters: Windhoek

Duration: 1 April 1989–21 March 1990

United Nations Angola Verification Mission I (UNAVEM I)

Authorization: Security Council resolution 626 (1988) of 20 December 1988

Function: Established on 20 December 1988 to verify the redeployment of Cuban troops northwards and their phased and total withdrawal from the territory of Angola in accordance with the timetable agreed between Angola and Cuba. The withdrawal was completed by 25 May 1991—more than one month before the scheduled date. On 6 June, the Secretary-General reported to the Council that UNAVEM I had carried out, fully and effectively, the mandate entrusted to it

Location: Angola

Headquarters: Luanda

Duration: 3 January 1989–30 May 1991

United Nations Angola Verification Mission II (UNAVEM II)

Authorization: Security Council resolutions:
696 (1991) of 30 May 1991
747 (1992) of 24 March 1992
785 (1992) of 30 October 1992
793 (1992) of 30 November 1992
804 (1993) of 29 January 1993
823 (1993) of 30 April 1993
834 (1993) of 1 June 1993
851 (1993) of 15 July 1993
864 (1993) of 15 September 1993
890 (1993) of 15 December 1993
903 (1994) of 16 March 1994
922 (1994) of 31 May 1994
932 (1994) of 30 June 1994
945 (1994) of 29 September 1994
952 (1994) of 27 October 1994
966 (1994) of 8 December 1994

Function: Established on 30 May 1991 to verify the arrangements agreed by the Angolan parties for the monitoring of the cease-fire and for the monitoring of the Angolan police during the cease-fire period and to observe and verify the elections in that country, in accordance with the Peace

Accords for Angola, signed by the Angolan Government and the União Nacional para a Independência Total de Angola (UNITA). Despite the United Nations verification that the elections—held in September 1992—had been generally free and fair, their results were contested by UNITA. After renewed fighting in October 1992 between the Government and UNITA forces, UNAVEM II's mandate was adjusted in order to help the two sides reach agreement on modalities for completing the peace process and, at the same time, to broker and help implement cease-fires at the national or local level. Following the signing on 20 November 1994 by the Government of Angola and UNITA of the Lusaka Protocol, UNAVEM II verified the initial stages of the peace agreement. In February 1995, the Security Council set up a new mission—UNAVEM III—to monitor and verify the implementation of the Protocol

Location: Angola

Headquarters: Luanda

Duration: 30 May 1991–8 February 1995

United Nations Angola Verification Mission III (UNAVEM III)

Authorization: Security Council resolutions:
976 (1995) of 8 February 1995
1008 (1995) of 7 August 1995
1045 (1996) of 8 February 1996

Function: Established to assist the Government of Angola and the União Nacional para a Independência Total de Angola (UNITA) in restoring peace and achieving national reconciliation on the basis of the 'Accordos de Paz' signed on 31 May 1991, the Lusaka Protocol signed on 20 November 1994, and relevant Security Council resolutions. Among the main features of UNAVEM III's mandate are the following: to provide good offices and meditation to the Angolan parties; to monitor and verify the extension of State administration throughout the country and the process of national reconciliation; to supervise, control and verify the disengagement of forces and to monitor the cease-fire; to verify information received from the Government and UNITA regarding their forces, as well as all troop movements; to assist in the establishment of quartering areas; to verify the withdrawal, quartering and demobilization of UNITA forces; to supervise the collection and storage of UNITA armaments; to verify the movement of Government forces (FAA) to barracks and the completion of the formation of FAA; to verify the free circulation of persons and goods; to verify and monitor the neutrality of the Angolan National Police, the disarming of civilians, the quartering of the rapid reaction police, and security arrangements for UNITA leaders; to coordinate, facilitate and support humanitarian activities directly linked to the peace process, as well as participating in mine-clearance activities; to declare formally that all essential requirements for the holding of the second round of presidential elections have been fulfilled, and to support, verify and monitor the electoral process

Location: Angola

Headquarters: Luanda

Duration: 8 February 1995 to date

United Nations Mission for the Referendum in Western Sahara (MINURSO)

Authorization: Security Council resolutions:
690 (1991) of 29 April 1991
907 (1994) of 29 March 1994
973 (1995) of 13 January 1995
995 (1995) of 26 May 1995
1002 (1995) of 30 June 1995
1017 (1995) of 22 September 1995
1042 (1996) of 31 January 1996
1056 (1996) of 29 May 1996

Function: Established in accordance with 'the settlement proposals', as accepted by Morocco and the Frente Popular para la Liberación de Saguia el-Hamra y de Río de Oro (Frente

POLISARIO) on 30 August 1988, to monitor a cease-fire, verify the reduction of Moroccan troops in the Territory, monitor the confinement of Moroccan and Frente POLISARIO troops to designated locations, ensure the release of all Western Saharan political prisoners or detainees, oversee the exchange of prisoners of war, implement the repatriation programme, identify and register qualified voters, organize and ensure a free referendum and proclaim the results. However, due to the parties' divergent views on some of the key elements of the settlement plan, in particular with regard to the criteria for eligibility to vote, it was not possible to implement the plan in conformity with the repeatedly revised timetable. In its limited deployment, the primary function of MINURSO was restricted to complementing the identification process, verifying the cease-fire and cessation of hostilities, and monitoring local police and ensuring security and order at identification and registration sites. In May 1996, the Security Council suspended the identification process, authorized the withdrawal of the civilian police component, except for a small number of officers to maintain contacts with the authorities on both sides, and decided to reduce the strength of the military component of MINURSO by 20 per cent. It also supported the Secretary-General's intention to maintain a political office in Laayoune, with a liaison office in Tindouf, to maintain a dialogue with the parties and the two neighbouring countries

Location: Western Sahara

Headquarters: Laayoune

Duration: 29 April 1991 to date

United Nations Operation in Somalia I (UNOSOM I)

Authorization: Security Council resolutions:
751 (1992) of 24 April 1992
775 (1992) of 28 August 1992
794 (1992) of 3 December 1992

Function: Established to monitor the cease-fire in Mogadishu, the capital of Somalia, and to provide protection and security for United Nations personnel, equipment and supplies at the seaports and airports in Mogadishu and escort deliveries of humanitarian supplies from there to distribution centres in the city and its immediate environs. In August 1992, UNOSOM I's mandate and strength were enlarged to enable it to protect humanitarian convoys and distribution centres throughout Somalia. In December 1992, after the situation in Somalia had further deteriorated, the Security Council authorized Member States to form the Unified Task Force (UNITAF) to establish a safe environment for the delivery of humanitarian assistance. UNITAF worked in coordination with UNOSOM I to secure major population centres and ensure that humanitarian assistance was delivered and distributed

Location: Somalia

Headquarters: Mogadishu

Duration: 24 April 1992–26 March 1993

United Nations Operation in Somalia II (UNOSOM II)

Authorization: Security Council resolutions:
814 (1993) of 26 March 1993
837 (1993) of 6 June 1993
865 (1993) of 22 September 1993
878 (1993) of 28 October 1993
886 (1993) of 18 November 1993
897 (1994) of 4 February 1994
923 (1994) of 31 May 1994
946 (1994) of 30 September 1994
953 (1994) of 31 October 1994
954 (1994) of 4 November 1994

Function: Established to take over from the Unified Task Force (UNITAF). [UNITAF was a multinational force, organized and led by the United States, which, in December 1992, had been authorized by the Security Council to use 'all necessary means' to establish a secure environment for humanitarian relief operations in Somalia.] The mandate of UNOSOM II was to take appropriate action, including enforcement measures, to establish throughout Somalia a secure environment for humanitarian assistance. To that end, UNOSOM II was to complete, through disarmament and reconciliation, the task begun by UNITAF for the restoration of peace, stability, law and order. Its main responsibilities included monitoring the cessation of hostilities, preventing resumption of violence, seizing unauthorized small arms, maintaining security at ports, airports and lines of communication required for delivery of humanitarian assistance, continuing mine-clearing, and assisting in repatriation of refugees in Somalia. UNOSOM II was also entrusted with assisting the Somali people in rebuilding their economy and social and political life, re-establishing the country's institutional structure, achieving national political reconciliation, recreating a Somali State based on democratic governance and rehabilitating the country's economy and infrastructure. In February 1994, after several violent incidents and attacks on United Nations soldiers, the Security Council revised UNOSOM II's mandate to exclude the use of coercive methods. UNOSOM II was withdrawn in early March 1995

Location: Somalia

Headquarters: Mogadishu

Duration: 26 March 1993–2 March 1995

United Nations Operation in Mozambique (ONUMOZ)

Authorization: Security Council resolutions:
797 (1992) of 16 December 1992
850 (1993) of 9 July 1993
879 (1993) of 29 October 1993
882 (1993) of 5 November 1993
898 (1994) of 23 February 1994
916 (1994) of 5 May 1994
957 (1994) of 15 November 1994

Function: Established to help implement the General Peace Agreement, signed on 4 October 1992 in Rome by the President of the Republic of Mozambique and the President of the Resistência Nacional Moçambicana (RENAMO). The mandate of ONUMOZ was: to facilitate impartially the implementation of the Agreement; to monitor and verify the cease-fire, the separation and concentration of forces, their demobilization and the collection, storage and destruction of weapons; to monitor and verify the complete withdrawal of foreign forces and to provide security in the transport corridors; to monitor and verify the disbanding of private and irregular armed groups; to authorize security arrangements for vital infrastructures; and to provide security for United Nations and other international activities in support of the peace process; to provide technical assistance and monitor the entire electoral process; to coordinate and monitor humanitarian assistance operations, in particular those relating to refugees, internally displaced persons, demobilized military personnel and the affected local population. After successful presidential and legislative elections in October 1994, and the installation of Mozambique's new Parliament and the inauguration of the President of Mozambique in early December, ONUMOZ's mandate formally came to an end at midnight on 9 December 1994. The Mission was formally liquidated at the end of January 1995

Location: Mozambique

Headquarters: Maputo

Duration: 16 December 1992–9 December 1994

United Nations Observer Mission Uganda-Rwanda (UNOMUR)

Authorization: Security Council resolutions:

846 (1993) of 22 June 1993
872 (1993) of 5 October 1993
891 (1993) of 20 December 1993
928 (1994) of 20 June 1994

Function: Established to monitor the border between Uganda and Rwanda and verify that no military assistance—lethal weapons, ammunition and other material of possible military use—was being provided across it. While the tragic turn of events in Rwanda in April 1994 prevented UNOMUR from fully implementing its mandate, the Observer Mission played a useful role as a confidence-building mechanism in the months following the conclusion of the Arusha Peace Agreement and during UNAMIR's initial efforts to defuse tensions between the Rwandese parties and to facilitate the implementation of that agreement. UNOMUR was officially closed on 21 September 1994

Location: Ugandan side of the Ugana-Rwanda border

Headquarters: Kabale, Uganda

Duration: 22 June 1993–21 September 1994

United Nations Assistance Mission for Rwanda (UNAMIR)

Authorization: Security Council resolutions:
872 (1993) of 5 October 1993
893 (1994) of 6 January 1994
909 (1994) of 5 April 1994
912 (1994) of 21 April 1994
918 (1994) of 17 May 1994
925 (1994) of 8 June 1994
965 (1994) of 30 November 1994
997 (1995) of 9 June 1995
1029 (1995) of 12 December 1995

Function: Originally established to help implement the Arusha Peace Agreement signed by the Rwandese parties on 4 August 1993. UNAMIR's mandate was: to assist in ensuring the security of the capital city of Kigali; monitor the cease-fire agreement, including establishment of an expanded demilitarized zone and demobilization procedures; monitor the security situation during the final period of the transitional Government's mandate leading up to elections; assist with mine-clearance; and assist in the coordination of humanitarian assistance activities in conjunction with relief operations. After renewed fighting in April 1994, the mandate of UNAMIR was adjusted so that it could act as an intermediary between the warring Rwandese parties in an attempt to secure their agreement to a cease-fire; assist in the resumption of humanitarian relief operations to the extent feasible; and monitor developments in Rwanda, including the safety and security of civilians who sought refuge with UNAMIR. After the situation in Rwanda deteriorated further, UNAMIR's mandate was expanded to enable it to contribute to the security and protection of refugees and civilians at risk, through means including the establishment and maintenance of secure humanitarian areas, and the provision of security for relief operations to the degree possible. Following the cease-fire and the installation of the new Government, the tasks of UNAMIR were further adjusted: to ensure stability and security in the north-western and south-western regions of Rwanda; to stabilize and monitor the situation in all regions of Rwanda to encourage the return of the displaced population; to provide security and support for humanitarian assistance operations inside Rwanda; and to promote, through mediation and good offices, national reconciliation in Rwanda. UNAMIR also contributed to the security in Rwanda of personnel of the International Tribunal for Rwanda and of human rights officers, and assisted in the establishment and training of a new, integrated, national police force. In December 1995, the Security Council further adjusted UNAMIR's mandate to focus primarily on facilitating the safe and voluntary return of refugees. UNAMIR's mandate came to an end on 8 March 1996. The withdrawal of the Mission was completed in April

Location: Rwanda

Headquarters: Kigali

Duration: 5 October 1993–8 March 1996

United Nations Observer Mission in Liberia (UNOMIL)

Authorization: Security Council resolutions:
866 (1993) of 22 September 1993
911 (1994) of 21 April 1994
950 (1994) of 21 October 1994
972 (1995) of 13 January 1995
985 (1995) of 13 April 1995
1001 (1995) of 30 June 1995
1014 (1995) of 15 September 1995
1020 (1995) of 10 November 1995
1041 (1996) of 29 January 1996
1059 (1996) of 31 May 1996

Function: To supervise and monitor, in cooperation with the Monitoring Group (ECOMOG) of the Economic Community of West African States (ECOWAS), the Cotonou Peace Agreement signed by the Liberian parties on 25 July 1993. In accordance with the Agreement, ECOMOG had primary responsibility for ensuring the implementation of the Agreement's provisions; UNOMIL's role was to monitor the implementation procedures in order to verify their impartial application. Delays in the implementation of the Peace Agreement and resumed fighting among Liberian factions made it impossible to hold elections in February–March 1994, as scheduled. In the following months, a number of supplementary peace agreements, amending and clarifying the Cotonou Agreement, were negotiated. In accordance with the peace agreements, ECOWAS is to continue to play the lead role in the peace process in Liberia, while ECOMOG retains the primary responsibility for assisting in the implementation of the military provisions of the agreements. For its part, UNOMIL is to continue to observe and monitor the implementation of the peace agreements. Its main functions are to exercise its good offices to support the efforts of ECOWAS and the Liberian National Transitional Government to implement the peace agreements; investigate allegations of reported cease-fire violations; recommend measures to prevent their recurrence and report to

	the Secretary-General accordingly; monitor compliance with the other military provisions of the agreements and verify their impartial application, especially disarming and demobilization of combatants; and assist in the maintenance of assembly sites and in the implementation of a programme for demobilization of combatants. UNOMIL has also been requested to support humanitarian assistance activities; investigate and report to the Secretary-General on violations of human rights; assist local human rights groups in raising voluntary assistance for training and logistic support; observe and verify the election process, including legislative and presidential elections
Location:	Liberia
Headquarters:	Monrovia
Duration:	22 September 1993 to date

United Nations Aouzou Strip Observer Group (UNASOG)

Authorization:	Security Council resolution 915 (1994) of 4 May 1994
Function:	Established to verify the withdrawal of the Libyan administration and forces from the Aouzou Strip in accordance with the decision of the International Court of Justice. UNASOG accomplished its mandate after both sides—the Republic of Chad and the Libyan Arab Jamahiriya—declared withdrawal to be complete
Location:	Aouzou Strip, Republic of Chad
Headquarters:	Aouzou Base
Duration:	May–June 1994

United Nations Observer Group in Central America (ONUCA)

Authorization:	Security Council resolutions:
	644 (1989) of 7 November 1989

650 (1990) of 27 March 1990
653 (1990) of 20 April 1990
654 (1990) of 4 May 1990
656 (1990) of 8 June 1990
675 (1990) of 5 November 1990
691 (1991) of 6 May 1991
719 (1991) of 6 November 1991
730 (1992) of 16 January 1992

Function: Established to verify compliance by the Governments of Costa Rica, El Salvador, Guatemala, Honduras and Nicaragua with their undertakings to cease aid to irregular forces and insurrectionist movements in the region and not to allow their territory to be used for attacks on other States. In addition, ONUCA played a part in the voluntary demobilization of the Nicaraguan Resistance and monitored a cease-fire and the separation of forces agreed by the Nicaraguan parties as part of the demobilization process

Location: Costa Rica, El Salvador, Guatemala, Honduras and Nicaragua

Headquarters: Tegucigalpa, Honduras

Duration: 7 November 1989 to 17 January 1992

United Nations Observer Mission in El Salvador (ONUSAL)

Authorization: Security Council resolutions:
693 (1991) of 20 May 1991
729 (1992) of 14 January 1992
784 (1992) of 30 October 1992
791 (1992) of 30 November 1992
832 (1993) of 27 May 1993
888 (1993) of 30 November 1993
920 (1994) of 26 May 1994
961 (1994) of 23 November 1994
991 (1995) of 28 April 1995

Function: Established to verify the implementation of all agreements between the Government of El Salvador and Frente

Farabundo Martí para la Liberación Nacional aimed at ending a decade-long civil war. The agreements involved a cease-fire and related measures, reform and reduction of the armed forces, creation of a new police force, reform of the judicial and electoral systems, human rights, land tenure and other economic and social issues. After the armed conflict had been formally brought to an end in December 1992, ONUSAL verified elections which were carried out successfully in March and April 1994. After ONUSAL completed its mandate on 30 April 1995, a small group of United Nations civilian personnel—known as the United Nations Mission in El Salvador (MINUSAL)—remained in El Salvador to provide good offices to the parties, to verify implementation of the outstanding points of the agreements and to provide a continuing flow of accurate and reliable information

Location: El Salvador

Headquarters: San Salvador

Duration: 26 July 1991 to 30 April 1995

United Nations Advance Mission in Cambodia (UNAMIC)

Authorization: Security Council resolutions:
717 (1991) of 16 October 1991
728 (1992) of 8 January 1992

Function: Established to assist the four Cambodian parties to maintain their cease-fire during the period prior to the establishment and deployment of the United Nations Transitional Authority in Cambodia, and to initiate mine-awareness training of civilian populations. Later, the mandate was enlarged to include a major training programme for Cambodians in mine-detection and mine-clearance and the mine-clearing of repatriation routes, reception centres and resettlement areas. UNAMIC was absorbed by UNTAC in March 1992

Location: Cambodia

Headquarters: Phnom Penh

Duration: 16 October 1991–15 March 1992

United Nations Transitional Authority in Cambodia (UNTAC)

Authorization: Security Council resolutions:

745 (1992) of 28 February 1992
860 (1993) of 27 August 1993
880 (1993) of 4 November 1993

Function: Established to ensure the implementation of the Agreements on a Comprehensive Political Settlement of the Cambodia Conflict, signed in Paris on 23 October 1991. Under the Agreements, the Supreme National Council of Cambodia (SNC) was 'the unique legitimate body and source of authority in which, throughout the transitional period, the sovereignty, independence and unity of Cambodia are enshrined'. SNC, which was made up of the four Cambodian factors, delegated to the United Nations 'all powers necessary' to ensure the implementation of the Agreements. The mandate given to UNTAC included aspects relating to human rights, the organization and conduct of free and fair general elections, military arrangements, civil administration, the maintenance of law and order, the repatriation and resettlement of the Cambodian refugees and displaced persons and the rehabilitation of essential Cambodian infrastructure during the transitional period. Upon becoming operational on 15 March 1992, UNTAC absorbed UNAMIC, which had been established immediately after the signing of the Agreements in October 1991. UNTAC's mandate ended in September 1993 with the promulgation of the Constitution for the Kingdom of Cambodia and the formation of the new Government

Location: Cambodia

Headquarters: Phnom Penh

Duration: 28 February 1992–24 September 1993

Appendix VI

UNITED NATIONS PROTECTION FORCE (UNPROFOR) (21 FEBRUARY 1992–31 MARCH 1995)

Authorization: Security Council resolutions:
743 (1992) of 21 February 1992
749 (1992) of 7 April 1992
758 (1992) of 8 June 1992
761 (1992) of 29 June 1992
762 (1992) of 30 June 1992
764 (1992) of 13 July 1992
769 (1992) of 7 August 1992
776 (1992) of 14 September 1992
779 (1992) of 6 October 1992
781 (1992) of 9 October 1992
786 (1992) of 10 November 1992
795 (1992) of 11 December 1992
807 (1993) of 19 February 1993
815 (1993) of 30 March 1993
819 (1993) of 16 April 1993
824 (1993) of 6 May 1993
836 (1993) of 4 June 1993
838 (1993) of 10 June 1993
842 (1993) of 18 June 1993
844 (1993) of 18 June 1993
847 (1993) of 30 June 1993
869 (1993) of 30 September 1993
870 (1993) of 1 October 1993
871 (1993) of 4 October 1993
900 (1994) of 4 March 1994
908 (1994) of 31 March 1994
914 (1994) of 27 April 1994
947 (1994) of 30 September 1994
982 (1995) of 31 March 1995

Function: Initially, established in Croatia as an interim arrangement to create the conditions of peace and security required for the negotiation of an overall settlement of the Yugoslav crisis. UNPROFOR's mandate was to ensure that the three 'United Nations Protected Areas' (UNPAs) in Croatia were demilitarized and that all persons residing in them were protected from fear of armed attack. In the course of

1992, UNPROFOR's mandate was enlarged to include monitoring functions in certain other areas of Croatia ('pink zones'); to enable the Force to control the entry of civilians into the UNPAs and to perform immigration and customs functions at the UNPA borders at international frontiers; and to include monitoring of the demilitarization of the Prevlaka Peninsula and to ensure control of the Peruca dam, situated in one of the 'pink zones'. In addition, UNPROFOR monitored implementation of a cease-fire agreement signed by the Croatian Government and local Serb authorities in March 1994 following a flare-up of fighting in January and September 1993. In June 1992, as the conflict intensified and extended to Bosnia and Herzegovina, UNPROFOR's mandate and strength were enlarged in order to ensure the security and functioning of the airport at Sarajevo, and the delivery of humanitarian assistance to that city and its environs. In September 1992, UNPROFOR's mandate was further enlarged to enable it to support efforts by the United Nations High Commissioner for Refugees to deliver humanitarian relief throughout Bosnia and Herzegovina, and to protect convoys of released civilian detainees if the International Committee of the Red Cross so requested. In addition, the Force monitored the 'no-fly' zone, banning all military flights in Bosnia and Herzegovina, and the United Nations 'safe areas' established by the Security Council around five Bosnian towns and the city of Sarajevo. UNPROFOR was authorized to use force in self-defence in reply to attacks against these areas, and to coordinate with the North Atlantic Treaty Organization (NATO) the use of air power in support of its activities. Similar arrangements were subsequently extended to the territory of Croatia. UNPROFOR also monitored the implementation of a cease-fire agreement signed by the Bosnian Government and Bosnian Croat forces in February 1994. In addition, UNPROFOR monitored cease-fire arrangements negotiated between Bosnian Government and Bosnian Serbs forces, which entered into force on 1 January 1995. In December 1992, UNPROFOR was also deployed in the former Yugoslav Republic of Macedonia, to monitor and report any developments in its border areas which could undermine confidence and stability in that Republic and threaten its territory. On 31 March 1995, the Security Council decided to restructure UNPROFOR, replacing it with three separate but interlinked peace-keeping operations [see UNPF below]

Location: Bosnia and Herzegovina, Croatia, the Federal Republic of Yugoslavia (Serbia and Montenegro) and the former Yugoslav Republic of Macedonia

Headquarters: Initially Sarajevo; later Zagreb

United Nations Peace Forces (UNPF)

Authorization: Security Council resolutions:
982 (1995) of 31 March 1995
1031 (1995) of 15 December 1995

Function: On 31 March 1995, the Security Council decided to restructure UNPROFOR, replacing it with three separate but interlinked peace-keeping operations. The Council extended the mandate of UNPROFOR in Bosnia and Herzegovina, established the United Nations Confidence Restoration Operation in Croatia (UNCRO), and decided that UNPROFOR within the former Yugoslav Republic of Macedonia should be known as the United Nations Preventive Deployment Force (UNPREDEP). Their joint theatre headquarters, known as United Nations Peace Forces headquarters (UNPF-HQ), was established in Zagreb, the capital of Croatia. UNPF-HQ was also responsible for liaison with the Government of the Federal Republic of Yugoslavia (Serbia and Montenegro), other concerned Governments and NATO. Each of the three operations was headed by a civilian Chief of Mission and had its own military commander. Overall command and control of the three operations was exercised by the Special Representative of the Secretary-General and the Theatre Force Commander. Eventually, following positive developments in the former Yugoslavia, the termination of the mandates of UNCRO and UNPROFOR and the establishment of two new United Nations missions in Bosnia and Herzegovina and Croatia, this arrangement came to an end on 31 January 1996 and UNPF-HQ was phased out.

Location: Bosnia and Herzegovina, Croatia, the Federal Republic of Yugoslavia (Serbia and Montenegro) and the former Yugoslav Republic of Macedonia

Headquarters: Zagreb

Duration: 31 March 1995–31 January 1996

United Nations Protection Force (UNPROFOR) (31 March–20 December 1995)

Authorization: Security Council resolutions:
982 (1995) of 31 March 1995
998 (1995) of 16 June 1995
1026 (1995) of 30 November 1995

Function: After the restructuring of UNPROFOR on 31 March 1995, the Force continued to perform the functions envisaged in Security Council resolutions relevant to the situation in Bosnia and Herzegovina. In November 1995, a United States initiative led to the Peace Agreement initialled and subsequently signed, in December 1995, by the leaders of Bosnia and Herzegovina, Croatia and the Federal Republic of Yugoslavia (Serbia and Montenegro). As requested by the Agreement, the Security Council authorized Member States to establish a NATO-led multinational Implementation Force (IFOR) to help ensure compliance with the provisions of the Agreement. After IFOR took over from UNPROFOR on 20 December 1995, the latter's mandate was terminated

Location: Bosnia and Herzegovina

Headquarters: Zagreb

Appendix VI

UNITED NATIONS CONFIDENCE RESTORATION OPERATION IN CROATIA (UNCRO)

Authorization: Security Council resolutions:
981 (1995) of 31 March 1995
990 (1995) of 28 April 1995
994 (1995) of 17 May 1995
1025 (1995) of 30 November 1995

Function: To perform the functions envisaged in the cease-fire agreement of 29 March 1994; facilitate implementation of the economic agreement of 2 December 1994; facilitate implementation of all relevant Security Council resolutions; assist in controlling, by monitoring and reporting, the crossing of military personnel, equipment, supplies and weapons, over the international borders between Croatia and Bosnia and Herzegovina, and Croatia and the Federal Republic of Yugoslavia (Serbia and Montenegro) at the border crossings; facilitate the delivery of international humanitarian assistance to Bosnia and Herzegovina through the territory of Croatia; and monitor the demilitarization of the Prevlaka peninsula. After Croatia's reintegration by force of Western Slavonia and the Krajina region in May and August 1995, the need for United Nations troops in those areas was effectively eliminated. However, in Eastern Slavonia—the last Serb-controlled territory in Croatia—the mandate of UNCRO remained essentially unchanged. The Government of Croatia and the Croatian Serb leadership agreed to resolve the issue of Eastern Slavonia through negotiation. United Nations-sponsored talks concluded with the signing of the Basic Agreement on the Region of Eastern Slavonia, Baranja and Western Sirmium on 12 November. The Agreement provided for the peaceful integration into Croatia of that region and requested the Security Council to establish a transitional administration to govern the region during the transitional period. Following the establishment of the United Nations administration, the mandate of UNCRO was terminated

Location: Croatia

Headquarters: Zagreb

Duration: 31 March 1995–15 January 1996

United Nations Preventive Deployment Force (UNPREDEP)

Authorization: Security Council resolutions:

983 (1995) of 31 March 1995
1027 (1995) of 30 November 1995
1046 (1996) of 13 February 1996

Function: To monitor and report any developments in the border areas (with Albania and the Federal Republic of Yugoslavia (Serbia and Montenegro)) which could undermine confidence and stability in the former Yugoslav Republic of Macedonia and threaten its territory

Location: The former Yugoslav Republic of Macedonia

Headquarters: Skopje

Duration: 31 March 1995 to date

United Nations Mission in Bosnia and Herzegovina (UNMIBH)

Authorization: Security Council resolution 1035 (1995) of 21 December 1995

Function: On 21 December 1995, the Security Council established, for a period of one year, the United Nations International Police Task Force (IPTF) and a United Nations civilian office. This was done in accordance with the Peace Agreement signed by the leaders of Bosnia and Herzegovina, Croatia and the Federal Republic of Yugoslavia (Serbia and Montenegro) on 14 December 1995. The operation has come to be known as the United Nations Mission in Bosnia and Herzegovina (UNMIBH). IPTF tasks include: (a) monitoring, observing and inspecting law enforcement activities and facilities, including associated judicial organizations, structures and proceedings; (b) advising law enforcement personnel and forces; (c) training law enforcement personnel; (d) facilitating, within the IPTF mission of assistance, the parties' law enforcement activities; (e) assessing threats to public order and advising on the capability of law enforcement agencies to deal with such threats; (f) advising government authorities in Bosnia and Herzegovina on the organization of effective civilian law enforcement agencies; and (g) assisting by accompanying the parties' law enforcement personnel as they carry out their responsibilities, as the Task Force deems appropriate. In addition, the Task Force is to consider requests from the parties or law enforcement agencies in Bosnia and Herzegovina for assistance, with priority being given to ensuring the existence of conditions for free and fair elections. The United Nations Coordinator, acting under the Secretary-General's authority, exercises authority over the IPTF Commissioner and coordinates other United Nations activities in Bosnia and Herzegovina relating to humanitarian relief and refugees; de-mining, human rights, elections, and rehabilitation of infrastructure and economic reconstruction. UNMIBH closely cooperates with a NATO-led multinational Implementation Force (IFOR), authorized by the Security Council to help ensure compliance with the provisions of the Peace Agreement, and with the High Representative, appointed by the Peace Implementation Conference and approved by the Security Council, and whose task is to mobilize and coordinate the activities of organizations and agencies involved in civilian aspects of the peace settlement in Bosnia and Herzegovina, and monitor the implementation of that settlement.

Location: Bosnia and Herzegovina

Headquarters: Sarajevo

Duration: December 1995 to date

United Nations Transitional Administration for Eastern Slavonia, Baranja and Western Sirmium (UNTAES)

Authorization: Security Council resolutions:
1037 (1996) of 15 January 1996
1043 (1996) of 31 January 1996

Function: The 12 November 1995 Basic Agreement on the Region of Eastern Slavonia, Baranja and Western Sirmium provides for the peaceful integration of that region into Croatia. The Agreement requested the Security Council to establish a transitional administration to govern the region during the transitional period of 12 months, which might be extended by up to a further 12 months and to authorize an international force to maintain peace and security during that period and to otherwise assist in the implementation of the Agreement. UNTAES was set up on 15 January 1996 for an initial period of 12 months, with both military and civilian components. The military component is to supervise and facilitate the demilitarization of the Region; monitor the voluntary and safe return of refugees and displaced persons to their home of origin in cooperation with UNHCR; contribute, by its presence, to the maintenance of peace and security in the region; and otherwise assist in implementation of the Basic Agreement. The civilian component is to establish a temporary police force, define its structure and size, develop a training programme and oversee its implementation, and monitor treatment of offenders and the prison system; undertake tasks relating to civil administration and to the functioning of public services; facilitate the return of refugees; organize elections, assist in their conduct, and certify the results. The component has also been requested to undertake other activities relevant to the Basic Agreement, including assistance in the coordination of plans for the development and economic reconstruction of the Region; and monitoring of the parties' compliance with their commitments to respect the highest standards of human rights and fundamental freedoms, promote an atmosphere of confidence among all local residents irrespective of their ethnic origin, monitor and facilitate the de-mining of territory within the Region, and maintain an active public affairs element. UNTAES is also to cooperate with the International Criminal Tribunal for the Former Yugoslavia in performing its mandate. Member States are authorized, acting nationally or through regional organizations, to take all necessary measures, including close air support to defend or help withdraw UNTAES, and that such actions would be based on UNTAES's request and procedures communicated to the United Nations.

Location: Eastern Slavonia, Baranja and Western Sirmium (Croatia)

Headquarters: Vukovar

Duration: January 1996 to date

United Nations Mission of Observers in Prevlaka (UNMOP)

Authorization: Security Council resolution 1038 (1996) of 15 January 1996

Function: United Nations military observers have been deployed in the strategically-important Prevlaka peninsula since October 1992, when the Security Council authorized UNPROFOR to assume responsibility for monitoring the demilitarization of that area. Following the restructuring of UNPROFOR in March 1995, those functions were carried out by UNCRO. With the termination of UNCRO's mandate in January 1996, the Council authorized United Nations military observers to continue monitoring the demilitarization of the peninsula for a period of three months, to be extended for an additional three months upon a report by the Secretary-General that an extension would continue to help decrease tension there. United Nations military observers are under the command and direction of a Chief Military Observer, who reports directly to United Nations Headquarters in New York.

Location: Prevlaka peninsula, Croatia

Duration: January 1996 to date

United Nations Observer Mission in Georgia (UNOMIG)

Authorization: Security Council resolutions:
849 (1993) of 9 July 1993
854 (1993) of 6 August 1993
858 (1993) of 24 August 1993
881 (1993) of 4 November 1993
892 (1993) of 22 December 1993
896 (1994) of 31 January 1994
901 (1994) of 4 March 1994
906 (1994) of 25 March 1994
934 (1994) of 30 June 1994
937 (1994) of 21 July 1994
971 (1995) of 12 January 1995
993 (1995) of 12 May 1995
1036 (1996) of 12 January 1996

Function: Originally established to verify compliance with the 27 July 1993 cease-fire agreement between the Government of Georgia and the Abkhaz authorities in Georgia with special attention to the situation in the city of Sukhumi; to investigate reports of cease-fire violations and to attempt to resolve such incidents with the parties involved; and to report to the Secretary-General on the implementation of its mandate, including, in particular, violations of the cease-fire agreement. After UNOMIG's original mandate had been invalidated by the resumed fighting in Abkhazia in September 1993, the Mission had an interim mandate to maintain contacts with both sides to the conflict and with Russian military contingents, and to monitor and report on the situation, with particular reference to developments relevant to United Nations efforts to promote a comprehensive political settlement. Following the signing, in May 1994, by the Georgian and Abkhaz sides of the Agreement on a Cease-fire and Separation of Forces, UNOMIG's tasks are: to monitor and verify the implementation of the Agreement; to observe the operation of the peace-keeping force of the Commonwealth of Independent States; to verify that troops do not remain in or re-enter the security zone and that heavy military equipment does not remain or is not reintroduced in the security zone or the restricted weapons zone; to monitor the storage areas for heavy military equipment withdrawn from the security zone and restricted weapons zone; to monitor the withdrawal of Georgian troops from the Kodori valley to places beyond the frontiers of Abkhazia; to patrol regularly the Kodori valley; and to investigate reported or alleged violations of the Agreement and attempt to resolve such incidents.

Location: Abkhazia, Georgia

Headquarters: Sukhumi

Duration: 24 August 1993 to date

United Nations Mission of Observers in Tajikistan (UNMOT)

Authorization: Security Council resolutions:
968 (1994) of 16 December 1994
999 (1995) of 16 June 1995
1030 (1995) of 14 December 1995
1061 (1996) of 14 June 1996

Function: Established with a mandate to assist the Joint Commission, composed of representatives of the Tajik Government and of the Tajik opposition, to monitor the implementation of the Agreement on a Temporary Cease-fire and the Cessation of Other Hostile Acts on the Tajik-Afghan Border and within the Country for the Duration of the Talks; to investigate reports of cease-fire violations and to report on them to the United Nations and to the Joint Commission; to provide its good offices as stipulated in the Agreement; to maintain close contact with the parties to the conflict, as well as close liaison with the Mission of the Conference on Security and Cooperation in Europe and with the Collective Peacekeeping Forces of the Commonwealth of Independent States in Tajikistan and with the border forces; to provide support for the efforts of the Secretary-General's Special Envoy; and to provide political liaison and coordination services, which could facilitate expeditious humanitarian assistance by the international community

Location: Tajikistan

Headquarters: Dushanbe

Duration: 16 December 1994 to date

United Nations Mission in Haiti (UNMIH)

Authorization: Security Council resolutions:
867 (1993) of 23 September 1993
905 (1994) of 23 March 1994
933 (1994) of 30 June 1994
940 (1994) of 31 July 1994
964 (1994) of 29 November 1994
975 (1995) of 30 January 1995
1007 (1995) of 31 July 1995
1048 (1996) of 19 February 1996

Function: Originally established to help implement certain provisions of the Governors Island Agreement signed by the Haitian parties on 3 July 1993. In 1993, UNMIH's mandate was to assist in modernizing the armed forces of Haiti and establishing a new police force. However, due to non-cooperation of the Haitian military authorities, UNMIH could not be fully deployed at that time and carry out that mandate. After the restoration, in October 1994, of the Haitian Constitutional Government with the help of a multinational force led by the United States and authorized by the Security Council, UNMIH's mandate was revised to enable the Mission to assist the democratic Government of Haiti in fulfilling its responsibilities in connection with: sustaining a secure and stable environment established during the multinational phase and protecting international personnel and key installations; and the professionalization of the Haitian armed forces and the creation of a separate police force. UNMIH was also to assist the legitimate constitutional authorities of Haiti in establishing an environment conductive to the organization of free and fair legislative elections to be called by those authorities. UNMIH assumed its functions in full on 31 March 1995. Democratic legislative elections were held in summer 1995, despite some logistical difficulties. The Presidential elections were held successfully on 17 December 1995 and the transfer of power to the new President took place on 7 February 1996. Upon receipt of a request by the President of Haiti, UNMIH's mandate was extended until the end of June 1996

Location: Haiti

Headquarters: Port-au-Prince

Duration: 23 September 1993–30 June 1996

United Nations Security Force in West New Guinea (West Irian) (UNSF)

Authorization: General Assembly resolution 1752 (XVII) of 21 September 1962

Function: Established to maintain peace and security in the territory under the United Nations Temporary Executive Authority (UNTEA), established by agreement between Indonesia and the Netherlands. UNSF monitored the cease-fire and helped ensure law and order during the transition period, pending transfer to Indonesia

Location: West New Guinea (West Irian)

Headquarters: Hollandia (now Jayaphra)

Duration: 3 October 1962–30 April 1963

Mission of the Representative of the Secretary-General in the Dominican Republic (DOMREP)

Authorization: Security Council resolution 203 (1965) of 14 May 1965

Function: Established to observe the situation and to report on breaches of the cease-fire between the two de facto authorities in the Dominican Republic. Following the agreement on a new Government, DOMREP was withdrawn

Location: Dominican Republic

Headquarters: Santo Domingo

Duration: 15 May 1965–22 October 1966

United Nations Good Offices Mission in Afghanistan and Pakistan (UNGOMAP)

Authorization: Letter of 25 April 1988 from the President of the Security Council addressed to the Secretary-General (S/19836)

Security Council resolutions:

622 (1988) of 31 October 1988
647 (1990) of 11 January 1990

Function: Established to assist the Personal Representative of the Secretary-General to lend his good offices to the parties in ensuring the implementation of the Agreements on the Settlement of the Situation Relating to Afghanistan and in this context to investigate and report possible violations of any of the provisions of the Agreements. When UNGOMAP's mandate ended, the Personal Representative remained in the country and served as Coordinator of the United Nations Office for the Coordination of Humanitarian Assistance to Afghanistan. In December 1994, the Secretary-General discontinued the function of the Personal Representative, creating in its place the Office of the Secretary-General in Afghanistan

Location: Afghanistan and Pakistan

Headquarters: Kabul and Islamabad

Duration: 15 May 1988–15 March 1990

United Nations Iran–Iraq Observer Group (UNIIMOG)

Authorization: Security Council resolutions:

598 (1987) of 20 July 1987
619 (1988) of 9 August 1988
631 (1989) of 8 February 1989
642 (1989) of 29 September 1989

	651 (1990) of 29 March 1990 671 (1990) of 27 September 1990 676 (1990) of 28 November 1990 685 (1991) of 31 January 1991
Function:	Established to verify, confirm and supervise the cease-fire and the withdrawal of all forces to the internationally recognized boundaries, pending a comprehensive settlement. UNIIMOG was terminated after Iran and Iraq had withdrawn fully their forces to the internationally recognized boundaries. Small civilian offices were established in Tehran and Baghdad to implement the remaining tasks which were essentially political. By the end of 1992, those offices were phased out
Location:	Iran and Iraq
Headquarters:	Tehran and Baghdad
Duration:	20 August 1988–28 February 1991

United Nations Iraq–Kuwait Observation Mission (UNIKOM)

Authorization:	Security Council resolutions: 687 (1991) of 3 April 1991 689 (1991) of 9 April 1991 806 (1993) of 5 February 1993
Function:	Established following the withdrawal of Iraq's forces from the territory of Kuwait. UNIKOM, set up initially as an unarmed observation mission, was to monitor a demilitarized zone (DMZ) along the boundary between Iraq and Kuwait and the Khawr 'Abd Allah waterway, to deter violations of the boundary, and to observe any hostile action mounted from the territory of one State against the other. In February 1993, following a series of incidents on the border, the Security Council decided to increase UNIKOM's strength and to extend its terms of reference to include the capacity to take physical action to prevent violations of the DMZ and of the newly demarcated boundary between Iraq and Kuwait

Location: Iraq/Kuwait

Headquarters: Umm Qasr, Iraq

Duration: 9 April 1991 to date

APPENDIX VII

MATTERS OF WHICH THE SECURITY COUNCIL IS SEIZED, 10 JANUARY 1997. S/1997/40.

As at 4 January 1997, the list of matters of which the Security Council is seized is as follows:

1. The Palestine question
2. The India–Pakistan question
3. The Hyderabad question
4. Letter dated 20 February 1958 from the representative of the Sudan addressed to the Secretary-General
5. Letter dated 11 July 1960 from the Minister for Foreign Affairs of Cuba addressed to the President of the Security Council
6. Letter dated 31 December 1960 from the Minister for External Affairs of Cuba addressed to the President of the Security Council
7. Letters dated 5 and 8 September 1964 from the Permanent Representative of Greece addressed to the President of the Security Council
8. The situation in the Middle East
9. The situation in the India/Pakistan subcontinent
10. Letter dated 3 December 1971 from the Permanent Representatives of Algeria, Iraq, the Libyan Arab Republic and the People's Democratic Republic of Yemen to the United Nations addressed to the President of the Security Council
11. Complaint by Cuba
12. Arrangements for the proposed Peace Conference on the Middle East
13. Complaint by Iraq concerning incidents on its frontier with Iran
14. The situation in Cyprus
15. The situation concerning Western Sahara
16. The situation in Timor
17. The Middle East problem including the Palestinian question
18. Request by the Libyan Arab Republic and Pakistan for consideration of the serious situation arising from recent developments in the occupied Arab territories
19. The situation in the occupied Arab territories
20. The question of the exercise by the Palestinian people of its inalienable rights

21. Complaint by Greece against Turkey

22. The situation between Iran and Iraq

23. Complaint by Iraq

24. Letter dated 19 February 1983 from the Permanent Representative of the Libyan Arab Jamahiriya to the United Nations addressed to the President of the Security Council

25. Letter dated 8 August 1983 from the Chargé d'affaires a.i. of the Permanent Mission of the Libyan Arab Jamahiriya to the United Nations addressed to the President of the Security Council

26. Letter dated 1 September 1983 from the Acting Permanent Representative of the United States of America to the United Nations addressed to the President of the Security Council

Letter dated 1 September 1983 from the Permanent Observer for the Republic of Korea to the United Nations addressed to the President of the Security Council

Letter dated 1 September 1983 from the Chargé d'affaires a.i. of the Permanent Mission of Canada to the United Nations addressed to the President of the Security Council

Letter dated 1 September 1983 from the Permanent Representative of Japan to the United Nations addressed to the President of the Security Council

Letter dated 2 September 1983 from the Acting Permanent Representative of Australia to the United Nations addressed to the President of the Security Council

27. Letter dated 22 March 1984 from the Chargé d'affaires a.i. of the Permanent Mission of the Libyan Arab Jamahiriya to the United Nations addressed to the President of the Security Council

28. Letter dated 1 October 1985 from the Permanent Representative of Tunisia to the United Nations addressed to the President of the Security Council

29. Letter dated 4 February 1986 from the Permanent Representative of the Syrian Arab Republic to the United Nations addressed to the President of the Security Council

30. Letter dated 15 April 1986 from the Chargé d'affaires a.i. of the Permanent Mission of the Libyan Arab Jamahiriya to the United Nations addressed to the President of the Security Council

Letter dated 15 April 1986 from the Chargé d'affaires a.i. of the Permanent Mission of Burkina Faso to the United Nations addressed to the President of the Security Council

Letter dated 15 April 1986 from the Chargé d'affaires a.i. of the Permanent Mission of the Syrian Arab Republic to the United Nations addressed to the President of the Security Council

Letter dated 15 April 1986 from the Permanent Representative of Oman to the United Nations addressed to the President of the Security Council

31. Letter dated 10 February 1988 from the Permanent Observer of the Republic of Korea to the United Nations addressed to the President of the Security Council

Letter dated 10 February 1988 from the Permanent Representative of Japan to the United Nations addressed to the President of the Security Council

32. Letter dated 19 April 1988 from the Permanent Representative of Tunisia to the United Nations addressed to the President of the Security Council

33. Letter dated 4 January 1989 from the Chargé d'affaires a.i. of the Permanent Mission of the Libyan Arab Jamahiriya to the United Nations addressed to the President of the Security Council

Letter dated 4 January 1989 from the Chargé d'affaires a.i. of the Permanent Mission of Bahrain to the United Nations addressed to the President of the Security Council

34. Central America: efforts towards peace

35. Letter dated 2 February 1990 from the Permanent Representative of Cuba to the United Nations addressed to the President of the Security Council

36. The situation between Iraq and Kuwait

37. The situation in Cambodia

38. The situation in Liberia

39. Letter dated 2 April 1991 from the Permanent Representative of Turkey to the United Nations addressed to the President of the Security Council

Letter dated 4 April 1991 from the Chargé d'affaires a.i. of the Permanent Mission of France to the United Nations addressed to the President of the Security Council

40. Letter dated 17 May 1991 from the Chargé d'affaires a.i. of the Permanent Mission of Angola to the United Nations addressed to the Secretary-General

Report of the Secretary-General on the United Nations Angola Verification Mission

41. Letter dated 19 September 1991 from the Permanent Representative of Austria to the United Nations addressed to the President of the Security Council

Letter dated 19 September 1991 from the Permanent Representative of Canada to the United Nations addressed to the President of the Security Council

Letter dated 20 September 1991 from the Permanent Representative of Hungary to the United Nations addressed to the President of the Security Council

Letter dated 24 September 1991 from the Permanent Representative of Yugoslavia to the United Nations addressed to the President of the Security Council

42. Letter dated 24 November 1991 from the Secretary-General addressed to the President of the Security Council

Letter dated 21 November 1991 from the Permanent Representative of Germany to the United Nations addressed to the President of the Security Council

Letter dated 26 November 1991 from the Permanent Representative of France to the United Nations addressed to the President of the Security Council

43. Report of the Secretary-General pursuant to Security Council resolution 721 (1991)

44. Oral report of the Secretary General pursuant to his report of 5 January 1992

45. Further reports of the Secretary-General pursuant to Security Council resolution 721 (1991)

46. Letter dated 20 January 1992 from the Chargé d'affaires a.i. of the Permanent Mission of Somalia to the United Nations addressed to the President of the Security Council

47. (a) The situation between Iraq and Kuwait

(b) Letter dated 2 April 1991 from the Permanent Representative of Turkey to the United Nations addressed to the President of the Security Council

Letter dated 4 April 1991 from the Chargé d'affaires a.i. of the Permanent Mission of France to the United Nations addressed to the President of the Security Council

Letter dated 5 March 1992 from the Chargé d'affaires a.i. of the Permanent Mission of Belgium to the United Nations addressed to the President of the Security Council

48. The situation in Somalia

49. Further report of the Secretary-General on the United Nations Angola Verification Mission (UNAVEM II)

50. Report of the Secretary-General pursuant to Security Council resolution 743 (1992)

51. Letter dated 23 April 1992 from the Chargé d'affaires a.i. of the Permanent Mission of Austria to the United Nations addressed to the President of the Security Council

Letter dated 24 April 1992 from the Permanent Representative of France to the United Nations addressed to the President of the Security Council

52. The situation relating to Nagorny Karabakh

53. Further report of the Secretary-General pursuant to Security Council resolution 749 (1992)

54. Report of the Secretary-General pursuant to Security Council resolution 752 (1992)

Letter dated 26 May 1992 from the Permanent Representative of Canada to the United Nations addressed to the President of the Security Council

Letter dated 27 May 1992 from the Minister for Foreign Affairs of Bosnia and Herzegovina addressed to the President of the Security Council

55. Report of the Secretary-General pursuant to Security Council resolution 757 (1992)

56. Report of the Secretary-General pursuant to paragraph 15 of Security Council resolution 757 (1992) and paragraph 10 of Security Council resolution 758 (1992)

57. Oral reports by the Secretary-General on 26 and 29 June 1992 pursuant to Security Council resolution 758 (1992)

58. Further report of the Secretary-General pursuant to Security Council resolution 752 (1992)

59. An agenda for peace: preventive diplomacy, peacemaking and peace-keeping

60. Further report of the Secretary-General pursuant to Security Council resolutions 757 (1992), 758 (1992) and 761 (1992)

61. Letter dated 11 July 1992 from the Minister for Foreign Affairs of Croatia addressed to the President of the Security Council

Letter dated 12 July 1992 from the Minister for Foreign Affairs of Croatia addressed to the President of the Security Council

Letter dated 13 July 1992 from the Permanent Representative of Bosnia and Herzegovina to the United Nations addressed to the President of the Security Council

Letter dated 13 July 1992 from the Chargé d'affaires a.i. of the Permanent Mission of Slovenia to the United Nations addressed to the President of the Security Council

Letter dated 17 July 1992 from the Permanent Representatives of Belgium, France and the United Kingdom of Great Britain and Northern Ireland to the United Nations addressed to the President of the Security Council

62. Report of the Secretary-General on the situation in Bosnia and Herzegovina

63. Letter dated 4 August 1992 from the Chargé d'affaires a.i. of the United States Mission to the United Nations addressed to the President of the Security Council

Letter dated 4 August 1992 from the Permanent Representative of Venezuela to the United Nations addressed to the President of the Security Council

64. Report of the Secretary-General pursuant to Security Council resolution 762 (1992)

65. Letter dated 7 August 1992 from the Chargé d'affaires a.i. of the Permanent Mission of Belgium to the United Nations addressed to the President of the Security Council

Letter dated 7 August 1992 from the Chargé d'affaires a.i. of the Permanent Mission of France to the United Nations addressed to the President of the Security Council

Letter dated 7 August 1992 from the Permanent Representative of the United Kingdom of Great Britain and Northern Ireland to the United Nations addressed to the President of the Security Council

Letter dated 7 August 1992 from the Chargé d'affaires a.i. of the United States Mission to the United Nations addressed to the President of the Security Council

66. Letter dated 10 August 1992 from the Permanent Representative of Bosnia and Herzegovina to the United Nations addressed to the President of the Security Council

Letter dated 10 August 1992 from the Chargé d'affaires a.i. of the Permanent Mission of Turkey to the United Nations addressed to the President of the Security Council

Letter dated 10 August 1992 from the Chargé d'affaires a.i. of the Permanent Mission of the Islamic Republic of Iran to the United Nations addressed to the President of the Security Council

Letter dated 10 August 1992 from the Permanent Representative of Malaysia to the United Nations addressed to the President of the Security Council

Letter dated 11 August 1992 from the Permanent Representative of Senegal to the United Nations addressed to the President of the Security Council

Letter dated 11 August 1992 from the Chargé d'affaires a.i. of the Permanent Mission of Saudi Arabia to the United Nations addressed to the President of the Security Council

Letter dated 10 August 1992 from the Chargé d'affaires a.i. of the

Permanent Mission of Kuwait to the United Nations addressed to the President of the Security Council

Letter dated 11 August 1992 from the Permanent Representative of Pakistan to the United Nations addressed to the President of the Security Council

Letter dated 12 August 1992 from the Permanent Representative of Egypt to the United Nations addressed to the President of the Security Council

Letter dated 13 August 1992 from the Permanent Representative of the United Arab Emirates to the United Nations addressed to the President of the Security Council

Letter dated 13 August 1992 from the Permanent representative of Bahrain to the United Nations addressed to the President of the Security Council

Letter dated 13 August 1992 from the Permanent Representative of the Comoros to the United Nations addressed to the President of the Security Council

Letter dated 13 August 1992 from the Permanent Representative of Qatar to the United Nations addressed to the President of the Security Council

67. Letter dated 28 August 1992 from the Secretary-General addressed to the President of the Security Council

68. Letter dated 24 August 1992 from the Secretary-General addressed to the President of the Security Council

69. The situation in Bosnia and Herzegovina[1]

70. Report of the Secretary-General on the situation in Bosnia and Herzegovina

71. Draft resolution contained in document S/24570

72. Further report of the Secretary-General pursuant to Security Council resolutions 743 (1992) and 762 (1992)

73. Letter dated 10 August 1992 from the Permanent Representative of Bosnia and Herzegovina to the United Nations addressed to the President of the Security Council

Letter dated 10 August 1992 from the Chargé d'affaires a.i. of the Permanent Mission of Turkey to the United Nations addressed to the President of the Security Council

Letter dated 10 August 1992 from the Chargé d'affaires a.i. of the Permanent Mission of the Islamic Republic of Iran to the United Nations addressed to the President of the Security Council

Letter dated 10 August 1992 from the Permanent Representative of

[1] As from the 3647th meeting, held on 4 April 1996, the previously used item 'The situation in the Republic of Bosnia and Herzegovina' was reformulated to read 'The situation in Bosnia and Herzegovina'.

Malaysia to the United Nations addressed to the President of the Security Council

Letter dated 11 August 1992 from the Permanent Representative of Senegal to the United Nations addressed to the President of the Security Council

Letter dated 11 August 1992 from the Chargé d'affaires a.i. of the Permanent Mission of Saudi Arabia to the United Nations addressed to the President of the Security Council

Letter dated 10 August 1992 from the Chargé d'affaires a.i. of the Permanent Mission of Kuwait to the Untied Nations addressed to the President of the Security Council

Letter dated 11 August 1992 from the Permanent Representative of Pakistan to the United Nations addressed to the President of the Security Council

Letter dated 12 August 1992 from the Permanent Representative of Egypt to the United Nations addressed to the President of the Security Council

Letter dated 13 August 1992 from the Permanent Representative of the United Arab Emirates to the United Nations addressed to the President of the Security Council

Letter dated 13 August 1992 from the Permanent Representative of Bahrain to the United Nations addressed to the President of the Security Council

Letter dated 13 August 1992 from the Permanent Representative of the Comoros to the United Nations addressed to the President of the Security Council

Letter dated 13 August 1992 from the Permanent Representative of Qatar to the United Nations addressed to the President of the Security Council

Letter dated 5 October 1992 from the Permanent Representatives of Egypt, the Islamic Republic of Iran, Pakistan, Saudi Arabia, Senegal and Turkey addressed to the President of the Security Council

74. Oral report of the Secretary-General on the United Nations Angola Verification Mission (UNAVEM II)

75. The situation in Georgia

76. The situation in Mozambique

77. Letter dated 27 October 1992 from the Secretary-General addressed to the President of the Security Council

78. Letter dated 29 October 1992 from the Secretary-General addressed to the President of the Security Council

79. The situation in Tajikistan

80. (a) The situation between Iraq and Kuwait

(b) Letter dated 2 April 1991 from the Permanent Representative of Turkey to the United Nations addressed to the President of the Security Council

Letter dated 4 April 1991 from the Chargé d'affaires a.i. of the Permanent Mission of France to the United Nations addressed to the President of the Security Council

Letter dated 5 March 1992 from the Chargé d'affaires a.i. of the Permanent Mission of Belgium to the United Nations addressed to the President of the Security Council

Letter dated 3 August 1992 from the Chargé d'affaires a.i. of the Permanent Mission of Belgium to the United Nations addressed to the President of the Security Council

Letter dated 19 November 1992 from the Permanent Representative of Belgium to the United Nations addressed to the President of the Security Council

81. Report of the Secretary-General on the former Yugoslav Republic of Macedonia

82. Letter dated 18 December 1992 from the Secretary-General addressed to the President of the Security Council

83. The situation prevailing in and adjacent to the United Nations Protected Areas in Croatia

84. The situation in Angola

85. Further report of the Secretary-General pursuant to Security Council resolution 743 (1992)

86. Establishment of an international tribunal for the prosecution of persons responsible for serious violations of international humanitarian law committed in the territory of the former Yugoslavia

87. The situation concerning Rwanda

88. Report of the Secretary-General pursuant to Security Council resolution 807 (1993)

89. Participation of the Federal Republic of Yugoslavia (Serbia and Montenegro) in the work of the Economic and Social Council

90. Letter dated 12 March 1993 from the Permanent Representative of the Democratic People's Republic of Korea to the United Nations addressed to the President of the Security Council

Letter dated 19 March 1993 from the Secretary-General addressed to the President of the Security Council

Note by the Secretary-General

91. The question concerning Haiti

92. The situation in the former Yugoslav Republic of Macedonia

93. Applications made under Article 50 of the Charter of the United

Nations as a consequence of the implementation of measures imposed against the former Yugoslavia

94. Follow-up to resolution 817 (1993)

95. United Nations Protection Force

96. Complaint by Ukraine regarding the decree of the Supreme Soviet of the Russian Federation concerning Sevastopol

97. Conference on Security and Cooperation in Europe missions in Kosovo, Sandjak and Vojvodina, the Federal Republic of Yugoslavia (Serbia and Montenegro)

98. The situation in Tajikistan and along the Tajik-Afghan border

99. The situation in Croatia

100. Security of United Nations operations

101. Navigation on the Danube river in the Federal Republic of Yugoslavia (Serbia and Montenegro)

102. The situation in Burundi

103. Letters dated 20 and 23 December 1991 from France, the United Kingdom of Great Britain and Northern Ireland and the United States of America

104. The situation in Afghanistan

105. Note by the Secretary-General (S/1994/254)
Note by the Secretary-General (S/1994/322)

106. Agreement signed on 4 April 1994 between the Governments of Chad and the Libyan Arab Jamahiriya concerning the practical modalities for the implementation of the Judgment delivered by the International Court of Justice on 3 February 1994

107. Note by the Secretary-General transmitting a letter dated 27 May 1994 from the Director-General of the International Atomic Energy Agency (IAEA) addressed to the Secretary-General (S/1994/631)

108. The situation in the Republic of Yemen

109. An agenda for peace: peacekeeping

110. Agreed framework of 21 October 1994 between the United States of America and the Democratic People's Republic of Korea

111. The situation prevailing in and around the safe area of Bihac

112. Letter dated 14 December 1994 from the Chairman of the Security Council Committee established pursuant to resolution 724 (1991) concerning Yugoslavia addressed to the President of the Security Council (S/1994/1418)

113. Security Council working methods and procedure

114. An agenda for peace

115. The proposal by China, France, the Russian Federation, the United Kingdom of Great Britain and Northern Ireland and the United States of America on security assurances

116. Navigation on the Danube river

117. The situation in the former Yugoslavia

118. The situation in Sierra Leone

119. Letter dated 9 January 1996 from the Permanent Representative of Ethiopia to the United Nations addressed to the President of the Security Council, concerning the extradition of the suspects wanted in the assassination attempt on the life of the President of the Arab Republic of Egypt in Addis Ababa on 26 June 1995 (S/1996/10)

120. Shooting down of two civil aircraft on 24 February 1996

121. International Tribunal for the Prosecution of Persons Responsible for Serious Violations of International Humanitarian Law Committed in the Territory of the Former Yugoslavia

International Tribunal for the Prosecution of Persons Responsible for Serious Violations of International Humanitarian Law Committed in the Territory of Rwanda and Rwandan Citizens Responsible for such Violations Committed in the Territory of Neighbouring States

Appointment of the Prosecutor

122. Signature of the African Nuclear-Weapon-Free Zone Treaty (Treaty of Pelindaba)

123. International Tribunal for the Prosecution of Persons Responsible for Serious Violations of International Humanitarian Law Committed in the Territory of the Former Yugoslavia

124. Demining in the context of United Nations peace-keeping

125. Letters dated 23 September and 3 and 11 October 1996 from the Permanent Representative of the Republic of Korea to the United Nations addressed to the President of the Security Council (S/1996/774, S/1996/824 and S/1996/847)

Letters from the Permanent Representative of the Democratic People's Republic of Korea to the United Nations addressed to the President of the Security Council and to the Secretary-General of 23 and 27 September 1996, respectively (S/1996/768 and S/1996/800)

126. The situation in the Great Lakes region

APPENDIX VIII

COMMUNICATIONS RECEIVED FROM PRIVATE INDIVIDUALS AND NON-GOVERNMENTAL BODIES RELATING TO MATTERS OF WHICH THE SECURITY COUNCIL IS SEIZED, 3 FEBRUARY 1997, S/NC/1996/4.

Sender	*Place*	*Date*
THE SITUATION IN AFGHANISTAN		
Daud Yaar, Council of Cooperation for Afghan National Organizations	Concord, CA, United States of America	18 October and 11 November 1996
Tajuddin Millatmal, Afghan Intellectual Community in North America[1]	Omaha, NE, United States of America	18 November 1996
THE SITUATION IN ANGOLA		
Jan Nico Scholten, European Parliamentarian for (Southern) Africa	Amsterdam, Netherlands	10 October 1996
THE SITUATION IN THE FORMER YUGOSLAVIA		
Andrew M. Patterson	Houston, TX, United States of America	14 October 1996
Kathleen Uhler, Franciscans International	New York, NY, United States of America	4 November 1996
Tony Devcich	Auckland, New Zealand	19 November 1996

[1] Plus 23 signatures.

Bryan J. Boyea	Plattsburgh, NY, United States of America	5 December 1996
Stephen Krolo, Canadian–Croatian Congress	Edmonton, Canada	27 December 1996

THE SITUATION IN BURUNDI

Kenneth Roth, Human Rights Watch	New York, NY, United States of America	28 October 1996
Andrea Orsini	Ripoli, Italy	19 December 1996

THE SITUATION IN CYPRUS

P. Petrou, Polemidia Lyceum	Limassol, Cyprus	18 October 1996
Stavros Ioannides	Limassol, Cyprus	29 November 1996

THE SITUATION IN GEORGIA

Konstantin Ozgan, Ministry of Foreign Affairs of the Republic of Abkhazia	Sukhumi, Georgia	29 November 1996

THE SITUATION BETWEEN IRAQ AND KUWAIT

Andreas Rentsch[2]	Leipzig, Germany	20 October 1996
Gordon Corey	Parchman, MS, United States of America	11 October 1996
Joan M. Wittreich	Center Moriches, NY, United States of America	21 November 1996
Yang Ling and Luo Zhi Qing	Chang Chin Province, China	Undated

[2] Plus 12 signatures.

THE SITUATION IN LIBERIA

Edwin G. K. Zoedua, Liberian Social Justice Foundation	Cincinnati, OH, United States of America	22 November 1996

THE SITUATION IN MOZAMBIQUE

Rafael Namachokola, Mozambique African National Union	Nairobi, Kenya	4 November 1996

LETTERS DATED 20 AND 23 DECEMBER 1991, FROM FRANCE, THE UNITED KINGDOM OF GREAT BRITAIN AND NORTHERN IRELAND AND THE UNITED STATES OF AMERICA

Daniel Orobedo	Benin City, Nigeria	28 November 1996

THE SITUATION CONCERNING RWANDA

Froduald Gasamunyiga	Nairobi, Kenya	23 October 1996
Claus Ladner, KOMERA e.V.	Reutlingen, Germany	19 November 1996
Claver Kanyarushoki, Rassemblement pour le Retour des Réfugiés et la Démocratie au Rwanda	Brussels, Belgium	10 December 1996

THE SITUATION IN SOMALIA

James Taylor	Brampton, Canada	11 November 1996

THE SITUATION IN THE GREAT LAKES REGION

Global Council Secretariat	Nairobi, Kenya	29 October and 18 November 1996
Ignacio Carreras, Foundation for the Third World	Madrid, Spain	30 October 1996

Paul Kanamby, Conseil de la Communauté zaïroise du Québec	Montreal, Canada	5 November 1996
Tony Devcich	Auckland, New Zealand	7 and 14 November 1996
Doctors without Borders	New York, NY, United States of America	8, 13 and 14 November 1996
Mario Weima, NOVIB (Nederlandse Organisatie voor Internationale Ontwikkelingssamenwerking)[3]	The Hague, Netherlands	14 November 1996
Gail Lerner, Commission of the Churches on International Affairs	New York, NY, United States of America	15 November 1996
T. Abdul-Raheem, Pan African Movement	Kampala, Uganda	15 November 1996

[3] Plus 496 identical petitions.

APPENDIX IX

THE SECRETARIAT'S TENTATIVE FORECAST OF THE PROGRAMME OF WORK OF THE SECURITY COUNCIL FOR THE MONTH OF AUGUST 1995

31 JULY 1995

For information only/not an official document

This tentative forecast of the programme of work of the Security Council has been prepared by the Secretariat for the President of the Council. The forecast covers in particular those matters that may be taken up during the month pursuant to earlier decisions of the Council. The fact that a matter is or is not included in the forecast carries no implication that it will or will not be taken up during the month: the actual programme of work will be determined by developments and the views of members of the Council.

Africa

Angola

By resolution 976 (1995) of 8 February 1995, the Security Council decided to establish UNAVEM III with an initial mandate *until 8 August 1995.*

Since February 1995, pursuant to the same resolution, the Secretary-General has kept the Council informed, on monthly basis, of progress in the deployment of UNAVEM III and in implementation of the Lusaka Protocol.

On 17 July 1995, the Secretary-General submitted to the Security Council *a comprehensive report* on UNAVEM III and on the implementation of the Lusaka Protocol (S/1995/588).

A meeting of Council members, troop-contributing countries and the Secretariat will be held in advance of the consideration of the mandate of UNAVEM III.

Burundi

In a statement made by the President of the Security Council at the 3497th, held meeting on 31 January 1995 (S/PRST/1995/5), the Council, which had been following closely developments in Burundi, indicated that it had learned with concern that the situation in the country had deteriorated considerably. In this regard, the Security Council requested the Secretary-General to continue *to keep it fully informed of developments in Burundi.*

In a statement made by the President of the Security Council at the 3511th meeting on 29 March 1995 (S/PRST/1995/13), the Council requested the Secretary-General *to report to it on an urgent basis* on what steps should be taken to establish an impartial international commission of inquiry into the October 1993 coup attempt and into the massacres that followed.

Pursuant to the above request, the Secretary-General, in his letter dated 28 July 1995 (S/1995/631), recommended that the Council adopt, as soon as possible, a resolution establishing such a commission, with a three-fold mandate, on the basis of the report annexed to his letter.

Rwanda

By its resolution 997 (1995) of 9 June 1995, the Security Council, in extending the mandate of UNAMIR until 8 December 1995, requested the Secretary-General *to report to the Council by 9 August 1995* on the discharge by UNAMIR of its mandate, the humanitarian situation and progress towards repatriation of refugees.

Somalia

In a statement made by the President of the Security Council at the 3513th meeting, on 6 April 1995 (S/PRST/1995/15), the Council supported the view of the Secretary-General that Somalia should not be abandoned by the United Nations. The Council requested the Secretary-General to continue to monitor the situation in Somalia and *to keep it informed about further developments.*

Western Sahara

By its resolution 1002 (1995) of 30 June 1995, the Security Council requested the Secretary-General, in addition to the reports called for in paragraph 48 of the report of the Security Council mission (S/1995/498), *to keep the Council fully informed of further developments* in the implementation of the Settlement Plan for Western Sahara during this period, in particular of any significant delays in the pace of the identification process or other developments that would call into question the Secretary-General's ability to set the start of the transitional period on 15 November 1995.

Asia

Situation on the Tajik–Afghan border

By its resolution 999 (1995) of 16 June 1995, the Security Council, having stressed the urgency of the cessation of all hostile acts on the Tajik–Afghan border and having called upon all States and others concerned to discourage any activities that could complicate or hinder the peace process in Tajikistan, *requested the Secretary-General to report to the Council* on his discussions with relevant Afghan authorities regarding a possible deployment of a small number of United Nations personnel in northern Afghanistan and expressed its willingness to consider a relevant recommendation of the Secretary-General in the context of the implementation of that resolution.

Europe

Bosnia and Herzegovina

In its resolution 1004 (1995) of 12 July 1995, the Security Council requested the Secretary-General to use all resources available to him to restore the status as defined by the Agreement of 18 April 1993 of the safe area of Srebrenica in accordance with the mandate of UNPROFOR, and called on the parties to cooperate to that end.

The Secretary-General accordingly decided to send Mr. Thorvald Stoltenberg immediately to Bosnia and Herzegovina, as his Special Envoy, to open negotiations with the parties on those matters.

The Secretary-General will keep the Security Council informed of the results of his Special Envoy's efforts.

ICFY Mission

In its resolution 1003 (1995) of 5 July 1995, the Council decided that the restrictions and other measures referred to in paragraph 1 of resolution 943 (1994) should be suspended *until 18 September 1995*.

In paragraph 2 of the same resolution, the Council decided also that the arrangements referred to in paragraphs 13, 14 and 15 of resolution 988 (1995) should continue to apply.

In paragraph 13 of its resolution 988 (1995), the Council requested that *every 30 days* and no fewer than ten days before the expiration of the period referred to in paragraph 1 of the resolution, *the Secretary-General submit to the Security Council for its review a report* as to whether the Co-Chairmen of the ICFY Steering Committee, on the basis of information made available to them from ICFY Mission and all other available sources deemed relevant by the ICFY Mission, certify that the authorities of the Federal Republic of Yugoslavia (Serbia and Montenegro) were implementing their decision to close the international border, on land and in the air, between the Federal Republic of Yugoslavia (Serbia and Montenegro) and the Republic of Bosnia and Herzegovina with respect to all goods, except foodstuffs, medical supplies and clothing for essential humanitarian needs, and were complying with the requirements of paragraph 3 of resolution 970 (1995) in respect to all shipments across the international border between the Federal Republic of Yugoslavia (Serbia and Montenegro) and the Republic of Bosnia and Herzegovina.

The Secretary-General transmitted the bi-annual report by the Co-Chairmen of the Steering Committee of the International Conference on the Former Yugoslavia on 26 July 1995 (S/1995/626).

The report concerning the operations of the International Conference's Mission to the Federal Republic of Yugoslavia (Serbia and Montenegro), as called for in paragraph 13 of resolution 988 (1995), is expected to be submitted in the *first week of August 1995*.

Croatia

In a statement made by the President of the Security Council at the 3545th meeting on 16 June 1995 (S/PRST/1995/30), the Council, having expressed its concern at the situation in Croatia and at the continuing failure of the parties to cooperate satisfactorily with UNCRO and to comply fully with the demands of the Council, *inter alia*, welcomed the Secretary-General's intention to monitor closely the parties' cooperation with UNCRO and their compliance with the cease-fire agreement of 29 March 1994, and requested the Secretary-General *to keep the Council fully informed.* The Council was of the opinion that such cooperation and compliance were essential for the implementation of UNCRO's mandate and for progress towards a negotiated settlement respecting fully the sovereignty and territorial integrity of the Republic of Croatia and which guaranteed the security and rights of all communities.

In paragraph 9 of resolution 981 (1995) the Security Council invited the Secretary-General 'to report as appropriate and not less than every four months on progress towards a peaceful political settlement and the situation on the ground including UNCRO's ability to implement its mandate as described above'. The report of the Secretary-General may be expected *in the first half of August 1995.*

Navigation on the Danube river

By its resolution 992 (1995) of 11 May 1995, the Security Council decided that the use of the locks of the Iron Gates I system on the left hand bank of the Danube by vessels (a) registered in the Federal Republic of Yugoslavia (Serbia and Montenegro) or (b) in which a majority or controlling interest is held by a person on undertaking in or operation from the Federal Republic of Yugoslavia (Serbia and Montenegro) should be permitted.

The Council further decided that the resolution should come into force on the day following the receipt by the Council from the Committee established pursuant to resolution 724 (1991) of a report by the Danube Commission that they were satisfied that preparations for the repairs to the locks of the Iron Gates I system on the right hand bank of the Danube had been completed. The required report by the Danube Commission was transmitted to the Council on 22 June 1995 (S/1995/502), thus the resolution entered into force the following day, i.e. 23 June 1995.

In paragraph 2 of the above resolution, the Council further decided, *inter alia*, that the resolution should remain in force for a period of 60 days from the date on which it came into force, and, unless the Council decided otherwise, for a further period of up to 60 days if the Council was notified by the Committee established pursuant to resolution 724 (1991) that each such further period was required for completion of the necessary repairs.

In this connection, the Council, in paragraph 7 of the resolution, requested the Executive Director of the Danube Commission to inform the Chairman of the Committee established pursuant to resolution 724 (1991) of the date of completion of the repairs, or, if the repairs have not been completed within 60 days of the entry into force of that resolution, or within the subsequent periods of up to 60 days for which the provisions of that resolution might be extended, *to provide the Chairman with a report on the state of the repairs 10 days before the expiry of any such period.*

The report by the Executive Director of the Danube Commission may be expected *by mid-August 1995*, if the repairs are not completed by that time.

Georgia

By its resolution 993 (1995) of 12 May 1995, the Security Council, in extending the mandate of UNOMIG until 12 January 1996, requested the Secretary-General *to report every three months* from the date of the adoption of that resolution on all aspects of the situation in Abkhazia, Republic of Georgia, including the operations of UNOMIG, and decided to undertake, on the basis of those reports, further reviews of the situation.

The first such report by the Secretary-General may be expected *by mid-August 1995.*

UNPREDEP

By its resolution 983 (1995) of 31 March 1995, the Security Council requested the Secretary-General *to keep the Council regularly informed* of any developments on the ground and other circumstances affecting the mandate of UNPREDEP.

31 July 1995

FORTHCOMING REPORTS BY THE SECRETARY-GENERAL AS REQUESTED BY THE SECURITY COUNCIL

(August 1995)

Item	Due date	Request contained in resolution or Presidential statement or letter from the President of the Security Council	Formulation of the request in the resolution or Presidential statement or letter from the President of the Security Council
Croatia (UNCRO)	First half of August 1995	S/RES/981 of 31 March 1995	'Invites the Secretary-General to report as appropriate and not less than every four months on progress towards a peaceful political settlement and the

Item	Due date	Request contained in resolution or Presidential statement or letter from the President of the Security Council	Formulation of the request in the resolution or Presidential statement or letter from the President of the Security Council
			situation on the ground including UNCRO's ability to implement its mandate . . ., and *undertakes* in this connection to examine without delay any recommendations that the Secretary-General may make in his reports and adopt appropriate decisions' (para. 9).
Rwanda (UNAMIR)	By 9 August 1995	S/RES/997 of 9 June 1995	'Requests the Secretary-General to report to the Council by 9 August 1995 . . . on the discharge by UNAMIR of its mandate, the humanitarian situation and progress towards repatriation of refugees' (para. 11).
Georgia (UNOMIG)	By 12 August 1995	S/RES/993 of 12 May 1995	'Requests the Secretary-General to report every three months from the date of the adoption of this resolution on all aspects of the situation in Abkhazia, Republic of Georgia, including the operations of UNOMIG . . .' (para. 12).
Haiti (UNMIH)	By mid-November 1995	S/RES/1007 of 31 July 1995	'Requests the Secretary-General to apprise the Council of progress in the fulfilment of UNMIH's mandate and, to this end, also requests the Secretary-General to report to the Council at the mid-point of this mandate' (para. 11).

Appendix IX

31 July 1995

SCHEDULE OF FORTHCOMING REVIEWS OR RENEWALS OF MANDATES

Subject	Date of Review/ Expiry of Mandate/ Review of Status*	Council Decision Providing for Current Mandate
UNAVEM III	8 August 1995	976 (1995) of 8 February 1995
UNOMIL	15 September 1995	1001 (1995) of 30 June 1995
MINURSO	30 September 1995	1002 (1995) of 30 June 1995
UNMIH	mid-November 1991[1]	1007 (1995) of 31 July 1995
UNIKOM	7 October 1995*	S/1995/280 of 7 April 1995
UNCRO	30 November 1995	981 (1995) of 31 March 1995
UNPROFOR	30 November 1995	982 (1995) of 31 March 1995
UNPREDEP	30 November 1995	983 (1995) of 31 March 1995
UNDOF	30 November 1995	996 (1995) of 30 May 1995
UNAMIR	8 December 1995	997 (1995) of 9 June 1995
UNMOT	15 December 1995	999 (1995) of 16 June 1995
UNFICYP	31 December 1995	1000 (1995) of 23 June 1995
UNOMIG	12 January 1996	993 (1995) of 12 May 1995
UNIFIL	31 January 1996	1006 (1995) of 28 July 1995
UNMIH	End of February 1996[2]	1007 (1995) of 31 July 1995

[1] In paragraph 11 of resolution 1007 (1995), the Secretary-General is requested to report to the Council at the mid-point of this mandate.

[2] In paragraph 9 of resolution 1007 (1995), the Council decided to extend the mandate of UNMIH for a period of seven months.

31 July 1995

REVIEW OF SANCTIONS REGIMES

Subject	Date of Next review	Explanatory Notes
Iraq	9 September 1995 (Saturday)	Under S/RES/687 (1991), paragraph 21, the Security Council is required to review every 60 days the provisions of paragraph 20 of that resolution. The last review, the 26th in the series, was undertaken on 11 July 1995 in consultations of the whole of the Council. No document was issued thereon.
	8 November 1995	Under S/RES/687 (1991), paragraph 28, the Security Council is required to review every 120 days the provisions set out in paragraphs 22, 23, 24 and 25 of that resolution. The required review does not apply to the provisions specified and

Subject	Date of Next review	Explanatory Notes
		defined in paragraphs 8 and 12 of resolution 687 (1991). The forthcoming review will be the 14th in the series. Under S/RES/700 (1991), paragraph 6, the Security Council decided to review the Guidelines for the implementation of the relevant provisions of resolution 687 (1991) at the same time as its regular reviews called for in paragraph 28 of that resolution. The forthcoming review will also be the 14th in the series.
Suspension of the restrictions and other measures against the Federal Republic of Yugoslavia (Serbia and Montenegro) referred to in paragraph 1 of Security Council resolution 943 (1994)	18 September 1995	Under S/RES/1003 (1995), paragraph 1, the Security Council decided that the restrictions and other measures referred to in paragraph 1 of resolution 943 (1994) shall be suspended until 18 September 1995.
Libyan Arab Jamahiriya	28 November 1995	Under S/RES/748 (1992), paragraph 13, the Security Council is required to review every 120 days or sooner, should the situation so require, the measures imposed by paragraphs 3 to 7. The last review took place in consultations of the whole of the Council on 28 July 1995, after which a Presidential statement was issued (S/PRST/1995/36).
Areas of the Republic of Bosnia and Herzegovina under the control of Bosnian Serb forces	23 September 1995	Under S/RES/942 (1994), paragraph 21, the Security Council is required to review the measures imposed by that resolution whenever appropriate and in any event every four months from the date of its adoption.

APPENDIX X (a)

PRESIDENTIAL NOTE OF 30 JUNE 1993 CONCERNING THE ANNUAL REPORT OF THE SECURITY COUNCIL TO THE GENERAL ASSEMBLY

On 30 June 1993, the President of the Security Council issued the following note:[1]

'The President of the Security Council wishes to refer to the issue of the format of the annual report of the Security Council to the General Assembly, which the Council has to submit under Article 24, paragraph 3, of the Charter of the United Nations and to certain other matters.

'The President wishes to state in this regard that all members of the Council have indicated their agreement with the following proposals:

'1. The Council should take all the necessary measures to ensure the timely submission of its report to the General Assembly. For that purpose:

'(*a*) The Council should retain the existing practice whereby the annual report is submitted to the General Assembly in a single volume covering the period from 16 June of one year to 15 June of the next year;

'(*b*) The Secretariat should submit the draft report to the members of the Council no later than 30 September immediately following the period covered by the report, so that the report may be adopted by the Council in time for consideration by the Assembly during the main part of its regular session.

'2. Presidential statements should be published, effective 1 January 1994, in an annual series using the prefix "S/PRST/—" followed by the year and the number of the statement. A new appendix should be included in the annual report of the Security Council to the General Assembly, starting with the report covering the period from 16 June 1992 to 15 June 1993, providing a chronological listing of presidential statements for the period under review and indicating the date when the statement was made or issued and the relevant agenda item or subject-matter. At the time of approval of presidential statements, the Council members should indicate the agenda item and, where none exists, an agreed formulation of the subject-matter under which the statement is being

[1] S/26015.

authorized. That should be reflected in the Council document circulating the presidential statement.

'3. The appendices in the annual report of the Council listing the resolutions and presidential statements should provide cross-references to the relevant chapter, section and subsection of the report, for each resolution and presidential statement.

'4. The draft annual report of the Council should no longer be issued as a confidential document; it should be a document with a "Limited distribution" designation, as is the common practice in other bodies of the United Nations.

'5. Henceforth, the draft annual report should be adopted at a public meeting of the Council. At that meeting, the document containing the draft report should be made available to interested delegations.

'6. Whenever inclusion of a reference to unpublished documentation in a draft resolution or a draft presidential statement is envisaged, the Secretariat should bring the matter to the attention of the President of the Council so that the President, in turn, could raise the matter with the members of the Council in order to determine whether or not to retain the reference in the draft text and, where the members of the Security Council decide that it is to be retained, whether that document should be published as an official document of the Council.

'7. The provisional agenda for formal meetings of the Council should be included in the *Journal* provided that it has been approved in informal consultations.

'8. The informal Working Group of the Security Council concerning the Council's documentation and other procedural matters discussed various possible options to establish new ways to provide information to States that are not members of the Council. It was agreed that the Council should keep this question under due consideration so as to enhance its practice in this respect.

'The members of the Council will continue their consideration of other suggestions concerning the Council's documentation and related matters.'

APPENDIX X (b)

PRESIDENTIAL NOTE OF 27 JULY 1993 CONCERNING THE FORECAST OF THE PROGRAMME OF WORK OF THE COUNCIL

On 27 July 1993, the President of the Security Council issued the following note:[1]

'Further to the note by the President of the Security Council concerning the Council's documentation and related matters, the President wishes to state that all members of the Council have indicated their agreement with the following proposals:

'1. The tentative forecast of the programme of work of the Council for each month should be made available to all Member States, for information. This should be done once the Secretariat has presented the forecast to the President of the Council and it has been transmitted to the members of the Council.

'2. The forecast should be prepared along the same lines as now, in conformity with the decisions of the Council.

'3. The forecast should be made available, in all official languages "For information only/not an official document", and there should be a footnote reading:

> 'This tentative forecast of the programme of work of the Security Council has been prepared by the Secretariat for the President of the Council. The forecast covers in particular those matters that may be taken up during the month pursuant to earlier decisions of the Council. The fact that a matter is or is not included in the forecast carries no implication that it will or will not be taken up during the month: the actual programme of work will be determined by developments and the views of members of the Council.

'The members of the Council will continue their consideration of other suggestions concerning the Council's documentation and related matters.'

[1] S/26176.

APPENDIX X (c)

PRESIDENTIAL NOTE OF 31 AUGUST 1993 CONCERNING COUNCIL DOCUMENTATION

On 31 August 1993, the President of the Security Council issued the following note:[1]

'Further to the notes by the President of the Security Council dated 30 June 1993 and 27 July 1993 concerning the Council's documentation and related matters, the President wishes to state that all members of the Council have indicated their agreement with the following proposals:

'1. Effective 1 January 1994, the documents of the Council should be published in an annual series. Accordingly, the first Security Council document for 1994 should be numbered "S/1994/1".

'2. The current system of numbering the adopted resolutions of the Security Council will continue unchanged.

'3. On the understanding that the verbatim record of each meeting of the Security Council will continue to be made available as provided in the Council's provisional rules of procedure, and subject to final agreement by the Council on the basis of a further report from the Secretariat in early December 1993, as of 1 January 1994 the verbatim records are to be issued in final form only.

'The members of the Council will continue to review the list of matters of which the Security Council is seized with a view to rationalizing it and to consider other suggestions concerning the Council's documentation and related matters.'

[1] S/26389.

APPENDIX X (d)

LETTER DATED 2 JUNE 1995 FROM ARGENTINA CONCERNING CHANGES TO THE NOMENCLATURE OF STATEMENTS MADE BY THE PRESIDENT OF THE SECURITY COUNCIL

Letter Dated 2 June 1995 from the Permanent Representative of Argentina to the United Nations Addressed to the President of the Security Council S/1995/456,* 9 June 1995

I have the honour to refer to the work of the informal Working Group of the Security Council concerning the Council's documentation and other procedural questions.

In this context, I shall draw attention, first of all, to the recent proposal by the United Kingdom to change the nomenclature of statements made by the President of the Security Council.

I shall then make some general observations on the basis of our preliminary analysis of the United Kingdom initiative.

1. With regard to the proposal by the United Kingdom to retitle Presidential statements made on behalf of the Security Council 'statements on behalf of the Security Council', we note that the original proposal has been modified, eliminating all reference to the stipulation that these statements be read out only in a formal meeting of the Council.

The new wording not only leaves open the possibility of invoking certain earlier experience related to the question but also maintains what is, in our understanding, the essential minimum of flexibility needed on this issue.

For these reasons, and expressly and formally subject to this condition, we would now be in a position to support the proposal by the United Kingdom on the basis of the terms of the consensus on the matter.

2. Notwithstanding the above, I should like to take this opportunity to open a discussion of some of my delegation's serious concerns which are directly linked to the question under review and have not yet been duly resolved.

* Reissued for technical reasons.

At present, the Security Council expresses itself through two principal channels.

First, it adopts 'resolutions', which can be defined, in short, as documents expressing the Council's will and giving rise to commitments.

It also issues 'statements' that express the opinion of those issuing them.

There are three types of statements, all of which, in accordance with established practice, are circulated as official documents of the Security Council.

These statements are generally submitted and debated in 'informal consultations'. Their texts must be unanimously agreed during these consultations.

The three types of statements are as follows: those released to the press, those submitted to the Secretariat to be directly circulated as Security Council documents and those which are read out at formal meetings of the Council.

It should be recalled that the President of the Council also makes 'statements to the press', which are defined at informal meetings on the basis of general guidelines; he may also issue statements on his own initiative.

The presentation of the United Kingdom proposal requires us to think about all the potential consequences of an initiative which, at face value, seems to be a simple change of nomenclature, but which might have more profound implications.

In this context, we should recall that 'statements' are, strictly speaking, a relatively new Security Council instrument whose use has increased considerably, in practice, in recent years.

Curiously, the Council has never defined the scope, content or nature of the documents it issues, not even in its rules of procedure or in its interpretive documents.

None the less, very recently—since 1993, to be more precise—a trend which we do not necessarily support has been emerging to regard the 'statements' that are read out during formal meetings as being made 'on behalf of the Council'. It is argued that those statements which simply arise out of the work of the Council during informal meetings should be made, on the other hand, 'on behalf of the members of the Council'.

Our delegation feels that the potential consequences of accepting this new 'distinction' should be duly evaluated in advance.

We must determine why an effort is being made to draw a conceptual distinction of such magnitude, in particular since it could have implications with regard to the very nature of the type of meeting from which, in each case, the 'statements' arise.

It is also time to address, in a serious manner, the issue of the very nature of 'informal' meetings, which are now the Council's primary working instrument, in terms of time.

Do the provisions of Article 31 of the Charter apply—as we, for example, would argue—to these meetings? For us, there is no doubt that they do.

It must be admitted that, whether we like it or not, some very momentous decisions are being adopted at these meetings on such matters as the sending of notes or letters, the definition of Security Council 'missions' and the negotiation and adoption of the actual texts of all the resolutions and 'statements' of the Security Council.

All these issues must be carefully evaluated, since they have much to do with the transparency and accountability of the Council's work.

We therefore propose that the Working Group undertake, without delay, a period of reflection on these matters, to enable it to harmonize criteria and perhaps adopt some guidelines, notwithstanding any parallel efforts being made in the General Assembly.

For all the foregoing reasons, we trust that the President will allow the Working Group to devote its attention to seeking to resolve the concerns expressed in this letter, to which we attach high priority.

In our view, this step has become essential, and it does not seem advisable to postpone—for perhaps secondary reasons—making the necessary effort to bring a minimum of clarity and transparency to a situation that could be defined as somewhat confused.

We should be grateful if you would arrange to have this letter distributed as a document of the Security Council.

(*Signed*) Emilio J. CARDENAS
Permanent Representative

APPENDIX X (e)

GENERAL ASSEMBLY RESOLUTION 51/193 OF 17 DECEMBER 1996 CONCERNING THE ANNUAL REPORT OF THE SECURITY COUNCIL

51/193. Report of the Security Council

The General Assembly,

Recalling its resolutions 47/233 of 17 August 1993 and 48/264 of 29 July 1994 on the revitalization of the work of the General Assembly,

Reiterating the importance of the objectives and principles relevant to the revitalization of the work of the General Assembly as set out in resolutions 47/233 and 48/264,

Reaffirming the need to improve the reporting procedures of the Security Council,

Bearing in mind the ongoing work of the Open-ended High-level Working Group on the Strengthening of the United Nations System and the Open-ended Working Group on the Question of Equitable Representation on and Increase in the Membership of the Security Council and Other Matters Related to the Security Council,

Taking note of the ongoing efforts of the Security Council to enhance the transparency of its working methods,

1. *Stresses* the importance of enhanced interaction and an effective relationship between the General Assembly and other principal organs, in particular the Security Council, in accordance with the relevant provisions of the Charter of the United Nations;

2. *Takes note* of the report of the Security Council to the General Assembly at its fifty-first session,[1] as well as the views expressed thereon in the course of the consideration of the report by the Assembly;

3. *Encourages* the Security Council, in the submission of its reports to the General Assembly, to provide in a timely manner a substantive, analytical and material account of its work;

4. *Calls upon* the Security Council to adopt the following measures, *inter alia*, in connection with the content of its future reports to the General Assembly:

[1] A/51/2; see *Official Records of the General Assembly, Fifty-first Session, Supplement No. 2.*

(*a*) To include, as appropriate, information on the consultations of the whole undertaken prior to action or deliberation by the Council on issues within its mandate and on the process leading to such action;

(*b*) To include the decisions, recommendations or progress of work of the subsidiary organs of the Council, in particular the sanctions committees;

(*c*) To highlight the extent to which resolutions of the General Assembly on issues falling within the scope of the General Assembly and the Security Council have been taken into account by the Council in its decision-making;

(*d*) To strengthen further the section in the report on the steps taken by the Council to improve its working methods;

(*e*) To include information on requests received under Article 50 of the Charter and actions taken by the Council thereon;

5. *Encourages* the Security Council to provide special reports in accordance with Articles 15 and 24 of the Charter;

6. *Requests* that the annual report of the Security Council be made available before the beginning of the general debate of the General Assembly;

7. *Requests* the President of the General Assembly to raise with the President of the Security Council during their monthly informal meetings and, when deemed appropriate, the matters covered by the present resolution and to report to the Assembly on the steps taken by the Council in this regard;

8. *Invites* the Security Council, through an appropriate procedure or mechanism, to update the General Assembly on a regular basis on the steps it has taken or is contemplating with respect to improving its reporting to the Assembly.

87th plenary meeting
17 December 1996

APPENDIX X (f)

NOTE BY THE PRESIDENT OF THE SECURITY COUNCIL [CONCERNING THE FORMAT OF THE ANNUAL REPORT OF THE COUNCIL TO THE GENERAL ASSEMBLY], 12 JUNE 1997. S/1997/451

1. Further to the notes by the President of the Security Council dated 30 June 1993 (S/26015), 27 July 1993 (S/26176), 31 August 1993 (S/26389), 29 November 1993 (S/26812), 28 February 1994 (S/1994/230), 23 March 1994 (S/1994/329), 28 July 1994 (S/1994/896), 29 March 1995 (S/1995/234), 31 May 1995 (S/1995/438), 31 May 1995 (S/1995/440), 24 January 1996 (S/1996/54), 24 January 1996 (S/1996/55), 30 July 1996 (S/1996/603) and 29 August 1996 (S/1996/704) concerning the Council's documentation and other procedural questions, the President of the Council wishes to state that all members of the Council have indicated their agreement with the following.

2. The members of the Security Council have reviewed the format of the annual report of the Council to the General Assembly, which is submitted by the Council in accordance with Article 24, paragraph 3, of the Charter of the United Nations. While the report covering the period from 16 June 1996 to 15 June 1997 will have to be in the same format as for the recently preceding years, the report of the Council for future years will be changed, taking into account views expressed on the existing format.

3. The Security Council will take the necessary action to ensure the timely submission of its report to the General Assembly. For that purpose:

(a) The Council should retain the existing practice whereby the annual report is submitted to the General Assembly in a single volume covering the period from 16 June of one year to 15 June of the next year;

(b) The Secretariat should submit the draft report to the members of the Council no later than 30 August immediately following the period covered by the report, so that the report may be adopted by the Council in time for consideration by the General Assembly during the main part of its regular session and where possible before the beginning of the general debate of the Assembly.

4. The report of the Security Council will include the following sections:

(a) In relation to each subject dealt with by the Council:

(i) As background, a descriptive list of the decisions, resolutions and presidential statements of the Council for the one-year period preceding the period covered by the report;

(ii) For the period covered by the report, a description in chronological order of the consideration by the Council of the matter in question and of actions taken by the Council on that item, including descriptions of the decisions, resolutions and presidential statements, and a list of communications received by the Council and reports of the Secretary-General;

(iii) Factual data, including dates of formal meetings and informal consultations at which a subject was discussed;

(b) Information regarding the work of the subsidiary organs of the Council, including the sanctions committees;

(c) Information regarding the documentation and working methods and procedures of the Council;

(d) Matters brought to the attention of the Council but not discussed by it during the period covered;

(e) Appendices as in the present report, but also:

(i) The full text of all resolutions, decisions and presidential statements adopted or voted upon by the Council during the year in question;

(ii) Information about meetings with troop-contributing countries.

5. There will also be attached, as an addendum to the report, brief assessments on the work of the Security Council, which representatives who have completed their functions as President of the Security Council may wish to prepare, under their own responsibility and following consultations with members of the Council for the month during which they presided and which should not be considered as representing the views of the Council.

The following disclaimer will appear at the beginning of the addendum containing the above-mentioned assessments:

> The attachment of the assessments of former Presidents on the work of the Security Council as an addendum to the report is intended to have an informative purpose and should not necessarily be considered as representing the views of the Security Council.

6. The members of the Security Council will continue to consider and to review ways to improve the Council's documentation and procedure, including the provision of special reports as referred to in Article 24, paragraph 3, of the Charter of the United Nations.

APPENDIX X (g)

INFORMAL BRIEFING NOTE ON BLUE DRAFT RESOLUTIONS, PREPARED BY THE SECRETARIAT, JULY 1995

Origin of 'Blue Draft Resolutions'

Blue draft resolutions have been in use since the 1960s in a number of UN organs including the General Assembly and ECOSOC. Originally they were envisaged as a means of distributing draft resolutions at very little notice, during the course of a meeting.

The Evolution of a Security Council Resolution

The first stage is a proposal. This will usually take the form of a 'working paper', in which case it will have no document symbol number and no official status. Occasionally a proposal will be in the form of an S/ document draft resolution from the outset. A proposal may emanate from the President, a member of the Council, a member from the United Nations invited in accordance with the rule 37 of the Council's provisional rules of procedure or a state invited under article 32 of the Charter to participate in the discussions of the Security Council. No matter how initiated, in the course of the consultations thereon, the members of the Council may agree that the text should be considered a Presidential text, that is a text implicitly sponsored by the 15 members of the Council.

The sponsor(s) of a draft resolution may request at any time during the negotiations that their draft resolution be issued by being put into 'blue'. Often at the point when either a text has been informally agreed among the 15 Council members, or where the negotiations have reached the point where no further progress will be achieved through negotiation and a Member still wishes to proceed with a vote on the resolution, then the President will usually ask 'may I take it that we are prepared to turn this draft into blue' or say 'the sponsors are requesting that this draft resolution be turned into blue this evening'. In cases where the draft resolution commands the support of all of the members of the Council and where the members of the Council wish to signify their unity, it would be proposed that the draft be a Presidential text, that is one with the heading 'Draft resolution' only; in other cases sponsors are indicated.

A blue draft resolution of the Security Council is a text printed with blue ink and issued in *provisional* form. It carries the word 'PROVISIONAL' in the symbol block. From a technical standpoint the emphasis is on the draft blue resolution being provisional in terms of accuracy of the different language versions rather than in terms of substance, and often minor translation alterations are subsequently necessary.

Unlike the General Assembly where 'blue' draft resolutions are automatically converted into 'black', in the Security Council they may remain in 'blue' indefinitely unless cancelled or turned into 'black', that is, into a document with the *general* distribution designation specified in the symbol block. The 'black' document carries the same symbol as the 'blue'. If not converted into 'black', the 'blue' document ceases to exist and the S/ symbol is vacated. While a blue draft resolution is provisional, it must be turned into 'black' if a reference is made to it at a formal meeting of the Council.

Physically, 'blue draft resolutions' are produced by the Secretariat in one room where a translator and word-processor operator (for each language) are brought together swiftly to produce a preliminary text. Low volume reproduction facilities are available nearby, and the resolution is then circulated in limited numbers in the Security Council Consultation Room, and since 1 March 1994, to the racks of the delegates' document distribution counter in the first basement of the Secretariat building.

Changes to a 'Blue Draft Resolution'

The vast majority of changes are undertaken at the level of the 'working papers'—ie. 'non-documents'. Working papers are identified only by title and date, and revisions to them specify the date and time of new versions. Once a draft resolution has been accepted as 'blue' it is rare to have any changes. If there are any, these are incorporated in a new version of the blue draft resolution. The symbol of a blue draft resolution will be in the following form: S/1997/*** where '***' stands for the next sequential number of Security Council documents issued that year. A revised version of that document will carry the same symbol with an asterisk following the symbol if issued the same day, or simply a new date if issued the next day. Unless the sponsors of a draft resolution undergoing revision specifically decided that there should be a revised version, the word 'revised' does not appear in the heading. If passed, the black version of the resolution will carry the identical document symbol.

When revisions are made by the sponsors of the text in 'blue' during a formal meeting, the President, in specifying the revisions made, explicitly states that 'they have been made to the text contained in document S/ . . . in its provisional form'. In such a case, when putting the text to the vote at the same meeting, the President refers to 'the draft resolution contained in document S/ . . ., as orally revised in its provisional form'. The said revisions are then incorporated in the 'black' version of the draft resolution. If the 'blue' draft resolution, as orally revised in its provisional form, is not put to the vote on that day, it is turned into 'black' overnight. If not adopted, 'blue' draft resolutions are nonetheless turned into 'black'.

While the Council normally takes a decision on the basis of a text issued in 'black', it can, as it has more and more frequently done, act on the basis of the 'blue' text. Draft resolutions are subject to the Council's Provisional Rules of Procedure. Although there is a requirement in the General Assembly Rules of Procedure for a resolution to be submitted at least 24 hours before voting is undertaken, there is nothing that specifies this in the Provisional Rules of Procedure of the Security Council. However a *de facto* '24-hour rule' exists in the Council to allow all members of the Council to receive instructions from their capitals. The sponsors may request that a decision be taken with application of the '24-hour rule'. The President may also indicate his intention to put the draft resolution to the vote in 24 hours. However, if in the view of members of the Council the situation so warrants, and if there is concurrence among them to that effect, a decision may be taken on a draft resolution within a shorter period.

Transparency and 'Blue Draft Resolutions'

The inter-linkage between 'blue draft resolutions', which were hitherto an administrative tool, and transparency measures, began when it was recommended by the *Informal Working Group on Documentation and Other Procedural Matters* of the Security Council that 'blue draft resolutions' should be made available to all Members of the organization. In a note by the President of the Security Council on 28 February 1994 (S/1994/230) the Council adopted the following practice:

> 'Effective 1 March 1994, draft resolutions in blue, that is, in provisional form, will be made available for collection by non-members of the Council at the time of consultations of the whole of the Council. Draft resolutions published in blue late at night will be made available for collection by non-members of the Council the following day.'

APPENDIX XI

AIDE-MÉMOIRE CONCERNING THE WORKING METHODS OF THE SECURITY COUNCIL FROM THE PERMANENT REPRESENTATIVE OF FRANCE, 11 NOVEMBER 1994

GENERAL ASSEMBLY A/49/667
Forty-ninth session S/1994/1279
Agenda item 11 11 November 1994
REPORT OF THE SECURITY COUNCIL

Letter dated 9 November 1994 from the Permanent Representative of France to the United Nations addressed to the Secretary-General

In his statement to the General Assembly, Mr. Alain Juppé, Minister for Foreign Affairs of the French Republic, expressed the wish for the Security Council to increase its reliance on public debate in reaching its decisions. The *aide-mémoire* annexed hereto sets forth in greater detail the grounds for this initiative and indicates some of the modalities through which it might be implemented. I should be grateful if you would have this text circulated as a document of the General Assembly, under agenda item 11, and of the Security Council.

(*Signed*) Jean-Bernard MERIMEE

ANNEX

Aide-mémoire concerning the working methods of the Security Council

I. SUMMARY

1. Many delegations believe that the working methods of the Security Council should allow for greater transparency. This criticism can, in our view, be explained basically by the fact that nearly all the work of the

Council takes place in the form of informal consultations to which States not members of the Council do not have access. This working method has been very useful at a time when, after a long period of paralysis owing to the cold war, the Security Council has had to learn to work as a unit in order to ensure prompt and effective action by the Organization in accordance with Article 24 of the Charter. However, now that the Council has, as it were, completed its basic training, it seems to us that the time has come to allow for fuller public debate in its work. The Council cannot be weakened but should, rather, be strengthened by meeting in public much more frequently than it does at present in order to hear the views of States not members of the Council and engage in a dialogue with them before taking positions on important questions—without, of course, giving up the essential informal consultations procedure. This, in our view, is the real solution to the dissatisfaction which many Member States experience and which we understand.

2. We believe that the key to the problem is rule 48 of the provisional rules of procedure of the Security Council, which provides as follows: 'Unless it decides otherwise, the Security Council shall meet in public'. There should be a dividing line between information, consultation and general exchanges of views, which should, in principle, remain public, and negotiation, the detailed preparation of a decision to be adopted, which is normally governed by other procedures.

3. In this context, France's proposal is to add to the only case currently applicable, that of a discussion organized on the occasion of the official announcement of a decision, two new cases in which the Council should meet in public:

(a) Orientation debates open to all Members of the Organization at a time when the Council is preparing to begin consideration of an important question;

(b) Public exchanges of views between members of the Security Council.

4. Speaking before the General Assembly at its forty-ninth session on the subject of the working methods of the Security Council, the Minister for Foreign Affairs of the French Republic stated that the Council must allow for fuller public debate in reaching its decisions than it currently did:

> 'Hence, we are in favour of the Council's holding official meetings—without of course giving up its informal consultations—to hear Members of the Organization and talk with them before taking positions on the important questions before it. We believe that this is the appropriate response to the demand for transparency made by many delegations.'

5. The purpose of this *aide-mémoire* is to specify the impact and consequences which this French initiative could have.

II. THE RECENT PRACTICE OF THE SECURITY COUNCIL DOES NOT ALLOW FOR SUFFICIENT PUBLIC DEBATE AND GIVES IT A STEREOTYPICAL ROLE

6. The Security Council, having been confronted since the early 1990s with a volume of business it had not experienced up to then, became accustomed to carrying out most of its work in the form of private consultations. This working method satisfied a legitimate concern with facilitating the search for a compromise among delegations in order to ensure prompt action by the Organization. It does not, of course, conflict with any rule or principle: all international negotiating bodies proceed similarly and, in addition to their plenary meetings, make it possible for the delegations concerned to meet in working groups or drafting groups in order to hammer out their differences in a more comfortable setting with a view to submitting to the body in plenary meeting a draft text likely to win its agreement. The General Assembly, its Main Committees and its subsidiary organs are perfectly familiar with this method, which is indispensable in cases where an agreement must be reached. It is especially necessary for the Security Council to have this tool at its disposal since it is required to reach decisions rapidly.

7. Probably in order to avoid the recurrence of the difficult public meetings punctuated by procedural disputes which had marked the cold war era, special attention has for several years been given to delivering only a finished product at official meetings of the Council. In other words, it is still customary nowadays to wait until all the differences of opinion within the Council have been settled, and a text has been negotiated down to the last comma, before holding an official meeting. The script for such a meeting has always been worked out beforehand in its tiniest details so as to leave no room for surprises. The consequence of this is, inevitably, the declaratory, rigid style of such meetings, at which delegations not members of the Council may be heard reading out their prepared statements before a decision is taken, with members presenting before and after the vote explanations which, of course, do not take into account the arguments put forth during the debate leading up to the vote.

8. This concept of public debate significantly impoverishes it and leads to a vicious circle. The fact that statements have no influence on the decision which, in general, has already been taken before the meeting is called to order, induces speakers to adopt a declaratory stance and not to seek dialogue; the conventional nature of the speeches renders the meeting far less

interesting. The consequence of this is that some delegations do not seem to be convinced spontaneously that increasing the frequency of public meetings would enhance the flow of discussion between members of the Security Council and other Members of the the Organization. Indeed, if all that was involved was increasing the number of meetings as currently organized, we would spend a great deal of time in them without gaining a clearer knowledge of the nuances of the position of each Member State. However, the search for a better balance between public and private meetings would certainly give a new impetus to public debate by eliminating the sterility from which it suffers today, a sterility closely linked to the expletive and marginal function to which such debate is currently relegated.

III. TWO TYPES OF SOLUTION ARE PROPOSED TO REDUCE THE OPACITY EXPERIENCED BY STATES MEMBERS OF THE ORGANIZATION

9. In the situation described above, the remedy most generally proposed is to give delegations which are not members of the Council greater access to the information concerning informal consultations. Much has already been done to that end, by announcing informal meetings in the *Journal* and by making available the documents submitted with a view to adoption, to cite but two examples. However, any attempt to proceed further in that direction, by disseminating the content of the discussion in informal meetings or by preparing verbatim records of those meetings, for instance, would negate the very purpose of the meetings. As has been pointed out, any negotiating body needs a place where it can conduct informal, exploratory and sometimes confidential exchanges of views. That is not, in principle, shocking and is, in any case, inevitable. If the informal meetings were no longer informal, new more or less secret working methods having the same purpose would necessarily emerge. Such a development would serve no practical purpose, for if informal meetings were to receive wide publicity they would be nothing more than a hybrid form of public meeting.

10. Recommending changes in the conditions in which informal consultations take place is certainly useful, but considering only such recommendations and nothing more would mean being satisfied with superficial and marginal improvements instead of tackling the problem at its source.

11. Rule 48 of the provisional rules of procedure provides as follows: 'Unless it decides otherwise, the Security Council shall meet in public'. The only type of meeting envisaged in this rule is the official meeting. In the procedural texts applicable to the Security Council this type of meeting is conceived of as a genuine debate, as can be seen from rules 27 to 39 of the rules

of procedure. Nothing imposes the current rigidity and nothing prevents any member of the Council from requesting a meeting, which must be called once it has been requested.

12. In this connection, it is necessary to beware of a tendency to regard informal consultations as another form of Council meeting. This runs directly counter to the rules of procedure in force, according to which informal consultations have no legal existence and are thus subject to no regulation. They are merely a convenient practice, a voluntary arrangement. As soon as the Council has reached a decision, it must be taken in a public meeting. That is, indeed, what happens now, but the public meetings of the Council are limited to the time necessary for the formal adoption of those decisions. Thus, a convenient practice has become the regular working method of the Council, which departs considerably from the spirit of the rules of procedure and is not conducive to the flow of information to and from the Council.

13. The view that the States concerned should be associated with the informal consultations of the Council is tantamount to considering that nothing useful can be done in public and that if a State wishes to influence a decision it must gain admittance to the private meetings or draw as close to them as possible. In our view, this reasoning is flawed, since it assumes that a debatable development in the practice of the Council is accepted, instead of seeking to correct that deviation: at least a significant part of the Council's work should be done in public, under the eyes of all delegations.

IV. A BETTER BALANCE BETWEEN OFFICIAL MEETINGS AND INFORMAL CONSULTATIONS IS DESIRABLE AND POSSIBLE WITHOUT REDUCING THE EFFICIENCY OF THE COUNCIL

14. Currently, there is only one form of public meeting of the Council: the meeting whose purpose is the adoption of a resolution or a decision or the reading out of a statement by the President. Two other types of situation in which the Council could meet in public should be envisaged in the light of the questions currently on its agenda.

15. The first formula is that of the orientation debate where the Council, on taking up a new question or beginning its consideration of an important matter, would give the floor to States Members of the Organization at their request so as to hear their views on the subject and discuss with them possible courses of action in that regard. It is quite clear that if this formula is to be viable, delegations which are not members of the Council will be expected to display a certain moderation as regards their requests to speak

and the length of their statements. A balance would have to be struck fairly quickly in the common interest of the Members of the Organization in order for the discussion to take place within a reasonable period of time. The provisional rules of procedure make it possible for the President of the Council to control the debate and guide it in a useful direction. Thus, the States of the region, other States concerned in a conflict or an emergency situation threatening international peace and security, troop-contributing States, and, in general, any Member State would have the opportunity to express its views on a problem, directly and publicly, to the Council before the latter defined its position. We feel that this is a veritable right for the Members of the Organization, since the Council exercises its powers on their behalf.

16. The second possibility which is not currently utilized is to hold public meetings where the Council, without giving the floor to delegations which are not members, holds an exchange of views on a matter which lends itself to this approach. There have been many recent cases where members of the Council have expressed their views in an informal meeting which could perfectly well have been held in public. In many cases, for example when beginning their consideration of a question, the members of the Council express in turn their general views on the course of a conflict or operation and there seems to be no particular reason why those views should remain confidential. The position of France is that recourse to informal consultations should not be general but limited to cases where a non-public working method is particularly useful, for example, when preparing a written document. But the basic principle should be that publicity is the rule, unless there is a need to act otherwise.

17. To that end, the French delegation is prepared, as soon as the occasion arises, to use its right, based on rule 2 of the provisional rules of procedure, to request a public meeting of the Council for a debate falling within either of the aforementioned categories. It invites other members of the Council wishing to achieve genuine transparency in accordance with the basic rules of the Organization to do likewise.

18. However, the French delegation is also well aware of the need to avoid unnecessarily increasing the workload of the Security Council. In order to strike the right balance between the requirements of publicity and efficiency, the President of the Security Council should undertake bilateral consultations at the beginning of the month and in the initial phase of each major debate in order to determine, on the basis of the suggestions made to him, the topics which could be discussed in a public meeting and the dates on which those meetings could take place. In our view, there is no question of establishing a principle of automaticity which would make it impossible to manage the way in which the Council allots its time. An effort must

undoubtedly be made as regards foresight and moderation. With the good will of all concerned, there is no doubt that things will rapidly fall into place.

19. A new phase could then begin in the existence of the Council and in the history of its relationship with the Members of the United Nations as a whole. After a long period of paralysis and relative inefficiency, followed by a phase marked by many multiform actions conducted in the interest of all but prepared in relative secrecy, the United Nations organ bearing the main responsibility for the maintenance of international peace and security could enter its maturity, combining a greater mastery of the means available to it with a constant concern to be the faithful interpreter of the interests of the Organization and its Members as a whole, free of complexes and any pointless desire for secrecy. It will thus strengthen the link of confidence which ought to bind it to those on behalf of whom it is supposed to act.

APPENDIX XII (a)

SECURITY COUNCIL PRESIDENTIAL STATEMENT

S/PRST/1994/22 Improving UN capacity for peace-keeping

Date: 3 May 1994 Meeting: 3372

Aware of its primary responsibility for the maintenance of international peace and security, the Security Council has begun its consideration of the report of the Secretary-General entitled 'Improving the capacity of the United Nations for peace-keeping' of 14 March 1994 (S/26450). The Security Council welcomes the useful account the report provides of the measures the Secretary-General has taken to strengthen the capacity of the United Nations to undertake peace-keeping operations. The Security Council notes that this report follows the report of the Secretary-General entitled 'An Agenda for Peace' (S/24111) and that it responds to the statements made by successive Presidents of the Security Council on 'An Agenda for Peace', including in particular the statement made by the President of the Security Council on 28 May 1993 (S/25859).

The Security Council notes that the report 'Improving the capacity of the United Nations for peace-keeping' has been transmitted to the General Assembly and also notes that the Special Committee on Peace-keeping Operations has made recommendations on the report.

Establishment of Peace-keeping Operations

The Security Council recalls that the statement made by its President on 28 May 1993 (S/25859) stated, *inter alia*, that United Nations peace-keeping operations should be conducted in accordance with a number of operational principles, consistent with the provisions of the Charter of the United Nations. In that context, the Security Council is conscious of the need for the political goals, mandate, costs, and, where possible, the estimated time-frame of United Nations peace-keeping operations to be clear and precise, and of the requirement for the mandates of peace-keeping operations to be subject to periodic review. The Council will respond to situations on a case-by-case basis. Without prejudice to its ability to do so and to respond rapidly and flexibly as circumstances require, the Council considers that the following factors, among others, should be taken into account when the establishment of new peace-keeping operations is under consideration:

—whether a situation exists the continuation of which is likely to endanger or constitute a threat to international peace and security;
—whether regional or subregional organizations and arrangements exist and are ready and able to assist in resolving the situation;
—whether a cease-fire exists and whether the parties have committed themselves to a peace process intended to reach a political settlement;
—whether a clear political goal exists and whether it can be reflected in the mandate;
—whether a precise mandate for a United Nations operation can be formulated;
—whether the safety and security of Untied Nations personnel can be reasonably ensured, including in particular whether reasonable guarantees can be obtained from the principal parties or factions regarding the safety and security of United Nations personnel; in this regard it reaffirms its statement of 31 March 1993 (S/25493) and its resolution 868 (1993) of 29 September 1993.

The Security Council should also be provided with an estimate of projected costs for the start-up phase (initial 90 days) of the operation and the first six months, as well as for the resulting increase in total projected annualized United Nations peace-keeping expenditures, and should be informed of the likely availability of resources for the new operation.

The Security Council emphasizes the need for the full cooperation of the parties concerned in implementing the mandates of peace-keeping operations as well as relevant decisions of the Security Council.

Ongoing Review of Operations

The Security Council notes that the increasing number and complexity of peace-keeping operations, and of situations likely to give rise to proposals for peace-keeping operations, may require measures to improve the quality and speed of the flow of information available to support Council decision-making. The Security Council will keep this question under consideration.

The Security Council welcomes the enhanced efforts made by the Secretariat to provide information to the Council and underlines the importance of further improving the briefing for Council members on matters of special concern.

Presidential Statement 3 May 1994

Communication with Non-Members of the Security Council (including Troop Contributors)

The Security Council recognizes the implications which its decisions on peace-keeping operations have for the Members of the United Nations and in particular for troop-contributing countries.

The Security Council welcomes the increased communication between members and non-members of the Council and believes that the practice of monthly consultations between the President of the Security Council and competent groups of Member States on the Council's programme of work (which includes matters relating to peace-keeping operations) should be continued.

The Security Council is conscious of the need for enhanced consultations and exchange of information with troop-contributing countries regarding peace-keeping operations, including their planning, management and coordination, particularly when significant extensions in an operation's mandate are in prospect. Such consultations can take a variety of forms involving Member States, troop-contributing countries, members of the Security Council and the Secretariat.

The Security Council believes that when major events occur regarding peace-keeping operations, including decisions to change or extend a mandate, there is a particular need for members of the Council to seek to exchange views with troop contributors, including by way of informal communications between the Council's President or its members and troop contributors.

The recent practice of the Secretariat convening meetings of troop contributors, in the presence, as appropriate, of Council members, is welcome and should be developed. The Council also encourages the Secretariat to convene regular meetings for troop contributors and Council members to hear reports from Special Representatives of the Secretary-General or Force Commanders and, as appropriate, to make situation reports on peace-keeping operations available at frequent and regular intervals.

The Security Council will keep under review arrangements for communication with non-members of the Council.

Stand-by Arrangements

The Security Council attaches great importance to improving the capacity of the United Nations to meet the need for rapid deployment and reinforcement of peace-keeping operations.

In this context the Security Council welcomes the recommendations in the Secretary-General's report of 14 March 1994 concerning stand-by arrangements and capabilities. The Security Council notes the intention of the Secretary-General to devise stand-by arrangements or capabilities which Member States could maintain at an agreed state of readiness as a possible contribution to a United Nations peace-keeping operation and welcomes the commitments undertaken by a number of Member States.

The Security Council welcomes the request by the Secretary-General to Member States to respond positively to this initiative and encourages Member States to do so in so far as possible.

The Security Council encourages the Secretary-General to continue his efforts to include civilian personnel, such as police, in the present stand-by arrangements planning initiative.

The Security Council also encourages the Secretary-General to ensure that the Stand-by Arrangements Management Unit carry on its work, including the periodic updating of the list of units and resources.

The Security Council requests the Secretary-General to report by 30 June 1994 and thereafter at least once a year on progress with this initiative.

The Council will keep this matter under review in order to make recommendations or take decisions required in this regard.

Civilian Personnel

The Security Council welcomes the observations made by the Secretary-General in his report in respect of civilian personnel, including civilian police, and invites Member States to respond positively to requests to contribute such personnel to United Nations peace-keeping operations.

The Security Council attaches importance to full coordination between the different components, military and civilian, of a peace-keeping operation, particularly a multifaceted one. This coordination should extend throughout the planning and implementation of the operation, both at United Nations Headquarters and in the field.

Training

The Security Council recognizes that the training of personnel for peace-keeping operations is essentially the responsibility of Member States, but encourages the Secretariat to continue the development of basic guidelines and performance standards and to provide descriptive materials.

The Security Council notes the recommendations of the Special Committee on Peace-keeping Operations on training of peace-keeping personnel. It invites Member States to cooperate with each other in the provision of facilities for this purpose.

Command and Control

The Security Council stresses that as a leading principle United Nations peace-keeping operations should be under the operational control of the United Nations.

The Security Council welcomes the call by the General Assembly (resolution 48/43) that the Secretary-General, in cooperation with the members of the Security Council, troop-contributing States and other interested Member States, take urgent action on the question of command and control, notes the comments of the Secretary-General in his report of 14 March 1994 and looks forward to his further report on the matter.

Financial and Administrative Issues

Bearing in mind the responsibilities of the General Assembly under Article 17 of the Charter, the Security Council notes the Secretary-General's observations and recommendations on budgetary matters relating to peace-keeping operations in his report of 14 March 1994 and notes also that his report has been referred to the General Assembly for its consideration.

The Security Council confirms that estimates of the financial implications of peace-keeping operations are required from the Secretariat before decisions on mandates or extensions are taken so that the Council is able to act in a financially responsible way.

Conclusion

The Security Council will give further consideration to the recommendations contained in the report of the Secretary-General.

APPENDIX XII (b)

SECURITY COUNCIL PRESIDENTIAL STATEMENT

S/PRST/1995/9 Consideration of Supplement to 'An Agenda for Peace'

Date: 22 February 1995 Meeting: 3503

The Security Council welcomes the Secretary-General's position paper entitled 'Supplement to an Agenda for Peace' (S/1995/1) as an important contribution to the debate on the development of the United Nations activities related to international peace and security in all its aspects at the beginning of the year in which the Organization celebrates its Fiftieth Anniversary. The Council notes that the paper contains a wide range of conclusions and recommendations with regard to instruments for resolving conflict. The Council is of the view that in the light of recent developments and experience gained, efforts should be made to further enhance the Organization's ability to perform the tasks laid down for it under the Charter. The Council reiterates that, in performing the above-mentioned tasks, the purposes and principles of the Charter should always be strictly observed.

The Security Council welcomes and shares the priority given by the Secretary-General to action to prevent conflict. It encourages all Member States to make the fullest possible use of instruments of preventive action, including the Secretary-General's good offices, the dispatch of special envoys of the Secretary-General and the deployment, with the consent as appropriate of the host country or countries, of small field missions for preventive diplomacy and peacemaking. The Council believes that adequate resources must be made available within the United Nations system for these actions. It notes the problem identified by the Secretary-General in finding senior persons to act as his special representative or special envoy and encourages Member States which have not yet done so to provide the Secretary-General with the names of persons who might be considered by him for such posts, together with other resources both human and material which might be useful to such missions. It encourages the Secretary-General to make full use of resources thus put at his disposal.

The Security Council endorses the view expressed by the Secretary-General concerning the crucial importance of economic and social development as a secure basis for lasting peace. Social and economic development can be as valuable in preventing conflicts as in healing the wounds after conflicts have occurred. The Council urges States to support the efforts of the United Nations system with regard to preventive and post-conflict peace-building activities and, in this context, to provide necessary assistance for the economic and social development of countries, especially those which have suffered or are suffering from conflicts.

The Security Council welcomes the Secretary-General's analysis regarding peace-keeping operations. It recalls the statement made by its President on 3 May 1994 (S/PRST/1994/22) which, *inter alia*, listed factors to be taken into account in establishing peace-keeping operations. It notes that in resolving conflicts, primary emphasis should continue to be placed on the use of peaceful means rather than force. Without prejudice to its ability to respond to situations on a case-by-case basis, and rapidly and flexibly as the circumstances require, it reiterates the principles of consent of the parties, impartiality and the non-use of force except in self-defence. It underlines the need to conduct peace-keeping operations with a clearly defined mandate, command structure, time-frame and secure financing, in support of efforts to achieve a peaceful solution to a conflict: it stresses the importance of the consistent application of these principles to the establishment and conduct of all peace-keeping operations. It stresses the importance it attaches to the provision of the fullest possible information to the Council to assist it in making decisions regarding the mandate, duration and termination of current operations. It also emphasizes the importance of providing troop contributors with the fullest possible information.

The Security Council shares the Secretary-General's concern regarding the availability of troops and equipment for peace-keeping operations. It recalls earlier statements by the President of the Council on the subject and reiterates the importance of improving the capacity of the United Nations for rapid deployment and reinforcement of operations. To that end, it encourages the Secretary-General to continue his study of options aimed at improving the capacity for such rapid deployment and reinforcement. The Council believes that the first priority in improving the capacity for rapid deployment should be the further enhancement of the existing stand-by arrangements, covering the full spectrum of resources, including arrangements for lift and headquarters capabilities, required to mount and execute peace-keeping operations. It strongly encourages the Secretary-General to take further steps in this regard, including the establishment of a comprehensive database to cover civilian as well as military resources. In this context, it considers that particular attention should be given to the greatest possible interoperability between elements identified in such arrangements. The Council reiterates its call to Member States not already doing so to participate in the stand-by arrangements. While affirming the principle that contributing Governments should ensure that their troops arrive with all the equipment needed to be fully operational, the Council also encourages the Secretary-General and Member States to continue to consider means, whether in the context of stand-by arrangements or more broadly, to address the requirements of contingents which may need additional equipment or training.

The Security Council strongly supports the Secretary-General's conclusion that peace-keeping operations need an effective information capacity, and his intention to address this requirement in future peace-keeping operations from the planning stage.

The Security Council welcomes the Secretary-General's ideas regarding post-conflict peace-building. It agrees that an appropriately strong overall United Nations contribution needs to be sustained after the successful conclusion of a peace-keeping operation, and encourages the Secretary-General to study ways and means of ensuring effective coordination between the United Nations and other agencies involved in post-conflict peace-building, and to take active steps to ensure that such coordination takes place in the immediate aftermath of a peace-keeping operation. The measures described by the Secretary-General may also be required, with the consent of the State or States concerned, after successful preventive action and in other cases where an actual peace-keeping deployment does not take place.

The Security Council shares the Secretary-General's assessment of the paramount importance of preventing the proliferation of weapons of mass destruction. Such proliferation is a threat to international peace and security. Appropriate measures will be taken in this respect in particular where international treaties provide for recourse to the Council when their provisions are violated. The Council underlines the need for all States to fulfil their obligations in respect of arms control and disarmament, in particular in regard to weapons of mass destruction.

The Security Council takes note of the assessment of the Secretary-General of the importance of 'micro-disarmament', as described in his paper, in the solution of conflicts with which the United Nations is currently dealing and of his view that small arms are probably responsible for most of the deaths in these conflicts. In shares the concern of the Secretary-General at the negative consequences for international peace and security which often arise from the illicit traffic in conventional weapons, including small arms, and takes note of his view that the search for effective solutions to this problem should begin now. In this context the Council stresses the vital importance of the strict implementation of existing arms embargo regimes. It welcomes and supports efforts with regard to international measures to curb the spread of anti-personnel land-mines and to deal with the land-mines already laid, and in this regard welcomes General Assembly resolutions 49/75 D of 15 December 1994 and 49/215 of 23 December 1994. It reaffirms its deep concern over the tremendous humanitarian problems caused by the presence of mines and other unexploded devices to the populations of mine-infested countries and emphasizes the need for an increase in mine-clearing efforts by the countries concerned and with the assistance of the international community.

The Security Council stresses the importance it attaches to the effective implementation of all measures taken by it to maintain or restore international peace and security including economic sanctions. It agrees that the object of economic sanctions is not to punish but to modify the behaviour of the country or party which represents a threat to international peace and security. The steps demanded of that country or party should be clearly defined in Council resolutions, and the sanctions regime in question should be subject to periodic review and it should be lifted when the objectives of the appropriate provisions of the relevant Security Council resolutions are achieved. The Council remains concerned that, within this framework, appropriate measures are taken to ensure that humanitarian supplies reach affected populations and appropriate consideration is given to submissions received from neighbouring or other States affected by special economic problems as a result of the imposition of sanctions. The Council urges the Secretary-General, when considering the allocation of resources available to him within the Secretariat, to take appropriate steps to reinforce those sections of the Secretariat dealing directly with sanctions and their various aspects so as to ensure that all these matters are addressed in as effective, consistent and timely a manner as possible. It welcomes the Secretary-General's efforts to study ways and means of addressing the various aspects related to sanctions in his report.

The Security Council reaffirms the importance it attaches to the role that regional organizations and arrangements can play in helping to maintain international peace and security. It underlines the need for effective coordination between their efforts and those of the United Nations in accordance with Chapter VIII of the Charter. It recognizes that the responsibilities and capacities of different regional organizations and arrangements vary, as well as the readiness and competence of regional organizations and arrangements, as reflected in their charters and other relevant documents, to participate in efforts to maintain international peace and security. It welcomes the Secretary-General's willingness to assist regional organizations and arrangements as appropriate in developing a capacity for preventive action, peacemaking and, where appropriate, peace-keeping. It draws particular attention in this regard to the needs of Africa. It encourages the Secretary-General and Member States to continue to consider ways and means of improving practical cooperation and coordination between the United Nations and regional organizations and arrangements in these areas. The Council encourages the Secretary-General to continue the practice of meetings on cooperation between the United Nations and regional and other organizations.

The Security Council recognizes the crucial importance of the availability of the necessary financial resources both for preventive action and operations undertaken to sustain international peace and security. It therefore urges Member States to honour their financial obligations to the United Nations. At the same time, the Council emphasizes the continuing necessity for careful control of peace-keeping costs and for the most efficient possible use of peace-keeping funds and other financial resources.

The Security Council will keep the Secretary-General's paper under consideration. The Council invites all interested Member States to present further reflections on United Nations peace-keeping operations, and in particular on ways and means to improve the capacity of the United Nations for rapid deployment. It invites the Secretary-General to keep it closely informed of the action he takes in follow-up to the paper and to the present statement. It hopes that the General Assembly, as well as other organizations and entities, will give consideration of the paper a high degree of priority and will take decisions on those matters which fall within their direct responsibility.

APPENDIX XII (c)

SECURITY COUNCIL PRESIDENTIAL STATEMENT

S/PRST/1994/62 Meetings between members of Security Council, troop-contributing countries and Secretariat

Date: 4 November 1994 Meeting: 3448

The Security Council has given further consideration to the question of communication between members and non-members of the Council, in particular troop contributing-countries, which was addressed in the statement of the President of the Council of 3 May 1994 (S/PRST/1994/22). The Council remains conscious of the implications that its decisions on peace-keeping operations have for troop-contributing countries. Having regard to the increase in the number and complexity of such operations, it believes that there is a need for further enhancement, in a pragmatic and flexible manner, of the arrangements for consultation and exchange of information with troop-contributing countries.

To this end, the Security Council has decided in future to follow the procedures set out in this statement:

(a) Meetings should be held as a matter of course between members of the Council, troop-contributing countries and the Secretariat to facilitate the exchange of information and views in good time before the Council takes decisions on the extension or termination of, or significant changes in, the mandate of a particular peace-keeping operation;

(b) Such meetings would be chaired jointly by the Presidency of the Council and a representative of the Secretariat nominated by the Secretary-General;

(c) The monthly tentative forecast of work of the Council made available to Member States will in future include an indication of the expected schedule of such meetings for the month;

(d) In the context of their review of the tentative forecast, the members of the Council will examine this schedule and communicate any suggested changes or proposals as to the timing of meetings to the Secretariat;

(e) Ad hoc meetings chaired jointly by the Presidency of the Security Council and a representative of the Secretariat nominated by the Secretary-

General may be convened in the event of unforeseen developments in a particular peace-keeping operation which could require action by the Council;

(f) Such meetings will be in addition to those convened and chaired solely by the Secretariat for troop contributors to meet with special representatives of the Secretary-General or force commanders or to discuss operational matters concerning particular peace-keeping operations, to which members of the Security Council will also be invited;

(g) An informal paper, including topics to be covered and drawing attention to relevant background documentation, will be circulated by the Secretariat to the participants well in advance of each of the various meetings referred to above;

(h) The time and venue of each meeting with members of the Council and troop contributors to a peace-keeping operation should, where possible, appear in advance in the *Journal of the United Nations*;

(i) The President of the Council will, in the course of informal consultations of members of the Council, summarize the views expressed by participants at each meeting with troop contributors.

The Security Council recalls that the arrangements described herein are not exhaustive. Consultations may take a variety of forms, including informal communication between the Council President or its members and troop-contributing countries and, as appropriate, with other countries especially affected, for example countries from the region concerned.

The Security Council will keep arrangements for the exchange of information and views with troop contributors under review and stands ready to consider further measures to enhance arrangements in the light of experience.

The Security Council will also keep under review arrangements to improve the quality and speed of the flow of information available to support Council decision-making, bearing in mind the conclusions contained in its statement of 3 May 1994 (S/PRST/1994/22).

APPENDIX XII (d)

SECURITY COUNCIL PRESIDENTIAL STATEMENT

S/PRST/1994/81 Increased recourse to open meetings of Security Council in order to improve flow of information and exchange of ideas between Security Council and other UN Member States

Date: 16 December 1994 Meeting: 3483

The Security Council has heard the views of members of the Council and many other United Nations Member States on the item under discussion. These have revealed widespread support for greater recourse to open meetings of the Council and a clear will on the part of the members of the Council to respond to this. It is therefore the intention of the Council, as part of its efforts to improve the flow of information and the exchange of ideas between members of the Council and other United Nations Member States, that there should be an increased recourse to open meetings, in particular at an early stage in its consideration of a subject. The Council will decide on a case-by-case basis when to schedule public meetings of this sort. The Security Council's working group on documentation and procedure will examine further this question in the light of the views expressed and submit a report without delay.

The Security Council will consider further this question.

APPENDIX XII (e)

SECURITY COUNCIL PRESIDENTIAL STATEMENT

S/PRST/1996/13 Strengthening consultation procedures with troop-contributing countries

Date: 28 March 1996 Meeting: 3645

The Security Council has reviewed the arrangements for consultation and exchange of information with troop-contributing countries, which were established by the statement of its President made on behalf of the Council on 4 November 1994 (S/PRST/1994/62). The Council has given careful consideration to the views expressed on this question in its debate under the item 'An Agenda for Peace: Peace-keeping' in its 3611th meeting on 20 December 1995, as well as to the views expressed in debates in the General Assembly.

The Security Council has noted the wish expressed in these debates that arrangements for consultation and exchange of information with troop-contributing countries should be improved. The Council shares this wish. It considers it essential for troop-contributing countries to be heard. It notes that many of the concerns expressed would be met if the arrangements set out in the statement of its President of 4 November 1994 were fully implemented. It is also of the view that those arrangements can be strengthened further as set forth below.

The Security Council will therefore follow in future the procedures here set out:

(a) Meetings will be held as a matter of course between members of the Council, troop-contributing countries and the Secretariat for the purpose of consultations and the exchange of information and views; the meetings will be chaired by the Presidency of the Council supported by a representative of the Secretariat;

(b) The meetings will be held as soon as practicable and in good time before the Council takes decisions on the extension or termination of, or significant changes in, the mandate of a particular peace-keeping operation;

(c) When the Council considers establishing a new peace-keeping operation, meetings will, unless it proves to be impracticable, be held with any prospective troop contributors who have already been approached by the Secretariat and who have indicated that they may be willing to contribute to the operation;

(d) The President of the Council will, in the course of informal consultations of members of the Council, report the views expressed by participants at each meeting with troop-contributing or prospective troop-contributing countries;

(e) The existing practice of inviting to these meetings Member States which make special contributions to peace-keeping operations other than troops—that is, contributions to trust funds, logistics and equipment—will continue;

(f) The monthly tentative forecast of work of the Council made available to Member States will include an indication of the expected schedule of such meetings for the month;

(g) Ad hoc meetings may be convened in the event of unforeseen developments in a particular peace-keeping operation which could require action by the Council;

(h) These meetings will be in addition to those convened and chaired by the Secretariat for troop contributors to meet with Special Representatives of the Secretary-General or Force Commanders, or to discuss operational matters concerning particular peace-keeping operations, to which members of the Security Council will also be invited;

(i) Background information and an agenda will be circulated by the Secretariat to the participants well in advance of each of the various meetings referred to above; members of the Council may also circulate information as appropriate;

(j) Interpretation services in all the official languages of the Organization will continue to be available; translation of written documents will continue to be available, if possible in advance of the meetings;

(k) The time and venue of each meeting should, where possible, appear in advance in the *Journal* of the United Nations;

(l) The Council will append to its annual report to the General Assembly information about these meetings.

The Security Council recalls that the arrangements described above are not exhaustive. They do not preclude consultations in a variety of forms, including informal communication between the Council President or its members and troop-contributing countries and, as appropriate, with other countries especially affected, for example, countries from the region concerned.

The Security Council will continue to keep arrangements for consultations and the exchange of information and views with troop contributors and prospective contributors under review and stands ready to consider further measures and new mechanisms to enhance further the arrangements in the light of experience.

APPENDIX XII (f)

SECURITY COUNCIL PRESIDENTIAL STATEMENT

S/PRST/1994/36 Stand-by arrangements for peace-keeping operations

Date: 27 July 1994 Meeting: 3408

The Security Council has considered the report of the Secretary-General of 30 June 1994 concerning stand-by arrangements for peace-keeping (S/1994/777), submitted pursuant to the statement by the President of the Council of 3 May 1994 (S/PRST/1994/22).

The Security Council reiterates the importance it attaches to improving the capacity of the United Nations for rapid deployment and reinforcement of peace-keeping operations. The recent history of United Nations peace-keeping operations demonstrates that such an effort is essential.

In this context, the Security Council is grateful for the efforts undertaken by the Secretary-General in respect of stand-by arrangements and welcomes the responses so far received from Member States. It also welcomes the intention of the Secretary-General to maintain a comprehensive database of the offers made, including the technical details of these offers.

The Security Council notes that one of the major limiting factors in the timely deployment of troops for United Nations peace-keeping is the lack of readily available equipment. It stresses the importance of urgently addressing the issue of availability of equipment both in the context of stand-by arrangements and more broadly.

The Security Council notes the Secretary-General's view that the commitments made so far do not yet cover adequately the spectrum of resources required to mount and execute future peace-keeping operations. It also notes that additional commitments are expected from other Member States. In this context, it welcomes the Secretary-General's call to those Member States which are not already doing so to participate in the arrangements.

The Security Council looks forward to a further and more comprehensive report on the progress of the stand-by arrangements initiative.

APPENDIX XII (g)

SECURITY COUNCIL PRESIDENTIAL STATEMENT

S/PRST/1995/61 Peace-keeping stand-by arrangements

Date: 19 December 1995 Meeting: 3609

The Security Council has noted with interest and appreciation the report of the Secretary-General of 10 November 1995 on stand-by arrangements for peace-keeping operations (S/1995/943). It recalls earlier statements by the President of the Security Council on this subject and strongly supports the efforts of the Secretary-General to enhance the capacity of the United Nations for the planning, rapid deployment and reinforcement and logistical support of peace-keeping operations.

The Security Council encourages Member States not yet doing so to participate in the stand-by arrangements. It invites them, and those States already participating in the arrangements, to provide information in as detailed a manner as possible on those elements which they are ready to make available to the United Nations. It also invites them to identify components, such as logistic support elements and sea/airlift resources, presently underrepresented in the arrangement. In this context the Security Council welcomes the initiative undertaken by the Secretariat for the creation of a stand-by Headquarters component within the Mission Planning Service of the Department of Peace-keeping Operations. The Security Council also joins with the Secretary-General in suggesting the establishment of partnerships between those troop-contributing countries that need equipment for units that may be provided to the United Nations and those Governments ready to provide such equipment and other support.

The Security Council looks forward to further reports from the Secretary-General on the progress of the stand-by arrangements initiative and undertakes to keep the matter under review.

APPENDIX XIII (a)

S/1995/234, 29 MARCH 1995

NOTE BY THE PRESIDENT OF THE SECURITY COUNCIL

1. Further to the notes by the President of the Security Council dated 30 June 1993 (S/26015), 27 July 1993 (S/26176), 31 August 1993 (S/26389), 29 November 1993 (S/26812), 28 February 1994 (S/1994/230) and 28 July 1994 (S/1994/896) concerning the Council's documentation and other procedural questions, the President of the Security Council wishes to state that all members of the Security Council have indicated their agreement with the following proposals:

The following improvements should be introduced to make the procedures of the Sanctions Committees more transparent:

—The practice of issuing press releases after meetings of the Committee should be increased;

—The Status of Communications lists under the 'No Objection' procedure prepared by the Secretariat should be made available to any delegation which wishes to have a copy;

—A list of all other decisions by each active Committee should be prepared by the Secretariat, on a regular basis, and be made available to any delegation which requests it;

—The annual report of the Security Council to the General Assembly should contain, in the Introduction, more information about each Committee than it does at present;

—An annual report to the Security Council should be prepared by each Committee, providing a concise indication of each Committee's activities;

—An effort should be made to expedite the preparation of the summary records of each Committee.

For the implementation of these measures, the existing procedures of the Committees should be respected.

Meetings of the Sanctions Committees should remain closed, as they are now, and the summary records of those meetings should continue to be distributed according to the existing pattern.

2. The members of the Council will continue their consideration of other suggestions concerning the Council's documentation and related matters.

APPENDIX XIII (b)

S/1995/438, 31 MAY 1995

Note by the President of the Security Council

1. Further to the note by the President of the Security Council dated 29 March 1995 (S/1995/234) concerning the Council's documentation and other procedural questions, the President of the Security Council wishes to state that all members of the Security Council have indicated their agreement with the following proposal:

> The practice of hearing comments by States and organizations concerned during closed meetings of the Sanctions Committees on issues arising from implementation of sanctions regimes imposed by the Security Council should be continued while respecting the existing procedures followed by such Committees.

2. The members of the Council will continue their consideration of other suggestions concerning the Council's documentation and related matters.

APPENDIX XIII (c)

S/1996/54, 24 JANUARY 1996

Note by the President of the Security Council

1. Further to the note by the President of the Security Council dated 31 May 1995 (S/1995/438) concerning the Council's documentation and other procedural questions, the President of the Security Council wishes to state that all members of the Security Council have indicated their agreement with the following proposals:

The following improvements should be introduced to make the procedures of the sanctions Committees more transparent:

> The Chairman of each Committee should give an oral briefing to interested Members of the United Nations after each meeting, in the same way as the President of the Security Council now gives oral briefings following informal consultations of Council members;
>
> The Chairman of each Committee should be asked to bring to the attention of its members and of the Members of the United Nations the improvements in procedures of the Committees which were agreed to by the members of the Council on 29 March and 31 May 1995 (see S/1995/234 and S/1995/438).

2. The members of the Council will continue their consideration of other suggestions concerning the Council's documentation and related matters.

APPENDIX XIV

Letter from the Permanent Members of the Security Council on the Humanitarian Aspects of Sanctions
S/1995/300, 13 April 1995

We have the honour to transmit to you the non-paper on the humanitarian impact of sanctions which has been agreed upon after consultations by China, France, the Russian Federation, the Untied Kingdom, and the Untied States.

ANNEX
HUMANITARIAN IMPACT OF SANCTIONS

The five permanent members emphasize the importance of the peaceful settlement of international disputes in accordance with the Charter of the United Nations. While recognizing the need to maintain the effectiveness of sanctions imposed in accordance with the Charter, further collective actions in the Security Council within the context of any future sanctions regime should be directed to minimize unintended adverse side-effects of sanctions on the most vulnerable segments of targeted countries. The structure and implementation of future sanctions regimes may vary according to the resource base of the targeted country. The relevant considerations include:

—To assess objectively the short- and long-term humanitarian consequences of sanctions in the context of the overall sanctions regime. The more information the Security Council and sanctions committees have on the humanitarian situation at any stage in existing or potential target countries, the better. In this respect, a coordinating role for the Department of Humanitarian Affairs would be welcomed. The Department should draw on the expertise and assistance of States, agencies, appropriate international bodies and non-governmental organizations, and report to sanctions committees. The committees could draw on those reports in making operational decisions and when necessary refer matters beyond their competence to the Security Council for decision (for example, recommendations which would require changes to Security Council resolutions).

—In case of emergencies or *force majeure* situations, the Security Council and/or the sanctions committees may review the application of sanctions and take appropriate actions.

—In reviewing sanctions in the Security Council, to give due regard to the humanitarian situation.

—To envisage in the sanctions regimes provision for all States, including targeted States, to allow unimpeded access to humanitarian aid. To elaborate measures aimed at discouraging the targeted States from impeding humanitarian aid and encouraging them to render their assistance in this respect.

—To ensure that procedures for consideration of humanitarian applications by sanctions committees are as expeditious as possible. The simplest possible authorization procedure should be developed in the case of essential humanitarian supplies—vital to the civilian population—with arrangements for monitoring by United Nations humanitarian agencies when it is necessary. Clearly defined categories of medical supplies and foodstuffs should be allowed to be supplied even without notification of relevant sanctions committees.

—To facilitate the expeditious process in the sanctions committees of applications from United Nations humanitarian agencies and the International Committee of the Red Cross.

—To pay particular attention to the improvement of the effectiveness of the sanctions committees by drawing on the experience and the work of different sanctions committees.

APPENDIX XV

S/1997/161, 26 FEBRUARY 1997

NOTE BY THE SECRETARY-GENERAL

1. At the 88th plenary meeting of its fifty-first session, on 17 December 1996, the General Assembly adopted resolution 51/208, entitled 'Implementation of the provisions of the Charter of the United Nations related to assistance to third States affected by the application of sanctions'.[1]

2. In paragraphs 1, 2 and 3 of the resolution, the General Assembly:

'1. *Underlines* the importance of consultations under Article 50 of the Charter of the United Nations, as early as possible, with third States which are or may be confronted with special economic problems arising from the carrying out of preventive or enforcement measures imposed by the Security Council under Chapter VII of the Charter and of early and regular assessments, as appropriate, of their impact on such States;

'2. *Invites* the Security Council to consider the establishment of further mechanisms or procedures, as appropriate, for such consultations with regard to a solution of those problems, including appropriate ways and means for increasing the effectiveness of its working methods and procedures applied in the consideration of the requests by the affected countries for assistance, in the context of Article 50 of the Charter;

'3. *Welcomes* the futher measures taken by the Security Council since the adoption of General Assembly resolution 50/51 and aimed at increasing the effectiveness and transparency of the sanctions committees, and strongly recommends that the Council continue its efforts further to enhance the functioning of those committees, to streamline their working procedures and to facilitate access to them by representatives of States which find themselves confronted with special economic problems arising from the carrying out of sanctions.'

[1] Not reproduced in the present document; for the full text, see A/RES/51/208.

APPENDIX XVI

SECURITY COUNCIL PRESIDENTIAL STATEMENT

S/PRST/1995/48 Fiftieth anniversary of United Nations

Date: 26 September 1995 Meeting: 3583

The Security Council has met on 26 September 1995, at the level of Foreign Ministers, to commemorate the Fiftieth Anniversary of the United Nations and to exchange views on the challenges which the Security Council faces.

Since its establishment the Security Council has played a crucial role in the maintenance of international peace and security on which development and cooperation among nations are based. The past few years in particular have been ones of momentous change, bringing fresh hope and new challenges. Operations mandated by the Council have assisted in the restoration of peace and stability to countries long-plagued by war. Although such operations have largely been successful, there are areas where success has not been achieved. The Council must continue to spare no effort in working for the maintenance of international peace and security, and build upon its experience of past and existing operations.

The Security Council recognizes that the challenges facing the international community demand a resolute response, based on the principles and purposes of the Charter of the United Nations. The members of the Security Council consider that the United Nations must be strengthened and revitalized to help meet these challenges. They take note of the conclusions of the Working Group of the General Assembly on the Question of Equitable Representation on and Increase in the Membership of the Security Council and other Matters Related to the Security Council, *inter alia*, that the Council should be expanded, and that its working methods should continue to be reviewed, in a way that further strengthens its capacity and effectiveness, enhances its representative character and improves its working efficiency and transparency; and that important differences on key issues continue to exist. The Council also believes that effective use should be made of instruments for preventive action, and the Organization's capacity to conduct effective peace-keeping operations should continue to be improved. The Council will continue to attach utmost importance to the safety and security of all who serve under the United Nations flag in the field.

The members of the Security Council reaffirm their commitment to the collective security system of the Charter. On the solemn occasion of the Fiftieth Anniversary of the United Nations, the Council, along with other United Nations bodies, commemorates what has been achieved so far, but also commits itself once again to the maintenance of international peace and security for which it has primary responsibility, and to working to save succeeding generations from the scourge of war.

APPENDIX XVII

SECURITY COUNCIL RESOLUTION 984 (1995) CONCERNING ASSURANCES TO NON-NUCLEAR WEAPONS STATES

S/RES/984 Assurances to non-nuclear weapon States

Date: 11 April 1995 Meeting: 3514 Vote: Unanimous

The Security Council,

Convinced that every effort must be made to avoid and avert the danger of nuclear war, to prevent the spread of nuclear weapons, to facilitate international cooperation in the peaceful uses of nuclear energy with particular emphasis on the needs of developing countries, and reaffirming the crucial importance of the Treaty on the Non-Proliferation of Nuclear Weapons to these efforts,

Recognizing the legitimate interest of non-nuclear-weapon States Parties to the Treaty on the Non-Proliferation of Nuclear Weapons to receive security assurances,

Welcoming the fact that more than 170 States have become Parties to the Treaty on the Non-Proliferation of Nuclear Weapons and stressing the desirability of universal adherence to it,

Reaffirming the need for all States Parties to the Treaty on the Non-Proliferation of Nuclear Weapons to comply fully with all their obligations,

Taking into consideration the legitimate concern of non-nuclear-weapon States that, in conjunction with their adherence to the Treaty on the Non-Proliferation of Nuclear Weapons, further appropriate measures be undertaken to safeguard their security,

Considering that the present resolution constitutes a step in this direction,

Considering further that, in accordance with the relevant provisions of the Charter of the United Nations, any aggression with the use of nuclear weapons would endanger international peace and security,

1. *Takes note* with appreciation of the statements made by each of the nuclear-weapon States (S/1995/261, S/1995/262, S/1995/263, S/1995/264, S/1995/265), in which they give security assurances against the use of nuclear weapons to non-nuclear-weapon States that are Parties to the Treaty on the Non-Proliferation of Nuclear Weapons;

2. *Recognizes* the legitimate interest of non-nuclear-weapon States Parties to the Treaty on the Non-Proliferation of Nuclear Weapons to receive assurances that the Security Council, and above all its nuclear-weapon State permanent members, will act immediately in accordance with the relevant provisions of the Charter of the United Nations, in the event that such States are the victim of an act of, or object of a threat of, aggression in which nuclear weapons are used;

3. *Recognizes further* that, in case of aggression with nuclear weapons or the threat of such aggression against a non-nuclear-weapon State Party to the Treaty on the Non-Proliferation of Nuclear Weapons, any State may bring the matter immediately to the attention of the Security Council to enable the Council to take urgent action to provide assistance, in accordance with the Charter, to the State victim of an act of, or object of a threat of, such aggression; and *recognizes also* that the nuclear-weapon State permanent members of the Security Council will bring the matter immediately to the attention of the Council and seek Council action to provide, in accordance with the Charter, the necessary assistance to the State victim;

4. *Notes* the means available to it for assisting such a non-nuclear-weapon State Party to the Treaty on the Non-Proliferation of Nuclear Weapons, including an investigation into the situation and appropriate measures to settle the dispute and restore international peace and security;

5. *Invites* Member States, individually or collectively, if any non-nuclear-weapon State Party to the Treaty on the Non-Proliferation of Nuclear Weapons is a victim of an act of aggression with nuclear weapons, to take appropriate measures in response to a request from the victim for technical, medical, scientific or humanitarian assistance, and affirms its readiness to consider what measures are needed in this regard in the event of such an act of aggression;

6. *Expresses* its intention to recommend appropriate procedures, in response to any request from a non-nuclear-weapon State Party to the Treaty on the Non-Proliferation of Nuclear Weapons that is the victim of such an act of aggression, regarding compensation under international law from the aggressor for loss, damage or injury sustained as a result of the aggression;

7. *Welcomes* the intention expressed by certain States that they will provide or support immediate assistance, in accordance with the Charter, to any non-nuclear-weapon State Party to the Treaty on the Non-Proliferation of Nuclear Weapons that is a victim of an act of, or an object of a threat of, aggression in which nuclear weapons are used;

8. *Urges* all States, as provided for in Article VI of the Treaty on the Non-Proliferation of Nuclear Weapons, to pursue negotiations in good

faith on effective measures relating to nuclear disarmament and on a treaty on general and complete disarmament under strict and effective international control which remains a universal goal;

9. *Reaffirms* the inherent right, recognized under Article 51 of the Charter, of individual and collective self-defence if an armed attack occurs against a member of the United Nations, until the Security Council has taken measures necessary to maintain international peace and security;

10. *Underlines* that the issues raised in this resolution remain of continuing concern to the Council.

APPENDIX XVIII

STATUTE OF THE INTERNATIONAL TRIBUNAL FOR RWANDA. ANNEX TO SECURITY COUNCIL RESOLUTION 955 (1994) OF 8 NOVEMBER 1994

Having been established by the Security Council acting under Chapter VII of the Charter of the United Nations, the International Criminal Tribunal for the Prosecution of Persons Responsible for Genocide and Other Serious Violations of International Humanitarian Law Committed in the Territory of Rwanda and Rwandan citizens responsible for genocide and other such violations committed in the territory of neighbouring States, between 1 January 1994 and 31 December 1994 (hereinafter referred to as 'the International Tribunal for Rwanda') shall function in accordance with the provisions of the present Statute.

Article 1

COMPETENCE OF THE INTERNATIONAL TRIBUNAL FOR RWANDA

The International Tribunal for Rwanda shall have the power to prosecute persons responsible for serious violations of international humanitarian law committed in the territory of Rwanda and Rwandan citizens responsible for such violations committed in the territory of neighbouring States, between 1 January 1994 and 31 December 1994, in accordance with the provisions of the present Statute.

Article 2

GENOCIDE

1. The International Tribunal for Rwanda shall have the power to prosecute persons committing genocide as defined in paragraph 2 of this article or of committing any of the other acts enumerated in paragraph 3 of this article.

2. Genocide means any of the following acts committed with intent to

destroy, in whole or in part, a national, ethnical, racial or religious group, as such:

(a) Killing members of the group;

(b) Causing serious bodily or mental harm to members of the group;

(c) Deliberately inflicting on the group conditions of life calculated to bring about its physical destruction in whole or in part;

(d) Imposing measures intended to prevent births within the group;

(e) Forcibly transferring children of the group to another group.

3. The following acts shall be punishable:

(a) Genocide;

(b) Conspiracy to commit genocide;

(c) Direct and public incitement to commit genocide;

(d) Attempt to commit genocide;

(e) Complicity in genocide.

Article 3

CRIMES AGAINST HUMANITY

The International Tribunal for Rwanda shall have the power to prosecute persons responsible for the following crimes when committed as part of a widespread or systematic attack against any civilian population on national, political, ethnic, racial or religious grounds:

(a) Murder;

(b) Extermination;

(c) Enslavement;

(d) Deportation;

(e) Imprisonment;

(f) Torture;

(g) Rape;

(h) Persecutions on political, racial and religious grounds;

(i) Other inhumane acts.

Article 4

VIOLATIONS OF ARTICLE 3 COMMON TO THE GENEVA CONVENTIONS AND OF ADDITIONAL PROTOCOL II

The International Tribunal for Rwanda shall have the power to prosecute persons committing or ordering to be committed serious violations of

Article 3 common to the Geneva Conventions of 12 August 1949 for the Protection of War Victims, and of Additional Protocol II thereto of 8 June 1977. These violations shall include, but shall not be limited to:

(a) Violence to life, health and physical or mental well-being of persons, in particular murder as well as cruel treatment such as torture, mutilation or any form of corporal punishment;

(b) Collective punishments;

(c) Taking of hostages;

(d) Acts of terrorism;

(e) Outrages upon personal dignity, in particular humiliating and degrading treatment, rape, enforced prostitution and any form of indecent assault;

(f) Pillage;

(g) The passing of sentences and the carrying out of executions without previous judgement pronounced by a regularly constituted court, affording all the judicial guarantees which are recognized as indispensable by civilized peoples;

(h) Threats to commit any of the foregoing acts.

Article 5

PERSONAL JURISDICTION

The International Tribunal for Rwanda shall have jurisdiction over natural persons pursuant to the provisions of the present Statute.

Article 6

INDIVIDUAL CRIMINAL RESPONSIBILITY

1. A person who planned, instigated, ordered, committed or otherwise aided and abetted in the planning, preparation or execution of a crime referred to in articles 2 to 4 of the present Statute, shall be individually responsible for the crime.

2. The official position of any accused person, whether as Head of State or Government or as a responsible Government official, shall not relieve such person of criminal responsibility nor mitigate punishment.

3. The fact that any of the acts referred to in articles 2 to 4 of the present Statute was committed by a subordinate does not relieve his or her superior of criminal responsibility if he or she knew or had reason to know that the subordinate was about to commit such acts or had done so and the

superior failed to take the necessary and reasonable measures to prevent such acts or to punish the perpetrators thereof.

4. The fact that an accused person acted pursuant to an order of a Government or of a superior shall not relieve him or her of criminal responsibility, but may be considered in mitigation of punishment if the International Tribunal for Rwanda determines that justice so requires.

Article 7

TERRITORIAL AND TEMPORAL JURISDICTION

The territorial jurisdiction of the International Tribunal for Rwanda shall extend to the territory of Rwanda including its land surface and airspace as well as to the territory of neighbouring States in respect of serious violations of international humanitarian law committed by Rwandan citizens. The temporal jurisdiction of the International Tribunal for Rwanda shall extend to a period beginning on 1 January 1994 and ending on 31 December 1994.

Article 8

CONCURRENT JURISDICTION

1. The International Tribunal for Rwanda and national courts shall have concurrent jurisdiction to prosecute persons for serious violations of international humanitarian law committed in the territory of Rwanda and Rwandan citizens for such violations committed in the territory of neighbouring States, between 1 January 1994 and 31 December 1994.

2. The International Tribunal for Rwanda shall have primacy over the national courts of all States. At any stage of the procedure, the International Tribunal for Rwanda may formally request national courts to defer to its competence in accordance with the present Statute and the Rules of Procedure and Evidence of the International Tribunal for Rwanda.

Article 9

NON BIS IN IDEM

1. No person shall be tried before a national court for acts constituting serious violations of international humanitarian law under the present Statute, for which he or she has already been tried by the International Tribunal for Rwanda.

2. A person who has been tried by a national court for acts constituting serious violations of international humanitarian law may be subsequently tried by the International Tribunal for Rwanda only if:

(a) The act for which he or she was tried was characterized as an ordinary crime; or

(b) The national court proceedings were not impartial or independent, were designed to shield the accused from international criminal responsibility, or the case was not diligently prosecuted.

3. In considering the penalty to be imposed on a person convicted of a crime under the present Statute, the International Tribunal for Rwanda shall take into account the extent to which any penalty imposed by a national court on the same person for the same act has already been served.

Article 10

ORGANIZATION OF THE INTERNATIONAL TRIBUNAL FOR RWANDA

The International Tribunal for Rwanda shall consist of the following organs:

(a) The Chambers, comprising two Trial Chambers and an Appeals Chamber;

(b) The Prosecutor; and

(c) A Registry.

Article 11

COMPOSITION OF THE CHAMBERS

The Chambers shall be composed of eleven independent judges, no two of whom may be nationals of the same State, who shall serve as follows:

(a) Three judges shall serve in each of the Trial Chambers;

(b) Five judges shall serve in the Appeals Chamber.

Article 12

QUALIFICATION AND ELECTION OF JUDGES

1. The judges shall be persons of high moral character, impartiality and integrity who possess the qualifications required in their respective countries

for appointment to the highest judicial offices. In the overall composition of the Chambers due account shall be taken of the experience of the judges in criminal law, international law, including international humanitarian law and human rights law.

2. The members of the Appeals Chamber of the International Tribunal for the Prosecution of Persons Responsible for Serious Violations of International Law Committed in the Territory of the Former Yugoslavia since 1991 (hereinafter referred to as 'the International Tribunal for the Former Yugoslavia') shall also serve as the members of the Appeals Chamber of the International Tribunal for Rwanda.

3. The judges of the Trial Chambers of the International Tribunal for Rwanda shall be elected by the General Assembly from a list submitted by the Security Council, in the following manner:

(a) The Secretary-General shall invite nominations for judges of the Trial Chambers from States Members of the United Nations and non-member States maintaining permanent observer missions at United Nations Headquarters;

(b) Within thirty days of the date of the invitation of the Secretary-General, each State may nominate up to two candidates meeting the qualifications set out in paragraph 1 above, no two of whom shall be of the same nationality and neither of whom shall be of the same nationality as any judge on the Appeals Chamber;

(c) The Secretary-General shall forward the nominations received to the Security Council. From the nominations received the Security Council shall establish a list of not less than twelve and not more than eighteen candidates, taking due account of adequate representation on the International Tribunal for Rwanda of the principal legal systems of the world;

(d) The President of the Security Council shall transmit the list of candidates to the President of the General Assembly. From that list the General Assembly shall elect the six judges of the Trial Chambers. The candidates who receive an absolute majority of the votes of the States Members of the United Nations and of the non-Member States maintaining permanent observer missions at United Nations Headquarters, shall be declared elected. Should two candidates of the same nationality obtain the required majority vote, the one who received the higher number of votes shall be considered elected.

4. In the event of a vacancy in the Trial Chambers, after consultation with the Presidents of the Security Council and of the General Assembly, the Secretary-General shall appoint a person meeting the qualifications of paragraph 1 above, for the remainder of the term of office concerned.

5. The judges of the Trial Chambers shall be elected for a term of four

years. The terms and conditions of service shall be those of the judges of the International Tribunal for the Former Yugoslavia. They shall be eligible for re-election.

Article 13

OFFICERS AND MEMBERS OF THE CHAMBERS

1. The judges of the International Tribunal for Rwanda shall elect a President.

2. After consultation with the judges of the International Tribunal for Rwanda, the President shall assign the judges to the Trial Chambers. A judge shall serve only in the Chamber to which he or she was assigned.

3. The judges of each Trial Chamber shall elect a Presiding Judge, who shall conduct all of the proceedings of that Trial Chamber as a whole.

Article 14

RULES OF PROCEDURE AND EVIDENCE

The judges of the International Tribunal for Rwanda shall adopt, for the purpose of proceedings before the International Tribunal for Rwanda, the rules of procedure and evidence for the conduct of the pre-trail phase of the proceedings, trials and appeals, the admission of evidence, the protection of victims and witnesses and other appropriate matters of the International Tribunal for the Former Yugoslavia with such changes as they deem necessary.

Article 15

THE PROSECUTOR

1. The Prosecutor shall be responsible for the investigation and prosecution of persons responsible for serious violations of international humanitarian law committed in the territory of Rwanda and Rwandan citizens responsible for such violations committed in the territory of neighbouring States, between 1 January 1994 and 31 December 1994.

2. The Prosecutor shall act independently as a separate organ of the International Tribunal for Rwanda. He or she shall not seek or receive instructions from any Government or from any other source.

3. The Prosecutor of the International Tribunal for the Former Yugoslavia shall also serve as the Prosecutor of the International Tribunal for Rwanda. He or she shall have additional staff, including an additional Deputy Prosecutor, to assist with prosecutions before the International Tribunal for Rwanda. Such staff shall be appointed by the Secretary-General on the recommendation of the Prosecutor.

Article 16

THE REGISTRY

1. The Registry shall be responsible for the administration and servicing of the International Tribunal for Rwanda.

2. The Registry shall consist of a Registrar and such other staff as may be required.

3. The Registrar shall be appointed by the Secretary-General after consultation with the President of the International Tribunal for Rwanda. He or she shall serve for a four-year term and be eligible for reappointment. The terms and conditions of service of the Registrar shall be those of an Assistant Secretary-General of the Untied Nations.

4. The staff of the Registry shall be appointed by the Secretary-General on the recommendation of the Registrar.

Article 17

INVESTIGATION AND PREPARATION OF INDICTMENT

1. The Prosecutor shall initiate investigations ex-officio or on the basis of information obtained from any source, particularly from Governments, United Nations organs, intergovernmental and non-governmental organizations. The Prosecutor shall assess the information received or obtained and decide whether there is sufficient basis to proceed.

2. The Prosecutor shall have the power to question suspects, victims and witnesses, to collect evidence and to conduct on-site investigations. In carrying out these tasks, the Prosecutor may, as appropriate, seek the assistance of the State authorities concerned.

3. If questioned, the suspect shall be entitled to be assisted by counsel of his or her own choice, including the right to have legal assistance assigned to the suspect without payment by him or her in any such case if he or she

does not have sufficient means to pay for it, as well as to necessary translation into and from a language he or she speaks and understands.

4. Upon a determination that a prima facie case exists, the Prosecutor shall prepare an indictment containing a concise statement of the facts and the crime or crimes with which the accused is charged under the Statute. The indictment shall be transmitted to a judge of the Trial Chamber.

Article 18

REVIEW OF THE INDICTMENT

1. The judge of the Trial Chamber to whom the indictment has been transmitted shall review it. If satisfied that a prima facie case has been established by the Prosecutor, he or she shall confirm the indictment. If not so satisfied, the indictment shall be dismissed.

2. Upon confirmation of an indictment, the judge may, at the request of the Prosecutor, issue such orders and warrants for the arrest, detention, surrender or transfer of persons and any other orders as may be required for the conduct of the trial.

Article 19

COMMENCEMENT AND CONDUCT OF TRIAL PROCEEDINGS

1. The Trial Chambers shall ensure that a trial is fair and expeditious and that proceedings are conducted in accordance with the rules of procedure and evidence, with full respect for the rights of the accused and due regard for the protection of victims and witnesses.

2. A person against whom an indictment has been confirmed shall, pursuant to an order or an arrest warrant of the International Tribunal for Rwanda, be taken into custody, immediately informed of the charges against him or her and transferred to the International Tribunal for Rwanda.

3. The Trial Chamber shall read the indictment, satisfy itself that the rights of the accused are respected, confirm that the accused understands the indictment, and instruct the accused to enter a plea. The Trial Chamber shall then set the date for trial.

4. The hearings shall be public unless the Trial Chamber decides to close the proceedings in accordance with its rules of procedure and evidence.

Article 20

RIGHTS OF THE ACCUSED

1. All persons shall be equal before the International Tribunal for Rwanda.

2. In the determination of charges against him or her, the accused shall be entitled to a fair and public hearing, subject to article 21 of the Statute.

3. The accused shall be presumed innocent until proved guilty according to the provisions of the present Statute.

4. In the determination of any charge against the accused pursuant to the present Statute, the accused shall be entitled to the following minimum guarantees, in full equality:

(a) To be informed promptly and in detail in a language which he or she understands of the nature and cause of the charge against him or her;

(b) To have adequate time and facilities for the preparation of his or her defence and to communicate with counsel of his or her own choosing;

(c) To be tried without undue delay;

(d) To be tried in his or her presence, and to defend himself or herself in person or through legal assistance of his or her own choosing; to be informed, if he or she does not have legal assistance, of this right; and to have legal assistance assigned to him or her, in any case where the interests of justice so require, and without payment by him or her in any such case if he or she does not have sufficient means to pay for it;

(e) To examine, or have examined, the witnesses against him or her and to obtain the attendance and examination of witnesses on his or her behalf under the same conditions as witnesses against him or her;

(f) To have the free assistance of an interpreter if he or she cannot understand or speak the language used in the International Tribunal for Rwanda;

(g) Not to be compelled to testify against himself or herself or to confess guilt.

Article 21

PROTECTION OF VICTIMS AND WITNESSES

The International Tribunal for Rwanda shall provide in its rules of procedure and evidence for the protection of victims and witnesses. Such protection measures shall include, but shall not be limited to, the conduct of in camera proceedings and the protection of the victim's identity.

Article 22

JUDGEMENT

1. The Trial Chambers shall pronounce judgements and impose sentences and penalties on persons convicted of serious violations of international humanitarian law.

2. The judgement shall be rendered by a majority of the judges of the Trial Chamber, and shall be delivered by the Trial Chamber in public. It shall be accompanied by a reasoned opinion in writing, to which separate or dissenting opinions may be appended.

Article 23

PENALTIES

1. The penalty imposed by the Trial Chamber shall be limited to imprisonment. In determining the terms of imprisonment, the Trial Chambers shall have recourse to the general practice regarding prison sentences in the courts of Rwanda.

2. In imposing the sentences, the Trial Chambers should take into account such factors as the gravity of the offence and the individual circumstances of the convicted person.

3. In addition to imprisonment, the Trial Chambers may order the return of any property and proceeds acquired by criminal conduct, including by means of duress, to their rightful owners.

Article 24

APPELLATE PROCEEDINGS

1. The Appeals Chamber shall hear appeals from persons convicted by the Trial Chambers or from the Prosecutor on the following grounds:

(a) An error on a question of law invalidating the decision; or

(b) An error of fact which has occasioned a miscarriage of justice.

2. The Appeals Chamber may affirm, reverse or revise the decisions taken by the Trial Chambers.

Article 25

REVIEW PROCEEDINGS

Where a new fact has been discovered which was not known at the time of the proceedings before the Trial Chambers or the Appeals Chamber and which could have been a decisive factor in reaching the decision, the convicted person or the Prosecutor may submit to the International Tribunal for Rwanda an application for review of the judgement.

Article 26

ENFORCEMENT OF SENTENCES

Imprisonment shall be served in Rwanda or any of the States on a list of States which have indicated to the Security Council their willingness to accept convicted persons, as designated by the International Tribunal for Rwanda. Such imprisonment shall be in accordance with the applicable law of the State concerned, subject to the supervision of the International Tribunal for Rwanda.

Article 27

PARDON OR COMMUTATION OF SENTENCES

If, pursuant to the applicable law of the State in which the convicted person is imprisoned, he or she is eligible for pardon or commutation of sentence, the State concerned shall notify the International Tribunal for Rwanda accordingly. There shall only be pardon or commutation of sentence if the President of the International Tribunal for Rwanda, in consultation with the judges, so decides on the basis of the interests of justice and the general principles of law.

Article 28

COOPERATION AND JUDICIAL ASSISTANCE

1. States shall cooperate with the International Tribunal for Rwanda in the investigation and prosecution of persons accused of committing serious violations of international humanitarian law.

2. States shall comply without undue delay with any request for assistance or an order issued by a Trial Chamber, including, but not limited to:

(a) The identification and location of persons;

(b) The taking of testimony and the production of evidence;

(c) The service of documents;

(d) The arrest or detention of persons;

(e) The surrender or the transfer of the accused to the International Tribunal for Rwanda.

Article 29

THE STATUS, PRIVILEGES AND IMMUNITIES OF THE INTERNATIONAL TRIBUNAL FOR RWANDA

1. The Convention on the Privileges and Immunities of the United Nations of 13 February 1946 shall apply to the International Tribunal for Rwanda, the judges, the Prosecutor and his or her staff, and the Registrar and his or her staff.

2. The judges, the Prosecutor and the Registrar shall enjoy the privileges and immunities, exemptions and facilities accorded to diplomatic enjoys, in accordance with international law.

3. The staff of the Prosecutor and of the Registrar shall enjoy the privileges and immunities accorded to officials of the United Nations under articles V and VII of the Convention referred to in paragraph 1 of this article.

4. Other persons, including the accused, required at the seat or meeting place of the International Tribunal for Rwanda shall be accorded such treatment as is necessary for the proper functioning of the International Tribunal for Rwanda.

Article 30

EXPENSES OF THE INTERNATIONAL TRIBUNAL FOR RWANDA

The expenses of the International Tribunal for Rwanda shall be expenses of the Organization in accordance with Article 17 of the Charter of the United Nations.

Article 31

WORKING LANGUAGES

The working languages of the International Tribunal shall be English and French.

Article 32

ANNUAL REPORT

The President of the International Tribunal for Rwanda shall submit an annual report of the International Tribunal for Rwanda to the Security Council and to the General Assembly.

APPENDIX XIX

THE FIRST SYDNEY BAILEY MEMORIAL LECTURE. ADDRESS GIVEN BY HIS ROYAL HIGHNESS CROWN PRINCE HASSAN BIN TALAL OF THE HASHEMITE KINGDOM OF JORDAN AT WESTMINSTER ABBEY, LONDON, 10 MARCH 1997

SCIENCE, FAITH AND PEACE

HASSAN BIN TALAL

It is hard to know where to begin in speaking about Sydney Bailey. The sheer breadth of his interests, and the profound depth of his knowledge, make it impossible to pay full tribute to his achievements. The huge range of his publications defies any easy summary.

This was, after all, a man who wrote some twenty books, several of which broke fresh ground in their fields. His knowledge of constitutional and international institutions and issues was unmatched. In what many regard as his greatest work, *How Wars End*, Sydney Bailey established connections between armed conflict and human rights issues which had never been made before. The phenomenal thoroughness of his scholarship was thus matched only by its diversity.

But I believe that there was a single uniting theme behind this bewildering diversity. This was his unshakeable belief in peace, which was itself underpinned by his faith. As he once wrote,

> Peace begins within ourselves. It is to be implemented within the family, in our meetings, in our work and leisure, in our own localities, and internationally.

At every level of his multi-faceted life, then, Sydney Bailey believed passionately in the idea of peace.

He was not just a theoretician of peace; he was a practitioner. He was a pragmatist who understood better than anyone I have met the difficulties and complexities of peace.

My own friendship with him was forged in the heat of the Gulf crisis of 1990–91. During those difficult and dangerous months, Sydney's was a voice of calm reason. As the calls for confrontation grew ever more strident, as the passions of war swelled across the world, voices such as his grew increasingly rare.

But as a great flood of human suffering streamed from and through the Middle East, the world was given ample evidence, if any were needed, that his was the only sane, the only viable, the only human and humane way to think and to act in the cauldron of conflict.

I therefore thought it appropriate that a memorial lecture for Sydney Bailey should explore this idea of peace; this inspirational idea which, I believe, motivated all that he did. I would like to start by enquiring into the meaning of peace. I would then like to survey some trends in the recent past. Finally, I would like to make some suggestions about the prospects for peace in the new millennium.

Some may think that the meaning of peace is self-evident. Peace is the opposite of war, is it not? On this view, in the absence of war, there must be peace.

But this is a shallow definition which does little to advance our understanding. I think of my own region, the Middle East. For the last half-century between relatively brief outbreaks of war, my region has existed in an uneasy, shadowy state. For long periods of time, there was no formal state of war; armies did not fight one another. But tension and hostility were ever-present. Both sides perceived the other as a hostile enemy. This was not a state of war, but by no means could it be described as a state of peace.

Perhaps we would do better, then, to define peace in a positive way. On this view, peace means more than the absence of war: it means the presence of justice. It means mutual respect; it means compassion and humility, tolerance and empathy. I think here of a recent survey which found that the sense of humiliation was a principal cause of the Palestinian *intifada*. Wherever our sense of human dignity is affronted, there can be no true peace.

Peace therefore means acknowledging that others have a valid viewpoint, and a self-validating sense of history, and a pain within their souls as deep as our own.

I have used the term 'the anthropology of suffering' to suggest that we must learn about, know and feel each other's pain if we are to avoid increasing it. This, to my mind, is the key to release from sequential historical grievances, to forgiveness if not forgetfulness, and to new beginnings.

Only if we truly comprehend what suffering means can we begin to overcome it. For such is the nature of redemption.

But peace, seen in this light, is not some destination, some final end which we can achieve, the conclusion of a linear process. It is, rather, a way of doing things that must permeate everything we do.

Sydney Bailey said, 'Peace is a process to engage in, not a goal to be reached.' He believed, as I believe, that peace is an ongoing commitment. It is something that must be built up and maintained, and not something that can just be made at the stroke of a pen and then forgotten.

As we might imagine, peace of this kind is rare in any historical period. But the twentieth century has been a particularly bad time for peace, however it is defined. This has been the bloodiest hundred years ever recorded. In our century alone, around 200 million people have been killed or allowed by human decision to perish. That is more than the entire human population has been for most of our history.

We could divide this murderous century into three periods. The first, which stretched until the mid-1940s, was one of great catastrophes. Two World Wars and an international economic crisis took a terrible toll on nations and individuals alike.

The second period, the era of the cold war, was one of fundamental instability and terror. Although parts of the world experienced prosperity amid rapid technological and cultural transformation, most of humanity did not. And the shadow of destruction hung over us all.

The final period began in 1989 with the fall of the Berlin Wall, which heralded the collapse of the Soviet Union. Many commentators believed this would be a golden age, in which the spectres of war and poverty would forever be eliminated. There was much talk of a 'New World Order', and a new code of conduct for relations between people and states.

And yet these years have been the most dangerous of all. For these are the years in which we have witnessed the emergence of new and disturbing phenomena: fear of peace, and fear of the future.

Indeed, I have just come from Amman, where I addressed a workshop on this very theme, attended by both Arabs and Israelis. Sydney Bailey would, I think, have approved of this approach as making a positive contribution to peace in itself. For such fears can only really be addessed when they are out in the open.

Not just in the Middle East, but all over the world, we can observe symptoms of the fear of peace, and the fear of the future. A kind of pre-millennium tension pervades popular discourse. The single and familiar fear of nuclear annihilation has been replaced by an entire spectrum of new and unfamiliar—or long-forgotten—dangers. We have already seen nations break down amid appalling bloodshed and hatred, neighbour raping and slaughtering neighbour, in the name of some atavistic ideal of racial purity. We have already seen the world stand idle while human beings lose everything: their homes, their livelihoods, their very lives.

The gap between rich and poor is wider than ever. One fifth of the world's population now lives in extreme poverty, while almost a third of our children are undernourished. And yet development is impeded by 'donor fatigue'.

It is perhaps unsurprising, then, that we should encounter a curious kind of nostalgia for bygone eras; eras when the world was divided into neat camps, and everyone knew where the boundaries were. Today there are no boundaries, and we are unsure what to do in their absence. The cold war is over, but this is not the state of global peace that we had envisaged. Something fundamental is lacking.

The twentieth century has been marked by the relentless quest for novelty, and the hope of open-ended progress. Its central vehicle and metaphor has been science. With science, with a scientific and rational approach to all things, we believed we could master the world.

But we who stand at the end of the twentieth century have been obliged to accept the existence of limits. Limits to the ability of science to describe, let alone improve or master the world. Limits to the capacity of governments and markets to solve social problems. Limits to the power of amoral reason to control human passion and prejudice.

Beyond these limits lies something greater and inconceivably more sophisticated than human intellect. And it is, ironically, science itself that has brought us to the verge of comprehension.

For science has now arrived at the understanding that nature is an interconnected, interdependent whole. Humanity could not exist apart from it. Where once we styled ourselves masters of nature, we must now acknowledge that we are but a part of it.

Science tells us that galaxies and quantum particles alike are best seen not as discrete entities possessing certain fixed qualities, but as aspects of a fluid field of existence. In both the macrocosm and the microcosm, everything that exists is part of the infinitely complex network of creation, in which everything is fundamentally related to everything else. And as part of this network, the very same holds true of human beings, and of our constructs: societies, nations, states. We are, by definition, our relationships.

From the certainties of the mechanical Newtonian–Cartesian universe, we now find ourselves in a universe where Relativity, Uncertainty and Chaos are the leading theories. At this point, science seems, like the serpent, to be devouring its own tail.

But from this morass emerge clear principles of interconnection and interdependence. What does this mean for human behaviour? What does this mean for peace?

If interdependence arising from interconnection is the underlying principle of the world, then each person stands at the centre of a triangle of relationships: human to human, human to nature and human to God.

The violation of peace begins when we hold the self to be more important than anything else; when we hold the centre of the triangle to be greater than its sides. When our horizon has shrunk to the point where we can only see our own shadows, we have lost the ability to live in true peace. And so begin the conflicts: human against human, human against nature, human against God.

Another great champion of peace, the Czech playwright and President Vaclav Havel, has written:

> We must recognize that we are related to more than the present moment, the present place, that we are related to the world as a whole and to eternity. We must recognize that by failing to reflect universal, superindividual and supertemporal interests, we do a disservice to our specific, local and immediate interests. Only people with a sense of responsibility for the world and to the world are truly responsible to and for themselves.

There now exists a unique opportunity for a quantum leap, a paradigm shift, in favour of peace. For these understandings are prefigured in our spiritual traditions and are now confirmed by science. They thus enjoy a powerful dual authority. When they spread through our societies, the differences between our traditions, our ideologies and our histories will seem far less significant than our fellowship.

Most religious traditions contain a golden rule: 'love your neighbour as yourself'. Now we must understand that our neighbour, in a very real way, is ourself.

When we grasp this insight, it becomes very difficult to hate our neighbour. Indeed, it becomes both possible and necessary to live in peace—not just the absence of war, but true peace.

And it may be that our fear of peace, and our fear of the future, will prove to be an asset, and not a handicap, in the search for peace, and the quest for a better future. For as I said earlier, only if we truly comprehend what suffering means can we begin to overcome it. Fear of the future could be exactly what we need to bring about a better future.

Sydney Bailey wrote,

> Reconciliation . . . is not about ideologies or beliefs but about people, their relationship and response to God, and their relationship and response to each other.

In ideas such as these lie our best hopes for peace in the new millennium.

SELECT BIBLIOGRAPHY

BAILEY, SYDNEY, D., *Voting in the Security Council*, Indiana University Press, Bloomington & London, 1969.

—— 'New Light on Abstentions in the UN Security Council', *International Affairs*, 50, no. 4 (Oct. 1974), pp. 554–73.

—— 'The UN Security Council: Evolving Practice', *World Today*, 34, no. 3 (Mar. 1978), pp. 100–6.

—— *How Wars End*, Clarendon Press, Oxford, 1982 (2 vols.).

—— *The UN Security Council and Human Rights*, Macmillan Press, 1994.

—— and DAWS, SAM, *The United Nations: A Concise Political Guide*, Macmillan Press, 1995.

BATRA, TARLOK SINGH, *UN Security Council: Snapping the Snare*, Metropolitan, New Delhi, 1977.

—— 'The Veto Power of the Security Council' *Indian Journal of International Law*, 18 (Jan.–March 1978), pp. 76–83.

BEDJAOUI, MOHAMMED, *The New World Order and the Security Council—Testing the Legality of its Acts*, Martinus Nijhoff Publishers, 1994.

BENNETT, A. LEROY, 'The Rejuvenation of the Security Council—Evidence and Reality', *Midwest Journal of Political Science*, 9 (1965), pp. 361–75.

BOYD, ANDREW, *Fifteen Men on a Powder Keg*, Methuen, London, 1971.

BRAND, RONALD A., 'Security Council Resolutions: When Do They Give Rise to Enforceable Legal Rights?' *Cornell International Law Journal*, 9 (May 1976), pp. 298–316.

CARON, DAVID D. 'The Legitimacy of the Collective Authority of the Security Council', *American Journal of International Law*, vol. 87:552 (1993), pp. 552–88.

CHAI, F. Y., *Consultation and Consensus in the Security Council*, UN Institute for Training and Research, New York and Geneva, 1971.

CLAUDE, INIS L., jun., 'The Security Council', in *The Evolution of International Organization*, ed. Evan Luard, Thames and Hudson, London, 1966, pp. 68–91.

CONFORTI, BENEDETTO, 'The Legal Effect of Non-Compliance with Rules of Procedure in the UN General Assembly and Security Council', *American Journal of International Law*, 63 (1969), pp. 479–89.

DUPUY, RENÉ-JEAN, *Le Développement du Rôle du Conseil de Sécurité*, Martinus Nijhoff Publishers, 1993.

FEUERLE, LOIE, 'Informal Consultation: A Mechanism in Security Council

Decision-Making', *New York University Journal of International Law and Politics*, 18 (1) fall (1985), pp. 267–308.

GILMOUR, DAVID R, 'Article 2(7) of the United Nations Charter and the Practice of the Permanent Members of the Security Council', *Australian Yearbook of International Law*, Butterworth, London, 1970, pp. 153–210.

GOODRICH, LELAND M., 'The UN Security Council', *International Organization*, no. 3 (1958), pp. 273–87.

—— and HAMBRO, EDVARD, *Charter of the United Nations: Commentary and Documents*, 3rd edn., World Peace Foundation, Boston, 1969.

—— and SIMONS, ANNE P. *The United Nations and the Maintenance of International Peace and Security*, Brookings Institution, Washington DC, 1955.

GREEN, L. C., Representation in the Security Council—A Survey', *Indian Year Book of International Affairs*, University of Madras, 1962, pp. 48–75.

GROSS, LEO, 'Voting in the Security Council: Abstention from Voting and Absence from Meetings', *Yale Law Journal*, 60 (1951), pp. 209–57.

—— 'The Double Veto and the Four-Power Statement on Voting in the Security Council', *Harvard Law Review*, 67 (1953), pp. 251–80.

—— 'The Question of Laos and the Double Veto in the Security Council', *American Journal of International Law*, 54 (1960), p. 118–31.

—— 'Voting in the Security Council and the PLO', *American Journal of International Law*, 70 (Dec. 1976), pp. 470–91.

HIGGINS, ROSAYLN, 'The Place of International Law in the Settlement of Disputes in the Security Council', *American Journal of International Law*, 64, no. 1 (1970), pp. 1–18.

HISCOCKS, RICHARD, The Security Council: A Study in Adolescence, Longman, London, 1973.

JIMÉNEZ DE ARÉCHAGA, EDUARDO, *Voting and the Handling of Disputes in the Security Council*, Carnegie Endowment for International Peace, New York, 1950.

JUNN, R. S., and PARK, T. W., 'Calculus for Voting Power in the UN Security Council', *Social Science Quarterly*, 58 (June 1977), pp. 104–10.

KAHNG, TAE JIN, *Law, Politics, and the Security Council*, Nijhoff, The Hague, 1964.

KELSEN, HANS, 'Organization and Procedure of the Security Council of the United Nations', *Harvard Law Review*, 59 (1946), pp. 1087–121.

—— *The Law of the United Nations*, Praeger, New York; Stevens, London, 1951.

KOO, WELLINGTON, jun., *Voting Procedures in International Political*

Organizations, Columbia University Press, New York; Oxford University Press, London, 1947.

KUYPER, P. J., 'The Limits of Supervision: The Security Council Watchdog Committee on Rhodesian Sanctions', *Netherlands International Law Review*, 25, no. 2 (1978), pp. 159–94.

LALL, ARTHUR, *The Security Council in a Universal United Nations*, Carnegie Endowment for International Peace, New York, 1971.

LEE, DWIGHT E., 'The Genesis of the Veto', *International Organization*, (1947), pp. 33–42.

LIANG, YUEN-LI, 'Abstention and Absence of a Permanent Member in Relation to the Voting Procedure in the Security Council', *American Journal of International Law*, 44 (1950), pp. 694–708.

LIE, TRYGVE, *In the Cause of Peace*, Macmillan, New York, 1954.

MURTI, B. S. N., 'Periodic Meetings of the Security Council: Article 28, paragraph 2 of the UN Charter', *Indian Journal of International Law*, (1970), pp. 283–99.

NICHOL, DAVIDSON (ed.), *Paths to Peace: The UN Security Council and its Presidency*, Pergamon, Oxford and New York, 1981.

—— with MARGARET CROKE and BABATUNDE ADENTRAN, *The United Nations Security Council: Towards Greater Effectiveness*, UN Institute for Training and Research, New York, 1982.

PADELFORD, NORMAN J.,'The Use of the Veto', *International Organization*, 2 (1948), pp. 227–46.

—— 'Politics and Change in the Security Council', *International Organization*, 14, no. 3 (1960), pp. 381–401.

PARSONS, ANTHONY, *From Cold War to Hot Peace: UN Interventions, 1947–1994*, London, Michael Joseph, 1995.

PETERSEN, KEITH S., 'The Business of the United Nations Security Council: History (1946–1963) and Prospects', *Journal of Politics*, 27 (1965), pp. 818–38.

PRANDLER, ARPAD, 'Rules of Procedure of the Security Council', *Questions of International Law*, Hungarian Branch of the International Law Association, Budapest, 1971, pp. 47–78.

—— 'The Security Council and International Law', *Acta Juridica*, 16 (1974), pp. 177–92.

PRZTACZNIK, FRANCISZEK, 'The Double Veto of the Security Council of the United Nations: A New Appraisal', *Revue de droit international de science diplomatiques et politiques*, 58 (July–Sept. 1980), pp. 153–81.

QURESHI, MOEEN, and VON WEIZSÄCKER, RICHARD, *The United Nations in its Second Half Century*, Ford Foundation/Yale University, 1995.

REISMAN, W. M., 'Case of the Non-permanent Vacancy', *American Journal of International Law*, 74, no. 4 (1980), pp. 907–13.

ROBERTS, ADAM, and KINGSBURY, BENEDICT, *United Nations, Divided World*, Oxford University Press, 2nd edn. 1993.

RUDZINSKI, ALEXANDER W., 'The So-Called Double Veto', *American Journal of International Law*, 45 (1951), pp. 443–61.

RUSSELL, RUTH B., assisted by Muther, Jeanette E., *A History of the United Nations Charter*, Brookings Institution, Washington DC; Faber, London, 1958.

RUSSETT, BRUCE, *The Once and Future Security Council*, New York, St Martin's Press, 1997.

—— and SUTTERLIN, JAMES S., 'The UN in a New World Order', *Foreign Affairs*, 70 (2), (spring 1991), pp. 69–83.

SCHACHTER, OSCAR, 'The Quasi-Judicial Role of the Security Council and the General Assembly', *American Journal of International Law*, 58, no. 4 (1964), pp. 959–66.

SIMMA, BRUNO (ed.), *The Charter of the United Nations: A Commentary,* Oxford, Oxford University Press, 1994.

SOHN, LOUIS B., 'The Security Council's Role in the Settlement of International Disputes', *American Journal of International Law*, 78, no. 2 (1984), pp. 402–4.

SONNENFELD, RENATA, 'The Obligation of UN Member-States "to Accept and Carry Out the Decisions of the Security Council" ', *Polish Yearbook of International Law*, 8 (1976), pp. 129–54.

STAVROPOLOUS, CONSTANTIN A., 'The Practice of Voluntary Abstentions by Permanent Members of the Security Council under Article 27 Paragraph 3 of the Charter of the United Nations', *American Journal of International Law*, 61 (July 1967).

SUBBARAO, M. V., *The Use of the Veto in Relation to Pacific Settlement of Disputes in the Security Council of the United Nations, 1946–1965*, New Heights, Delhi, 1976.

TAYLOR, P., DAWS, S., and ADAMCZICK-GERTEIS, U., *Documents on Reform of the United Nations*, Dartmouth, 1997.

TEJA, JASKARAN S., 'Expansion of the Security Council and its Consensus Procedure', *Nederlands Tijdschrift voor International Recht*, 16, no. 4 (1969), pp. 349–63.

THANT, U [MAUNG], *View from the UN*, David & Charles, London, 1978.

TIEWUL, S. AZADON, 'Namibia and the Unanimity Principle in the Security Council: Is an Abstention a Concurring Vote?', *University of Ghana Law Journal*, 11 (1974), pp. 20–42.

—— 'Binding Decisions of the Security Council within the Meaning of Art.

25 of the UN Charter', *Indian Journal of International Law*, 15 (1976), pp. 195–215.

TODD, J. B., 'An Analysis of Security Council Voting Behaviour', *Western Political Quarterly*, 22 (1969), pp. 61–78.

UDECHUKU, E. C., 'The Problem of the Veto in the Security Council', *International Relations*, 4 (1972), pp. 187–217.

UNITED NATIONS, *Handbook on the Peaceful Settlement of Disputes between States*, UN, New York, 1992.

URQUHART, BRIAN, *Hammarskjöld*, Bodley Head, London, 1972.

—— *A Life in Peace and War*, Weidenfeld & Nicholson, London, 1987.

VALLAT, FRANCIS, 'The General Assembly and the Security Council of the United Nations', *British Yearbook of International Law*, pp. 63–104, Oxford University Press (under the auspices of the Royal Institute of International Affairs), New York, 1953.

WALDHEIM, KURT, *In the Eye of the Storm*, Weidenfeld & Nicholson, London, 1985.

WERNERS, S. E., *The Presiding Officers of the United Nations*, Bohn, Haarlem, 1967.

WILCOX, FRANCIS, 'The Rule of Unanimity in the Security Council', *Proceedings of the American Society of International Law*, 1946, pp. 51–83.

WOOD, MICHAEL C., 'Security Council Working Methods and Procedure: Recent Developments', *The International and Comparative Law Quarterly*, vol. 45 (Jan. 1996), pp. 150–61.

REFERENCES

for pp. 1–9
CHAPTER 1

1. PC/20, 23 Dec. 1945, pp. 24–7; SCOR, 1st year, 1st series, 1st mtg (17 Jan, 1946), pp. 1–2.
2. Preamble and Arts. 1.1, 2.3, 2.6, 11.1, 11.2, 11.3, 12.2, 18.2, 23.1, 24.1, 26, 33.1, 34, 37.2, 42, 43.1, 47.1 48.1, 51, 52.1, 54, 73, 73c, 76a, 84, 106.
3. Preamble and Arts. 1.2, 13.1b, 55c, 62.2, 68, 76c.
4. GAOR, 27th Session, Supplement no. 1A, A/8701/Add.1, pp. 1–2.
5. See, for example, U Thant's speech on 28 Oct. 1969, printed in *UN Monthly Chronicle*, 6, no. 10 (Nov. 1969), p. 85.
6. A/RES/50/52, 15 December 1995.
7. Hearings before the Committee on Foreign Relations, United States Senate: submission of the Vietnam Conflict to the United Nations, 90th Congress, first session, 26 Oct. 1967, p. 50.
8. Robert E. Riggs, 'Overselling the UN Charter—Fact and Myth', *International Organization,* vol. 14, no. 2 (spring 1960), pp. 277–90.
9. *The Papers of Adlai E. Stevenson, vol. ii, 1941–1948*, ed. Walter Johnson and Carol Evans, Boston, Mass., Little Brown, 1973 (hereafter cited as 'Stevenson') pp. 306–8.
10. Foreign Relations of the United States, 1946, 1, Washington DC, Government Printing Office, 1972, pp. 314, 342, 352; ibid. 1947, 1973, p. 69; Paul-Henri Spaak, *The Continuing Battle*, trans. Ray Steding and Henry Fox, London, Weidenfeld & Nicolson, 1971, p. 109.
11. Sydney D. Bailey, *Peace is a Process*, London, Quaker Home Service and Woodbrooke College (Swarthmore Lecture). 1993, p. 173.
12. SCOR, 9th meeting (6 Feb. 1946), p. 148.
13. Sydney D. Bailey *The General Assembly of the United Nations*, 2nd edn., reprint, 1978, New York and London, Greenwood, p. 111.
14. Elcott Reid, *On Duty: A Canadian at the Making of the United Nations, 1945-46*, Ohio, Kent State University Press, 1983, p. 143.
15. SCOR, 9th meeting (6 Feb. 1946) p. 143.
16. Arpad Prandler, 'Rules of Procedure of the Security Council', *Questions of International Law*, Budapest, Hungarian Branch of the International Law Association, 1971, p. 147.

17. A/9128, 25 Oct. 1973 (mimeo.), pp. 3–4.
18. See Benedetto Conforti, 'The Legal Effect of Non-compliance with the Rules of Procedure of the UN General Assembly and Security Council', *American Journal of International Law*, 63 (July 1969) pp. 479–89.
19. PC/EX/113/Rev.1, 12 Nov. 1945, p. 45; see also SCOR, first year, first series, Supplement no. 2, p. 42, S/88.
20. PC/20, 23 Dec. 1945, pp. 25–7.
21. Ibid. pp. 125–9.
22. SCOR, 1st meeting (17 Jan. 1946), p. 11
23. Ibid., Supplement no. 2, pp. 1–8. S/6.
24. Ibid. pp. 8–15.
25. Ibid., 31st meeting (9 Apr. 1946), pp. 100–18.
26. FRUS, 1946, vol. 1, pp. 251–92; SCOR, 1st year, 1st series, Supplement no. 2, p. 23, S/57.
27. Ibid., 41st meeting (16 May 1946), pp. 253–69; 42nd meeting (17 May 1946), pp. 270–8; 44th meeting (6 June 1946), p. 311; 48th meeting (24 June 1946), p. 382.
28. Elcott Reid op. cit. p. 144.
29. SCOR, 138th meeting (4 June 1947), pp. 949–52; 222nd meeting (9 Dec. 1947), p. 2771; SC res. 26 (S/368), 4 June 1947; SC res. 37 (S/612), 9 Dec. 1947.
30. SCOR, 462nd meeting (17 Jan. 1950), pp. 10–13; 468th meeting (28 Feb. 1950), pp. 9–11.
31. SC res. 263 (S/8976), 24 Jan. 1969; 345 (S/11192), 17 Jan. 1974; 528 (S/15531), 21 Dec. 1982.
32. SCOR, 1350th meeting (3 April 1982), paras., 185–7; SC res. 502 (S/14947/Rev. 1), 3 April 1982.
33. *Repertoire VI*, pp. 168, 217; SC res. 346 (S/8429), 14 March 1968. NB ten volumes of the *Repertoire* have been issued, and will be cited as follows:

Form of citation	Period covered	UN doc. ref.	Year of publication
Repertoire I	1946–51	ST/PSCA/I	1954
Repertoire II	1952–5	ST/PSCA/I/Add.1	1957
Repertoire III	1956–8	ST/PSCA/I/Add.2	1959
Repertoire IV	1959–63	ST/PSCA/I/Add.3	1965
Repertoire V	1964–5	ST/PSCA/I/Add.4	1968
Repertoire VI	1966–8	ST/PSCA/I/Add.5	1971
Repertoire VII	1969–71	ST/PSCA/I/Add.6	1976
Repertoire VIII	1972–4	ST/PSCA/I/Add.7	1979

Repertoire IX	1975–80	ST/PSCA/I/Add.8	1987
Repertoire X	1981–4	ST/PSCA/I/Add.9	1992

Volumes II to X were issued as supplements.

CHAPTER 2

1. A/AC. 18/SC. 4 (mimeo.), 18 May 1948, para. 4.
2. *Repertoire of the Practice of the Security Council 1946–1951* (ST/PSC/1), 1954, p. 8.
3. SCOR, 4th year, 424th meeting (May 1949), pp. 2 and 8.
4. SCOR, 11th year, 746th meeting (28 Oct. 1956), paras. 1–4; 752nd meeting (2 Nov. 1956), paras. 3–5; 22nd year, 1341st meeting (24 May 1967), para. 1.
5. SCOR, 14th year, Supplement for July to Sept. 1959, pp. 6–8, S/4212, S/4213; 847th meeting (7 Sept. 1959), paras. 5, 14–22, and 30; 848th meeting (7 Sept. 1959), paras. 12 and 22.
6. SCOR, 20th year, 1237th meeting (4 Sept. 1965), paras. 5–10 and 19–63.
7. The following are examples of meetings called by different Presidents without the agreement of all Council members:

the Soviet representative	SCOR, 16th year, 973rd meeting (13 Nov. 1961), paras. 17–19;
the Malaysian representative	SCOR, 20th year, 1208th meeting (14 May 1965, paras. 2–4;
the Dutch representative	SCOR, 20th year, 1220th meeting (3 June 1965), paras. 8–24.

8. SCOR, 24th year, Supplement for July to Sept. 1969, p. 159, S/9394; 1503rd meeting (20 Aug. 1969).
9. SCOR, 3rd year, 390th meeting (23 Dec. 1948), pp. 5 and 17.
10. SCOR, 21st year, Supplement for Apr. to June 1966, pp. 29–33, S/7237, S/7238, S/7240, S/7241; 1276th meeting (9 Apr. 1966), paras. 10, 11, 14, 38–41, 82–5; 1277th meeting (9 Apr. 1966), paras. 5–10, 36–9. Also oral communications from diplomats and officials.
11. SCOR, 21st year, Supplement for Apr. to June 1966, pp. 46–9 and 62–3, S/7261 and S/7272.
12. *Repertoire V*, pp. 5–6.
13. *Repertoire of the Practice of the Security Council, Supplement 1966–1968*, ST/PSCA/1/Add.5, p. 5.
14. S/PV. 2966, 8 December 1990, p. 12.
15. S/22135, 23 January 1991.
16. S/22138, 23 January 1991.

17. S/22144, 24 January 1991.
18. S/22147, 25 January 1991.
19. S/22157, 28 January 1991.
20. Cuba stated the following in praising the President's work during January 1991: 'Although the public work of the Council had not been as intense as in the last few months, during this period we have in fact worked rather hard at other levels' S/PV. 2976, 31 January 1991, p. 12.
21. S/PV.2977 (Part I), 13 February 1991, pp. 52–3.
22. S/PV.2976, 31 January 1991, p. 11.
23. Ibid. p. 13.
24. S/22185, 31 January 1991, p. 1.
25. S/PV.2976, 31 January 1991, p. 51.
26. S/25607.
27. PV.3201, 19 April 1993, p. 27.
28. Keith S. Petersen, 'The Business of the United Nations Security Council: History (1946–1963) and Prospects', *Journal of Politics*, 27 (1965), p. 821.
29. SCOR, 26th year, 1601st meeting (24 Nov. 1971), para. 128.
30. Remarks of Ambassador Fulci of Italy on his Presidency, made to the NGO Working Group on the Security Council, reported in the minutes of the High-Level NGO Consultation; held at 777 UN Plaza (11th Floor), 13 January 1997, published on the Internet by Global Policy Forum; and Verbatim Records for the month of December 1996.
31. S/PV.2953, 7 May 1990.
32. S/540, 2 Sept. 1947 (mimeo.).
33. The Council met at 4.45 a.m. on 2 August 1990, S/PV.2932; at 10.45 p.m. on Saturday and 12.35 a.m. on Sunday 18–19 August 1990, S/PV.2937; at 3.15 a.m. on Saturday 25 August 1990, S/PV. 2938; at 10.35 p.m. on 14 September 1990, S/PV.2939; and at 2.15 a.m. on Sunday 16 September 1990, S/PV. 2940.
34. SCOR, 2nd year, 90th meeting (9 Jan. 19947), pp. 21–4; 92nd meeting (15 Jan. 1947), pp. 63–4.
35. SCOR, 3rd year, 356th meeting (30 Aug. 1948), pp. 1–10.
36. SCOR, 3rd year, 387th meeting (20 Dec. 1948), p. 5; 385th meeting (17 Dec. 1948), pp. 18–19; 386th meeting (17 Dec. 1948), pp. 19–23, and 37.
37. SCOR, 4th year, 454th meeting (18 Nov. 1949).
38. SCOR, 15th year, 911th meeting (3/4 Dec. 1960), paras. 3–98.
39. SCOR, 17th year, Supplement for Jan. to Mar. 1962, pp. 52–3, S/5064; 989th meeting (30 Jan. 1962), paras. 26–75.

40. SCOR, 24th year, 1503rd meeting (20 Aug. 1969).
41. SCOR, 3rd year, 365th meeting (14 Oct. 1948), pp. 1–4.
42. S/PV. 2562, 9 Nov. 1984, pp. 2–5, 27.
43. SCOR, 9th year, 657th meeting (4 Feb. 1954), paras. 3–114.
44. SCOR, 15th year, Supplement for July to Sept. 1960, p. 145, S/4486; 896th meeting (9/10 Sept. 1960), paras. 9–81; 16th year, 941st meeting (20 Feb. 1961), paras. 23–4; 942nd meeting (20/1 Feb. 1961), paras. 246–7.
45. SCOR, 20th year, 1225th meeting (16 June 1965), paras. 107–20; 1226th meeting (18 June 1965), paras. 11, 30–2, 68–70, 85.
46. SCOR, 27th year, Supplement for Jan. to Mar. 1972, pp. 80–2, S/10602/Rev. 2, S/10604, S/10605; 1632nd meeting (1 Feb. 1972), paras. 7–11; 1633rd meeting (1 Feb. 1972), paras. 1–2.
47. SC res. 309 (S/10376/Rev. 2); 310 (S/10608/Rev. 1); 311 (S/10609/Rev. 1); 312 (S/10607/Rev. 1); S/10535; all dated 4 Feb. 1972.
48. SCOR, 27th year, Supplement for Jan. to Mar. 1972, pp. 82–3, S/10606.
49. A/8775, 5 Oct. 1972, pp. 31–2; A/8847, 8 Dec. 1972, p. 2; A/8847/Add. 1, 12 Dec. 1972, pp. 10–11; A/PV. 2205, 18 Dec. 1973, pp. 68, 77 (all mimeo.).
50. S/PV. 1631, 31 Jan. 1972, pp. 3–16. The official printed version (SCOR, 27th year, 1631st meeting (31 Jan. 1972), paras. 1–41) is garbled at a crucial point.
51. S/10858, 9 Jan. 1973; S/10859, 9 Jan. 1973; S/10872, 30 Jan. 1973; S/10878, 2 Feb. 1973 (all mimeo.).
52. S/10868, 25 Jan. 1973 (mimeo.); SC res. 325, 26 Jan. 1973.
53. S/10931/Rev. 1, 21 Mar. 1973 (mimeo.); SC res. 330, 21 March 1973.
54. Letter dated 21 May 1990, S/21300.
55. S/21309, 22 May 1990.
56. Resolutions and decisions of the Security Council 1990, SCOR: 45th Year, pp. 5–6; S/INF/46.
57. Press Feature no. 214, July 1971 (mimeo.); SC res. 330, 21 March 1973.
58. See B. S. N. Murti, 'Periodic Meetings of the Security Council, Art. 28, paragraph 2 of the UN Charter', *Indian Journal of International Law*, 10 (1970), pp. 283–98.
59. GAOR, 5th session, Supplement no. 1, A/1287, pp. xii–xiii; Annexes, Agenda item 60, pp. 1–4, A/1304; 6th session, Supplement no. 1A, A/1844/Add. 1, p. 6; Trygve Lie, *In the Cause of Peace*, London and New York, Macmillan, 1954, pp. 279, 431; GAOR, 10th session, Supplement no. 1A, A/2911 p. xii; 14th session, supplement no. 1A, A/4132/Add. 1, p. 3; 22nd session, Supplement no. 1A, A/6701/Add.

1, paras. 157–60; 23rd session, Supplement no. 1A, A/7201/Add. 1, para. 169; *UN Monthly Chronicle*, 7, no. 8 (Aug.–Sept. 1970), p. 90; GAOR, 25th session, Supplement no. 1A, A/8001/Add. 1, para. 64; A/8431, 24 Sept. 1971 (mimeo.), p. 4, para. 9: GA res. 494(V), 20 Nov. 1950; 503B (VI), 12 Jan. 1952; 817 (IX), 23 Nov. 1954; 2606 (XXIV), 16 Dec. 1969. See also Goodrich, p. 287.

60. S/PV. 1247, 25 Oct. 1964, p. 81; SCOR, 20th year, 1247th meeting (25 Oct. 1965), para. 141.
61. Ibid., 1257th–1263rd meetings (12–17 Nov. 1965).
62. This meeting was not numbered; the verbatim record is contained in a Supplement to the Council's official records, SCOR, 24th year, Supplement for Apr. to June 1969, pp. 331–4, S/9259.
63. SCOR, 13th year, Supplement for July to Sept., 1958, pp. 97–110, S/4071–5.
64. GAOR, 24th session, Annexes, Agenda item 103, p. 2, A/7654; GA res. 2606 (XXIV), 16 Dec. 1969.
65. SCOR, 25th year, Supplement for Apr. to June 1970, pp. 153–6 and 207, S/9799 and S/9824.
66. SCOR, 25th year, 1544th meeting (12 June 1970), paras. 19–89; A/7922, 15 May 1970 (mimeo.), pp. 50–1, 62, 70, 88; A/7922/Add. 1, 4 June 1970 (mimeo.), pp. 5, 16; A/7922/Add. 2, 1 July 1970 (mimeo.), p. 3.
67. SCOR, 25th year, 1544th meeting (12 June 1970), para. 2; Supplement for Apr. to June 1970, p. 210, S/9835.
68. SCOR, 25th year, 1555th meeting (21 Oct. 1970).
69. GA res. 2734 (XXV), 16 Dec. 1970.
70. GAOR, 26th session, Supplement no. 1A, A/8401/Add. 1, para. 99. See also A/8431, 24 Sept. 1971 (mimeo.), p. 4.
71. A/8847, 8 Dec. 1972 (mimeo.), p. 2 and Annex, pp. 3, 10, 11, and 18; A/8847/Add. 1, 12 Dec. 1972 (mimeo.), pp. 9–10; A/9128, 25 Oct. 1973 (mimeo.), pp. 9, 23; A/9143, 30 Nov. 1973 (mimeo.), pp. 10, 21; see also A/PV. 2205, 18 Dec. 1973, p. 72.
72. S/17427, 29 Aug. 1985; (mimeo.).
73. S/PV. 2608, 26 Sept. 1985, pp. 118–28; S/17501, 26 Sept. 1985 (mimeo.).
74. S/PV.2750.
75. S/PV.2818, 14 July 1988.
76. S/PV.3499, 8 February 1995.
77. S/PV.3698, 27 September 1996.
78. S/PV.2943.
79. S/PV.2963.
80. S/PV.3009.

81. S/PV.3583.
82. S/PV.3046, 31 Jan.1992; S/24111–A/47/277, 17 Jan.1992; A/INF/47/5, 7 Oct. 1992; S/25944 – A/47/965, 15 June 1993.
83. S/PV.3483, 16 December 1994, p. 3.
84. Ibid.
85. S/PRST/1994/81, 16 December 1994.
86. S/PV.3621, 25 January 1996, p. 9.
87. S/PV.3628, 6 February 1996, p. 29.
88. S/PV.3641, 15 March 1996.
89. S/PV.3650, 9 April 1996; and David Travers 'The United Nations and its Agencies' *The Annual Register 1996,* Cartermill, 1997, p. 372.
90. UN *Journal* No. 1997/52 (Part II), 15 March 1997.
91. Spaak, p. 102.
92. *The First Assembly*, ed. by Oliver Brett, London, Macmillan, 1921, p. 239.
93. Goodrich, p. 287.
94. *Repertoire I*, p. 218.
95. SCOR, 5th year, 510th meeting (12 Oct. 1950); Lie, pp. 376–7.
96. S/PV. 612, 13 March 1953.
97. Ibid.
98. Ibid.
99. S/PV. 614, 19 March 1953.
100. S/PV. 613, 13 March 1953.
101. SCOR, 8th year, 613th meeting (13 Mar. 1953); Lie, p. 415.
102. SCOR, 26th year, 1620th meeting (21 Dec. 1971).
103. S/PV.3714, 19 November 1996.
104. S/PV.3725, 13 December 1996.
105. SCOR, 28th year, 1752nd meeting (27 Oct. 1973), paras. 117–18, 128, 130–1, 133–8, and personal communication.
106. See the review of the relevant official records of this case by Davidson Nicol in 'The United Nations Security Council: Towards Greater Effectiveness', UNITAR, 1982, pp. 75–6.
107. See *Repertoire of the Practice of the Security Council, Supplement 1946–1951*, p. 201 and p. 227.
108. SCOR 739th to 741st meetings, 9 to 12 October 1956.
109. *Repertoire of the Practice of the Security Council, Supplement 1956–1958*, p. 22.
110. October 1970.
111. 1784th meeting, 24 July 1974.
112. S/PV. 1759, 14 Dec. 1973, p. 86; SCOR, 28th year, 1760th meeting (15 Dec. 1973), paras. 1, 34–45; SC res. 344 (S/11156), 15 Dec. 1973.

113. *Repertoire of the Practice of the Security Council, Supplement 1975–1980*, p. 246.
114. S/22110/Add.6, 5 March 1991.
115. This reference was as much a consequence of the influence of wider CNN coverage of the Gulf War, which diplomats watched assiduously, as it was of the presence of CNN at Council meetings.
116. Simma, Bruno, *The UN Charter: A Commentary*, 1994, Oxford University Press, p. 474.
117. Davidson Nicol, op. cit. p. 77.
118. See 'The case for a new interpretation of Article 31 of the UN Charter' by Ambassador Kovanda of the Czech Republic, paper presented to the General Assembly *Open-ended Working Group on the Question of Equitable Representation on and Increase in the Membership of the Security Council*. He derived the statistics from Loie Feuerle, 'Informal Consultations: A Mechanism in Security Council Decision-Making', *New York University Journal of International Law and Politics*, vol. 18, No. 1, fall 1985, pp. 267–308.
119. 5 August 1991 (S/22904); 6 December 1991 (S/23305); and 28 January and 5 February 1992 (S/23517).
120. 27 March 1992 (S/23761); 27 May 1992 (S/24010); 27 July 1992 (S/24352); 24 September 1992 (S/24584); 24 November 1992 (S/24843); 25 January 1993 (S/25157); 23 and 29 March 1993 (S/25480); 24 May 1993 (S/25830); 21 July 1993 (S/26126); 20 September 1993 (S/26474); 18 November 1993 (S/26768); 18 January 1994 (S/PRST/1994/3).
121. 12 August 1992, 9 December 1992, 8 April 1993, 13 August 1993, 10 December 1993.
122. S/PRST/3, 18 January 1994.
123. S/PRST/1994/18, 8 April 1994; S/PRST/1994/41, 5 August 1994; S/PRST/1994/76, 30 November 1994; S/PRST/1995/14, 30 March 1995; S/PRST/1995/36, 28 July 1995; S/PRST/1995/56, 22 November 1995.
124. S/23803.
125. S/23609.
126. UN *Journal* 18 March 1997 No. 1997/53 (part II) p. 1.
127. S/PV. 3483, 16 December 1994.
128. A proposal that participation of a non-member in informal consultations be allowed on a discretionary basis, (and in fact the participation of non-members in *formal* meetings is always discretionary, albeit seldom opposed) when its' interests were specifically affected, was made by the Czech Republic in 1996, and is discussed in detail in Chapter 3.6.

129. S/PV.3483, 16 December 1994, pp. 10–11.
130. Occasional exceptions to this practice have occurred when statements prepared for an informal meeting have ended up being read at a formal meeting, and vice versa. After hours or days of intricate negotiation of the wording of a statement, Council members are understandably reluctant to risk opening a statement to further amendment by proposing a correction to reflect the type of meeting from which the statement has emerged.
131. David D. Caron 'The Legitimacy of the Collective Authority of the Security Council', *The American Journal of International Law*, vol. 87, 1993, pp. 552–78.
132. Procedure adopted through a Note by the President on 28 February 1994 (S/1994/230).
133. Michael C. Wood 'Security Council Working Methods and Procedure: Recent Developments', *The International and Comparative Law Quarterly*, vol. 45, January 1996, p. 157.
134. Davidson Nicol 'The United Nations Security Council: Towards Greater Effectiveness', 1982, UNITAR, p. 76.
135. See the chapter by Anthony Aust on 'The Procedure and Practice of the Security Council Today' in *Le Développement du Rôle du Conseil de Sécurité*, 1993, Martinus Nijhoff Publishers, pp. 368–9, from which some of the information in this section has been derived. Aust reports that the permanent five often use the Council Caucus Room for the purpose of drafting complex resolutions. This has not recently been the case, with the Caucus Room being used more generally for expert level meetings of all members or those particularly interested in an issue.
136. S/1995/827.
137. S/1995/275, 11 April 1995, S/1995/300, 13 April 1995, and S/1995/827, 27 September 1995.
138. Such co-operation has included the issuing of a tripartite declaration on 5 August 1994, A/49/299–S/1994/938 and joint letters—see 29 January 1997, S/PRST/1997/2.
139. As of 1 January 1997. Figure derived from British Foreign and Commonwealth Office circular No. 45/97, 31 December 1997.
140. S/PV.3247, 29 June 1993.
141. S/PV.3245, 27 June 1993.
142. Draft resolution contained in S/1995/394 on the Occupied Arab Territories; S/PV.3538, 17 May 1995.
143. A meeting of the Joint Co-ordinating Committee was held on 25 January 1997 and listed in the UN *Journal* no. 1997/18.

144. An example of this was highlighted by the United Kingdom when it stated that 'the co-sponsors of the draft resolution [on Israel] accepted all the amendments proposed by the European Union members of the Council' S/PV.3538, 17 May 1995.
145. Italy spoke on behalf of the European Union in a debate on 'The Situation in Burundi' on 29 January 1996, S/PV.3623, as did Ireland in a debate on 12 July 1996, S/PV.3680/Corr.1.
146. This information on Contact Groups is derived from a Discussion Paper by Helen Leigh-Phippard 'Coalitions and Contact Groups in Multilateral Diplomacy', Centre for the Study of Diplomacy, Leicester University, Discussion Paper No. 21, September 1996, pp. 9–11.
147. S/PV. 3201; 19 April 1993 and letter contained in S/25607.
148. 6 May 1994.
149. S/PV.3488, 12 January 1995, p. 2.
150. S/PV.3528, 28 April 1995.
151. A/51/790, 31 January 1997.
152. UN Office of the Spokesman for the Secretary-General, Daily Press Briefing, 4 March 1997.
153. UN Office of the Spokesman for the Secretary-General, Daily Press Briefing, 5 March 1997; S/PV.3765 (Resumption 1), 15 April 1997.
154. S/PRST/1994/62, 4 November 1994.
155. SCOR, 1st year, 1st series, 31st meeting (9 Apr. 1946), p. 101.
156. Ibid. pp. 109–10.
157. SCOR, 2nd series, 77th meeting (16 Oct. 1946), p. 483; 2nd year, 202nd meeting (15 Sept. 1947), pp. 2405–6.
158. The notification for 1986 was issued on 18 Sept. as doc. A/41/613 (mimeo.).
159. SCOR, 1st year, 1st series, Supplement no. 2, pp. 46–7, S/30.
160, Ibid., Supplement no. I, pp. 16–17, Annex 2A.
161. SC res. 2, 30 Jan. 1946; res. 3, 4 Apr. 1946.
162. SCOR, 1st year, 1st series, Supplement no. 2, p. 47, S/33; 32nd meeting (15 Apr. 1946), pp. 122–3.
163. Ibid., 33rd meeting (16 Apr. 1946), pp. 142–3.
164. Ibid. pp. 143–5, A/39.
165. Lie, pp. 79–80.
166. Ibid. pp. 80–3.
167. SCOR, 1st year, 1st series, 33rd meeting (16 Apr. 1946), p. 145.
168. ICJ Reports 1971, paras. 24 and 26.
169. SCOR, 1st year, 1st series, Supplement no. 2, pp. 47–50, S/42.
170. Ibid., 36th meeting (23 Apr. 1946), pp. 213–14.
171. SC res. 5, 8 May 1946.

172. SCOR, 1st year, 1st series, Supplement no. 2, pp. 52–4, S/66 and S/68.
173. Ibid., 43rd meeting (22 May 1946), p. 305.
174. SCOR, 29th year, 1810th meeting (13 Dec. 1974), para. 367.
175. S/1996/55, 24 January 1996.
176. S/1996/603, 30 July 1996 replaced by S/1996/603*, 13 August 1996. The replacement document is a Corrigendum and was referred to by a number of Member States as Corr.1; but this identification did not appear in the document's symbol block.
177. S/1996/649, 13 August 1996.
178. Ibid.
179. S/1996/655, 14 August 1996.
180. S/1996/693, 26 August 1996.
181. S/1996/704.
182. S/1996/747, 12 September 1996.
183. Ibid.
184. S/1996/748, 13 September 1996.
185. S/1996/751, 13 September 1996.
186. S/1997/40, 10 January 1997.
187. Vratislav Pechota, *Complementary Structures of Third Party Settlement of International Disputes*, UNITAR (PS3), 1971, p. 22.
188. SCOR, 5th year, 473rd meeting (25 June 1950), p. 1.
189. Ibid. p. 2.
190. SCOR, 7th year, 577th meeting (18 June 1952), p. 1.
191. Ibid. paras. 2–89.
192. See, for example, SCOR, 3rd year, 231st meeting (22 Jan. 1948), pp. 143–64; 19th year, 1127th meeting (8 June 1964), paras. 1–2. Since 5 Aug. 1968, South West Africa has been known as Namibia in official documents of the Security Council; the title of the agenda item was changed at the 1464th meeting of the Council on 20 Mar. 1969.
193. SCOR, 26th year, 1614th meeting (14/15 Dec. 1971), paras. 3–9.
194. SCOR, 1st year, 2nd series, 59th meeting (3 Sept. 1946), pp. 175–6.
195. See, for example, SCOR, 3rd year, 268th meeting (17 Mar. 1948), p. 100; 6th year, 559th meeting (1 Oct. 1951), para. 5; 7th year, 574th meeting (4 Apr. 1952), paras. 46, 51, and 96; 575th meeting (10 April 1952), para. 25; 576th meeting (14 Apr. 1952), para. 29; 11th year, 730th meeting (26 June 1956), paras. 14–15; 17th year, 991st meeting (27 Feb. 1962), para. 65.
196. David R. Gilmour, 'Article 2(7) of the United Nations Charter and the Practice of the Permanent Members of the Security Council', *Australian Yearbook of International Law, 1967*, London, Butterworth, 1970, p. 162.

197. SCOR, 3rd year, 361st meeting (4 Oct. 1948), pp. 16–17.
198. Ibid., 357th meeting (16 Sept. 1948), p. 8.
199. SCOR, 2nd year, 171st meeting (31 July 1947).
200. SCOR, 3rd year, 357th meeting (16 Sept. 19948), p. 10.
201. Ibid. p. 4.
202. SCOR, 30th year, 1834th meeting (6 Aug. 1975), paras. 3–5, 86; 1842nd meeting (26 Sept. 1975), paras. 5–9.
203. S/Agenda/1651, 18 July 1972 (mimeo.).
204. SC res. 316 (S/10722), 26 June 1972.
205. S/Agenda/1651, 18 July 1972 (mimeo.).
206. SCOR, 27th year, 1651st meeting (18 July 1972), paras. 3–53.
207. SCOR, 3rd year, 356th meeting (30 Aug. 1948), pp. 7–10; 5th year, 502nd meeting (18 Sept. 1950), pp. 11–14. See also SCOR, 3rd year, 327th meeting (25 June 1948), p. 6.
208. SCOR, 27th year, 1651st meeting (18 July 1972), paras. 54–139. For other examples of difficulties over formulating the agenda when the Council is convened to consider the situation in the Middle East, see SCOR, 21st year, 1288th meeting (25 July 1966), paras. 6–45; 1305th meeting (14 Oct. 1966), paras. 1–131; 22nd year, 1365th meeting (8 July 1967), paras. 4–53.
209. SCOR, 24th year, Supplement for Apr. to June 1969, pp. 331–4, S/9259.
210. S/PV. 1703, 21 Mar. 1972.
211. SCOR, 1st year, 1st series, 31st meeting (9 Apr. 1946), pp. 101–2.
212. *Repertoire III*, p. 47; *Repertoire IV*, p. 28; *Repertoire V*, p. 47; *Repertoire VI*, p. 38.
213. SCOR, 3rd year, 383rd meeting (2 Dec. 1948), pp. 2–7.
214. SCOR, 5th year, 480th meeting (1 Aug. 1950), pp. 12–21; 481st meeting (2 Aug. 1950), pp. 1–7, 10–18; 482nd meeting (3 Aug. 1950), pp. 1–23; 504th meeting (27 Sept. 1950), pp. 1–3; 7th year, 594th meeting (2 Sept. 1952), paras. 6–26; 16th year, 973rd meeting (13 Nov. 1961), paras. 2–16.
215. See, for example, SCOR, 7th year, 599th meeting (12 Sept. 1952), paras. 2–3, 6–11, 26–31; 21st year, 1305th meeting (14 Oct. 1966), paras. 94 and 121.
216. SCOR, 9th year, 676th meeting (25 June 1954), paras. 140 and 195.
217. SCOR, 1st year, 2nd series, 71st meeting (23 Sept. 1946), pp. 426–8; 72nd meeting (24 Sept. 1946), pp. 453–5; see also 12th year, 783rd meeting (20 Aug. 1957), paras. 32 and 58. The President has not always convened a meeting when asked to do so. In two cases he has taken no action: concerning relations between Siam (Thailand) and

France in 1946 (S/72, 31 May 1946 mimeo.) and in 1976 when Sudan complained of 'armed banditry' by Libya (SCOR, 31st year, Supplement for July to Sept. 1976, pp. 2–3, S/12122). In three cases, the President simply took note of the requests: two about Cyprus (SCOR, 29th year, Supplement for July to Sept. 1974, pp. 53, 57, S/11358, S/11366; 1782nd meeting (21 July 1974), para. 4; 1783rd meeting (23 July 1974), para. 3) and a complaint by Somalia of French aggression (SCOR, 31st year, Supplement for Jan. to Mar. 1976, p. 103, S/11987; 1889th meeting (18 Feb. 1976), para. 4). In one case a meeting was convened but a letter of request from Cyprus was not included in the agenda (SCOR, 29th year, Supplement for July to Sept. 1974, p. 66, S/11384; 1785th meeting (27 July 1974), p. 1) and in another case a proposal to delete from the provisional agenda a communication from Israel asking for an urgent meeting was rejected and it was decided to consider it at a future meeting—which was never, in fact, held (SCOR, 27th year, Supplement for July to Sept. 1972, p. 72, S/10739; 1651st meeting (18 July 1972), paras. 71–139).

218. SCOR, 7th year, 574th meeting (4 Apr. 1952), paras. 27 and 34; see also SCOR, 12th year, 783rd meeting (20 Aug. 1957), paras. 35 and 50; 784th meeting (20 Aug. 1957), para. 22.

219. SCOR, 1st year, 2nd series, 71st meeting (23 Sept. 1946), p. 425; 72nd meeting (24 Sept. 1946), pp. 448–9; 7th year, 574th meeting (4 Apr. 1952), para. 34; 575th meeting (10 Apr. 1952), paras. 9, 11, 18, 58–62, 68; 576th meeting (14 Apr. 1952), paras. 58 and 63; 8th year, 620th meeting (27 Aug. 1953), paras. 26–7; 621st meeting (31 Aug. 1953), paras. 7–8; 623rd meeting (2 Sept. 1953), para. 18; 11th year, 730th meeting (26 June 1956), paras. 48–9, 57, 84; 755th meeting (5 Nov. 1956), paras. 28–9, 56; 17th year, 991st meeting (27 Feb. 1962), paras. 15 and 19; 24th year, 1503rd meeting (20 Aug. 1969), paras. 8 and 10.

220. SCOR, 3rd year, 327th meeting (25 June 1948), p. 3; 6th year, 559th meeting (1 Oct. 1951), paras. 2–4, 9–10; 8th year, 619th meeting (26 Aug. 1953), paras. 5–6, 24–8; 620th meeting (27 Aug. 1953), paras. 16–23; 623rd meeting (2 Sept. 1953), paras. 11–12, 29; 624th meeting (3 Sept. 1953), paras. 12–15; 11th year, 729th meeting (26 June 1956), paras. 29, 95–101; 730th meeting (26 June 1956), paras. 36–40, 52–3, 60–5; 12th year, 783rd meeting (20 Aug. 1957), paras. 57, 64, 73–7; 784th meeting (20 Aug. 1957), para. 30; 24th year, 1503rd meeting (20 Aug. 1969), paras. 2–9.

221. See, for example, SCOR, 1st year, 2nd series, 71st meeting (23 Sept. 1946), p. 425; 17th year, 991st meeting (27 Feb. 1962), paras. 2–3, 94–5, 100.

222. Gilmour, op. cit. p. 175.
223. GA res. 2479 (XXIII), 21 Dec. 1968; SC res. 263 (S/8976). 24 Jan. 1969.
224. GA res. 3189 (XXVIII), 18 Dec. 1973; SC res. 345 (S/11192), 17 Jan. 1974.
225. GA res. 3190 (XXVIII), 18 Dec. 1973; 35/219, 17 Dec. 1980; SC res. 528 (S/15531), 21 Dec. 1982; S/PV. 2411, 18 Jan. 1983, pp. 12–17.
226. H. A. L. Fisher, *An International Experiment*, Oxford, Clarendon Press, 1921, p. 25.
227. SCOR, 7th year, 575th meeting (10 Apr. 1952), para. 13.
228. S/PV.2977 (Part II) (Closed-resumption 4), 26 February 1991; and (Closed-resumption 2) /Corr.1, 25 February 1991.
229. A/9143, 30 Nov. 1973 (mimeo.); SCOR, 239th year, Supplement for Oct. to Dec. 1974, p. 72, S/11586; 30th year, Supplement no. 2 (A/10002), paras. 495–6.
230. S/16913, 29 Jan. 1985 (mimeo.); Resolutions and Decisions of the Security Council, 1985, p. 27.
231. S/26015, 30 June 1993.
232. S/PV.3440, 18 October 1994.
233. S/PV.3593, 13 November 1995.
234. S/PV.3711, 13 November 1996.
235. A/AC.182/L.87, 21 February 1996.
236. Para 4 (f) of General Assembly resolution 50/52 of 11 December 1995.
237. Its full title is 'the Special Committee on the Charter of the United Nations and on the Strengthening of the Role of the Organization'
238. A/AC.182/L.87, 21 February 1996, pp. 13–15.
239. SCOR, 1st year, 1st series, Supplement no. 1, pp. 19–24, S/1.
240. S/PV.3492, 18 Jan. 1995.
241. *Information for Delegations* (ST/CS/23), Sept. 1973, pp. 19–20.
242. SCOR, 5th year, 524th meeting (17 Nov. 1950), p. 2. The statement is in ibid., 523rd meeting (16 Nov. 1950), pp. 27–30, S/1902.
243. SCOR, 7th year, 576th meeting (14 Apr. 1952), paras. 5–13.
244. See, for example, SCOR, 12th year, Supplement for Jan. to Mar. 1957, pp. 12–20 (S/PV. 761/Add. 1) and 21–82 (S/PV. 762/Add. 1); 23rd year, 1326th meeting (23 Nov. 1966), Annex; 1408th meeting (26 Mar. 1968) p. 13; 1418th meeting (1 May 1968), paras. 124–5; 1421st meeting (3 May 1968), paras. 52, 174–5; S/PV. 1421/Adds. 1 and 2, 6 May and 24 June 1968.
245. SCOR, 26th year, 1589th meeting (6 Oct. 1971), paras. 2–43.
246. SCOR, 34th year, 2147th meeting (12 June 1979), paras. 18, 187.
247. S/PV. 2471, 6 Sept. 1983, pp. 6–10.

248. S/PV. 2567, 30 January 1985, pp. 2, 19–21.
249. S/PV.2874, 11 August 1989.
250. S/PV.2896, 30 November 1989.
251. S/PV.2953, 7 November 1990.
252. S/PV.2959, 27 November 1990.
253. See *The InterNet—An Introductory Guide for United Nations Organizations*, ACCIS, Geneva, March 1994, Doc. no. ACCIS/94/1.
254. SCOR, 1st year, 1st series, 31st meeting (9 Apr. 1946), pp. 117–18.
255. See, for example, the communication from the Zimbabwe African People's Union about the Rhodesian question, circulated at the request of Algeria, SCOR, 21st year, Supplement for Apr. to June 1966, p. 102, S/7313.
256. S/17959, 31 Mar. 1986 (mimeo.).
257. See, for example, SCOR, 11th year, 742nd meeting (13 Oct. 1956), paras. 5–6.
258. See, for example, SCOR, 3rd year, Supplement for Sept. 1948, pp. 5–7, S/986, S/998, S/1000; 4th year, 409th meeting (15 Feb. 1949), pp. 12–15, 18, S/1247 and S/1256.
259. SCOR, 2nd year, Supplement no. 1, pp. 1–2, S/224; 143rd meeting (20 June 1947), p. 1043, S/374; 3rd year, Supplement for Aug. 1948, pp. 79–84, S/927.
260. SCOR, 13th year, Supplement for Jan. to Mar. 1958, pp. 12–13, S/3951.
261. SCOR, 27th year, Supplement for Apr. to June 1972, pp. 44–7, S/10631 (text also in *US Department of State Bulletin*, vol. 66, pp. 750–1).
262. SCOR, 30th year, Supplement for Apr. to June 1975, pp. 24–5, S/11689.
263. S/17938, 25 Mar. 1986; S/17983, 12 Apr. 1986; S/17986 and S/17990, 14 Apr. 1986 (all mimeo.).
264. SCOR, 6th year, 550th meeting (1 Aug. 1951), paras. 34–42; 553rd meeting (16 Aug. 1951), para. 60.
265. SCOR, 13th year, 827th meeting (15 July 1958), para. 84; 833rd meeting (18 July 1958), para. 10; 836th meeting (22 July 1958), para. 7.
266. SCOR, 22nd year, 1347th meeting (5 June 1967), paras. 30–2, 134; S/PV. 1736, 13 Aug. 1973, p. 96.
267. SCOR, 28th year, 1733rd meeting (20 July 1973), para. 75; 29th year, 1767th meeting (16 Apr. 1974), para. 160.
268. S/PV.2835, 5 January 1989.
269. S/PV.2902, 23 December 1989.
270. S/PV.2835, 5 January 1989 pp. 13–15; S/PV.2899, 20 December 1989.

271. S/PV.3247, 29 June 1993; the draft resolution contained in document S/25997 failed by six votes in favour, none against, and nine abstentions.
272. S/PV.3245, 27 June 1993.
273. SCOR, 17th year, 995th meeting (20 Mar. 1962), para. 59.
274. SCOR, 15th year, 920th meeting (13/14 Dec. 1960), para. 78.
275. SCOR, 16th year, Supplement for July to Sept. 1961, pp. 52–7, S/4908–S/4911/Adds. 1 and 2.
276. Ibid., 976th meeting (17 Nov. 1961), paras. 114–17; Supplement for Oct. to Dec. 1961, pp. 135–6, S/4988.
277. SCOR, 18th year, Supplement for Jan. to Mar. 1963, pp. 116–29, S/5259, paras. 9, 13, 17, and 60.
278. Ibid. pp. 130–2, 141–7, S/5260, S/5264, S/5266, S/5268, S/5271, S/5272.
279. Ibid. pp. 133, 143–5, 147, S/5262, S/5267, S/5269, S/5273.
280. SCOR, 22nd year, Supplement for Jan. to Mar. 1967, pp. 233–4, S/7822.
281. Ibid., Supplement for Apr. to June 1967, pp. 103–4, S/7891. See also GAOR, 26th session, Supplement no. 1A, A/8401/Add. 1, para. 101.
282. SCOR, 22nd year, Supplement for Apr. to June 1967, pp. 98–9, S/7888.
283. SCOR, 24th year, Supplement for July to Sept. 1969, p. 186, S/9455; 25th year, Supplement for Apr. to June 1970, p. 153, S/9579; Supplement for July to Sept. 1970, pp. 130–1, S/9909; 26th year Supplement for Oct. to Dec. 1971, pp. 34–5, S/10389; 27th year, Supplement for Jan. to Mar. 1972, pp. 63–4, 72–3, 80–1, S/10563, S/10577, S/10603; Supplement for Apr. to June 1972, p. 139, S/10718; Supplement for Oct. to Dec. 1972, pp. 31–2, S/10831.
284. SCOR, 23rd year, 1445th meeting (24 Aug. 1968), paras. 3–157; 24th year, Supplement for Oct. to Dec. 1969, pp. 95–6, S/9486; 1514th meeting (23 Oct. 1969), paras. 6–40; 25th year, Supplement for Jan. to Mar. 1970, p. 115, S/9624; 27th year, Supplement for Apr. to June 1972, p. 50, S/10637.
285. SCOR, 24th year, Supplement for Oct. to Dec. 1969, p. 104, S/9498; 25th year, Supplement for Jan. to Mar. 1970, p. 149, S/9674; Supplement for Oct. to Dec. 1970, p. 85, S/10042; 27th year, Supplement for Apr. to June 1972, p. 69, S/10660.
286. SCOR, 24th year, Supplement for Oct. to Dec. 1969, pp. 117–18, S/9515.
287. SCOR, 23rd year, 1445th meeting (24 Aug. 1968), paras. 16–19, 23–34.
288. SCOR, 25th year, Supplement for Jan. to Mar. 1970, pp. 151–2, 163, 170–1, 173, S/9680, S/9704, S/9718, S/9723.

289. SCOR, 26th year, Supplement for Jan. to Mar. 1971, p. 61, S/10104.
290. SCOR, 26th year, Supplement for Oct. to Dec. 1971, p. 89, S/10415; 27th year, Supplement for July to Sept. 1972, pp. 94–5, S/10774.
291. SCOR, 29th year, Supplement for July to Sept. 1974, p. 104, S/11447.
292. SCOR, 30th year, Supplement for Apr. to June 1975, pp. 41–2, S/11706.
293. SCOR, 31st year, Supplement for Jan. to Mar. 1976, pp. 134–5, S/12029.
294. S/17919 and S/17959, 14 and 31 Mar. 1986 (both mimeo.).
295. A/8987, 18 Dec. 1972; A/8991, 4 Jan. 1973; A/9037, 23 Jan. 1973; A/9040, 30 Jan. 1973; A/9047, 21 Feb. 1973; A/9115, 7 Aug. 1973; A/9118, 10 Aug. 1973; A/9210, 10 Dec. 1973; see also A/9052, 29 Mar. 1973 (all mimeo.).
296. GAOR, 28th session, Annexes, Agenda item 83, A/9399, para. 4.
297. S/PV.3116.
298. GA 7th Plenary meeting; resolution 47/1.

CHAPTER 3

1. GAOR, 5th session, 289th plenary meeting (28 Sept. 1950), para. 40.
2. SCOR, 11th year, 751st meeting (31 Oct. 1956), para. 1.
3. Ibid., 754th meeting (4 Nov. 1956), para. 76.
4. SCOR, 15th year, 873rd meeting (13/14 July 1960), para. 26. For Hammarskjold's understanding of Art. 99, see Urquhart pp. 254–5, 310, 343, 396–7, 533, 538.
5. Address at the annual luncheon of the Dag Hammarskjold Memorial Scholarship Fund on 16 Sept. 1971, printed in *UN Monthly Chronicle*, 8, no. 9 (Oct. 1971), p. 184.
6. Press Release SG/SM/1516, 2 Aug. 1971, later reproduced in SCOR, 26th year, Supplement for Oct. to Dec. 1971, p. 80, S/10410, para. 3; Press Release SG/SM/1530, 14 Sept. 1971, p. 15.
7. SCOR, 34th year, Supplement for Oct. to Dec. 1979, p. 83, S/13646; 2172nd meeting (27 Nov. 1979), para. 9.
8. SCOR, 1st year, 2nd series, 70th meeting (20 Sept. 1946), p. 404.
9. GAOR, 15th session, 5th Committee, 769th meeting (18 Oct. 1960), paras. 10 and 17.
10. SCOR, 16th year, 964th meeting (28 July 1961), paras. 86; see also A/9128, 25 Oct. 1973 (mimeo.), p. 9.
11. GAOR, 26th session, Supplement no. 1A, A/8401/Add. 1, para. 126.
12. GAOR, 26th session, Supplement no. 1A, A/8401/Add. 1, para. 127; Pechota, *The Quiet Approach*, p. 10.

13. GAOR, 23rd session, Supplement no. 1A. A/7201/Add. 1, paras. 201–4; 24th session, Supplement no. 1A, A/7601/Add. 1, para. 205; 27th session, Supplement no. 1, A/8701, pp. 75–6; Pechota, pp. 67, 77; Vratislav Pechota, *Complementary Structures of Third Party Settlement of International Disputes.*
14. Boutros Boutros-Ghali 'An Agenda for Democratization', United Nations, New York, 1996, p. 50, para. 112. A/51/761.
15. Boutros Boutros-Ghali 'Annual Report on the Work of the Organization', United Nations, New York, 1995, p. 39, para. 100. See also Boutros Boutros-Ghali 'A Grotian Moment', *Fordham International Law Journal*, May 1995, vol. 18 no. 5, pp. 1609–16.
16. SCOR, 3rd year, 331st meeting (7 July 1948), pp. 32–4; 338th meeting (15 July 1948), pp. 63–5. The resolution of the General Assembly was no. 186 (S–2), 14 May 1948.
17. SCOR, 13th year, 837th meeting (22 July 1958), paras. 10–16.
18. SC res. 203 (S/6355), 14 May 1965; SCOR, 20th year, 1209th meeting (14 May 1965), paras. 56–7; 1227th meeting (18 June 1965), paras. 4–5.
19. S/PV. 1755, 12 Nov. 1973, pp. 2–3.
20. 'A Quiet United Nations Road to Accord', *UN Monthly Chronicle*, 7, no. 7 (July 1970), pp. 122–31. See also GAOR, 22nd session, Supplement no. 1A, A/6701/Add. 1, para. 156; 24th session, Supplement no. 1A, A/7601/Add. 1, paras. 176–86; 26th session, Supplement no. 1A/A/8401/Add. 1, paras. 129–35.
21. A/3934/Rev. 1, 29 Sept. 1958 (mimeo.), paras. 26–38.
22. GAOR, 15th session, Supplement no. 1, A/4390, p. 23.
23. SCOR, 22nd year, Supplement for July to Sept. 1967, pp. 199–209, S/8124; Supplement for Oct. to Dec. 1967, pp. 80–154, S/8158.
24. Ibid., Supplement for July to Sept. 1967, p. 195, S/8121; pp. 232–86, S/8146.
25. SCOR, 25th year, Supplement for Jan. to Mar. 1970, pp. 175–6, S/9726; Supplement for Apr. to June, pp. 143, 166–70, 175, 178, S/9737, S/9738, S/9772, S/9779, S/9783.
26. S/11229.
27. SC Resolution 415, 29 September 1977.
28. SC Resolution 568, 21 June 1985.
29. SC Resolution 621, 20 September 1988.
30. SC Resolution 747, 24 April 1992.
31. SC Resolution 849, 9 July 1993.
32. SCOR, 11th year, Supplement for Jan. to Mar. 1956, pp. 20–1, S/3561 and S/3562.

33. Ibid., 720th meeting (3 Apr. 1956), para. 9. Eisenhower was under the impression that 'the Soviets supported Arab opposition' to Hammarskjold's trip, and he also gives the date of the Security Council decision as March rather than April, Dwight D. Eisenhower, *Waging Peace 1956–1961*, New York, Doubleday, 1965: London, Heinemann, 1966, pp. 28–9.
34. SCOR, 11th year, 722nd meeting (4 Apr. 1956), paras. 36–46; SC res. 113 (S/3575), 4 April 1956. See also Urquhart, pp. 138–53.
35. See, for example, Boutros-Ghali's reports on the situation in Rwanda immediately prior to the genocide (April 1994), on withdrawal of the UN peace-keeping operation from Somalia (October 1994), on the future of the UN operation in Bosnia (May 1995), and on the establishment of a Transitional Administration in Croatia (November 1995).
36. 'An Agenda for Peace', A/47/277–S/24111.
37. 'Report on An Agenda for Development' A/48/935, 6 May 1994; and 'An Agenda for Development: Recommendations' A/49/665, 11 November 1994.
38. 'Supplement to An Agenda for Peace'. A/50/60–S/1995/1.
39. Boutros Boutros-Ghali, 'Global Leadership After the Cold War', *Foreign Affairs*, vol. 75, no. 2 (March/April 1996), p. 98.
40. S. E. Werners, *Presiding Officers in the United Nations*, Haarlem (Netherlands), De Erven F. Bohn, 1967, pp. 41–3.
41. PC/EX/113/Rev. 1 (12 Nov. 1945), p. 46.
42. SCOR, 1st year, 1st series, 31st meeting (9 Apr. 1946), pp. 115–16.
43. PC/EX/113/Rev. 1 (12 Nov. 1945), pp. 24 and 40.
44. SCOR, 1st year, 1st series, 1st meeting (17 Jan. 1946), p. 4.
45. SCOR, 1st year, 2nd series, 84th meeting (16 Dec. 1946), pp. 585–7; SC. res. 14 (S/212), 16 Dec. 1946.
46. PC/EX/113/Rev. 1, 12 Nov. 1945, p. 45; SCOR, 1st year, 1st series, Supplement no. 2, p. 42, S/88.
47. SCOR, 5th year, 461st meeting (13 Jan. 1950), pp. 11–16; 462nd meeting (17 Jan. 1950), pp. 1–3, 13–16; 6th year, 566th meeting (10 Nov. 1951), paras. 1–3; 10th year, 700th meeting (8 Sept. 1955) paras. 1–5.
48. SCOR, 13th year, 814th meeting (29 Apr. 1958), paras. 2–15.
49. SCOR, 15th year, 912th meeting (7 Dec. 1960), paras. 3–122.
50. SCOR, 3rd year, 354th meeting (19 Aug. 1948), p. 29.
51. S/PV.2907, 9 February 1990, p. 6. Letter contained in document S/21120.
52. S/PV.3420, 25 Aug. 1994; S/PRST/1994/48.
53. S/PV.3426, 16 Sept. 1994; S/PRST/1994/55.

54. S/PV.3481, 15 Dec. 1994.
55. SCOR, 33rd year, 2056th meeting (26 Jan. 1978), paras. 9–28.
56. PC/EX/113/Rev. 1, (12 Nov. 1945), p. 46.
57. F. Y. Chai, *Consultation and Consensus in the Security Council*, UNITAR (PS4), 1971, pp. 13–27. Examples of draft resolutions being submitted by or for the President include SC res. 233 (S/7935), 6 June 1967; 235 (S/7960), 9 June 1967; 240, 25 Oct. 1967; 251, 2 May 1968; 258, 18 Sept. 1968; 266, 10 June 1969; 270, 26 Aug. 1969; 274, 11 Dec. 1969; 278, 11 May 1970; 281, 9 June 1970; 286, 9 Sept. 1970; 291 (S/10036), 10 Dec. 1970; 293 (S/10209), 26 May 1971; 305 (S/10441), 13 Dec. 1971); 315 (S/10699), 15 June 1972; 324 (S/10847), 12 Dec. 1972.
58. Prandler, p. 166.
59. See, for example, SCOR, 16th year, 963rd meeting (22 July 1961), paras. 142–4; 23rd year, 1412th meeting (4 Apr. 1968), para. 122.
60. SCOR, 34th year, 2140th meeting (5 Apr. 1979), para. 5.
61. SCOR, 31st year, 1955th meeting (10 Sept. 1976), paras. 1–6.
62. S/PV. 2221, 8 May 1980, p. 2.
63. SCOR, 35th year, 2243rd meeting (29 July 1980), para. 2.
64. S/PV. 2401, 12 Nov. 1982, p. 2.
65. S/PV. 2561, 7 Nov. 1984, p. 2.
66. S/PV. 2667, 21 Mar. 1986, p. 2.
67. S/PV.2839, 9 January 1989.
68. S/PV.3589, 6 November 1995.
69. S/PV.3617, 8 January 1996.
70. S/PV.3620, 24 January 1996.
71. S/PV. 2279, 4 June 1981, p. 37.
72. S/PV. 2290, 8 July 1981, p. 2.
73. SCOR, 31st year, 1944th meeting (27 July 1976), paras. 4–5.
74. S/PV. 2648, 28 Jan. 1986, pp. 2–5; S/PV.3647, 4 April 1996; S/PV.3682, 24 July 1996.
75. SCOR, 31st year, 1945th meeting (28 July 1976), para. 8; 32nd year, 1988th meeting (21 Mar. 1977), para. 2; S/PV. 2250, 15 Oct. 1980, p. 2; S/PV.3284, 30 September 1993; S/PV. 3330, 24 January 1994; S/PV.3492, 18 January 1995.
76. S/PV.3692, 28 August 1996.
77. E.g. S/PV.3524, 15 July 1993 and S/PV.2966, 8 December 1990, p. 26.
78. S/PV.2966, 8 December 1990
79. S/PV. 2981, 3 April 1991.
80. S/PV. 2328, 14 Jan. 1982, pp. 43–7.
81. SCOR, 31st year, 1882nd meeting (28 Jan. 1976), para. 31; 1889th meeting (18 Feb. 1976), para. 103; S/PV. 2199, 22 Feb. 1980, p. 57.

82. SCOR, 31st year, 1942nd meeting (13 July 1976), paras. 60–72; S/PV. 2675, 15 Apr. 1986, p. 21; S/PV. 2677, 16 Apr. 1986, p. 47.
83. S/PV. 2396, 19 Sept. 1982, pp. 71–2.
84. S/PV. 2675, 15 Apr. 1986, pp. 38, 54; S/PV. 2676, 16 Apr. 1986, p. 3.
85. S/PV. 2427, 27 Mar. 1983, pp. 36–7.
86. S/PV.2981, 3 April 1991, p. 137.
87. Ibid.
88. S/PV. 2665, 20 Feb. 1986, pp. 37–40; S/PV. 2666, 24 Feb. 1986, pp. 2–6.
89. S/PV. 2334, 24 Mar. 1982, pp. 63–7; S/PV. 2355, 16 Apr. 1982, pp. 21–3, 28–31; S/PV. 2388, 4 Aug. 1982, pp. 58–60.
90. S/PV. 2357, 20 Apr. 1982, p. 22; see also S/PV. 2390, 6 Aug. 1982, pp. 21–6.
91. SCOR, 29th year, 1788th meeting (31 July 1974), para. 284; 1906th meeting Mar. 1976), paras. 316–20.
92. GA res. 268b(III), 28 Apr. 1949; SC res. 81 (S/1486), 24 May 1950.
93. SCOR, 3rd year, 387th meeting (20 Dec. 1948), pp. 3–5.
94. SCOR, 1st year, 1st series, 48th meeting (24 June 1946), p. 400; SC res. 47 (S/726), 21 Apr. 1948; SCOR, 3rd year, 289th meeting (7 May 1948), p. 8; SC res. 276 (S/9620/Rev. 1), 30 Jan. 1970; SCOR, 25th year, Supplement for Mar. to July 1970, p. 148, S/9748; SC res. 283 (S/9891), 29 July 1970; SCOR, 25th year, Supplement for July to Sept. 1970, p. 147, S/9951.
95. SCOR, 2nd year, 174th meeting (4 Aug. 1947), pp. 1717–18; SC res. 289 (S/9990)/Rev. 1), 23 Nov. 1970; res. 294 (S/10266), 15 July 1971; res. 295 (S/10281), 3 Aug. 1971.
96. SCOR, 16th year, 960th meeting (7 July 1961), para. 82; 962nd meeting (22 July 1961), para. 62; 19th year, 1086th meeting (10 Jan. 1964), paras. 59–60, 104–5; 1143rd meeting (9/11 Aug. 1964), paras. 11–14; 21st year, 1300th meeting (16 Aug. 1966), para. 2; 22nd year, 1383rd meeting (24/25 Nov. 1967), para. 151; 23rd year, 1448th meeting (8/9 Sept. 1968), para. 37.
97. SCOR, 3rd year, 229th meeting (17 Jan. 1948), pp. 125–8; 230th meeting (20 Jan. 1948), pp. 132–3; 235th meeting (24 Jan. 1948), pp. 259, 262–4; 277th meeting (1 Apr. 1948), pp. 2 and 36–41; 282nd meeting (15 Apr. 1948), p. 2; 4th year, 457th meeting (17 Dec. 1949), pp. 4–8; 458th meeting (29 Dec. 1948), pp. 4–22.
98. SCOR, 19th year, 1140th meeting (5 Aug. 1946), paras. 88–91; 1141st meeting (7 Aug. 1964), paras. 22–3.
99. SC res. 290 (S/10030), 8 Dec. 1970; res. 298 (S/10337, S/10338/Add. 1), 25 Sept. 1971; res. 302 (S/10395, as amended), 24 Nov. 1971; res. 317 (S/10742), 21 July 1972.

100. SCOR, 3rd year, 226th meeting (6 Jan. 1948), pp. 4–5, S/636.
101. SC res. 43 (S/714, I), 1 Apr. 1948; SCOR, 3rd year, 282nd meeting (15 Apr. 1948), pp. 2–4; SC res. 46 (S/723), 17 Apr. 1948.
102. GAOR, 4th session, Supplement no. 1. A/930, pp. 17–18; Supplement no. 2, A/945, p. 65; S/1182, 4 Jan. 1948 (mimeo.); Press Release SC/908, 15 Mar. 1949 (mimeo.); Lie, p. 216.
103. SC res. 132 (S/4216), 7 Sept. 1959.
104. S/PRST/1994/3, 18 January 1994.
105. S/PRST/1994/18, 8 April 1994; S/PRST/1994/41, 5 August 1994; S/PRST/1994/76, 30 November 1994; S/PRST/1995/14, 30 March 1995; S/PRST/1995/36, 28 July 1995; S/PRST/1995/56, 22 November 1995.
106. S/PRST/1995/3, 24 January 1995; S/PRST/1996/10, 4 March 1996.
107. S/PRST/1994/40, 29 July 1994.
108. S/PRST/1994/24, 11 May 1994; S/PRST/1994/49, 30 August 1994.
109. S/PRST/1996/3, 22 January 1996.
110. SCOR, 12th year, 768th meeting (15 Feb. 1957) to 773rd meeting (20 Feb. 1957), para. 126; Supplement for Jan. to Mar. 1957, pp. 7–8, S/3787 and S/3789.
111. Ibid., 773rd meeting (20 Feb. 1957), paras. 127–53; 774th meeting (21 Feb. 1957), paras. 1–82; SC res. 123 (S/3793), 21 Feb. 1957; Supplement for Apr. to June 1957, pp. 12–16, S/3821.
112. Ibid., 797th meeting (25 Oct. 1957), paras. 1, 25, 45, 55; 798th meeting (29 Oct. 1957), paras. 1, 14, 24, 25.
113. SCOR, 34th year, 2118th meeting (28 Feb. 1979), paras. 63–7.
114. UNCIO, 1945, 10 pp. 710–14, reproduced in Appendix III.
115. See Sydney D. Bailey, *Voting in the Security Council*, pp. 48–50, 112–35.
116. A revised version of this working paper appears in A/50/47/Add.1, 9 September 1996.
117. General Assembly *Open-ended Working Group on the Question of Equitable Representation on and Increase in the Membership of the Security Council and Other Matters Related to the Security Council.*
118. GA res. 1619 (XV), 21 Apr. 1961; 1732 (XVI), 20 Dec. 1961; 1854B (XVII), 19 Dec. 1962; 1874 (S–IV), 27 June 1963; 2053B (XX), 15 Dec. 1965.
119. Press Release of the Permanent Mission of Germany to the UN, No.17/97, 21 March 1997.
120. S/1995/261, S/1995/262, S/1995/263, S/1995/264, and S/1995/265.
121. GA res. 1991 (A/XVIII), 17 Dec. 1963.
122. Ruth B. Russell, assisted by Jeanette E. Muther, *A History of the*

United Nations Charter, Washington, DC, Brookings Institution; London, Faber, 1958, p. 444.
123. Ibid. pp. 648–9.
124. FRUS, 1946, 1 (1972), pp. 117–250.
125. GAOR, 1st session, Part I, 4th and 5th plenary meetings (12 Jan. 1946).
126. FRUS, 1947, 1 (1973), pp. 135, 154, 157.
127. GAOR, 8th session, 450th plenary meeting (5 Oct. 1953), para. 19. See also 4th session, 231st plenary meeting (20 Oct. 19994), para. 10; 6th session, 353rd plenary meeting (7 Dec. 1951), paras. 10–13; 11th session, 612th plenary meeting (7 Dec. 1956), pars. 17–22; SCOR, 20th year, Supplement for Jan. to Mar. 1965, pp. 264–5, S/6264.
128. FRUS, 1947, 1 (1973), pp. 102–65.
129. GAOR, 2nd session, 109th plenary meeting (13 Nov. 1947), p. 750.
130. GAOR, 10th session, 551st plenary meeting (6 Dec. 1955), para. 64.
131. Ibid., 559th plenary meeting (16 Dec. 1955), paras. 197–201.
132. Ibid. paras. 172, 301–2.
133. GAOR, 11th session, Annexes, Agenda item 68, A/3332.
134. Ibid., 612th plenary meeting (7 Dec. 1956), paras. 18–22.
135. GAOR, 14th session 857th plenary meeting (12 Dec. 1959), paras. 305–6.
136. GA res. 1991 (XVIII), 17 Dec. 1963.
137. GAOR, 18th session, Annexes, Agenda items 82 and 12, A/5686, paras. 18–21.
138. GAOR, 20th session, Annexes, Agenda items 15 and 16, A/6019, pp. 1–3.
139. SCOR, 18th year, Supplement for July to Sept. 1963, pp. 6–10, S/5347.
140. S/PV. 2451, 1 June 1983, p. 3; S/PV. 2595, 19 June 1985, pp. 3–4.
141. S/22319, 2 March 1991.
142. S/PV.1870–1879, 12–26 January 1976.
143. SCOR, 26th year, 1606th meeting (4 Dec. 1971), paras. 3–4, 10, 16, 18, 23, 29–30, 43–4.
144. *Repertoire I*, p. 101.
145. S/PV. 2185, 5 Jan. 1980, pp. 17–18; S/PV. 2202, 27 Feb. 1980, pp. 48–52.
146. SCOR, 26th year, 1607th meeting (5 Dec. 1971), para. 260; 1608th meeting (6 Dec. 1971), paras. 15–27.
147. S/PV. 2241, 30 June 1980, p. 3; S/PV. 2242, 30 June 1980, p. 5.
148. S/PV. 2461, 2 Aug. 1983, p. 96.
149. S/PV. 2580, 10 May 1985, p. 117.
150. SCOR, 30th year, 1859th to 1862nd meetings (4–8) Dec. 1975); see also SCOR, 3rd year, 278th meeting (6 Apr. 1948), pp. 1–7; 5th year,

520th meeting (8 Nov. 1950), p. 8; 10th year, 690th meeting (31 Jan. 1955), para. 143; 15th year, 851st meeting (30 Mar. 1960), paras. 80–1; 887th meeting (21 Aug. 1960), paras. 1–2; 18th year, 1040th meeting (22 July 1963), paras. 10–12; 1041st meeting (23 July 1960), para. 89; 1050th meeting (31 July 1960), paras. 5–6; 19th year, 1141st meeting (7 Aug. 1964), para. 22; 21st year, 1248th meeting (27 Oct. 1965), paras. 1–8; 1261st meeting (15 Nov. 1965), paras. 63–4; 1262nd meeting (16 Nov. 1965), para. 35.

151. S/PV. 2409, 16 Dec. 1982, p. 53.
152. SCOR, 6th year, 558th meeting (1 Sept. 1951), paras. 7–11; 8th year, 643rd meeting (25 Nov. 1953), paras. 1–13; 9th year, 664th meeting (29 Mar. 1954), paras. 117–37.
153. See, for example, SCOR, 2nd year, 96th meeting (28 Jan. 1947), p. 133; 171st meeting (31 July 1947), p. 1619; 5th year, 520th meeting (8 Nov. 1950), p. 9.
154. SCOR, 3rd year, 231st meeting (22 Jan. 1948), paras. 144–64.
155. SCOR, 24th year, Supplement for July to Sept. 1969, p. 159, S/9394; 1503rd meeting (20 Aug. 1969).
156. SCOR, 21st year, 1312th meeting (28 Oct. 1966), paras. 125–6, 133, 135, 139; 26th year, 1606th meeting (4 Dec. 1971), paras. 51–3, 140; 1607th meeting (5 Dec. 1971), paras. 41, 67.
157. SCOR, 2nd year, 192nd meeting (22 Aug. 1947), p. 2152. See also 11th year, 746th meeting (28 Oct. 1956), paras. 39–41.
158. SCOR, 6th year, 540th meeting (2 Apr. 1951), paras. 10–13; 16th year, 962nd meeting (22 July 1961), para. 57; 19th year, 1142nd meeting (8 Aug. 1964), para. 50; 20th year, 1247th meeting (25 Oct. 1965), paras. 77–86, 102–9, 112–21, 129–35, 138–40; S/PV. 1613, 13 Dec. 1971, pp. 51, 53–5, 63.
159. SCOR, 31st year, 1894th meeting (22 Mar. 1976), paras. 194–5; Kurt Waldheim, *In the Eye of the Storm*, London, Weidenfeld & Nicolson, 1985, p. 41.
160. GA res. 3210 (XXIV), 14 Oct. 1974; A/AV. 2282, 13 Nov. 1974, pp. 2–51.
161. SCOR, 30th year, Supplement for Oct. to Dec. 1975, p. 50, S/11893; 1859th meeting (4 Dec. 1975), para. 3.
162. S/PV.3340, 28 February 1994.
163. Resolution 777 (1992) adopted on 19 September 1992 at its 3116th meeting.
164. In a letter dated 29 September 1992 addressed to the Permanent Representatives of Bosnia and Herzegovina and Croatia to the United Nations, A/47/485, annex.

165. Meeting nos. 3135th, 13 November 1992; 3174th, 19 February 1993; 3200th, 17 April 1993; 3201st, 19 April 1993; 3247th, 3262th, 9 August 1993; 29 June 1993; 3336th, 14 February 1994; 3367th, 21 April 1994; 3370th, 27 April 1994; 3428th, 23 September 1994; 3434th, 30 September 1994; 3454th, 8 November 1994 and 3487th, 12 January 1995.
166. 'The case for a new interpretation of Article 31 of the UN Charter' Paper submitted to the General Assembly's *Open-ended Working Group on the Question of Equitable Representation on and Increase in the Membership of the Security Council.* A/AC.247/1996/CRP.13, 12 June 1996.
167. See B. Simma, *The Charter of the United Nations: A Commentary*, Oxford, Oxford University Press, 1994, p. 641.
168. S/PRST/1996/13, 28 March 1996.
169. For example S/PV.3711, 13 November 1996.
170. S/PV.2222, 20 May 1980, pp. 4–5 (S/13942).
171. S/PV.2959, 27 November 1990, p. 22.
172. Ibid. p. 23.
173. S/PV.3105, 11 August 1992.
174. S/PV.3134, 13 November 1992.
175. S/PV.3139, 25 November 1992.
176. See Richard F. Pedersen, 'National Representation in the United Nations', *International Organization*, 15, no. 2 (Spring 1961), pp. 256–66.
177. GA res. 257A (III), 3 Dec. 1948.
178. UNTS, 1, p. 15; 2, p. 11; and 500, p. 108.
179. ST/SG/SER.A/278, January 1997.
180. Address to the Students' Association, Copenhagen, SG/812, 1 May 1959, p. 2; GAOR, 14th session, Supplement no. 1A, A/4132/Add. 1, p. 2.
181. FRUS, 1947, 1 (1973), p. 511.
182. GA res. 1990 (XVIII) and 1991A (XVIII), 17 Dec. 1963.
183. *Journal*, no. 5203, 1 July 1971, p. 4.
184. SCOR, 21st year, 1307th meeting (14/15 Oct. 1966), para. 3.
185. SCOR, 28th year, Supplement for Jan. to Mar. 1973, p. 48, S/10889.
186. SCOR, 33rd year, 2082nd meeting (27 July 1978), p. 283.
187. S/PV.2237, 26 June 1980, p. 62; S/PV.2245, 20 Aug. 1980, p. 7.
188. S/PV.2596, 20 June 1985, p. 41; S/PV.2607, 20 Sept. 1985, pp. 9–10.
189. SCOR, 28th year, Supplement for Jan. to Mar. 1973, p. 28, S/10859; S/PV.2597, 20 June 1985, p. 3; S/PV.2598, 21 June 1985, p. 28.
190. S/PV.2597, 20 June 1985, p. 42.

191. SCOR, 34th year, 2111th meeting (15 Jan. 1979), para. 4; S/PV.2461, 2 Aug. 1983, p. 96.
192. See, for example, vol. XXIII, no. 4 (Autumn 1986), inside back cover. (This table omits Brunei-Darussalam and fails to give Upper Volta its new name of Burkina Faso.)
193. Mar. 1972, Nov. 1973, Sept. 1975, July 1977, May 1979, Mar. 1981, Jan. 1983, Nov. 1984, Sept. 1986, etc.
194. Turkey chaired this group in Dec. 1972, June 1976, May 1980, June 1982, Dec. 1983, Dec. 1985.
195. Source: British Foreign and Commonwealth Office. 'Major UN groups and major groupings relating to the UN System', FCO Circular No. 45/97, 31 January 1997.
196. A/41/173, 21 Feb. 1986.
197. Stevenson, p. 342.
198. S/PV.3046, 31 January 1992, p. 69.
199. See Karen E. Smith 'Regional Agencies and the Yugoslav Crisis: The Application of Chapter VIII of the United Nations Charter' in P. Taylor, S. Daws, and U. Adamczick-Gerteis, *Documents on Reform of the United Nations*, Dartmouth, 1997.
200. A/C.6/49/L.12, 15 November 1994.
201. SCOR, 1st year, 1st series, Supplement no. 2, Annex 1a, pp. 2 and 4, S/6.
202. Ibid., 31st meeting (9 Apr. 1946), pp. 111–15.
203. SCOR, 5th year, Supplement for Jan. to May. 1950, pp. 2–3, and 16–18, S/1447 and S/1457 and Corr. 1; 468th meeting (28 Feb. 1950), pp. 9–11.
204. See, for example, SCOR, 2nd year, 171st meeting (31 July 1947), p. 1618; 181st meeting (12 Aug. 1947), p. 1940; 184th meeting (14 Aug. 1947), p. 1980; see also *Juridical Yearbook 1971*, p. 194.
205. *Juridical Yearbook 1977*, p. 157.
206. SCOR, 11th year, 752nd meeting (2 Nov. 1956), paras. 7–44.
207. SCOR, 13th year, 827th meeting (15 July 1958), paras. 1–29; 834th meeting. (18 July 1958), paras. 2–42; Supplement for July to Sept., pp. 54–6 and 124–5, S/4060, S/4080, and S/4081; 838th meeting (7 Aug. 1958), para. 1.
208. SCOR, 29th year, 1780th meeting (19 July 1974), paras. 2–3; Supplement for July to Sept. 1974, pp. 30–1, S/11349.
209. SCOR, 15th year, 899th meeting (14 Sept. 1960), paras. 5–38; 900th meeting (14 Sept. 1960), paras. 53–87.
210. SCOR, 20th year, 1207th meeting (13 May 1965), paras. 4–109; 1209th meeting (14 May 1965), paras. 3–49; Supplement for Apr. to June 1965, pp. 118–22, S/6353.

211. SCOR, 23rd year, Supplement for Jan. to Mar. 1968, pp. 143–5, S/8365 and Corr. 1, paras 2–3.
212. Ibid., 1387th meeting (25 Jan. 1968), paras. 11–37; Supplement for Jan. to Mar. 1968; pp. 143–5, S/8365 and Corr. 1, para. 5.
213. S/PV. 2469, 31 Aug. 1983, pp. 41–50.
214. See Sydney Bailey's monograph *Chinese Representation in the Security Council and the General Assembly of the United Nations*, Brighton, Institute for the Study of International Organization, 1970.
215. A/1123, 21 Nov. 1949 (mimeo.).
216. GAOR, 4th session, 227th plenary meeting (24 Sept. 1950), p. 48.
217. SCOR, 4th year, 458th meeting (29 Dec. 1949), pp. 1–3.
218. S/1462, 24 Feb. 1950 (mimeo.), p. 2; SCOR, 5th year, 459th meeting (10 Jan. 1950), pp. 1–4.
219. SCOR, 5th year, 460th meeting (12 Jan. 1950) and 461st meeting (13 Jan. 1950), pp. 1–10.
220. S/1462, 24 Feb. 1950 (mimeo.), pp. 2–3.
221. Lie, p. 254.
222. Ibid. pp. 254–5, 258–60.
223. Ibid. pp. 256–7, 261; SCOR, 5th year, Supplement for Jan. to May 1950, pp. 18–23, S/1466.
224. Ibid. pp. 23–6, S/1470. See also Lie, pp. 249–74.
225. SCOR, 5th year, Supplement for Jan. to May 1950, pp. 23–6, S/1470.
226. Ibid., 459th meeting (10 Jan. 1950), pp. 8–9; 460th meeting (12 Jan. 1950), pp. 6–7; 462nd meeting (17 Jan. 1950), pp. 1–12; Supplement for Jan. to May 1950, pp. 2–3, and 16–18, S/1447 and S/1457 and Corr. 1, paras. 4–12; 468th meeting (28 Feb. 1950), paras. 9–11.
227. Ibid., 480th meeting (1 Aug. 1950), pp. 1–12; 481st meeting (2 Aug. 1950); 482nd meeting (3 Aug. 1950), pp. 1–22.
228. SCOR, 6th year, 566th meeting (10 Nov. 1951), p. 1; 10th year, 689th meeting (31 Jan. 1955), paras. 1–27; 700th meeting (8 Sept. 1955), paras. 1–5; 22nd year, 1341st meeting (24 May 1967), paras. 8–59.
229. SCOR, 26th year, 1565th meeting (9 Feb. 1971), paras. 51–101; see also S/10378, 26 Oct. 1971, and S/10382, 2 Nov. 1971 (both mimeo.).
230. International Documents Review, Vol. 7 No. 36. 14 October 1996. P. 3. reports that the diplomat in question, Ambassador Salim A. Salim claims that the dance was a Western media myth.
231. GA res. 2758 (XXVI), 25 Oct. 1971.
232. A/PV. 1983, 15 Nov. 1971, pp. 87–101.
233. SCOR, 5th year, 525th meeting (27 Nov. 1950), p. 20; 526th meeting (28 Nov. 1950), p. 2; 527th meeting (28 Nov. 1950), pp. 1–26; 528th

meeting (29 Nov. 1950), pp. 8 and 11; 529th meeting (30 Nov. 1950), p. 1; 530th meeting (30 Nov. 1950), pp. 1 and 19–20.

234. S/10391, 19 Nov. 1971 (mimeo.); SCOR, 26th year, 1599th meeting (23 Nov. 1971), paras. 1–94.
235. See, for example, SCOR, 23rd year, 1417th meeting (27 Apr. 1968), paras. 71–2; 25th year, 1530th meeting (6 Mar. 1970), para. 5.
236. A/48/191, 9 August 1993.
237. S/1997/18, 10 January 1997.
238. The insurgent movement 'Unidad Revolucionaria Nacional Guatemalteca'.
239. S/PV.3730, 10 January 1997.
240. S/1997/49, 20 January 1997.
241. S/1997/53*, 20 January 1997.
242. A/52/143, 16 July 1997.
243. *Yearbook of the International Law Commission* 11 (1968), p. 163; *Satow's Guide to Diplomatic Practice*, ed. Lord Gore-Booth, 5th edn., London and New York, Longman, 1979, ch. 4, 21–2; letter from the Chief of Protocol at the United Nations, 20 Jan. 1987.

CHAPTER 4

1. SCOR, 27th year, Supplement for Apr. to June 1972, pp. 32–3, S/10611, S/10612.
2. John P. Humphrey, *Human Rights and the United Nations: A Great Adventure*, New York, Transnational, 1984, p. 122.
3. SCOR, 19th year, 1136th meeting (18 June 1964), para. 16.
4. SCOR, 21st year, 1316th meeting (3 Nov. 1966), paras. 3–4; 26th year, 1608th meeting (6 Dec. 1971); paras. 212–13.
5. SCOR, 19th year, 1136th meeting (18 June 1964), para. 15.
6. SCOR, 3rd year, 330th meeting (7 July 1948), pp. 6, 10–11; 15th year, 893rd meeting (8 Sept. 1960), para. 71; 22nd year, 1373rd meeting (9/10 Nov. 1967), para. 8; 28th year, 1747th meeting (21/22 Oct. 1973), paras. 89–99; 1749th meeting (24 Oct. 1973), paras. 106–7, 116; 32rd year, 2005th meeting (14 Apr. 1977), para. 4; S/PV. 2248, 28th Sept. 1980, pp. 7–10, 42, 47; S/PV. 2409, 16 Dec. 1982, pp. 53, 68.
7. SCOR, 22nd year, 1355th meeting (10 June 1967), paras. 47–8; 1373rd meeting (9/10 Nov. 1967), paras. 15, 34, 45; 28th year, 1748th meeting (23 Oct. 1973), paras. 124a–124c, 154.
8. SCOR, 28th year, 1744th meeting (9 Oct. 1973), para. 107.
9. SCOR, 5th year, 519th meeting (8 Nov. 1950), pp. 1–14.

10. SCOR, 3rd year, 357th meeting (16 Sept. 1948), pp. 11–18.
11. SCOR, 5th year, 525th meeting (27 Nov. 1950), pp. 21–2; 526th meeting (28 Nov. 1950), pp. 2–10.
12. SCOR, 19th year, 1095th meeting (18 Feb. 1964), paras. 2–32.
13. SCOR, 22nd year, 1373rd meeting (9/10 Nov. 1967), paras. 5–45.
14. SCOR, 9th year, 656th meeting (22 Jan. 1954), para. 19; 33rd year, 2056th meeting (26 Jan. 1978), paras. 4–28; S/PV. 2465, 12 Aug. 1983, pp. 68–70, 76.
15. SCOR, 17th year, 1025th meeting (25 Oct. 1962), paras. 49, 51.
16. SCOR, 11th year, 753rd meeting (3 Nov. 1956), paras. 15, 23–31; 22nd year, 1355th meeting (to June 1967), paras. 18–58.
17. SCOR, 15th year, 874th meeting (18 July 1960), paras. 4–5; 893rd meeting (8 Sept. 1960), paras. 27, 71; 16th year, 975th meeting (16 Nov. 1961), paras. 122, 124–30; 20th year, 1263rd meeting (17 Nov. 1965), paras. 22–4; S/PV. 2465, 12 Aug. 1983, p. 66.
18. SCOR, 19th year, 1142nd meeting (8 Aug. 1964), paras. 8–46; 20th year, 1210th meeting (18 May 1965), para. 5.
19. Cited in Sydney D. Bailey, *The General Assembly of the United Nations*, 2nd edn., 1964, p. 121.
20. SCOR, 2nd year, 185th meeting (15 Aug. 1947), p. 2024.
21. GAOR, 26th session, Supplement no. 26, A/8426, p. 44, para. 229(a) (Reference inserted by the author).
22. Ibid. p. 45, para. 229(d).
23. SCOR, 31st year, 1940th meeting (12 July 1976) paras. 14–16.
24. SCOR, 1st year, 2nd series, 67th meeting (16 Sept. 1946), p. 338.
25. SCOR, 17th year, 989th meeting (30 Jan. 1962), paras. 32–41, 45, 49.
26. Ibid., paras. 54–5, 62, 67–74. For an exception to this practice, see SCOR, 23rd year, 1448th meeting (8/9th Sept. 1968), paras 67–72.
27. GAOR, 26th session, Supplement no. 26, A/8426, pp. 44–5, paras. 229(a) and (c).
28. SCOR, 28th year, 1748th meeting (23 Oct. 1973), para. 51.
29. GAOR, 26th session, Supplement no. 26 (A/8426), para. 229(c).
30. SCOR, 11th year, 751st meeting (31 Oct. 1956), paras. 126–7.
31. *Repertoire I*, p. 32, n. 22.
32. For an exception, see SCOR, 17th year, 998th meeting (23 Mar. 1962), paras. 154–6.
33. GAOR, 26th session, Supplement no. 26, A/8426, p. 45, para. 229(c).
34. SCOR, 26th year, 1606th meeting (4 Dec. 1971), paras. 46–67.
35. Ibid., 1613rd meeting (13 Dec. 1971), paras. 76–138.
36. SCOR, 1st year, 2nd series, 67th meeting (16 Sept. 1946), pp. 336–8; 5th year, 525th meeting (27 Nov. 1950), pp. 20–1.

37. SCOR, 2nd year, 202nd meeting (15 Sept. 1947), p. 2402; 20th year, 1247th meeting (25 Oct. 1965), paras. 78, 102–9, 112–19; 21st year, 1295th meeting (3 Aug. 1966), para. 133. See also 25th year, 1537th meeting (12 May 1970), paras. 55–6.
38. SCOR, 2nd year, 213rd meeting (22 Oct. 1947), pp. 2619–20.
39. SCOR, 3rd year, 3429th meeting (6 July 1948), pp. 20–1.
40. See, for example, SCOR, 5th year, 480th meeting (1 Aug. 1950), p. 1.
41. John P. Humphrey, *Human Rights and the United Nations: A Great Adventure*, New York, Transnational, 1984, p. 60.
42. Rules 75 and 116.
43. SCOR, 15th year, 874th meeting (18 July 1960), pp. 4–5; 16th year, 975th meeting (16 Nov. 1961), para. 126; 28th year, 1717th meeting (6 June 1973), paras. 140–3; S/PV. 2465, 12 Aug. 1983, pp. 66, 68–70, 76; S/PV. 2495, 11 Nov. 1983, p. 6.
44. S/PV. 2655, 16 Dec. 1987.
45. See, for example, S/PV. 2480 18 Oct. 1983.
46. SCOR, 1st year, 1st series, Supplement no. 2, p. 22, S/57.
47. SCOR, 1st year, 1st series, 41st meeting (16 May 1946), p. 257.
48. See, for example, SCOR, 25th year, 1537th meeting (12 May 1970), paras. 113–31.
49. SCOR, 1st year, 1st series, 41st meeting (16 May 1946), pp. 255, 257 (our italics).
50. SCOR, 26th year, 1606th meeting (4 Dec. 1971), pp. 391–2; 27th year, 1637th meeting (3 Feb. 1972), paras. 9, 115, 119, 124, 133, 171; 1639th meeting (4 Feb. 1972), paras. 1–2; 28th year, 1710th meeting (20 Apr. 1973), paras. 5–8.
51. See, for example, SCOR, 24th year, 1481st meeting (24 June 1969), paras. 50, 57; 27th year, 1677th meeting (22 Nov. 1972), paras. 76–82.
52. SCOR, 1st year 1st series, 7th meting (4 Feb. 1946), pp. 123–4.
53. For discussion of the application of Rule 31, see SCOR, 3rd year, 328th meeting (1 July 1948), p. 25; 329th meeting (6 July 1948), pp. 27–30; 337th meeting (15 July 1948), p. 42; 9th year, 655th meeting (21 Jan. 1954), paras. 76, 79, 83, 85; 16th year, 942nd meeting (20/21 Feb. 1961), para. 170; 966th meeting (29 July 1961), paras. 62–3.
54. See, for example, SCOR, 10th year, 690th meeting (31 Jan. 1955), para. 138; 20th year, 1214th meeting (21 May 1965), paras. 64–7.
55. SCOR, 29th year, 1788th meeting (31 July 1974), paras. 134–200.
56. SCOR, 2nd year, 194th meeting (25 Aug. 1947), pp. 2193–6; 3rd year, 381st meeting (16 Nov. 1948), pp. 50–1; 4th year, 408th meeting (10 Feb. 1949), pp. 16–19; 447th meeting (16 Sept. 1949), pp. 22–3; 8th year, 653rd meeting (22 Dec. 1953), paras. 65–76.

57. See, for example, SCOR, 5th year, 492nd meeting (29 Aug. 1950), pp. 15–16; 497th meeting (7 Sept. 1950), pp. 27–9; 501st meeting (12 Sept. 1950), pp. 2–13; 10th year, 702nd meeting (10 Dec. 1955), paras. 17, 22–6; 703rd meeting (13 Dec. 1955), paras. 62–6.
58. Ibid., 709th meeting (22 Dec. 1955), para. 43; 11th year, Supplement for Jan. to Mar. 1956, pp. 1–2, S/3528; 715th meeting (19 Jan. 1956), paras. 120–30.
59. SCOR, 34th year, 2115th meeting (24 Feb. 1979), para. 3.
60. SCOR, 4th year, 405th meeting (27 Jan. 1949), pp. 31–2.
61. GAOR, 26th session, Supplement no. 26, A/8426, p. 45, para. 229(b).
62. For examples of the correct procedure (by the Soviet Union, Tunisia, and the United States respectively), see SCOR, 11th year, 746th meeting (28 Oct. 1956), paras. 47–8; 15th year, 897th meeting (10 Sept. 1960), paras. 78–9; 898th meeting (12 Sept. 1960), paras. 7–8.
63. SCOR, 1st year, 1st series, Supplement no. 2, p. 22, S/57; 41st meeting (16 May 1946), pp. 259–60.
64. SCOR, 2nd year, 160th meeting (17 July 1947), p. 1387; 193rd meeting (22 Aug. 1947), pp. 2171–3; 9th year, 656th meeting (22 Jan. 1954), paras. 14–22.
65. SCOR, 32nd year, 2054th meeting (15 Dec. 1977), para. 17; S/PV. 2319, 17 Dec. 1981, p. 16; S/PV. 2455, 29 June 1983, p. 16; S/PV. 2456, 10 July 1983.
66. SCOR, 19th year, 1143rd meeting (9/11 Aug. 1964), para. 180; 35th year, 2190th meeting (7 Jan. 1980), para. 141; 2191st meeting (11 Jan. 1980), para. 141; 2191st meeting (11 Jan. 1980), para. 9.
67. SCOR, 19th year, 1143rd meeting (9/11 Aug. 1964), paras. 149–50; S/PV.2350, 3 Apr. 1982, pp. 77–81; S/PV.2677, 16 Apr. 1986, p. 16; S/PV.2682, 21 Apr. 1986, p. 26.
68. SCOR, 1st year, 1st series, 8th meeting (5 Feb. 1946), p. 133; 9th meeting (6 Feb. 1946), pp. 136–63.
69. SCOR, 1st year, 2nd series, 57th meeting (29 Aug. 1946), pp. 113–15.
70. SCOR, 7th year, 591st meeting (9 July 1952), para. 43; 8th year, 653rd meeting (22 Dec. 1953), para. 38; 10th year, 706th meeting (15 Dec. 1955), para. 123; 12th year, 788th meeting (6 Sept. 1957), paras. 54 and 67.
71. SCOR, 16th year, 982nd meeting (24 Nov. 1961), paras. 87–94.
72. SCOR, 19th year, 1143rd meeting (9/11 Aug. 1964), paras. 144, 149–50, 169–70, 180.
73. S/PV.2923, 29 May 1990.
74. S/PV.2926, 31 May 1990, p. 35.
75. PV.2970 (Part II)*, 20 December 1990.

76. S/PV.2977 (Part I), 13 February 1991.
77. S/PV.2977 (Parts II closed resumptions 1–5; 14, 15, 16, 23, 26 February and 2 March 1991)
78. S/PV.3652 (and Resumption 1), 15 April 1996. The announcement of the President, Ambassador Somavía of Chile, that he intended to suspend the meeting 'in view of the lateness of the hour' is a typical formulation used.
79. S/PV.3536 and Resumptions 1 and 2; 12, 15 and 16 May 1995.
80. S/PV.3538, 17 May 1995; Draft resolution contained in document S/1995/394.
81. SCOR, 5th year, 507th meeting (29 Sept. 1950), pp. 15–17.
82. SCOR, 22nd year, 1358th meeting (13 June 1967), paras. 329–33 and 334.
83. SCOR, 17th year, 989th meeting (30 Jan. 1962), paras. 30–75.
84. Conforti, p. 485.
85. SCOR, 1093rd meeting (17 Feb. 1964), paras. 4, 16, 22; 1104th meeting (17 Mar. 1964), paras. 2–89; 1105th meeting (20 Mar. 1964), paras. 2–51.
86. SCOR, 15th year, 898th meeting (12 Sept. 1960), paras. 16–26.
87. SCOR, 11th year, 714th meeting (18 Jan. 1956), paras. 107–27.
88. S/PV.2966.
89. S/21952, 20 November 1990.
90. S/21933/Rev.1–3.
91. S/PV.2966, 8 December 1990.
92. Ibid.
93. S/PV.2967, 10 December 1990.
94. S/PV.2968, 12 December 1990.
95. S/PV.2970 (Part I)*, 17 December 1990 and S/PV.2970 (Part II)*, 20 December 1990.
96. S/PV.2972, 22 December 1990.
97. See, for example, SCOR, 2nd year, 121st meeting (21 July 1947), p. 590; 122nd meeting (25 Mar. 1947), pp. 609–11; 5th year, 459th meeting (10 Jan. 1950), p. 10; 17th year, 989th meeting (30 Jan. 1962), paras. 30–75.
98. SCOR, 1st year, 2nd series, 57th meeting (29 Aug. 1946), p. 113; 11th year, 714th meeting (18 Jan. 1956), para. 110; 22nd year, 1349th meeting (7 June 1967), para. 23.
99. SCOR, 1st year, 1st series, 19th meeting (14 Feb. 1946), p. 278; 2nd year, 93rd meeting (15 Jan. 1947), p. 82.
100. SCOR, 1st year, 2nd series, 55th meeting (28 Aug. 1946), p. 55.
101. Ibid., 57th meeting (29 Aug. 1946), p. 116; 3rd year, 384th meeting (15 Dec. 1948), p. 14.

102. SCOR, 8th year, 651st meeting (21 Dec. 1953), para. 30; 12th year, 790th meeting (9 Sept. 1957), paras. 45, 47.
103. SCOR, 11th year, 746th meeting (28 Oct. 1956), paras. 48–53.
104. SCOR, 12th year, 788th meeting (6 Sept. 1957), para. 97.
105. SCOR, 7th year, 577th meeting (18 June 1952), para. 138; 582nd meeting (25 June 1952), paras. 96–8; 583rd meeting (26 June 1962), para. 6.
106. SCOR, 1st year, 1st series, 19th meeting (14 Feb. 1946), pp. 275–81.
107. SCOR, 1st year, 2nd series, 55th meeting (28 Aug. 1946), pp. 55, 68; 57th meeting (29 Aug. 1946), pp. 117–19, 125–7, 135–6, 138; see also FRUS, 1 (1947), pp. 236, 238–46, 252.
108. See, for example, SCOR, 2nd year, 93rd meeting (15 Jan. 1947), pp. 83, 85–6; 95th meeting (20 Jan. 1947), pp. 122–3; 3rd year, 384th meeting (15 Dec. 1948), pp. 13–14, 22, 28; 5th year, 506th meeting (29 Sept. 1950), p. 5; 6th year, 565th meeting (19 Oct. 1951), paras. 10–16, 19–26, 28–9, 34, 47–8, 62; 7th year, 590th meeting (9 July 1952), paras. 38–58, 77; 591st meeting (9 July 1952), paras. 1–96; 8th year, 628th meeting (20 Oct. 1953), paras. 4–5, 43–9, 79–82, 90, 131–3; 634th meeting (2 Nov. 1953), paras. 14, 20, 53, 56, 88–9; 641st meeting (23 Nov. 1953), paras. 6–8, 54, 77, 101; 647th meeting (14 Dec. 1943), paras. 3–5, 9–10, 40–3; 13th year, 820th meeting (2 June 1958), para. 109; 821st meeting (4 June 1958), para. 62.
109. SCOR, 2nd year, 90th meeting (9 Jan. 1947), p. 24.
110. SCOR, 10th year, 689th meeting (31 Jan. 1955), paras. 2–26.
111. See Appendix III.
112. SCOR, 5th year, 484th to 488th meetings (8–17 Aug. 1950).
113. See, for example, SCOR, 1st year, 2nd series, 55th meeting (28 Aug. 1946), p. 62; 2nd year, 132nd meeting (30 Apr. 1947), pp. 820–1.
114. SCOR, 3rd year, 330th meeting (7 July 1948), pp. 2–9; 4th year, 443rd meeting (13 Sept. 1949), pp. 22–7; 5th year, 480th meeting (1 Aug. 1950), p. 9; 482nd meeting (3 Aug. 1950), pp. 18–20; 494th meeting (1 Sept. 1950), pp. 2–11; 7th year, 581st meeting (25 June 1952), paras. 31–4; 9th year, 676th meeting (25 June 1954), paras 29–63; 17th year, 989th meeting (30 Jan. 1962), paras. 32–74; 998th meeting (23 Mar. 1962), paras. 145–56; 19th year, 1143rd meeting (9–11 Aug. 1964), paras. 174–7.
115. SCOR, 5th year, 484th meeting (8 Aug. 1950), p. 16; 492nd meeting (29 Aug. 1950), pp. 15–16.
116. SCOR, 1st year, 1st series, 49th meeting (26 June 1946), pp. 410–13.
117. Ibid., 41st meeting (16 May 1946), p. 260; 49th meeting (26 June 1946), p. 411.

118. S/PV.2978.
119. S/22298.
120. SCOR, 2nd year, 169th meeting (29 July 1947), pp. 1585–95.
121. SCOR, 10th year, Supplement for Oct. to Dec. 1955, pp. 20 and 22, S/3502 and S/3506.
122. Ibid., 704th meeting (13 Dec. 1955), paras. 24–48.
123. SCOR, 1st year, 1st series, 17th meeting (12 Feb. 1946), pp. 251–3; 18th meeting (13 Feb. 1946), p. 257; 7th year, 590th meeting (9 July 1952), paras. 38–43, 56–8; 591st meeting (9 July 1952), paras. 10, 25–34, 38.
124. SCOR, 32nd year, 2054th meeting (15 Dec. 1977), paras. 4–17.
125. S/PV.3351, 18 March 1994. The draft resolution became Resolution 904 (1994).
126. Draft resolution contained in document S/1997/18.
127. S/PV.3730, 10 January 1997, p. 20.

CHAPTER 5

1. SCOR, 15th year, 863rd meeting (27 May 1960), paras. 43, 45–6.
2. SCOR, 2nd year, 131st meeting (18 Apr. 1947), p. 807.
3. SCOR, 17th year, 998th meeting (23 Mar. 1962), paras. 113–58.
4. SCOR, 2nd year, 206th meeting (1 Oct. 1947), pp. 2465, 2469; 9th year, 655th meeting (21 Jan. 1954), paras. 58, 87–8; 656th meeting (22 Jan. 1954), paras. 107–35; 11th year, 715th meeting (19 Jan. 1956), paras. 140–1; 722nd meeting (4 Apr. 1956), para. 43; 749th meeting (30 Oct. 1956), para. 124; 21st year, 1319th meeting (4 Nov. 1966), paras. 52–4; 24th year, 1481st meeting (24 June 1968), paras. 50, 57; 27th year, 1677th meeting (22 Nov. 1972), paras. 76–86.
5. See, for example, SCOR, 3rd year, 286th meeting (21 Apr. 1948), pp. 39–40.
6. SCOR, 2nd year, 170th meeting (29 July 1947), p. 1612; 174th meeting (4 Aug. 1947), pp. 1723–6; 9th year, 670th meeting (4 May 1954), paras. 72–3.
7. SCOR, 2nd year, 174th meeting (4 Aug. 1947), p. 1724.
8. SCOR, 5th year, 530th meeting (30 Nov. 1950), pp. 24–5.
9. SCOR, 17th year, 998th meeting (23 Mar. 1962), paras. 78–110.
10. SCOR, 1st year, 1st series, 16th meeting (11 Feb. 1946), pp. 223–32; 18th meeting (13 Feb. 1946), p. 258.
11. SCOR, 2nd year, 206th meeting (1 Oct. 1947), pp. 2465–75.

12. SCOR, 10th year, 706th meeting (15 Dec. 1955), paras. 90, 99, 119.
13. SCOR, 2nd year, 132nd meeting (30 Apr. 1947), p. 821; 194th meeting (25 Aug. 1947), p. 2195; 4th year, 408th meeting (10 Feb. 1949), p. 19; 26th year, 1606th meeting (4 Dec. 1971), paras. 391–2; 27th year, 1637th meeting (3 Feb. 1972), paras. 9, 115, 119, 124, 133, 171; 1639th meeting (4 Feb. 1972), paras. 1–2; 28th year, 1710th meeting (20 Apr. 1973), paras. 5–8; 31st year, 1963rd meeting (19 Oct. 1976), paras. 115–20; S/PV.2580, 10 May 1985, p. 117; S/PV.2686, 23 May 1986, p. 126.
14. SCOR, 23rd year, 2074th meeting (19 Mar. 1978), paras. 4–41.
15. GA res. 2101 (XX), 20 Dec. 1965.
16. UN Conference on International Organization, 1945, 11, p. 713.
17. Richard Hiscocks, *The Security Council: A Study in Adolescence*, Longman, 1973, p. 109.
18. Draft resolution S/1995/394; S/PV.3538, 17 May 1995.
19. Draft resolution S/1995/952; 18 November 1996.
20. GA resolution 377 (V), 3 November 1950.
21. FRUS, 1950, Vol. II, pp. 307 n.1, 311 n.1, 317–24, 330–1, 343–4.
22. GA res. 40(I), 13 Dec. 1946; 117(II), 21 Nov. 1947; 267(III), 14 Apr. 1949; 296K(IV), 2 Nov. 1949.
23. SCOR, 30th year, 1836th meeting (11 Aug. 1975), paras. 110–16.
24. SCOR, 31st year, 1879th meeting (26 Jan. 1976), paras. 74–6.
25. SCOR, 1st year, 1st series, 49th meeting (26 June 1946), pp. 401, 412, 422.
26. SCOR, 1st year, 2nd series, 55th meeting (28 Aug. 1946), pp. 55, 68; 57th meeting (29 Aug. 1946), pp. 132–5.
27. SCOR, 1st year, 2nd series, 70th meeting (20 Sept. 1946), pp. 396, 410–12.
28. SCOR, 2nd year, 114th meeting (27 Feb. 1947), pp. 425–7.
29. SCOR, 2nd year, 202nd meeting (15 Sept. 1947), pp. 2369, 2390–2401.
30. SCOR, 3rd year, 268th meeting (17 Mar. 1948), pp. 90–3; 273rd meeting (23 Mar. 1948), pp. 208–25; 281st meeting (12 Apr. 1948), pp. 2–21; 288th meeting (29 Apr. 1948), pp. 19, 21–8; 300th meeting (21 May 1948), pp. 30–43; 303rd meeting (24 May 1948), pp. 4–29, 33.
31. SCOR, 5th year, 505th meeting (8 Sept. 1950), pp. 17, 20–9; 507th meeting (29 Sept. 1950), pp. 4–8.
32. SCOR, 14th year, 848th meeting (7 Sept. 1959), pp. 12, 22.
33. SCOR, 4th year, 428th meeting (21 June 1949), p. 16; 21st year, 1340th meeting (16 Dec. 1966), para. 154; GAOR, 3rd session, 1st part, *ad Hoc* Political Committee, 20th meeting (30 Nov. 1948), p. 227.

34. SCOR, 16th year, 960th meeting (7 July 1961), para. 61 and see 998th meeting (23 Mar, 1962) para. 154.
35. SCOR, 31st year, 1943rd meeting (14 July 1976), para. 162.
36. S/25997.
37. S/PV.3247, 29 June 1993.
38. See Sydney Bailey's article, 'New Light on Abstentions in the Security Council', *International Affairs*, 50, No. 4 (Oct. 1974), pp. 554–73.
39. UN Conference on International Organization, 1945, 11, pp. 707, 713.
40. FRUS 1945, 1(1967), pp. 1258–60; Wellington Koo, jun., *Voting Procedures in International Organizations*, New York, Columbia University Press, 1947, pp. 153–7.
41. FRUS, 1946, 1(1972), pp. 258–9, 262–4, 266, 271–3, 332, 334.
42. SCOR, 1st year, 1st series, 39th meeting (29 Apr. 1946), p. 243.
43. The Soviet Union abstained on res. 4 (Spanish question), the UK on res. 30 (Indonesia), China on res. 51 (Kashmir), France on res. 63 (Indonesia), and the United States on res. 66 (Palestine).
44. ICJ Reports, 1971, p. 22.
45. See, for example, SCOR, 1st year, 1st series, 3rd meeting (28 Jan. 1946), p. 44; 7th meeting (4 Feb. 1946), pp. 125, 129; 19th meeting (14 Feb. 1946), pp. 272, 277–81; 23rd meeting (16 Feb. 1946), pp. 357, 360–4; 2nd year, 173rd meeting (1 Aug. 1947), p. 1703, 12th year, 169th meeting (15 Feb. 1957), paras. 136–7; 774th meeting (21 Feb. 1957), para. 13.
46. SCOR, 1st year, 1st series, Supplement no. 1, pp. 82–3, S/5; 20th meeting (15 Feb. 1946), pp. 284–9, 292; 21st meeting (15 Feb. 1946), pp. 300, 317; 22nd meeting (16 Feb. 1946), pp. 319, 323 ff.; 23rd meeting (16 Feb. 1946), pp. 360–3.
47. SCOR, 1st year, 1st series, Supplement no. 2, pp. 43–4, S/15; 26th meeting (26 Mar. 1946), p. 30; 27th meeting (27 Mar. 1946), pp. 56, 58, 61; 28th meeting (29 Mar. 1946), pp. 75–6, 82; 30th meeting (4 Apr. 1946), pp. 88–9, 97; 33rd meeting (16 Apr. 1946), pp. 142–3; 36th meeting (23 Apr. 1946), pp. 213–14.
48. S/72, 25 May 1946 (mimeo.); SCOR, 1st year, 2nd series, 81st meeting (29 Nov. 1946), pp. 505–7; 83rd meeting (12 Dec. 1946), pp. 561–3; Supplement nos. 4, 9, 10, S/73, S/114, S/121, S/132, S/139, S/199–201.
49. SCOR, 2nd year, Supplement no. 3, pp. 35–6, S/247; 107th meeting (18 Feb. 1947), p. 306; 111th meeting (24 Feb. 1947), pp. 364–5; 114th meeting (27 Feb. 1947), pp. 418, 422, 425–32, 438.
50. SCOR, 2nd year, 120th meeting (20 Mar. 1947), p. 567; 121st meeting (21 Mar. 1947), p. 589; 122nd meeting (25 Mar. 1947), pp. 595–7, 608–9; 125th meeting (3 Apr. 1947), pp. 685–6; 127th meeting (9 Apr. 1947), pp. 726–7.

51. SCOR, 2nd year, 159th meeting (17 July 1947), pp. 1343–5, S/410; 182nd meeting (13 Aug. 1947), p. 1965; 189th meeting (20 Aug. 1947), pp. 2108–9, 2112, 2115; 193rd meeting (22 Aug. 1947), p. 2169; 196th meeting (26 Aug. 1947), p. 2249; 198th meeting (28 Aug. 1947), pp. 2301–5; 200th meeting (29 Aug. 1947), pp. 2338–40; 201st meeting 910 Sept. 1947), pp. 2344, 2362.
52. SCOR, 3rd year, Supplement for Nov. 1948, pp. 67–87, 139–44, S/646 and Corr. 1, S/628; 5th year, 470th meeting (15 Mar. 1950), p. 4; 471st meeting (12 Apr. 1950), pp. 5–6; 6th year, Supplement for Jan. to Mar. 1951, pp. 23–5, S/2017 and Special Supplement no. 2, pp. 24–6, S/2107/Rev. 1; 539th meeting (30 Mar. 1951), p. 15; 543rd meeting (30 Apr. 1951), p. 4; 548th meeting (29 May 1951), pp. 21–2; 566th meeting (10 Nov. 1951), p. 13; 7th year, 572nd meeting (31 Jan. 1952), paras. 34–5; Supplement for Oct. to Dec. 1952, pp. 54–5, S/2839 and Corr. 1; 611th meeting (23 Dec. 1952), paras. 72, 111.
53. SCOR, 3rd year, Supplement for Sept. 1948, p. 5, S/986.
54. SCOR, 6th year, Supplement for July to Sept. 1951, pp. 9–10, S/2241; 553rd meeting (16 Aug. 1951), paras. 98–110; 555th meeting (27 Aug. 1951), paras. 3–14, 67–72; 556th meeting (29 Aug. 1951), para. 18; 558th meeting (1 Sept. 1951), para. 6.
55. SCOR, 15th year, 865th meeting (2 June 1960), para. 47; 866th meeting (22 June 1960), paras. 78–9; 868th meeting (23 June 1960), paras. 43, 51–2; Supplement for Apr. to June 1960, pp. 24–6, S/4345.
56. SCOR, 29th year, 1801st meeting (24 Oct. 1974), para. 24.
57. SCOR, 31st year, 1888th meeting (6 Feb. 1976), paras. 247, 266–310; Supplement for Jan. to Mar. 1976, pp. 80, 85, S/11953, S/11967.
58. SCOR, 37th year, Supplement for Apr. to June 1982, p. 4, S/14947; S/PV.2350, 3 Apr. 1982, pp. 81–5.
59. S/PV.2466, 12 Aug. 1983, pp. 31, 38–40.
60. SCOR, 3rd year, 386th meeting (17 Dec. 1948), p. 37; 387th meeting (20 Dec. 1948), pp. 1–2; 392nd meeting (24 Dec. 1948), p. 30; 393rd meeting (27 Dec. 1948), p. 3.
61. SCOR, 1st year, 1st series, 27th meeting (27 Mar. 1946), p. 58; 32nd meeting (15 Apr. 1946), p. 128; 40th meeting (8 May 1946), p. 252; 43rd meeting (22 May 1946), p. 305; Supplement no. 2, pp. 46–7, S/30.
62. SCOR, 5th year, 459th meeting (10 Jan. 1950), pp. 1–4; 460th meeting (12 Jan. 1950); 461st meeting (13 Jan. 1950), pp. 1–10.
63. SCOR, 1st year, 1st series, 32nd meeting (15 Apr. 1946), p. 128; 40th meeting (8 May 1946), pp. 249–52; 5th year, 462nd meeting (17 Jan. 1950), pp. 7–8, 10; 475th meeting (30 June 1950), pp. 7–8, 15; 476th meeting (7 July 1950), p. 7; 486th meeting (11 Aug. 1950), pp. 6–7;

487th meeting (14 Aug. 1950), pp. 8, 11–12; 488th meeting (17 Aug. 1950, p. 3; 494th meeting (1 Sept. 1950), pp. 3, 20; 526th meeting (28 Nov. 1950), p. 16; S/PV. 2306, 5 Nov. 1981, p. 36.

64. Resolutions 937 (1994), 21 July 1994; 938 (1994), 28 July 1994; 939 (1994), 29 July 1994; and 940 (1994), 31 July 1994.
65. SC res. 79 (S/1455), 17 Jan. 1950; 83 (S/1508/Rev. 1, S/1511), 27 June 1950; 166 (S/4968), 25 Oct. 1961.
66. SC res. 22 (S/324), 9 Apr. 1947; 98 (S/2883), 23 Dec. 1952; 138 (S/4349), 23 Jan. 1960; 164 (S/4882), 22 July 1961.
67. See F. Y. Chai, *Consultation and Consensus in the Security Council*, New York, UN Institute for Training and Research, 1971.
68. SCOR, 20th year, 1227th meeting (18 June 1965), para. 36.
69. SCOR, 24th year, 1504th meeting (26 Aug. 1969), paras. 2–3; SC res. 270 (S/9410).
70. SCOR, 25th year, 1557th meeting (17 Nov. 1970), paras. 1–3; SC res. 288 (S/9980).
71. GAOR, 5th session, Annexes, agenda item 49, A/1356, paras. 23–4.
72. *Repertoire I*, p. 2. This information is repeated in abbreviated form in later volumes of the *Repertoire*.
73. *Resolutions and Decisions of the Security Council* . . . (published annually), ii.
74. ICJ Reports 1962, p. 163.
75. SC res. 246 (S/8429), 14 Mar. 1968; *Repertoire VI*, p. 217.
76. See, for example, SC res. 67 (S/1234), 28 Jan. 1949; 91 (S/2017/Rev. 1), 30 Mar. 1951; 144 (S/4395), 19 July 1960; 353 (S/11350), 20 July 1974; 417 (S/12309/Rev. 1), 31 Oct. 1977.
77. ICJ Reports 1971, pp. 52–4. See also SCOR, 30th year, 1856th meeting (30 Nov. 1975), para. 102.
78. Helmut Freudenschuß 'Article 39 of the UN Charter Revisited: Threats to the Peace and the Recent Practice of the UN Security Council', *Austrian Journal of Public and International Law* (1993) vol. 46, p. 33–4. Freudenschuß cites Delbrück in support of this position, nevertheless Delbrück has cautioned that some authors have 'over-emphasised the importance of the intention of the SC with regard to the question of the binding force of [a] particular decision' ('Article 25' in Bruno Simma, *The United Nations Charter: A Commentary*, Oxford: Oxford University Press, 1994, p. 416).
79. SCOR, 2nd year, 162nd meeting (22 July 1947), p. 1419; 134th meeting (16 May 1947), p. 843; 135th meeting (20 May 1947), p. 875; 162nd meeting (22 July 1947), p. 1422; 167th meeting (25 July 1947), p. 1530.
80. SCOR, 2nd year, 156th meeting (11 July 1947), p. 1280; 160th

meeting (17 July 1947), pp. 1379, 1383; 167th meeting (25 July 1947), pp. 1541–2.

81. SCOR, 3rd year, 293rd meeting (17 May 1948), p. 2; 296th meeting (19 May 1948), pp. 2–12, 22; 298th meeting (20 May 1948), pp. 14–15, 32.
82. SCOR, 12th year, 767th meeting (8 Feb. 1957), paras. 92–3; 774th meeting (21 Feb. 1957), para. 31; 805th meeting (21 Nov. 1957), para. 52.
83. Sc res. 145 (S/4405), 22 July 1960, para. 3; 146 (S/4426), 9 Aug. 1960, para. 5; SCOR, 15th year, Supplement for July to Sept. 1960, pp. 139–40, S/4482 Add. 1; Supplement for Oct. to Dec. 1960, pp. 100–3, S/4599; 16th year, Supplement for Jan. to Mar. 1961, pp. 261–5, S/4775, sect. I.
84. SC res. 161 (S/4741), 21 Feb. 1961, paras. 1 and 5; SCOR, 16th year, Supplement for Jan. to Mar. 1961, pp. 178–9, S/4752, Annex 1; pp. 182–3, 190–7, 269–71, S/4752, Annex III, S/4775, sect. IV.
85. GAOR, 16th session, Supplement no. 1A, A/4800/Add. 1, p. 4; U Thant expressed a similar view in a speech on 28 Oct. 1969, see *UN Monthly Chronicle*, 6, no. 10 (Nov. 1969), p. 86.
86. SCOR, 23rd year, Supplement for Jan. to Mar. 1968, pp. 284–7, S/8495. See also Sydney Bailey, *The Making of Resolution 242*, Dordrecht, Netherlands, Nijhoff, 1985.
87. SCOR, 26th year, 1589th meeting (6 Oct. 1971), para. 116.
88. Ibid., 1588th meeting (5 Oct. 1971), para. 18; 1589th meeting (6 Oct. 1971, para. 51–3.
89. Helmut Freudenschuß, op. cit., p. 31.

CHAPTER 6

1. GAOR, 4th session, Supplement no. 1, A/930, p. 46.
2. SCOR, 1st year, 1st series, Supplement no. 1, pp. 2 and 3; 2nd meeting (25 Jan. 1946), pp. 12–14; SC res. 1, 25 Jan. 1946.
3, S/10, 14 Feb. 1946 (restricted). There is some uncertainty as to the precise date on which the Military Staff Committee held its first meeting. Some UN documents give 4 Feb. 1946 (GAOR, 1st session, 2nd part, A/65, p. 9; *Repertoire I*, p. 239); see also FRUS, 1946, 1(1972), p. 734, fn. 46. The first report of the Security Council, however, gives 3 Feb. (GAOR, 1st session, Supplement no. 1, A/93, p. 84).
4. SCOR, 1st year, 1st series, 23rd meeting (16 Feb. 1946), p. 369; 25th meeting (16 Mar. 1946), p. 10.

5. FRUS, 1946, 1(1972), pp. 790, 895, 914–15, 931, 1036; 1947, vol. 1, p. 447.
6. S/124 and Corr. 1 and Add. 1, 8 Aug. 1946 (restricted).
7. S/115, 1 Aug. 1946 (restricted). There is again some uncertainty about dates, some documents giving 1 Aug. (*Repertoire I*, p. 238), others giving 24 July (ibid. p. 191; GAOR, 2nd session, Supplement no. 2, A/366, p. 103). The document which presumably gives the correct date (S/115) is restricted.
8. S/165, 20 Sept. 1946; S/187; 28 Oct. 1946; S/325, 9 Apr. 1947; S/356, 19 May 1947 (all restricted).
9. S/421, 17 July 1947 (restricted).
10. GA res. 41(1) and 42(1), 14 Dec. 1946; SC res. 18 (S/268/Rev. 1/Corr. 1), 13 Feb. 1947.
11. SCOR, 2nd year, Special Supplement no. 1, S/336.
12. FRUS, 1947, 1(1973), p. 468, fn. 3, and p. 495. A convenient annotated text of the principles approved by the Security Council, with alternative formulations of the articles not agreed, is in *Repertoire II*, pp. 296–408; see also Lie, pp. 95–8.
13. SCOR, 2nd year, 142nd meeting (18 June 1947), pp. 1027–41; 143rd meeting (20 June 1947), pp. 1053–4, 1061–2; 145th meeting (24 June 1947), pp. 1078–91; 146th meeting (25 June 1947), pp. 1104–13; 149th meeting (30 June 1947), pp. 1158 and 1175–9; 154th meeting (10 July 1947), p. 1267), Special Supplement no. 13, pp. 133–40, S/394.
14. Ibid., 141st meeting (16 June 1947), pp. 1018–19.
15. S/879, 2 July 1948 (mimeo.).
16. GAOR, 4th session, Supplement no. 2, A/945, p. 95; MS/417, 6 Aug. 1948; MS/420, 16 Aug. 1948.
17. GAOR, 5th session, Supplement no. 2, A/1361, p. 62; 6th session, Supplement no. 2, A/1873, p. 88.
18. GAOR, 19th session, Annexes, item 21, A/5721 section 3; 5th special session, Annexes, agenda item 8, A/6654, paras. 117, 119–20, 13. See also A/42/574–S/19143, 18 Sept. 1987.
19. SC Res. 665 (S/21640), 25 Aug. 1990.
20. SCOR 2938th meeting, 25 Aug. 1990.
21. Ibid. p. 43.
22. Francis Delon, former first Counsellor (legal affairs), Permanent Mission of France, 'Le rôle joué par les Membres Permanents dans L'action du Conseil de Sécurité', in Dupuy op. cit. p. 360.
23. Goodrich, pp. 276, 279, 283–4.
24. Speech on 28 Oct. 1969, published in *UN Monthly Chronicle*, 6, no. 10, p. 86.

25. GAOR, 26th session, Supplement no. 1A, A/8401/Add. 1, para. 96.
26. Russell, pp. 154–5; Cordell Hull, p. 1684.
27. General Assembly resolutions 2864 (XXVI) and 2991 (XXVII).
28. A/8447 and Add.1; A/9243; and resolution 3186 (XXVIII).
29. GAOR, 42nd plenary meeting, 28 October 1994, p. 3, Spain.
30. General Assembly resolution 47/233 of 17 August 1993.
31. See GAOR, 41st plenary meeting, 28 October 1994, p. 4, Malaysia.
32. GAOR, 41st plenary meeting, 28 October 1994, p. 7, Colombia.
33. Ibid. p. 8.
34. A/50/PV.73, 29 November 1995, p. 6, New Zealand.
35. A/51/PV.65, 26 November 1996, p. 10.
36. Algeria, Colombia, Cuba, Egypt, Indonesia, Iran, Malaysia, Mexico, and the Philippines.
37. A/48/2, p. 29.
38. GAOR, 41st plenary meeting, 28 October 1994, p. 9, Malaysia.
39. GAOR, 41st plenary meeting, 28 October 1994, p. 15, the Philippines.
40. GAOR, 41st plenary meeting, 28 October 1994, p. 12, Cuba and p. 15 the Philippines.
41. GAOR, 41st plenary meeting, 28 October 1994, p. 11, Cuba.
42. GAOR, 41st plenary meeting, 28 October 1994, p. 9, Malaysia.
43. GAOR, 41st plenary meeting, 28 October 1994, p. 7, Colombia.
44. A/49/2, 18 Oct. 1994, pp. 26–32, 439–442; GAOR, 49th session, 48th plenary meeting (31 Oct. 1994); 49th plenary meeting (1 Nov. 1994); S/1994/1279—A/49/667, 11 Nov. 1994.
45. GAOR, 41st plenary meeting, 28 October 1994, p. 19, Egypt.
46. A/51/PV.65, 26 November 1996, p. 10.
47. GAOR, 41st plenary meeting, 28 October 1994, p. 13, Algeria.
48. GAOR, 48th plenary meeting, 31 October 1994.
49. GA res. 181(11); SCOR, 2nd year, Supplement no. 20, p. 172, S/614; 222nd meeting (9 Dec. 1947), pp. 2776–88.
50. GA res. 268B(111), 28 Apr. 1949; S/1323, 13 May 1949 (mimeo.); SC res. 81 (S/1486), 24 May 1950.
51. GA res. 1(1), 24 Jan. 1946; 41(1), 14 Dec. 1946; 42(1), 14 Dec. 1946; 191(111), 4 Nov. 1948; 192(111), 19 Nov. 1948; 299(IV), 23 Nov. 1949; 300(IV), 5 Dec. 1949; 502(VI), 11 Jan. 1952.
52. SCOR, 5th year, 503rd meeting (26 Sept. 1950), pp. 29–33; 504th meeting (27 Sept. 1950), pp. 5–6; 505th meeting (28 Sept. 1950), p. 22; 506th meeting (29 Sept. 1950), pp. 4–5.
53. *Juridical Yearbook 1964*, p. 229, 237; *Juridical Yearbook 1968*, p. 185.

54. SCOR, 1st year, 1st series, 48th meeting (24 June 1946), p. 398.
55. SCOR, 1st year, 2nd series, 79th meeting (4 Nov. 1956), p. 497.
56. *Juridical Yearbook 1964*, p. 237.
57. *Juridical Yearbook 1968*, p. 185 (we have changed the verbs to the present tense).
58. GA res. 377(V), 3 Nov. 1950.
59. FRUS, 1947, 1(1973), p. 201; ICJ Reports 1962, pp. 155, 163–5; see also ICJ Reports 1971, p. 50.
60. GA res. 34(1), 9 Nov. 1946; 35(1) and 36(1), 19 Nov. 1946; 113(11), 17 Nov. 1947; 197(III), 8 Dec. 1948; 296(IV), 22 Nov. 1949; 495(V), 4 Dec. 1950; 506(VI), 1 Feb. 1951; 620(VII), 21 Dec. 1952; 718(VIII), 23 Oct 1953; 816(IX) and 817(IX), 23 Nov. 1954; 917(X) and 918(X), 8 Dec. 1955; 1017(XI), 23 Feb. 1957; 1144(XII), 23 Oct. 1957; see also res. 550(VI), 7 Dec. 1951.
61. SCOR, 20th year, 1244th meeting (22 Sept. 1965), para. 30.
62. GAOR, 19th session, Annexes, Item 11, p. 1, A/5844; SCOR, 20th year, Supplement for Jan. to Mar. 1965, pp. 20–2, S/6157.
63. A/5861, 25 Jan. 1965 (mimeo.); *Juridical Yearbook, 1966*, pp. 222–3; SCOR, 20th year, Supplement for Jan. to Mar. 1965, pp. 73 and 174–5, S/6202 and S/6229; 1190th meeting (15 Mar. 1965), para. 128; Supplement for April to June 1965, pp. 6–8 and 124–6, S/6269 and S/6356.
64. Ibid., 1190th meeting (15 Mar. 1965), para. 113; Supplement for Jan. to Mar. 1965, pp. 264–5, S/6264.
65. SCOR, 21st year, Supplement for July to Sept. 1966, p. 127, S/7498; *Juridical Yearbook, 1966*, p. 223; GAOR, 21st session, 1402th plenary meeting (28 Sept. 1966), paras. 1–8.
66. *General Assembly of the United Nations*, pp. 221–38.
67. SCOR, 18th year, 1039th meeting (1 June 1963), paras. 19–25; 19th year, 1102nd meeting (4 Mar. 1964), para. 11; 20th year, 1247th meeting (25 Oct. 1965), para. 243.
68. SCOR, 28th year, 1750th meeting (25 Oct. 1973), paras. 42, 45–6, 87–8.
69. S/PV. 3211, 11 May 1993, p6 (S/25693); SC res. 831, 27 May 1993.
70. *Juridical Yearbook 1979*, pp. 164–6.
71. See ECOSOC res. 214B (viii), 16 Feb. 1949, concerning human rights in Palestine, circulated to the Security Council as S/1291, 14 Mar. 1949 (mimeo.); SCOR, 3rd year, 354th meeting (19 Aug. 1948), pp. 55–6 (Palestine refugees); SC res. 85 (S/1657), 31 July 1950, para. 4 (relief and support for the civilian population of Korea).
72. A/8775/Add. 4. 19 Dec. 1972 (mimeo.).

73. SC res. 329 (S/10899/Rev. 1), 10 Mar. 1973.
74. SC res. 330 (S/10932/Rev. 2), 21 Mar. 1973.
75. A/47/277–S/24111, 17 June 1992.
76. GA/50/697, 27 October 1995, p. 23.
77. These proposals are enumerated in Frances Stewart and Sam Daws 'Global Challenges: The Case for a United Nations Economic and Social Security Council', Christian Aid Viewpoint, No. 10 January 1996.
78. SCOR, 2nd year, 113th meeting (26 Feb. 1947), p. 410.
79. SC res. 21 (S/318), 2 Apr. 1947; see also FRUS, 1(1947), pp. 258–78.
80. SCOR, 2nd year, 220th meeting (15 Nov. 1947), p. 2763.
81. SC res. 70 (S/1280), 7 Mar. 1949. The President of the Trusteeship Council's interpretation of the procedure, also approved by the Security Council on 7 Mar. 1949, is in SCOR, 4th year, Supplement for Mar. 1949, pp. 1–3, S/916.
82. See Sydney Bailey, *General Assembly of the United Nations*, pp. 176–84 and 'The Future Composition of the Trusteeship Council', *International Organization* 8, no. 3 (summer 1959), pp. 412–21.
83. UNCIO, 1945, 3, pp. 600 and 619.
84. PC/EX/TC/4, 15 Sept. 1945 (mimeo.), para. 5.
85. SCOR, 23rd year, Supplement for Jan. to Mar. 1968, pp. 71–2, S/8355 and Add. 1 and 2.
86. GA res. 2145(xxi), 25 Jan. 1968.
87. SC res. 245, 25 Jan. 1968; 246 (S/8429), 14 Mar. 1968.
88. SC res. 264 (S/9100), 20 Mar. 1969.
89. SC res. 956 (1994), 10 Nov. 1994.
90. T/RES/2200 (LXI), 25 May 1994.
91. S/PV.3455, 10 November 1994, pp. 2–3.
92. A/50/142, 16 June 1995.
93. Ibid.
94. A/50/646, 1 December 1995.
95. A/50/1011, 1 August 1996.
96. Statute of the Court, Articles 8 and 10; 1st year, 1st series, 9th meeting (6 Feb. 1946), pp. 134–5.
97. Statute, Art. 12.
98. SCOR, 1st year, 1st series, 9th meeting (6 Feb. 1946), pp. 146–56; 138th meeting (4 June 1947), pp. 949–52. It is now Rule 61; the equivalent rule for the Assembly is 152.
99. Statute, Arts. 2, 3, 9, and 13.
100. S/PV.3552, 12 July 1995.
101. GAOR 15th session, 915th plenary meeting (16 Nov. 1960) paras. 23–45.
102. Statute, Arts. 4, 8, 10, and 11.

103. Statute, Art. 12.
104. SCOR, 6th year, 567th meeting (6 Dec. 1951), paras. 23, 26–8, 52–4, 59–60, 63, 70, 114, 116–18.
105. SCOR, 9th year, 681st meeting (7 Oct. 1954).
106. SCOR, 18th year, 1071st and 1072nd meetings (21 Oct. 1963).
107. SCOR, 18th year, Supplement for Oct. to Dec. 1963, pp. 42–3, S/5445; pp. 86–8, 95–9, S/5449, S/5461.
108. SCOR, 20th year, 1262nd meeting (16 Nov. 1965), paras. 1–6.
109. SCOR, 21st year, 1315th meeting (2 Nov. 1966); 1318th meeting (3 Nov. 1966).
110. S/PV. 2306, 5 Nov. 1981; S/PV. 2321, 21 Dec. 1981, p. 3.
111. *Juridical Yearbook 1981*, pp. 145–8; S/PV. 2321, 21 Dec. 1981. pp. 2–3.
112. S/PV.2333, 19 Mar. 1982, pp. 6–10.
113. S/PV.3309, 10 November 1993, p. 3
114. S/PV.3310, 10 November 1993.
115. S/PV.3311, 10 November 1993.
116. S/1996/722.
117. S/PV. 3709, 6 November 1996; pp. 2–5.
118. SCOR, 2nd year, 189th meeting (20 Aug. 1947), p. 2115; 3rd year, 363rd meeting (6 Oct. 1948), p. 10; 9th year, 679th meeting (10 Sept. 1954), paras. 38–9.
119. SCOR, 2nd year, Supplement no. 3, pp. 35–50, S/247, S/250; Supplement no. 6; 95th meeting (20 Jan. 1947), pp. 123–4; SC res. 19, 27 Feb. 1947; SCOR, 2nd year, Supplement no. 10, pp. 77–118, S/300, S/298, S/304; 122nd meeting (25 Mar. 1947), p. 609; 127th meeting (9 Apr. SC res. 22 (S/324), 9 Apr. 1947.
120. SC res. 395 (S/12187), 25 Aug. 1976.
121. ICJ Reports 1951, p. 100.
122. SCOR, 6th year, Supplement for Oct. to Dec. 1951, pp. 1–5, S/2357, S/2358 and Revs. 1 and 2.
123. SCOR, 6th year, 559th meeting (1 Oct. 1951); 560th meeting (15 Oct. 1951); 561st meeting (16 Oct. 1951); 562nd and 563rd meetings (17 Oct. 1951); 565th meeting (19 Oct. 1951).
124. S/18187, 28 June 1986, S/18250, 31 July 1986, and S/18415, 20 Oct. 1986 (all mimeo.); S/PV. 2704, 31 July 1986, pp. 54–5; S/PV. 2718, 28 Oct. 1986, p. 51.
125. Cases Concerning Questions of Interpretation and Application of the 1971 Montreal Convention Arising from the Aerial Incident at *Lockerbie*, Request for the indication of interim measures, Order of 14 April 1992; and A/51/4 p. 14. Report of the International Court of Justice, 1 August 1995–31 July 1996.

126. Marc Weller 'The *Lockerbie* Case: A Premature End to the "New World Order"', *African Journal of International and Comparative Law*, 1992, vol. 4, Part 2. p. 321. This contains a good analysis of the legal issues surrounding the initial findings of the Court on the *Lockerbie* Case.
127. Ibid. p. 322.
128. Vaughan Lowe '*Lockerbie*—Changing the Rules during the Game', *The Cambridge Law Journal* (Case and Comment section), vol. 51, Part 3, Nov. 1992. p. 410.
129. Ibid.
130. E.g. Weller (1992), op. cit.; Vera Gowlland-Debbas, 'The Relationship between the International Court of Justice and the Security Council in the Light of the *Lockerbie* Case', *The American Journal of International Law*, 1994, vol. 88, pp. 643–77.
131. E.g. Keith Harper, 'Does the United Nations Security Council have the Competence to Act as Court and Legislature?', *International Law and Politics*, 1994, vol. 27, pp. 103–57; Ebere Osieke, 'The Legal Validity of *Ultra Vires* Decisions of International Organizations', *The American Journal of International Law*, 1983, vol. 77, pp. 239–56; Thomas M. Franck, 'Editorial Comment—The Powers of Appreciation: Who is the Ultimate Guardian of UN Legality?', *The American Journal of International Law*, 1992, vol. 86, pp. 519–523; W. Michael Reisman, 'Notes and Comments on The Constitutional Crisis in the United Nations', *The American Journal of International Law*, 1993, vol. 87, pp. 83–100.
132. Lowe (1992) op. cit.
133. Mohammed Bedjaoui, *The New World Order and the Security Council—Testing the Legality of its Acts*, (Martinus Nijhoff Publishers, 1994), pp. 127–8.
134. Boutros Boutros-Ghali 'An Agenda for Democratization', United Nations, New York, 1996, p. 50, para. 112. Circulated as an official document (A/51/761) of the 51st session of the General Assembly.
135. SCOR, 6th meeting (1 Feb. 1946), p. 72; 31st meeting (9 April 1946), pp. 116–18.
136. S/NC/1996/4, 3 February 1997.
137. GA res. 11 (I), 24 Jan. 1946.
138. SCOR, 1st year, 1st series, 41st meeting (16 May 1946), p. 261; GA res. 11(I), 24 Jan. 1946. It now forms the second sentence of Rule 48 of the Provisional Rules of Procedure of the Security Council.
139. Provisional Rules of Procedure of the Security Council, Rule 55.
140. GA res. 11(I), 24 Jan. 1946.

141. SCOR, 1st year, 1st series, 4th meeting (29 Jan. 1946), p. 44; GAOR, 1st session, part I, 20th plenary meeting (1 Feb. 1946). See also Trygve Lie, *In the Cause of Peace*, New York, Macmillan, 1954, pp. 1–17; Stephen M. Schwebel, *The Secretary-General of the United Nations*, Cambridge, Mass., Harvard University Press, 1952, pp. 49–53; Sydney D. Bailey, *The General Assembly of the United Nations*, 2nd edn., New York, Praeger; London, Pall Mall Press, 1964, pp. 53–4, 188–9.
142. Lie, pp. 367–74.
143. GA res. 492(V), 1 Nov. 1950; Lie, pp. 382–5.
144. GAOR, 7th session, 392nd plenary meeting (10 Nov. 1952), paras. 2–10; Annexes, agenda item 74, A/2253, 12 Nov. 1952; Lie, pp. 406–7, 412–13.
145. S/PV. 613, 13 March 1953.
146. Ibid.
147. S/PV. 614, 19 March 1953.
148. SCOR, 8th year, 617th meeting (31 Mar. 1953); GAOR, 7th session, 423rd plenary meeting (7 Apr. 1953); GA res. 709 (VII), 7 Apr. 1953.
149. SCOR, 12th year, 792nd meeting (26 Sept. 1957); GAOR, 12th session, 690th plenary meeting (26 Sept. 1957), paras. 57–166.
150. SC res. 168 (S/4972), 3 Nov. 1961; GA res. 1640 (XVI), 3 Nov. 1961; SCOR, 17th year, 1026th meeting (30 Nov. 1962); GA res. 1771 (XVII), 30 Nov. 1962; U Thant, *View from the UN*, London, David & Charles, 1978, pp. 3–19.
151. GAOR, 21st session, Annexes, agenda item 18, A/6400, 1 Sept. 1966; SG/SM/567, 19 Sept., pp. 2–4, 8.
152. SCOR, 21st year, 1301st meeting (29 Sept. 1966); SC res. 227, 28 Oct. 1966; GA res. 2147 (XXI), 1 Nov. 1966.
153. SCOR, 21st year, 1329th meeting (2 Dec. 1966); SC res. 229, 2 Dec. 1966; GA res. 2161 (XXI), 2 Dec. 1966.
154. Thant, pp. 437–8; Kurt Waldheim, *In the Eye of the Storm*, London, Weidenfeld & Nicholson, 1985, pp. 35–40; SC res. 306, 21 Dec. 1971; GA res. 2903 (XXVI), 22 Dec. 1971.
155. SC res. 400, 7 Dec. 1976; GA res. 31/60, 8 Dec. 1976.
156. It has been reported that Jeanne Kirkpatrick, former US envoy, had remarked that she had only vetoed Salim Salim twice. It has been suggested instead that the French, who objected to the fact that Salim Salim did not speak French, may have cast at least some of the remainder of the vetoes. See *International Documents Review*, 23 December 1996, vol. 7, No. 45, p. 1.
157. Waldheim, pp. 230–5; SC res. 494, 11 Dec. 1981; GA res. 36/137, 15 Dec. 1981; SC res. 589, 10 Oct. 1986; GA. res. 41/1, 10 Oct. 1986.

158. The main source for the elections of Pérez de Cuéllar and Boutros-Ghali was *International Documents Review*, vol. 7, No. 36, 14 October 1996, edited by Mr Bhaskar Menon. We are very grateful to Mr Menon for permission to reproduce this material.
159. Resolution 720 (1991).
160. GA resolution 46/21.
161. Much of the information for this section on Boutros-Ghali and Annan was derived from two sources: (1) an article entitled 'Chronology of the Secretary-General Election 1996', published on the Internet in February 1997 by the Global Policy Forum at www.globalpolicy.org, edited by James Paul; (2) *International Documents Review*, 23 December 1996, vol. 7, No. 45, pp. 1–2, edited by Mr Bhaskar Menon. We are grateful to Mr Paul and to Mr Menon for permission to reproduce this material. Other sources included official UN documentation, interviews with diplomats, and media articles.
162. 7 May 1996.
163. S/PV. 3714, 19 November 1996.
164. Ibid.
165. Of 30 January 1946.
166. See Bruno Simma *et al.*, *The United Nations Charter: A Commentary*, Oxford, Oxford University Press, 1994, p. 1029.
167. Associated Press Wire Service. 5 December 1996. 'New candidates expected to emerge after Boutros-Ghali suspends candidacy'.
168. S/1996/1020, 9 December 1996.
169. S/1996/1021, 9 December 1996.
170. S/1996/1022, 9 December 1996.
171. S/1996/1023, 9 December 1996.
172. See speculation in the *Daily Telegraph*, 14 Dec. 1996, p. 14, David Sapsted 'Ghanaian wins UN job as French cave in'.
173. S/Res/1090 (1996), and S/PV.3725 both 13 December 1996.
174. S/Res/1091 (1996), and S/PV.3725, both 13 December 1996.
175. A/51/732, 13 December 1996.
176. Press Release GA/9204, 13 December 1996.
177. Sir Brian Urquhart and Erskine Childers 'A world in need of leadership: tomorrow's United Nations: a fresh appraisal', Dag Hammarsjold Foundation, Uppsala, Sweden, 1996.

CHAPTER 7

1. SCOR, 1st year, 1st series, 1st meeting (1 Feb. 1946), p. 11.

2. SCOR, 2nd year, 138th meeting (4 June 1947), pp. 950–1; 3rd year, 305th meeting (26 May 1948), p. 35; Supplement for May 1948, p. 99, S/782.
3. SCOR, 1st year, 1st series, 31st meeting (9 Apr. 1946), pp. 100–2, 110, 115–16, 117–18; 41st meeting (16 May 1946), pp. 253–4, 255, 256, 260; 42nd meeting (17 May 1946), p. 270; 44th meeting (6 June 1946), pp. 310–11; 1st year, 2nd series 76th meeting (15 Oct. 1946), p. 466; 80th meeting (15 Nov. 1946), p. 502; 2nd year, 197th meeting (27 Aug. 1947), p. 2256; 3rd year, 320th meeting (15 June 1948), p. 13; 4th year, 432nd meeting (27 July 1949), pp. 1–2; 5th year, 468th meeting (28 Feb. 1950), pp. 9–11.
4. SCOR, 15th year, Supplement for July to Sept. 1960, p. 145, S/4486; 16th year, 941st meeting (20 Feb. 1961), para. 23; 20th year, 1225th meeting (16 June 1965), paras. 107–9.
5. SCOR, 27th year, Supplement for Jan. to Mar. 1972, pp. 20–7, S/10514; S/10868, 25 Jan. 1973 (mimeo.).
6. SCOR, 1st year, 1st series, Supplement no. 1, pp. 5–6.
7. SCOR, Supplement no. 2, S/57, pp. 25, 38–9.
8. SCOR, 41st meeting (16 May 1946), pp. 261–7; 42nd meeting (17 May 1946), pp. 275–7.
9. SCOR, p. 277; see also FRUS, 1 (1946), pp. 386–454.
10. *Repertoire I*, p. 261; SCOR, 2nd year, Supplement no. 19, pp. 157–62, S/520; 197th meeting (27 Aug. 1947), pp. 2256–64; GAOR, 2nd session, First Committee, pp. 550–1, A/384, 12 Sept. 1947; ICJ Reports, 1950, p. 10.
11. SCOR, 2nd year, Supplement no. 19, pp. 164–5, S/520/Add. 1; FRUS, 1 (1947), pp. 236–47; SCOR, 2nd year, 197th meeting (27 Aug. 1947); 222nd meeting (9 Dec. 1947), p. 2771.
12. SCOR, 7th year, 598th meeting (10 Sept. 1952), paras. 48, 84, 95; 599th meeting (12 Sept. 1952), paras. 63–4, 104–87.
13. SCOR, 2nd year, 206th meeting (1 Oct. 1947), pp. 2461–4, 2476.
14. Ibid., 186th meeting (18 Aug. 1947), pp. 2029–30.
15. SCOR, 4th year, 410th meeting (16 Feb. 1949), p. 15.
16. *Repertoire I*, p. 272. A comprehensive survey of the practice of United Nations organs regarding the admission of new Members can be found in A/C. 64/L. 1, 22 Apr. 1953 (mimeo.).
17. SCOR, 3rd year, Supplement for Dec. 1948, S/1110 and Corr. 1, pp. 119–20.
18. SCOR, 4th year, Supplement for Sept. to Dec. 1949, S/1382, pp. 10–12.
19. SCOR, 25th year, Supplement for Apr. to June 1970, pp. 210–11, S/9836, para. 5; 1554th meeting (10 Oct. 1970).

20. Ibid. 1565th meeting (9 Feb. 1971), para. 126.
21. SCOR, 1st year, 2nd series, 54th meeting (28 Aug. 1946), pp. 39–40; 2nd year, 186th meeting (18 Aug. 1947), pp. 2030–1; 3rd year, 279th meeting (10 Apr. 1948), pp. 2–3; 351st meeting (18 Aug. 1948), p. 351.
22. SCOR, 26th year, 1587th meeting (30 Sept. 1971), paras. 86–106.
23. SC res. 99 (S/10345, para. 4), 30 Sept. 1971; GA res. 2754 (XXVI), 7 Oct. 1971.
24. SCOR, 27th year, Supplement for July to Sept. 1972, pp. 85–6, 90–2, 93–5, S/10759, S/10766, S/10768, S/10771, S/10773, S/10774; S/PV. 1660, 25 Aug. 1972, p. 47; GA res. 2937 (XVII), 29 Nov. 1972.
25. SCOR, 35th year, 2244th meeting (30 July 1980), paras. 4–5; SC res. 477 (S/14076), 30 July 1980; GA res. S11/1, 25 Aug. 1980.
26. GAOR, 5th year, Supplement no. 2, A/1361, p. 48; 26th year, Supplement no. 2, A/8402, p. 57.
27. S/25545, 7 April 1993.
28. GAOR, 22nd session, Supplement no. 1A, A/6701/Add. 1, paras. 163–6. See also GAOR 23rd session, Supplement no. 1A, A/7201/Add. 1 para. 172; 24th session, Supplement no. 1A, A/7601/Add. 1, para. 163; 26th session, Supplement no. 1A, A/8401/Add. 1, para. 105.
29. SCOR, 22nd year, Supplement for Oct. to Dec. 1967, pp. 321–2, S/8296.
30. Ibid., p. 333, S/8316; 23rd year, Supplement for Jan. to Mar. 1968, pp. 156 and 208, S/8376 and S/8437; Supplement for Apr. to June 1968, pp. 108–9, S/8520.
31. SCOR, 24th year, Supplement for July to Sept. 1969, pp. 124, 159–60, and 164, S/9327, S/9397, S/9414.
32. Ibid., 1505th and 1506th meetings, 27 and 29 Aug. 1969.
33. SCOR, 25th year, Supplement for Apr. to June 1970, pp. 210–11, S/9836; GAOR, 27th session, Supplement no. 2, A/8702, p. 134.
34. SCOR, 25th year, Supplement for April to June 1970, pp. 210–11, S/9836 Annexes I and II; A/8746, 22 Aug. 1972 (mimeo.), pp. 15–16; A/8746/Add. 1, 13 Sept. 1972 (mimeo.), p. 14; Stephen M. Schwebel, 'Mini-States and a More Effective United Nations', *American Journal of International Law*, 67, no. 1 (Jan. 1973), pp. 110 and 112.
35. E.g. Liechtenstein, population 29,000, admitted into membership on 18 Sept. 1990; San Marino, population 24,000, admitted on 2 March 1992; Monaco, population 28,000, admitted 28 May 1993; and Palau, 12,000, admitted, 15 Dec. 1994.
36. Dr Peter D. Maynard 'Universality and the United Nations', Address to the UN Congress on Public International Law, UN Headquarters, 17 March 1995, pp. 8–9.

37. 'UN Fact-Finding and Human Rights Complaints', *International Affairs*, pp. 250–66.
38. FRUS, 1946, I (1972), pp. 294, 303, 305, 339.
39. UNCIO, 11 (1945), pp. 710–14. The full text of the San Francisco statement is to be found in Appendix III.
40. SCOR, 1st year, 1st series, 35th meeting (18 Apr. 1946), p. 198; 37th meeting (25 Apr. 1946), p. 216; SC res. 4, 29 Apr. 1946.
41. SCOR, 1st year, 2nd series, 70th meeting (20 Sept. 1946), pp. 396, 410–12. The full text of the vetoed proposal is in Sydney Bailey, *Voting in the Security Council*, p. 161.
42. SCOR, 2nd year, 114th meeting (27 Feb. 1947), pp. 425–32; SC res. 19, 27 Feb. 1947. For further discussion of the procedural confusion on this occasion, see *Voting in the Security Council*, pp. 20–1 and 65–6.
43. SCOR, 3rd year, 288th meeting (29 Apr. 1948), pp. 19–23; 303rd meeting (24 May 1948), pp. 4–29; full text of vetoed proposal in *Voting in the Security Council*, p. 168; see also pp. 22–3.
44. SCOR, 14th year, 848th meeting (7 Sept. 1959); see also Urquhart, pp. 329–67.
45. Leland M. Goodrich, Eduard Hambro, and Anne Patricia Simons, *Charter of the United Nations: Commentary and Documents*, 3rd edn., Columbia University Press, 1969, p. 224.
46. S/19836.
47. 622 (1988) of 31 October 1988 and 647 (1990) of 11 January 1990.
48. SC resolution 161 (1961), 21 February 1961.
49. SC resolution 169 (1961), 24 November 1961.
50. SC resolution 836 (1993), 4 June 1993.
51. 9 December 1994.
52. This meeting was referred to by France in S/PV.3611, 20 December 1995, p. 5.
53. In 1992, Spain made proposals for the promotion of more frequent and more regular consultations between members of the Security Council, countries that provide contingents to a given peace-keeping operation, and the Secretariat. This is referred to in S/PV.3449, 4 November 1994, p. 8. Malaysia pointed particularly to the importance of close consultations between the Council and troop-contributors in decisions to change the mandate of the UN Operation in Somalia. See S/1994/120.
54. S/PRST/1994/22, 3 May 1994.
55. 15 September 1994.
56. The Nordic countries (S/1994/1136), Benelux countries (S/1994/1193), Uruguay (S/1994/1201), Austria (S/1994/1219), Ireland (S/1994/1221*),

Egypt (S/1994/1231) Turkey (S/1994/1237) and Portugal (S/1994/1238).

57. S/PV.3449, 4 November 1994, p. 10.
58. Paper prepared following a meeting in Ottawa, Canada. See S/PV.3449, 4 November 1994, p. 18.
59. Ibid.
60. A/50/60–S/1995/1.
61. S/PV.3492 and Resumptions 1 and 2, 18–19 January 1995.
62. Chile, S/1996/224; Egypt, S/1996/234.
63. Resolution 780 (1992).
64. Resolution 808 (1993).
65. Resolution 955 (1994).
66. See The United Nations and Rwanda 1993–1996, UN Blue Book Series, Volume X, DPI, New York, 1996, p. 65 from which the information in this section was obtained.
67. Ibid.
68. Aust, op. cit. p. 373.
69. Boutros Boutros-Ghali 'The 50th Anniversary Report on the Work of the Organization 1996', New York, 1996, p. 18.
70. A/50/203, 15 July 1995.
71. See, for example, GA Press Release L/2821, 7 February 1997.
72. Resolution 943 of 23 September 1994.
73. Resolution 942 of 23 September 1994.
74. 22 November 1995.
75. 7 September 1995.
76. Presidential statement read out at the Council's 3314th meeting, 15 November 1993.
77. Resolution 917 (1994).
78. United Nations, Introduction by Boutros Boutros-Ghali in 'Blue Helmets', 1996, p. 6.

CHAPTER 8

1. SCOR, 39th mtg. (29 April 1946), p. 243; SC res. 4, 29 April 1946; SC res. 30 (S/525, I), 25 Aug. 1947; SC res. 51 (S/819), 3 June 1948; SC res. 63 (S/1150), 24 Dec. 1948; SC res. 66 (S/1169), 29 Dec. 1948. This was confirmed by the International Court of Justice in the Namibia Advisory Opinion.
2. Resolutions and Decisions of the Security Council 1991, S/INF/47, p. v., n.

3. Carolyn L. Wilson, 'Changing the Charter: The United Nations Prepares for the Twenty-first Century', in Current Developments, *American Journal of International Law*, vol. 90, 1996, p. 118.
4. A/47/675—S/24816, annex, document NAC 10/Doc. 1/Rev. 2, sect. C.
5. General Assembly Resolution 47/62, 11 December 1992; Draft A/47/26/Rev. 1 and Add. 1.
6. Algeria, Barbados, Bhutan, Brazil, Chile, Colombia, Cuba, Egypt, Gabon, Guyana, Honduras, India, Indonesia, Jamaica, Japan, Jordan, Lebanon, Liberia, Libyan Arab Jamahiriya, Lithuania, Malaysia, Mali, Mauritius, Mexico, Nepal, Nicaragua, Nigeria, Pakistan, Paraguay, Peru, Senegal, Togo, Tunisia, Uganda, Venezuela, Viet Nam and Zimbabwe.
7. A/RES/48/26, 10 December 1993.
8. Ibid.
9. A/48/47, 2 September 1994, p. 3.
10. A/49/47, 15 September 1995. In 1995 the full name of the Working Group became the *Open-ended Working Group on the Question of Equitable Representation on and Increase in the Membership of the Security Council and other matters related to the Security Council.*
11. Page 1 of a Statement by the Permanent Representative of Italy, Ambassador Francesco Paolo Fulci on the Question of Equitable Representation and Increase in the Membership of the Security Council, made to the *Open-Ended Working Group* on 13 March 1997 and make public by the Italian Government on its UN Permanent Mission World Wide Web Page. Http:///www.undp.org/missions/italy/statemen/reform/130397.htm.
12. Ibid; Ambassador Jayanama of Thailand briefed the Working Group on the findings of the Vice-Chairmen on 10 March 1997—UN Press Release GA/9222 10 March 1997, p. 2.
13. European Parliament session document A3–0331/93, 8 November 1993; Report of the Committee on Foreign Affairs and Security on the role of the Union within the UN and the problems of reforming the UN. Rapportuer: Mr Renzo Trivelli.
14. Sir David Hannay 'Anyone for the Roller-Coaster', *The World Today*, vol. 52, No. 2 Feb. 1996, p. 49.
15. Reports of the Interim Committee of the General Assembly, 5 January to 5 August 1948; General Assembly Official Records: Third Session. Supplement No.10 (A/578, A/583, A/605, A/606).
16. Paper on Cluster II issues contained in A/49/965, 18 September 1995, pp. 97–103.

17. 'The case for a reinterpretation of Article 31 of the Charter of the United Nations' Working paper by the Czech Republic, 12 June 1996, A/AC.247/1996/CRP.12.
18. Working methods and procedures of the Security Council: working paper by Argentina and New Zealand, 17 May 1996, A/AC.247/1996/CRP.8.
19. Boutros Boutros-Ghali 'Magisterial Lecture on Security Council Reform', Ministry of Foreign Affairs, Mexico City, Mexico, 4 March 1996.
20. GAOR, 1st year, 1st series, Supplement no. 2, p. 2, S/6.
21. Ibid., 31st meeting (9 Apr. 1946), pp. 103–6.
22. Ibid., 41st meeting (16 May 1946), p. 261.
23. GA res. 88(1), 19 Nov. 1946; SC res. 26 (S/368), 4 June 1947.
24. A/AC.247/1997/CRP.8, 29 May 1997.
25. SCOR, 1st year, 1st series, 31st meeting (9 Apr. 1946), p. 101.
26. S/10770, 22 Aug. 1972 (mimeo.), p. 1.
27. SCOR, 1st year, 1st series, 31st meeting (9 Apr. 1946), pp. 102 ff.
28. SCOR, 5th year, Supplement for Jan. to May 1950, pp. 2–3, S/1447.
29. Ibid. pp. 16–18, S/1457 and [in English only] Corr. 1; 462nd meeting (17 Jan. 1950), pp. 10–13; 468th meeting (28 Feb. 1950), pp. 9–11.
30. GA res. 396(V), 14 Dec. 1950.
31. PC/EX/113/Rev. 1, 12 Nov. 1945, p. 45.
32. *Yearbook of the International Law Commission* 1968, vol. ii, p. 164 (A/CN. 4/L. 129, 3 July 1968).
33. PC/EX/113/Rev. 1, 12 Nov. 1945, p. 45.
34. SCOR, 1st year, 1st series, Supplement no. 2, p. 42, S/88.
35. Ibid. p. 8.
36. Ibid. p. 42, S/88.
37. Ibid. p. 39, S/71.
38. Ibid. pp. 39–40, S/71.
39. Ibid. p. 22, S/57.
40. Ibid. p. 13.
41. FRUS, 1945, 1(1967), 1967, p. 1495.
42. There have been five occasions when a President put his ruling to the vote as a proposal to uphold the ruling: 49th meeting, pp. 421–2; 57th meeting, p. 132; 224th meeting, pp. 2816–17; 459th meeting, pp. 3–4; 998th meeting, and ten occasions when the President put his ruling to the vote as a proposal to overrule (i.e. the challenge was voted upon): 303rd meeting, pp. 26–7; 330th meeting, pp. 8–9; 443rd meeting, pp. 27–8; 480th meeting, p. 9; 483nd meeting, pp. 19–20; 492nd meeting, p. 16; 494th meeting, pp. 8, 11; 507th meeting, pp. 7–8; 989th meet-

ing, 1016th meeting. With the exception of the 1606th meeting of 4 Dec. 1971 where the procedure followed is unclear, the *Repertoire of the Practice of the Security Council* does not list any votes on Presidential rulings under Rule 30 from 1964 to 1984.

43. 989th meeting, 30 Jan. 1962; *Repertoire* 1959–93, pp. 27–8.
44. SCOR, 1st year, 1st series, Supplement no. 2, p. 25, Rule 25; 41st meeting (16 May 1946), pp. 254–5.
45. SC res. 81 (S/1486), 24 May 1950.
46. SCOR, 5th year, 472nd meeting (24 May 1950), p. 4.
47. GAOR, 1st session, 1st part, Supplement no. 1, A/93, p. 88.
48. PC/EX/113/Rev. 1, 12 Nov. 1945, p. 45.
49. See Appendix III.
50. SCOR, 1st year, 1st series, Supplement no. 2, p. 23, S/57.
51. Part of the new UN Department of General Assembly Affairs and Conference Services from mid-1997.
52. A/52/6 (Sect.27E), 9 June 1997. General Assembly Proposed programme budget for the biennium, 1998–9, Part VIII Common Support Services. Section 27E Conference Services, Table 27E.16 p. 19.
53. SCOR, 1st year, 1st series, Supplement no. 2, p. 24, S/57.
54. Ibid.
55. Ibid., 31st meeting (9 Apr. 1946), p. 118.
56. Ibid., Supplement no. 2, p. 10.
57. Ibid. pp. 38–9, S/57.
58. Ibid., 41st meeting (16 May 1946), pp. 261–7; 42nd meeting (17 May 1946) pp. 270–7.
59. SCOR, 2nd year, Supplement no. 19, pp. 157–60, S/520; 222nd meeting (9 Dec. 1947), p. 2771.
60. SCOR, 1st year, 1st series, Supplement no. 2, p. 23, S/57.
61. Ibid., p. 22; 41st meeting (16 May 1946), pp. 259–60.
62. *An Essay towards the Present and Future Peace of Europe.*

INDEX

Abdullah, Sheikh Mohammad 156
Abkhazia, Georgia 175, 538, 539
abstention by permanent member 7, 12, 16–17
access, right of 141–2, 154–9
action threshold 389–90
Addis Ababa 41, 91; meeting in 335
Afghanistan 52, 157, 529, 535; civil war 73; United Nations Good Offices Mission (UNGOMAP) 356, 515
Africa 41–2; Great Lakes region 75, 321, 373, 531–2; regionalism 571–2
African Group 42, 170, 171
Afro–Asian Group 171
Aga Khan, Prince Sadruddin 326–7
agenda 1; adoption of the Agenda 76; changes in 395–7; discussion of 158; informal consultations 395; and order of speakers 189; placing items on 84; provisional 76, 85–9, 395, 442–3; rejection of items 89–91; Rules on 395–7, 442–3; and Summary Statement 76, 77; titles of items 83–4
Agnelli, Mrs 50
Ahmed Salim, Salim 326, 330
Al-Khussaiby, Salim Bin Mohammed 287
Albania 3; application for UN membership 211, 218, 242–3; *see also* Corfu Channel case
Albright, Madeleine 52, 168
Algeria 30, 150, 151; and credentials 178–9; on transparency 291
All Africa Conference of Churches 42, 164
amendments 212–18, 221, 404–5, 436, 440, 448; introduction of 212; ordering of 213, 215–18; and proposals 224
Amman 116, 608
Ammoun, Fouad 311–12
Amr, Abdel Fattah 2
Anglo–Iranian Oil Company 316
Angola 49, 52, 116, 520, 529; and Cuba 487; Lusaka Protocol (1994) 489, 533; sanctions 365, 372–3; situation in 464–5, 467; UNITA 271, 365, 372–3, 488–90; United Nations Verification Missions (UNAVEM) 360, 487–90, 520, 521, 533
Annan, Kofi 55–6, 117, 124, 327, 330–2
annual reports 284–93, 420, 434, 542–3, 549–52; sanctions committees 366
Anti-Apartheid Movement 164
apartheid 42, 467–9; *see also* South Africa
Arab Group 82, 171
Arab Higher Committee 134, 164
Arab League 157, 172, 175
Arab Maghreb Union 30
Arab Occupied Territories 49, 76, 203–4, 219, 518
Arab States: self–defence 103
Arab–Asian Group 171
Arafat, Yasser 43, 73, 97 n., 160, 335
Argentina 64, 71, 86–7, 148, 149, 150, 151, 245–6, 389; abstention 255; on consultations with troop-contributors 361; on documentation 546–8; and Falklands (Malvinas) 16–17, 256; on permanent membership 139–40; as President 134; terrorism in 135
Aristide, Jean-Bertrand 374
arms control 570
arms embargoes 104, 570–1
Arnenberg, Arenstein 44
Arria, Diego 73
'Arria formula' meetings 68, 73–4, 75, 393
Asian Group 170, 171
Association of South-East Asian Nations (ASEAN) 172
Atomic Energy Commission 38, 167, 211

attitudes to UN 7–8
Auriol, Vincent 1–2
Austin, Warren 8, 138
Australia 1, 2, 10, 13, 79–80, 143, 144–5, 148, 149, 150, 151, 519; on applications for membership 345–6; as President 125, 190, 211, 394; on procedure 409; and Spanish question (1946) 354; on terminology 199
Australian House of Representatives 164
Austria 30–3, 42, 48, 150, 151, 520, 521; as President 132
Azerbaijan 77–80
Aziz, Tariq 204

Badawi, Abdel Hamid 2
Bahrain 116, 520
Bailey, Sydney 299, 606–7; *How Wars End* 606
Bandung Conference (1955) 171
Bangladesh 84, 108, 113, 150, 195; application for membership 348; war (1971) 76
Baroody, Jamil 159, 184
Barre de Nanteuil, Luc de la 256
Bedjaoui, Mohammed 319–20
Belaunde, Victor Andres 93
Belgium 46, 48, 148, 149, 150, 151, 156, 521, 523; on competence of Council 85; as President 134, 244, 253
Benin 150, 258
Berard, Armand 138
Berlin 83, 134, 608
Bernadotte, Count Folke 115
Bevin, Ernest 1, 2, 8, 275
Bhutan: application for membership 348
Bidault, Georges 2
binding decisions *see* decisions
biological weapons 121, 210, 377
Bishara, Abdalla Yaccoub 200
Blix, Hans 204
'Blue Helmets' (UN publication) 477 n.
Bolivia 149, 150
bombings, aircraft 69–70
Boncour, Paul 2
Borneo 156
Bosnia and Herzegovina 156, 175, 522, 523; arms embargo 104; Contact Group on 33, 72; Dayton peace agreement (1995) 371; and hidden veto 249–50; ICFY Mission 536; Implementation Force (IFOR) 376; international tribunal on atrocities 363–4; peace-enforcement action 122, 123, 358, 374, 376, 384; sanctions against Bosnian Serbs 373; Stabilization Force (SFOR) 376; United Nations Mission (UNMIBH) 507–8; United Nations Protection Force (UNPROFOR) 502–4, 505, 535
Botswana 52, 116, 151
Bourguiba, Habib 113
Boutros-Ghali, Boutros 50, 55, 327–30, 331; on enforcement action 374–7; on International Tribunal for Rwanda 364–5; peace-making initiatives 113–14, 121–4; re-appointment vetoed 229, 328–9; and regionalism 174–5; on sanctions 366–8; and United States 327–8; UNPROFOR report (1995) 123; on voting threshold 390; 'An Agenda for Democratization' (1996) 124, 320; 'An Agenda for Peace' (1992) 123–4, 174–5, 302, 358, 576; 'Global Leadership After the Cold War' 328; 'Improving the capacity of the UN for peace-keeping' 358–9, 563–7; 'Report on an Agenda for Development' (1994) 123–4; 'Supplement to an Agenda for Peace' 362, 568–72
boycotts 257
Brandt, W. 108
Brazil 1, 2, 65, 71, 79–80, 143, 148, 149, 150, 151; as President 106
Briefing Room 67
briefings 63, 66; by NGOs 75; oral 67; on work of Council 287, 288, 553–5
budget contributions: permanent members 140
Bulgaria 150, 151; membership application 224; as President 106–7

Burke, Edmund 168
Burkina Faso 151, 519
Burma 46
Burundi 52, 150, 530, 534; sanctions against 271
Bush, George 49, 104
Buthelezi, Mangosuthu 204
Byelorussian SSR 6, 150, 258

Cable News Network (CNN) 60, 67
Cabral, Amilcar 42
Cadogan, Sir Alexander 2, 196, 199, 222–3, 405; on China 181
Cambodia 520; mine-clearance 500; United Nations Advance Mission (UNAMIC) 500–1; United Nations Transitional Authority in (UNTAC) 500, 501; and United States 103
Cameroon 150
Canada 9, 72, 143, 148, 149, 150, 151, 519, 520, 522; on convening meetings 46; as President 180
Cape Verde 151
Caradon, Sir Hugh Foot, Baron 46, 138
Caron, David D. 66
Carr, Canon Burgess 164
caucuses 68–71
Cecil, Lord Robert 53
Central America, United Nations Observer Group (ONUCA) 498–9
Ceylon 149
Chad 256; and Libya 179; United Nations Aouzou Strip Observer Group (UNASOG) 498; use of audio-visual records 99
chain of events theory 240–1, 248, 353–4
Chang Wen-t'ien 181
Chapultepec, Act of 173
Charter (*numbers in bold type refer to individual Articles of the Charter*) 1; amendments 6–7, 152–3; Article **1** 414; **2** 2; **4** 19, 297; **5** 19; **6** 6; **7** 399, 416; **8** 168; **10** 416; **11** 11–12, 281, 292–4; **12** 110–11, 123, 292–6; **13** 417–18; **14** 418; **15** 282; **17** 418, 567, 604; **18** 142; **19** 19–20, 419; **20** 20, 22, 137, 419; **24** 4, 267–8; **25** 4; **26** 23, 266, 275, 281, 421; **27** 4, 79 n., 138, 225, 226, 244, 250, 254, 263, 380–1, 387, 421; **28** 4–5, 40, 45, 48, 50, 75, 138, 335, 353, 392, 421; **29** 353, 361, 405, 422; **30** 5, 124, 156, 188–9, 353, 422; **31** 65, 154, 157, 161, 162, 288, 353, 389, 401, 422; **32** 65, 154, 157, 161, 353, 389, 401, 410, 553; **33** 3, 78–9, 113, 173–4, 266, 307, 314, 353, 422; **34** 78, 154, 245, 353, 423; **35** 30, 154, 241, 252, 401, 417; **36** 18, 78–9, 252–3, 266–7, 307, 423; **37** 18–19, 263, 267, 314, 423–4; **38** 19, 78–9, 267, 314, 424; **39** 19, 263, 267, 269, 424; **40** 17, 223, 256, 263, 267, 424; **41** 19, 263, 267, 284, 424; **42** 19, 267, 284, 424; **43** 20, 138, 163, 275–6, 361, 402, 425–6; **44** 154, 162–3, 263, 361, 401, 425; **45** 275, 425–6; **46** 46–7, 275, 426; **47** 137, 275, 281, 421; **48** 263, 426; **49** 4, 22, 138, 263, 267, 270, 427; **50** 369, 372, 427, 550, 586; **51** 103–5, 173, 427, 591; **52** 5, 173, 250, 267, 421; **53** 6, 105, 173, 267, 380, 428; **54** 19, 103, 166, 173, 428; **55** 65, 428–9; **56** 6, 429; **65** 302, 429; **73** 429–30; **76** 430; **77** 6, 77, 303, 430; **82** 303, 431; **83** 431; **84** 431; **86** 304, 432; **87** 166 n., 307; **88** 304; **92** 5, 432; **93** 282, 307, 432–3; **94** 19, 266, 315–16, 433; **95** 433; **96** 113, 307, 320, 433; **97** 19, 115–16, 282, 321, 400, 433; **98** 110, 115, 117, 120, 400, 434; **99** 25, 111–13, 117, 282, 391, 434; **100** 111, 124, 434; **101** 110, 111, 400, 434; **103** 318, 435; **106** 138, 435; **107** 6, 380, 435; **108** 4, 138, 436; **109** 225, 436; changes to 379–81; Chapter I 19, 414–15; Chapter II 415–16; Chapter III 416; Chapter IV 416–19; Chapter V 3, 118, 267, 420–2; Chapter VI 3, 5, 17, 78, 227, 244, 263, 266, 269, 420, 422–4, 455–6; Chapter VII 3, 5, 19–20, 32, 63, 163, 173, 227, 263, 264, 267, 269–73, 287, 357–8, 364–5, 373,

Chapter, Chapter VII (*cont.*): 374, 380, 415, 420, 424–7, 455, 592; Chapter VIII 3, 173–4, 267, 268, 420, 427–8, 455–6; Chapter X 418, 429; Chapter XI 429–30, 469; Chapter XII 430–1; Chapter XIII 432; Chapter XIV 432–3; Chapter XV 433–4; Chapter XVI 435; Chapter XVII 435; Chapter XVIII 436; and responsibilities of Secretary-General 110–14; reviews of 225; signing 5; Special Committee on 6, 96, 369, 380
Chauvel, Jean 405
chemical and biological weapons 121, 210; UN Special Commission 377
Ch'iao Kuan-hua 184
Childers, Erskine 332
Chile 149, 151, 245–6
China 1, 2, 13, 16, 46, 59, 79–80, 86; and documentation 98; and Guatemala 186–7; and Korea 213–14, 216–18; as President 126, 165; representation of 137–41, 178, 179–87, 211–12, 397–8; and Soviet Union 152–3, 180–1, 183, 185–6, 190, 257; and Vietnam 216–18
China, People's Republic of 381; as permanent member 137–41; and Taiwan 211–12, 246–7, 248, 258; use of veto 218, 219–20, 224, 229, 230
China, Republic of (Nationalist China) 179–87, 381
Christian Institute of South Africa 164
Christopher, Warren 328
Chronicle 172
Churchill, Winston 173
CIS 175
Cisse, Jeanne Martin 168
Cold War 8, 357, 608; early issues 3; end of 139; thawing 49
Colombia 39, 46, 88, 148, 149, 150, 151, 347 n.; as President 108, 134
Commission on Human Rights 165, 302–3
Commission for Indonesia 333
Committee on Admission of New Members 338–50
Committee on Council meetings away from Headquarters 337–8
Committee of Experts 3, 11, 79–80, 175–6, 183, 202, 334–5, 336–7, 378; and Military Staff Committee (MSC) 275–6; on presidency 400; on rapporteurs 405–6
Committee of Good Offices on Indonesia 196
Committee on New Members 351
Commonwealth 171, 172
Commonwealth Prime Ministers' Conference (1971) 139
Commonwealth States 171
communications, abusive 105–6, 132–3; circulation of 102–9; *see also* documentation; language
communiqués 47–8, 54–60, 117
Comoros, The 255–6; and France 258
Compensation Commission 377
competence 84–5
conciliation procedures 133
conduct of business: Rules on 401–6, 446–9
Conference on Security and Co-operation in Europe (CSCE) 175
confidentiality 408–9
Conforti, Benedetto 205
Congo 39, 41, 105, 120, 151, 155, 269–70, 461, 466–7; adjournment of meeting on 205; and credentials 176, 178; crisis (1960) 111, 126, 127–8; meeting in 335; UN Subcommittee on 333–4; United Nations Operation in (ONUC) 357, 486–7; *see also* Zaire
consensus and unanimity 259–63, 264–5
Consultation Room 44
consultations, informal 22, 29, 32, 35, 50–1, 60–8, *see also* informal consultations; Contact Groups 68, 72; European Union 71; formalization 61–4; 'Groups of Friends' 68, 72; measures supplementing 67, 68; non-aligned (NAM) 70–1; non-non-aligned 71; 'of the whole' 61–8; permanent five ('P5') 69; and private meetings 56–7; and sanctions 63–4; Western permanent members ('P3') 69–70

'Contact Groups' 68, 72
Cordova, Roberto 2
Corfu Channel case (1947) 244, 252–3, 314–15, 355
Cornut-Gentille, Bernard 209, 399
Costa Rica 70, 71, 106, 150, 151
Cote d'Ivoire (Ivory Coast) 149, 151
Council Chamber 44
Council of Foreign Ministers 103
credentials 167, 175–9, 397–8; presentation of 443–4; Rules on 397–8, 443–4
criminal tribunals 114, 363–5, 496, 510, 592–605
Croatia 156, 509–10, 522; United Nations Confidence Restoration Operation (UNCRO) 506–7, 536–7, 538–9; United Nations Mission of Observers in Prevlaka (UNMOP) 510; United Nations Protection Force (UNPROFOR) 502–4
Crowe, Sir Colin 188
Cuba 10, 29–30, 30, 39, 59, 83, 144–5, 148, 149, 151, 174, 180, 205, 518, 520; and Angola 487; attacks on United States 132; and Iraq/Kuwait 215; missile crisis (1962) 191; and Organization of American States 104–5, 223; as President 128, 210; on recognition of governments 398; and Soviet Union 221–2
custom and usage 17–18; and responsibilities of Secretary-General 110, 121–4
Cyprus 108, 174, 518, 530; credentials 178; Turkish community 164; and United Kingdom 191; United Nations Peace-Keeping Force in (UNFICYP) 229, 300–1, 484–6
Czech Republic 151, 161, 349, 389
Czechoslovakia 148, 149, 150, 170, 245–6, 349, 355; and Malaysia 298, 299; and Soviet Union 103

Danube river 537–8
Dayton peace agreement 72
Dean, Sir Patrick 205
debates: closure of 202, 410; interrupting speaker 192–6; order of speakers 189–91; purposes of 188; right of reply 196–7; statements before or after vote 218–20; *see also* meetings
decisions: binding 263–73; definitions 263–4; substantive 4, 12, 226–7, 241, 248–9
Delon, Francis 280
Denmark 149, 150, 151
Diaz, Alfonso de Rosenzweig 2
disarmament 37–8, 276–7, 281, 570; General Assembly and 292; negotiating body 292; Non-Proliferation of Nuclear Weapons Treaty (NPT) 69, 140–1, 589–91
dispute: definition 79–80
Dixon, Sir Pierson 138, 194, 212
Djibouti 82, 151
Djokic, Dragomir 161
Djukic, Ilija 161
documentation 94–100, 581–3; access to 401, 452; annual Index 95; annual reports 366, 420, 434, 542–3, 549–52; audio-visual 99–100; confidentiality 408–9; corrections 97–8, 100, 117, 131, 407–8, 554–5; nomenclature 106–9, 545–8; Presidential statements 95, 542–3; provisional records 97–9; reports to General Assembly 95–6; resolutions and decisions 95; responsibilities of Secretary-General 114; Rules on 450–2; S/-letters and reports 94–5, 542–3; subsidiary organs 96–7, 101; verbatim records 94, 545; working group on 81, 286, 377–8, 389, 410–11, 543, 555
domestic jurisdiction 90, 158–9, 205
Dominican Republic 41, 115, 174; credentials 178; Mission of the Representative of the Secretary-General (DOMREP) 514–15; UN meeting in 335
double veto 240–9, 406
Douglas, Lewis 229
draft resolutions *see under* resolutions

Index

Dumbarton Oaks meeting (1945) 5, 142, 227

Eastern Europe: representation of 133, 143, 152, 169–70
Economic Commission for Europe 108
Economic Community of West African States (ECOWAS) 175, 497–8
Economic and Social Council (ECOSOC) 75, 118, 139, 152, 165, 166, 171, 301–3, 429; enlargement 379
Ecuador 59, 148, 149, 151
Eden, Anthony 173
Egypt 1, 2, 79–80, 103, 143, 148, 149, 151, 191, 223, 349; 1967 war 103; on consultations with troop-contributors 361; invasion of 253, 461, 465–6, 478; and Israel 38, 40; and Lebanon 103; and Palestine Liberation Organization (PLO) 160
Eichmann, Adolf 255
Ekeus, Rolf 204
El Salvador: 'friends' group 72; United Nations Mission in (MINUSAL) 500; United Nations Observer Mission (ONUSAL) 499–500; use of audio-visual records 99
elections: non-permanent members 142–52
emergency sessions 460–1, 464, 466
enemy state clauses 428, 435
enlargement of Security Council 135, 152–3, 225, 283, 356, 379, 382–90
Entebbe hijack 249
equality 168
equality of States 6
Estonia 172
Ethiopia 150, 151
European Parliament, Committee on Foreign Affairs and Security 386
European Union 172, 175, 386; as group 71

fact-finding missions 113, 353–6
Falklands (Malvinas) 16–17, 256, 258
Farah, Ambassador 35
Feller, Abe 181
Fiji: application for membership 347; and peace-keeping operations 352
filibustering 196, 200, 201, 213–14
film: as documentation 99–100
Finland 46, 48, 150, 151; membership application 224, 346–7
Fisher, H. A. L. 92
Fisheries Jurisdiction 316–17
Foo Ping-sheung 2
France 1, 10, 48, 64, 68, 72, 78, 79, 80, 86, 127, 520, 521, 522, 523; on Charter 105; and the Comoros 255–6, 258; on competence of Council 85; on convening meetings 46; and enlargement 153; and Kofi Annan 330–1; and Lebanon 211; as permanent member 137–41; as President 179, 246, 256; on public meetings 51; and Siam (Thailand) 252; and Syria 211; and Tunisia 89–90, 103, 464; use of veto 230
Freitas-Valle, Cyro de 2
Freudenschuß, Helmut 268, 271
Fry, Ken 164
Fulci, Paolo 330–1

Gabon 150
Garba, John 191
General Armistic Agreement (1949) 40, 477
General Assembly 1, 2, 118, 281–2; annual and special reports to 21, 284–93, 420, 434, 542–3, 549–52; and appointment of Secretary-General 321–32; and disarmament 281, 292; elections and appointments 283–4; elections to Security Council 142, 301; emergency sessions 226; evolving role 134; and financing of peace-keeping operations 299–301; influence 281–2; Open-ended Working Group 73–4, 140, 227, 382–90; on Palestine 292; and peace-keeping initiatives 122–4; on permanent members 140; recommendations by 295–6; recommendations to 19; relationship with Security Council 3; reports to 95–6; and reviews of

Charter 225; and SC meetings in Africa 41; special sessions 296–7; subsidiary organs 297; and threats to peace and security 292–6; and UN membership 297–9; and veto 230
Geneva 41, 43
Geneva Convention (1949) 593–4
Geneva Protocol (1925) 84, 210
genocide 592–3
Georgia 116, 530; and Abkhazia 175, 538, 539; 'friends' group 72; United Nations Observer Mission (UNOMIG) 511–12, 538
German Democratic Republic 106–8, 150
Germany 72, 151, 349, 520; and permanent membership 140, 387, 390; re-unification 108, 608
Germany, Federal Republic 72, 106–8, 150, 151
Ghana 149, 151
Gilmour, David 90
Gizenga, Antoine 105
Goldberg, Arthur 191
Greece 3, 48, 144, 148, 149, 269, 518; frontier incidents (1947) 244–5, 461–2; and Turkey 315, 519; and Ukrainian SSR 243, 354–5
Grenada: credentials 178
Gromyko, Andrei 1, 2, 196, 215, 243, 245
'Group of 77' (G77) group of developing countries 70, 71, 172
groups 168–73
'Groups of Friends' 68, 72
Guatemala 174; and China 186–7, 229; 'friends' group 72; Human Rights Verification Mission 219–20; military observers 229; and Taiwan 220
Guinea 42, 86, 150; female representative 168
Guinea-Bissau 151
Guiringaud, Louis de 399
Gulf Co-operation Council 172
Gulf War (1991) 30–3, 58–60, 201, 606–7
Guyana 150, 151
Haile Selassie, Emperor of Ethiopia 41–2
Haiti 135; 'friends' group 72; Governors Island Agreement (1993) 374, 376, 513; human rights 175; peace-enforcement action 374, 376; sanctions against 271, 365, 373–4; United Nations Mission (UNMIH) 360, 513–14, 539
Hammarskjold, Dag 25, 55, 105, 323–4; and Article 99 111–13; and communications 105; and Congo 117, 269–70; and Lebanon 115; and Middle East 119–20; on permanent representation 167; and role of Secretary-General 120–1, 283
Hannay, Sir David 39, 58, 287, 386–7
Havel, Vaclav 610
Headquarters Agreement 166
Hebron massacre (1994) 219
Herzegovina *see* Bosnia and Herzegovina
Higgins, Rosalyn 309
hijacking 249
Hiscocks 228
Hodgson, W. R. 2, 196
Honduras 128, 151
Hoppenot, Henri 212
Howe, Sir Geoffrey 49
human rights 4, 6, 302–3; Bosnia and Herzegovina 508; Cambodia 501; Croatia 509–10; Haiti 175; Iraq 165; Liberia 498; and peace-keeping operations 357; Rwanda 496, 592–605
Human Rights Verification Mission, Guatemala 219–20
Humanitarian Affairs, Department of 75, 584
humanitarian aid 492–3, 496, 512, 584–5
humanity, crimes against 593
Humphrey, John 189
Hungary 150, 151, 461, 520; application for UN membership 209, 224; credentials 178; crisis (1956) 75–6, 111, 209
Hyderabad: and India 190, 254, 518

Index to Proceedings of the Security Council 378
India 38, 59, 86, 108, 144, 148, 150, 151, 197; and Bangladesh 348; on credentials 176, 183; and Hyderabad 190, 254, 518; and Kashmir 103, 206; and Pakistan 135–6, 158, 253–4, 316, 518; as President 126; on recognition of governments 397–8; Representatives for 333; United Nations India–Pakistan Observation Mission (UNIPOM) 300, 483–4; United Nations Military Observer Group (UNMOGIP) 483
Indonesia 3, 26, 38, 148, 150, 151, 156, 224, 349, 462–4; application for membership 338; Commission for 333; Committee of Good Offices 196; withdrawal from UN 298–9
Indonesia, East 156
informal consultations 60–8, 136, 286, 390–1, 393–4, 557–62; agenda 395; non-members and 288, 291, 402; and suspension of meetings 203
International Atomic Energy Agency 166, 377
International Conference on the Former Yugoslavia (ICFY) 536
International Court of Justice 2, 113, 266, 267, 307–20, 423, 432–3; on abstentions 251; cases referred to 314–15; definition of dispute 79 n.; election to 13–16, 19 77, 225, 266, 282, 307–14, 394–5, 437–9, 474–6; Lockerbie case 317–19; and Namibia 268–9, 271; Statute 5, 19, 282, 432, 437–40, 454; suspension of election meetings 203
International Defence and Aid Fund 42
international tribunals 363–5; for the Former Yugoslavia 510, 598; Rwanda 364–5, 496, 592–605
Internet site 100
interpretation 407; simultaneous 91–3; *see also* translation
Iran 3, 48, 49, 79–80, 97, 149, 256, 523; Anglo–Iranian Oil Company 316; and Azerbaijan 77–9; and Iraq 49, 116, 121, 518; and Soviet Union 251–2; United Nations Iran–Iraq Observer Group (UNIIMOG) 515–16; and United States 104; US hostage crisis (1979) 112, 121, 317
Iraq 30–3, 37, 63–4, 94, 149, 150, 258, 519; chemical and biological weapons 377; compensation due from 377; credentials 178; human rights 165; and Iran 49, 116, 121, 518; and Kuwait 49–50, 58–9, 132, 155, 164–5, 215, 370–1, 520, 530; peace-keeping forces 301, 374, 375; sanctions against 135, 271, 365–6, 370–1; United Nations Iran–Iraq Observer Group (UNIIMOG) 515–16; United Nations Iraq–Kuwait Observation Mission (UNIKOM) 64, 516–17; and United States 104
Iraq–Kuwait Boundary Demarcation Commission 377
Ireland 26, 39, 46, 90, 148, 149, 150, 151, 158–9
Ireland, Northern 158–9, 205
Islamic Conference 166, 172, 175
Ismail, Razali 331–2
Israel 29, 38, 87, 191, 197, 229; 1967 war 103; application for membership 347; described by Arab states 133; and Egypt 38, 40, 477–9; and Entebbe 121; and geographical groups 172; Hebron massacre (1994) 219; land occupied by 157; orientation debate on 52; and Palestine question 254–5; self-defence 103–4; and Soviet Union 108–9; and Syria 480; terrorist attacks in 135; U Thant and 121
Italy 149, 150, 151; membership application 224
Ivory Coast 149, 151

Jakobson, Max 326
Jamaica 150
Jammu and Kashmir *see* Kashmir
Japan 70, 71, 86, 87, 149, 150, 151, 519, 520; on enemy State clauses 380;

and International Court of Justice 334; membership application 218, 224; and permanent membership 387, 390
Jarring, Gunnar 135–6
Jebb, Sir Gladwyn 246–7
Jennings, Sir Robert Yewdall 309
Jerusalem 229
Jesus, José Luis 313–14
Jewish Agency for Palestine 134, 164
Jordan 30, 46, 149, 150, 151, 157; and Israel 133; and Lebanon 461
Journal of the United Nations 23, 36, 40, 53, 62, 65, 66, 75, 171, 361, 395, 543, 574
Jovanovic, Vladislav 109, 161
Juppe, Alain 556
Juridicial Yearbook 113
Just War doctrine 368, 607

Kagame, Paul 129
Kamanda wa Kamanda 256
Kampuchea, Democratic: credentials 178; *see also* Cambodia
Kasavubu, Joseph 176
Kashmir 25–6, 35, 103, 158, 269, 483–4; adjournment of meeting on 205–6
Keita, Ambassador 27–8
Kennedy, John F. 353
Kenya 150, 151
Kerno, Ivan 181
Kiribati 352
Kleffens, E. van 2
Koo, Wellington 1–2
Korea, war in 83–4, 111, 201, 257, 374–5
Korea, Democratic People's Republic of (North Korea) 347; application for membership 216–18
Korea, Republic of (South Korea) 70, 71, 83, 108, 151, 213–14 519, 520; application for membership 216–18; UN military support 181
Koroma, Abdul G. 313–14
Kovanda, Ambassador 161–2
Krishna Menon, V. K. 269
Krogh, Per 44
Kuwait 30–3, 37, 104, 150, 524; and Iraq 49–50, 58–9, 132, 155, 164–5, 215, 370–1, 520, 530; as President 136–7; United Nations Iraq–Kuwait Observation Mission (UNIKOM) 64, 516–17; use of audio-visual records 100

land-mines 500, 510, 571
Lange, Oscar 194, 242–3
Langehove, Fernand van 244, 253
language: abusive 105–6, 132–3; and ambiguities 403
languages: additional 16; rules on 10, 11, 407–9, 449–50; *see also* translation
Laos 25, 116, 247, 355–6; UN Subcommittee on 333
Latin American group 169, 173
League of Arab States 43, 166, 173, 372
League of Nations 124, 142, 405, 457; mandate system 303, 305
Lebanon 40, 46, 86–7, 115, 144, 149, 174; British and French troops in 211, 251; and Egypt 103; on elections to ICJ 311–12; and Jordan 461; United Nations Interim Force (UNIFIL) 480–2; United Nations Observation Group (UNOGIL) 188, 333, 482; use of audio-visual records 99
Lee Kuan Yew 139
Legal Counsel 113–14, 295–6, 459–73; on credentials 177–8
Legwaila, Ambassador 52
Leigh-Phippard, Helen 72
liberation movements 43, 108, 157, 160, 164, 197, 402
Liberia 52, 148, 149, 175, 520, 530; Cotonou Peace Agreement (1993) 497; sanctions against 271, 365, 373; United Nations Observer Mission (UNOMIL) 497–8
Libya 30, 63–4, 69–70, 83, 108, 132–3, 150, 256, 258; and Chad 179; Libyan Arab Jamahiriya, Socialist People's 69–70, 518, 519, 520; Lockerbie case 69–70, 317–19, 371–2; sanctions against 135, 271, 365–6, 371–2; and United States 103, 104

Lie, Trygve 2, 54–5, 78–80, 211, 322–3; and Article 99 111, 112, 113; on credentials 167; and Military Staff Committee (MSC) 276; and Palestine 115; and representation of China 179–83; and role of Secretary-General 121; and Soviet Union 322
Liu Chieh 138
Lodge, Henry Cabot 127, 138, 207, 212
London 41
Lopez-Bravo, Gregorio 47
Lowe, Vaughan 318–19
Lumumba, Patrice 176
Luxembourg 46

Maastricht Treaty 386
Macedonia 350; United Nations Preventive Deployment Force (UNPREDEP) 504, 507; United Nations Protection Force (UNPROFOR) 503–4
McIntyre, Sir Laurence 194
McNair, Sir Arnold 316
Madagascar 151
Makin, Norman 2, 125
Malaysia 33–4, 39, 148, 149, 151, 523; on consultations with troop-contributors 362; and Czechoslovakia 298, 299; and Indonesia 298–9; on reports to General Assembly 289
Mali 27–9, 150
Malik, Yakov 23, 138, 190, 210, 300; and Korea 213–14
Malta 151; on Trusteeship Council 306
Malta summit (1945) 5
mandatory decisions 19–20
Marshall Islands 305–6
Massigli, René 2
Mauritania 30, 38–9, 150
Maynard, Peter D. 352
Mazowiecki, Mr 165
meetings 4–5; absence from 257–8; adjournment of 204–8; Arria formula 68, 73–4, 75, 393; away from Headquarters 335, 392; changes to 391–5; closed 10, 13, 53–60, 581; 'commemorative' 50, 587–8; convening 22–37; duration of 75–6; emergency 24–6; 'exchange of views' 50–3; notice of 37–40; open 575; order of speakers 189–91, 403; 'orientation' 50–3; participation of individuals 163–5; 'periodic' 45–50; place of 40–4; postponement of 210–12; private 21–2, 33, 100, 117, 321, 392; public 21, 33, 51, 401–2; quorum 410; Rules on 391–5, 441–2; sanctions committees 367–8; suspension of 201, 202–4; timing 22–37; with troop-contributing countries 74, 287, 288, 360–3, 565, 569, 573–4, 576–8; verbatim records 21–2; *see also* consultations, informal
membership 4; changes to 379, 382–90; Council size 388; geographical distribution 171; growth in 153; non-permanent 387–8; permanent 386–7; working group on 382–90
membership: applications for 10, 114, 117, 130, 209, 211, 216–18, 224, 242–3, 297–9; Committee on 338–50, 351, 410; criteria 350; mini-States 350–2; Rules on 409–10, 415–16, 452–3
Merrem, G. 64
Mexico 1, 79–80, 143, 148, 150; as President 242
Michiels van Verduynen, Jonkheer 2
Micronesian Federation 305–6
Middle East 91, 103, 518, 607; discussion of (1972) 86–8; General Armistic Agreements 119; human rights in 121; individual speakers on 164; October War 201; resolution 242 270–1; Six Day War 201; UN Emergency Force 300
Military Staff Committee (MSC) 137, 274–81, 285, 380, 421; chronology 275–8; and disarmament 276–7, 281; functions 274–5; and Gulf War 280
mine clearance 500, 510, 571
mini-States 348 n., 350–2
Minty, Abdul 164
Mission of the Representative of the Secretary-General in the

Dominican Republic (DOMREP) 514–15
Modzelewski, Zygmunt 2
Mongolia 39, 42; application for membership 211, 218, 224, 242–3
Montreal Convention (1971) 317–18
Morocco 30, 89, 149, 151, 156, 205; and Western Sahara 490–1
Moscow Declaration (1943) 435
motions: precedence 201–12; principal 198–9, 404; procedural 213, 225–6, 241–2, 248–9; substantive 198–9, 213, 404
motions of order 198
Movement of Non-Aligned States 372, 389
Moynihan, Daniel P. 256
Mozambique 531; sanctions against 271; United Nations Operation in (ONUMOZ) 493–4
Muslims 72

Nagorny Karabakh 175, 522
Najera, Castillo 242
Namibia 42, 69, 91, 99, 120, 267, 303, 305; Contact Group on 72; debates on 155; and International Court of Justice 268–9, 271; United Nations Transition Assistance Group (UNTAG) 487
national policies, changes in 411–12
NATO (North Atlantic Treaty Organization) 103, 172, 175, 503, 504
Nauru, Republic of 334, 474
Nepal 150, 151; application for membership 347
Nervo, Padilla 2
Netherlands 1, 2, 13, 48, 79–80, 143, 148, 149, 150, 151; on postponement of meetings 211
New Guinea, West (West Irian), United Nations Security Force (UNSF) 514
New York 40–1
New Zealand 52, 65, 104, 149, 150, 151, 389; on consultations with troop-contributors 361; as President 216–18, 224
Nicaragua 40, 91, 150, 151; and Taiwan 186; and United States 317; use of audio-visual records 99
Nicol, Davidson 61, 68
Niger 70, 150
Nigeria 150, 151; civil war 113; as President 129
Nobel Peace Prize 2
Noel-Baker, Philip 2, 8
Non-Aligned Movement (NAM) 70–1, 104, 172, 288; Co-ordinating Committee 71
non-government organizations (NGOs) 75, 320–1; Rules on 454
non-permanent members 141–53; geographical distribution 142–4
Non-Proliferation of Nuclear Weapons, Treaty on (NPT) 69, 140–1, 589–91
North Atlantic Treaty Organization (NATO) 103, 172, 175, 503, 504
Norway 10, 148, 149, 150
Nsanze, Mr (Burundi) 132
Nuclear Test cases 317
nuclear weapons, *see* Non-Proliferation of Nuclear Weapons 69, 140–1, 589–91
Nyerere, President Julius 139

O'Brien, Conor Cruise 168
observer missions 299, 300, 333
Occupied Arab Territories 49, 76, 219, 518; suspension of meetings on 203–4
Oman 70, 89, 151, 520; application for membership 348
order of speakers 403
Organization of African Unity (OAU) 41–2, 43, 49, 90–1, 103, 166, 172, 175, 372; and Boutros-Ghali 328, 329–30
Organization of American States (OAS) 103, 104–5, 172, 175, 223
Organization of the Islamic Conference 166, 172, 175
Organization for Security and Co-operation in Europe (OSCE) 172
Ortona, Egidio 247
Ould Daddah, Moktar 42
Owen–Stoltenberg initiative 72

Pacific Islands 303–4
Pakistan 38, 46, 73, 82, 149, 150, 151, 156, 298, 524; application for membership 347; and India 135–6, 158, 253–4, 316, 518; and Kashmir 103, 205–6; as President 179; Representatives for 333; United Nations Good Offices Mission (UNGOMAP) 356, 515; United Nations India–Pakistan Observation Mission (UNIPOM) 300, 483–4; United Nations Military Observer Group (UNMOGIP) 483
Palau 167, 208, 262, 306
Palestine 29, 35, 36, 38, 39, 40, 254–5, 269, 461, 465, 477, 518; adjournment of meeting on 207–8; elections (1996) 135; General Assembly committees for 297; General Assembly recommendations 292; *intifada* 607; Jewish Agency for 134; Permanent Observer 160; suspension of meetings on 203–4; use of audio-visual records 99–100
Palestine Liberation Organization (PLO) 43, 108, 157, 160, 197, 402
Palme, Olof 164
Panama 69, 128, 149, 150, 151, 174; credentials 178; meetings in 41, 42–3; Panama City, UN meeting in 41, 42–3, 88; use of audio-visual records 99
Pandit, Mrs V. L. 55, 323
Paraguay 106, 150
Paris 41
Parodi, Alexandre 246
Parsons, Sir Anthony 16–17
Peace Observation Commission 230
peace-keeping operations 20, 52, 266–8, 287, 356–63, 374–7, 380, 477–517, 563–7, 568–72; authorization 356; Bosnia 384; civilian personnel 566; command and control 567; financing of 140, 299–301, 564, 567, 572; and human rights 302, 357; informal consultations and 65–6; mandates 357–8, 360, 564; mini–States 352; and regionalism 174–5, 571–2, *see also under* individual countries; Special Committee on 359; stand-by arrangements 359–60, 565–6, 569–70, 579–80; 'sunset clause' 66; training 566–7; troop-contributors 74, 162–3, 287, 288, 360–3, 401, 565, 573–4, 576–8
Pearson, Lester B. 55
Penn, William 411–12
Pérez de Cuéllar, Javier 32, 55, 326–7; and Iran–Iraq war 121; peace-making initiatives 113
periodic reviews 390
permanent members 137–41
permanent missions 166–8, 177–8
Permanent Missions to the United Nations 167
Peru 149, 150, 151; as President 207
Philippines 145–6, 148, 149, 150, 156
Pinies, Jaime de 262–3
points of order 192–6, 403–4
Poland 1, 2, 13, 46, 79, 143, 145, 147–8, 148, 149, 150, 151; on competence of Council 85; as President 211, 216
Portugal 52, 150, 151; and Angola 467; and enlargement 153; territories administered by 469–70, 473; U Thant and 121
precedence 187
Preparatory Commission 1; Executive Committee 9–10
presidency: ceding of chair 125–9; discretionary role 130–1; duties of 130; of European Union 71; formal tasks 131–2; management of meetings 132–3; powers of 398–9; role of 9–10, 120, 124–37; rotation of 16, 23, 124–6, 398; Rules on 398–400, 445
Presidential Statements 63–4, 74, 95, 563–80, 587–8
Primakov, Yevgeny 59
procedure: discussions on 8–9; rules of 2, 5, 9–17
propaganda 90
proposals: and amendments 224;

sponsors 221–2; submission of 221; *see also* amendments
Provisional Rules of Procedure (*numbers in bold type refer to individual Rule numbers*) **1** 29, 130, 391–2, 399, 441; **2** 11, 16, 17, 29, 30; **3** 29, 130, 391, 399, 441; **4** 11–12, 45, 391, 392, 441; **5** 16, 17, 40, 335, 392, 400, 442; **6** 114, 396, 400, 408, 442; **7** 76, 89, 114, 130, 395, 399, 400, 442; **8** 16, 114, 395, 400, 442; **9** 17, 76, 395, 443; **10** 88–9, 391, 396–7, 442; **11** 16, 77, 114, 396, 400, 443; **12** 12, 16, 45, 391, 392, 395, 443; **13** 12, 16, 117, 397, 400, 443–4; **14** 16, 117, 397, 400, 444; **15** 16, 114, 117, 178–9, 397, 400, 444; **16** 16, 397, 444; **17** 16, 178, 397, 444; **18** 11, 16, 126, 129, 398, 445; **19** 11, 128, 130, 189, 399, 445; **20** 10, 11, 13, 16, 125–6, 127, 130, 313, 445, 399–400; **21** 11, 116, 391, 400, 445; **22** 11, 13, 116–17, 400, 446; **23** 11, 13, 117, 391, 401, 446; **24** 11, 114, 115–16, 118, 391, 400, 446; **25** 11, 13, 37, 114, 400, 446; **26** 11, 13, 114, 400, 446; **27** 11, 16, 130, 189, 399, 401, 403, 446; **28** 11, 13, 117, 333, 369, 372, 391, 401, 405, 446; **29** 11, 13, 131, 189, 399, 401, 403, 447; **30** 12, 16, 130, 193, 208–9, 213, 399, 400, 401, 403, 447; **31** 13, 16, 31, 118–19, 391, 401, 404, 447; **32** 11, 13, 16, 25, 198, 200, 209, 214, 222–3, 224, 391, 401, 404, 447; **33** 12, 193, 198, 201–12, 391, 401, 404–5, 410, 447–8; **34** 12, 16, 198, 401, 404, 448; **35** 16, 198, 221–2, 401, 404, 448, **36** 11, 130, 198, 212–15, 391, 399, 401, 405, 448; **37** 11, 16, 154, 160, 189, 401–2, 448–9, 553; **38** 11, 157, 189, 198, 200, 221, 401, 449; **39** 42, 118, 154–5, 160, 163–4, 165, 189, 320, 400, 401, 402, 449; **40** 406–7; **41** 407, 449; **42** 407, 450; **43** 407; **44** 16, 407, 450; **45** 16, 97, 407, 450; **46** 16, 407, 450; **47** 407, 450; **48** 53, 56, 321; **49** 408, 451; **50** 16, 97, 117, 130, 400, 408, 451; **51** 54, 58, 100, 114, 130, 393, 400, 408, 451; **52** 16, 97, 131, 399, 408, 451; **53** 56, 98, 130, 391, 399, 408, 451; **54** 98, 408, 452; **55** 47, 54, 58, 117, 393, 400, 452; **56** 54, 100, 117, 393, 400, 452; **57** 114, 391, 400, 452; **58** 13, 117, 400, 409–10, 452; **59** 13, 16, 114, 130, 346, 399, 400, 453; **60** 13, 297–8, 410, 453; **61** 13–16, 307, 394–5, 454; **73** 193; **85** 142; **90** 193; amendments 13–16, 390–1; Appendix 15, 16, 118, 408, 454; breaches 192; Chapter V 400; Chapter VII 406–7; 'Conduct of Business' 188; and Council practice 25–7; on credentials 175–7; and custom 17; and informal consultations 64–5; motions of order 198; obstruction 13; points of order 192–6, 208; Presidential interpretations 213–14; and responsibilities of Secretary-General 110, 114–18

Quiet Room 67
Quo, Tai-chi 209, 221

racial discrimination 88
rapporteurs 210, 292, 401, 403, 405–6, 447
Razali, Ambassador 390
recognition of states 157
recommendations: to disputing parties 18–19; to General Assembly 19
Red Cross 585
refugees 496; Bosnia and Herzegovina 503; Cambodia 501; Croatia 509; UN High Commissioner for 503
regional agencies 103
regional organizations 166
regionalism 166, 173–5; and peace-keeping initiatives 174–5, 571–2
Repertoire of Practice 20, 23, 54, 89, 96, 194–5, 256, 263–6, 267
reports: to General Assembly 284–93, 420, 434, 542–3, 549–52; on membership applications 297–8; sanctions committees 366
representation, Rules on 397–8, 443–4

resolutions, Security Council (*numbers in bold type refer to individual resolution numbers*) **1** 240; **83** 375; **84** 375; **95** 255; **113** 119; **169** 120; **217** 369; **232** 369; **242** 270–1; **246** 20; **253** 369; **257** 177; **294** 120; **295** 120; **298** 120; **302** 120; **310** 120; **385** 72; **418** 369–70; **421** 369–70; **460** 369; **476** 157; **562** 157; **598** 49, 515; **660** 258–9, 375; **661** 59, 104, 280, 370–1; **665** 59, 280; **670** 49, 280; **678** 32, 49, 59, 375; **681** 208; **687** 271, 370, 377, 516, 540–1; **689** 66, 516; **692** 377; **712** 370; **713** 49–50, 104, 250, 371; **724** 271, 371, 537; **727**, 371; **731** 318, 371–2; **733** 372; **748** 318–19, 371–2, 541; **751** 372, 491; **771** 271; **777** 109; **788** 373; **794** 375, 491; **819** 271, 502; **820** 271; **824** 271, 502; **827** 364; **833** 271; **841** 373–4; **844** 271, 502; **864** 372–3, 488; **918** 373, 495; **919** 370; **925** 376, 495; **929** 375; **940** 376, 513; **944** 374; **948** 374; **955** 364, 592; **984** 141, 589–91; **985** 373, 497; **986** 53, 370; **1013** 373; **1021** 371; **1022** 371; **1031** 376, 504; **1051** 377; **1074** 371; **1080** 376; **1088** 376; **1092** 240; **1127** 373; 'blue draft' 553–5; on CD-Rom 100; for cease-fire 201; database 100; on disarmament 276–7; draft 66–7, 198, 200, 221–2, 259, 553–5; evolution of 553–5; proposed 198; 'sunset clause' 66; Uniting for Peace (1950) 229–30, 296, 460–1
Resolutions and Decisions of the Security Council 266
Rhodesia, South 27, 42, 46, 91, 116, 156, 462, 470–1; peace-enforcement action 374, 375; sanctions against 106–7, 121, 302, 365, 369, 473; *see also* Zimbabwe
Richard, Ivor 225
Riggs, Robert E. 7
Romania 148, 149, 150, 151; membership application 224
Romulo, Carlos P. 55
Ross, John 13
Russian Federation 72, 166, 381; on peace-keeping financing 300; as permanent member 137; use of veto 229; *see also* Soviet Union
Rwanda 151, 161–2, 257, 531; credentials 178; International Tribunal for 364–5, 496, 592–605; peace-keeping operations 358, 374, 375–6; as President 126, 128–9, 162, 398; sanctions against 271, 365, 373; United Nations Assistance Mission (UNAMIR) 495–6, 534, 539; United Nations Observer Mission (UNOMUR) 494–5
San Francisco Conference (1945) 5, 169, 226–7, 240, 241, 250
San Francisco declaration 406, 413
San Marino: and International Court of Justice 334
sanctions 27, 53, 260, 271, 286, 424–5, 571, 586; against Bosnian Serbs 373, 541; against Iraq 135, 370–1, 540–1; against Libya 135; against Rhodesia 302, 369; Angola 372–3; committees *see* sanctions committees; disadvantages 366–8; Haiti 373–4; humanitarian aspects 584–5; implementation 114; informal consultations and 63–4, 65–6; Liberia 373; Libya 371–2; P5 on 69; Rhodesia 369; Rwanda 373; Somalia 372; South Africa 369–70, 468–9, 473; Yugoslavia 365–6, 371, 541
sanctions committees 67, 288, 289, 334, 365–74, 552, 581–3; Angola 365; annual reports 366; Haiti 365; Iraq 365, 365–6; Liberia 365; Libya 365, 365–6, 541; meetings 367–8; Rwanda 365; Somalia 365; South Africa 365; Southern Rhodesia 365; Sudan 365; transparency 366; Yugoslavia 365–6
Sardenberg, Ambassador 286
Saudi Arabia 159, 523
SCOR (Security Council Official Records) 97–9

secret diplomacy 10–11
Secretariat 1, 285, 400–1, 433–4; role of 118; Rules on 400–1, 445–6; Security Council Affairs Division 164; working languages 407
Secretary-General, and agenda 76; appointment 19, 21, 53–6, 77, 266, 282, 321–2, 392–3; appointment of staff 114–16; convening meetings 37; and credentials 176–7; deputy 400, 445–6; discretionary powers 120; evolving role 118–19, 134; illness 399; oral interventions by 117; receiving credentials 117; responsibilities 110–24, 282; and UN decisions 118–21
self-defence 103–4, 173
Senegal 150, 151, 523
Siam (Thailand), and Francc 252
Sierra Leone 150; on documentation 99; sanctions against 271
Siilasvuo, Ensio 115
Simma, Bruno 61
Skrzeszewski, Stanislaw 55
Slavonia, Eastern *see* United Nations Transitional Administration
Slovakia 349
Slovenia 522
Smith, Ian 369
Sobolev, Arkady 93, 138, 207, 209, 211–12; and Korea and Vietnam 216–18
Somalia 42, 52, 86, 150, 175, 521, 531, 534; and China 183; peace-keeping operations 122, 358, 374, 375, 384; Presidency 90–1; sanctions against 271, 365, 372; United Nations Operations in (UNOSOM) 491–3
Somavía, Juan 75, 321
South Africa 69, 91, 157, 255, 467–9; and enlargement 153; individual speakers on 164; and Namibia 305; sanctions 365, 369–70, 468–9, 473; U Thant and 121
South Pacific Forum 172
Soviet Union 1, 6, 12, 86; and Azerbaijan 77–80; and Bangladesh 195; boycotts 257, 280; break-up 153, 381, 608; challenges by 25–6; and China 152–3, 180–1, 183, 185–6, 190, 257; on convening meetings 46, 59; and Cuba 221–2; and Czechoslovakia 103, 245–6; and Dag Hammarskjold 105; on documentation 98; and enlargement 152–3; filibustering 200; and German Democratic Republic 106–8; groups opposing 170–1; and India 135–6; and Iran 3, 251–2; and Israel 108–9; and Korea 83–4; leaving Chamber 180–1; on limitation of veto 227; and membership applications 224; on non-permanent members 143; on peace-keeping forces 299–300; as permanent member 137–41; and Presidency by United States 126–7; as President 126, 127–8, 197, 243, 245, 355; and role of Secretary-General 120–1; and Taiwan 280; and Trygve Lie 322; U Thant and 121; use of veto 54–5, 217–18, 224, 228, 230–7, 251, 283, 323, 326, 329; *see also* Russian Federation
Spaak, Paul-Henri 8, 53, 322, 394–5
Spain 46, 150, 151, 354, 461; and double veto 242
Special Committee on Apartheid 468
Special Committee on Peace-keeping Operations 566–7
Special Committee on Territories under Portuguese Administration 469–70
Special Representatives and Envoys 64, 334
sponsors 221–2
staff appointments, by Secretary-General 114–16
Stalin, Josef 227
Stettinius, Edward, Jr. 1, 2, 3, 224, 410
Stevenson, Adlai 7–8, 39, 173, 191, 205
Stewart, Michael 46
Stoltenberg, Thorvald 72, 535
subsidiary organs 333–78, 405, 416, 552
Sudan 30, 86, 150, 518; Presidency 90–1; sanctions 365
Suez Canal 103, 254–5
Suez crisis (1956) 75–6, 111, 127, 194, 201

suggestions 199–200
Sukarno, Achmed 298–9
Summary Statements 396; and agenda 76, 77; deletion of items 77–83
summit diplomacy 45
Sweden 48, 149, 150, 151
Switzerland 474
Syria 10, 38, 40, 46, 86–7, 148, 150, 200, 349, 519; British and French troops in 211, 251; and Israel 480

Taiwan 185–7, 211–12, 461; armed invasion of (1950) 246–7, 248; and China 258; and Guatemala 220
Tajikistan 64, 175, 535; United Nations Mission of Observers (UNMOT) 512–13
Taliban, Afghanistan 73
Tanzania 150, 349
Taylor-Kamara, J. B. 195
terrorism 594; Lockerbie bombing 69–70, 317–19, 371–2
Thailand 151; and France 252
Thant, U 27, 48, 55, 105, 107, 324–6; Annual Reports 283; appointment of staff 115, 116; and Article 99 112, 113; on China 185; and Congo 120; on credentials 178; and Dominican Republic 115; and enlargement 153; and Indonesia 298–9; and Israel 121; on mini-States 351; and Nigeria 113; and Portugal 121; and South Africa 121; and Soviet Union 121; and United States 121
Tickell, Sir Crispin 197
Timor 164, 518
Togo 151
Tomeh, George J. 263
Tonkin, Gulf of 103
translation: and interpretation 91–4; official and working languges 91–2; *see also* interpretation
transparency 10–11, 50–1, 66, 162, 388–9, 393–4, 556–62, 581; and reports to General Assembly 286–91; sanctions committees 366, 581
tribunals, international 114, 363–5, 496, 510, 592–605
Trieste 103
Trinidad and Tobago 151
troop-contributing countries 162–3, 401; consultations with 74, 287, 288, 360–3, 565, 569, 573–4, 576–8
trusteeship 430–1
Trusteeship Council 118, 119, 166, 303–7, 431, 432; composition 304–5
Tshombe, Moise 105
Tsiang, T. F. 138, 181
Tunisia 30, 42, 48, 83, 89–90, 113, 149, 150, 156, 157, 464, 519, 520; and France 103
Turkey 108, 144, 147–8, 148, 149, 520, 521, 523; and Cyprus 164, 229, 300, 484–6; and geographical groups 172; and Greece 315, 519
Tutu, Bishop Desmond 164

Uganda 150, 151, 258; and Israel 121; United Nations Observer Mission (UNOMUR) 494–5
Ukraine 144
Ukrainian SSR 3, 6, 148, 151, 196, 224, 246; absence 257; and Greece 243, 354–5
UN Preparatory Commission 2
Unified Task Force (UNITAF) 492–3
Union of Soviet Socialist Republics *see* Soviet Union
UNITA, Angola 365, 372–3, 488–90; sanctions against 271
United Arab Emirates 82, 151
United Arab Republic 149, 349
United Kingdom 1, 2, 10, 13, 72, 79–80, 258, 522, 523; Anglo-Iranian Oil Company 316; on competence of Council 85; on convening meetings 46; and Corfu Channel 252–3, 314–15; and Cyprus 191; and documentation 546; and double veto 244; and Egypt 253; and enlargement 153; and Falklands (Malvinas) 16–17, 256; and foundation of UN 7, 8; and Greece 3; and Gulf War 58–9; and Ireland 158–9; and Lebanon 211; Lockerbie case 317–18; and

Northern Ireland 39; as permanent member 137–41; as President 132, 160, 246–7; and Rhodesia 27, 462, 470–1; and Syria 211; terrorism in 135; and United States 167–8; and Uniting for Peace resolution (1950) 229–30; use of veto 230
United Nations Advance Mission in Cambodia (UNAMIC) 500–1
United Nations Angola Verification Missions (UNAVEM) 487–90, 533, 540
United Nations Aouzou Strip Observer Group (UNASOG) 498
United Nations Assistance Mission for Rwanda (UNAMIR) 495–6, 534, 539, 540
United Nations Confidence Restoration Operation in Croatia (UNCRO) 506–7, 536–7, 538–9, 540
United Nations Disengagement Observation Force (UNDOF) 479–80, 540
United Nations Emergency Force (UNEF) 356, 357, 478–9
United Nations Good Offices Mission in Afghanistan and Pakistan (UNGOMAP) 356, 515
United Nations High Commissioner for Refugees 503
United Nations India–Pakistan Observation Mission (UNIPOM) 483–4
United Nations Interim Force in Lebanon (UNIFIL) 480–2, 540
United Nations International Police Task Force (IPTF) 507–8
United Nations Iran–Iraq Observer Group (UNIIMOG) 515–16
United Nations Iraq–Kuwait Observation Mission (UNIKOM) 516–17, 540
United Nations Military Observer Group in India and Pakistan (UNMOGIP) 483
United Nations Mission in Bosnia and Herzegovina (UNMIBH) 507–8
United Nations Mission in Haiti (UNMIH) 513–14, 539, 540
United Nations Mission of Observers in Prevlaka (UNMOP) 510
United Nations Mission of Observers in Tajikistan (UNMOT) 512–13, 540
United Nations Mission for the Referendum in Western Sahara (MINURSO) 490–1, 540
United Nations Observation Group in Lebanon (UNOGIL) 482
United Nations Observer Group in Central America (ONUCA) 498–9
United Nations Observer Mission in El Salvador (ONUSAL) 499–500
United Nations Observer Mission in Georgia (UNOMIG) 511–12, 538, 539, 540
United Nations Observer Mission in Liberia (UNOMIL) 497–8, 540
United Nations Observer Mission Uganda-Rwanda (UNOMUR) 494–5
United Nations Operation in the Congo (ONUC) 357, 486–7
United Nations Operation in Mozambique (ONUMOZ) 493–4
United Nations Operations in Somalia (UNOSOM) 491–3
United Nations Peace Forces (UNPF) 504–5
United Nations Peace-Keeping Force in Cyprus (UNFICYP) 484–6, 540
United Nations Preventive Deployment Force (UNPREDEP) 504, 507, 538, 540
United Nations Protection Force (UNPROFOR) 156, 175, 357–8, 502–4, 505, 540
United Nations Security Force (UNSF) 356, 514
United Nations Transition Assistance Group (UNTAG) 487
United Nations Transitional Administration for Eastern Slavonia, Baranja and Western Sirmium (UNTAES) 509–10
United Nations Transitional Authority in Cambodia (UNTAC) 500, 501
United Nations Truce Supervision Organization (UNTSO) 356, 477–8

United Nations Yemen Observation Mission (UNYOM) 482–3
United States 1, 40, 72, 79–80, 519, 523; and Boutros-Ghali 327–8; and Cambodia 103; and China 185, 212; on competence of Council 85; on convening meetings 46; and enlargement 153; and foundation of UN 7–8; in Gulf of Tonkin 103; hostage crisis (1979) 112, 121, 317; hostages in Iran 317; and Iran 104; and Iraq 104; and Korea 83–4, 210; and Libya 103, 104; Lockerbie case 317–19; and Mali 28–9; and Nicaragua 317; on non-permanent members 143–4; and Pacific Islands 303–4; and Palestine Liberation Organization (PLO) 160; and Panama 41, 43, 104; as permanent member 137–41; as President 108, 126–7, 256; U Thant and 121; on UN contributions 140; and United Kingdom 167–8; Uniting for Peace resolution (1950) 229–30, 296, 460–1; use of audio-visual records 99; use of veto 219, 229, 230, 327–8; and Vietnam 103; and Yasser Arafat 43
Uniting for Peace *see under* resolutions
Urquhart, Sir Brian 332
Uruguay 149, 150
USSR *see* Soviet Union

Valle, Henrique 2
van der Stoel, Max 165, 204
Vance–Owen initiative 72
Venezuela 106, 149, 150, 151, 523; as President 222
veto 43, 139, 141, 157, 227–39, 379, 386–7, 406–7, 457; and appointment of Secretary-General 54–6; by P3 group 69–70; changing use of 18; Chinese use of 218, 219–20, 224, 229, 230; collective 390; double 9, 213, 240–9, 406; draft resolutions 230; and expansion of Council 228; and fact–finding missions 353–6; French use of 230; General Assembly and 230; hidden 139, 249–50, 389–90; indirect 249–50; limitations 227; open 139; of preliminary question 213; right of 3, 6, 7, 12, 45; Russian Federation use of 229; Soviet use of 54–5, 217–18, 224, 228, 230–7, 251, 283, 323, 326, 329; United Kingdom use of 230; United States use of 219, 229, 230, 327–8
Vienna Convention on Diplomatic Relations 187
Vietnam 108, 121; and United States 103
Vietnam, Democratic Republic of (North) 347; application for membership 216–18
Vietnam, South 353; application for membership 216–18
Vinci, Piero 193
Visiting Missions 166 n.
voting: absence 257; absolute majority 225; abstentions 12, 250–7; affirmative 380–1, 389–90; binding decisions 263–73; consensus and unanimity 259–63, 264–5; explanation of 218–20; non-participation 258–9; procedural motions 225–6; provisional 12; Rules on 406–7, 449; substantive decisions 226–7; unanimous 226–7; Yalta formula 455–8
Vyshinsky, Andrei 2, 275

Waldheim, Kurt 42, 55, 326; appointment of staff 115; and Article 99 112; and Bangladesh 113; and Entebbe 121; and Portugal 121; and South Africa 121; and US hostages in Iran 121
Walter, Harold 219
West New Guinea (West Irian) 356
Western Europe and other States Group (WEOG) 169–70, 172
Western Sahara 58, 116, 518, 534–5; United Nations Mission for the Referendum in (MINURSO) 490–1
Weston, Sir John 52
Wilson, Woodrow 53

Wisnumurti, Ambassador 288, 290
women representatives 168
Woods, Donald 164
working groups: on documentation 81, 286, 377–8, 389, 410–11, 543, 555; on membership 382–90; Open-ended 383–90, 391, 411
working methods, *aide-mémoire* 556–62; changes to 388–9
World Council of Churches 164
World Wide Web UN Home Page 92, 100
Wu Hsiu-ch'uan 184

Yalta formula (1945) 225–6, 240–1, 248–9, 455–8; on veto 139
Yalta summit (1945) 5
Yeltsin, Boris 381
Yemen 30–2, 59, 148, 151, 349; as President 207; United Nations Observation Mission (UNYOM) 299–300, 482–3
Yemen, Democratic 151, 348
Yost, Charles 7, 351
Yugoslavia 10, 42, 70–1, 86, 144, 145–6, 148, 149, 150, 151, 170, 520, 529–30; break-up 109, 153; on documentation 98; International Criminal Tribunal 363–4, 510, 598; as President 190; sanctions against 50, 271, 365–6, 371
Yugoslavia, Federal Republic of (Serbia and Montenegro) 156, 371, 502–5; in Council meetings 160–1; Danube river 537–8; ICFY Mission 536; membership application 298; UN Protection Force (UNPROFOR) 357–8

Zaire 94, 97, 151; peace-enforcement action 374, 376; as President 30–2, 91, 256; *see also* Congo
Zambia 39, 150, 151
Zhou Enlai 179, 180–1
Zimbabwe 59, 151; application for membership 348; Presidency 32, 91; *see also* Rhodesia, South
Zorin, Valerian 191, 205